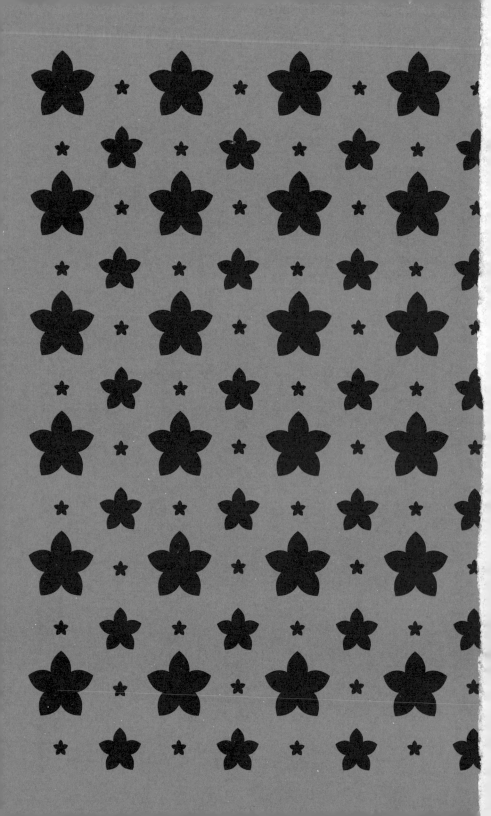

THE
RAMAYAN

Translated by RALPH T.H. GRIFFITH

VALMIKI

CLASSICS

First Published 2024

FiNGERPRINT! **CLASSiCS**

An imprint of Prakash Books India Pvt. Ltd

113/A, Darya Ganj,
New Delhi-110 002
Email: info@prakashbooks.com/sales@prakashbooks.com

Fingerprint Publishing
@FingerprintP
@fingerprintpublishingbooks
www.fingerprintpublishing.com

ISBN: 978 93 6214 413 3

Contents

Invocation

Praise to Válmíki, bird of charming song,
Who mounts on Poesy's sublimest spray,
And sweetly sings with accent clear and strong
Ráma, aye Ráma, in his deathless lay.
Where breathes the man can listen to the strain
That flows in music from Válmíki's tongue,
Nor feel his feet the path of bliss attain
When Ráma's glory by the saint is sung!
The stream Rámáyan leaves its sacred fount
The whole wide world from sin and stain to free.
The Prince of Hermits is the parent mount,
The lordly Ráma is the darling sea.
Glory to him whose fame is ever bright!
Glory to him, Prachetas' holy son!
Whose pure lips quaff with ever new delight
The nectar-sea of deeds by Ráma done.
Hail, arch-ascetic, pious, good, and kind!
Hail, Saint Válmíki, lord of every lore!
Hail, holy Hermit, calm and pure of mind!
Hail, First of Bards, Válmíki, hail once more!

BOOK

I

BOOK

I

CANTO

I

Nárad

OM

To sainted Nárad, prince of those
Whose lore in words of wisdom flows.
Whose constant care and chief delight
Were Scripture and ascetic rite,
The good Válmíki, first and best
Of hermit saints, these words addressed:
"In all this world, I pray thee, who
Is virtuous, heroic, true?
Firm in his vows, of grateful mind,
To every creature good and kind?
Bounteous, and holy, just, and wise,
Alone most fair to all men's eyes?
Devoid of envy, firm, and sage,
Whose tranquil soul ne'er yields to rage?
Whom, when his warrior wrath is high,
Do Gods embattled fear and fly?
Whose noble might and gentle skill
The triple world can guard from ill?
Who is the best of princes, he
Who loves his people's good to see?
The store of bliss, the living mine
Where brightest joys and virtues shine?

Queen Fortune's best and dearest friend,
Whose steps her choicest gifts attend?
Who may with Sun and Moon compare,
With Indra, Vishṇu, Fire, and Air?
Grant, Saint divine, the boon I ask,
For thee, I ween, an easy task,
To whom the power is given to know
If such a man breathe here below."
Then Nárad, clear before whose eye
The present, past, and future lie,
Made ready answer: "Hermit, where
Are graces found so high and rare?
Yet listen, and my tongue shall tell
In whom alone these virtues dwell.
From old Ikshváku's line he came,
Known to the world by Ráma's name:
With soul subdued, a chief of might,
In Scripture versed, in glory bright,
His steps in virtue's paths are bent,
Obedient, pure, and eloquent.
In each emprise he wins success,
And dying foes his power confess.
Tall and broad-shouldered, strong of limb,
Fortune has set her mark on him.
Graced with a conch-shell's triple line,
His throat displays the auspicious sign.
High destiny is clear impressed
On massive jaw and ample chest,
His mighty shafts he truly aims,
And foemen in the battle tames.
Deep in the muscle, scarcely shown,
Embedded lies his collar-bone.
His lordly steps are firm and free,
His strong arms reach below his knee;
All fairest graces join to deck
His head, his brow, his stately neck,
And limbs in fair proportion set:
The manliest form e'er fashioned yet.
Graced with each high imperial mark,
His skin is soft and lustrous dark.
Large are his eyes that sweetly shine

18

With majesty almost divine.
His plighted word he ne'er forgets;
On erring sense a watch he sets.
By nature wise, his teacher's skill
Has trained him to subdue his will.
Good, resolute and pure, and strong,
He guards mankind from scathe and wrong,
And lends his aid, and ne'er in vain,
The cause of justice to maintain.
Well has he studied o'er and o'er
The Vedasand their kindred lore.
Well skilled is he the bow to draw,
Well trained in arts and versed in law;
High-souled and meet for happy fate,
Most tender and compassionate;
The noblest of all lordly givers,
Whom good men follow, as the rivers
Follow the King of Floods, the sea:
So liberal, so just is he.
The joy of Queen Kauśalyá'sheart,
In every virtue he has part:
Firm as Himálaya's snowy steep,
Unfathomed like the mighty deep:
The peer of Vishṇu's power and might,
And lovely as the Lord of Night;
Patient as Earth, but, roused to ire,
Fierce as the world-destroying fire;
In bounty like the Lord of Gold,
And Justice self in human mould.
With him, his best and eldest son,
By all his princely virtues won
King Daśaratha willed to share
His kingdom as the Regent Heir.
But when Kaikeyí, youngest queen,
With eyes of envious hate had seen
The solemn pomp and regal state
Prepared the prince to consecrate,
She bade the hapless king bestow
Two gifts he promised long ago,
That Ráma to the woods should flee,
And that her child the heir should be.

19

By chains of duty firmly tied,
The wretched king perforce complied.
Ráma, to please Kaikeyí went
Obedient forth to banishment.
Then Lakshmaṇ's truth was nobly shown,
Then were his love and courage known,
When for his brother's sake he dared
All perils, and his exile shared.
And Sítá, Ráma's darling wife,
Loved even as he loved his life,
Whom happy marks combined to bless,
A miracle of loveliness,
Of Janak's royal lineage sprung,
Most excellent of women, clung
To her dear lord, like Rohiṇí
Rejoicing with the Moon to be.
The King and people, sad of mood,
The hero's car awhile pursued.
But when Prince Ráma lighted down
At Śringavera's pleasant town,
Where Gangá's holy waters flow,
He bade his driver turn and go.
Guha, Nishádas' king, he met,
And on the farther bank was set.
Then on from wood to wood they strayed,
O'er many a stream, through constant shade,
As Bharadvája bade them, till
They came to Chitrakúṭa's hill.
And Ráma there, with Lakshmaṇ's aid,
A pleasant little cottage made,
And spent his days with Sítá, dressed
In coat of bark and deerskin vest.
And Chitrakúṭa grew to be
As bright with those illustrious three
As Meru's sacred peaks that shine
With glory, when the Gods recline
Beneath them: Śiva's self between
The Lord of Gold and Beauty's Queen.

The aged king for Ráma pined,
And for the skies the earth resigned.

Bharat, his son, refused to reign,
Though urged by all the twice-born train.
Forth to the woods he fared to meet
His brother, fell before his feet,
And cried, "Thy claim all men allow:
O come, our lord and king be thou."
But Ráma nobly chose to be
Observant of his sire's decree.
He placed his sandals in his hand
A pledge that he would rule the land:
And bade his brother turn again.
Then Bharat, finding prayer was vain,
The sandals took and went away;
Nor in Ayodhyá would he stay.
But turned to Nandigráma, where
He ruled the realm with watchful care,
Still longing eagerly to learn
Tidings of Ráma's safe return.

Then lest the people should repeat
Their visit to his calm retreat,
Away from Chitrakúṭa's hill
Fared Ráma ever onward till

Beneath the shady trees he stood
Of Daṇḍaká's primeval wood,
Virádha, giant fiend, he slew,
And then Agastya's friendship knew.
Counselled by him he gained the sword
And bow of Indra, heavenly lord:
A pair of quivers too, that bore
Of arrows an exhaustless store.
While there he dwelt in greenwood shade
The trembling hermits sought his aid,
And bade him with his sword and bow
Destroy the fiends who worked them woe:
To come like Indra strong and brave,
A guardian God to help and save.
And Ráma's falchion left its trace
Deep cut on Śúrpaṇakhá's face:
A hideous giantess who came

21

Burning for him with lawless flame.
Their sister's cries the giants heard.
And vengeance in each bosom stirred:
The monster of the triple head.
And Dúshaṇ to the contest sped.
But they and myriad fiends beside
Beneath the might of Ráma died.

When Rávaṇ, dreaded warrior, knew
The slaughter of his giant crew:
Rávaṇ, the king, whose name of fear
Earth, hell, and heaven all shook to hear:
He bade the fiend Márícha aid
The vengeful plot his fury laid.
In vain the wise Márícha tried
To turn him from his course aside:
Not Rávaṇ's self, he said, might hope
With Ráma and his strength to cope.
Impelled by fate and blind with rage
He came to Ráma's hermitage.
There, by Márícha's magic art,
He wiled the princely youths apart,
The vulture slew, and bore away
The wife of Ráma as his prey.
The son of Raghu came and found
Jaṭáyu slain upon the ground.
He rushed within his leafy cot;
He sought his wife, but found her not.
Then, then the hero's senses failed;
In mad despair he wept and wailed.
Upon the pile that bird he laid,
And still in quest of Sítá strayed.
A hideous giant then he saw,
Kabandha named, a shape of awe.
The monstrous fiend he smote and slew,
And in the flame the body threw;
When straight from out the funeral flame
In lovely form Kabandha came,
And bade him seek in his distress
A wise and holy hermitess.
By counsel of this saintly dame

To Pampá's pleasant flood he came,
And there the steadfast friendship won
Of Hanumán the Wind-God's son.
Counselled by him he told his grief
To great Sugríva, Vánar chief,
Who, knowing all the tale, before
The sacred flame alliance swore.
Sugríva to his new-found friend
Told his own story to the end:
His hate of Báli for the wrong
And insult he had borne so long.
And Ráma lent a willing ear
And promised to allay his fear.
Sugríva warned him of the might
Of Báli, matchless in the fight,
And, credence for his tale to gain,
Showed the huge fiend by Báli slain.
The prostrate corse of mountain size
Seemed nothing in the hero's eyes;
He lightly kicked it, as it lay,
And cast it twenty leagues away.
To prove his might his arrows through
Seven palms in line, uninjured, flew.
He cleft a mighty hill apart,
And down to hell he hurled his dart.
Then high Sugríva's spirit rose,
Assured of conquest o'er his foes.
With his new champion by his side
To vast Kishkindhá's cave he hied.
Then, summoned by his awful shout,
King Báli came in fury out,
First comforted his trembling wife,
Then sought Sugríva in the strife.
One shaft from Ráma's deadly bow
The monarch in the dust laid low.
Then Ráma bade Sugríva reign
In place of royal Báli slain.
Then speedy envoys hurried forth
Eastward and westward, south and north,
Commanded by the grateful king
Tidings of Ráma's spouse to bring.

Then by Sampáti's counsel led,
Brave Hanumán, who mocked at dread,
Sprang at one wild tremendous leap
Two hundred leagues across the deep.
To Lanká's town he urged his way,
Where Rávaṇ held his royal sway.

There pensive 'neath Aśoka boughs
He found poor Sítá, Ráma's spouse.
He gave the hapless girl a ring,
A token from her lord and king.
A pledge from her fair hand he bore;
Then battered down the garden door.
Five captains of the host he slew,
Seven sons of councillors o'erthrew;
Crushed youthful Aksha on the field,
Then to his captors chose to yield.
Soon from their bonds his limbs were free,
But honouring the high decree
Which Brahmá had pronounced of yore,
He calmly all their insults bore.
The town he burnt with hostile flame,
And spoke again with Ráma's dame,
Then swiftly back to Ráma flew
With tidings of the interview.

Then with Sugríva for his guide,
Came Ráma to the ocean side.
He smote the sea with shafts as bright
As sunbeams in their summer height,
And quick appeared the Rivers' King
Obedient to the summoning.
A bridge was thrown by Nala o'er
The narrow sea from shore to shore.
They crossed to Lanká's golden town,
Where Ráma's hand smote Rávaṇ down.
Vibhishaṇ there was left to reign
Over his brother's wide domain.
To meet her husband Sítá came;
But Ráma, stung with ire and shame,
With bitter words his wife addressed

Before the crowd that round her pressed.
But Sítá, touched with noble ire,
Gave her fair body to the fire.
Then straight the God of Wind appeared,
And words from heaven her honour cleared.
And Ráma clasped his wife again,
Uninjured, pure from spot and stain,
Obedient to the Lord of Fire
And the high mandate of his sire.
Led by the Lord who rules the sky,
The Gods and heavenly saints drew nigh,
And honoured him with worthy meed,
Rejoicing in each glorious deed.
His task achieved, his foe removed,
He triumphed, by the Gods approved.
By grace of Heaven he raised to life
The chieftains slain in mortal strife;
Then in the magic chariot through
The clouds to Nandigráma flew.
Met by his faithful brothers there,
He loosed his votive coil of hair:
Thence fair Ayodhyá's town he gained,
And o'er his father's kingdom reigned.
Disease or famine ne'er oppressed
His happy people, richly blest
With all the joys of ample wealth,
Of sweet content and perfect health.
No widow mourned her well-loved mate,
No sire his son's untimely fate.
They feared not storm or robber's hand;
No fire or flood laid waste the land:
The Golden Age had come again
To bless the days of Ráma's reign.

From him, the great and glorious king,
Shall many a princely scion spring.
And he shall rule, beloved by men,
Ten thousand years and hundreds ten,
And when his life on earth is past
To Brahmá's world shall go at last."

Whoe'er this noble poem reads
That tells the tale of Ráma's deeds,
Good as the Scriptures, he shall be
From every sin and blemish free.
Whoever reads the saving strain,
With all his kin the heavens shall gain.
Bráhmans who read shall gather hence
The highest praise for eloquence.
The warrior, o'er the land shall reign,
The merchant, luck in trade obtain;
And Súdras listening ne'er shall fail
To reap advantage from the tale.

CANTO

II

Brahmá's Visit

Válmíki, graceful speaker, heard,
    To highest admiration stirred.
    To him whose fame the tale rehearsed
He paid his mental worship first;
Then with his pupil humbly bent
Before the saint most eloquent.
Thus honoured and dismissed the seer
Departed to his heavenly sphere.
Then from his cot Válmíki hied
To Tamasá's sequestered side,
Not far remote from Gangá's tide.
He stood and saw the ripples roll
Pellucid o'er a pebbly shoal.
To Bharadvája by his side
He turned in ecstasy, and cried:
"See, pupil dear, this lovely sight,
The smooth-floored shallow, pure and bright,
With not a speck or shade to mar,

And clear as good men's bosoms are.
Here on the brink thy pitcher lay,
And bring my zone of bark, I pray.
Here will I bathe: the rill has not,
To lave the limbs, a fairer spot.
Do quickly as I bid, nor waste
The precious time; away, and haste."

Obedient to his master's hest
Quick from the cot he brought the vest;
The hermit took it from his hand,
And tightened round his waist the band;
Then duly dipped and bathed him there,
And muttered low his secret prayer.
To spirits and to Gods he made
Libation of the stream, and strayed
Viewing the forest deep and wide
That spread its shade on every side.
Close by the bank he saw a pair
Of curlews sporting fearless there.
But suddenly with evil mind
An outcast fowler stole behind,
And, with an aim too sure and true,
The male bird near the hermit slew.
The wretched hen in wild despair
With fluttering pinions beat the air,
And shrieked a long and bitter cry
When low on earth she saw him lie,
Her loved companion, quivering, dead,
His dear wings with his lifeblood red;
And for her golden crested mate
She mourned, and was disconsolate.

The hermit saw the slaughtered bird,
And all his heart with ruth was stirred.
The fowler's impious deed distressed
His gentle sympathetic breast,
And while the curlew's sad cries rang
Within his ears, the hermit sang:
"No fame be thine for endless time,
Because, base outcast, of thy crime,

Whose cruel hand was fain to slay
One of this gentle pair at play!"
E'en as he spoke his bosom wrought
And laboured with the wondering thought
What was the speech his ready tongue
Had uttered when his heart was wrung.
He pondered long upon the speech,
Recalled the words and measured each,
And thus exclaimed the saintly guide
To Bharadvája by his side:
"With equal lines of even feet,
With rhythm and time and tone complete,
The measured form of words I spoke
In shock of grief be termed a śloke."
And Bharadvája, nothing slow
His faithful love and zeal to show,
Answered those words of wisdom,
"Be the name, my lord, as pleases thee."

As rules prescribe the hermit took
Some lustral water from the brook.
But still on this his constant thought
Kept brooding, as his home he sought;
While Bharadvája paced behind,
A pupil sage of lowly mind,
And in his hand a pitcher bore
With pure fresh water brimming o'er.
Soon as they reached their calm retreat
The holy hermit took his seat;
His mind from worldly cares recalled,
And mused in deepest thought enthralled.

Then glorious Brahmá, Lord Most High,
Creator of the earth and sky,

The four-faced God, to meet the sage
Came to Válmíki's hermitage.
Soon as the mighty God he saw,
Up sprang the saint in wondering awe.
Mute, with clasped hands, his head he bent,
And stood before him reverent.

His honoured guest he greeted well,
Who bade him of his welfare tell;
Gave water for his blessed feet,
Brought offerings, and prepared a seat.
In honoured place the God Most High
Sate down, and bade the saint sit nigh.
There sate before Válmíki's eyes
The Father of the earth and skies;
But still the hermit's thoughts were bent
On one thing only, all intent
On that poor curlew's mournful fate
Lamenting for her slaughtered mate;
And still his lips, in absent mood,
The verse that told his grief, renewed:
"Woe to the fowler's impious hand
That did the deed that folly planned;
That could to needless death devote
The curlew of the tuneful throat!"

The heavenly Father smiled in glee,
And said, "O best of hermits, see,
A verse, unconscious, thou hast made;
No longer be the task delayed.
Seek not to trace, with labour vain,
The unpremeditated strain.
The tuneful lines thy lips rehearsed
Spontaneous from thy bosom burst.
Then come, O best of seers, relate
The life of Ráma good and great,
The tale that saintly Nárad told,
In all its glorious length unfold.
Of all the deeds his arm has done
Upon this earth, omit not one,
And thus the noble life record
Of that wise, brave, and virtuous lord.
His every act to day displayed,
His secret life to none betrayed:
How Lakshman, how the giants fought;
With high emprise and hidden thought:
And all that Janak's child befell
Where all could see, where none could tell.

The whole of this shall truly be
Made known, O best of saints, to thee.
In all thy poem, through my grace,
No word of falsehood shall have place.
Begin the story, and rehearse
The tale divine in charming verse.
As long as in this firm-set land
The streams shall flow, the mountains stand,
So long throughout the world, be sure,
The great Rámáyan shall endure.
While the Rámáyan's ancient strain
Shall glorious in the earth remain,
To higher spheres shalt thou arise
And dwell with me above the skies."

He spoke, and vanished into air,
And left Válmíki wondering there.
The pupils of the holy man,
Moved by their love of him, began
To chant that verse, and ever more
They marvelled as they sang it o'er:
"Behold, the four-lined balanced rime,
Repeated over many a time,
In words that from the hermit broke
In shock of grief, becomes a śloke."
This measure now Válmíki chose
Wherein his story to compose.
In hundreds of such verses, sweet
With equal lines and even feet,
The saintly poet, lofty-souled,
The glorious deeds of Ráma told.

CANTO
III

The Argument

The hermit thus with watchful heed
    Received the poem's pregnant seed,
    And looked with eager thought around
If fuller knowledge might be found.

His lips with water first bedewed,
He sate, in reverent attitude
On holy grass, the points all bent
Together toward the orient;
And thus in meditation he
Entered the path of poesy.
Then clearly, through his virtue's might,
All lay discovered to his sight,
Whate'er befell, through all their life,
Ráma, his brother, and his wife:
And Daśaratha and each queen
At every time, in every scene:
His people too, of every sort;
The nobles of his princely court:
Whate'er was said, whate'er decreed,
Each time they sate each plan and deed:
For holy thought and fervent rite
Had so refined his keener sight
That by his sanctity his view
The present, past, and future knew,
And he with mental eye could grasp,
Like fruit within his fingers clasp,
The life of Ráma, great and good,
Roaming with Sítá in the wood.
He told, with secret-piercing eyes,
The tale of Ráma's high emprise,

Each listening ear that shall entice,
A sea of pearls of highest price.
Thus good Válmíki, sage divine,
Rehearsed the tale of Raghu's line,
As Nárad, heavenly saint, before
Had traced the story's outline o'er.
He sang of Ráma's princely birth,
His kindness and heroic worth;
His love for all, his patient youth,
His gentleness and constant truth,
And many a tale and legend old
By holy Viśvámitra told.
How Janak's child he wooed and won,
And broke the bow that bent to none.
How he with every virtue fraught
His namesake Ráma met and fought.
The choice of Ráma for the throne;
The malice by Kaikeyí shown,
Whose evil counsel marred the plan
And drove him forth a banisht man.
How the king grieved and groaned, and cried,
And swooned away and pining died.
The subjects' woe when thus bereft;
And how the following crowds he left:
With Guha talked, and firmly stern
Ordered his driver to return.
How Gangá's farther shore he gained;
By Bharadvája entertained,
By whose advice he journeyed still
And came to Chitrakúṭa's hill.
How there he dwelt and built a cot;
How Bharat journeyed to the spot;
His earnest supplication made;
Drink-offerings to their father paid;
The sandals given by Ráma's hand,
As emblems of his right, to stand:
How from his presence Bharat went
And years in Nandigráma spent.
How Ráma entered Daṇḍak wood
And in Sutíkhṇa's presence stood.
The favour Anasúyá showed,

The wondrous balsam she bestowed.
How Śarabhanga's dwelling-place
They sought; saw Indra face to face;
The meeting with Agastya gained;
The heavenly bow from him obtained.
How Ráma with Virádha met;
Their home in Panchavaṭa set.
How Śúrpaṇakhá underwent
The mockery and disfigurement.
Of Triśirá's and Khara's fall,
Of Rávaṇ roused at vengeance call,
Márícha doomed, without escape;
The fair Videhan lady's rape.
How Ráma wept and raved in vain,
And how the Vulture-king was slain.
How Ráma fierce Kabandha slew;
Then to the side of Pampá drew,
Met Hanumán, and her whose vows
Were kept beneath the greenwood boughs.
How Raghu's son, the lofty-souled,
On Pampá's bank wept uncontrolled,
Then journeyed, Rishyamúk to reach,
And of Sugríva then had speech.
The friendship made, which both had sought:
How Báli and Sugríva fought.
How Báli in the strife was slain,
And how Sugríva came to reign.
The treaty, Tára's wild lament;
The rainy nights in watching spent.
The wrath of Raghu's lion son;
The gathering of the hosts in one.
The sending of the spies about,
And all the regions pointed out.
The ring by Ráma's hand bestowed;
The cave wherein the bear abode.
The fast proposed, their lives to end;
Sampati gained to be their friend.

The scaling of the hill, the leap
Of Hanumán across the deep.
Ocean's command that bade them seek

33

Maináka of the lofty peak.
The death of Sinhiká, the sight
Of Lanká with her palace bright
How Hanumán stole in at eve;
His plan the giants to deceive.
How through the square he made his way
To chambers where the women lay,
Within the Aśoka garden came
And there found Ráma's captive dame.
His colloquy with her he sought,
And giving of the ring he brought.
How Sítá gave a gem o'erjoyed;
How Hanumán the grove destroyed.
How giantesses trembling fled,
And servant fiends were smitten dead.
How Hanumán was seized; their ire
When Lanká blazed with hostile fire.
His leap across the sea once more;
The eating of the honey store.
How Ráma he consoled, and how
He showed the gem from Sítá's brow.
With Ocean, Ráma's interview;
The bridge that Nala o'er it threw.
The crossing, and the sitting down
At night round Lanká's royal town.
The treaty with Vibhíshan made:
The plan for Rávan's slaughter laid.
How Kumbhakarṇa in his pride
And Meghanáda fought and died.
How Rávaṇ in the fight was slain,
And captive Sítá brought again.
Vibhíshaṇ set upon the throne;
The flying chariot Pushpak shown.
How Brahmá and the Gods appeared,
And Sítá's doubted honour cleared.
How in the flying car they rode
To Bharadvája's cabin abode.
The Wind-God's son sent on afar;
How Bharat met the flying car.
How Ráma then was king ordained;
The legions their discharge obtained.

How Ráma cast his queen away;
How grew the people's love each day.
Thus did the saint Válmíki tell
Whate'er in Ráma's life befell,
And in the closing verses all
That yet to come will once befall.

The Rhapsodists

When to the end the tale was brought,
Rose in the sage's mind the thought;
"Now who throughout this earth will go,
And tell it forth that all may know?"
As thus he mused with anxious breast,
Behold, in hermit's raiment dressed,
Kuśá and Lava came to greet
Their master and embrace his feet.
The twins he saw, that princely pair
Sweet-voiced, who dwelt beside him there
None for the task could be more fit,
For skilled were they in Holy Writ;
And so the great Rámáyan, fraught
With lore divine, to these he taught:
The lay whose verses sweet and clear
Take with delight the listening ear,
That tell of Sítá's noble life
And Rávan's fall in battle strife.
Great joy to all who hear they bring,
Sweet to recite and sweet to sing.
For music's sevenfold notes are there,
And triple measure, wrought with care
With melody and tone and time,
And flavours that enhance the rime;

Heroic might has ample place,
And loathing of the false and base,
With anger, mirth, and terror, blent
With tenderness, surprise, content.
When, half the hermit's grace to gain,
And half because they loved the strain,
The youth within their hearts had stored
The poem that his lips outpoured,
Válmíki kissed them on the head,
As at his feet they bowed, and said;
"Recite ye this heroic song
In tranquil shades where sages throng:
Recite it where the good resort,
In lowly home and royal court."

The hermit ceased. The tuneful pair,
Like heavenly minstrels sweet and fair,
In music's art divinely skilled,
Their saintly master's word fulfilled.
Like Ráma's self, from whom they came,
They showed their sire in face and frame,

As though from some fair sculptured stone
Two selfsame images had grown.
Sometimes the pair rose up to sing,
Surrounded by a holy ring,
Where seated on the grass had met
Full many a musing anchoret.
Then tears bedimmed those gentle eyes,
As transport took them and surprise,
And as they listened every one
Cried in delight, Well done! Well done!
Those sages versed in holy lore
Praised the sweet minstrels more and more:
And wondered at the singers' skill,
And the bard's verses sweeter still,
Which laid so clear before the eye
The glorious deeds of days gone by.
Thus by the virtuous hermits praised,
Inspirited their voice they raised.
Pleased with the song this holy man

Would give the youths a water-can;
One gave a fair ascetic dress,
Or sweet fruit from the wilderness.
One saint a black-deer's hide would bring,
And one a sacrificial string:
One, a clay pitcher from his hoard,
And one, a twisted munja cord.
One in his joy an axe would find,
One braid, their plaited locks to bind.
One gave a sacrificial cup,
One rope to tie their fagots up;
While fuel at their feet was laid,
Or hermit's stool of fig-tree made.
All gave, or if they gave not, none
Forgot at least a benison.
Some saints, delighted with their lays,
Would promise health and length of days;
Others with surest words would add
Some boon to make their spirit glad.
In such degree of honour then
That song was held by holy men:
That living song which life can give,
By which shall many a minstrel live.
In seat of kings, in crowded hall,
They sang the poem, praised of all.
And Ráma chanced to hear their lay,
While he the votive steed would slay,
And sent fit messengers to bring
The minstrel pair before the king.
They came, and found the monarch high
Enthroned in gold, his brothers nigh;
While many a minister below,
And noble, sate in lengthened row.
The youthful pair awhile he viewed
Graceful in modest attitude,
And then in words like these addressed
His brother Lakshmaṇ and the rest:
"Come, listen to the wondrous strain
Recited by these godlike twain,
Sweet singers of a story fraught
With melody and lofty thought."

The pair, with voices sweet and strong,
Rolled the full tide of noble song,
With tone and accent deftly blent
To suit the changing argument.
Mid that assembly loud and clear
Rang forth that lay so sweet to hear,
That universal rapture stole
Through each man's frame and heart and soul.
"These minstrels, blest with every sign
That marks a high and princely line,
In holy shades who dwell,
Enshrined in Saint Válmíki's lay,
A monument to live for aye,
My deeds in song shall tell."
Thus Ráma spoke: their breasts were fired,
And the great tale, as if inspired,
The youths began to sing,
While every heart with transport swelled,
And mute and rapt attention held
The concourse and the king.

CANTO
V

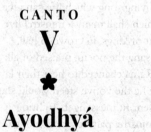

Ayodhyá

"Ikshváku's sons from days of old
Were ever brave and mighty-souled.
The land their arms had made their own
Was bounded by the sea alone.
Their holy works have won them praise,
Through countless years, from Manu's days.
Their ancient sire was Sagar, he
Whose high command dug out the sea:
With sixty thousand sons to throng
Around him as he marched along.

From them this glorious tale proceeds:
The great Rámáyan tells their deeds.
This noble song whose lines contain
Lessons of duty, love, and gain,
We two will now at length recite,
While good men listen with delight.

On Sarjú's bank, of ample size,
The happy realm of Kośal lies,

With fertile length of fair champaign
And flocks and herds and wealth of grain.
There, famous in her old renown,
Ayodhyá stands, the royal town,
In bygone ages built and planned
By sainted Manu's princely hand.
Imperial seat! her walls extend
Twelve measured leagues from end to end,
And three in width from side to side,
With square and palace beautified.
Her gates at even distance stand;
Her ample roads are wisely planned.
Right glorious is her royal street
Where streams allay the dust and heat.
On level ground in even row
Her houses rise in goodly show:
Terrace and palace, arch and gate
The queenly city decorate.
High are her ramparts, strong and vast,
By ways at even distance passed,
With circling moat, both deep and wide,
And store of weapons fortified.

King Daśaratha, lofty-souled,
That city guarded and controlled,
With towering Sál trees belted round,
And many a grove and pleasure ground,
As royal Indra, throned on high,
Rules his fair city in the sky.
She seems a painted city, fair
With chess-board line and even square.

And cool boughs shade the lovely lake
Where weary men their thirst may slake.
There gilded chariots gleam and shine,
And stately piles the Gods enshrine.
There gay sleek people ever throng
To festival and dance and song.
A mine is she of gems and sheen,
The darling home of Fortune's Queen.
With noblest sort of drink and meat,
The fairest rice and golden wheat,
And fragrant with the chaplet's scent
With holy oil and incense blent.
With many an elephant and steed,
And wains for draught and cars for speed.
With envoys sent by distant kings,
And merchants with their precious things
With banners o'er her roofs that play,
And weapons that a hundred slay;
All warlike engines framed by man,
And every class of artisan.
A city rich beyond compare
With bards and minstrels gathered there,
And men and damsels who entrance
The soul with play and song and dance.
In every street is heard the lute,
The drum, the tabret, and the flute,
The Veda chanted soft and low,
The ringing of the archer's bow;
With bands of godlike heroes skilled
In every warlike weapon, filled,
And kept by warriors from the foe,
As Nágas guard their home below.
There wisest Bráhmans evermore
The flame of worship feed,
And versed in all the Vedas' lore,
Their lives of virtue lead.
Truthful and pure, they freely give;
They keep each sense controlled,
And in their holy fervour live
Like the great saints of old.

40

VI

The King

There reigned a king of name revered,
To country and to town endeared,
Great Daśaratha, good and sage,
Well read in Scripture's holy page:

Upon his kingdom's weal intent,
Mighty and brave and provident;
The pride of old Ikshváku's seed
For lofty thought and righteous deed.
Peer of the saints, for virtues famed,
For foes subdued and passions tamed:
A rival in his wealth untold
Of Indra and the Lord of Gold.
Like Manu first of kings, he reigned,
And worthily his state maintained.
For firm and just and ever true
Love, duty, gain he kept in view,
And ruled his city rich and free,
Like Indra's Amarávatí.
And worthy of so fair a place
There dwelt a just and happy race
With troops of children blest.
Each man contented sought no more,
Nor longed with envy for the store
By richer friends possessed.
For poverty was there unknown,
And each man counted as his own
Kine, steeds, and gold, and grain.
All dressed in raiment bright and clean,
And every townsman might be seen
With earrings, wreath, or chain.

None deigned to feed on broken fare,
And none was false or stingy there.
A piece of gold, the smallest pay,
Was earned by labour for a day.
On every arm were bracelets worn,
And none was faithless or forsworn,
A braggart or unkind.
None lived upon another's wealth,
None pined with dread or broken health,
Or dark disease of mind.
High-souled were all. The slanderous word,
The boastful lie, were never heard.
Each man was constant to his vows,
And lived devoted to his spouse.
No other love his fancy knew,
And she was tender, kind, and true.
Her dames were fair of form and face,
With charm of wit and gentle grace,
With modest raiment simply neat,
And winning manners soft and sweet.
The twice-born sages, whose delight
Was Scripture's page and holy rite,
Their calm and settled course pursued,
Nor sought the menial multitude.
In many a Scripture each was versed,
And each the flame of worship nursed,
And gave with lavish hand.
Each paid to Heaven the offerings due,
And none was godless or untrue
In all that holy band.
To Bráhmans, as the laws ordain,
The Warrior caste were ever fain
The reverence due to pay;
And these the Vaiśyas' peaceful crowd,
Who trade and toil for gain, were proud
To honour and obey;
And all were by the Śúdras served,
Who never from their duty swerved,
Their proper worship all addressed
To Bráhman, spirits, God, and guest.
Pure and unmixt their rites remained,

Their race's honour ne'er was stained.
Cheered by his grandsons, sons, and wife,
Each passed a long and happy life.
Thus was that famous city held
By one who all his race excelled,
Blest in his gentle reign,
As the whole land aforetime swayed
By Manu, prince of men, obeyed
Her king from main to main.
And heroes kept her, strong and brave,
As lions guard their mountain cave:
Fierce as devouring flame they burned,
And fought till death, but never turned.
Horses had she of noblest breed,
Like Indra's for their form and speed,
From Váhlí's hills and Sindhu's sand,
Vanáyu and Kámboja's land.

Her noble elephants had strayed
Through Vindhyan and Himálayan shade,
Gigantic in their bulk and height,
Yet gentle in their matchless might.
They rivalled well the world-spread fame
Of the great stock from which they came,
Of Váman, vast of size,
Of Mahápadma's glorious line,
Thine, Anjan, and, Airávat, thine.
Upholders of the skies.
With those, enrolled in fourfold class,
Who all their mighty kin surpass,
Whom men Matangas name,
And Mrigas spotted black and white,
And Bhadras of unwearied might,
And Mandras hard to tame.
Thus, worthy of the name she bore,
Ayodhyá for a league or more
Cast a bright glory round,
Where Daśaratha wise and great
Governed his fair ancestral state,
With every virtue crowned.
Like Indra in the skies he reigned

In that good town whose wall contained
High domes and turrets proud,
With gates and arcs of triumph decked,
And sturdy barriers to protect
Her gay and countless crowd.

CANTO
VII

★

The Ministers

T wo sages, holy saints, had he,
    His ministers and priests to be:
    Vaśishṭha, faithful to advise,
And Vámadeva, Scripture-wise.
Eight other lords around him stood,
All skilled to counsel, wise and good:
Jayanta, Vijay, Dhrishṭi bold
In fight, affairs of war controlled:
Siddhárth and Arthasádhak true
Watched o'er expense and revenue,
And Dharmapál and wise Aśok
Of right and law and justice spoke.
With these the sage Sumantra, skilled
To urge the car, high station filled.
All these in knowledge duly trained
Each passion and each sense restrained:
With modest manners, nobly bred
Each plan and nod and look they read,
Upon their neighbours' good intent,
Most active and benevolent:
As sit the Vasus round their king,
They sate around him counselling.
They ne'er in virtue's loftier pride
Another's lowly gifts decried.
In fair and seemly garb arrayed,

44

No weak uncertain plans they made.
Well skilled in business, fair and just,
They gained the people's love and trust,
And thus without oppression stored
The swelling treasury of their lord.
Bound in sweet friendship each to each,
They spoke kind thoughts in gentle speech.
They looked alike with equal eye
On every caste, on low and high.
Devoted to their king, they sought,
Ere his tongue spoke, to learn his thought,
And knew, as each occasion rose,
To hide their counsel or disclose.
In foreign lands or in their own
Whatever passed, to them was known.
By secret spies they timely knew
What men were doing or would do.
Skilled in the grounds of war and peace
They saw the monarch's state increase,
Watching his weal with conquering eye
That never let occasion by,
While nature lent her aid to bless
Their labours with unbought success.
Never for anger, lust, or gain,
Would they their lips with falsehood stain.
Inclined to mercy they could scan
The weakness and the strength of man.
They fairly judged both high and low,
And ne'er would wrong a guiltless foe;
Yet if a fault were proved, each one
Would punish e'en his own dear son.
But there and in the kingdom's bound
No thief or man impure was found:
None of loose life or evil fame,
No tempter of another's dame.
Contented with their lot each caste

Calm days in blissful quiet passed;
And, all in fitting tasks employed,
Country and town deep rest enjoyed,
With these wise lords around his throne

The monarch justly reigned,
And making every heart his own
The love of all men gained.
With trusty agents, as beseems,
Each distant realm he scanned,
As the sun visits with his beams
Each corner of the land.
Ne'er would he on a mightier foe
With hostile troops advance,
Nor at an equal strike a blow
In war's delusive chance.
These lords in council bore their part
With ready brain and faithful heart,
With skill and knowledge, sense and tact,
Good to advise and bold to act.
And high and endless fame he won
With these to guide his schemes,
As, risen in his might, the sun
Wins glory with his beams.

CANTO
VIII

Sumantra's Speech

But splendid, just, and great of mind,
The childless king for offspring pined.
No son had he his name to grace,
Transmitter of his royal race.
Long had his anxious bosom wrought,
And as he pondered rose the thought:
"A votive steed 'twere good to slay,
So might a son the gift repay."
Before his lords his plan he laid,
And bade them with their wisdom aid:
Then with these words Sumantra, best

46

Of royal counsellors, addressed:
"Hither, Vaśishṭha at their head,
Let all my priestly guides be led."
To him Sumantra made reply:
"Hear, Sire, a tale of days gone by.
To many a sage in time of old,
Sanatkumár, the saint, foretold
How from thine ancient line, O King,
A son, when years came round, should spring.
"Here dwells," 'twas thus the seer began,
"Of Kaśyap's race, a holy man,
Vibhâṇdak named: to him shall spring
A son, the famous Rishyaśring.
Bred with the deer that round him roam,
The wood shall be that hermit's home.
To him no mortal shall be known
Except his holy sire alone.
Still by those laws shall he abide
Which lives of youthful Bráhmans guide,
Obedient to the strictest rule
That forms the young ascetic's school:
And all the wondering world shall hear
Of his stern life and penance drear;
His care to nurse the holy fire
And do the bidding of his sire.
Then, seated on the Angas' throne,
Shall Lomapád to fame be known.
But folly wrought by that great king
A plague upon the land shall bring;
No rain for many a year shall fall
And grievous drought shall ruin all.
The troubled king with many a prayer
Shall bid the priests some cure declare:
"The lore of Heaven 'tis yours to know,
Nor are ye blind to things below:
Declare, O holy men, the way
This plague to expiate and stay."
Those best of Bráhmans shall reply:
"By every art, O Monarch, try
Hither to bring Vibhâṇdak's child,
Persuaded, captured, or beguiled.

And when the boy is hither led
To him thy daughter duly wed."

But how to bring that wondrous boy
His troubled thoughts will long employ,
And hopeless to achieve the task
He counsel of his lords will ask,
And bid his priests and servants bring
With honour saintly Rishyaśring.
But when they hear the monarch's speech,
All these their master will beseech,
With trembling hearts and looks of woe,
To spare them, for they fear to go.
And many a plan will they declare
And crafty plots will frame,
And promise fair to show him there,
Unforced, with none to blame.
On every word his lords shall say,
The king will meditate,
And on the third returning day
Recall them to debate.
Then this shall be the plan agreed,
That damsels shall be sent
Attired in holy hermits' weed,
And skilled in blandishment,
That they the hermit may beguile
With every art and amorous wile

Whose use they know so well,
And by their witcheries seduce
The unsuspecting young recluse
To leave his father's cell.
Then when the boy with willing feet
Shall wander from his calm retreat
And in that city stand,
The troubles of the king shall end,
And streams of blessed rain descend
Upon the thirsty land.
Thus shall the holy Rishyaśring
To Lomapád, the mighty king,
By wedlock be allied;

For Śántá, fairest of the fair,
In mind and grace beyond compare,
Shall be his royal bride.
He, at the Offering of the Steed,
The flames with holy oil shall feed,
And for King Daśaratha gain
Sons whom his prayers have begged in vain."
"I have repeated, Sire, thus far,
The words of old Sanatkumár,
In order as he spoke them then
Amid the crowd of holy men."
Then Daśaratha cried with joy,
"Say how they brought the hermit boy."

CANTO

IX

Rishyasring

T he wise Sumantra, thus addressed,
     Unfolded at the king's behest
     The plan the lords in council laid
To draw the hermit from the shade:
"The priest, amid the lordly crowd,
To Lomapád thus spoke aloud:
"Hear, King, the plot our thoughts have framed,
A harmless trick by all unblamed.
Far from the world that hermit's child
Lives lonely in the distant wild:
A stranger to the joys of sense,
His bliss is pain and abstinence;
And all unknown are women yet
To him, a holy anchoret.
The gentle passions we will wake
That with resistless influence shake
The hearts of men; and he

Drawn by enchantment strong and sweet
Shall follow from his lone retreat,
And come and visit thee.
Let ships be formed with utmost care
That artificial trees may bear,
And sweet fruit deftly made;
Let goodly raiment, rich and rare,
And flowers, and many a bird be there
Beneath the leafy shade.
Upon the ships thus decked a band
Of young and lovely girls shall stand,
Rich in each charm that wakes desire,
And eyes that burn with amorous fire;
Well skilled to sing, and play, and dance
And ply their trade with smile and glance
Let these, attired in hermits' dress,
Betake them to the wilderness,
And bring the boy of life austere
A voluntary captive here."
He ended; and the king agreed,
By the priest's counsel won.
And all the ministers took heed
To see his bidding done.
In ships with wondrous art prepared
Away the lovely women fared,
And soon beneath the shade they stood
Of the wild, lonely, dreary wood.
And there the leafy cot they found
Where dwelt the devotee,
And looked with eager eyes around
The hermit's son to see.
Still, of Vibhándak sore afraid,
They hid behind the creepers' shade.
But when by careful watch they knew
The elder saint was far from view,
With bolder steps they ventured nigh
To catch the youthful hermit's eye.
Then all the damsels, blithe and gay,
At various games began to play.
They tossed the flying ball about
With dance and song and merry shout,

And moved, their scented tresses bound
With wreaths, in mazy motion round.
Some girls as if by love possessed,
Sank to the earth in feigned unrest,
Up starting quickly to pursue
Their intermitted game anew.
It was a lovely sight to see
Those fair ones, as they played,
While fragrant robes were floating free,
And bracelets clashing in their glee
A pleasant tinkling made.
The anklet's chime, the Koïl's cry
With music filled the place
As 'twere some city in the sky
Which heavenly minstrels grace.
With each voluptuous art they strove
To win the tenant of the grove,
And with their graceful forms inspire
His modest soul with soft desire.
With arch of brow, with beck and smile,
With every passion-waking wile

Of glance and lotus hand,
With all enticements that excite
The longing for unknown delight
Which boys in vain withstand.
Forth came the hermit's son to view
The wondrous sight to him so new,
And gazed in rapt surprise,
For from his natal hour till then
On woman or the sons of men
He ne'er had cast his eyes.
He saw them with their waists so slim,
With fairest shape and faultless limb,
In variegated robes arrayed,
And sweetly singing as they played.
Near and more near the hermit drew,
And watched them at their game,
And stronger still the impulse grew
To question whence they came.
They marked the young ascetic gaze

With curious eye and wild amaze,
And sweet the long-eyed damsels sang,
And shrill their merry laughter rang.
Then came they nearer to his side,
And languishing with passion cried:
"Whose son, O youth, and who art thou,
Come suddenly to join us now?
And why dost thou all lonely dwell
In the wild wood? We pray thee, tell,
We wish to know thee, gentle youth;
Come, tell us, if thou wilt, the truth."
He gazed upon that sight he ne'er
Had seen before, of girls so fair,
And out of love a longing rose
His sire and lineage to disclose:
"My father," thus he made reply,
"Is Kaśyap's son, a saint most high,
Vibhándak styled; from him I came,
And Rishyaśring he calls my name.
Our hermit cot is near this place:
Come thither, O ye fair of face;
There be it mine, with honour due,
Ye gentle youths, to welcome you."
They heard his speech, and gave consent,
And gladly to his cottage went.
Vibhándak's son received them well
Beneath the shelter of his cell
With guest-gift, water for their feet,
And woodland fruit and roots to eat,
They smiled, and spoke sweet words like these,
Delighted with his courtesies:
"We too have goodly fruit in store,
Grown on the trees that shade our door;
Come, if thou wilt, kind Hermit, haste
The produce of our grove to taste;
And let, O good Ascetic, first
This holy water quench thy thirst."
They spoke, and gave him comfits sweet
Prepared ripe fruits to counterfeit;
And many a dainty cate beside
And luscious mead their stores supplied.

The seeming fruits, in taste and look,
The unsuspecting hermit took,
For, strange to him, their form beguiled
The dweller in the lonely wild.
Then round his neck fair arms were flung,
And there the laughing damsels clung,
And pressing nearer and more near
With sweet lips whispered at his ear;
While rounded limb and swelling breast
The youthful hermit softly pressed.
The pleasing charm of that strange bowl,
The touch of a tender limb,
Over his yielding spirit stole
And sweetly vanquished him.
But vows, they said, must now be paid;
They bade the boy farewell,
And, of the aged saint afraid,
Prepared to leave the dell.
With ready guile they told him where
Their hermit dwelling lay:
Then, lest the sire should find them there,
Sped by wild paths away.
They fled and left him there alone
By longing love possessed;
And with a heart no more his own
He roamed about distressed.
The aged saint came home, to find
The hermit boy distraught,
Revolving in his troubled mind
One solitary thought.
"Why dost thou not, my son," he cried,
"Thy due obeisance pay?
Why do I see thee in the tide
Of whelming thought to-day?
A devotee should never wear
A mien so sad and strange.
Come, quickly, dearest child, declare
The reason of the change."
And Rishyaśring, when questioned thus,
Made answer in this wise:
"O sire, there came to visit us

53

Some men with lovely eyes.
About my neck soft arms they wound
And kept me tightly held
To tender breasts so soft and round,
That strangely heaved and swelled.
They sing more sweetly as they dance
Than e'er I heard till now,
And play with many a sidelong glance
And arching of the brow."
"My son," said he, "thus giants roam
Where holy hermits are,
And wander round their peaceful home
Their rites austere to mar.
I charge thee, thou must never lay
Thy trust in them, dear boy:
They seek thee only to betray,
And woo but to destroy."
Thus having warned him of his foes
That night at home he spent.
And when the morrow's sun arose

Forth to the forest went.
But Rishyaśring with eager pace
Sped forth and hurried to the place
Where he those visitants had seen
Of daintly waist and charming mien.
When from afar they saw the son
Of Saint Vibhándak toward them run,
To meet the hermit boy they hied,
And hailed him with a smile, and cried:
"O come, we pray, dear lord, behold
Our lovely home of which we told
Due honour there to thee we'll pay,
And speed thee on thy homeward way."
Pleased with the gracious words they said
He followed where the damsels led.
As with his guides his steps he bent,
That Bráhman high of worth,
A flood of rain from heaven was sent
That gladdened all the earth.

Vibhándak took his homeward road,
And wearied by the heavy load
Of roots and woodland fruit he bore
Entered at last his cottage door.
Fain for his son he looked around,
But desolate the cell he found.
He stayed not then to bathe his feet,
Though fainting with the toil and heat,
But hurried forth and roamed about
Calling the boy with cry and shout,
He searched the wood, but all in vain;
Nor tidings of his son could gain.
One day beyond the forest's bound
The wandering saint a village found,
And asked the swains and neatherds there
Who owned the land so rich and fair,
With all the hamlets of the plain,
And herds of kine and fields of grain.
They listened to the hermit's words,
And all the guardians of the herds,
With suppliant hands together pressed,
This answer to the saint addressed:
"The Angas' lord who bears the name
Of Lomapád, renowned by fame,
Bestowed these hamlets with their kine
And all their riches, as a sign
Of grace, on Rishyaśring: and he
Vibhándak's son is said to be."
The hermit with exulting breast
The mighty will of fate confessed,
By meditation's eye discerned;
And cheerful to his home returned.

A stately ship, at early morn,
The hermit's son away had borne.
Loud roared the clouds, as on he sped,
The sky grew blacker overhead;
Till, as he reached the royal town,
A mighty flood of rain came down.
By the great rain the monarch's mind
The coming of his guest divined.

To meet the honoured youth he went,
And low to earth his head he bent.
With his own priest to lead the train,
He gave the gift high guests obtain.
And sought, with all who dwelt within
The city walls, his grace to win.
He fed him with the daintiest fare,
He served him with unceasing care,
And ministered with anxious eyes
Lest anger in his breast should rise;
And gave to be the Bráhman's bride
His own fair daughter, lotus-eyed.

Thus loved and honoured by the king,
The glorious Bráhman Rishyaśring
Passed in that royal town his life
With Śántá his beloved wife."

CANTO

X

Rishyasring Invited

"Again, O best of kings, give ear:
My saving words attentive hear,
And listen to the tale of old
By that illustrious Bráhman told.
"Of famed Ikshváku's line shall spring
('Twas thus he spoke) a pious king,
Named Daśaratha, good and great,
True to his word and fortunate.
He with the Angas' mighty lord
Shall ever live in sweet accord,
And his a daughter fair shall be,
Śántá of happy destiny.
But Lomapád, the Angas' chief,

Still pining in his childless grief,
To Daśaratha thus shall say:
"Give me thy daughter, friend, I pray,
Thy Śántá of the tranquil mind,
The noblest one of womankind."

The father, swift to feel for woe,
Shall on his friend his child bestow;
And he shall take her and depart
To his own town with joyous heart.
The maiden home in triumph led,
To Rishyaśring the king shall wed.
And he with loving joy and pride
Shall take her for his honoured bride.
And Daśaratha to a rite
That best of Bráhmans shall invite
With supplicating prayer,
To celebrate the sacrifice
To win him sons and Paradise,
That he will fain prepare.

From him the lord of men at length
The boon he seeks shall gain,
And see four sons of boundless strength
His royal line maintain."
"Thus did the godlike saint of old
The will of fate declare,
And all that should befall unfold
Amid the sages there.
O Prince supreme of men, go thou,
Consult thy holy guide,
And win, to aid thee in thy vow,
This Bráhman to thy side."
Sumantra's counsel, wise and good,
King Daśaratha heard,
Then by Vaśishṭha's side he stood
And thus with him conferred:
"Sumantra counsels thus: do thou
My priestly guide, the plan allow."
Vaśishṭha gave his glad consent,
And forth the happy monarch went

With lords and servants on the road
That led to Rishyaśring's abode.
Forests and rivers duly past,
He reached the distant town at last
Of Lomapád the Angas' king,
And entered it with welcoming.
On through the crowded streets he came,
And, radiant as the kindled flame,
He saw within the monarch's house
The hermit's son most glorious.
There Lomapád, with joyful breast,
To him all honour paid,
For friendship for his royal guest
His faithful bosom swayed.
Thus entertained with utmost care
Seven days, or eight, he tarried there,
And then that best of men thus broke
His purpose to the king, and spoke:
"O King of men, mine ancient friend,
(Thus Daśaratha prayed)
Thy Śántá with her husband send
My sacrifice to aid."
Said he who ruled the Angas, Yea,
And his consent was won:
And then at once he turned away
To warn the hermit's son.
He told him of their ties beyond
Their old affection's faithful bond:
"This king," he said, "from days of old
A well beloved friend I hold.
To me this pearl of dames he gave
From childless woe mine age to save,
The daughter whom he loved so much,
Moved by compassion's gentle touch.
In him thy Śántás father see:
As I am even so is he.
For sons the childless monarch yearns:
To thee alone for help he turns.
Go thou, the sacred rite ordain
To win the sons he prays to gain:

Go, with thy wife thy succour lend,
And give his vows a blissful end."
The hermit's son with quick accord
Obeyed the Angas' mighty lord,
And with fair Śántá at his side
To Daśaratha's city hied.
Each king, with suppliant hands upheld,
Gazed on the other's face:
And then by mutual love impelled
Met in a close embrace.
Then Daśaratha's thoughtful care,
Before he parted thence,
Bade trusty servants homeward bear
The glad intelligence:
"Let all the town be bright and gay
With burning incense sweet;
Let banners wave, and water lay
The dust in every street."
Glad were the citizens to learn
The tidings of their lord's return,
And through the city every man
Obediently his task began.
And fair and bright Ayodhyá showed,
As following his guest he rode
Through the full streets where shell and drum
Proclaimed aloud the king was come.
And all the people with delight
Kept gazing on their king,
Attended by that youth so bright,
The glorious Rishyaśring.
When to his home the king had brought
The hermit's saintly son,
He deemed that all his task was wrought,
And all he prayed for won.
And lords who saw that stranger dame
So beautiful to view,
Rejoiced within their hearts, and came
And paid her honour too.
There Rishyaśring passed blissful days,
Graced like the king with love and praise

And shone in glorious light with her,
Sweet Śántá, for his minister,
As Brahmá's son Vaśishṭha, he
Who wedded Saint Arundhatí.

The Sacrifice Decreed

The Dewy Season came and went;
 The spring returned again:
 Then would the king, with mind intent,
His sacrifice ordain.

He came to Rishyaśring, and bowed
To him of look divine,
And bade him aid his offering vowed
For heirs, to save his line.
Nor would the youth his aid deny:
He spake the monarch fair,
And prayed him for that rite so high
All requisites prepare.
The king to wise Sumantra cried
Who stood aye ready near;
"Go summon quick each holy guide,
To counsel and to hear."
Obedient to his lord's behest
Away Sumantra sped,
And brought Vaśishṭha and the rest,
In Scripture deeply read.
Suyajña, Vámadeva came,
Jávali, Kaśyap's son,
And old Vaśishṭha, dear to fame,
Obedient every one.
King Daśaratha met them there

And duly honoured each,
And spoke in pleasant words his fair
And salutary speech:
"In childless longing doomed to pine,
No happiness, O lords, is mine.
So have I for this cause decreed
To slay the sacrificial steed.
Fain would I pay that offering high
Wherein the horse is doomed to die,
With Rishyaśring his aid to lend,
And with your glory to befriend."
With loud applause each holy man
Received his speech, approved the plan,
And, by the wise Vaśishtha led,
Gave praises to the king, and said:
"The sons thou cravest shalt thou see,
Of fairest glory, born to thee,
Whose holy feelings bid thee take
This righteous course for offspring's sake."
Cheered by the ready praise of those
Whose aid he sought, his spirits rose,
And thus the king his speech renewed
With looks of joy and gratitude:
"Let what the coming rites require
Be ready as the priests desire,
And let the horse, ordained to bleed,
With fitting guard and priest, be freed,
Yonder on Sarjú's northern side
The sacrificial ground provide;
And let the saving rites, that naught
Ill-omened may occur, be wrought.
The offering I announce to-day
Each lord of earth may claim to pay,
Provided that his care can guard
The holy rite by flaws unmarred.
For wandering fiends, whose watchful spite
Waits eagerly to spoil each rite,
Hunting with keenest eye detect
The slightest slip, the least neglect;
And when the sacred work is crossed
The workman is that moment lost.

Let preparation due be made:
Your powers the charge can meet:
That so the noble rite be paid
In every point complete."
And all the Bráhmans answered, Yea,
His mandate honouring,
And gladly promised to obey
The order of the king.
They cried with voices raised aloud:
"Success attend thine aim!"
Then bade farewell, and lowly bowed,
And hastened whence they came.
King Daśaratha went within,
His well loved wives to see:
And said: "Your lustral rites begin,
For these shall prosper me.
A glorious offering I prepare
That precious fruit of sons may bear."
Their lily faces brightened fast
Those pleasant words to hear,
As lilies, when the winter's past,
In lovelier hues appear.

CANTO
XII

The Sacrifice Begun

Again the spring with genial heat
Returning made the year complete.
To win him sons, without delay
His vow the king resolved to pay:
And to Vaśishṭha, saintly man,
In modest words this speech began:
"Prepare the rite with all things fit
As is ordained in Holy Writ,

And keep with utmost care afar
Whate'er its sacred forms might mar.
Thou art, my lord, my trustiest guide,
Kind-hearted, and my friend beside;
So is it meet thou undertake
This heavy task for duty's sake."
Then he, of twice-born men the best,
His glad assent at once expressed:
"Fain will I do whate'er may be
Desired, O honoured King, by thee."
To ancient priests he spoke, who, trained
In holy rites, deep skill had gained:
"Here guards be stationed, good and sage
Religious men of trusted age.
And various workmen send and call,
Who frame the door and build the wall:
With men of every art and trade,
Who read the stars and ply the spade,

And mimes and minstrels hither bring,
And damsels trained to dance and sing."
Then to the learned men he said,
In many a page of Scripture read:
"Be yours each rite performed to see
According to the king's decree.
And stranger Bráhmans quickly call
To this great rite that welcomes all.
Pavilions for the princes, decked
With art and ornament, erect,
And handsome booths by thousands made
The Bráhman visitors to shade,
Arranged in order side by side,
With meat and drink and all supplied.
And ample stables we shall need
For many an elephant and steed:
And chambers where the men may lie,
And vast apartments, broad and high,
Fit to receive the countless bands
Of warriors come from distant lands.
For our own people too provide
Sufficient tents, extended wide,

And stores of meat and drink prepare,
And all that can be needed there.
And food in plenty must be found
For guests from all the country round.
Of various viands presents make,
For honour, not for pity's sake,
That fit regard and worship be
Paid to each caste in due degree.
And let not wish or wrath excite
Your hearts the meanest guest to slight;
But still observe with special grace
Those who obtain the foremost place,
Whether for happier skill in art
Or bearing in the rite their part.
Do you, I pray, with friendly mind
Perform the task to you assigned,
And work the rite, as bids the law,
Without omission, slip, or flaw."
They answered: "As thou seest fit
So will we do and naught omit."
The sage Vaśiṣṭha then addressed
Sumantra called at his behest:
"The princes of the earth invite,
And famous lords who guard the rite,
Priest, Warrior, Merchant, lowly thrall,
In countless thousands summon all.
Where'er their home be, far or near,
Gather the good with honour here,
And Janak, whose imperial sway
The men of Míthilá obey.
The firm of vow, the dread of foes,
Who all the lore of Scripture knows,
Invite him here with honour high,
King Daśaratha's old ally.
And Káśi's lord of gentle speech,
Who finds a pleasant word for each,
In length of days our monarch's peer,
Illustrious king, invite him here.
The father of our ruler's bride,
Known for his virtues far and wide,

The king whom Kekaya's realms obey,
Him with his son invite, I pray.
And Lomapád the Angas' king,
True to his vows and godlike, bring.
For be thine invitations sent
To west and south and orient.
Call those who rule Suráshtra's land,
Suvíra's realm and Sindhu's strand,
And all the kings of earth beside
In friendship's bonds with us allied:
Invite them all to hasten in
With retinue and kith and kin."
Vaśishtha's speech without delay
Sumantra bent him to obey.
And sent his trusty envoys forth
Eastward and westward, south and north.
Obedient to the saint's request
Himself he hurried forth, and pressed
Each nobler chief and lord and king
To hasten to the gathering.
Before the saint Vaśishtha stood
All those who wrought with stone and wood,
And showed the work which every one
In furtherance of the rite had done,
Rejoiced their ready zeal to see,
Thus to the craftsmen all said he:
"I charge ye, masters, see to this,
That there be nothing done amiss,
And this, I pray, in mind be borne,
That not one gift ye give in scorn:
Whenever scorn a gift attends
Great sin is his who thus offends."
And now some days and nights had past,
And kings began to gather fast,
And precious gems in liberal store
As gifts to Daśaratha bore.
Then joy thrilled through Vaśishtha's breast
As thus the monarch he addressed:
"Obedient to thy high decree
The kings, my lord, are come to thee.

65

And it has been my care to greet
And honour all with reverence meet.
Thy servants' task is ended quite,
And all is ready for the rite.
Come forth then to the sacred ground
Where all in order will be found."
Then Rishyaśring confirmed the tale:
Nor did their words to move him fail.
The stars propitious influence lent
When forth the world's great ruler went.
Then by the sage Vaśishṭha led
The priest begun to speed
Those glorious rites wherein is shed
The lifeblood of the steed.

CANTO
XIII

The Sacrifice Finished

The circling year had filled its course,
And back was brought the wandering horse:
Then upon Sarjú's northern strand
Began the rite the king had planned.
With Rishyaśring the forms to guide,
The Bráhmans to their task applied,
At that great offering of the steed
Their lofty-minded king decreed.
The priests, who all the Scripture knew,
Performed their part in order due,
And circled round in solemn train
As precepts of the law ordain.
Pravargya rites were duly sped:
For Upasads the flames were fed.
Then from the plant the juice was squeezed,
And those high saints with minds well pleased

Performed the mystic rites begun
With bathing ere the rise of sun
They gave the portion Indra's claim,
And hymned the King whom none can blame.
The mid-day bathing followed next,
Observed as bids the holy text.
Then the good priests with utmost care,
In form that Scripture's rules declare,
For the third time pure water shed
On high souled Daśaratha's head.
Then Rishyaśring and all the rest
To Indra and the Gods addressed
Their sweet-toned hymn of praise and prayer,
And called them in the rite to share.
With sweetest song and hymn entoned
They gave the Gods in heaven enthroned,
As duty bids, the gifts they claim,
The holy oil that feeds the flame.
And many an offering there was paid,
And not one slip in all was made.
For with most careful heed they saw
That all was done by Veda law.
None, all those days, was seen oppressed
By hunger or by toil distressed.
Why speak of human kind? No beast
Was there that lacked an ample feast.
For there was store for all who came,
For orphan child and lonely dame;
The old and young were well supplied,
The poor and hungry satisfied.
Throughout the day ascetics fed,
And those who roam to beg their bread:
While all around the cry was still,
"Give forth, give forth," and "Eat your fill."
"Give forth with liberal hand the meal,
And various robes in largess deal."
Urged by these cries on every side
Unweariedly their task they plied:
And heaps of food like hills in size
In boundless plenty met the eyes:
And lakes of sauce, each day renewed,

Refreshed the weary multitude.
And strangers there from distant lands,
And women folk in crowded bands
The best of food and drink obtained
At the great rite the king ordained.
Apart from all, the Bráhmans there,
Thousands on thousands, took their share
Of various dainties sweet to taste,
On plates of gold and silver placed,
All ready set, as, when they willed,
The twice-born men their places filled.
And servants in fair garments dressed
Waited upon each Bráhman guest.
Of cheerful mind and mien were they,
With gold and jewelled earrings gay.
The best of Bráhmans praised the fare
Of countless sorts, of flavour rare:
And thus to Raghu's son they cried:
"We bless thee, and are satisfied."
Between the rites some Bráhmans spent
The time in learned argument,

With ready flow of speech, sedate,
And keen to vanquish in debate.
There day by day the holy train
Performed all rites as rules ordain.
No priest in all that host was found
But kept the vows that held him bound:
None, but the holy Vedas knew,
And all their six-fold science too.
No Bráhman there was found unfit
To speak with eloquence and wit.
And now the appointed time came near
The sacrificial posts to rear.
They brought them, and prepared to fix
Of Bel and Khádir six and six;
Six, made of the Paláśa tree,
Of Fig-wood one, apart to be:
Of Sleshmát and of Devadár
One column each, the mightiest far:

So thick the two, the arms of man
Their ample girth would fail to span.
All these with utmost care were wrought
By hand of priests in Scripture taught,
And all with gold were gilded bright
To add new splendour to the rite:
Twenty-and-one those stakes in all,
Each one-and-twenty cubits tall:
And one-and-twenty ribbons there
Hung on the pillars, bright and fair.
Firm in the earth they stood at last,
Where cunning craftsmen fixed them fast;
And there unshaken each remained,
Octagonal and smoothly planed.
Then ribbons over all were hung,
And flowers and scent around them flung.
Thus decked they cast a glory forth
Like the great saints who star the north.
The sacrificial altar then
Was raised by skilful twice-born men,
In shape and figure to behold
An eagle with his wings of gold,
With twice nine pits and formed three-fold
Each for some special God, beside
The pillars were the victims tied;
The birds that roam the wood, the air,
The water, and the land were there,
And snakes and things of reptile birth,
And healing herbs that spring from earth:
As texts prescribe, in Scripture found,
Three hundred victims there were bound.
The steed devoted to the host
Of Gods, the gem they honour most,
Was duly sprinkled. Then the Queen
Kauśalyá, with delighted mien,
With reverent steps around him paced,
And with sweet wreaths the victim graced;
Then with three swords in order due
She smote the steed with joy, and slew.
That night the queen, a son to gain,

With calm and steady heart was fain
By the dead charger's side to stay
From evening till the break of day.
Then came three priests, their care to lead
The other queens to touch the steed,
Upon Kauśalyá to attend,
Their company and aid to lend.
As by the horse she still reclined,
With happy mien and cheerful mind,
With Rishyaśring the twice-born came
And praised and blessed the royal dame.
The priest who well his duty knew,
And every sense could well subdue,
From out the bony chambers freed
And boiled the marrow of the steed.
Above the steam the monarch bent,
And, as he smelt the fragrant scent,
In time and order drove afar
All error that his hopes could mar.
Then sixteen priests together came
And cast into the sacred flame
The severed members of the horse,
Made ready all in ordered course.
On piles of holy Fig-tree raised

The meaner victims' bodies blazed:
The steed, of all the creatures slain,
Alone required a pile of cane.
Three days, as is by law decreed,
Lasted that Offering of the Steed.
The Chatushṭom began the rite,
And when the sun renewed his light,
The Ukthya followed: after came
The Atirátra's holy flame.
These were the rites, and many more
Arranged by light of holy lore,
The Aptoryám of mighty power,
And, each performed in proper hour,
The Abhijit and Viśvajit
With every form and service fit;
And with the sacrifice at night

The Jyotishṭom and Áyus rite.
The task was done, as laws prescribe:
The monarch, glory of his tribe,
Bestowed the land in liberal grants
Upon the sacred ministrants.
He gave the region of the east,
His conquest, to the Hotri priest.
The west, the celebrant obtained:
The south, the priest presiding gained:
The northern region was the share
Of him who chanted forth the prayer,
Thus did each priest obtain his meed
At the great Slaughter of the Steed,
Ordained, the best of all to be,
By self-existent deity.
Ikshváku's son with joyful mind
This noble fee to each assigned,
But all the priests with one accord
Addressed that unpolluted lord:
'Tis thine alone to keep the whole
Of this broad earth in firm control.

No gift of lands from thee we seek:
To guard these realms our hands were weak.
On sacred lore our days are spent:
Let other gifts our wants content."
The chief of old Ikshváku's line
Gave them ten hundred thousand kine,
A hundred millions of fine gold,
The same in silver four times told.
But every priest in presence there
With one accord resigned his share.
To Saint Vaśishṭha, high of soul,
And Rishyaśring they gave the whole.
That largess pleased those Bráhmans well,
Who bade the prince his wishes tell.
Then Daśaratha, mighty king,
Made answer thus to Rishyaśring:
"O holy Hermit, of thy grace,
Vouchsafe the increase of my race."
He spoke; nor was his prayer denied:

71

The best of Bráhmans thus replied:
"Four sons, O Monarch, shall be thine,
Upholders of thy royal line."

CANTO
XIV

Rávan Doomed

The saint, well read in holy lore,
   Pondered awhile his answer o'er,
   And thus again addressed the king,
His wandering thoughts regathering:
"Another rite will I begin
Which shall the sons thou cravest win,
Where all things shall be duly sped
And first Atharva texts be read."

Then by Vibhándak's gentle son
Was that high sacrifice begun,
The king's advantage seeking still
And zealous to perform his will.
Now all the Gods had gathered there,
Each one for his allotted share:
Brahmá, the ruler of the sky,
Sthánu, Náráyan, Lord most high,
And holy Indra men might view
With Maruts for his retinue;
The heavenly chorister, and saint,
And spirit pure from earthly taint,
With one accord had sought the place
The high-souled monarch's rite to grace.
Then to the Gods who came to take
Their proper share the hermit spake:
"For you has Daśaratha slain
The votive steed, a son to gain;

Stern penance-rites the king has tried,
And in firm faith on you relied,
And now with undiminished care
A second rite would fain prepare.
But, O ye Gods, consent to grant
The longing of your supplicant.
For him beseeching hands I lift,
And pray you all to grant the gift,
That four fair sons of high renown
The offerings of the king may crown."
They to the hermit's son replied:
"His longing shall be gratified.
For, Bráhman, in most high degree
We love the king and honour thee."

These words the Gods in answer said,
And vanished thence by Indra led.
Thus to the Lord, the worlds who made,
The Immortals all assembled prayed:
"O Brahmá, mighty by thy grace,
Rávan, who rules the giant race,
Torments us in his senseless pride,
And penance-loving saints beside.
For thou well pleased in days of old
Gavest the boon that makes him bold,
That God nor demon e'er should kill
His charmed life, for so thy will.
We, honouring that high behest,
Bear all his rage though sore distressed.
That lord of giants fierce and fell
Scourges the earth and heaven and hell.
Mad with thy boon, his impious rage
Smites saint and bard and God and sage.
The sun himself withholds his glow,
The wind in fear forbears to blow;
The fire restrains his wonted heat
Where stand the dreaded Rávan's feet,
And, necklaced with the wandering wave,
The sea before him fears to rave.
Kuvera's self in sad defeat
Is driven from his blissful seat.

We see, we feel the giant's might,
And woe comes o'er us and affright.
To thee, O Lord, thy suppliants pray
To find some cure this plague to stay."
Thus by the gathered Gods addressed
He pondered in his secret breast,
And said: "One only way I find
To slay this fiend of evil mind.
He prayed me once his life to guard
From demon, God, and heavenly bard,
And spirits of the earth and air,
And I consenting heard his prayer.
But the proud giant in his scorn
Recked not of man of woman born.
None else may take his life away,
But only man the fiend may slay."
The Gods, with Indra at their head,
Rejoiced to hear the words he said.
Then crowned with glory like a flame,
Lord Vishṇu to the council came;
His hands shell, mace, and discus bore,
And saffron were the robes he wore.

Riding his eagle through the crowd,
As the sun rides upon a cloud,
With bracelets of fine gold, he came
Loud welcomed by the Gods' acclaim.
His praise they sang with one consent,
And cried, in lowly reverence bent:
"O Lord whose hand fierce Madhu slew,
Be thou our refuge, firm and true;
Friend of the suffering worlds art thou,
We pray thee help thy suppliants now."
Then Vishṇu spake: "Ye Gods, declare,
What may I do to grant your prayer?"

"King Daśaratha," thus cried they,
"Fervent in penance many a day,
The sacrificial steed has slain,
Longing for sons, but all in vain.
Now, at the cry of us forlorn,

Incarnate as his seed be born.
Three queens has he: each lovely dame
Like Beauty, Modesty, or Fame.
Divide thyself in four, and be
His offspring by these noble three.
Man's nature take, and slay in fight
Rávaṇ who laughs at heavenly might:
This common scourge, this rankling thorn
Whom the three worlds too long have borne
For Rávaṇ in the senseless pride
Of might unequalled has defied
The host of heaven, and plagues with woe
Angel and bard and saint below,
Crushing each spirit and each maid
Who plays in Nandan's heavenly shade.
O conquering Lord, to thee we bow;
Our surest hope and trust art thou.
Regard the world of men below,
And slay the Gods' tremendous foe."

When thus the suppliant Gods had prayed,
His wise reply Náráyaṇ made:
"What task demands my presence there,
And whence this dread, ye Gods declare."

The Gods replied: "We fear, O Lord,
Fierce Rávaṇ, ravener abhorred.
Be thine the glorious task, we pray,
In human form this fiend to slay.
By thee of all the Blest alone
This sinner may be overthrown.
He gained by penance long and dire
The favour of the mighty Sire.
Then He who every gift bestows
Guarded the fiend from heavenly foes,
And gave a pledge his life that kept
From all things living, man except.
On him thus armed no other foe
Than man may deal the deadly blow.
Assume, O King, a mortal birth,
And strike the demon to the earth."

75

Then Vishṇu, God of Gods, the Lord
Supreme by all the worlds adored,
To Brahmá and the suppliants spake:
"Dismiss your fear: for your dear sake
In battle will I smite him dead,
The cruel fiend, the Immortal's dread.
And lords and ministers and all
His kith and kin with him shall fall.
Then, in the world of mortal men,
Ten thousand years and hundreds ten
I as a human king will reign,
And guard the earth as my domain."

God, saint, and nymph, and minstrel throng
With heavenly voices raised their song
In hymns of triumph to the God
Whose conquering feet on Madhu trod:
"Champion of Gods, as man appear,
This cruel Rávaṇ slay,
The thorn that saints and hermits fear,
The plague that none can stay.
In savage fury uncontrolled
His pride for ever grows:
He dares the Lord of Gods to hold
Among his deadly foes."

CANTO

XV

The Nectar

When wisest Vishṇu thus had given
His promise to the Gods of heaven,
He pondered in his secret mind
A suited place of birth to find,
Then he decreed, the lotus-eyed,

In four his being to divide,
And Daśaratha, gracious king,
He chose as sire from whom to spring.
That childless prince of high renown,
Who smote in war his foemen down,
At that same time with utmost care
Prepared the rite that wins an heir.
Then Vishṇu, fain on earth to dwell,
Bade the Almighty Sire farewell,
And vanished while a reverent crowd
Of Gods and saints in worship bowed.

The monarch watched the sacred rite,
When a vast form of awful might,
Of matchless splendour, strength, and size
Was manifest before his eyes.

From forth the sacrificial flame,
Dark, robed in red, the being came.
His voice was drumlike, loud and low,
His face suffused with rosy glow.
Like a huge lion's mane appeared
The long locks of his hair and beard.
He shone with many a lucky sign,
And many an ornament divine;
A towering mountain in his height,
A tiger in his gait and might.
No precious mine more rich could be,
No burning flame more bright than he.
His arms embraced in loving hold,
Like a dear wife, a vase of gold
Whose silver lining held a draught
Of nectar as in heaven is quaffed:
A vase so vast, so bright to view,
They scarce could count the vision true.
Upon the king his eyes he bent,
And said: "The Lord of life has sent
His servant down, O Prince, to be
A messenger from heaven to thee."
The king with all his nobles by
Raised reverent hands and made reply:

77

"Welcome, O glorious being! Say
How can my care thy grace repay."
Envoy of Him whom all adore
Thus to the king he spake once more:
"The Gods accept thy worship: they
Give thee the blessed fruit to-day.
Approach and take, O glorious King,
This heavenly nectar which I bring,
For it shall give thee sons and wealth,
And bless thee with a store of health.
Give it to those fair queens of thine,
And bid them quaff the drink divine:
And they the princely sons shall bear
Long sought by sacrifice and prayer."

"Yea, O my lord," the monarch said,
And took the vase upon his head,
The gift of Gods, of fine gold wrought,
With store of heavenly liquor fraught.
He honoured, filled with transport new,
That wondrous being, fair to view,
As round the envoy of the God
With reverential steps he trod.
His errand done, that form of light
Arose and vanished from the sight.
High rapture filled the monarch's soul,
Possessed of that celestial bowl,
As when a man by want distressed
With unexpected wealth is blest.
And rays of transport seemed to fall
Illuminating bower and hall,
As when the autumn moon rides high,
And floods with lovely light the sky.
Quick to the ladies' bower he sped,
And thus to Queen Kauśalyá said:
"This genial nectar take and quaff,"
He spoke, and gave the lady half.
Part of the nectar that remained
Sumitrá from his hand obtained.
He gave, to make her fruitful too,
Kaikeyí half the residue.

A portion yet remaining there,
He paused awhile to think.
Then gave Sumitrá, with her share.
The remnant of the drink.
Thus on each queen of those fair three
A part the king bestowed,
And with sweet hope a child to see
Their yearning bosoms glowed.
The heavenly bowl the king supplied
Their longing souls relieved,
And soon, with rapture and with pride,
Each royal dame conceived.
He gazed upon each lady's face,
And triumphed as he gazed,
As Indra in his royal place
By Gods and spirits praised.

CANTO
XVI

The Vánars

When Vishṇu thus had gone on earth,
From the great king to take his birth,
The self-existent Lord of all
Addressed the Gods who heard his call:
"For Vishṇu's sake, the strong and true,
Who seeks the good of all of you,
Make helps, in war to lend him aid,
In forms that change at will, arrayed,
Of wizard skill and hero might,
Outstrippers of the wind in flight,
Skilled in the arts of counsel, wise,
And Vishṇu's peers in bold emprise;
With heavenly arts and prudence fraught,
By no devices to be caught;

Skilled in all weapon's lore and use
As they who drink the immortal juice.
And let the nymphs supreme in grace,
And maidens of the minstrel race,
Monkeys and snakes, and those who rove
Free spirits of the hill and grove,
And wandering Daughters of the Air,
In monkey form brave children bear.
So erst the lord of bears I shaped,
Born from my mouth as wide I gaped."

Thus by the mighty Sire addressed
They all obeyed his high behest,
And thus begot in countless swarms
Brave sons disguised in sylvan forms.
Each God, each sage became a sire,
Each minstrel of the heavenly quire,
Each faun, of children strong and good
Whose feet should roam the hill and wood.
Snakes, bards, and spirits, serpents bold
Had sons too numerous to be told.
Báli, the woodland hosts who led,
High as Mahendra's lofty head,
Was Indra's child. That noblest fire,
The Sun, was great Sugríva's sire,
Tára, the mighty monkey, he
Was offspring of Vrihaspati:
Tára the matchless chieftain, boast
For wisdom of the Vánar host.
Of Gandhamádan brave and bold
The father was the Lord of Gold.
Nala the mighty, dear to fame,
Of skilful Viśvakarmá came.
From Agni, Nila bright as flame,
Who in his splendour, might, and worth,
Surpassed the sire who gave him birth.
The heavenly Aśvins, swift and fair,
Were fathers of a noble pair,
Who, Dwivida and Mainda named,
For beauty like their sires were famed,
Varuṇ was father of Susheṇ,

Of Sarabh, he who sends the rain,
Hanúmán, best of monkey kind,
Was son of him who breathes the wind:
Like thunderbolt in frame was he,
And swift as Garuḍ's self could flee.
These thousands did the Gods create
Endowed with might that none could mate,
In monkey forms that changed at will;
So strong their wish the fiend to kill.
In mountain size, like lions thewed,
Up sprang the wondrous multitude,
Auxiliar hosts in every shape,
Monkey and bear and highland ape.
In each the strength, the might, the mien
Of his own parent God were seen.
Some chiefs of Vánar mothers came,
Some of she-bear and minstrel dame,
Skilled in all arms in battle's shock;
The brandished tree, the loosened rock;
And prompt, should other weapons fail,
To fight and slay with tooth and nail.
Their strength could shake the hills amain,
And rend the rooted trees in twain,
Disturb with their impetuous sweep
The Rivers' Lord, the Ocean deep,
Rend with their feet the seated ground,
And pass wide floods with airy bound,
Or forcing through the sky their way
The very clouds by force could stay.
Mad elephants that wander through
The forest wilds, could they subdue,
And with their furious shout could scare
Dead upon earth the birds of air.
So were the sylvan chieftains formed;
Thousands on thousands still they swarmed.
These were the leaders honoured most,
The captains of the Vánar host,
And to each lord and chief and guide
Was monkey offspring born beside.
Then by the bears' great monarch stood
The other roamers of the wood,

And turned, their pathless homes to seek,
To forest and to mountain peak.
The leaders of the monkey band
By the two brothers took their stand,
Sugríva, offspring of the Sun
And Báli, Indra's mighty one.
They both endowed with Garuḍ's might,
And skilled in all the arts of fight,
Wandered in arms the forest through,
And lions, snakes, and tigers, slew.
But every monkey, ape, and bear
Ever was Báli's special care;
With his vast strength and mighty arm
He kept them from all scathe and harm.
And so the earth with hill, wood, seas,
Was filled with mighty ones like these,
Of various shape and race and kind,
With proper homes to each assigned,
With Ráma's champions fierce and strong
The earth was overspread,
High as the hills and clouds, a throng
With bodies vast and dread.

CANTO

XVII

Rishyasring's Return

Now when the high-souled monarch's rite,
The Aśvamedh, was finished quite,
Their sacrificial dues obtained,
The Gods their heavenly homes regained.
The lofty-minded saints withdrew,
Each to his place, with honour due,
And kings and chieftains, one and all,
Who came to grace the festival.

And Daśaratha, ere they went,
Addressed them thus benevolent:
"Now may you, each with joyful heart,
To your own realms, O Kings, depart.
Peace and good luck attend you there,
And blessing, is my friendly prayer;
Let cares of state each mind engage
To guard his royal heritage.
A monarch from his throne expelled
No better than the dead is held.
So he who cares for power and might
Must guard his realm and royal right.
Such care a meed in heaven will bring
Better than rites and offering.
Such care a king his country owes
As man upon himself bestows,
When for his body he provides
Raiment and every need besides.
For future days should kings foresee,
And keep the present error-free."

Thus did the king the kings exhort:
They heard, and turned them from the court
And, each to each in friendship bound,
Went forth to all the realms around.
The rites were o'er, the guests were sped:
The train the best of Bráhmans led,
In which the king with joyful soul,
With his dear wives, and with the whole
Of his imperial host and train
Of cars and servants turned again,
And, as a monarch dear to fame,
Within his royal city came.

Next, Rishyaśring, well-honoured sage,
And Śántá, sought their hermitage.
The king himself, of prudent mind,
Attended him, with troops behind.
And all her men the town outpoured
With Saint Vaśishtha and their lord.
High mounted on a car of state,

O'er canopied fair Śántá sate.
Drawn by white oxen, while a band
Of servants marched on either hand.
Great gifts of countless price she bore,
With sheep and goats and gems in store.
Like Beauty's self the lady shone
With all the jewels she had on,
As, happy in her sweet content,
Peerless amid the fair she went.
Not Queen Paulomí's self could be
More loving to her lord than she.
She who had lived in happy ease,
Honoured with all her heart could please,
While dames and kinsfolk ever vied
To see her wishes gratified,
Soon as she knew her husband's will
Again to seek the forest, still
Was ready for the hermit's cot,
Nor murmured at her altered lot.
The king attended to the wild
That hermit and his own dear child,
And in the centre of a throng
Of noble courtiers rode along.
The sage's son had let prepare
A lodge within the wood, and there
While they lingered blithe and gay.
Then, duly honoured, went their way.
The glorious hermit Rishyaśring
Drew near and thus besought the king:

"Return, my honoured lord, I pray,
Return, upon thy homeward way."
The monarch, with the waiting crowd,
Lifted his voice and wept aloud,
And with eyes dripping still to each
Of his good queens he spake this speech:

"Kauśalyá and Sumitrá dear,
And thou, my sweet Kaikeyí, hear.
All upon Śántá feast your gaze,
The last time for a length of days."

To Śántá's arms the ladies leapt,
And hung about her neck and wept,
And cried, "O, happy be the life
Of this great Bráhman and his wife.
The Wind, the Fire, the Moon on high,
The Earth, the Streams, the circling Sky,
Preserve thee in the wood, true spouse,
Devoted to thy husband's vows.
And O dear Śántá, ne'er neglect
To pay the dues of meek respect
To the great saint, thy husband's sire,
With all observance and with fire.
And, sweet one, pure of spot and blame,
Forget not thou thy husband's claim;
In every change, in good and ill,
Let thy sweet words delight him still,
And let thy worship constant be:
Her lord is woman's deity.
To learn thy welfare, dearest friend,
The king will many a Bráhman send.
Let happy thoughts thy spirit cheer,
And be not troubled, daughter dear."

These soothing words the ladies said.
And pressed their lips upon her head.
Each gave with sighs her last adieu,
Then at the king's command withdrew.
The king around the hermit went
With circling footsteps reverent,
And placed at Rishyaśring's command
Some soldiers of his royal band.
The Bráhman bowed in turn and cried,
"May fortune never leave thy side.
O mighty King, with justice reign,
And still thy people's love retain."
He spoke, and turned away his face,
And, as the hermit went,
The monarch, rooted to the place,
Pursued with eyes intent.
But when the sage had past from view
King Daśaratha turned him too,

Still fixing on his friend each thought.
With such deep love his breast was fraught.
Amid his people's loud acclaim
Home to his royal seat he came,
And lived delighted there,
Expecting when each queenly dame,
Upholder of his ancient fame,
Her promised son should bear.
The glorious sage his way pursued
Till close before his eyes he viewed
Sweet Champá, Lomapád's fair town,
Wreathed with her Champacs' leafy crown.
Soon as the saint's approach he knew,
The king, to yield him honour due,
Went forth to meet him with a band
Of priests and nobles of the land:
"Hail, Sage," he cried, "O joy to me!
What bliss it is, my lord, to see
Thee with thy wife and all thy train
Returning to my town again.
Thy father, honoured Sage, is well,
Who hither from his woodland cell
Has sent full many a messenger
For tidings both of thee and her."
Then joyfully, for due respect,
The monarch bade the town be decked.
The king and Rishyaśring elate
Entered the royal city's gate:
In front the chaplain rode.
Then, loved and honoured with all care
By monarch and by courtier, there
The glorious saint abode.

CANTO
XVIII

Rishyasring's Departure

The monarch called a Bráhman near
And said, "Now speed away
To Kaśyap's son, the mighty seer,
And with all reverence say
The holy child he holds so dear,
The hermit of the noble mind,
Whose equal it were hard to find,
Returned, is dwelling here.
Go, and instead of me do thou
Before that best of hermits bow,
That still he may, for his dear son,
Show me the favour I have won."
Soon as the king these words had said,
To Kaśyap's son the Bráhman sped.
Before the hermit low he bent
And did obeisance, reverent;
Then with meek words his grace to crave
The message of his lord he gave:
"The high-souled father of his bride
Had called thy son his rites to guide:
Those rites are o'er, the steed is slain;
Thy noble child is come again."
Soon as the saint that speech had heard
His spirit with desire was stirred
To seek the city of the king
And to his cot his son to bring.

With young disciples at his side
Forth on his way the hermit hied,
While peasants from their hamlets ran
To reverence the holy man.

Each with his little gift of food,
Forth came the village multitude,
And, as they humbly bowed the head,
"What may we do for thee?" they said.
Then he, of Bráhmans first and best,
The gathered people thus addressed:
"Now tell me for I fain would know,
Why is it I am honoured so?"
They to the high-souled saint replied:
"Our ruler is with thee allied.
Our master's order we fulfil;
O Bráhman, let thy mind be still."

With joy the saintly hermit heard
Each pleasant and delightful word,
And poured a benediction down
On king and ministers and town.
Glad at the words of that high saint
Some servants hastened to acquaint
Their king, rejoicing to impart
The tidings that would cheer his heart.
Soon as the joyful tale he knew
To meet the saint the monarch flew,
The guest-gift in his hand he brought,
And bowed before him and besought:
"This day by seeing thee I gain
Not to have lived my life in vain,
Now be not wroth with me, I pray,
"Because I wiled thy son away.
The best of Bráhmans answer made:
"Be not, great lord of kings, afraid.
Thy virtues have not failed to win
My favour, O thou pure of sin."
Then in the front the saint was placed,
The king came next in joyous haste,
And with him entered his abode,
Mid glad acclaim as on they rode.
To greet the sage the reverent crowd
Raised suppliant hands and humbly bowed.
Then from the palace many a dame
Following well-dressed Śántá came,

Stood by the mighty saint and cried:
"See, honour's source, thy son's dear bride."
The saint, who every virtue knew,
His arms around his daughter threw,
And with a father's rapture pressed
The lady to his wondering breast.
Arising from the saint's embrace
She bowed her low before his face,
And then, with palm to palm applied,
Stood by her hermit father's side.
He for his son, as laws ordain,
Performed the rite that frees from stain,
And, honoured by the wise and good,
With him departed to the wood.

CANTO
XIX

The Birth of the Princes

The seasons six in rapid flight
Had circled since that glorious rite.
Eleven months had passed away;
'Twas Chaitra's ninth returning day.
The moon within that mansion shone
Which Aditi looks kindly on.
Raised to their apex in the sky
Five brilliant planets beamed on high.
Shone with the moon, in Cancer's sign,
Vṛihaspati with light divine.
Kauśalyá bore an infant blest
With heavenly marks of grace impressed;
Ráma, the universe's lord,
A prince by all the worlds adored.
New glory Queen Kauśalyá won
Reflected from her splendid son.

So Aditi shone more and more,
The Mother of the Gods, when she
The King of the Immortals bore,
The thunder-wielding deity.

The lotus-eyed, the beauteous boy,
He came fierce Rávan to destroy;
From half of Vishnu's vigour born,
He came to help the worlds forlorn.
And Queen Kaikeyí bore a child
Of truest valour, Bharat styled,
With every princely virtue blest,
One fourth of Vishnu manifest.
Sumitrá too a noble pair,
Called Lakshman and Śatrughna, bare,
Of high emprise, devoted, true,
Sharers in Vishnu's essence too.
'Neath Pushya's mansion, Mina's sign,
Was Bharat born, of soul benign.
The sun had reached the Crab at morn
When Queen Sumitrá's babes were born,
What time the moon had gone to make
His nightly dwelling with the Snake.
The high-souled monarch's consorts bore
At different times those glorious four,
Like to himself and virtuous, bright
As Proshthapadá's four-fold light.
Then danced the nymphs' celestial throng,
The minstrels raised their strain;
The drums of heaven pealed loud and long,
And flowers came down in rain.
Within Ayodhyá, blithe and gay,
All kept the joyous holiday.
The spacious square, the ample road
With mimes and dancers overflowed,
And with the voice of music rang
Where minstrels played and singers sang,
And shone, a wonder to behold,
With dazzling show of gems and gold.
Nor did the king his largess spare,
For minstrel, driver, bard, to share;

Much wealth the Bráhmans bore away,
And many thousand dine that day.

Soon as each babe was twelve days old
'Twas time the naming rite to hold.
When Saint Vaśishṭha, rapt with joy,
Assigned a name to every boy.
Ráma, to him the high-souled heir,
Bharat, to him Kaikeyí bare:
Of Queen Sumitrá one fair son
Was Lakshmaṇ, and Śatrughna one
Ráma, his sire's supreme delight,
Like some proud banner cheered his sight,
And to all creatures seemed to be
The self-existent deity.
All heroes, versed in holy lore,
To all mankind great love they bore.
Fair stores of wisdom all possessed,
With princely graces all were blest.
But mid those youths of high descent,
With lordly light preëminent.
Like the full moon unclouded, shone
Ráma, the world's dear paragon.
He best the elephant could guide.
Urge the fleet car, the charger ride:
A master he of bowman's skill,
Joying to do his father's will.
The world's delight and darling, he
Loved Lakshmaṇ best from infancy
And Lakshmaṇ, lord of lofty fate,
Upon his elder joyed to wait,
Striving his second self to please
With friendship's sweet observances.
His limbs the hero ne'er would rest
Unless the couch his brother pressed;
Except beloved Ráma shared
He could not taste the meal prepared.
When Ráma, pride of Reghu's race,
Sprang on his steed to urge the chase,
Behind him Lakshmaṇ loved to go
And guard him with his trusty bow.

As Ráma was to Lakshmaṇ dear
More than his life and ever near,
So fond Śatrughna prized above
His very life his Bharat's love.
Illustrious heroes, nobly kind
In mutual love they all combined,
And gave their royal sire delight
With modest grace and warrior might:
Supported by the glorious four
Shone Daśaratha more and more,
As though, with every guardian God
Who keeps the land and skies,
The Father of all creatures trod
The earth before men's eyes.

CANTO

XX

Visvámitra's Visit

Now Daśaratha's pious mind
    Meet wedlock for his sons designed;
With priests and friends the king began
To counsel and prepare his plan.
Such thoughts engaged his bosom, when,
To see Ayodhyá's lord of men,
A mighty saint of glorious fame,
The hermit Viśvámitra came.
For evil fiends that roam by night
Disturbed him in each holy rite,
And in their strength and frantic rage
Assailed with witcheries the sage.
He came to seek the monarch's aid
To guard the rites the demons stayed,

Unable to a close to bring
One unpolluted offering.
Seeking the king in this dire strait
He said to those who kept the gate:
"Haste, warders, to your master run,
And say that here stands Gádhi's son."

Soon as they heard the holy man,
To the king's chamber swift they ran
With minds disordered all, and spurred
To wildest zeal by what they heard.
On to the royal hall they sped,
There stood and lowly bowed the head,
And made the lord of men aware
That the great saint was waiting there.
The king with priest and peer arose
And ran the sage to meet,
As Indra from his palace goes
Lord Brahmá's self to greet.
When glowing with celestial light
The pious hermit was in sight,
The king, whose mien his transport showed,
The honoured gift for guests bestowed.
Nor did the saint that gift despise,
Offered as holy texts advise;
He kindly asked the earth's great king
How all with him was prospering.
The son of Kuśik bade him tell
If all in town and field were well,
All well with friends, and kith and kin,
And royal treasure stored within:
"Do all thy neighbours own thy sway?
Thy foes confess thee yet?
Dost thou continue still to pay
To Gods and men each debt?"
Then he, of hermits first and best,
Vaśishṭha with a smile addressed,
And asked him of his welfare too,
Showing him honour as was due.
Then with the sainted hermit all

Went joyous to the monarch's hall,
And sate them down by due degree,
Each one, of rank and dignity.
Joy filled the noble prince's breast
Who thus bespoke the honoured guest:
"As amrit by a mortal found,
As rain upon the thirsty ground,
As to an heirless man a son
Born to him of his precious one,
As gain of what we sorely miss,
As sudden dawn of mighty bliss,
So is thy coming here to me:
All welcome, mighty Saint, to thee.
What wish within thy heart hast thou?
If I can please thee, tell me how.
Hail, Saint, from whom all honours flow,
Worthy of all I can bestow.
Blest is my birth with fruit to-day,
Nor has my life been thrown away.
I see the best of Bráhman race
And night to glorious morn gives place.
Thou, holy Sage, in days of old
Among the royal saints enrolled,
Didst, penance-glorified, within
The Bráhman caste high station win.
'Tis meet and right in many a way
That I to thee should honour pay.
This seems a marvel to mine eyes:
All sin thy visit purifies;
And I by seeing thee, O Sage,
Have reaped the fruit of pilgrimage.
Then say what thou wouldst have me do,
That thou hast sought this interview.
Favoured by thee, my wish is still,
O Hermit, to perform thy will.
Nor needest thou at length explain
The object that thy heart would gain.
Without reserve I grant it now:
My deity, O Lord, art thou."

The glorious hermit, far renowned,
With highest fame and virtue crowned,
Rejoiced these modest words to hear
Delightful to the mind and ear.

CANTO

XXI

Visvámitra's Speech

The hermit heard with high content
That speech so wondrous eloquent,
And while each hair with joy arose,

He thus made answer at the close:
"Good is thy speech O noble King,
And like thyself in everything.
So should their lips be wisdom-fraught
Whom kings begot, Vaśishṭha taught.
The favour which I came to seek
Thou grantest ere my tongue can speak.
But let my tale attention claim,
And hear the need for which I came.
O King, as Scripture texts allow,
A holy rite employs me now.
Two fiends who change their forms at will
Impede that rite with cursed skill.
Oft when the task is nigh complete,
These worst of fiends my toil defeat,
Throw bits of bleeding flesh, and o'er
The altar shed a stream of gore.
When thus the rite is mocked and stayed,
And all my pious hopes delayed,
Cast down in heart the spot I leave,
And spent with fruitless labour grieve.

Nor can I, checked by prudence, dare
Let loose my fury on them there:
The muttered curse, the threatening word,
In such a rite must ne'er be heard.
Thy grace the rite from check can free.
And yield the fruit I long to see.
Thy duty bids thee, King, defend
The suffering guest, the suppliant friend.
Give me thy son, thine eldest born,
Whom locks like raven's wings adorn.
That hero youth, the truly brave,
Of thee, O glorious King, I crave.
For he can lay those demons low
Who mar my rites and work me woe:
My power shall shield the youth from harm,
And heavenly might shall nerve his arm.
And on my champion will I shower
Unnumbered gifts of varied power,
Such gifts as shall ensure his fame
And spread through all the worlds his name.
Be sure those fiends can never stand
Before the might of Ráma's hand,
And mid the best and bravest none
Can slay that pair but Raghu's son.
Entangled in the toils of Fate
Those sinners, proud and obstinate,
Are, in their fury overbold,
No match for Ráma mighty-souled.
Nor let a father's breast give way
Too far to fond affection's sway.
Count thou the fiends already slain:
My word is pledged, nor pledged in vain.
I know the hero Ráma well
In whom high thoughts and valour dwell;
So does Vaśishṭha, so do these
Engaged in long austerities.
If thou would do the righteous deed,
And win high fame, thy virtue's meed,
Fame that on earth shall last and live,
To me, great King, thy Ráma give.
If to the words that I have said,

With Saint Vaśishṭha at their head
Thy holy men, O King, agree,
Then let thy Ráma go with me.
Ten nights my sacrifice will last,
And ere the stated time be past
Those wicked fiends, those impious twain,
Must fall by wondrous Ráma slain.
Let not the hours, I warn thee, fly,
Fixt for the rite, unheeded by;
Good luck have thou, O royal Chief,
Nor give thy heart to needless grief."

Thus in fair words with virtue fraught
The pious glorious saint besought.
But the good speech with poignant sting
Pierced ear and bosom of the king,
Who, stabbed with pangs too sharp to bear,
Fell prostrate and lay fainting there.

XXII

Dasaratha's Speech

His tortured senses all astray,
While the hapless monarch lay,
Then slowly gathering thought and strength
To Viśvámitra spoke at length:
"My son is but a child, I ween;
This year he will be just sixteen.
How is he fit for such emprise,
My darling with the lotus eyes?
A mighty army will I bring
That calls me master, lord, and king,
And with its countless squadrons fight
Against these rovers of the night.

My faithful heroes skilled to wield
The arms of war will take the field;
Their skill the demons' might may break:
Ráma, my child, thou must not take.
I, even I, my bow in hand,
Will in the van of battle stand,
And, while my soul is left alive,
With the night-roaming demons strive.
Thy guarded sacrifice shall be
Completed, from all hindrance free.
Thither will I my journey make:
Ráma, my child, thou must not take.
A boy unskilled, he knows not yet
The bounds to strength and weakness set.
No match is he for demon foes
Who magic arts to arms oppose.

O chief of saints, I have no power,
Of Ráma reft, to live one hour:
Mine aged heart at once would break:
Ráma, my child, thou must not take.
Nine thousand circling years have fled
With all their seasons o'er my head,
And as a hard-won boon, O sage,
These sons have come to cheer mine age.
My dearest love amid the four
Is he whom first his mother bore,
Still dearer for his virtues' sake:
Ráma, my child, thou must not take.
But if, unmoved by all I say,
Thou needs must bear my son away,
Let me lead with him, I entreat,
A four-fold army all complete.
What is the demons' might, O Sage?
Who are they? What their parentage?
What is their size? What beings lend
Their power to guard them and befriend?
How can my son their arts withstand?
Or I or all my armed band?
Tell me the whole that I may know

To meet in war each evil foe
Whom conscious might inspires with pride."

And Viśvámitra thus replied:
"Sprung from Pulastya's race there came
A giant known by Rávaṇ's name.
Once favoured by the Eternal Sire
He plagues the worlds in ceaseless ire,
For peerless power and might renowned,
By giant bands encompassed round.
Viśravas for his sire they hold,
His brother is the Lord of Gold.
King of the giant hosts is he,
And worst of all in cruelty.
This Rávaṇ's dread commands impel
Two demons who in might excel,
Márícha and Suváhu hight,
To trouble and impede the rite."
Then thus the king addressed the sage:
"No power have I, my lord, to wage
War with this evil-minded foe;
Now pity on my darling show,
And upon me of hapless fate,
For thee as God I venerate.
Gods, spirits, bards of heavenly birth,
The birds of air, the snakes of earth
Before the might of Rávaṇ quail,
Much less can mortal man avail.
He draws, I hear, from out the breast
The valour of the mightiest.
No, ne'er can I with him contend,
Or with the forces he may send.
How can I then my darling lend,
Godlike, unskilled in battle? No,
I will not let my young child go.
Foes of thy rite, those mighty ones,
Sunda and Upasunda's sons,
Are fierce as Fate to overthrow:
I will not let my young child go.
Márícha and Suváhu fell

Are valiant and instructed well.
One of the twain I might attack.
With all my friends their lord to back."

Vasishtha's Speech

While thus the hapless monarch spoke,
Paternal love his utterance broke.
Then words like these the saint returned,
And fury in his bosom burned:
"Didst thou, O King, a promise make,
And wishest now thy word to break?
A son of Raghu's line should scorn
To fail in faith, a man forsworn.
But if thy soul can bear the shame
I will return e'en as I came.
Live with thy sons, and joy be thine,
False scion of Kakutstha's line."

As Viśvámitra, mighty sage,
Was moved with this tempestuous rage,
Earth rocked and reeled throughout her frame,
And fear upon the Immortals came.
But Saint Vaśishṭha, wisest seer,
Observant of his vows austere,
Saw the whole world convulsed with dread,
And thus unto the monarch said:
"Thou, born of old Ikshváku's seed,
Art Justice' self in mortal weed.
Constant and pious, blest by fate,
The right thou must not violate.
Thou, Raghu's son, so famous through
The triple world as just and true,

100

Perform thy bounden duty still,
Nor stain thy race by deed of ill.
If thou have sworn and now refuse
Thou must thy store of merit lose.
Then, Monarch, let thy Ráma go,
Nor fear for him the demon foe.
The fiends shall have no power to hurt
Him trained to war or inexpert,
Nor vanquish him in battle field,
For Kuśik's son the youth will shield.
He is incarnate Justice, he
The best of men for bravery.
Embodied love of penance drear,
Among the wise without a peer.

Full well he knows, great Kuśik's son,
The arms celestial, every one,
Arms from the Gods themselves concealed,
Far less to other men revealed.
These arms to him, when earth he swayed,
Mighty Kriśáśva, pleased, conveyed.
Kriśáśva's sons they are indeed,
Brought forth by Daksha's lovely seed,
Heralds of conquest, strong and bold,
Brilliant, of semblance manifold.
Jayá and Vijayá, most fair,
And hundred splendid weapons bare.
Of Jayá, glorious as the morn,
First fifty noble sons were born,
Boundless in size yet viewless too,
They came the demons to subdue.
And fifty children also came
Of Vijayá the beauteous dame,
Sanháras named, of mighty force,
Hard to assail or check in course.
Of these the hermit knows the use,
And weapons new can he produce.
All these the mighty saint will yield
To Ráma's hand, to own and wield;
And armed with these, beyond a doubt
Shall Ráma put those fiends to rout.

For Ráma and the people's sake,
For thine own good my counsel take,
Nor seek, O King, with fond delay,
The parting of thy son to stay."

CANTO
XXIV

The Spells

Vaśishṭha thus was speaking still:
    The monarch, of his own free will,
    Bade with quick zeal and joyful cheer
Ráma and Lakshmaṇ hasten near.
Mother and sire in loving care
Sped their dear son with rite and prayer:
Vaśishṭha blessed him ere he went;
O'er his loved head the father bent,
And then to Kuśik's son resigned
Ráma with Lakshmaṇ close behind.
Standing by Viśvámitra's side,
The youthful hero, lotus-eyed,
The Wind-God saw, and sent a breeze
Whose sweet pure touch just waved the trees.
There fell from heaven a flowery rain,
And with the song and dance the strain
Of shell and tambour sweetly blent
As forth the son of Raghu went.
The hermit led: behind him came
The bow-armed Ráma, dear to fame,
Whose locks were like the raven's wing:
Then Lakshmaṇ, closely following.
The Gods and Indra, filled with joy,
Looked down upon the royal boy,
And much they longed the death to see
Of their ten-headed enemy.

Ráma and Lakshman paced behind
That hermit of the lofty mind,
As the young Aśvins, heavenly pair,
Follow Lord Indra through the air.
On arm and hand the guard they wore,
Quiver and bow and sword they bore;
Two fire-born Gods of War seemed they.
He, Śiva's self who led the way.

Upon fair Sarjú's southern shore
They now had walked a league and more,
When thus the sage in accents mild
To Ráma said: "Beloved child,
This lustral water duly touch:
My counsel will avail thee much.
Forget not all the words I say,
Nor let the occasion slip away.
Lo, with two spells I thee invest,
The mighty and the mightiest.
O'er thee fatigue shall ne'er prevail,
Nor age or change thy limbs assail.
Thee powers of darkness ne'er shall smite
In tranquil sleep or wild delight.
No one is there in all the land
Thine equal for the vigorous hand.

Thou, when thy lips pronounce the spell,
Shalt have no peer in heaven or hell.
None in the world with thee shall vie,
O sinless one, in apt reply,
In fortune, knowledge, wit, and tact,
Wisdom to plan and skill to act.
This double science take, and gain
Glory that shall for aye remain.
Wisdom and judgment spring from each
Of these fair spells whose use I teach.
Hunger and thirst unknown to thee,
High in the worlds thy rank shall be.
For these two spells with might endued,
Are the Great Father's heavenly brood,
And thee, O Chief, may fitly grace,

Thou glory of Kakutstha's race.
Virtues which none can match are thine,
Lord, from thy birth, of gifts divine,
And now these spells of might shall cast
Fresh radiance o'er the gifts thou hast."
Then Ráma duly touched the wave,
Raised suppliant hands, bowed low his head,
And took the spells the hermit gave,
Whose soul on contemplation fed.
From him whose might these gifts enhanced,
A brighter beam of glory glanced:
So shines in all his autumn blaze
The Day-God of the thousand rays.
The hermit's wants those youths supplied,
As pupils use to holy guide.
And then the night in sweet content
On Sarjú's pleasant bank they spent.

CANTO
XXV

The Hermitage of Love

Soon as appeared the morning light
Up rose the mighty anchorite,
And thus to youthful Ráma said,
Who lay upon his leafy bed:
"High fate is hers who calls thee son:
Arise, 'tis break of day;
Rise, Chief, and let those rites be done
Due at the morning's ray."
At that great sage's high behest
Up sprang the princely pair,
To bathing rites themselves addressed,
And breathed the holiest prayer.
Their morning task completed, they

To Viśvámitra came
That store of holy works, to pay
The worship saints may claim.
Then to the hallowed spot they went
Along fair Sarjú's side
Where mix her waters confluent
With three-pathed Gangá's tide.
There was a sacred hermitage
Where saints devout of mind
Their lives through many a lengthened age
To penance had resigned.
That pure abode the princes eyed
With unrestrained delight,
And thus unto the saint they cried,
Rejoicing at the sight:
"Whose is that hermitage we see?
Who makes his dwelling there?
Full of desire to hear are we:
O Saint, the truth declare."
The hermit smiling made reply
To the two boys' request:
"Hear, Ráma, who in days gone by
This calm retreat possessed.
Kandarpa in apparent form,
Called Káma by the wise,
Dared Umá's new-wed lord to storm
And make the God his prize.
'Gainst Stháṇu's self, on rites austere
And vows intent, they say,
His bold rash hand he dared to rear,
Though Stháṇu cried, Away!
But the God's eye with scornful glare
Fell terrible on him.
Dissolved the shape that was so fair

And burnt up every limb.
Since the great God's terrific rage
Destroyed his form and frame,
Káma in each succeeding age
Has borne Ananga's name.
So, where his lovely form decayed,

105

This land is Anga styled:
Sacred to him of old this shade,
And hermits undefiled.
Here Scripture-talking elders sway
Each sense with firm control,
And penance-rites have washed away
All sin from every soul.
One night, fair boy, we here will spend,
A pure stream on each hand,
And with to-morrow's light will bend
Our steps to yonder strand.
Here let us bathe, and free from stain
To that pure grove repair,
Sacred to Káma, and remain
One night in comfort there."
With penance' far-discerning eye
The saintly men beheld
Their coming, and with transport high
Each holy bosom swelled.
To Kuśik's son the gift they gave
That honoured guest should greet,
Water they brought his feet to lave,
And showed him honor meet.
Ráma and Lakshmaṇ next obtained
In due degree their share.
Then with sweet talk the guests remained,
And charmed each listener there.
The evening prayers were duly said
With voices calm and low:
Then on the ground each laid his head
And slept till morning's glow.

XXVI

The Forest of Tádaká

When the fair light of morning rose
 The princely tamers of their foes
 Followed, his morning worship o'er,
The hermit to the river's shore.
The high-souled men with thoughtful care
A pretty barge had stationed there.
All cried, "O lord, this barge ascend,
And with thy princely followers bend
To yonder side thy prosperous way
With naught to check thee or delay."
Nor did the saint their rede reject:
He bade farewell with due respect,
And crossed, attended by the twain,
That river rushing to the main.
When now the bark was half way o'er,
Ráma and Lakshmaṇ heard the roar,
That louder grew and louder yet,
Of waves by dashing waters met.
Then Ráma asked the mighty seer:
"What is the tumult that I hear
Of waters cleft in mid career?"
Soon as the speech of Ráma, stirred
By deep desire to know, he heard,
The pious saint began to tell
What paused the waters' roar and swell:
"On high Kailása's distant hill
There lies a noble lake
Whose waters, born from Brahmá's will,
The name of Mánas take.
Thence, hallowing where'er they flow,
The streams of Sarjú fall,

And wandering through the plains below
Embrace Ayodhyá's wall.
Still, still preserved in Sarjú's name
Sarovar's fame we trace.
The flood of Brahma whence she came
To run her holy race.
To meet great Gangá here she hies
With tributary wave:
Hence the loud roar ye hear arise,
Of floods that swell and rave.
Here, pride of Raghu's line, do thou
In humble adoration bow."

He spoke. The princes both obeyed,
And reverence to each river paid.
They reached the southern shore at last,
And gaily on their journey passed.
A little space beyond there stood
A gloomy awe-inspiring wood.
The monarch's noble son began
To question thus the holy man:
"Whose gloomy forest meets mine eye
Like some vast cloud that fills the sky?
Pathless and dark it seems to be,
Where birds in thousands wander free;
Where shrill cicadas' cries resound,

And fowl of dismal note abound.
Lion, rhinoceros, and bear,
Boar, tiger, elephant, are there,
There shrubs and thorns run wild:
Dháo, Sál, Bignonia, Bel, are found,
And every tree that grows on ground.
How is the forest styled?"
The glorious saint this answer made:
"Dear child of Raghu, hear
Who dwells within the horrid shade
That looks so dark and drear.
Where now is wood, long ere this day
Two broad and fertile lands,
Malaja and Karúsha lay,

Adorned by heavenly hands.
Here, mourning friendship's broken ties,
Lord Indra of the thousand eyes
Hungered and sorrowed many a day,
His brightness soiled with mud and clay,
When in a storm of passion he
Had slain his dear friend Namuchi.
Then came the Gods and saints who bore
Their golden pitchers brimming o'er
With holy streams that banish stain,
And bathed Lord Indra pure again.
When in this land the God was freed
From spot and stain of impious deed
For that his own dear friend he slew,
High transport thrilled his bosom through.
Then in his joy the lands he blessed,
And gave a boon they long possessed:
"Because these fertile lands retain
The washings of the blot and stain,"
'Twas thus Lord Indra sware,
"Malaja and Karúsha's name
Shall celebrate with deathless fame
My malady and care."
"So be it," all the Immortals cried,
When Indra's speech they heard,
And with acclaim they ratified
The names his lips conferred.
Long time, O victor of thy foes,
These happy lands had sweet repose,
And higher still in fortune rose.
At length a spirit, loving ill,
Táḍaká, wearing shapes at will,
Whose mighty strength, exceeding vast,
A thousand elephants, surpassed,
Was to fierce Sunda, lord and head
Of all the demon armies, wed.
From her, Lord Indra's peer in might
Giant Márícha sprang to light:
And she, a constant plague and pest,
These two fair realms has long distressed.
Now dwelling in her dark abode

109

A league away she bars the road:
And we, O Ráma, hence must go
Where lies the forest of the foe.
Now on thine own right arm rely,
And my command obey:
Smite the foul monster that she die,
And take the plague away.
To reach this country none may dare
Fallen from its old estate,
Which she, whose fury naught can bear,
Has left so desolate.
And now my truthful tale is told
How with accursed sway
The spirit plagued this wood of old,
And ceases not to-day."

CANTO
XXVII

The Birth of Tádaká

When thus the sage without a peer
Had closed that story strange to hear,
Ráma again the saint addressed
To set one lingering doubt at rest:
"O holy man, 'tis said by all
That spirits' strength is weak and small:
How can she match, of power so slight,
A thousand elephants in might?"
And Viśvámitra thus replied
To Raghu's son the glorified:
"Listen, and I will tell thee how
She gained the strength that arms her now.
A mighty spirit lived of yore;
Suketu was the name he bore.
Childless was he, and free from crime

In rites austere he passed his time.
The mighty Sire was pleased to show
His favour, and a child bestow.
Táḍaká named, most fair to see,
A pearl among the maids was she,
And matched, for such was Brahmá's dower,
A thousand elephants in power.
Nor would the Eternal Sire, although
The spirit longed, a son bestow
That maid in beauty's youthful pride
Was given to Sunda for a bride.
Her son, Márícha was his name,
A giant, through a curse, became.
She, widowed, dared with him molest

Agastya, of all saints the best.
Inflamed with hunger's wildest rage,
Roaring she rushed upon the sage.
When the great hermit saw her near,
On speeding in her fierce career,
He thus pronounced Márícha's doom:
"A giant's form and shape assume."
And then, by mighty anger swayed,
On Táḍaká this curse he laid:
"Thy present form and semblance quit,
And wear a shape thy mood to fit;
Changed form and feature by my ban,
A fearful thing that feeds on man."

She, by his awful curse possessed,
And mad with rage that fills her breast,
Has on this land her fury dealt
Where once the saint Agastya dwelt.
Go, Ráma, smite this monster dead,
The wicked plague, of power so dread,
And further by this deed of thine
The good of Bráhmans and of kine.
Thy hand alone can overthrow,
In all the worlds, this impious foe.
Nor let compassion lead thy mind
To shrink from blood of womankind;

111

A monarch's son must ever count
The people's welfare paramount,
And whether pain or joy he deal
Dare all things for his subjects' weal;
Yea, if the deed bring praise or guilt,
If life be saved or blood be spilt:
Such, through all time, should be the care
Of those a kingdom's weight who bear.
Slay, Ráma, slay this impious fiend,
For by no law her life is screened.
So Manthará, as bards have told,
Virochan's child, was slain of old
By Indra, when in furious hate
She longed the earth to devastate.
So Kávya's mother, Bhrigu's wife,
Who loved her husband as her life,
When Indra's throne she sought to gain,
By Vishṇu's hand of yore was slain.
By these and high-souled kings beside,
Struck down, have lawless women died."

CANTO

XXVIII

The Death of Tádaká

Thus spoke the saint. Each vigorous word
The noble monarch's offspring heard,
And, reverent hands together laid,
His answer to the hermit made:
"My sire and mother bade me aye
Thy word, O mighty Saint, obey
So will I, O most glorious, kill
This Tádaká who joys in ill,
For such my sire's, and such thy will.
To aid with mine avenging hand

The Bráhmans, kine, and all the land,
Obedient, heart and soul, I stand."

Thus spoke the tamer of the foe,
And by the middle grasped his bow.
Strongly he drew the sounding string
That made the distant welkin ring.
Scared by the mighty clang the deer
That roamed the forest shook with fear,
And Tádaká the echo heard,
And rose in haste from slumber stirred.
In wild amaze, her soul aflame
With fury toward the spot she came.
When that foul shape of evil mien
And stature vast as e'er was seen
The wrathful son of Raghu eyed,
He thus unto his brother cried:
"Her dreadful shape, O Lakshman, see,
A form to shudder at and flee.
The hideous monster's very view
Would cleave a timid heart in two.
Behold the demon hard to smite,
Defended by her magic might.
My hand shall stay her course to-day,
And shear her nose and ears away.
No heart have I her life to take:
I spare it for her sex's sake.
My will is but, with minished force,
To check her in her evil course."
While thus he spoke, by rage impelled
Roaring as she came nigh,
The fiend her course at Ráma held
With huge arms tossed on high.
Her, rushing on, the seer assailed
With a loud cry of hate;
And thus the sons of Raghu hailed:
"Fight, and be fortunate."
Then from the earth a horrid cloud
Of dust the demon raised,
And for awhile in darkling shroud
Wrapt Raghu's sons amazed.

113

Then calling on her magic power
The fearful fight to wage,
She smote him with a stony shower,
Till Ráma burned with rage.
Then pouring forth his arrowy rain
That stony flood to stay,

With winged darts, as she charged amain,
He shore her hands away.
As Táḍaká still thundered near
Thus maimed by Ráma's blows,
Lakshmaṇ in fury severed sheer
The monster's ears and nose.
Assuming by her magic skill
A fresh and fresh disguise,
She tried a thousand shapes at will,
Then vanished from their eyes.
When Gádhi's son of high renown
Still saw the stony rain pour down
Upon each princely warrior's head,
With words of wisdom thus he said:
"Enough of mercy, Ráma, lest
This sinful evil-working pest,
Disturber of each holy rite,
Repair by magic arts her might.
Without delay the fiend should die,
For, see, the twilight hour is nigh.
And at the joints of night and day
Such giant foes are hard to slay."
Then Ráma, skilful to direct
His arrow to the sound,
With shafts the mighty demon checked
Who rained her stones around.
She sore impeded and beset
By Ráma and his arrowy net,
Though skilled in guile and magic lore,
Rushed on the brothers with a roar.
Deformed, terrific, murderous, dread,
Swift as the levin on she sped,
Like cloudy pile in autumn's sky,
Lifting her two vast arms on high,

114

When Ráma smote her with a dart,
Shaped like a crescent, to the heart.
Sore wounded by the shaft that came
With lightning speed and surest aim,
Blood spouting from her mouth and side,
She fell upon the earth and died.
Soon as the Lord who rules the sky
Saw the dread monster lifeless lie,
He called aloud, Well done! well done!
And the Gods honoured Raghu's son.
Standing in heaven the Thousand-eyed,
With all the Immortals, joying cried:
"Lift up thine eyes, O Saint, and see
The Gods and Indra nigh to thee.
This deed of Ráma's boundless might
Has filled our bosoms with delight,
Now, for our will would have it so,
To Raghu's son some favour show.
Invest him with the power which naught
But penance gains and holy thought,
Those heavenly arms on him bestow
To thee entrusted long ago
By great Krišášva best of kings,
Son of the Lord of living things.
More fit recipient none can be
Than he who joys it following thee;
And for our sakes the monarch's seed
Has yet to do a mighty deed."

He spoke; and all the heavenly train
Rejoicing sought their homes again,
While honour to the saint they paid.
Then came the evening's twilight shade,
The best of hermits overjoyed
To know the monstrous fiend destroyed,
His lips on Ráma's forehead pressed,
And thus the conquering chief addressed:
"O Ráma gracious to the sight.
Here will we pass the present night,
And with the morrow's earliest ray
Bend to my hermitage our way."

The son of Daśaratha heard,
Delighted, Viśvámitra's word,
And as he bade, that night he spent
In Táḍaká's wild wood, content.
And the grove shone that happy day,
Freed from the curse that on it lay,
Like Chaitraratha fair and gay.

CANTO
XXIX

The Celestial Arms

That night they slept and took their rest;
And then the mighty saint addressed,
With pleasant smile and accents mild
These words to Raghu's princely child:
"Well pleased am I. High fate be thine,
Thou scion of a royal line.
Now will I, for I love thee so,
All heavenly arms on thee bestow.
Victor with these, whoe'er oppose,
Thy hand shall conquer all thy foes,
Though Gods and spirits of the air,
Serpents and fiends, the conflict dare.
I'll give thee as a pledge of love
The mystic arms they use above,
For worthy thou to have revealed
The weapons I have learnt to wield.

First, son of Raghu, shall be thine
The arm of Vengeance, strong, divine:
The arm of Fate, the arm of Right,
And Vishṇu's arm of awful might:
That, before which no foe can stand,
The thunderbolt of Indra's hand;

116

And Śiva's trident, sharp and dread,
And that dire weapon Brahmá's Head.
And two fair clubs, O royal child,
One Charmer and one Pointed styled
With flame of lambent fire aglow,
On thee, O Chieftain, I bestow.
And Fate's dread net and Justice' noose
That none may conquer, for thy use:
And the great cord, renowned of old,
Which Varuṇ ever loves to hold.
Take these two thunderbolts, which I
Have got for thee, the Moist and Dry.
Here Śiva's dart to thee I yield,
And that which Vishṇu wont to wield.
I give to thee the arm of Fire,
Desired by all and named the Spire.
To thee I grant the Wind-God's dart,
Named Crusher, O thou pure of heart,
This arm, the Horse's Head, accept,
And this, the Curlew's Bill yclept,
And these two spears, the best e'er flew,
Named the Invincible and True.
And arms of fiends I make thine own,
Skull-wreath and mace that smashes bone.
And Joyous, which the spirits bear,
Great weapon of the sons of air.
Brave offspring of the best of lords,
I give thee now the Gem of swords,
And offer next, thine hand to arm,
The heavenly bards' beloved charm.
Now with two arms I thee invest
Of never-ending Sleep and Rest,
With weapons of the Sun and Rain,
And those that dry and burn amain;
And strong Desire with conquering touch,
The dart that Káma prizes much.
I give the arm of shadowy powers
That bleeding flesh of men devours.
I give the arms the God of Gold
And giant fiends exult to hold.
This smites the foe in battle-strife,

And takes his fortune, strength, and life.
I give the arms called False and True,
And great Illusion give I too;
The hero's arm called Strong and Bright
That spoils the foeman's strength in fight.
I give thee as a priceless boon
The Dew, the weapon of the Moon,
And add the weapon, deftly planned,
That strengthens Viśvakarmá's hand.
The Mortal dart whose point is chill,
And Slaughter, ever sure to kill;
All these and other arms, for thou
Art very dear, I give thee now.
Receive these weapons from my hand,
Son of the noblest in the land."

Facing the east, the glorious saint
Pure from all spot of earthly taint,
To Ráma, with delighted mind,
That noble host of spells consigned.
He taught the arms, whose lore is won
Hardly by Gods, to Raghu's son.
He muttered low the spell whose call
Summons those arms and rules them all
And, each in visible form and frame,
Before the monarch's son they came.
They stood and spoke in reverent guise
To Ráma with exulting cries:
"O noblest child of Raghu, see,
Thy ministers and thralls are we."
With joyful heart and eager hand
Ráma received the wondrous band,
And thus with words of welcome cried:
"Aye present to my will abide."
Then hasted to the saint to pay
Due reverence, and pursued his way.

CANTO

XXX

The Mysterious Powers

Pure, with glad cheer and joyful breast,
Of those mysterious arms possessed,
Ráma, now passing on his way,
Thus to the saint began to say:
"Lord of these mighty weapons, I
Can scarce be harmed by Gods on high;
Now, best of saints, I long to gain
The powers that can these arms restrain."
Thus spoke the prince. The sage austere,
True to his vows, from evil clear,
Called forth the names of those great charms
Whose powers restrain the deadly arms.
"Receive thou True and Truly famed,
And Bold and Fleet: the weapons named

Warder and Progress, swift of pace,
Averted-head and Drooping-face;
The Seen, and that which Secret flies;
The weapon of the thousand eyes;
Ten-headed, and the Hundred-faced,
Star-gazer and the Layer-waste:
The Omen-bird, the Pure-from-spot,
The pair that wake and slumber not:
The Fiendish, that which shakes amain,
The Strong-of-Hand, the Rich-in-Gain:
The Guardian, and the Close-allied,
The Gaper, Love, and Golden-side:
O Raghu's son receive all these,
Bright ones that wear what forms they please;
Kriśáśva's mystic sons are they,
And worthy thou their might to sway."

With joy the pride of Raghu's race
Received the hermit's proffered grace,
Mysterious arms, to check and stay,
Or smite the foeman in the fray.
Then, all with heavenly forms endued,
Nigh came the wondrous multitude.
Celestial in their bright attire
Some shone like coals of burning fire;
Some were like clouds of dusky smoke;
And suppliant thus they sweetly spoke:
"Thy thralls, O Ráma, here we stand:
Command, we pray, thy faithful band"
"Depart," he cried, "where each may list,
But when I call you to assist,
Be present to my mind with speed,
And aid me in the hour of need."

To Ráma then they lowly bent,
And round him in due reverence went,
To his command, they answered, Yea,
And as they came so went away.
When thus the arms had homeward flown,
With pleasant words and modest tone,
E'en as he walked, the prince began
To question thus the holy man:
"What cloudlike wood is that which near
The mountain's side I see appear?
O tell me, for I long to know;
Its pleasant aspect charms me so.
Its glades are full of deer at play,
And sweet birds sing on every spray,
Past is the hideous wild; I feel
So sweet a tremor o'er me steal,
And hail with transport fresh and new
A land that is so fair to view.
Then tell me all, thou holy Sage,
And whose this pleasant hermitage
In which those wicked ones delight
To mar and kill each holy rite.
And with foul heart and evil deed
Thy sacrifice, great Saint, impede.

To whom, O Sage, belongs this land
In which thine altars ready stand!
'Tis mine to guard them, and to slay
The giants who the rites would stay.
All this, O best of saints, I burn
From thine own lips, my lord, to learn."

CANTO

XXXI

The Perfect Hermitage

Thus spoke the prince of boundless might,
And thus replied the anchorite:
"Chief of the mighty arm, of yore
Lord Vishṇu whom the Gods adore,
For holy thought and rites austere
Of penance made his dwelling here.
This ancient wood was called of old
Grove of the Dwarf, the mighty-souled,
And when perfection he attained
The grove the name of Perfect gained.
Bali of yore, Virochan's son,
Dominion over Indra won,
And when with power his proud heart swelled,
O'er the three worlds his empire held.
When Bali then began a rite,
The Gods and Indra in affright
Sought Vishṇu in this place of rest,
And thus with prayers the God addressed:
"Bali. Virochan's mighty son,
His sacrifice has now begun:
Of boundless wealth, that demon king
Is bounteous to each living thing.
Though suppliants flock from every side
The suit of none is e'er denied.

Whate'er, where'er howe'er the call,
He hears the suit and gives to all.
Now with thine own illusive art
Perform, O Lord, the helper's part:
Assume a dwarfish form, and thus
From fear and danger rescue us."

Thus in their dread the Immortals sued:
The God a dwarflike shape indued:
Before Virochan's son he came,
Three steps of land his only claim.
The boon obtained, in wondrous wise
Lord Vishṇu's form increased in size;
Through all the worlds, tremendous, vast,
God of the Triple Step, he passed.
The whole broad earth from side to side
He measured with one mighty stride,
Spanned with the next the firmament,
And with the third through heaven he went.

Thus was the king of demons hurled
By Vishṇu to the nether world,
And thus the universe restored
To Indra's rule, its ancient lord.
And now because the immortal God
This spot in dwarflike semblance trod,
The grove has aye been loved by me
For reverence of the devotee.
But demons haunt it, prompt to stay
Each holy offering I would pay.
Be thine, O lion-lord, to kill
These giants that delight in ill.
This day, beloved child, our feet
Shall rest within the calm retreat:
And know, thou chief of Raghu's line,
My hermitage is also thine."

He spoke; and soon the anchorite,
With joyous looks that beamed delight,
With Ráma and his brother stood

Within the consecrated wood.
Soon as they saw the holy man,
With one accord together ran
The dwellers in the sacred shade,
And to the saint their reverence paid,
And offered water for his feet,
The gift of honour and a seat;
And next with hospitable care
They entertained the princely pair.
The royal tamers of their foes
Rested awhile in sweet repose:
Then to the chief of hermits sued
Standing in suppliant attitude:
"Begin, O best of saints, we pray,
Initiatory rites to-day.
This Perfect Grove shall be anew
Made perfect, and thy words be true."

Then, thus addressed, the holy man,
The very glorious sage, began
The high preliminary rite.
Restraining sense and appetite.
Calmly the youths that night reposed,
And rose when morn her light disclosed,
Their morning worship paid, and took
Of lustral water from the brook.
Thus purified they breathed the prayer,
Then greeted Viśvámitra where
As celebrant he sate beside
The flame with sacred oil supplied.

Visvámitra's Sacrifice

That conquering pair, of royal race,
   Skilled to observe due time and place,
   To Kuśik's hermit son addressed,
In timely words, their meet request:
"When must we, lord, we pray thee tell,
Those Rovers of the Night repel?
Speak, lest we let the moment fly,
And pass the due occasion by."
Thus longing for the strife, they prayed,
And thus the hermits answer made:
"Till the fifth day be come and past,
O Raghu's sons, your watch must last.
The saint his Dikshá has begun,
And all that time will speak to none."
Soon as the steadfast devotees
Had made reply in words like these,
The youths began, disdaining sleep,
Six days and nights their watch to keep.
The warrior pair who tamed the foe,
Unrivalled benders of the bow,
Kept watch and ward unwearied still
To guard the saint from scathe and ill.
'Twas now the sixth returning day,
The hour foretold had past away.
Then Ráma cried: "O Lakshman, now
Firm, watchful, resolute be thou.
The fiends as yet have kept afar
From the pure grove in which we are:
Yet waits us, ere the day shall close,
Dire battle with the demon foes."

While thus spoke Ráma borne away
By longing for the deadly fray,
See! bursting from the altar came
The sudden glory of the flame.
Round priest and deacon, and upon
Grass, ladles, flowers, the splendour shone,
And the high rite, in order due,
With sacred texts began anew.
But then a loud and fearful roar
Re-echoed through the sky;
And like vast clouds that shadow o'er
The heavens in dark July,
Involved in gloom of magic might
Two fiends rushed on amain,
Márícha, Rover of the Night,
Suváhu, and their train.
As on they came in wild career
Thick blood in rain they shed;
And Ráma saw those things of fear
Impending overhead.
Then soon as those accursed two
Who showered down blood be spied,
Thus to his brother brave and true
Spoke Ráma lotus-eyed:
"Now, Lakshman, thou these fiends shalt see,
Man-eaters, foul of mind,
Before my mortal weapon flee
Like clouds before the wind."
He spoke. An arrow, swift as thought,
Upon his bow he pressed,
And smote, to utmost fury wrought,
Márícha on the breast.
Deep in his flesh the weapon lay
Winged by the mystic spell,

And, hurled a hundred leagues away,
In ocean's flood he fell.
Then Ráma, when he saw the foe
Convulsed and mad with pain
Neath the chill-pointed weapon's blow,
To Lakshman spoke again:

125

"See, Lakshmaṇ, see! this mortal dart
That strikes a numbing chill,
Hath struck him senseless with the smart,
But left him breathing still.
But these who love the evil way,
And drink the blood they spill,
Rejoicing holy rites to stay,
Fierce plagues, my hand shall kill."
He seized another shaft, the best,
Aglow with living flame;
It struck Suváhu on the chest,
And dead to earth he came.
Again a dart, the Wind-God's own,
Upon his string he laid,
And all the demons were o'erthrown,
The saints no more afraid.
When thus the fiends were slain in fight,
Disturbers of each holy rite,
Due honour by the saints was paid
To Ráma for his wondrous aid:
So Indra is adored when he
Has won some glorious victory.
Success at last the rite had crowned,
And Viśvámitra gazed around,
And seeing every side at rest,
The son of Raghu thus addressed:
"My joy, O Prince, is now complete:
Thou hast obeyed my will:
Perfect before, this calm retreat
Is now more perfect still."

CANTO
XXXIII

The Sone

Their task achieved, the princes spent
That night with joy and full content.
Ere yet the dawn was well displayed
Their morning rites they duly paid,
And sought, while yet the light was faint,
The hermits and the mighty saint.
They greeted first that holy sire
Resplendent like the burning fire,
And then with noble words began
Their sweet speech to the sainted man:
"Here stand, O Lord, thy servants true:
Command what thou wouldst have us do."

The saints, by Viśvámitra led,
To Ráma thus in answer said:
"Janak the king who rules the land
Of fertile Míthilá has planned
A noble sacrifice, and we
Will thither go the rite to see.
Thou, Prince of men, with us shalt go,
And there behold the wondrous bow,
Terrific, vast, of matchless might,
Which, splendid at the famous rite,
The Gods assembled gave the king.
No giant, fiend, or God can string
That gem of bows, no heavenly bard:
Then, sure, for man the task were hard.
When lords of earth have longed to know
The virtue of that wondrous bow,
The strongest sons of kings in vain
Have tried the mighty cord to strain.

This famous bow thou there shalt view,
And wondrous rites shalt witness too.
The high-souled king who lords it o'er
The realm of Míthilá of yore
Gained from the Gods this bow, the price
Of his imperial sacrifice.
Won by the rite the glorious prize
Still in the royal palace lies,
Laid up in oil of precious scent
With aloe-wood and incense blent."

Then Ráma answering, Be it so,
Made ready with the rest to go.
The saint himself was now prepared,
But ere beyond the grove he fared,
He turned him and in words like these
Addressed the sylvan deities:
"Farewell! each holy rite complete,
I leave the hermits' perfect seat:
To Gangá's northern shore I go
Beneath Himálaya's peaks of snow."
With reverent steps he paced around
The limits of the holy ground,
And then the mighty saint set forth
And took his journey to the north.
His pupils, deep in Scripture's page,
Followed behind the holy sage,
And servants from the sacred grove
A hundred wains for convoy drove.
The very birds that winged that air,
The very deer that harboured there,
Forsook the glade and leafy brake
And followed for the hermit's sake.
They travelled far, till in the west
The sun was speeding to his rest,
And made, their portioned journey o'er,
Their halt on Śona's distant shore.
The hermits bathed when sank the sun,
And every rite was duly done,
Oblations paid to Fire, and then
Sate round their chief the holy men.

Ráma and Lakshmaṇ lowly bowed
In reverence to the hermit crowd,
And Ráma, having sate him down
Before the saint of pure renown,

With humble palms together laid
His eager supplication made:
"What country, O my lord, is this,
Fair-smiling in her wealth and bliss?
Deign fully, O thou mighty Seer,
To tell me, for I long to hear."
Moved by the prayer of Ráma, he
Told forth the country's history.

CANTO
XXXIV

Brahmadatta

"A king of Brahmá's seed who bore
The name of Kuśa reigned of yore.
Just, faithful to his vows, and true,
He held the good in honour due.
His bride, a queen of noble name,
Of old Vidarbha's monarchs came.
Like their own father, children four,
All valiant boys, the lady bore.
In glorious deeds each nerve they strained,
And well their Warrior part sustained.
To them most just, and true, and brave,
Their father thus his counsel gave:
"Beloved children, ne'er forget
Protection is a prince's debt:
The noble work at once begin,
High virtue and her fruits to win."
The youths, to all the people dear,

Received his speech with willing ear;
And each went forth his several way,
Foundations of a town to lay.
Kuśámba, prince of high renown,
Was builder of Kauśámbí's town,
And Kuśanábha, just and wise,
Bade high Mahodaya's towers arise.
Amúrtarajas chose to dwell
In Dharmáraṇya's citadel,
And Vasu bade his city fair
The name of Girivraja bear.
This fertile spot whereon we stand
Was once the high-souled Vasu's land.
Behold! as round we turn our eyes,
Five lofty mountain peaks arise.
See! bursting from her parent hill,
Sumágadhí, a lovely rill,
Bright gleaming as she flows between
The mountains, like a wreath is seen,
And then through Magadh's plains and groves
With many a fair mæander roves.
And this was Vasu's old domain,
The fertile Magadh's broad champaign,
Which smiling fields of tilth adorn
And diadem with golden corn.

The queen Ghritáchí, nymph most fair,
Married to Kuśanábha, bare
A hundred daughters, lovely-faced,
With every charm and beauty graced.
It chanced the maidens, bright and gay
As lightning-flashes on a day
Of rain time, to the garden went
With song and play and merriment,
And there in gay attire they strayed,
And danced, and laughed, and sang, and played.
The God of Wind who roves at will
All places, as he lists, to fill,
Saw the young maidens dancing there,
Of faultless shape and mien most fair.
"I love you all, sweet girls," he cried,

130

"And each shall be my darling bride.
Forsake, forsake your mortal lot,
And gain a life that withers not.
A fickle thing is youth's brief span,
And more than all in mortal man.
Receive unending youth, and be
Immortal, O my loves, with me."

The hundred girls, to wonder stirred,
The wooing of the Wind-God heard,
Laughed, as a jest, his suit aside,
And with one voice they thus replied:
"O mighty Wind, free spirit who
All life pervadest, through and through,
Thy wondrous power we maidens know;
Then wherefore wilt thou mock us so?
Our sire is Kuśanábha, King;
And we, forsooth, have charms to bring
A God to woo us from the skies;
But honour first we maidens prize.
Far may the hour, we pray, be hence,
When we, O thou of little sense,
Our truthful father's choice refuse,
And for ourselves our husbands choose.
Our honoured sire our lord we deem,
He is to us a God supreme,
And they to whom his high decree
May give us shall our husbands be."

He heard the answer they returned,
And mighty rage within him burned.
On each fair maid a blast he sent:
Each stately form he bowed and bent.
Bent double by the Wind-God's ire
They sought the palace of their sire,

There fell upon the ground with sighs,
While tears and shame were in their eyes.
The king himself, with troubled brow,
Saw his dear girls so fair but now,
A mournful sight all bent and bowed,

131

And grieving thus he cried aloud:
"What fate is this, and what the cause?
What wretch has scorned all heavenly laws?
Who thus your forms could curve and break?
You struggle, but no answer make."

They heard the speech of that wise king
Of their misfortune questioning.
Again the hundred maidens sighed,
Touched with their heads his feet, and cried:
"The God of Wind, pervading space,
Would bring on us a foul disgrace,
And choosing folly's evil way
From virtue's path in scorn would stray.
But we in words like these reproved
The God of Wind whom passion moved:
"Farewell, O Lord! A sire have we,
No women uncontrolled and free.
Go, and our sire's consent obtain
If thou our maiden hands wouldst gain.
No self-dependent life we live:
If we offend, our fault forgive."
But led by folly as a slave,
He would not hear the rede we gave,
And even as we gently spoke
We felt the Wind-God's crushing stroke."

The pious king, with grief distressed,
The noble hundred thus addressed:
"With patience, daughters, bear your fate,
Yours was a deed supremely great
When with one mind you kept from shame
The honour of your father's name.
Patience, when men their anger vent,
Is woman's praise and ornament;
Yet when the Gods inflict the blow
Hard is it to support the woe.
Patience, my girls, exceeds all price:
'Tis alms, and truth, and sacrifice.
Patience is virtue, patience fame:
Patience upholds this earthly frame.

And now, I think, is come the time
To wed you in your maiden prime.
Now, daughters, go where'er you will:
Thoughts for your good my mind shall fill."

The maidens went, consoled, away:
The best of kings, that very day,
Summoned his ministers of state
About their marriage to debate.
Since then, because the Wind-God bent
The damsels' forms for punishment,
That royal town is known to fame
By Kanyákubja's borrowed name.

There lived a sage called Chúli then,
Devoutest of the sons of men;
His days in penance rites he spent,
A glorious saint, most continent.
To him absorbed in tasks austere
The child of Urmilá drew near,
Sweet Somadá, the heavenly maid
And lent the saint her pious aid.
Long time near him the maiden spent,
And served him meek and reverent,
Till the great hermit, pleased with her,
Thus spoke unto his minister:
"Grateful am I for all thy care:
Blest maiden, speak, thy wish declare."
The sweet-voiced nymph rejoiced to see
The favour of the devotee,
And to that eloquent old man,
Most eloquent she thus began:
"Thou hast, by heavenly grace sustained,
Close union with the Godhead gained.
I long, O Saint, to see a son
By force of holy penance won.
Unwed, a maiden life I live:
A son to me, thy suppliant, give."
The saint with favour heard her prayer,
And gave a son exceeding fair.
Him, Chúli's spiritual child,

133

His mother Brahmadatta styled.
King Brahmadatta, rich and great,
In Kámpilí maintained his state,
Ruling, like Indra in his bliss,
His fortunate metropolis.
King Kuśanábha planned that he
His hundred daughters' lord should be.
To him, obedient to his call,
The happy monarch gave them all.
Like Indra then he took the hand
Of every maiden of the band.
Soon as the hand of each young maid
In Brahmadatta's palm was laid,
Deformity and cares away,
She shone in beauty bright and gay.
Their freedom from the Wind-God's might
Saw Kuśanábha with delight.
Each glance that on their forms he threw
Filled him with raptures ever new.
Then when the rites were all complete,
With highest marks of honour meet
The bridegroom with his brides he sent
To his great seat of government.

The nymph received with pleasant speech
Her daughters; and, embracing each,
Upon their forms she fondly gazed,
And royal Kuśanábha praised.

CANTO
XXXV

Visvámitra's Lineage

"The rites were o'er, the maids were wed,
The bridegroom to his home was sped.
The sonless monarch bade prepare
A sacrifice to gain an heir.
Then Kuśa, Brahmá's son, appeared,
And thus King Kuśanábha cheered:
"Thou shalt, my child, obtain a son
Like thine own self, O holy one.
Through him for ever, Gádhi named,
Shalt thou in all the worlds be famed."
He spoke, and vanished from the sight
To Brahmá's world of endless light.
Time fled, and, as the saint foretold,
Gádhi was born, the holy-souled.
My sire was he; through him I trace
My line from royal Kuśa's race.
My sister—elder-born was she—
The pure and good Satyavatí,
Was to the great Richíka wed.
Still faithful to her husband dead,
She followed him, most noble dame,
And, raised to heaven in human frame,
A pure celestial stream became.
Down from Himálaya's snowy height,
In floods for ever fair and bright,
My sister's holy waves are hurled
To purify and glad the world.
Now on Himálaya's side I dwell
Because I love my sister well.
She, for her faith and truth renowned,
Most loving to her husband found,

135

High-fated, firm in each pure vow,
Is queen of all the rivers now.
Bound by a vow I left her side
And to the Perfect convent hied.
There, by the aid 'twas thine to lend,
Made perfect, all my labours end.
Thus, mighty Prince, I now have told
My race and lineage, high and old,
And local tales of long ago
Which thou, O Ráma, fain wouldst know.
As I have sate rehearsing thus
The midnight hour is come on us.
Now, Ráma, sleep, that nothing may
Our journey of to-morrow stay.
No leaf on any tree is stirred:
Hushed in repose are beast and bird:
Where'er you turn, on every side,
Dense shades of night the landscape hide,
The light of eve is fled: the skies,
Thick-studded with their host of eyes,
Seem a star-forest overhead,
Where signs and constellations spread.
Now rises, with his pure cold ray,
The moon that drives the shades away,
And with his gentle influence brings
Joy to the hearts of living things.
Now, stealing from their lairs, appear
The beasts to whom the night is dear.
Now spirits walk, and every power
That revels in the midnight hour."

The mighty hermit's tale was o'er,
He closed his lips and spoke no more.
The holy men on every side,
"Well done! well done," with reverence cried;
"The mighty men of Kuśa's seed
Were ever famed for righteous deed.
Like Brahmá's self in glory shine
The high-souled lords of Kuśa's line,
And thy great name is sounded most,

136

O Saint, amid the noble host.
And thy dear sister—fairest she
Of streams, the high-born Kauśikí—
Diffusing virtue where she flows,
New splendour on thy lineage throws."
Thus by the chief of saints addressed
The son of Gádhi turned to rest;
So, when his daily course is done,
Sinks to his rest the beaming sun.
Ráma with Lakshmaṇ, somewhat stirred
To marvel by the tales they heard,
Turned also to his couch, to close
His eyelids in desired repose.

XXXVI

The Birth of Gangá

The hours of night now waning fast
  On Śona's pleasant shore they passed.
  Then, when the dawn began to break,
To Ráma thus the hermit spake:
"The light of dawn is breaking clear,
The hour of morning rites is near.
Rise, Ráma, rise, dear son, I pray,
And make thee ready for the way."

Then Ráma rose, and finished all
His duties at the hermit's call,
Prepared with joy the road to take,
And thus again in question spake:
"Here fair and deep the Śona flows,
And many an isle its bosom shows:
What way, O Saint, will lead us o'er

And land us on the farther shore?"
The saint replied: "The way I choose
Is that which pious hermits use."

For many a league they journeyed on
Till, when the sun of mid-day shone,
The hermit-haunted flood was seen
Of Jáhnaví, the Rivers' Queen.
Soon as the holy stream they viewed,
Thronged with a white-winged multitude
Of sárases and swans, delight
Possessed them at the lovely sight;
And then prepared the hermit band
To halt upon that holy strand.
They bathed as Scripture bids, and paid
Oblations due to God and shade.
To Fire they burnt the offerings meet,
And sipped the oil, like Amrit sweet.
Then pure and pleased they sate around
Saint Viśvámitra on the ground.
The holy men of lesser note,
In due degree, sate more remote,
While Raghu's sons took nearer place
By virtue of their rank and race.
Then Ráma said: "O Saint, I yearn
The three-pathed Gangá's tale to learn."

Thus urged, the sage recounted both
The birth of Gangá and her growth:
"The mighty hill with metals stored,
Himálaya, is the mountains' lord,
The father of a lovely pair
Of daughters fairest of the fair:
Their mother, offspring of the will
Of Meru, everlasting hill,
Mená, Himálaya's darling, graced
With beauty of her dainty waist.
Gangá was elder-born: then came
The fair one known by Umá's name.
Then all the Gods of heaven, in need
Of Gangá's help their vows to speed,

To great Himálaya came and prayed
The mountain King to yield the maid.
He, not regardless of the weal
Of the three worlds, with holy zeal
His daughter to the Immortals gave,
Gangá whose waters cleanse and save,
Who roams at pleasure, fair and free,
Purging all sinners, to the sea.
The three-pathed Gangá thus obtained,
The Gods their heavenly homes regained.
Long time the sister Umá passed
In vows austere and rigid fast,
And the king gave the devotee
Immortal Rudra's bride to be,
Matching with that unequalled Lord
His Umá through the worlds adored.
So now a glorious station fills
Each daughter of the King of Hills:
One honoured as the noblest stream,
One mid the Goddesses supreme.
Thus Gangá, King Himálaya's child,
The heavenly river, undefiled,
Rose bearing with her to the sky
Her waves that bless and purify."

[I am compelled to omit Cantos XXXVII and XXXVIII, The Glory
of Umá, and the Birth of Kártikeya, as both in subject and language
offensive to modern taste. They will be found in Schlegel's Latin
translation.]

The Sons of Sagar

The saint in accents sweet and clear
Thus told his tale for Ráma's ear,
And thus anew the holy man
A legend to the prince began:
"There reigned a pious monarch o'er
Ayodhyá in the days of yore:
Sagar his name: no child had he,
And children much he longed to see.
His honoured consort, fair of face,
Sprang from Vidarbha's royal race,
Keśini, famed from early youth
For piety and love of truth.
Aríshṭanemi's daughter fair,
With whom no maiden might compare
In beauty, though the earth is wide,
Sumati, was his second bride.
With his two queens afar he went,
And weary days in penance spent,
Fervent, upon Himálaya's hill
Where springs the stream called Bhrigu' rill.
Nor did he fail that saint to please
With his devout austerities.
And, when a hundred years had fled,
Thus the most truthful Bhrigu said:
"From thee, O Sagar, blameless King,
A mighty host of sons shall spring,
And thou shalt win a glorious name
Which none, O Chief, but thou shall claim.
One of thy queens a son shall bear,
Maintainer of thy race and heir;

And of the other there shall be
Sons sixty thousand born to thee."

Thus as he spake, with one accord,
To win the grace of that high lord,
The queens, with palms together laid,
In humble supplication prayed:
"Which queen, O Bráhman, of the pair,
The many, or the one shall bear?
Most eager, Lord, are we to know,
And as thou sayest be it so."

With his sweet speech the saint replied:
"Yourselves, O Queens, the choice decide.
Your own discretion freely use
Which shall the one or many choose:
One shall the race and name uphold,
The host be famous, strong, and bold.
Which will have which?" Then Keśini
The mother of one heir would be.
Sumati, sister of the king
Of all the birds that ply the wing,
To that illustrious Bráhman sued
That she might bear the multitude
Whose fame throughout the world should sound
For mighty enterprise renowned.
Around the saint the monarch went,
Bowing his head, most reverent.
Then with his wives, with willing feet,
Resought his own imperial seat.
Time passed. The elder consort bare
A son called Asamanj, the heir.
Then Sumati, the younger, gave
Birth to a gourd, O hero brave,
Whose rind, when burst and cleft in two,
Gave sixty thousand babes to view.
All these with care the nurses laid
In jars of oil; and there they stayed,
Till, youthful age and strength complete,
Forth speeding from each dark retreat,

141

All peers in valour, years, and might,
The sixty thousand came to light.
Prince Asamanj, brought up with care,
Scourge of his foes, was made the heir.
But liegemen's boys he used to cast
To Sarjú's waves that hurried past,
Laughing the while in cruel glee
Their dying agonies to see.
This wicked prince who aye withstood
The counsel of the wise and good,
Who plagued the people in his hate,
His father banished from the state.
His son, kind-spoken, brave, and tall,
Was Anśumán, beloved of all.

Long years flew by. The king decreed
To slay a sacrificial steed.
Consulting with his priestly band
He vowed the rite his soul had planned,
And, Veda skilled, by their advice
Made ready for the sacrifice.

CANTO
XL

The Cleaving of The Earth

The hermit ceased: the tale was done:
Then in a transport Raghu's son
Again addressed the ancient sire
Resplendent as a burning fire:
"O holy man, I fain would hear
The tale repeated full and clear
How he from whom my sires descend
Brought the great rite to happy end."
The hermit answered with a smile:

"Then listen, son of Raghu, while
My legendary tale proceeds
To tell of high-souled Sagar's deeds.
Within the spacious plain that lies
From where Himálaya's heights arise
To where proud Vindhya's rival chain
Looks down upon the subject plain—
A land the best for rites declared—
His sacrifice the king prepared.
And Anśumán the prince—for so
Sagar advised—with ready bow
Was borne upon a mighty car
To watch the steed who roamed afar.
But Indra, monarch of the skies,
Veiling his form in demon guise,
Came down upon the appointed day
And drove the victim horse away.
Reft of the steed the priests, distressed,
The master of the rite addressed:
"Upon the sacred day by force
A robber takes the victim horse.
Haste, King! now let the thief be slain;
Bring thou the charger back again:
The sacred rite prevented thus
Brings scathe and woe to all of us.
Rise, monarch, and provide with speed
That naught its happy course impede."
King Sagar in his crowded court
Gave ear unto the priests' report.
He summoned straightway to his side
His sixty thousand sons, and cried:
"Brave sons of mine, I knew not how
These demons are so mighty now:
The priests began the rite so well
All sanctified with prayer and spell.
If in the depths of earth he hide,
Or lurk beneath the ocean's tide,

Pursue, dear sons, the robber's track;
Slay him and bring the charger back.
The whole of this broad earth explore,

Sea-garlanded, from shore to shore:
Yea, dig her up with might and main
Until you see the horse again.
Deep let your searching labour reach,
A league in depth dug out by each.
The robber of our horse pursue,
And please your sire who orders you.
My grandson, I, this priestly train,
Till the steed comes, will here remain."

Their eager hearts with transport burned
As to their task the heroes turned.
Obedient to their father, they
Through earth's recesses forced their way.
With iron arms' unflinching toil
Each dug a league beneath the soil.
Earth, cleft asunder, groaned in pain,
As emulous they plied amain
Sharp-pointed coulter, pick, and bar,
Hard as the bolts of Indra are.
Then loud the horrid clamour rose
Of monsters dying neath their blows,
Giant and demon, fiend and snake,
That in earth's core their dwelling make.
They dug, in ire that naught could stay,
Through sixty thousand leagues their way,
Cleaving the earth with matchless strength
Till hell itself they reached at length.
Thus digging searched they Jambudvip
With all its hills and mountains steep.
Then a great fear began to shake
The heart of God, bard, fiend, and snake,
And all distressed in spirit went
Before the Sire Omnipotent.
With signs of woe in every face
They sought the mighty Father's grace,
And trembling still and ill at ease
Addressed their Lord in words like these:
"The sons of Sagar, Sire benign,
Pierce the whole earth with mine on mine,
And as their ruthless work they ply

144

Innumerable creatures die.
"This is the thief," the princes say,
"Who stole our victim steed away.
This marred the rite, and caused us ill,
And so their guiltless blood they spill."

CANTO

XLI

Kapil

The father lent a gracious ear
        And listened to their tale of fear,
        And kindly to the Gods replied
Whom woe and death had terrified:
"The wisest Vásudeva, who
The Immortals' foe, fierce Madhu, slew,
Regards broad Earth with love and pride
And guards, in Kapil's form, his bride.
His kindled wrath will quickly fall
On the king's sons and burn them all.
This cleaving of the earth his eye
Foresaw in ages long gone by:
He knew with prescient soul the fate
That Sagar's children should await."
The Three-and-thirty, freed from fear,
Sought their bright homes with hopeful cheer.
Still rose the great tempestuous sound
As Sagar's children pierced the ground.
When thus the whole broad earth was cleft,
And not a spot unsearched was left,
Back to their home the princes sped,
And thus unto their father said:
"We searched the earth from side to side,
While countless hosts of creatures died.
Our conquering feet in triumph trod

145

On snake and demon, fiend and God;
But yet we failed, with all our toil,
To find the robber and the spoil.
What can we more? If more we can,
Devise, O King, and tell thy plan."

His children's speech King Sagar heard,
And answered thus, to anger stirred:
"Dig on, and ne'er your labour stay
Till through earth's depths you force your way.
Then smite the robber dead, and bring
The charger back with triumphing."

The sixty thousand chiefs obeyed:
Deep through the earth their way they made.
Deep as they dug and deeper yet
The immortal elephant they met,
Famed Vírúpáksha vast of size,
Upon whose head the broad earth lies:
The mighty beast who earth sustains
With shaggy hills and wooded plains.
When, with the changing moon, distressed,
And longing for a moment's rest,
His mighty head the monster shakes,
Earth to the bottom reels and quakes.
Around that warder strong and vast
With reverential steps they passed.
Nor, when the honour due was paid,
Their downward search through earth delayed.
But turning from the east aside
Southward again their task they plied.
There Mahápadma held his place,
The best of all his mighty race,
Like some huge hill, of monstrous girth,
Upholding on his head the earth.
When the vast beast the princes saw,
They marvelled and were filled with awe.
The sons of high-souled Sagar round
That elephant in reverence wound.
Then in the western region they
With might unwearied cleft their way.

146

There saw they with astonisht eyes
Saumanas, beast of mountain size.
Round him with circling steps they went
With greetings kind and reverent.

On, on—no thought of rest or stay—
They reached the seat of Soma's sway.
There saw they Bhadra, white as snow,
With lucky marks that fortune show,
Bearing the earth upon his head.
Round him they paced with solemn tread,
And honoured him with greetings kind,
Then downward yet their way they mined.
They gained the tract 'twixt east and north
Whose fame is ever blazoned forth,
And by a storm of rage impelled,
Digging through earth their course they held.

Then all the princes, lofty-souled,
Of wondrous vigour, strong and bold,
Saw Vásudeva standing there
In Kapil's form he loved to wear,
And near the everlasting God
The victim charger cropped the sod.
They saw with joy and eager eyes
The fancied robber and the prize,
And on him rushed the furious band
Crying aloud, Stand, villain! stand!
"Avaunt! avaunt!" great Kapil cried,
His bosom flusht with passion's tide;
Then by his might that proud array
All scorcht to heaps of ashes lay.

CANTO
XLII

Sagar's Sacrifice

Then to the prince his grandson, bright
With his own fame's unborrowed light,
King Sagar thus began to say,
Marvelling at his sons' delay:
"Thou art a warrior skilled and bold,
Match for the mighty men of old.
Now follow on thine uncles' course
And track the robber of the horse.

To guard thee take thy sword and bow,
for huge and strong are beasts below.
There to the reverend reverence pay,
And kill the foes who check thy way;
Then turn successful home and see
My sacrifice complete through thee."

Obedient to the high-souled lord
Grasped Anśumán his bow and sword,
And hurried forth the way to trace
With youth and valour's eager pace.
On sped he by the path he found
Dug by his uncles underground.
The warder elephant he saw
Whose size and strength pass Nature's law,
Who bears the world's tremendous weight,
Whom God, fiend, giant venerate,
Bird, serpent, and each flitting shade,
To him the honour meet he paid
With circling steps and greeting due,
And further prayed him, if he knew,
To tell him of his uncles' weal,

148

And who had dared the horse to steal.
To him in war and council tried
The warder elephant replied:
"Thou, son of Asamanj, shalt lead
In triumph back the rescued steed."

As to each warder beast he came
And questioned all, his words the same,
The honoured youth with gentle speech
Drew eloquent reply from each,
That fortune should his steps attend,
And with the horse he home should wend.
Cheered with the grateful answer, he
Passed on with step more light and free,
And reached with careless heart the place
Where lay in ashes Sagar's race.
Then sank the spirit of the chief
Beneath that shock of sudden grief,
And with a bitter cry of woe
He mourned his kinsmen fallen so.
He saw, weighed down by woe and care,
The victim charger roaming there.
Yet would the pious chieftain fain
Oblations offer to the slain:
But, needing water for the rite,
He looked and there was none in sight
His quick eye searching all around
The uncle of his kinsmen found,
King Garuḍ, best beyond compare
Of birds who wing the fields of air.
Then thus unto the weeping man
The son of Vinatá began:
"Grieve not, O hero, for their fall
Who died a death approved of all.
Of mighty strength, they met their fate
By Kapil's hand whom none can mate.
Pour forth for them no earthly wave,
A holier flood their spirits crave.
If, daughter of the Lord of Snow,
Gangá would turn her stream below,
Her waves that cleanse all mortal stain

Would wash their ashes pure again.
Yea, when her flood whom all revere
Rolls o'er the dust that moulders here,
The sixty thousand, freed from sin,
A home in Indra's heaven shall win.
Go, and with ceaseless labour try
To draw the Goddess from the sky.
Return, and with thee take the steed;
So shall thy grandsire's rite succeed."

Prince Anśumán the strong and brave
Followed the rede Suparṇa gave.
The glorious hero took the horse,
And homeward quickly bent his course.
Straight to the anxious king he hied,
Whom lustral rites had purified,
The mournful story to unfold
And all the king of birds had told.
The tale of woe the monarch heard,
Nor longer was the rite deferred:
With care and just observance he
Accomplished all, as texts decree.
The rites performed, with brighter fame,
Mighty in counsel, home he came.
He longed to bring the river down,
But found no plan his wish to crown.
He pondered long with anxious thought
But saw no way to what he sought.
Thus thirty thousand years he spent,
And then to heaven the monarch went.

CANTO
XLIII

Bhagírath

When Sagar thus had bowed to fate,
The lords and commons of the state
Approved with ready heart and will
Prince Anśumán his throne to fill.
He ruled, a mighty king, unblamed,
Sire of Dilípa justly famed.
To him, his child and worthy heir,
The king resigned his kingdom's care,
And on Himálaya's pleasant side
His task austere of penance plied.
Bright as a God in clear renown
He planned to bring pure Gangá down.
There on his fruitless hope intent
Twice sixteen thousand years he spent,
And in the grove of hermits stayed
Till bliss in heaven his rites repaid.
Dilípa then, the good and great,
Soon as he learnt his kinsmen's fate,
Bowed down by woe, with troubled mind,

Pondering long no cure could find.
"How can I bring," the mourner sighed,
"To cleanse their dust, the heavenly tide?
How can I give them rest, and save
Their spirits with the offered wave?"
Long with this thought his bosom skilled
In holy discipline was filled.
A son was born, Bhagírath named,
Above all men for virtue famed.
Dilípa many a rite ordained,
And thirty thousand seasons reigned.

151

But when no hope the king could see
His kinsmen from their woe to free,
The lord of men, by sickness tried,
Obeyed the law of fate, and died;
He left the kingdom to his son,
And gained the heaven his deeds had won.
The good Bhagírath, royal sage,
Had no fair son to cheer his age.
He, great in glory, pure in will,
Longing for sons was childless still.
Then on one wish, one thought intent,
Planning the heavenly stream's descent,
Leaving his ministers the care
And burden of his state to bear,
Dwelling in far Gokarna he
Engaged in long austerity.
With senses checked, with arms upraised,
Five fires around and o'er him blazed.
Each weary month the hermit passed
Breaking but once his awful fast.
In winter's chill the brook his bed,
In rain, the clouds to screen his head.
Thousands of years he thus endured
Till Brahmá's favour was assured,
And the high Lord of living things
Looked kindly on his sufferings.
With trooping Gods the Sire came near
The king who plied his task austere:
"Blest Monarch, of a glorious race,
Thy fervent rites have won my grace.
Well hast thou wrought thine awful task:
Some boon in turn, O Hermit, ask."

Bhagírath, rich in glory's light,
The hero with the arm of might,
Thus to the Lord of earth and sky
Raised suppliant hands and made reply:
"If the great God his favour deigns,
And my long toil its fruit obtains,
Let Sagar's sons receive from me
Libations that they long to see.

152

Let Gangá with her holy wave
The ashes of the heroes lave,
That so my kinsmen may ascend
To heavenly bliss that ne'er shall end.
And give, I pray, O God, a son,
Nor let my house be all undone.
Sire of the worlds! be this the grace
Bestowed upon Ikshváku's race."
The Sire, when thus the king had prayed,
In sweet kind words his answer made.
"High, high thy thought and wishes are,
Bhagírath of the mighty car!
Ikshváku's line is blest in thee,
And as thou prayest it shall be.
Gangá, whose waves in Swarga flow,
Is daughter of the Lord of Snow.
Win Śiva that his aid be lent
To hold her in her mid descent,
For earth alone will never bear
Those torrents hurled from upper air;
And none may hold her weight but He,
The Trident wielding deity."
Thus having said, the Lord supreme
Addressed him to the heavenly stream;
And then with Gods and Maruts went
To heaven above the firmament.

CANTO
XLIV

The Descent of Gangá

The Lord of life the skies regained:
The fervent king a year remained
With arms upraised, refusing rest
While with one toe the earth he pressed,

Still as a post, with sleepless eye,
The air his food, his roof the sky.
The year had past. Then Umá's lord,
King of creation, world adored,
Thus spoke to great Bhagírath: "I,
Well pleased thy wish will gratify,
And on my head her waves shall fling
The daughter of the Mountains' King!"

He stood upon the lofty crest
That crowns the Lord of Snow,
And bade the river of the Blest
Descend on earth below.
Himálaya's child, adored of all,
The haughty mandate heard,
And her proud bosom, at the call,
With furious wrath was stirred.
Down from her channel in the skies
With awful might she sped
With a giant's rush, in a giant's size,
On Śiva's holy head.
"He calls me," in her wrath she cried,
"And all my flood shall sweep
And whirl him in its whelming tide
To hell's profoundest deep."
He held the river on his head,
And kept her wandering, where,
Dense as Himálaya's woods, were spread
The tangles of his hair.

No way to earth she found, ashamed,
Though long and sore she strove,
Condemned, until her pride were tamed,
Amid his locks to rove.
There, many lengthening seasons through,
The wildered river ran:
Bhagírath saw it, and anew
His penance dire began.
Then Śiva, for the hermit's sake,
Bade her long wanderings end,
And sinking into Vindu's lake

154

Her weary waves descend.
From Gangá, by the God set free,
Seven noble rivers came;
Hládiní, Pávaní, and she
Called Naliní by name:
These rolled their lucid waves along
And sought the eastern side.
Suchakshu, Sítá fair and strong,
And Sindhu's mighty tide—
These to the region of the west
With joyful waters sped:
The seventh, the brightest and the best,
Flowed where Bhagírath led.
On Śiva's head descending first
A rest the torrents found:
Then down in all their might they burst
And roared along the ground.
On countless glittering scales the beam
Of rosy morning flashed,
Where fish and dolphins through the stream
Fallen and falling dashed.
Then bards who chant celestial lays
And nymphs of heavenly birth
Flocked round upon that flood to gaze
That streamed from sky to earth.
The Gods themselves from every sphere,
Incomparably bright,
Borne in their golden cars drew near
To see the wondrous sight.
The cloudless sky was all aflame
With the light of a hundred suns
Where'er the shining chariots came
That bore those holy ones.
So flashed the air with crested snakes
And fish of every hue
As when the lightning's glory breaks
Through fields of summer blue.
And white foam-clouds and silver spray
Were wildly tossed on high,
Like swans that urge their homeward way
Across the autumn sky.

Now ran the river calm and clear
With current strong and deep:
Now slowly broadened to a mere,
Or scarcely seemed to creep.
Now o'er a length of sandy plain
Her tranquil course she held;
Now rose her waves and sank again,
By refluent waves repelled.
So falling first on Śiva's head,
Thence rushing to their earthly bed,
In ceaseless fall the waters streamed,
And pure with holy lustre gleamed.
Then every spirit, sage, and bard,
Condemned to earth by sentence hard,
Pressed eagerly around the tide
That Śiva's touch had sanctified.
Then they whom heavenly doom had hurled,
Accursed, to this lower world,
Touched the pure wave, and freed from sin
Resought the skies and entered in.
And all the world was glad, whereon
The glorious water flowed and shone,
For sin and stain were banished thence
By the sweet river's influence.
First, in a car of heavenly frame,
The royal saint of deathless name,
Bhagírath, very glorious rode,
And after him fair Gangá flowed.
God, sage, and bard, the chief in place
Of spirits and the Nága race,
Nymph, giant, fiend, in long array
Sped where Bhagírath led the way;
And all the hosts the flood that swim
Followed the stream that followed him.
Where'er the great Bhagírath led,
There ever glorious Gangá fled,
The best of floods, the rivers' queen,
Whose waters wash the wicked clean.

It chanced that Jahnu, great and good,
Engaged with holy offerings stood;

156

The river spread her waves around
Flooding his sacrificial ground.
The saint in anger marked her pride,
And at one draught her stream he dried.
Then God, and sage, and bard, afraid,
To noble high-souled Jahnu prayed,
And begged that he would kindly deem
His own dear child that holy stream.
Moved by their suit, he soothed their fears
And loosed her waters from his ears.
Hence Gangá through the world is styled
Both Jáhnavi and Jahnu's child.
Then onward still she followed fast,
And reached the great sea bank at last.
Thence deep below her way she made
To end those rites so long delayed.
The monarch reached the Ocean's side,
And still behind him Gangá hied.
He sought the depths which open lay
Where Sagar's sons had dug their way.
So leading through earth's nether caves
The river's purifying waves,

Over his kinsmen's dust the lord
His funeral libation poured.
Soon as the flood their dust bedewed,
Their spirits gained beatitude,
And all in heavenly bodies dressed
Rose to the skies' eternal rest.

Then thus to King Bhagírath said
Brahmá, when, coming at the head
Of all his bright celestial train,
He saw those spirits freed from stain:
"Well done! great Prince of men, well done!
Thy kinsmen bliss and heaven have won.
The sons of Sagar mighty-souled,
Are with the Blest, as Gods, enrolled,
Long as the Ocean's flood shall stand
Upon the border of the land,
So long shall Sagar's sons remain,

And, godlike, rank in heaven retain.
Gangá thine eldest child shall be,
Called from thy name Bhágirathí;
Named also—for her waters fell
From heaven and flow through earth and hell—
Tripathagá, stream of the skies,
Because three paths she glorifies.
And, mighty King, 'tis given thee now
To free thee and perform thy vow.
No longer, happy Prince, delay
Drink-offerings to thy kin to pay.
For this the holiest Sagar sighed,
But mourned the boon he sought denied.
Then Ansumán, dear Prince! although
No brighter name the world could show,
Strove long the heavenly flood to gain
To visit earth, but strove in vain.
Nor was she by the sages' peer,
Blest with all virtues, most austere,
Thy sire Dilípa, hither brought,
Though with fierce prayers the boon he sought.
But thou, O King, earned success,
And won high fame which God will bless.
Through thee, O victor of thy foes,
On earth this heavenly Gangá flows,
And thou hast gained the meed divine
That waits on virtue such as thine.
Now in her ever holy wave
Thyself, O best of heroes, lave:
So shalt thou, pure from every sin,
The blessed fruit of merit win.
Now for thy kin who died of yore
The meet libations duly pour.
Above the heavens I now ascend:
Depart, and bliss thy steps attend."

Thus to the mighty king who broke
His foemens' might, Lord Brahmá spoke,
And with his Gods around him rose
To his own heaven of blest repose.

The royal sage no more delayed,
But, the libation duly paid,
Home to his regal city hied
With water cleansed and purified.
There ruled he his ancestral state,
Best of all men, most fortunate.
And all the people joyed again
In good Bhagírath's gentle reign.
Rich, prosperous, and blest were they,
And grief and sickness fled away.
Thus, Ráma, I at length have told
How Gangá came from heaven of old.
Now, for the evening passes swift,
I wish thee each auspicious gift.
This story of the flood's descent
Will give—for 'tis most excellent—
Wealth, purity, fame, length of days,
And to the skies its hearers raise"

CANTO
XLV

The Quest of The Amrit

High and more high their wonder rose
As the strange story reached its close,
And thus, with Lakshmaṇ, Ráma, best
Of Raghu's sons, the saint addressed:
"Most wondrous is the tale which thou
Hast told of heavenly Gangá, how
From realms above descending she
Flowed through the land and filled the sea.
In thinking o'er what thou hast said
The night has like a moment fled,
Whose hours in musing have been spent

Upon thy words most excellent:
So much, O holy Sage, thy lore
Has charmed us with this tale of yore."

Day dawned. The morning rites were done
And the victorious Raghu's son
Addressed the sage in words like these,
Rich in his long austerities:
"The night is past: the morn is clear;
Told is the tale so good to hear:
Now o'er that river let us go,
Three-pathed, the best of all that flow.
This boat stands ready on the shore
To bear the holy hermits o'er,
Who of thy coming warned, in haste,
The barge upon the bank have placed."

And Kuśik's son approved his speech,
And moving to the sandy beach,
Placed in the boat the hermit band,
And reached the river's further strand.
On the north bank their feet they set,
And greeted all the saints they met.
On Gangá's shore they lighted down,
And saw Viśálá's lovely town.
Thither, the princes by his side,
The best of holy hermits hied.
It was a town exceeding fair

That might with heaven itself compare.
Then, suppliant palm to palm applied,
Famed Ráma asked his holy guide:
"O best of hermits, say what race
Of monarchs rules this lovely place.
Dear master, let my prayer prevail,
For much I long to hear the tale."
Moved by his words, the saintly man
Viśálá's ancient tale began:
"List, Ráma, list, with closest heed
The tale of Indra's wondrous deed,
And mark me as I truly tell

What here in ancient days befell.
Ere Krita's famous Age had fled,
Strong were the sons of Diti bred;
And Aditi's brave children too
Were very mighty, good, and true.
The rival brothers fierce and bold
Were sons of Kaśyap lofty-souled.
Of sister mothers born, they vied,
Brood against brood, in jealous pride.
Once, as they say, band met with band,
And, joined in awful council, planned
To live, unharmed by age and time,
Immortal in their youthful prime.
Then this was, after due debate,
The counsel of the wise and great,
To churn with might the milky sea
The life-bestowing drink to free.
This planned, they seized the Serpent King,
Vásuki, for their churning-string,
And Mandar's mountain for their pole,
And churned with all their heart and soul.
As thus, a thousand seasons through,
This way and that the snake they drew,
Biting the rocks, each tortured head,
A very deadly venom shed.
Thence, bursting like a mighty flame,
A pestilential poison came,
Consuming, as it onward ran,
The home of God, and fiend, and man.
Then all the suppliant Gods in fear
To Śankar, mighty lord, drew near.
To Rudra, King of Herds, dismayed,
"Save us, O save us, Lord!" they prayed.
Then Vishṇu, bearing shell, and mace,
And discus, showed his radiant face,
And thus addressed in smiling glee
The Trident wielding deity:
"What treasure first the Gods upturn
From troubled Ocean, as they churn,
Should—for thou art the eldest—be
Conferred, O best of Gods, on thee.

161

Then come, and for thy birthright's sake,
This venom as thy first fruits take."
He spoke, and vanished from their sight,
When Śiva saw their wild affright,
And heard his speech by whom is borne
The mighty bow of bending horn,
The poisoned flood at once he quaffed
As 'twere the Amrit's heavenly draught.
Then from the Gods departing went
Śiva, the Lord pre-eminent.
The host of Gods and Asurs still
Kept churning with one heart and will.
But Mandar's mountain, whirling round,
Pierced to the depths below the ground.
Then Gods and bards in terror flew
To him who mighty Madhu slew.
"Help of all beings! more than all,
The Gods on thee for aid may call.
Ward off, O mighty-armed! our fate,
And bear up Mandar's threatening weight."
Then Vishṇu, as their need was sore,
The semblance of a tortoise wore,
And in the bed of Ocean lay
The mountain on his back to stay.
Then he, the soul pervading all,
Whose locks in radiant tresses fall,
One mighty arm extended still,
And grasped the summit of the hill.
So ranged among the Immortals, he
Joined in the churning of the sea.

A thousand years had reached their close,
When calmly from the ocean rose
The gentle sage with staff and can,
Lord of the art of healing man.
Then as the waters foamed and boiled,
As churning still the Immortals toiled,
Of winning face and lovely frame,
Forth sixty million fair ones came.
Born of the foam and water, these
Were aptly named Apsarases.

162

Each had her maids. The tongue would fail—
So vast the throng—to count the tale.
But when no God or Titan wooed
A wife from all that multitude,
Refused by all, they gave their love
In common to the Gods above.
Then from the sea still vext and wild
Rose Surá, Varuṇ's maiden child.
A fitting match she sought to find:
But Diti's sons her love declined,
Their kinsmen of the rival brood
To the pure maid in honour sued.
Hence those who loved that nymph so fair
The hallowed name of Suras bear.
And Asurs are the Titan crowd
Her gentle claims who disallowed.
Then from the foamy sea was freed
Uchchaihśravas, the generous steed,
And Kaustubha, of gems the gem,
And Soma, Moon God, after them.

At length when many a year had fled,
Up floated, on her lotus bed,
A maiden fair and tender-eyed,
In the young flush of beauty's pride.
She shone with pearl and golden sheen,
And seals of glory stamped her queen,
On each round arm glowed many a gem,
On her smooth brows, a diadem.
Rolling in waves beneath her crown
The glory of her hair flowed down,
Pearls on her neck of price untold,
The lady shone like burnisht gold.
Queen of the Gods, she leapt to land,
A lotus in her perfect hand,
And fondly, of the lotus-sprung,
To lotus-bearing Vishṇu clung.
Her Gods above and men below
As Beauty's Queen and Fortune know.
Gods, Titans, and the minstrel train
Still churned and wrought the troubled main.

At length the prize so madly sought,
The Amrit, to their sight was brought.
For the rich spoil, 'twixt these and those
A fratricidal war arose,
And, host 'gainst host in battle, set,
Aditi's sons and Diti's met.
United, with the giants' aid,
Their fierce attack the Titans made,
And wildly raged for many a day
That universe-astounding fray.
When wearied arms were faint to strike,
And ruin threatened all alike,
Vishṇu, with art's illusive aid,
The Amrit from their sight conveyed.
That Best of Beings smote his foes
Who dared his deathless arm oppose:
Yea, Vishṇu, all-pervading God,
Beneath his feet the Titans trod
Aditi's race, the sons of light,
slew Diti's brood in cruel fight.
Then town-destroying Indra gained
His empire, and in glory reigned
O'er the three worlds with bard and sage
Rejoicing in his heritage.

CANTO
XLVI

Diti's Hope

B ut Diti, when her sons were slain,
Wild with a childless mother's pain,
To Kaśyap spake, Marícha's son,
Her husband: "O thou glorious one!

Dead are the children, mine no more,
The mighty sons to thee I bore.
Long fervour's meed, I crave a boy
Whose arm may Indra's life destroy.
The toil and pain my care shall be:
To bless my hope depends on thee.
Give me a mighty son to slay
Fierce Indra, gracious lord! I pray."
Then glorious Kaśyap thus replied
To Diti, as she wept and sighed:
"Thy prayer is heard, dear saint! Remain
Pure from all spot, and thou shalt gain
A son whose arm shall take the life
Of Indra in the battle strife.
For full a thousand years endure
Free from all stain, supremely pure;
Then shall thy son and mine appear,
Whom the three worlds shall serve with fear."
These words the glorious Kaśyap said,
Then gently stroked his consort's head,
Blessed her, and bade a kind adieu,
And turned him to his rites anew.
Soon as her lord had left her side,
Her bosom swelled with joy and pride.
She sought the shade of holy boughs,
And there began her awful vows.
While yet she wrought her rites austere,
Indra, unbidden, hastened near,
With sweet observance tending her,
A reverential minister.
Wood, water, fire, and grass he brought,
Sweet roots and woodland fruit he sought,
And all her wants, the Thousand-eyed,
With never-failing care, supplied,
With tender love and soft caress
Removing pain and weariness.

When, of the thousand years ordained,
Ten only unfulfilled remained,
Thus to her son, the Thousand-eyed,

The Goddess in her triumph cried:
"Best of the mighty! there remain
But ten short years of toil and pain;
These years of penance soon will flee,
And a new brother thou shalt see.
Him for thy sake I'll nobly breed,
And lust of war his soul shall feed;
Then free from care and sorrow thou
Shalt see the worlds before him bow."

CANTO

XLVII

Sumati

Thus to Lord Indra, Thousand-eyed,
    Softly beseeching Diti sighed.
    When but a blighted bud was left,
Which Indra's hand in seven had cleft:
"No fault, O Lord of Gods, is thine;
The blame herein is only mine.
But for one grace I fain would pray,
As thou hast reft this hope away.
This bud, O Indra, which a blight
Has withered ere it saw the light—
From this may seven fair spirits rise
To rule the regions of the skies.
Be theirs through heaven's unbounded space
On shoulders of the winds to race,
My children, drest in heavenly forms,
Far-famed as Maruts, Gods of storms.
One God to Brahmá's sphere assign,
Let one, O Indra, watch o'er thine;
And ranging through the lower air,
The third the name of Váyu bear.

166

Gods let the four remaining be,
And roam through space, obeying thee."

The Town-destroyer, Thousand-eyed,
Who smote fierce Bali till he died,
Joined suppliant hands, and thus replied:
"Thy children heavenly forms shall wear;
The names devised by thee shall bear,
And, Maruts called by my decree,
Shall Amrit drink and wait on me.
From fear and age and sickness freed,
Through the three worlds their wings shall speed."

Thus in the hermits' holy shade
Mother and son their compact made,
And then, as fame relates, content,
Home to the happy skies they went.
This is the spot—so men have told—
Where Lord Mahendra dwelt of old,
This is the blessed region where
His votaress mother claimed his care.
Here gentle Alambúshá bare
To old Ikshváku, king and sage,
Visála, glory of his age,
By whom, a monarch void of guilt,
Was this fair town Visálá built.

His son was Hemachandra, still
Renowned for might and warlike skill.
From him the great Suchandra came;
His son, Dhúmráśva, dear to fame.
Next followed royal Srinjay; then
Famed Sahadeva, lord of men.
Next came Kuśáśva, good and mild,
Whose son was Somadatta styled,
And Sumati, his heir, the peer
Of Gods above, now governs here.
And ever through Ikshváku's grace,
Visálá's kings, his noble race,
Are lofty-souled, and blest with length

167

Of days, with virtue, and with strength.
This night, O prince, we here will sleep;
And when the day begins to peep,
Our onward way will take with thee,
The king of Míthilá to see."

Then Sumati, the king, aware
Of Viśvámitra's advent there,
Came quickly forth with honour meet
The lofty-minded sage to greet.
Girt with his priest and lords the king
Did low obeisance, worshipping,
With suppliant hands, with head inclined,
Thus spoke he after question kind;
"Since thou hast deigned to bless my sight,
And grace awhile thy servant's seat,
High fate is mine, great Anchorite,
And none may with my bliss compete."

CANTO

XLVIII

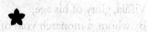

Indra and Ahalyá

W hen mutual courtesies had past,
Viśálá's ruler spoke at last:
"These princely youths, O Sage, who vie
In might with children of the sky,
Heroic, born for happy fate,
With elephants' or lions' gait,
Bold as the tiger or the bull,
With lotus eyes so large and full,
Armed with the quiver, sword, and bow,
Whose figures like the Aśvins show,
Like children of the deathless Powers,
Come freely to these shades of ours,—

How have they reached on foot this place?
What do they seek, and what their race?
As sun and moon adorn the sky,
This spot the heroes glorify.
Alike in stature, port, and mien,
The same fair form in each is seen,"

He spoke; and at the monarch's call
The best of hermits told him all,
How in the grove with him they dwelt,
And slaughter to the demons dealt.
Then wonder filled the monarch's breast,
Who tended well each royal guest.
Thus entertained, the princely pair
Remained that night and rested there,
And with the morn's returning ray
To Mithilá pursued their way.

When Janak's lovely city first
Upon their sight, yet distant, burst,
The hermits all with joyful cries
Hailed the fair town that met their eyes.
Then Ráma saw a holy wood,
Close, in the city's neighbourhood,
O'ergrown, deserted, marked by age,
And thus addressed the mighty sage:
"O reverend lord. I long to know
What hermit dwelt here long ago."
Then to the prince his holy guide,
Most eloquent of men, replied:
"O Ráma, listen while I tell
Whose was this grove, and what befell
When in the fury of his rage
The high saint cursed the hermitage.
This was the grove—most lovely then—
Of Gautam, O thou best of men,
Like heaven itself, most honoured by
The Gods who dwell above the sky.
Here with Ahalyá at his side
His fervid task the ascetic plied.
Years fled in thousands. On a day

It chanced the saint had gone away,
When Town-destroying Indra came,
And saw the beauty of the dame.
The sage's form the God endued,
And thus the fair Ahalyá wooed:
"Love, sweet! should brook no dull delay
But snatch the moments when he may."
She knew him in the saint's disguise,
Lord Indra of the Thousand Eyes,
But touched by love's unholy fire,
She yielded to the God's desire.

"Now, Lord of Gods!" she whispered, "flee,
From Gautam save thyself and me."
Trembling with doubt and wild with dread
Lord Indra from the cottage fled;
But fleeing in the grove he met
The home-returning anchoret,
Whose wrath the Gods and fiends would shun,
Such power his fervent rites had won.
Fresh from the lustral flood he came,
In splendour like the burning flame,
With fuel for his sacred rites,
And grass, the best of eremites.
The Lord of Gods was sad of cheer
To see the mighty saint so near,
And when the holy hermit spied
In hermit's garb the Thousand-eyed,

He knew the whole, his fury broke
Forth on the sinner as he spoke:
"Because my form thou hast assumed,
And wrought this folly, thou art doomed,
For this my curse to thee shall cling,
Henceforth a sad and sexless thing."

No empty threat that sentence came,
It chilled his soul and marred his frame,
His might and godlike vigour fled,
And every nerve was cold and dead.

Then on his wife his fury burst,
And thus the guilty dame he cursed:
"For countless years, disloyal spouse,
Devoted to severest vows,
Thy bed the ashes, air thy food,
Here shalt thou live in solitude.
This lonely grove thy home shall be,
And not an eye thy form shall see.
When Ráma, Daśaratha's child,
Shall seek these shades then drear and wild,
His coming shall remove thy stain,
And make the sinner pure again.
Due honour paid to him, thy guest,
Shall cleanse thy fond and erring breast,
Thee to my side in bliss restore,
And give thy proper shape once more."
Thus to his guilty wife he said,
Then far the holy Gautam fled,
And on Himálaya's lovely heights
Spent the long years in sternest rites."

CANTO

XLIX

Ahalyá Freed

Then Ráma, following still his guide,
Within the grove, with Lakshman, hied,
Her vows a wondrous light had lent
To that illustrious penitent.
He saw the glorious lady, screened
From eye of man, and God, and fiend,
Like some bright portent which the care
Of Brahmá launches through the air,
Designed by his illusive art
To flash a moment and depart:

Or like the flame that leaps on high
To sink involved in smoke and die:
Or like the full moon shining through
The wintry mist, then lost to view:
Or like the sun's reflection, cast
Upon the flood, too bright to last:
So was the glorious dame till then
Removed from Gods' and mortals' ken,
Till—such was Gautam's high decree—
Prince Ráma came to set her free.

Then, with great joy that dame to meet,
The sons of Raghu clapped her feet;
And she, remembering Gautam's oath,
With gentle grace received them both;
Then water for their feet she gave,
Guest-gift, and all that strangers crave.

The prince, of courteous rule aware,
Received, as meet, the lady's care.
Then flowers came down in copious rain,
And moving to the heavenly strain
Of music in the skies that rang,
The nymphs and minstrels danced and sang:
And all the Gods with one glad voice
Praised the great dame, and cried, "Rejoice!
Through fervid rites no more defiled,
But with thy husband reconciled."
Gautam, the holy hermit knew—
For naught escaped his godlike view—
That Ráma lodged beneath that shade,
And hasting there his homage paid.
He took Ahalyá to his side,
From sin and folly purified,
And let his new-found consort bear
In his austerities a share.

Then Ráma, pride of Raghu's race,
Welcomed by Gautam, face to face,
Who every highest honour showed,
To Mithilá pursued his road.

Janak

The sons of Raghu journeyed forth,
　　Bending their steps 'twixt east and north.
　　Soon, guided by the sage, they found,
Enclosed, a sacrificial ground.
Then to the best of saints, his guide,
In admiration Ráma cried:

"The high-souled king no toil has spared,
But nobly for his rite prepared,
How many thousand Bráhmans here,
From every region, far and near,
Well read in holy lore, appear!
How many tents, that sages screen,
With wains in hundreds, here are seen!
Great Bráhman, let us find a place
Where we may stay and rest a space."
The hermit did as Ráma prayed,
And in a spot his lodging made,

Far from the crowd, sequestered, clear,
With copious water flowing near.

Then Janak, best of kings, aware
Of Viśvámitra lodging there,
With Śatánanda for his guide—
The priest on whom he most relied,
His chaplain void of guile and stain—
And others of his priestly train,
Bearing the gift that greets the guest,
To meet him with all honour pressed.
The saint received with gladsome mind

Each honour and observance kind:
Then of his health he asked the king,
And how his rites were prospering,
Janak, with chaplain and with priest,
Addressed the hermits, chief and least,
Accosting all, in due degree,
With proper words of courtesy.
Then, with his palms together laid,
The king his supplication made:
"Deign, reverend lord, to sit thee down
With these good saints of high renown."
Then sate the chief of hermits there,
Obedient to the monarch's prayer.
Chaplain and priest, and king and peer,
Sate in their order, far or near.
Then thus the king began to say:
"The Gods have blest my rite to-day,
And with the sight of thee repaid
The preparations I have made.
Grateful am I, so highly blest,
That thou, of saints the holiest,
Hast come, O Bráhman, here with all
These hermits to the festival.
Twelve days, O Bráhman Sage, remain—
For so the learned priests ordain—
And then, O heir of Kuśik's name,
The Gods will come their dues to claim."

With looks that testified delight
Thus spake he to the anchorite,
Then with his suppliant hands upraised,
He asked, as earnestly he gazed:
"These princely youths, O Sage, who vie
In might with children of the sky,
Heroic, born for happy fate,
With elephants' or lions' gait,
Bold as the tiger and the bull,
With lotus eyes so large and full,
Armed with the quiver, sword and bow,
Whose figures like the Aśvins show,
Like children of the heavenly Powers,

174

Come freely to these shades of ours,—
How have they reached on foot this place?
What do they seek, and what their race?
As sun and moon adorn the sky,
This spot the heroes glorify:
Alike in stature, port, and mien,
The same fair form in each is seen."

Thus spoke the monarch, lofty-souled,
The saint, of heart unfathomed, told
How, sons of Daśaratha, they
Accompanied his homeward way,
How in the hermitage they dwelt,
And slaughter to the demons dealt:
Their journey till the spot they neared
Whence fair Viśálá's towers appeared:
Ahalyá seen and freed from taint;
Their meeting with her lord the saint;
And how they thither came, to know
The virtue of the famous bow.

Thus Viśvámitra spoke the whole
To royal Janak, great of soul,
And when this wondrous tale was o'er,
The glorious hermit said no more.

CANTO
LI

Visvámitra

Wise Viśvámitra's tale was done:
Then sainted Gautam's eldest son,
Great Śatánanda, far-renowned,
Whom long austerities had crowned
With glory—as the news he heard

The down upon his body stirred,—
Filled full of wonder at the sight
Of Ráma, felt supreme delight.
When Śatánanda saw the pair
Of youthful princes seated there,
He turned him to the holy man
Who sate at ease, and thus began:
"And didst thou, mighty Sage, in truth
Show clearly to this royal youth
My mother, glorious far and wide,
Whom penance-rites have sanctified?
And did my glorious mother—she,
Heiress of noble destiny—
Serve her great guest with woodland store,
Whom all should honour evermore?
Didst thou the tale to Ráma tell
Of what in ancient days befell,
The sin, the misery, and the shame
Of guilty God and faithless dame?
And, O thou best of hermits, say,
Did Ráma's healing presence stay
Her trial? was the wife restored
Again to him, my sire and lord?
Say, Hermit, did that sire of mine
Receive her with a soul benign,
When long austerities in time
Had cleansed her from the taint of crime?

And, son of Kuśik, let me know,
Did my great-minded father show
Honour to Ráma, and regard,
Before he journeyed hitherward?"
The hermit with attentive ear
Marked all the questions of the seer:
To him for eloquence far-famed,
His eloquent reply he framed:
"Yea, 'twas my care no task to shun,
And all I had to do was done;
As Reṇuká and Bhrigu's child,
The saint and dame were reconciled."

176

When the great sage had thus replied,
To Ráma Śatánanda cried:
"A welcome visit, Prince, is thine,
Thou scion of King Raghu's line.
With him to guide thy way aright,
This sage invincible in might,
This Bráhman sage, most glorious-bright,
By long austerities has wrought
A wondrous deed, exceeding thought:
Thou knowest well, O strong of arm,
This sure defence from scathe and harm.
None, Ráma, none is living now
In all the earth more blest than thou,
That thou hast won a saint so tried
In fervid rites thy life to guide.
Now listen, Prince, while I relate
His lofty deeds and wondrous fate.
He was a monarch pious-souled.
His foemen in the dust he rolled;
Most learned, prompt at duty's claim,
His people's good his joy and aim.

Of old the Lord of Life gave birth
To mighty Kuśa, king of earth.
His son was Kuśanábha, strong,
Friend of the right, the foe of wrong.
Gádhi, whose fame no time shall dim,
Heir of his throne was born to him,
And Viśvámitra, Gádhi's heir,
Governed the land with kingly care.
While years unnumbered rolled away
The monarch reigned with equal sway.
At length, assembling many a band,
He led his warriors round the land—
Complete in tale, a mighty force,
Cars, elephants, and foot, and horse.
Through cities, groves, and floods he passed,
O'er lofty hills, through regions vast.
He reached Vaśishṭha's pure abode,
Where trees, and flowers, and creepers glowed,
Where troops of sylvan creatures fed;

Which saints and angels visited.
Gods, fauns, and bards of heavenly race,
And spirits, glorified the place;
The deer their timid ways forgot,
And holy Bráhmans thronged the spot.
Bright in their souls, like fire, were these,
Made pure by long austerities,
Bound by the rule of vows severe,
And each in glory Brahmá's peer.
Some fed on water, some on air,
Some on the leaves that withered there.
Roots and wild fruit were others' food;
All rage was checked, each sense subdued,
There Bálakhilyas went and came,
Now breathed the prayer, now fed the flame:
These, and ascetic bands beside,
The sweet retirement beautified.
Such was Vaśishṭha's blest retreat,
Like Brahmá's own celestial seat,
Which gladdened Viśvámitra's eyes,
Peerless for warlike enterprise.

CANTO
LII

Vasishtha's Feast

R ight glad was Viśvámitra when
He saw the prince of saintly men.
Low at his feet the hero bent,
And did obeisance, reverent.

The king was welcomed in, and shown
A seat beside the hermit's own,
Who offered him, when resting there,

178

Fruit in due course, and woodland fare.
And Viśvámitra, noblest king,
Received Vaśishṭha's welcoming,
Turned to his host, and prayed him tell
That he and all with him were well.
Vaśishṭha to the king replied
That all was well on every side,
That fire, and vows, and pupils throve,
And all the trees within the grove.
And then the son of Brahmá, best
Of all who pray with voice suppressed,
Questioned with pleasant words like these
The mighty king who sate at ease:
"And is it well with thee? I pray;
And dost thou win by virtuous sway
Thy people's love, discharging all
The duties on a king that fall?
Are all thy servants fostered well?
Do all obey, and none rebel?
Hast thou, destroyer of the foe,
No enemies to overthrow?
Does fortune, conqueror! still attend
Thy treasure, host, and every friend?
Is it all well? Does happy fate
On sons and children's children wait?"

He spoke. The modest king replied
That all was prosperous far and wide.

Thus for awhile the two conversed,
As each to each his tale rehearsed,
And as the happy moments flew,
Their joy and friendship stronger grew.
When such discourse had reached an end,
Thus spoke the saint most reverend
To royal Viśvámitra, while
His features brightened with a smile:
"O mighty lord of men. I fain
Would banquet thee and all thy train
In mode that suits thy station high:

179

And do not thou my prayer deny.
Let my good lord with favour take
The offering that I fain would make,
And let me honour, ere we part,
My royal guest with loving heart."

Him Viśvámitra thus addressed:
"Why make, O Saint, this new request?
Thy welcome and each gracious word
Sufficient honour have conferred.
Thou gavest roots and fruit to eat,
The treasures of this pure retreat,
And water for my mouth and feet;
And—boon I prize above the rest—
Thy presence has mine eyesight blest.
Honoured by thee in every way,
To whom all honour all should pay,
I now will go. My lord, Good-bye!
Regard me with a friendly eye."

Him speaking thus Vaśishṭha stayed,
And still to share his banquet prayed.
The will of Gádhi's son he bent,
And won the monarch to consent,
Who spoke in answer. "Let it be,
Great Hermit, as it pleases thee."
When, best of those who breathe the prayer,
He heard the king his will declare,
He called the cow of spotted skin,
All spot without, all pure within.
"Come, Dapple-skin," he cried, "with speed;
Hear thou my words and help at need.
My heart is set to entertain
This monarch and his mighty train
With sumptuous meal and worthy fare;
Be thine the banquet to prepare.
Each dainty cate, each goodly dish,
Of six-fold taste as each may wish—
All these, O cow of heavenly power,
Rain down for me in copious shower:
Viands and drink for tooth and lip,

To eat, to suck, to quaff, to sip—
Of these sufficient, and to spare,
O plenty-giving cow, prepare."

CANTO
LIII

Visvámitra's Request

Thus charged, O slayer of thy foes,
    The cow from whom all plenty flows,
    Obedient to her saintly lord,
Viands to suit each taste, outpoured.
Honey she gave, and roasted grain,
Mead sweet with flowers, and sugar-cane.
Each beverage of flavour rare,
An food of every sort, were there:
Hills of hot rice, and sweetened cakes,
And curdled milk and soup in lakes.
Vast beakers foaming to the brim
With sugared drink prepared for him,
And dainty sweetmeats, deftly made,
Before the hermit's guests were laid.
So well regaled, so nobly fed,
The mighty army banqueted,
And all the train, from chief to least,
Delighted in Vaśishṭha's feast.
Then Viśvámitra, royal sage,
Surrounded by his vassalage,
Prince, peer, and counsellor, and all
From highest lord to lowest thrall,
Thus feasted, to Vaśishṭha cried
With joy, supremely gratified:
"Rich honour I, thus entertained,
Most honourable lord, have gained:
Now hear, before I journey hence,

181

My words, O skilled in eloquence.
Bought for a hundred thousand kine,
Let Dapple-skin, O Saint, be mine.
A wondrous jewel is thy cow,
And gems are for the monarch's brow.
To me her rightful lord resign
This Dapple-skin thou callest thine."

The great Vaśishṭha, thus addressed,
Arch-hermit of the holy breast,
To Viśvámitra answer made,
The king whom all the land obeyed:
"Not for a hundred thousand,—nay,
Not if ten million thou wouldst pay,
With silver heaps the price to swell,—
Will I my cow, O Monarch, sell.
Unmeet for her is such a fate.
That I my friend should alienate.
As glory with the virtuous, she
For ever makes her home with me.
On her mine offerings which ascend
To Gods and spirits all depend:
My very life is due to her,
My guardian, friend, and minister.

The feeding of the sacred flame,
The dole which living creatures claim.
The mighty sacrifice by fire,
Each formula the rites require,
And various saving lore beside,
Are by her aid, in sooth, supplied.
The banquet which thy host has shared,
Believe it, was by her prepared,
In her mine only treasures lie,
She cheers mine heart and charms mine eye.
And reasons more could I assign
Why Dapple-skin can ne'er be thine."

The royal sage, his suit denied,
With eloquence more earnest cried:
"Tusked elephants, a goodly train,

182

Each with a golden girth and chain,
Whose goads with gold well fashioned shine—
Of these be twice seven thousand thine.
And four-horse cars with gold made bright,
With steeds most beautifully white,
Whose bells make music as they go,
Eight hundred, Saint, will I bestow.
Eleven thousand mettled steeds
From famous lands, of noble breeds—
These will I gladly give, O thou
Devoted to each holy vow.
Ten million heifers, fair to view,
Whose sides are marked with every hue—
These in exchange will I assign;
But let thy Dapple-skin be mine.
Ask what thou wilt, and piles untold
Of priceless gems and gleaming gold,
O best of Bráhmans, shall be thine;
But let thy Dapple-skin be mine."

The great Vaśishṭha, thus addressed,
Made answer to the king's request:
"Ne'er will I give my cow away,
My gem, my wealth, my life and stay.
My worship at the moon's first show,
And at the full, to her I owe;
And sacrifices small and great,
Which largess due and gifts await.
From her alone, their root, O King,
My rites and holy service spring.
What boots it further words to say?
I will not give my cow away
Who yields me what I ask each day."

183

CANTO
LIV

The Battle

As Saint Vaśishṭha answered so,
Nor let the cow of plenty go,
The monarch, as a last resource,
Began to drag her off by force.
While the king's servants tore away
Their moaning, miserable prey,
Sad, sick at heart, and sore distressed,
She pondered thus within her breast:
"Why am I thus forsaken? why
Betrayed by him of soul most high.
Vaśishṭha, ravished by the hands
Of soldiers of the monarch's bands?
Ah me! what evil have I done
Against the lofty-minded one,
That he, so pious, can expose
The innocent whose love he knows?"
In her sad breast as thus she thought,
And heaved deep sighs with anguish fraught,
With wondrous speed away she fled,
And back to Saint Vaśishṭha sped.
She hurled by hundreds to the ground
The menial crew that hemmed her round,
And flying swifter than the blast
Before the saint herself she cast.
There Dapple-skin before the saint
Stood moaning forth her sad complaint,
And wept and lowed: such tones as come
From wandering cloud or distant drum.
"O son of Brahmá," thus cried she,
"Why hast thou thus forsaken me,

That the king's men, before thy face,
Bear off thy servant from her place?"

Then thus the Bráhman saint replied
To her whose heart with woe was tried,
And grieving for his favourite's sake,
As to a suffering sister spake:
"I leave thee not: dismiss the thought;
Nor, duteous, hast thou failed in aught.
This king, o'erweening in the pride
Of power, has reft thee from my side.
Little, I ween, my strength could do
'Gainst him, a mighty warrior too.
Strong, as a soldier born and bred,—
Great, as a king whom regions dread.
See! what a host the conqueror leads,
With elephants, and cars, and steeds.
O'er countless bands his pennons fly;
So is he mightier far than I."

He spoke. Then she, in lowly mood,
To that high saint her speech renewed:
"So judge not they who wisest are:
The Bráhman's might is mightier far.
For Bráhmans strength from Heaven derive,
And warriors bow when Bráhmans strive.
A boundless power 'tis thine to wield:
To such a king thou shouldst not yield,
Who, very mighty though he be,—
So fierce thy strength,—must bow to thee.
Command me, Saint. Thy power divine
Has brought me here and made me thine;
And I, howe'er the tyrant boast,
Will tame his pride and slay his host."
Then cried the glorious sage: "Create
A mighty force the foe to mate."

She lowed, and quickened into life,
Pahlavas, burning for the strife,
King Viśvámitra's army slew

185

Before the very leader's view.
The monarch in excessive ire,
His eyes with fury darting fire,
Rained every missile on the foe
Till all the Pahlavas were low.
She, seeing all her champions slain,
Lying by thousands on the plain.
Created, by her mere desire,
Yavans and Śakas, fierce and dire.
And all the ground was overspread
With Yavans and with Śakas dread:
A host of warriors bright and strong,
And numberless in closest throng:
The threads within the lotus stem,
So densely packed, might equal them.
In gold-hued mail 'against war's attacks,
Each bore a sword and battle-axe,
The royal host, where'er these came,
Fell as if burnt with ravening flame.

The monarch, famous through the world
Again his fearful weapons hurled,
That made Kámbojas, Barbars, all,
With Yavans, troubled, flee and fall.

CANTO
LV

The Hermitage Burnt

So o'er the field that host lay strown,
    By Viśvámitra's darts o'erthrown.
    Then thus Vaśishṭha charged the cow:
"Create with all thy vigour now."

Forth sprang Kámbojas, as she lowed;
Bright as the sun their faces glowed,
Forth from her udder Barbars poured,—
Soldiers who brandished spear and sword,—
And Yavans with their shafts and darts,
And Śakas from her hinder parts.
And every pore upon her fell,
And every hair-producing cell,
With Mlechchhas and Kirátas teemed,
And forth with them Hárítas streamed.
And Viśvámitra's mighty force,
Car, elephant, and foot, and horse,
Fell in a moment's time, subdued
By that tremendous multitude.
The monarch's hundred sons, whose eyes
Beheld the rout in wild surprise,
Armed with all weapons, mad with rage,
Rushed fiercely on the holy sage.
One cry he raised, one glance he shot,
And all fell scorched upon the spot:
Burnt by the sage to ashes, they
With horse, and foot, and chariot, lay.
The monarch mourned, with shame and pain,
His army lost, his children slain,
Like Ocean when his roar is hushed,
Or some great snake whose fangs are crushed:

Or as in swift eclipse the Sun
Dark with the doom he cannot shun:
Or a poor bird with mangled wing—
So, reft of sons and host, the king
No longer, by ambition fired,
The pride of war his breast inspired.
He gave his empire to his son—
Of all he had, the only one:
And bade him rule as kings are taught
Then straight a hermit-grove he sought.
Far to Himálaya's side he fled,
Which bards and Nágas visited,
And, Mahádeva's grace to earn,

He gave his life to penance stern.
A lengthened season thus passed by,
When Śiva's self, the Lord most High,
Whose banner shows the pictured bull,
Appeared, the God most bountiful:

"Why fervent thus in toil and pain?
What brings thee here? what boon to gain?
Thy heart's desire, O Monarch, speak:
I grant the boons which mortals seek."
The king, his adoration paid,
To Mahádeva answer made:
"If thou hast deemed me fit to win
Thy favour, O thou void of sin,
On me, O mighty God, bestow
The wondrous science of the bow,
All mine, complete in every part,
With secret spell and mystic art.
To me be all the arms revealed
That Gods, and saints, and Titans wield,
And every dart that arms the hands
Of spirits, fiends and minstrel bands,
Be mine, O Lord supreme in place,
This token of thy boundless grace."

The Lord of Gods then gave consent,
And to his heavenly mansion went.
Triumphant in the arms he held,
The monarch's breast with glory swelled.
So swells the ocean, when upon
His breast the full moon's beams have shone.
Already in his mind he viewed
Vaśishṭha at his feet subdued.
He sought that hermit's grove, and there
Launched his dire weapons through the air,
Till scorched by might that none could stay
The hermitage in ashes lay.
Where'er the inmates saw, aghast,
The dart that Viśvámitra cast,
To every side they turned and fled
In hundreds forth disquieted.

Vaśishṭha's pupils caught the fear,
And every bird and every deer,
And fled in wild confusion forth
Eastward and westward, south and north,
And so Vaśishṭha's holy shade
A solitary wild was made,
Silent awhile, for not a sound
Disturbed the hush that was around.

Vaśishṭha then, with eager cry,
Called, "Fear not, friends, nor seek to fly.
This son of Gádhi dies to-day,
Like hoar-frost in the morning's ray."
Thus having said, the glorious sage
Spoke to the king in words of rage:
"Because thou hast destroyed this grove
Which long in holy quiet throve,
By folly urged to senseless crime,
Now shalt thou die before thy time."

CANTO
LVI

Visvámitra's Vow

B ut Viśvámitra, at the threat
Of that illustrious anchoret,
Cried, as he launched with ready hand
A fiery weapon, "Stand, O Stand!"
Vaśishṭha, wild with rage and hate,
Raising, as 'twere the Rod of Fate,
His mighty Bráhman wand on high,
To Viśvámitra made reply:
"Nay, stand, O Warrior thou, and show
What soldier can, 'gainst Bráhman foe.
O Gádhi's son, thy days are told;

Thy pride is tamed, thy dart is cold.
How shall a warrior's puissance dare
With Bráhman's awful strength compare?
To-day, base Warrior, shalt thou feel
That God-sent might is more than steel."
He raised his Bráhman staff, nor missed
The fiery dart that near him hissed:
And quenched the fearful weapon fell,
As flame beneath the billow's swell.

Then Gádhi's son in fury threw
Lord Varuṇ's arm and Rudra's too:
Indra's fierce bolt that all destroys;
That which the Lord of Herds employs:
The Human, that which minstrels keep,
The deadly Lure, the endless Sleep:
The Yawner, and the dart which charms;
Lament and Torture, fearful arms:
The Terrible, the dart which dries,
The Thunderbolt which quenchless flies,
And Fate's dread net, and Brahmá's noose,
And that which waits for Varuṇ's use:
The dart he loves who wields the bow
Pináka, and twin bolts that glow
With fury as they flash and fly,
The quenchless Liquid and the Dry:
The dart of Vengeance, swift to kill:
The Goblins' dart, the Curlew's Bill:

The discus both of Fate and Right,
And Vishṇu's, of unerring flight:
The Wind-God's dart, the Troubler dread,
The weapon named the Horse's Head.
From his fierce hand two spears were thrown,
And the great mace that smashes bone;
The dart of spirits of the air,
And that which Fate exults to bear:
The Trident dart which slaughters foes,
And that which hanging skulls compose:
These fearful darts in fiery rain
He hurled upon the saint amain,

An awful miracle to view.
But as the ceaseless tempest flew,
The sage with wand of God-sent power
Still swallowed up that fiery shower.

Then Gádhi's son, when these had failed,
With Brahmá's dart his foe assailed.
The Gods, with Indra at their head,
And Nágas, quailed disquieted,
And saints and minstrels, when they saw
The king that awful weapon draw;
And the three worlds were filled with dread,
And trembled as the missile sped.

The saint, with Bráhman wand, empowered
By lore divine that dart devoured.
Nor could the triple world withdraw
Rapt gazes from that sight of awe;
For as he swallowed down the dart
Of Brahmá, sparks from every part,
From finest pore and hair-cell, broke
Enveloped in a veil of smoke.
The staff he waved was all aglow
Like Yáma's sceptre, King below,
Or like the lurid fire of Fate
Whose rage the worlds will desolate.

The hermits, whom that sight had awed,
Extolled the saint, with hymn and laud:
"Thy power, O Sage, is ne'er in vain:
Now with thy might thy might restrain.
Be gracious, Master, and allow
The worlds to rest from trouble now;
For Viśvámitra, strong and dread,
By thee has been discomfited."

Then, thus addressed, the saint, well pleased,
The fury of his wrath appeased.
The king, o'erpowered and ashamed,
With many a deep-drawn sigh exclaimed:
"Ah! Warriors' strength is poor and slight;

A Bráhman's power is truly might.
This Bráhman staff the hermit held
The fury of my darts has quelled.
This truth within my heart impressed,
With senses ruled and tranquil breast
My task austere will I begin,
And Bráhmanhood will strive to win."

Trisanku

Then with his heart consumed with woe,
 Still brooding on his overthrow
 By the great saint he had defied,
At every breath the monarch sighed.
Forth from his home his queen he led,
And to a land far southward fled.
There, fruit and roots his only food,
He practised penance, sense-subdued,
And in that solitary spot
Four virtuous sons the king begot:
Havishyand, from the offering named,
And Madhushyand, for sweetness famed,
Mahárath, chariot-borne in fight,
And Driḍhanetra strong of sight.

A thousand years had passed away,
When Brahmá, Sire whom all obey,
Addressed in pleasant words like these
Him rich in long austerities:
"Thou by the penance, Kuśik's son,
A place 'mid royal saints hast won.
Pleased with thy constant penance, we
This lofty rank assign to thee."

192

Thus spoke the glorious Lord most High
Father of earth and air and sky,
And with the Gods around him spread
Home to his changeless sphere he sped.
But Viśvámitra scorned the grace,
And bent in shame his angry face.
Burning with rage, o'erwhelmed with grief,
Thus in his heart exclaimed the chief:
"No fruit, I ween, have I secured
By strictest penance long endured,
If Gods and all the saints decree
To make but royal saint of me."
Thus pondering, he with sense subdued,
With sternest zeal his vows renewed.

Then reigned a monarch, true of soul,
Who kept each sense in firm control;
Of old Ikshváku's line he came,
That glories in Triśanku's name.
Within his breast, O Raghu's child,
Arose a longing, strong and wild,
Great offerings to the Gods to pay,
And win, alive, to heaven his way.
His priest Vaśishṭha's aid he sought,
And told him of his secret thought.
But wise Vaśishṭha showed the hope
Was far beyond the monarch's scope.
Triśanku then, his suit denied,
Far to the southern region hied,
To beg Vaśishṭha's sons to aid
The mighty plan his soul had made.
There King Triśanku, far renowned,
Vaśishṭha's hundred children found,
Each on his fervent vows intent,
For mind and fame preëminent.
To these the famous king applied,
Wise children of his holy guide.
Saluting each in order due.
His eyes, for shame, he downward threw,
And reverent hands together pressed,
The glorious company addressed:

"I as a humble suppliant seek
Succour of you who aid the weak.
A mighty offering I would pay,
But sage Vaśishṭha answered, Nay.
Be yours permission to accord,
And to my rites your help afford.
Sons of my guide, to each of you
With lowly reverence here I sue;
To each, intent on penance-vow,
O Bráhmans, low my head I bow,
And pray you each with ready heart
In my great rite to bear a part,
That in the body I may rise
And dwell with Gods within the skies.
Sons of my guide, none else I see
Can give what he refuses me.
Ikshváku's children still depend
Upon their guide most reverend;
And you, as nearest in degree
To him, my deities shall be!"

CANTO

LVIII

Trisanku Cursed

Triśanku's speech the hundred heard,
And thus replied, to anger stirred:
"Why foolish King, by him denied,
Whose truthful lips have never lied,
Dost thou transgress his prudent rule,
And seek, for aid, another school?
Ikshváku's sons have aye relied
Most surely on their holy guide:
Then how dost thou, fond Monarch, dare
Transgress the rule his lips declare?

"Thy wish is vain," the saint replied,
And bade thee cast the plan aside.
Then how can we, his sons, pretend
In such a rite our aid to lend?
O Monarch, of the childish heart,
Home to thy royal town depart.
That mighty saint, thy priest and guide,
At noblest rites may well preside:
The worlds for sacrifice combined
A worthier priest could never find."

Such speech of theirs the monarch heard,
Though rage distorted every word,
And to the hermits made reply:
"You, like your sire, my suit deny.
For other aid I turn from you:
So, rich in penance, Saints, adieu!"

Vaśishṭha's children heard, and guessed
His evil purpose scarce expressed,
And cried, while rage their bosoms burned,
"Be to a vile Chaṇḍála turned!"

This said, with lofty thoughts inspired,
Each to his own retreat retired.

That night Triśanku underwent
Sad change in shape and lineament.
Next morn, an outcast swart of hue,
His dusky cloth he round him drew.
His hair had fallen from his head,
And roughness o'er his skin was spread.
Such wreaths adorned him as are found
To flourish on the funeral ground.
Each armlet was an iron ring:
Such was the figure of the king,
That every counsellor and peer,
And following townsman, fled in fear.

Alone, unyielding to dismay,
Though burnt by anguish night and day,

Great Viśvámitra's side he sought,
Whose treasures were by penance bought.
The hermit with his tender eyes
Looked on Triśanku's altered guise,
And grieving at his ruined state
Addressed him thus, compassionate:
"Great King," the pious hermit said,
"What cause thy steps has hither led,
Ayodhyá's mighty Sovereign, whom
A curse has plagued with outcast's doom?"
In vile Chaṇḍála shape, the king
Heard Viśvámitra's questioning,
And, suppliant palm to palm applied,
With answering eloquence he cried:
"My priest and all his sons refused
To aid the plan on which I mused.
Failing to win the boon I sought,
To this condition I was brought.
I, in the body, Saint, would fain
A mansion in the skies obtain.
I planned a hundred rites for this,
But still was doomed the fruit to miss.
Pure are my lips from falsehood's stain,
And pure they ever shall remain,—
Yea, by a Warrior's faith I swear,—
Though I be tried with grief and care.
Unnumbered rites to Heaven I paid,
With righteous care the sceptre swayed;
And holy priest and high-souled guide
My modest conduct gratified.
But, O thou best of hermits, they
Oppose my wish these rites to pay;
They one and all refuse consent,
Nor aid me in my high intent.
Fate is, I ween, the power supreme,
Man's effort but an idle dream,
Fate whirls our plans, our all away;
Fate is our only hope and stay;
Now deign, O blessed Saint, to aid
Me, even me by Fate betrayed,
Who come, a suppliant, sore distressed,

One grace, O Hermit, to request.
No other hope or way I see:
No other refuge waits for me.
Oh, aid me in my fallen state,
And human will shall conquer Fate."

The Sons of Vasishtha

T hen Kuśik's son, by pity warmed,
    Spoke sweetly to the king transformed:
    "Hail! glory of Ikshváku's line:
I know how bright thy virtues shine.
Dismiss thy fear, O noblest Chief,
For I myself will bring relief.
The holiest saints will I invite
To celebrate thy purposed rite:
So shall thy vow, O King, succeed,
And from thy cares shalt thou be freed.
Thou in the form which now thou hast,
Transfigured by the curse they cast,—
Yea, in the body, King, shalt flee,
Transported, where thou fain wouldst be.
O Lord of men, I ween that thou
Hast heaven within thy hand e'en now,
For very wisely hast thou done,
And refuge sought with Kuśik's son."

Thus having said, the sage addressed
His sons, of men the holiest,
And bade the prudent saints whate'er
Was needed for the rite prepare.
The pupils he was wont to teach
He summoned next, and spoke this speech:

197

"Go bid Vaśishṭha'a sons appear,
And all the saints be gathered here.
And what they one and all reply
When summoned by this mandate high,
To me with faithful care report,
Omit no word and none distort."

The pupils heard, and prompt obeyed,
To every side their way they made.
Then swift from every quarter sped
The sages in the Vedas read.
Back to that saint the envoys came,
Whose glory shone like burning flame,
And told him in their faithful speech
The answer that they bore from each:
"Submissive to thy word, O Seer,
The holy men are gathering here.
By all was meet obedience shown:
Mahodaya refused alone.

And now, O Chief of hermits, hear
What answer, chilling us with fear,
Vaśishṭha's hundred sons returned,
Thick-speaking as with rage they burned:
"How will the Gods and saints partake
The offerings that the prince would make,
And he a vile and outcast thing,
His ministrant one born a king?
Can we, great Bráhmans, eat his food,
And think to win beatitude,
By Viśvámitra purified?"
Thus sire and sons in scorn replied,
And as these bitter words they said,
Wild fury made their eyeballs red.

Their answer when the arch-hermit heard,
His tranquil eyes with rage were blurred;
Great fury in his bosom woke,
And thus unto the youths he spoke:
"Me, blameless me they dare to blame,
And disallow the righteous claim

My fierce austerities have earned:
To ashes be the sinners turned.
Caught in the noose of Fate shall they
To Yáma's kingdom sink to-day.
Seven hundred times shall they be born
To wear the clothes the dead have worn.
Dregs of the dregs, too vile to hate,
The flesh of dogs their maws shall sate.
In hideous form, in loathsome weed,
A sad existence each shall lead.
Mahodaya too, the fool who fain
My stainless life would try to stain,
Stained in the world with long disgrace
Shall sink into a fowler's place.
Rejoicing guiltless blood to spill,
No pity through his breast shall thrill.
Cursed by my wrath for many a day,
His wretched life for sin shall pay."

Thus, girt with hermit, saint, and priest,
Great Viśvámitra spoke—and ceased.

CANTO
LX

Trisanku's Ascension

So with ascetic might, in ire,
He smote the children and the sire.
Then Viśvámitra, far-renowned,
Addressed the saints who gathered round:
"See by my side Triśanku stand,
Ikshváku's son, of liberal hand.
Most virtuous and gentle, he
Seeks refuge in his woe with me.
Now, holy men, with me unite,

And order so his purposed rite
That in the body he may rise
And win a mansion in the skies."

They heard his speech with ready ear
And, every bosom filled with fear
Of Viśvámitra, wise and great,
Spoke each to each in brief debate:
"The breast of Kuśik's son, we know,
With furious wrath is quick to glow.
Whate'er the words he wills to say,
We must, be very sure, obey.
Fierce is our lord as fire, and straight
May curse us all infuriate.
So let us in these rites engage,
As ordered by the holy sage.
And with our best endeavour strive
That King Ikshváku's son, alive,
In body to the skies may go
By his great might who wills it so."
Then was the rite begun with care:
All requisites and means were there:
And glorious Viśvámitra lent
His willing aid as president.
And all the sacred rites were done
By rule and use, omitting none.
By chaplain-priest, the hymns who knew,
In decent form and order due.
Some time in sacrifice had past,
And Viśvámitra made, at last,
The solemn offering with the prayer
That all the Gods might come and share.
But the Immortals, one and all,
Refused to hear the hermit's call.

Then red with rage his eyeballs blazed:
The sacred ladle high he raised,
And cried to King Ikshváku's son:
"Behold my power, by penance won:
Now by the might my merits lend,
Ikshváku's child, to heaven ascend.

200

In living frame the skies attain,
Which mortals thus can scarcely gain.
My vows austere, so long endured,
Have, as I ween, some fruit assured.
Upon its virtue, King, rely,
And in thy body reach the sky."

His speech had scarcely reached its close,
When, as he stood, the sovereign rose,
And mounted swiftly to the skies
Before the wondering hermits' eyes.

But Indra, when he saw the king
His blissful regions entering,
With all the army of the Blest
Thus cried unto the unbidden guest:
"With thy best speed, Triśanku, flee:
Here is no home prepared for thee.
By thy great master's curse brought low,
Go, falling headlong, earthward go."

Thus by the Lord of Gods addressed,
Triśanku fell from fancied rest,
And screaming in his swift descent,
"O, save me, Hermit!" down he went.
And Viśvámitra heard his cry,
And marked him falling from the sky,
And giving all his passion sway,
Cried out in fury, "Stay, O stay!"

By penance-power and holy lore,
Like Him who framed the worlds of yore,
Seven other saints he fixed on high
To star with light the southern sky.
Girt with his sages forth he went,
And southward in the firmament
New wreathed stars prepared to set
In many a sparkling coronet.
He threatened, blind with rage and hate,
Another Indra to create,
Or, from his throne the ruler hurled,

All Indraless to leave the world.
Yea, borne away by passion's storm,
The sage began new Gods to form.
But then each Titan, God, and saint,
Confused with terror, sick and faint,
To high souled Viśvámitra hied,
And with soft words to soothe him tried:
"Lord of high destiny, this king,
To whom his master's curses cling,
No heavenly home deserves to gain,
Unpurified from curse and stain."

The son of Kuśik, undeterred,
The pleading of the Immortals heard,
And thus in haughty words expressed
The changeless purpose of his breast:
"Content ye, Gods: I soothly sware
Triśanku to the skies to bear
Clothed in his body, nor can I
My promise cancel or deny.
Embodied let the king ascend
To life in heaven that ne'er shall end.
And let these new-made stars of mine
Firm and secure for ever shine.
Let these, my work, remain secure
Long as the earth and heaven endure.
This, all ye Gods, I crave: do you
Allow the boon for which I sue."
Then all the Gods their answer made:
"So be it, Saint, as thou hast prayed.
Beyond the sun's diurnal way
Thy countless stars in heaven shall stay:
And 'mid them hung, as one divine,
Head downward shall Triśanku shine;
And all thy stars shall ever fling
Their rays attendant on the king."

The mighty saint, with glory crowned,
With all the sages compassed round,
Praised by the Gods, gave full assent,
And Gods and sages homeward went.

CANTO
LXI

Sunahsepha

Then Viśvámitra, when the Blest
  Had sought their homes of heavenly rest,
  Thus, mighty Prince, his counsel laid
Before the dwellers of the shade:
"The southern land where now we are
Offers this check our rites to bar:
To other regions let us speed,
And ply our tasks from trouble freed.
Now turn we to the distant west.
To Pushkar's wood where hermits rest,
And there to rites austere apply,
For not a grove with that can vie."

The saint, in glory's light arrayed,
In Pushkar's wood his dwelling made,
And living there on roots and fruit
Did penance stern and resolute.

The king who filled Ayodhyá's throne,
By Ambarísha's name far known,
At that same time, it chanced, began
A sacrificial rite to plan.
But Indra took by force away
The charger that the king would slay.
The victim lost, the Bráhman sped
To Ambarísha's side, and said:
"Gone is the steed, O King, and this
Is due to thee, in care remiss.

Such heedless faults will kings destroy
Who fail to guard what they enjoy.

The flaw is desperate: we need
The charger, or a man to bleed.
Quick! bring a man if not the horse,
That so the rite may have its course."

The glory of Ikshváku's line
Made offer of a thousand kine,
And sought to buy at lordly price
A victim for the sacrifice.
To many a distant land he drove,
To many a people, town, and grove,
And holy shades where hermits rest,
Pursuing still his eager quest.
At length on Bhrigu's sacred height
The saint Richíka met his sight
Sitting beneath the holy boughs.
His children near him, and his spouse.

The mighty lord drew near, assayed
To win his grace, and reverence paid;
And then the sainted king addressed
The Bráhman saint with this request:
"Bought with a hundred thousand kine,
Give me, O Sage, a son of thine
To be a victim in the rite,
And thanks the favour shall requite.
For I have roamed all countries round,
Nor sacrificial victim found.
Then, gentle Hermit, deign to spare
One child amid the number there."

Then to the monarch's speech replied
The hermit, penance-glorified:
"For countless kine, for hills of gold,
Mine eldest son shall ne'er be sold."
But, when she heard the saint's reply,
The children's mother, standing nigh,
Words such as these in answer said
To Ambarísha, monarch dread:
"My lord, the saint, has spoken well:
His eldest child he will not sell.

And know, great Monarch, that above
The rest my youngest born I love.
'Tis ever thus: the father's joy
Is centred in his eldest boy.
The mother loves her darling best
Whom last she rocked upon her breast:
My youngest I will ne'er forsake."

As thus the sire and mother spake,
Young Śunahśepha, of the three
The midmost, cried unurged and free:
"My sire withholds his eldest son,
My mother keeps her youngest one:
Then take me with thee, King: I ween
The son is sold who comes between."
The king with joy his home resought,
And took the prize his kine had bought.
He bade the youth his car ascend,
And hastened back the rites to end.

CANTO
LXII

Ambarísha's Sacrifice

As thus the king that youth conveyed,
His weary steeds at length he stayed
At height of noon their rest to take
Upon the bank of Pushkar's lake.
There while the king enjoyed repose
The captive Śunahśepha rose,
And hasting to the water's side
His uncle Viśvámitra spied,
With many a hermit 'neath the trees
Engaged in stern austerities.

Distracted with the toil and thirst,
With woeful mien, away he burst,
Swift to the hermit's breast he flew,
And weeping thus began to sue:
"No sire have I, no mother dear,
No kith or kin my heart to cheer:
As justice bids, O Hermit, deign
To save me from the threatened pain.
O thou to whom the wretched flee,
And find a saviour, Saint, in thee,
Now let the king obtain his will,
And me my length of days fulfil,
That rites austere I too may share,
May rise to heaven and rest me there.
With tender soul and gentle brow
Be guardian of the orphan thou,
And as a father pities, so
Preserve me from my fear and woe."

When Viśvámitra, glorious saint,
Had heard the boy's heart-rending plaint.
He soothed his grief, his tears he dried,

Then called his sons to him, and cried:
"The time is come for you to show
The duty and the aid bestow
For which, regarding future life,
A man gives children to his wife.
This hermit's son, whom here you see
A suppliant, refuge seeks with me.
O sons, the friendless youth befriend,
And, pleasing me, his life defend.
For holy works you all have wrought,
True to the virtuous life I taught.
Go, and as victims doomed to bleed,
Die, and Lord Agni's hunger feed.
So shall the rite completed end,
This orphan gain a saving friend,
Due offerings to the Gods be paid,
And your own father's voice obeyed."

Then Madhushyand and all the rest
Answered their sire with scorn and jest:
"What! aid to others' sons afford,
And leave thine own to die, my lord!
To us it seems a horrid deed,
As 'twere on one's own flesh to feed."

The hermit heard his sons' reply,
And burning rage inflamed his eye.
Then forth his words of fury burst:
"Audacious speech, by virtue cursed!
It lifts on end each shuddering hair—
My charge to scorn! my wrath to dare!
You, like Vaśishṭha's evil brood,
Shall make the flesh of dogs your food
A thousand years in many a birth,
And punished thus shall dwell on earth."

Thus on his sons his curse he laid.
Then calmed again that youth dismayed,
And blessed him with his saving aid:
"When in the sacred fetters bound,
And with a purple garland crowned,
At Vishṇu's post thou standest tied,
With lauds be Agni glorified.
And these two hymns of holy praise
Forget not, Hermit's son, to raise
In the king's rite, and thou shalt be
Lord of thy wish, preserved, and free."

He learnt the hymns with mind intent,
And from the hermit's presence went.
To Ambarísha thus he spake:
"Let us our onward journey take.
Haste to thy home, O King, nor stay
The lustral rites with slow delay."
The boy's address the monarch cheered,
And soon the sacred ground he neared.
The convocation's high decree
Declared the youth from blemish free;
Clothed in red raiment he was tied

A victim at the pillar's side.
There bound, the Fire-God's hymn he raised,
And Indra and Upendra praised.
Thousand-eyed Vishṇu, pleased to hear
The mystic laud, inclined his ear,
And won by worship, swift to save,
Long life to Śunahśepha gave.
The king in bounteous measure gained
The fruit of sacrifice ordained,
By grace of Him who rules the skies,
Lord Indra of the thousand eyes.

And Viśvámitra evermore.
Pursued his task on Pushkar's shore
Until a thousand years had past
In fierce austerity and fast.

CANTO
LXIII

Menaká

A thousand years had thus flown by
When all the Gods within the sky,
Eager that he the fruit might gain
Of fervent rite and holy pain,
Approached the great ascetic, now
Bathed after toil and ended vow.
Then Brahmá speaking for the rest
With sweetest words the sage addressed:
"Hail, Saint! This high and holy name
Thy rites have won, thy merits claim."

Thus spoke the Lord whom Gods revere,
And sought again his heavenly sphere.
But Viśvámitra, more intent,

His mind to sterner penance bent.
So many a season rolled away,
When Menaká, fair nymph, one day
Came down from Paradise to lave
Her perfect limbs in Pushkar's wave,
The glorious son of Kuśik saw
That peerless shape without a flaw
Flash through the flood's translucent shroud
Like lightning gleaming through a cloud.
He saw her in that lone retreat,
Most beautiful from head to feet,
And by Kandarpa's might subdued
He thus addressed her as he viewed:
"Welcome, sweet nymph! O deign, I pray,
In these calm shades awhile to stay.
To me some gracious favour show,
For love has set my breast aglow."

He spoke. The fairest of the fair
Made for awhile her dwelling there,
While day by day the wild delight
Stayed vow austere and fervent rite
There as the winsome charmer wove
Her spells around him in the grove,
And bound him in a golden chain,
Five sweet years fled, and five again.
Then Viśvámitra woke to shame,
And, fraught with anguish, memory came
For quick he knew, with anger fired,
That all the Immortals had conspired

To lap his careless soul in ease,
And mar his long austerities.
"Ten years have past, each day and night
Unheeded in delusive flight.
So long my fervent rites were stayed,
While thus I lay by love betrayed."
As thus long sighs the hermit heaved,
And, touched with deep repentance, grieved,
He saw the fair one standing nigh
With suppliant hands and trembling eye.

With gentle words he bade her go,
Then sought the northern hills of snow.
With firm resolve he vowed to beat
The might of love beneath his feet.
Still northward to the distant side
Of Kauśikí, the hermit hide,
And gave his life to penance there
With rites austere most hard to bear.
A thousand years went by, and still
He laboured on the northern hill
With pains so terrible and drear
That all the Gods were chilled with fear,
And Gods and saints, for swift advice,
Met in the halls of Paradise.
"Let Kuśik's son," they counselled, "be
A Mighty saint by just decree."
His ear to hear their counsel lent
The Sire of worlds, omnipotent.
To him enriched by rites severe
He spoke in accents sweet to hear:
"Hail, Mighty Saint! dear son, all hail!
Thy fervour wins, thy toils prevail.
Won by thy vows and zeal intense
I give this high preëminence."
He to the General Sire replied,
Not sad, nor wholly satisfied:
"When thou, O Brahmá, shalt declare
The title, great beyond compare,
Of Bráhman saint my worthy meed,
Hard earned by many a holy deed,
Then may I deem in sooth I hold
Each sense of body well controlled."
Then Brahmá cried, "Not yet, not yet:
Toil on awhile O Anchoret!"

Thus having said to heaven he went,
The saint, upon his task intent,
Began his labours to renew,
Which sterner yet and fiercer grew.
His arms upraised, without a rest,
With but one foot the earth he pressed;

The air his food, the hermit stood
Still as a pillar hewn from wood.
Around him in the summer days
Five mighty fires combined to blaze.
In floods of rain no veil was spread
Save clouds, to canopy his head.
In the dank dews both night and day
Couched in the stream the hermit lay.
Thus, till a thousand years had fled,
He plied his task of penance dread.
Then Vishṇu and the Gods with awe
The labours of the hermit saw,
And Śakra, in his troubled breast,
Lord of the skies, his fear confessed.
And brooded on a plan to spoil
The merits of the hermit's toil.
Encompassed by his Gods of Storm
He summoned Rambhá, fair of form,
And spoke a speech for woe and weal,
The saint to mar, the God to heal.

CANTO
LXIV

Rambhá

"A great emprise, O lovely maid,
To save the Gods, awaits thine aid:
To bind the son of Kuśik sure,
And take his soul with love's sweet lure."
Thus order'd by the Thousand-eyed
The suppliant nymph in fear replied:
"O Lord of Gods, this mighty sage
Is very fierce and swift to rage.
I doubt not, he so dread and stern
On me his scorching wrath will turn.

Of this, my lord, am I afraid:
Have mercy on a timid maid."
Her suppliant hands began to shake,
When thus again Lord Indra spake:
"O Rambhá, drive thy fears away,
And as I bid do thou obey.
In Koïl's form, who takes the heart
When trees in spring to blossom start,
I, with Kandarpa for my friend,
Close to thy side mine aid will lend.

Do thou thy beauteous splendour arm
With every grace and winsome charm,
And from his awful rites seduce
This Kuśik's son, the stern recluse."

Lord Indra ceased. The nymph obeyed:
In all her loveliest charms arrayed,
With winning ways and witching smile
She sought the hermit to beguile.
The sweet note of that tuneful bird
The saint with ravished bosom heard,
And on his heart a rapture passed
As on the nymph a look he cast.
But when he heard the bird prolong
His sweet incomparable song,
And saw the nymph with winning smile,
The hermit's heart perceived the wile.
And straight he knew the Thousand-eyed
A plot against his peace had tried.
Then Kuśik's son indignant laid
His curse upon the heavenly maid:
"Because thou wouldst my soul engage
Who fight to conquer love and rage,
Stand, till ten thousand years have flown,
Ill-fated maid, transformed to stone.
A Bráhman then, in glory strong,
Mighty through penance stern and long,
Shall free thee from thine altered shape;
Thou from my curse shalt then escape."
But when the saint had cursed her so,

His breast was burnt with fires of woe,
Grieved that long effort to restrain
His mighty wrath was all in vain.
Cursed by the angry sage's power,
She stood in stone that selfsame hour.
Kandarpa heard the words he said,
And quickly from his presence fled.
His fall beneath his passion's sway
Had reft the hermit's meed away.
Unconquered yet his secret foes,
The humbled saint refused repose:
"No more shall rage my bosom till,
Sealed be my lips, my tongue be still.
My very breath henceforth I hold
Until a thousand years are told:
Victorious o'er each erring sense,
I'll dry my frame with abstinence,
Until by penance duly done
A Bráhman's rank be bought and won.
For countless years, as still as death,
I taste no food, I draw no breath,
And as I toil my frame shall stand
Unharmed by time's destroying hand."

CANTO
LXV

Visvámitra's Triumph

Then from Himálaya's heights of snow,
   The glorious saint prepared to go,
      And dwelling in the distant east
His penance and his toil increased.
A thousand years his lips he held
Closed by a vow unparalleled,
And other marvels passing thought,

Unrivalled in the world, he wrought.
In all the thousand years his frame
Dry as a log of wood became.
By many a cross and check beset,
Rage had not stormed his bosom yet.
With iron will that naught could bend
He plied his labour till the end.
So when the weary years were o'er,
Freed from his vow so stern and sore,
The hermit, all his penance sped,
Sate down to eat his meal of bread.
Then Indra, clad in Bráhman guise,
Asked him for food with hungry eyes.
The mighty saint, with steadfast soul,
To the false Bráhman gave the whole,
And when no scrap for him remained,
Fasting and faint, from speech refrained.
His silent vow he would not break:
No breath he heaved, no word he spake,
Then as he checked his breath, behold!
Around his brow thick smoke-clouds rolled
And the three worlds, as if o'erspread
With ravening flames, were filled with dread.
Then God and saint and bard, convened,
And Nága lord, and snake, and fiend,
Thus to the General Father cried,
Distracted, sad, and terrified:
"Against the hermit, sore assailed,
Lure, scathe, and scorn have naught availed,
Proof against rage and treacherous art
He keeps his vow with constant heart.
Now if his toils assist him naught
To gain the boon his soul has sought,
He through the worlds will ruin send
That fixt and moving things shall end,
The regions now are dark with doom,
No friendly ray relieves the gloom.
Each ocean foams with maddened tide,
The shrinking hills in fear subside.
Trembles the earth with feverous throe
The wind in fitful tempest blows.

No cure we see with troubled eyes:
And atheist brood on earth may rise.
The triple world is wild with care,
Or spiritless in dull despair.
Before that saint the sun is dim,
His blessed light eclipsed by him.
Now ere the saint resolve to bring
Destruction on each living thing,
Let us appease, while yet we may,
Him bright as fire, like fire to slay.
Yea, as the fiery flood of Fate
Lays all creation desolate,
He o'er the conquered Gods may reign:
O, grant him what he longs to gain."

Then all the Blest, by Brahmá led,
Approached the saint and sweetly said:
"Hail, Bráhman Saint! for such thy place:
Thy vows austere have won our grace.
A Bráhman's rank thy penance stern
And ceaseless labour richly earn.
I with the Gods of Storm decree
Long life, O Bráhman Saint, to thee.
May peace and joy thy soul possess:
Go where thou wilt in happiness."

Thus by the General Sire addressed,
Joy and high triumph filled his breast.
His head in adoration bowed,
Thus spoke he to the Immortal crowd:
"If I, ye Gods, have gained at last
Both length of days and Bráhman caste,
Grant that the high mysterious name,
And holy Vedas, own my claim,
And that the formula to bless
The sacrifice, its lord confess.
And let Vaśishṭha, who excels
In Warriors' art and mystic spells,
In love of God without a peer,
Confirm the boon you promise here."

With Brahmá's son Vaśishṭha, best
Of those who pray with voice repressed,
The Gods by earnest prayer prevailed,
And thus his new-made friend he hailed:
"Thy title now is sure and good
To rights of saintly Bráhmanhood."
Thus spake the sage. The Gods, content,
Back to their heavenly mansions went.
And Viśvámitra, pious-souled,
Among the Bráhman saints enrolled,
On reverend Vaśishṭha pressed
The honours due to holy guest.
Successful in his high pursuit,
The sage, in penance resolute,
Walked in his pilgrim wanderings o'er
The whole broad land from shore to shore.
'Twas thus the saint, O Raghu's son,
His rank among the Bráhmans won.
Best of all hermits, Prince, is he;
In him incarnate Penance see.
Friend of the right, who shrinks from ill,
Heroic powers attend him still."

The Bráhman, versed in ancient lore,
Thus closed his tale, and said no more,
To Śatánanda Kuśik's son
Cried in delight, Well done! well done!
Then Janak, at the tale amazed,
Spoke thus with suppliant hands upraised:
"High fate is mine, O Sage, I deem,
And thanks I owe for bliss supreme,
That thou and Raghu's children too
Have come my sacrifice to view.
To look on thee with blessed eyes
Exalts my soul and purifies.
Yea, thus to see thee face to face
Enriches me with store of grace.
Thy holy labours wrought of old,
And mighty penance, fully told,
Ráma and I with great delight
Have heard, O glorious Anchorite.

216

Unrivalled thine ascetic deeds:
Thy might, O Saint, all might exceeds.
No thought may scan, no limit bound
The virtues that in thee are found.
The story of thy wondrous fate
My thirsty ears can never sate.
The hour of evening rites is near:
The sun declines in swift career.
At early dawn, O Hermit, deign
To let me see thy face again.
Best of ascetics, part in bliss:
Do thou thy servant now dismiss."

The saint approved, and glad and kind
Dismissed the king with joyful mind
Around the sage King Janak went
With priests and kinsmen reverent.
Then Viśvámitra, honoured so,
By those high-minded, rose to go,
And with the princes took his way
To seek the lodging where they lay.

CANTO

LXVI

Janak's Speech

With cloudless lustre rose the sun;
The king, his morning worship done,
Ordered his heralds to invite
The princes and the anchorite.
With honour, as the laws decree,
The monarch entertained the three.
Then to the youths and saintly man
Videha's lord this speech began:
"O blameless Saint, most welcome thou!

If I may please thee tell me how.
Speak, mighty lord, whom all revere,
'Tis thine to order, mine to hear."

Thus he on mighty thoughts intent;
Then thus the sage most eloquent:
"King Daśaratha's sons, this pair
Of warriors famous everywhere,
Are come that best of bows to see
That lies a treasure stored by thee.
This, mighty Janak, deign to show,
That they may look upon the bow,
And then, contented, homeward go."
Then royal Janak spoke in turn:
"O best of Saints, the story learn
Why this famed bow, a noble prize,
A treasure in my palace lies.
A monarch, Devarát by name,
Who sixth from ancient Nimi came,
Held it as ruler of the land,
A pledge in his successive hand.
This bow the mighty Rudra bore

At Daksha's sacrifice of yore,
When carnage of the Immortals stained
The rite that Daksha had ordained.
Then as the Gods sore wounded fled,
Victorious Rudra, mocking, said:
"Because, O Gods, ye gave me naught
When I my rightful portion sought,
Your dearest parts I will not spare,
But with my bow your frames will tear."

The Sons of Heaven, in wild alarm,
Soft flatteries tried his rage to charm.
Then Bhava, Lord whom Gods adore,
Grew kind and friendly as before,
And every torn and mangled limb
Was safe and sound restored by him.
Thenceforth this bow, the gem of bows,
That freed the God of Gods from foes,

Stored by our great forefathers lay
A treasure and a pride for aye.
Once, as it chanced, I ploughed the ground,
When sudden, 'neath the share was found
An infant springing from the earth,
Named Sítá from her secret birth.
In strength and grace the maiden grew,
My cherished daughter, fair to view.
I vowed her, of no mortal birth,
Meet prize for noblest hero's worth.
In strength and grace the maiden grew,
And many a monarch came to woo.
To all the princely suitors I
Gave, mighty Saint, the same reply:
"I give not thus my daughter, she
Prize of heroic worth shall be.
To Míthilá the suitors pressed
Their power and might to manifest.
To all who came with hearts aglow
I offered Śiva's wondrous bow.
Not one of all the royal band
Could raise or take the bow in hand.
The suitors' puny might I spurned,
And back the feeble princes turned.
Enraged thereat, the warriors met,
With force combined my town beset.
Stung to the heart with scorn and shame,
With war and threats they madly came,
Besieged my peaceful walls, and long
To Míthilá did grievous wrong.
There, wasting all, a year they lay,
And brought my treasures to decay,
Filling my soul, O Hermit chief,
With bitter woe and hopeless grief.
At last by long-wrought penance I
Won favour with the Gods on high,
Who with my labours well content
A four-fold host to aid me sent.
Then swift the baffled heroes fled
To all the winds discomfited—
Wrong-doers, with their lords and host,

And all their valour's idle boast.
This heavenly bow, exceeding bright,
These youths shall see, O Anchorite.
Then if young Ráma's hand can string
The bow that baffled lord and king,
To him I give, as I have sworn,
My Sítá, not of woman born."

CANTO

LXVII

The Breaking of The Bow

Then spoke again the great recluse:
  "This mighty bow, O King, produce."
  King Janak, at the saint's request,
This order to his train addressed:
"Let the great bow be hither borne,
Which flowery wreaths and scents adorn."
Soon as the monarch's words were said,
His servants to the city sped;
Five thousand youths in number, all
Of manly strength and stature tall,
The ponderous eight-wheeled chest that held
The heavenly bow, with toil propelled.
At length they brought that iron chest,
And thus the godlike king addressed:
"This best of bows, O lord, we bring,
Respected by each chief and king,
And place it for these youths to see,
If, Sovereign, such thy pleasure be."

With suppliant palm to palm applied
King Janak to the strangers cried:
"This gem of bows, O Bráhman Sage,
Our race has prized from age to age,

Dasaratha's Visit

S oon as the shades of night had fled,
    Thus to the wise Sumantra said
    The happy king, while priest and peer,
Each in his place, were standing near:
"Let all my treasurers to-day,
Set foremost in the long array,
With gold and precious gems supplied
In bounteous store, together ride.
And send you out a mighty force,
Foot, chariot, elephant, and horse.
Besides, let many a car of state,
And noblest steeds, my will await.
Vaśishṭha, Vámadeva sage,
And Márkaṇḍeya's reverend age,
Jáváli, Kaśyap's godlike seed,
And wise Kátyáyana, shall lead.
Thy care, Sumantra, let it be
To yoke a chariot now for me,
That so we part without delay:
These envoys hasten me away."

So fared he forth. That host, with speed,
Quadruple, as the king decreed,
With priests to head the bright array,
Followed the monarch on his way.
Four days they travelled on the road,
And eve Videha's kingdom showed.
Janak had left his royal seat
The venerable king to greet,
And, noblest, with these words addressed
That noblest lord, his happy guest:

"Hail, best of kings: a blessed fate
Has led thee, Monarch, to my state.
Thy sons, supreme in high emprise,
Will gladden now their father's eyes.
And high my fate, that hither leads
Vaśishṭha, bright with holy deeds,
Girt with these sages far-renowned,
Like Indra with the Gods around.
Joy! joy! for vanquished are my foes:
Joy! for my house in glory grows,
With Raghu's noblest sons allied,
Supreme in strength and valour's pride.
To-morrow with its early light
Will shine on my completed rite.
Then, sanctioned by the saints and thee,
The marriage of thy Ráma see."

Then Daśaratha, best of those
Whose speech in graceful order flows,
With gathered saints on every side,
Thus to the lord of earth replied:
"A truth is this I long have known,
A favour is the giver's own.
What thou shalt bid, O good and true,
We, as our power permits, will do."

That answer of the truthful lord,
With virtuous worth and honour stored,
Janak, Videha's noble king,
Heard gladly, greatly marvelling.
With bosoms filled with pleasure met
Long-parted saint and anchoret,
And linked in friendship's tie they spent
The peaceful night in great content.

Ráma and Lakshmaṇ thither sped,
By sainted Viśvámitra led,
And bent in filial love to greet
Their father, and embraced his feet.
The aged king, rejoiced to hear
And see again his children dear,

226

Honoured by Janak's thoughtful care,
With great enjoyment rested there.
King Janak, with attentive heed,
Consulted first his daughters' need,
And ordered all to speed the rite;
Then rested also for the night.

CANTO
LXX

The Maidens Sought

Then with the morn's returning sun.
King Janak, when his rites were done,
Skilled all the charms of speech to know,
Spoke to wise Śatánanda so:
"My brother, lord of glorious fame,
My younger, Kuśadhwaj by name,
Whose virtuous life has won renown,
Has settled in a lovely town,
Sánkáśyá, decked with grace divine,
Whose glories bright as Pushpak's shine,
While Ikshumatí rolls her wave
Her lofty rampart's foot to lave.
Him, holy priest, I long to see:
The guardian of my rite is he:
That my dear brother may not miss
A share of mine expected bliss."
Thus in the presence of the priest
The royal Janak spoke, and ceased.
Then came his henchmen, prompt and brave,

To whom his charge the monarch gave.
Soon as they heard his will, in haste
With fleetest steeds away they raced,
To lead with them that lord of kings,

227

As Indra's call Lord Vishṇu brings.
Sánkásyá's walls they duly gained,
And audience of the king obtained.
To him they told the news they brought
Of marvels past and Janak's thought.
Soon as the king the story knew
From those good envoys swift and true,
To Janak's wish he gave assent,
And swift to Míthilá he went.
He paid to Janak reverence due,
And holy Śatánanda too,
Then sate him on a glorious seat
For kings or Gods celestial meet.
Soon as the brothers, noble pair
Peerless in might, were seated there,
They gave the wise Sudáman, best
Of councillors, their high behest:
"Go, noble councillor," they cried,
"And hither to our presence guide
Ikshváku's son, Ayodhyá's lord,
Invincible by foeman's sword,
With both his sons, each holy seer,
And every minister and peer."
Sudáman to the palace flew,
And saw the mighty king who threw
Splendour on Raghu's splendid race,
Then bowed his head with seemly grace:
"O King, whose hand Ayodhyá sways,
My lord, whom Míthilá obeys,
Yearns with desire, if thou agree,
Thee with thy guide and priest to see."
Soon as the councillor had ceased,
The king, with saint and peer and priest,
Sought, speeding through the palace gate,
The hall where Janak held his state.
There, with his nobles round him spread,
Thus to Videha's lord be said:
"Thou knowest, King, whose aid divine
Protects Ikshváku's royal line.
In every need, whate'er befall,
The saint Vaśishṭha speaks for all.

If Viśvámitra so allow,
And all the saints around me now,
The sage will speak, at my desire,
As order and the truth require."

Soon as the king his lips had stilled,
Up rose Vaśishṭha, speaker skilled.
And to Videha's lord began
In flowing words that holy man:
"From viewless Nature Brahmá rose,
No change, no end, no waste he knows.
A son had he Maríchi styled,
And Kaśyap was Maríchi's child.
From him Vivasvat sprang: from him
Manu whose fame shall ne'er be dim.
Manu, who life to mortals gave,
Begot Ikshváku good and brave.
First of Ayodhyá's kings was he,
Pride of her famous dynasty.
From him the glorious Kukshi sprang,
Whose fame through all the regions rang.
Rival of Kukshi's ancient fame,
His heir, the great Vikukshi, came,
His son was Váṇa, lord of might;
His Anaraṇya, strong to fight.
His son was Prithu, glorious name;
From him the good Triśanku came.
He left a son renowned afar,
Known by the name of Dhundhumár.
His son, who drove the mighty car,
Was Yuvanáśva, feared in war.
He passed away. Him followed then
His son Mándhátá, king of men.
His son was blest in high emprise,
Susandhi, fortunate and wise.
Two noble sons had he, to wit
Dhruvasandhi and Prasenajit.
Bharat was Dhruvasandhi's son,
And glorious fame that monarch won.
The warrior Asit he begot.
Asit had warfare, fierce and hot,

229

With rival kings in many a spot,
Haihayas, Tálajanghas styled,
And Śaśivindus, strong and wild.
Long time he strove, but forced to yield
Fled from his kingdom and the field.
With his two wives away he fled
Where high Himálaya lifts his head,
And, all his wealth and glory past,
He paid the dues of Fate at last.
The wives he left had both conceived—
So is the ancient tale believed—
One, of her rival's hopes afraid
Fell poison in her viands laid.
It chanced that Chyavan, Bhrigu's child,
Had wandered to that pathless wild,
And there Himálaya's lovely height
Detained him with a strange delight.
There came the other widowed queen,
With lotus eyes and beauteous mien,
Longing a noble son to bear,
And wooed the saint with earnest prayer.
When thus Kálindi, fairest dame,
With reverent supplication came,
To her the holy sage replied:
"Born with the poison from thy side,
O happy Queen, shall spring ere long
An infant fortunate and strong.
Then weep no more, and check thy sighs,
Sweet lady of the lotus eyes."
The queen, who loved her perished lord,
For meet reply, the saint adored,
And, of her husband long bereaved,
She bore a son by him conceived.
Because her rival mixed the bane

To render her conception vain,
And fruit unripened to destroy,
Sagar she called her darling boy.
To Sagar Asamanj was heir:
Bright Anśumán his consort bare.
Anśumán's son, Dilípa famed,

Begot a son Bhagírath named.
From him the great Kakutstha rose:
From him came Raghu, feared by foes,
Of him sprang Purushádak bold,
Fierce hero of gigantic mould:
Kalmáshapáda's name he bore,
Because his feet were spotted o'er.
From him came Śankaṇ, and from him
Sudarśan, fair in face and limb.
From beautiful Sudarśan came
Prince Agnivarṇa, bright as flame.
His son was Śíghraga, for speed
Unmatched; and Maru was his seed.
Praśuśruka was Maru's child;
His son was Ambarísha styled.
Nahush was Ambarísha's heir,
The mighty lord of regions fair:
Nahush begot Yayáti: he,
Nábhág of happy destiny.
Son of Nábhág was Aja: his,
The glorious Daśaratha is,
Whose noble children boast to be
Ráma and Lakshmaṇ, whom we see.
Thus do those kings of purest race
Their lineage from Ikshváku trace:
Their hero lives the right maintained,
Their lips with falsehood ne'er were stained.
In Ráma's and in Lakshmaṇ's name
Thy daughters as their wives I claim,
So shall in equal bands be tied
Each peerless youth with peerless bride."

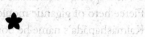

Janak's Pedigree

Then to the saint supremely wise
King Janak spoke in suppliant guise:
"Deign, Hermit, with attentive ear,
My race's origin to hear.
When kings a daughter's hand bestow,
'Tis right their line and fame to show.
There was a king whose deeds and worth
Spread wide his name through heaven and earth,
Nimi, most virtuous e'en from youth,
The best of all who love the truth.
His son and heir was Mithi, and
His Janak, first who ruled this land.
He left a son Udávasu,
Blest with all virtues, good and true.
His son was Nandivardhan, dear
For pious heart and worth sincere.
His son Suketu, hero brave,
To Devarát, existence gave.
King Devarát, a royal sage,
For virtue, glory of the age,
Begot Vrihadratha; and he
Begot, his worthy heir to be,
The splendid hero Mahábír
Who long in glory governed here.
His son was Sudhriti, a youth
Firm in his purpose, brave in sooth,
His son was Dhristaketu, blest
With pious will and holy breast.
The fame of royal saint he won:
Haryaśva was his princely son.
Haryaśva's son was Maru, who

232

Begot Pratíndhak, wise and true.
Next Kírtiratha held the throne,
His son, for gentle virtues known.
Then followed Devamidha, then
Vibudh, Mahándhrak, kings of men.
Mahándhrak's son, of boundless might,
Was Kírtirát, who loved the right.
He passed away, a sainted king,
And Maháromá following
To Swarṇaromá left the state.
Then Hraśvaromá, good and great,
Succeeded, and to him a pair
Of sons his royal consort bare,
Elder of these I boast to be:
Brave Kuśadhwaj is next to me.
Me then, the elder of the twain,
My sire anointed here to reign.
He bade me tend my brother well,
Then to the forest went to dwell.
He sought the heavens, and I sustained
The burden as by law ordained,
And noble Kuśadhwaj, the peer
Of Gods, I ever held most dear.
Then came Sánkáśyá's mighty lord,
Sudhanvá, threatening siege and sword,
And bade me swift on him bestow
Śiva's incomparable bow,

And Sítá of the lotus eyes:
But I refused each peerless prize.
Then, host to host, we met the foes,
And fierce the din of battle rose,
Sudhanvá, foremost of his band,
Fell smitten by my single hand.
When thus Sánkáśyá's lord was slain,
I sanctified, as laws ordain,
My brother in his stead to reign,
Thus are we brothers, Saint most high
The younger he, the elder I.
Now, mighty Sage, my spirit joys
To give these maidens to the boys.

233

Let Sítá be to Ráma tied.
And Urmilá be Lakshman's bride.
First give, O King, the gift of cows,
As dowry of each royal spouse,
Due offerings to the spirits pay,
And solemnize the wedding-day.
The moon tonight, O royal Sage,
In Maghá's House takes harbourage;
On the third night his rays benign
In second Phálguni will shine:
Be that the day, with prosperous fate,
The nuptial rites to celebrate."

CANTO
LXXII

The Gift of Kine

When royal Janak's words were done,
Joined with Vaśishṭha Kuśik's son,
The mighty sage began his speech:
"No mind may soar, no thought can reach
The glories of Ikshváku's line,
Or, great Videha's King, of thine:
None in the whole wide world may vie
With them in fame and honours high.
Well matched, I ween, in holy bands,
These peerless pairs will join their hands.
But hear me as I speak once more;
Thy brother, skilled in duty's lore,
Has at his home a royal pair
Of daughters most divinely fair.
I for the hands of these sweet two
For Bharat and Śatrughna sue,
Both princes of heroic mould,
Wise, fair of form, and lofty-souled.

All Daśaratha's sons, I ween,
Own each young grace of form and mien:
Brave as the Gods are they, nor yield
To the great Lords the worlds who shield.
By these, good Prince of merits high,
Ikshváku's house with thine ally."
The suit the holy sage preferred,
With willing ear the monarch heard:
Vaśishtha's lips the counsel praised:
Then spake the king with hands upraised:
"Now blest indeed my race I deem,
Which your high will, O Saints supreme,
With Daśaratha's house unites
In bonds of love and marriage rites.
So be it done. My nieces twain
Let Bharat and Śatrughna gain,
And the four youths the selfsame day
Four maiden hands in theirs shall lay.
No day so lucky may compare,
For marriage—so the wise declare—
With the last day of Phálguni
Ruled by the genial deity."
Then with raised hands in reverence due
To those arch-saints he spoke anew:
"I am your pupil, ever true:
To me high favour have ye shown;
Come, sit ye on my royal throne,
For Daśaratha rules these towers
E'en as Ayodhyá now is ours.
Do with your own whate'er ye choose:
Your lordship here will none refuse."

He spoke, and to Videha's king
Thus Daśaratha, answering:
"Boundless your virtues, lords, whose sway
The realms of Mithilá obey.
With honouring care you entertain
Both holy sage and royal train.
Now to my house my steps I bend—
May blessings still on you at end—
Due offerings to the shades to pay."

235

Thus spoke the king, and turned away:
To Janak first he bade adieu,
Then followed fast those holy two.
The monarch reached his palace where
The rites were paid with solemn care.
When the next sun began to shine
He rose and made his gift of kine.
A hundred thousand cows prepared
For each young prince the Bráhmans shared.
Each had her horns adorned with gold;
And duly was the number told,
Four hundred thousand perfect tale:
Each brought a calf, each filled a pail.
And when that glorious task was o'er,
The monarch with his children four,
Showed like the Lord of Life divine
When the worlds' guardians round him shine.

CANTO

LXXIII

The Nuptials

On that same day that saw the king
His gift of kine distributing,
The lord of Kekaya's son, by name
Yudhájit, Bharat's uncle, came,
Asked of the monarch's health, and then
Addressed the reverend king of men:
"The lord of Kekaya's realm by me
Sends greeting, noble King, to thee:
Asks if the friends thy prayers would bless
Uninterrupted health possess.
Right anxious, mighty King, is he
My sister's princely boy to see.
For this I sought Ayodhyá fair

The message of my sire to bear.
There learning, O my liege, that thou
With sons and noble kinsmen now
Wast resting here, I sought the place
Longing to see my nephew's face."
The king with kind observance cheered
His friend by tender ties endeared,
And every choicest honour pressed
Upon his honourable guest.

That night with all his children spent,
At morn King Daśaratha went,
Behind Vaśishṭha and the rest,
To the fair ground for rites addressed.
Then when the lucky hour was nigh
Called Victory, of omen high,
Came Ráma, after vow and prayer
For nuptial bliss and fortune fair,
With the three youths in bright attire,
And stood beside his royal sire.
To Janak then Vaśishṭha sped,
And to Videha's monarch said:
"O King, Ayodhyá's ruler now
Has breathed the prayer and vowed the vow,
And with his sons expecting stands
The giver of the maidens' hands.
The giver and the taker both
Must ratify a mutual oath.
Perform the part for which we wait,
And rites of marriage celebrate."

Skilled in the laws which Scriptures teach,
He answered thus Vaśishṭha's speech:
"O Saint, what warder bars the gate?
Whose bidding can the king await?
In one's own house what doubt is shown?
This kingdom, Sage, is all thine own.
E'en now the maidens may be found
Within the sacrificial ground:
Each vow is vowed and prayed each prayer,
And they, like fire, are shining there.

237

Here by the shrine my place I took
Expecting thee with eager look,
No bar the nuptial rites should stay:
What cause have we for more delay?"
When Janak's speech the monarch heard,
To sons and saints he gave the word,
And set them in the holy ring,
Then to Vaśishṭha spoke the king
Of Mithilá: "O mighty Sage,
Now let this task thy care engage,
And lend thine aid and counsel wise
The nuptial rites to solemnize."

The saint Vaśishṭha gave assent,
And quickly to the task he went,
With Viśvámitra, nothing loth,
And Śatánanda aiding both.
Then, as the rules prescribe, they made
An altar in the midst, and laid
Fresh wreaths of fragrant flowers thereon.
The golden ladles round it shone;
And many a vase, which branches hid
Fixed in the perforated lid,
And sprays, and cups, and censers there
Stood filled with incense rich and rare;
Shell-bowls, and spoons, and salvers dressed
With gifts that greet the honoured guest;
Piles of parched rice some dishes bore,
Others with corn prepared ran o'er;
And holy grass was duly spread
In equal lengths, while prayers were said.
Next chief of saints, Vaśishṭha came
And laid the offering in the flame.
Then by the hand King Janak drew
His Sítá, beautiful to view,
And placed her, bright in rich attire,
Ráma to face, before the fire,
Thus speaking to the royal boy
Who filled Kauśalyá's heart with joy:
"Here Sítá stands, my daughter fair,
The duties of thy life to share.

238

Take from her father, take thy bride;
Join hand to hand, and bliss betide!
A faithful wife, most blest is she,
And as thy shade will follow thee."

Thus as he spoke the monarch threw
O'er her young limbs the holy dew,
While Gods and saints were heard to swell
The joyous cry, 'Tis well! 'Tis well!
His daughter Sítá thus bestowed,
O'er whom the sacred drops had flowed.
King Janak's heart with rapture glowed.
Then to Prince Lakshmaṇ thus he cried:
"Take Urmilá thine offered bride,
And clasp her hand within thine own
Ere yet the lucky hour be flown."
Then to Prince Bharat thus cried he;
"Come, take the hand of Mándavi."
Then to Śatrughna: "In thy grasp
The hand of Srutakírti clasp.
Now, Raghu's sons, may all of you
Be gentle to your wives and true;

Keep well the vows you make to-day,
Nor let occasion slip away."

King Janak's word the youths obeyed;
The maidens' hands in theirs they laid.
Then with their brides the princes went
With ordered steps and reverent
Round both the fire and Janak, round
The sages and the sacred ground.

A flowery flood of lucid dyes
In rain descended from the skies,
While with celestial voices blent
Sweet strains from many an instrument,
And the nymphs danced in joyous throng
Responsive to the minstrel's song.
Such signs of exultation they
Saw on the princes' wedding day.

Still rang the heavenly music's sound
When Raghu's sons thrice circled round
The fire, each one with reverent head,
And homeward then their brides they led.
They to the sumptuous palace hied
That Janak's care had seen supplied.
The monarch girt with saint and peer
Still fondly gazing followed near.

LXXIV

Ráma with The Axe

Soon as the night had reached its close
The hermit Viśvámitra rose;
To both the kings he bade adieu
And to the northern hill withdrew.
Ayodhyá's lord of high renown
Received farewell, and sought his town.
Then as each daughter left her bower
King Janak gave a splendid dower,
Rugs, precious silks, a warrior force,
Cars, elephants, and foot, and horse,
Divine to see and well arrayed;
And many a skilful tiring-maid,
And many a young and trusty slave
The father of the ladies gave.
Silver and coral, gold and pearls
He gave to his beloved girls.
These precious gifts the king bestowed
And sped his guest upon his road.
The lord of Mithilá's sweet town
Rode to his court and lighted down.
Ayodhyá's monarch, glad and gay,
Led by the seers pursued his way

240

With his dear sons of lofty mind:
The royal army marched behind.
As on he fared the voice he heard
Around of many a dismal bird,
And every beast in wild affright
Began to hurry to the right.
The monarch to Vaśishṭha cried:
"What strange misfortune will betide?
Why do the beasts in terror fly,
And birds of evil omen cry?
What is it shakes my heart with dread?
Why is my soul disquieted?"

Soon as he heard, the mighty saint
Thus answered Daśaratha's plaint
In sweetest tone: "Now, Monarch, mark,
And learn from me the meaning dark.
The voices of the birds of air
Great peril to the host declare:
The moving beasts the dread allay,
So drive thy whelming fear away,"
As he and Daśaratha spoke
A tempest from the welkin broke,
That shook the spacious earth amain
And hurled high trees upon the plain.
The sun grew dark with murky cloud,
And o'er the skies was cast a shroud,
While o'er the army, faint with dread,
A veil of dust and ashes spread.
King, princes, saints their sense retained,
Fear-stupefied the rest remained.
At length, their wits returning, all
Beneath the gloom and ashy pall
Saw Jamadagni's son with dread,
His long hair twisted round his head,
Who, sprung from Bhrigu, loved to beat
The proudest kings beneath his feet.
Firm as Kailása's hill he showed,
Fierce as the fire of doom he glowed.
His axe upon his shoulder lay,
His bow was ready for the fray,

With thirsty arrows wont to fly
Like Lightnings from the angry sky.
A long keen arrow forth he drew,
Invincible like those which flew
From Śiva's ever-conquering bow
And Tripura in death laid low.

When his wild form, that struck with awe,
Fearful as ravening flame, they saw,
Vaśishṭha and the saints whose care
Was sacrifice and muttered prayer,
Drew close together, each to each,
And questioned thus with bated speech:
"Indignant at his father's fate
Will he on warriors vent his hate,
The slayers of his father slay,
And sweep the loathed race away?
But when of old his fury raged
Seas of their blood his wrath assuaged:

So doubtless now he has not planned
To slay all warriors in the land."

Then with a gift the saints drew near
To Bhrigu's son whose look was fear,
And Ráma! Ráma! soft they cried.
The gift he took, no word replied.
Then Bhrigu's son his silence broke
And thus to Ráma Ráma spoke:

CANTO
LXXV

The Parle

"Heroic Ráma, men proclaim
The marvels of thy matchless fame,
And I from loud-voiced rumour know
The exploit of the broken bow,
Yea, bent and broken, mighty Chief,
A feat most wondrous, past belief.
Stirred by thy fame thy face I sought:
A peerless bow I too have brought.
This mighty weapon, strong and dire,
Great Jamadagni owned, my sire.
Draw with its shaft my father's bow,
And thus thy might, O Ráma, show.
This proof of prowess let me see—
The weapon bent and drawn by thee;
Then single fight our strength shall try,
And this shall raise thy glory high."

King Daśaratha heard with dread
The boastful speech, and thus he said;
Raising his hands in suppliant guise,
With pallid cheek and timid eyes:
"Forgetful of the bloody feud
Ascetic toils hast thou pursued;
Then, Bráhman, let thy children be
Untroubled and from danger free.
Sprung of the race of Bhrigu, who
Read holy lore, to vows most true,
Thou swarest to the Thousand-eyed
And thy fierce axe was cast aside.
Thou turnedst to thy rites away
Leaving the earth to Kaśyap's sway,

243

And wentest far a grove to seek
Beneath Mahendra's mountain peak.
Now, mighty Hermit, art thou here
To slay us all with doom severe?
For if alone my Ráma fall,
We share his fate and perish all."

As thus the aged sire complained
The mighty chief no answer deigned.
To Ráma only thus he cried:
"Two bows, the Heavenly Artist's pride,
Celestial, peerless, vast, and strong,
By all the worlds were honoured long.
One to the Three-eyed God was given,
By glory to the conflict driven,
Thus armed fierce Tripura he slew:
And then by thee 'twas burst in two.
The second bow, which few may brave,
The highest Gods to Vishṇu gave.
This bow I hold; before it fall
The foeman's fenced tower and wall.
Then prayed the Gods the Sire Most High
By some unerring proof to try
Were praise for might Lord Vishṇu's due,
Or his whose Neck is stained with Blue.
The mighty Sire their wishes knew,
And he whose lips are ever true
Caused the two Gods to meet as foes.
Then fierce the rage of battle rose:
Bristled in dread each starting hair
As Śiva strove with Vishṇu there.
But Vishṇu raised his voice amain.
And Śiva's bowstring twanged in vain;
Its master of the Three bright Eyes
Stood fixt in fury and surprise.
Then all the dwellers in the sky,
Minstrel, and saint, and God drew nigh,
And prayed them that the strife might cease,
And the great rivals met in peace.
'Twas seen how Śiva's bow has failed

244

Bharat's Departure

Then Ráma with a cheerful mind
     The bow to Varuṇ's hand resigned.
     Due reverence to the saints he paid,
And thus addressed his sire dismayed:
"As Bhrigu's son is far from view,
Now let the host its march pursue,
And to Ayodhyá's town proceed
In four-fold bands, with thee to lead."

King Daśaratha thus addressed
His lips to Ráma's forehead pressed,
And held him to his aged breast.
Rejoiced in sooth was he to know
That Bhrigu's son had parted so,
And hailed a second life begun
For him and his victorious son.
He urged the host to speed renewed,
And soon Ayodhyá's gates he viewed.
High o'er the roofs gay pennons played;
Tabour and drum loud music made;
Fresh water cooled the royal road,
And flowers in bright profusion glowed.
Glad crowds with garlands thronged the ways
Rejoicing on their king to gaze
And all the town was bright and gay
Exalting in the festive day.
People and Bráhmans flocked to meet
Their monarch ere he gained the street.
The glorious king amid the throng
Rode with his glorious sons along,

And passed within his dear abode
That like Himálaya's mountain showed.
And there Kauśalyá, noble queen,
Sumitrá with her lovely mien,
Kaikeyí of the dainty waist,
And other dames his bowers who graced,
Stood in the palace side by side
And welcomed home each youthful bride:
Fair Sítá, lofty-fated dame,
Urmilá of the glorious fame,
And Kuśadhwaj's children fair,
With joyous greeting and with prayer,
As all in linen robes arrayed
With offerings at the altars prayed.
Due reverence paid to God above,
Each princess gave her soul to love,
And hidden in her inmost bower
Passed with her lord each blissful hour.
The royal youths, of spirit high,
With whom in valor none could vie,
Lived each within his palace bounds
Bright as Kuvera's pleasure-grounds,
With riches, troops of faithful friends,
And bliss that wedded life attends:
Brave princes trained in warlike skill,
And duteous to their father's will.
At length the monarch called one morn
Prince Bharat, of Kaikeyí born,
And cried: "My son, within our gates
Lord Yudhájit thine uncle waits.
The son of Kekaya's king is he,
And came, my child, to summon thee."
Then Bharat for the road prepared,
And with Śatrughna forth he fared.
First to his sire he bade adieu,
Brave Ráma, and his mothers too.
Lord Yudhájit with joyful pride
Went forth, the brothers by his side,
And reached the city where he dwelt:
And mighty joy his father felt.

Ráma and Lakshman honoured still
Their godlike sire with duteous will.
Two constant guides for Ráma stood,
His father's wish, the people's good.
Attentive to the general weal
He thought and wrought to please and heal.
His mothers too he strove to please
With love and sonly courtesies.
At every time, in every spot,
His holy guides he ne'er forgot.
So for his virtues kind and true
Dearer and dearer Ráma grew
To Daśaratha, Bráhmans, all
In town and country, great and small.
And Ráma by his darling's side
Saw many a blissful season glide,
Lodged in her soul, each thought on her,
Lover, and friend, and worshipper.
He loved her for his father's voice
Had given her and approved the choice:
He loved her for each charm she wore
And her sweet virtues more and more.
So he her lord and second life
Dwelt in the bosom of his wife,
In double form, that, e'en apart,
Each heart could commune free with heart.

Still grew that child of Janak's race,
More goddess-fair in form and face,
The loveliest wife that e'er was seen,
In mortal mould sweet Beauty's Queen.
Then shone the son Kauśalyá bore,
With this bright dame allied,
Like Vishnu whom the Gods adore,
With Lakshmi by his side.

CANTO
I

The Heir Apparent

S o Bharat to his grandsire went
   Obedient to the message sent,
   And for his fond companion chose
Śatrughna slayer of his foes.
There Bharat for a time remained
With love and honour entertained,
King Aśvapati's constant care,
Beloved as a son and heir.
Yet ever, as they lived at ease,
While all around combined to please,
The aged sire they left behind
Was present to each hero's mind.
Nor could the king's fond memory stray
From his brave children far away,
Dear Bharat and Śatrughna dear,
Each Varuṇ's match or Indra's peer.

To all the princes, young and brave,
His soul with fond affection clave;
Around his loving heart they clung
Like arms from his own body sprung.
But best and noblest of the four,
Good as the God whom all adore,
Lord of all virtues, undefiled,

His darling was his eldest child.
For he was beautiful and strong,
From envy free, the foe of wrong,
With all his father's virtues blest,
And peerless in the world confessed.
With placid soul he softly spoke:
No harsh reply could taunts provoke.
He ever loved the good and sage
Revered for virtue and for age,
And when his martial tasks were o'er
Sate listening to their peaceful lore.
Wise, modest, pure, he honoured eld,
His lips from lying tales withheld;
Due reverence to the Bráhmans gave,
And ruled each passion like a slave.
Most tender, prompt at duty's call,
Loved by all men he loved them all.
Proud of the duties of his race,
With spirit meet for Warrior's place.
He strove to win by glorious deed,
Throned with the Gods, a priceless meed.
With him in speech and quick reply
Vrihaspati might hardly vie,
But never would his accents flow
For evil or for empty show.
In art and science duly trained,
His student vow he well maintained;
He learnt the lore for princes fit,
The Vedas and their Holy Writ,
And with his well-drawn bow at last
His mighty father's fame surpassed.
Of birth exalted, truthful, just,
With vigorous hand, with noble trust,
Well taught by aged twice-born men
Who gain and right could clearly ken,
Full well the claims and bounds he knew
Of duty, gain, and pleasure too:
Of memory keen, of ready tact,
In civil business prompt to act.
Reserved, his features ne'er disclosed
What counsel in his heart reposed.

All idle rage and mirth controlled,
He knew the times to give and hold,
Firm in his faith, of steadfast will,
He sought no wrong, he spoke no ill:
Not rashly swift, not idly slow,
His faults and others' keen to know.
Each merit, by his subtle sense;
He matched with proper recompense.
He knew the means that wealth provide,
And with keen eye expense could guide.
Wild elephants could he reclaim,
And mettled steeds could mount and tame.
No arm like his the bow could wield,
Or drive the chariot to the field.
Skilled to attack, to deal the blow,
Or lead a host against the foe:
Yea, e'en infuriate Gods would fear
To meet his arm in full career.
As the great sun in noontide blaze
Is glorious with his world of rays,
So Ráma with these virtues shone
Which all men loved to gaze upon.

The aged monarch fain would rest,
And said within his weary breast,
"Oh that I might, while living yet,
My Ráma o'er the kingdom set.
And see, before my course be run,
The hallowed drops anoint my son;
See all this spacious land obey,
From side to side, my first-born's sway,
And then, my life and joy complete,
Obtain in heaven a blissful seat!"
In him the monarch saw combined
The fairest form, the noblest mind,
And counselled how his son might share,
The throne with him as Regent Heir.
For fearful signs in earth and sky,
And weakness warned him death was nigh:
But Ráma to the world endeared
By every grace his bosom cheered,

The moon of every eye, whose ray
Drove all his grief and fear away.
So duty urged that hour to seize,
Himself, his realm, to bless and please.

From town and country, far and near,
He summoned people, prince, and peer.
To each he gave a meet abode,
And honoured all and gifts bestowed.
Then, splendid in his king's attire,
He viewed them, as the general Sire,
In glory of a God arrayed,
Looks on the creatures he has made.
But Kekaya's king he called not then
For haste, nor Janak, lord of men;
For after to each royal friend
The joyful tidings he would send.
Mid crowds from distant countries met
The king upon his throne was set;
Then honoured by the people, all
The rulers thronged into the hall.
On thrones assigned, each king in place
Looked silent on the monarch's face.
Then girt by lords of high renown
And throngs from hamlet and from town
He showed in regal pride,
As, honoured by the radiant band
Of blessed Gods that round him stand,
Lord Indra, Thousand-eyed.

CANTO
III

Dasaratha's Precepts

The monarch with the prayer complied
   Of suppliant hands, on every side
   Uplifted like a lotus-bed:
And then these gracious words he said:
"Great joy and mighty fame are mine
Because your loving hearts incline,
In full assembly clearly shown
To place my Ráma on the throne."
Then to Vaśishṭha, standing near,
And Vámadeva loud and clear
The monarch spoke that all might hear:
"'Tis pure and lovely Chaitra now
When flowers are sweet on every bough;
All needful things with haste prepare
That Ráma be appointed heir."

Then burst the people's rapture out
In loud acclaim and joyful shout;
And when the tumult slowly ceased
The king addressed the holy priest:
"Give order, Saint, with watchful heed
For what the coming rite will need.
This day let all things ready wait
Mine eldest son to consecrate."
Best of all men of second birth
Vaśishṭha heard the lord of earth,
And gave commandment to the bands
Of servitors with lifted hands
Who waited on their master's eye:
"Now by to-morrow's dawn supply
Rich gold and herbs and gems of price

263

And offerings for the sacrifice,
Wreaths of white flowers and roasted rice,
And oil and honey, separate;
New garments and a car of state,
An elephant with lucky signs,
A fourfold host in ordered lines,
The white umbrella, and a pair
Of chowries, and a banner fair;
A hundred vases, row on row,
To shine like fire in splendid glow,
A tiger's mighty skin, a bull
With gilded horns most beautiful.
All these, at dawn of coming day,
Around the royal shrine array,
Where burns the fire's undying ray.
Each palace door, each city gate
With wreaths of sandal decorate.
And with the garlands' fragrant scent
Let clouds of incense-smoke be blent.
Let food of noble kind and taste
Be for a hundred thousand placed;
Fresh curds with streams of milk bedewed
To feed the Bráhman multitude.

With care be all their wants supplied.
And mid the twice-born chiefs divide
Rich largess, with the early morn,
And oil and curds and roasted corn.
Soon as the sun has shown his light
Pronounce the prayer to bless the rite,
And then be all the Bráhmans called
And in their ordered seats installed.
Let all musicians skilled to play,
And dancing-girls in bright array
Stand ready in the second ring
Within the palace of the king.
Each honoured tree, each holy shrine
With leaves and flowery wreaths entwine,
And here and there beneath the shade
Be food prepared and presents laid.
Then brightly clad, in warlike guise,

With long swords girt upon their thighs,
Let soldiers of the nobler sort
March to the monarch's splendid court."

Thus gave command the twice-born pair
To active servants stationed there.
Then hastened to the king and said
That all their task was duly sped,
The king to wise Sumantra spake:
"Now quick, my lord, thy chariot take,
And hither with thy swiftest speed
My son, my noble Ráma lead."

Sumantra, ere the word was given,
His chariot from the court had driven,
And Ráma, best of all who ride
In cars, came sitting by his side.
The lords of men had hastened forth
From east and west and south and north,
Áryan and stranger, those who dwell
In the wild wood and on the fell,
And as the Gods to Indra, they
Showed honour to the king that day.

Like Vásav, when his glorious form
Is circled by the Gods of storm,
Girt in his hall by kings he saw
His car-borne Ráma near him draw,
Like him who rules the minstrel band
Of heaven; whose valour filled the land,
Of mighty arm and stately pride
Like a wild elephant in stride,
As fair in face as that fair stone
Dear to the moon, of moonbeams grown,
With noble gifts and grace that took
The hearts of all, and chained each look,
World-cheering as the Lord of Rain
When floods relieve the parching plain.
The father, as the son came nigh,
Gazed with an ever-thirstier eye.
Sumantra helped the prince alight

From the good chariot passing bright,
And as to meet his sire he went
Followed behind him reverent.
Then Ráma clomb, the king to seek
That terrace like Kailása's peak,
And reached the presence of the king,
Sumantra closely following.
Before his father's face he came,
Raised suppliant hands and named his name,
And bowing lowly as is meet
Paid reverence to the monarch's feet.
But soon as Daśaratha viewed
The prince in humble attitude,
He raised him by the hand in haste
And his beloved son embraced,
Then signed him to a glorious throne,
Gem-decked and golden, near his own.
Then Ráma, best of Raghu's line,
Made the fair seat with lustre shine
As when the orient sun upsprings
And his pure beam on Meru flings.
The glory flashed on roof and wall,
And with strange sheen suffused the hall,
As when the moon's pure rays are sent
Through autumn's star-lit firmament.
Then swelled his breast with joy and pride
As his dear son the father eyed,
E'en as himself more fair arrayed
In some clear mirror's face displayed.
The aged monarch gazed awhile,
Then thus addressed him with a smile,
As Kaśyap, whom the worlds revere,
Speaks for the Lord of Gods to hear:
"O thou of all my sons most dear,
In virtue best, thy father's peer,
Child of my consort first in place,
Mine equal in her pride of race,
Because the people's hearts are bound
To thee by graces in thee found,
Be thou in Pushya's favouring hour
Made partner of my royal power.

Sítá in haste was summoned too.
Absorbed, with half-shut eyes, the queen
Attended by the three was seen.
She knew that Pushya's lucky hour
Would raise her son to royal power,
So fixed with bated breath each thought
On God supreme, by all men sought.
To her, as thus she knelt and prayed,
Ráma drew near, due reverence paid,
And then to swell his mother's joy,
Thus spoke her own beloved boy;
"O mother dear, my sire's decree
Entrusts the people's weal to me.
To-morrow I, for so his will,
Anointed king, the throne shall fill.
The few last hours till night shall end
Sítá with me must fasting spend,
For so my father has decreed,
And holy priests with him agreed.
What vows soever thou mayst deem
My consecration's eve beseem,
Do thou, sweet mother, for my sake
And for beloved Sítá's make."

When the glad news Kauśalyá heard,
So long desired, so long deferred,
While tears of joy her utterance broke,
In answer to her son she spoke:
"Long be thy life, my darling: now
Thy prostrate foes before thee bow.
Live long and with thy bright success
My friends and dear Sumitrá's bless.
Surely the stars were wondrous fair
When thee, sweet son, thy mother bare,
That thy good gifts such love inspire
And win the favour of thy sire.
With thee I travailed not in vain;
Those lotus eyes reward my pain,
And all the glory of the line
Of old Ikshváku will be thine."

He smiled, and on his brother gazed
Who sate with reverent hands upraised,
And said: "My brother, thou must be
Joint-ruler of this land with me.
My second self thou, Lakshmaṇ, art,
And in my fortune bearest part.
Be thine, Sumitrá's son, to know
The joys from regal power that flow.
My life itself, the monarch's seat,
For thy dear sake to me are sweet."

Thus Ráma to his brother said,
To both his mothers bowed his head,
And then with Sítá by his side
To his own house the hero hied.

CANTO

V

Ráma's Fast

T hen Saint Vaśishṭha to the king
  Came ready at his summoning.
  "Now go," exclaimed the monarch, "thou
Enriched by fervent rite and vow,
For Ráma and his wife ordain
The fast, that joy may bless his reign."
The best of those who Scripture know
Said to the king, "My lord, I go."
To Ráma's house Vaśishṭha hied,
The hero's fast by rule to guide,
And skilled in sacred texts to tell
Each step to him instructed well.
Straight to Prince Ráma's high abode,
That like a cloud pale-tinted showed,
Borne in his priestly car he rode.

Two courts he passed, and in the third
He stayed his car. Then Ráma heard
The holy sage was come, and flew
To honour him with honour due.
He hastened to the car and lent
His hand to aid the priest's descent.
Then spoke Vaśishṭha words like these,
Pleased with his reverent courtesies,
With pleasant things his heart to cheer
Who best deserved glad news to hear:
"Prince, thou hast won thy father's grace,
And thine will be the Regent's place:
Now with thy Sítá, as is right,
In strictest fasting spend the night,

For when the morrow's dawn is fair
The king will consecrate his heir:
So Nahush, as the wise relate,
Yayáti joyed to consecrate."

Thus having said, Vaśishṭha next
Ordained the fast by rule and text,
For Ráma faithful to his vows
And the Videhan dame his spouse.
Then from the prince's house he hied
With courteous honours gratified.
Round Ráma gathered every friend
In pleasant talk a while to spend.
He bade good night to all at last,
And to his inner chamber passed.
Then Ráma's house shone bright and gay
With men and maids in glad array,
As in the morning some fair lake
When all her lotuses awake,
And every bird that loves the flood
Flits joyous round each opening bud.

Forth from the house Vaśishṭha drove,
That with the king's in splendour strove,
And all the royal street he viewed
Filled with a mighty multitude

273

The eager concourse blocked each square,
Each road and lane and thoroughfare,
And joyous shouts on every side
Rose like the roar of Ocean's tide,
As streams of men together came
With loud huzza and glad acclaim.
The ways were watered, swept and clean,
And decked with flowers and garlands green
And all Ayodhyá shone arrayed
With banners on the roofs that played.
Men, women, boys with eager eyes,
Expecting when the sun should rise,
Stood longing for the herald ray
Of Ráma's consecration day,
To see, a source of joy to all,
The people-honoured festival.

The priest advancing slowly through
The mighty crowd he cleft in two,
Near to the monarch's palace drew.
He sought the terrace, by the stair,
Like a white cloud-peak high in air,
The reverend king of men to meet
Who sate upon his splendid seat:
Thus will Vṛihaspati arise
To meet the monarch of the skies.
But when the king his coming knew,
He left his throne and near him drew
Questioned by him Vaśishṭha said
That all his task was duly sped.
Then all who sate there, honouring
Vaśishṭha, rose as rose the king.
Vaśishṭha bade his lord adieu,
And all the peers, dismissed, withdrew.
Then as a royal lion seeks
His cave beneath the rocky peaks,
So to the chambers where abode
His consorts Daśaratha strode.
Full-thronged were those delightful bowers
With women richly dressed,
And splendid as the radiant towers

"Does Ráma's mother give away
Rich largess to the crowds to-day,
On some dear object fondly bent,
Or blest with measureless content?
What mean these signs of rare delight
On every side that meet my sight?
Say, will the king with joy elate
Some happy triumph celebrate?"

The nurse, with transport uncontrolled,
Her glad tale to the hump-back told:
"Our lord the king to-morrow morn
Will consecrate his eldest-born,
And raise, in Pushya's favouring hour,
Prince Ráma to the royal power."
As thus the nurse her tidings spoke,
Rage in the hump-back's breast awoke.
Down from the terrace, like the head
Of high Kailása's hill, she sped.
Sin in her thoughts, her soul aflame,
Where Queen Kaikeyí slept, she came:

"Why sleepest thou?" she cried, "arise,
Peril is near, unclose thine eyes.
Ah, heedless Queen, too blind to know
What floods of sin above thee flow!
Thy boasts of love and grace are o'er:
Thine is the show and nothing more.
His favour is an empty cheat,
A torrent dried by summer's heat."

Thus by the artful maid addressed
In cruel words from raging breast,
The queen, sore troubled, spoke in turn;
"What evil news have I to learn?
That mournful eye, that altered cheek
Of sudden woe or danger speak."

Such were the words Kaikeyí said:
Then Manthará, her eyeballs red
With fury, skilled with treacherous art

279

To grieve yet more her lady's heart,
From Ráma, in her wicked hate,
Kaikeyí's love to alienate,
Upon her evil purpose bent
Began again most eloquent:
"Peril awaits thee swift and sure,
And utter woe defying cure;
King Daśaratha will create
Prince Ráma Heir Associate.
Plunged in the depths of wild despair,
My soul a prey to pain and care,
As though the flames consumed me, zeal
Has brought me for my lady's weal,
Thy grief, my Queen, is grief to me:
Thy gain my greatest gain would be.
Proud daughter of a princely line,
The rights of consort queen are thine.
How art thou, born of royal race,
Blind to the crimes that kings debase?
Thy lord is gracious, to deceive,
And flatters, but thy soul to grieve,
While thy pure heart that thinks no sin
Knows not the snares that hem thee in.
Thy husband's lips on thee bestow
Soft soothing word, an empty show:
The wealth, the substance, and the power
This day will be Kauśalyá's dower.
With crafty soul thy child he sends
To dwell among thy distant friends,
And, every rival far from sight,
To Ráma gives the power and might.
Ah me! for thou, unhappy dame,
Deluded by a husband's name,
With more than mother's love hast pressed
A serpent to thy heedless breast,
And cherished him who works thee woe,
No husband but a deadly foe.
For like a snake, unconscious Queen,
Or enemy who stabs unseen,
King Daśaratha all untrue
Has dealt with thee and Bharat too.

Ah, simple lady, long beguiled
By his soft words who falsely smiled!
Poor victim of the guileless breast,
A happier fate thou meritest.
For thee and thine destruction waits
When he Prince Ráma consecrates.
Up, lady, while there yet is time;
Preserve thyself, prevent the crime.
Up, from thy careless ease, and free
Thyself, O Queen, thy son, and me!"
Delighted at the words she said,
Kaikeyí lifted from the bed,
Like autumn's moon, her radiant head,
And joyous at the tidings gave
A jewel to the hump-back slave;
And as she gave the precious toy
She cried in her exceeding joy:
"Take this, dear maiden, for thy news
Most grateful to mine ear, and choose
What grace beside most fitly may
The welcome messenger repay.
I joy that Ráma gains the throne:
Kauśalyá's son is as mine own."

CANTO

VIII

Manthará's Speech

The damsel's breast with fury burned:
     She answered, as the gift she spurned:
     "What time, O simple Queen, is this
For idle dreams of fancied bliss?
Hast thou not sense thy state to know,
Engulfed in seas of whelming woe;
Sick as I am with grief and pain

281

My lips can scarce a laugh restrain
To see thee hail with ill-timed joy
A peril mighty to destroy.
I mourn for one so fondly blind:
What woman of a prudent mind
Would welcome, e'en as thou hast done,
The lordship of a rival's son,
Rejoiced to find her secret foe
Empowered, like death, to launch the blow;
I see that Ráma still must fear
Thy Bharat, to his throne too near.
Hence is my heart disquieted,
For those who fear are those we dread.
Lakshman, the mighty bow who draws,
With all his soul serves Ráma's cause;
And chains as strong to Bharat bind
Śatrughna, with his heart and mind,
Now next to Ráma, lady fair,
Thy Bharat is the lawful heir:
And far remote, I ween, the chance
That might the younger two advance.
Yes, Queen, 'tis Ráma that I dread,
Wise, prompt, in warlike science bred;
And oh, I tremble when I think
Of thy dear child on ruin's brink.

Blest with a lofty fate is she,
Kauśalyá; for her son will be
Placed, when the moon and Pushya meet,
By Bráhmans on the royal seat,
Thou as a slave in suppliant guise
Must wait upon Kauśalyá's eyes,
With all her wealth and bliss secured
And glorious from her foes assured.
Her slave with us who serve thee, thou
Wilt see thy son to Ráma bow,
And Sítá's friends exult o'er all,
While Bharat's wife shares Bharat's fall."

As thus the maid in wrath complained,
Kaikeyí saw her heart was pained,

Thou for no favour then wouldst sue,
The gifts reserved for season due;
And he, thy high-souled lord, agreed
To give the boons when thou shouldst need.
Myself I knew not what befell,
But oft the tale have heard thee tell,
And close to thee in friendship knit
Deep in my heart have treasured it.
Remind thy husband of his oath,
Recall the boons and claim them both,
That Bharat on the throne be placed
With rites of consecration graced,
And Ráma to the woods be sent
For twice seven years of banishment.
Go, Queen, the mourner's chamber seek,
With angry eye and burning cheek;
And with disordered robes and hair
On the cold earth lie prostrate there.
When the king comes still mournful lie,
Speak not a word nor meet his eye,
But let thy tears in torrent flow,
And lie enamoured of thy woe.
Well do I know thou long hast been,
And ever art, his darling queen.
For thy dear sake, O well-loved dame,
The mighty king would brave the flame,
But ne'er would anger thee, or brook
To meet his favourite's wrathful look.
Thy loving lord would even die
Thy fancy, Queen, to gratify,
And never could he arm his breast
To answer nay to thy request.
Listen and learn, O dull of sense,
Thine all-resistless influence.
Gems he will offer, pearls and gold:
Refuse his gifts, be stern and cold.
Those proffered boons at length recall,
And claim them till he grants thee all.
And O my lady, high in bliss,
With heedful thought forget not this.
When from the ground his queen he lifts

And grants again the promised gifts,
Bind him with oaths he cannot break
And thy demands unflinching, make.
That Ráma travel to the wild
Five years and nine from home exiled,
And Bharat, best of all who reign,
The empire of the land obtain.
For when this term of years has fled
Over the banished Ráma's head,
Thy royal son to vigour grown
And rooted firm will stand alone.
The king, I know, is well inclined,
And this the hour to move his mind.
Be bold: the threatened rite prevent,
And force the king from his intent."

She ceased. So counselled to her bane
Disguised beneath a show of gain,
Kaikeyí in her joy and pride
To Manthará again replied:
"Thy sense I envy, prudent maid;
With sagest lore thy lids persuade.
No hump-back maid in all the earth,
For wise resolve, can match thy worth.
Thou art alone with constant zeal
Devoted to thy lady's weal.
Dear girl, without thy faithful aid
I had not marked the plot he laid.

Full of all guile and sin and spite
Misshapen hump-backs shock the sight:
But thou art fair and formed to please,
Bent like a lily by the breeze.
I look thee o'er with watchful eye,
And in thy frame no fault can spy;
The chest so deep, the waist so trim,
So round the lines of breast and limb.
Thy cheeks with moonlike beauty shine,
And the warm wealth of youth is thine.
Thy legs, my girl, are long and neat,
And somewhat long thy dainty feet,

288

While stepping out before my face
Thou seemest like a crane to pace.
The thousand wiles are in thy breast
Which Śambara the fiend possessed,
And countless others all thine own,
O damsel sage, to thee are known.
Thy very hump becomes thee too,
O thou whose face is fair to view,
For there reside in endless store
Plots, wizard wiles, and warrior lore.
A golden chain I'll round it fling
When Ráma's flight makes Bharat king:
Yea, polished links of finest gold,
When once the wished for prize I hold
With naught to fear and none to hate,
Thy hump, dear maid, shall decorate.
A golden frontlet wrought with care,
And precious jewels shalt thou wear:
Two lovely robes around thee fold,
And walk a Goddess to behold,
Bidding the moon himself compare
His beauty with a face so fair.
With scent of precious sandal sweet
Down to the nails upon thy feet,
First of the household thou shalt go
And pay with scorn each battled foe."
Kaikeyí's praise the damsel heard,
And thus again her lady stirred,
Who lay upon her beauteous bed
Like fire upon the altar fed:
"Dear Queen, they build the bridge in vain
When swollen streams are dry again.
Arise, thy glorious task complete,
And draw the king to thy retreat."

The large-eyed lady left her bower
Exulting in her pride of power,
And with the hump-back sought the gloom
And silence of the mourner's room.
The string of priceless pearls that hung
Around her neck to earth she flung,

With all the wealth and lustre lent
By precious gem and ornament.
Then, listening to her slave's advice,
Lay, like a nymph from Paradise.
As on the ground her limbs she laid
Once more she cried unto the maid:
"Soon must thou to the monarch say
Kaikeyí's soul has past away,
Or, Ráma banished as we planned,
My son made king shall rule the land.
No more for gold and gems I care,
For brave attire or dainty fare.
If Ráma should the throne ascend,
That very hour my life will end."

The royal lady wounded through
The bosom with the darts that flew
Launched from the hump-back's tongue
Pressed both her hands upon her side,
And o'er and o'er again she cried
With wildering fury stung:
"Yes, it shall be thy task to tell
That I have hurried hence to dwell
In Yáma's realms of woe,
Or happy Bharat shall be king,
And doomed to years of wandering
Kauśalyá's son shall go.
I heed not dainty viands now
Fair wreaths of flowers to twine my brow,
Soft balm or precious scent:
My very life I count as naught,
Nothing on earth can claim my thought
But Ráma's banishment."
She spoke these words of cruel ire;
Then stripping off her gay attire,
The cold bare floor she pressed.
So, falling from her home on high,
Some lovely daughter of the sky
Upon the ground might rest.
With darkened brow and furious mien,
Stripped of her gems and wreath, the queen

In spotless beauty lay,
Like heaven obscured with gathering cloud,
When shades of midnight darkness shroud
Each star's expiring ray.

CANTO

X

Dasaratha's Speech

A s Queen Kaikeyí thus obeyed
The sinful counsel of her maid
She sank upon the chamber floor,
As sinks in anguish, wounded sore,
An elephant beneath the smart
Of the wild hunter's venomed dart.
The lovely lady in her mind
Revolved the plot her maid designed,
And prompt the gain and risk to scan
She step by step approved the plan.
Misguided by the hump-back's guile
She pondered her resolve awhile,
As the fair path that bliss secured
The miserable lady lured,

Devoted to her queen, and swayed
By hopes of gain and bliss, the maid
Rejoiced, her lady's purpose known,
And deemed the prize she sought her own.
Then bent upon her purpose dire,
Kaikeyí with her soul on fire,
Upon the floor lay, languid, down,
Her brows contracted in a frown.
The bright-hued wreath that bound her hair,
Chains, necklets, jewels rich and rare,
Stripped off by her own fingers lay

Spread on the ground in disarray,
And to the floor a lustre lent
As stars light up the firmament.
Thus prostrate in the mourner's cell,
In garb of woe the lady fell,
Her long hair in a single braid,
Like some fair nymph of heaven dismayed.

The monarch, Ráma to install,
With thoughtful care had ordered all,
And now within his home withdrew,
Dismissing first his retinue.
Now all the town has heard, thought he,
What joyful rite the morn will see.
So turned he to her bower to cheer
With the glad news his darling's ear.
Majestic, as the Lord of Night,
When threatened by the Dragon's might,
Bursts radiant on the evening sky
Pale with the clouds that wander by,
So Daśaratha, great in fame,
To Queen Kaikeyí's palace came.
There parrots flew from tree to tree,
And gorgeous peacocks wandered free,
While ever and anon was heard
The note of some glad water-bird.
Here loitered dwarf and hump-backed maid,
There lute and lyre sweet music played.
Here, rich in blossom, creepers twined
O'er grots with wondrous art designed,
There Champac and Aśoka flowers
Hung glorious o'er the summer bowers,
And mid the waving verdure rose
Gold, silver, ivory porticoes.
Through all the months in ceaseless store
The trees both fruit and blossom bore.
With many a lake the grounds were graced;
Seats gold and silver, here were placed;
Here every viand wooed the taste,
It was a garden meet to vie
E'en with the home of Gods on high.

Within the mansion rich and vast
The mighty Daśaratha passed:
Not there was his beloved queen
On her fair couch reclining seen.
With love his eager pulses beat
For the dear wife he came to meet,
And in his blissful hopes deceived,
He sought his absent love and grieved.
For never had she missed the hour
Of meeting in her sumptuous bower,
And never had the king of men
Entered the empty room till then.
Still urged by love and anxious thought
News of his favourite queen he sought,
For never had his loving eyes
Found her or selfish or unwise.
Then spoke at length the warder maid,
With hands upraised and sore afraid:
"My Lord and King, the queen has sought
The mourner's cell with rage distraught."

The words the warder maiden said
He heard with soul disquieted,
And thus as fiercer grief assailed,
His troubled senses wellnigh failed.
Consumed by torturing fires of grief
The king, the world's imperial chief,
His lady lying on the ground
In most unqueenly posture, found.
The aged king, all pure within,
Saw the young queen resolved on sin,
Low on the ground, his own sweet wife,
To him far dearer than his life,
Like some fair creeping plant uptorn,
Or like a maid of heaven forlorn,
A nymph of air or Goddess sent
From Swarga down in banishment.

As some wild elephant who tries
To soothe his consort as she lies
Struck by the hunter's venomed dart,

So the great king disturbed in heart,
Strove with soft hand and fond caress
To soothe his darling queen's distress,
And in his love addressed with sighs
The lady of the lotus eyes:
"I know not, Queen, why thou shouldst be
Thus angered to the heart with me.
Say, who has slighted thee, or whence
Has come the cause of such offence
That in the dust thou liest low,
And rendest my fond heart with woe,
As if some goblin of the night
Had struck thee with a deadly blight,
And cast foul influence on her
Whose spells my loving bosom stir?
I have Physicians famed for skill,
Each trained to cure some special ill:
My sweetest lady, tell thy pain,
And they shall make thee well again.
Whom, darling, wouldst thou punished see?
Or whom enriched with lordly fee?

Weep not, my lovely Queen, and stay
This grief that wears thy frame away;
Speak, and the guilty shall be freed.
The guiltless be condemned to bleed,
The poor enriched, the rich abased,
The low set high, the proud disgraced.
My lords and I thy will obey,
All slaves who own thy sovereign sway;
And I can ne'er my heart incline
To check in aught one wish of thine.
Now by my life I pray thee tell
The thoughts that in thy bosom dwell.
The power and might thou knowest well,
Should from thy breast all doubt expel.
I swear by all my merit won,
Speak, and thy pleasure shall be done.
Far as the world's wide bounds extend
My glorious empire knows no end.

Mine are the tribes in eastern lands,
And those who dwell on Sindhu's sands:
Mine is Suráshtra, far away,
Suvíra's realm admits my sway.
My best the southern nations fear,
The Angas and the Vangas hear.
And as lord paramount I reign
O'er Magadh and the Matsyas' plain,
Kośal, and Káśi's wide domain:
All rich in treasures of the mine,
In golden corn, sheep, goats, and kine.
Choose what thou wilt. Kaikeyí, thence:
But tell me, O my darling, whence
Arose thy grief, and it shall fly
Like hoar-frost when the sun is high."

She, by his loving words consoled,
Longed her dire purpose to unfold,
And sought with sharper pangs to wring
The bosom of her lord the king.

CANTO

XI

The Queen's Demand

To him enthralled by love, and blind,
 Pierced by his darts who shakes the mind,
 Kaikeyí with remorseless breast
Her grand purpose thus expressed:
"O King, no insult or neglect
Have I endured, or disrespect.
One wish I have, and faith would see
That longing granted, lord, by thee.
Now pledge thy word if thou incline

To listen to this prayer of mine,
Then I with confidence will speak,
And thou shalt hear the boon I seek."

Ere she had ceased, the monarch fell,
A victim to the lady's spell,
And to the deadly snare she set
Sprang, like a roebuck to the net.
Her lover raised her drooping head,
Smiled, playing with her hair, and said:
"Hast thou not learnt, wild dame, till now
That there is none so dear as thou
To me thy loving husband, save
My Ráma bravest of the brave?
By him my race's high-souled heir,
By him whom none can match, I swear,
Now speak the wish that on thee weighs:
By him whose right is length of days,
Whom if my fond paternal eye
Saw not one hour I needs must die,—
I swear by Ráma my dear son,
Speak, and thy bidding shall be done.
Speak, darling; if thou choose, request
To have the heart from out my breast;
Regard my words, sweet love, and name
The wish thy mind thinks fit to frame.
Nor let thy soul give way to doubt:
My power should drive suspicion out.
Yea, by my merits won I swear,
Speak, darling, I will grant thy prayer."
The queen, ambitious, overjoyed
To see him by her plot decoyed,
More eager still her aims to reach,
Spoke her abominable speech:
"A boon thou grantest, nothing loth,
And swearest with repeated oath.
Now let the thirty Gods and three
My witnesses, with Indra, be.
Let sun and moon and planets hear,
Heaven, quarters, day and night, give ear.
The mighty world, the earth outspread,

296

With bards of heaven and demons dread;
The ghosts that walk in midnight shade,
And household Gods, our present aid,
A every being great and small
To hear and mark the oath I call."

When thus the archer king was bound,
With treacherous arts and oaths enwound,
She to her bounteous lord subdued
By blinding love, her speech renewed:
"Remember, King, that long-past day
Of Gods' and demons' battle fray.
And how thy foe in doubtful strife
Had nigh bereft thee of thy life.
Remember, it was only I
Preserved thee when about to die,
And thou for watchful love and care
Wouldst grant my first and second prayer.
Those offered boons, pledged with thee then,
I now demand, O King of men,

Of thee, O Monarch, good and just,
Whose righteous soul observes each trust.
If thou refuse thy promise sworn,
I die, despised, before the morn.
These rites in Ráma's name begun—
Transfer them, and enthrone my son.
The time is come to claim at last
The double boon of days long-past,
When Gods and demons met in fight,
And thou wouldst fain my care requite.
Now forth to Daṇḍak's forest drive
Thy Ráma for nine years and five,
And let him dwell a hermit there
With deerskin coat and matted hair.
Without a rival let my boy
The empire of the land enjoy,
And let mine eyes ere morning see
Thy Ráma to the forest flee."

CANTO
XII

Dasaratha's Lament

The monarch, as Kaikeyí pressed
    With cruel words her dire request,
    Stood for a time absorbed in thought
While anguish in his bosom wrought.
"Does some wild dream my heart assail?
Or do my troubled senses fail?
Does some dire portent scare my view?
Or frenzy's stroke my soul subdue?"
Thus as he thought, his troubled mind
In doubt and dread no rest could find,
Distressed and trembling like a deer
Who sees the dreaded tigress near.
On the bare ground his limbs he threw,
And many a long deep sigh he drew,
Like a wild snake, with fury blind,
By charms within a ring confined.
Once as the monarch's fury woke,
"Shame on thee!" from his bosom broke,
And then in sense-bewildering pain
He fainted on the ground again.
At length, when slowly strength returned,
He answered as his eyeballs burned
With the wild fury of his ire
Consuming her, as 'twere, with fire:
"Fell traitress, thou whose thoughts design
The utter ruin of my line,
What wrong have I or Ráma done?
Speak murderess, speak thou wicked one,
Seeks he not evermore to please
Thee with all sonlike courtesies?
By what persuasion art thou led

298

To bring this ruin on his head?
Ah me, that fondly unaware
I brought thee home my life to share,
Called daughter of a king, in truth
A serpent with a venomed tooth!
What fault can I pretend to find
In Ráma praised by all mankind,
That I my darling should forsake?
No, take my life, my glory take:
Let either queen be from me torn,
But not my well-loved eldest-born.
Him but to see is highest bliss,
And death itself his face to miss.
The world may sunless stand, the grain
May thrive without the genial rain,
But if my Ráma be not nigh
My spirit from its frame will fly.
Enough, thine impious plan forgo,
O thou who plottest sin and woe.
My head before thy feet, I kneel,
And pray thee some compassion feel.
O wicked dame, what can have led
Thy heart to dare a plot so dread?
Perchance thy purpose is to sound
The grace thy son with me has found;
Perchance the words that, all these days,
Thou still hast said in Ráma's praise,
Were only feigned, designed to cheer
With flatteries a father's ear.
Soon as thy grief, my Queen, I knew,
My bosom felt the anguish too.
In empty halls art thou possessed,
And subject to anothers' hest?
Now on Ikshváku's ancient race
Falls foul disorder and disgrace,
If thou, O Queen, whose heart so long
Has loved the good should choose the wrong.
Not once, O large-eyed dame, hast thou
Been guilty of offence till now,
Nor said a word to make me grieve,
Now will I now thy sin believe.

With thee my Ráma used to hold
Like place with Bharat lofty-souled.
As thou so often, when the pair
Were children yet, wouldst fain declare.
And can thy righteous soul endure
That Ráma glorious, pious, pure,
Should to the distant wilds be sent
For fourteen years of banishment?
Yea, Ráma Bharat's self exceeds
In love to thee and sonlike deeds,
And, for deserving love of thee,
As Bharat, even so is he.
Who better than that chieftain may
Obedience, love, and honour pay,
Thy dignity with care protect,
Thy slightest word and wish respect?
Of all his countless followers none
Can breathe a word against my son;
Of many thousands not a dame
Can hint reproach or whisper blame.
All creatures feel the sweet control
Of Ráma's pure and gentle soul.
The pride of Manu's race he binds
To him the people's grateful minds.
He wins the subjects with his truth,

The poor with gifts and gentle ruth,
His teachers with his docile will,
The foemen with his archer skill.
Truth, purity, religious zeal,
The hand to give, the heart to feel,
The love that ne'er betrays a friend,
The rectitude that naught can bend,
Knowledge, and meek obedience grace
My Ráma pride of Raghu's race.
Canst thou thine impious plot design
'Gainst him in whom these virtues shine,
Whose glory with the sages vies,
Peer of the Gods who rule the skies!
From him no harsh or bitter word
To pain one creature have I heard,

And how can I my son address,
For thee, with words of bitterness?
Have mercy, Queen: some pity show
To see my tears of anguish flow,
And listen to my mournful cry,
A poor old man who soon must die.
Whate'er this sea-girt land can boast
Of rich and rare from coast to coast,
To thee, my Queen, I give it all:
But O, thy deadly words recall:
O see, my suppliant hands entreat,
Again my lips are on thy feet:
Save Ráma, save my darling child,
Nor kill me with this sin defiled."
He grovelled on the ground, and lay
To burning grief a senseless prey,
And ever and anon, assailed
By floods of woe he wept and wailed,
Striving with eager speed to gain
The margent of his sea of pain.

With fiercer words she fiercer yet
The hapless father's pleading met:
"O Monarch, if thy soul repent
The promise and thy free consent,
How wilt thou in the world maintain
Thy fame for truth unsmirched with stain?
When gathered kings with thee converse,
And bid thee all the tale rehearse,
What wilt thou say, O truthful King,
In answer to their questioning?
"She to whose love my life I owe,
Who saved me smitten by the foe,
Kaikeyí, for her tender care,
Was cheated of the oath I sware."
Thus wilt thou answer, and forsworn
Wilt draw on thee the princes' scorn.
Learn from that tale, the Hawk and Dove,
How strong for truth was Saivya's love.
Pledged by his word the monarch gave
His flesh the suppliant bird to save.

So King Alarka gave his eyes,
And gained a mansion in the skies.
The Sea himself his promise keeps,
And ne'er beyond his limit sweeps.
My deeds of old again recall,
Nor let thy bond dishonoured fall.
The rights of truth thou wouldst forget,
Thy Ráma on the throne to set,
And let thy days in pleasure glide,
Fond King, Kauśalyá by thy side.
Now call it by what name thou wilt,
Justice, injustice, virtue, guilt,
Thy word and oath remain the same,
And thou must yield what thus I claim.
If Ráma be anointed, I
This very day will surely die,
Before thy face will poison drink,
And lifeless at thy feet will sink.
Yea, better far to die than stay
Alive to see one single day
The crowds before Kauśalyá stand
And hail her queen with reverent hand.
Now by my son, myself, I swear,
No gift, no promise whatsoe'er
My steadfast soul shall now content,
But only Ráma's banishment."

So far she spake by rage impelled,
And then the queen deep silence held.
He heard her speech full fraught with ill,
But spoke no word bewildered still,
Gazed on his love once held so dear
Who spoke unlovely rede to hear;
Then as he slowly pondered o'er
The queen's resolve and oath she swore.
Once sighing forth, Ah Ráma! he
Fell prone as falls a smitten tree.
His senses lost like one insane,
Faint as a sick man weak with pain,
Or like a wounded snake dismayed,
So lay the king whom earth obeyed.

Long burning sighs he slowly heaved,
As, conquered by his woe, he grieved,
And thus with tears and sobs between
His sad faint words addressed the queen:

"By whom, Kaikeyí, wast thou taught
This flattering hope with ruin fraught?
Have goblins seized thy soul, O dame,
Who thus canst speak and feel no shame?
Thy mind with sin is sicklied o'er,
From thy first youth ne'er seen before.
A good and loving wife wast thou,
But all, alas! is altered now.
What terror can have seized thy breast
To make thee frame this dire request,
That Bharat o'er the land may reign,
And Ráma in the woods remain?
Turn from thine evil ways, O turn,
And thy perfidious counsel spurn,
If thou would fain a favour do
To people, lord, and Bharat too.
O wicked traitress, fierce and vile,
Who lovest deeds of sin and guile,

What crime or grievance dost thou see,
What fault in Ráma or in me?
Thy son will ne'er the throne accept
If Ráma from his rights be kept,
For Bharat's heart more firmly yet
Than Ráma's is on justice set.
How shall I say, Go forth, and brook
Upon my Ráma's face to look,
See his pale cheek and ashy lips
Dimmed like the moon in sad eclipse?
How see the plan so well prepared
When prudent friends my counsels shared,
All ruined, like a host laid low
Beneath some foeman's murderous blow.
What will these gathered princes say,
From regions near and far away?
"O'erlong endures the monarch's reign,

or now he is a child again."
When many a good and holy sage
In Scripture versed, revered for age,
Shall ask for Ráma, what shall I
Unhappy, what shall I reply?
"By Queen Kaikeyí long distressed
I drove him forth and dispossessed."
Although herein the truth I speak,
They all will hold me false and weak.
What will Kauśalyá say when she
Demands her son exiled by me?
Alas! what answer shall I frame,
Or how console the injured dame?
She like a slave on me attends,
And with a sister's care she blends
A mother's love, a wife's, a friend's.
In spite of all her tender care,
Her noble son, her face most fair,
Another queen I could prefer
And for thy sake neglected her,
But now, O Queen, my heart is grieved
For love and care by thee received,
E'en as the sickening wretch repents
His dainty meal and condiments.
And how will Queen Sumitrá trust
The husband whom she finds unjust,
Seeing my Ráma driven hence
Dishonoured, and for no offence?
Ah! the Videhan bride will hear
A double woe, a double fear,
Two whelming sorrows at one breath,
Her lord's disgrace, his father's death.
Mine aged bosom she will wring
And kill me with her sorrowing,
Sad as a fair nymph left to weep
Deserted on Himálaya's steep.
For short will be my days, I ween,
When I with mournful eyes have seen
My Ráma wandering forth alone
And heard dear Sítá sob and moan.
Ah me! my fond belief I rue.

CANTO
XIII

Dasaratha's Distress

Unworthy of his mournful fate,
The mighty king, unfortunate,
Lay prostrate in unseemly guise,
As, banished from the blissful skies,
Yayáti, in his evil day.
His merit all exhausted, lay.
The queen, triumphant in the power
Won by her beauty's fatal dower,
Still terrible and unsubdued,
Her dire demand again renewed:
"Great Monarch, 'twas thy boast till now
To love the truth and keep the vow;
Then wherefore would thy lips refuse
The promised boon 'tis mine to choose?"

King Daśaratha, thus addressed,
With anger raging in his breast,
Sank for a while beneath the pain,
Then to Kaikeyí spoke again:

"Childless so long, at length I won,
With mighty toil, from Heaven a son,
Ráma, the mighty-armed; and how
Shall I desert my darling now?
A scholar wise, a hero bold,
Of patient mood, with wrath controlled,
How can I bid my Ráma fly,
My darling of the lotus eye?
In heaven itself I scarce could bear,
When asking of my Ráma there,
To hear the Gods his griefs declare,

309

And O, that death would take me hence
Before I wrong his innocence!"
As thus the monarch wept and wailed,
And maddening grief his heart assailed,
The sun had sought his resting-place,
And night was closing round apace.
But yet the moon-crowned night could bring
No comfort to the wretched king.
As still he mourned with burning sighs
And fixed his gaze upon the skies:
"O Night whom starry fires adorn,
I long not for the coming morn.
Be kind and show some mercy: see,
My suppliant hands are raised to thee.
Nay, rather fly with swifter pace;
No longer would I see the face
Of Queen Kaikeyí, cruel, dread,
Who brings this woe upon mine head."
Again with suppliant hands he tried
To move the queen, and wept and sighed:
"To me, unhappy me, inclined
To good, sweet dame, thou shouldst be kind;
Whose life is well-nigh fled, who cling
To thee for succour, me thy king.
This, only this, is all my claim:
Have mercy, O my lovely dame.
None else have I to take my part,
Have mercy: thou art good at heart.
Hear, lady of the soft black eye,
And win a name that ne'er shall die:
Let Ráma rule this glorious land,
The gift of thine imperial hand.
O lady of the dainty waist,
With eyes and lips of beauty graced,
Please Ráma, me, each saintly priest,
Bharat, and all from chief to least."
She heard his wild and mournful cry,
She saw the tears his speech that broke,
Saw her good husband's reddened eye,
But, cruel still, no word she spoke.

His eyes upon her face he bent,
And sought for mercy, but in vain:
She claimed his darling's banishment,
He swooned upon the ground again.

CANTO
XIV

Ráma Summoned

The wicked queen her speech renewed,
When rolling on the earth she viewed
Ikshváku's son, Ayodhyá's king,
For his dear Ráma sorrowing:
"Why, by a simple promise bound,
Liest thou prostrate on the ground,
As though a grievous sin dismayed
Thy spirit! Why so sore afraid?
Keep still thy word. The righteous deem
That truth, mid duties, is supreme:
And now in truth and honour's name
I bid thee own the binding claim.
Śaivya, a king whom earth obeyed,
Once to a hawk a promise made,
Gave to the bird his flesh and bone,
And by his truth made heaven his own.
Alarka, when a Bráhman famed
For Scripture lore his promise claimed,
Tore from his head his bleeding eyes
And unreluctant gave the prize.
His narrow bounds prescribed restrain
The Rivers' Lord, the mighty main,
Who, though his waters boil and rave,
Keeps faithful to the word he gave.
Truth all religion comprehends,

Through all the world its might extends:
In truth alone is justice placed,
On truth the words of God are based:
A life in truth unchanging past
Will bring the highest bliss at last.
If thou the right would still pursue,
Be constant to thy word and true:
Let me thy promise fruitful see,
For boons, O King, proceed from thee.
Now to preserve thy righteous fame,
And yielding to my earnest claim—
Thrice I repeat it—send thy child,
Thy Ráma, to the forest wild.
But if the boon thou still deny,
Before thy face, forlorn, I die."

Thus was the helpless monarch stung
By Queen Kaikeyí's fearless tongue,
As Bali strove in vain to loose
His limbs from Indra's fatal noose.
Dismayed in soul and pale with fear,
The monarch, like a trembling steer
Between the chariot's wheel and yoke,
Again to Queen Kaikeyí spoke,
With sad eyes fixt in vacant stare,
Gathering courage from despair:
"That hand I took, thou sinful dame,
With texts, before the sacred flame,
Thee and thy son, I scorn and hate,
And all at once repudiate.

The night is fled: the dawn is near:
Soon will the holy priests be here
To bid me for the rite prepare
That with my son the throne will share,
The preparation made to grace
My Ráma in his royal place—
With this, e'en this, my darling for
My death the funeral flood shall pour.
Thou and thy son at least forbear
In offerings to my shade to share,

312

Kine, Bráhmans, teachers fill the court,
And bird and beast of purest sort.
From town and village, far and near,
The noblest men are gathered here;
Here merchants with their followers crowd,
And men in joyful converse loud,
And kings from many a distant land
To view the consecration stand.
The dawn is come, the lucky day;
Go bid the monarch haste away,
That now Prince Ráma may obtain
The empire, and begin his reign."

Soon as he heard the high behest
The driver of the chariot pressed
Within the chambers of the king,
His lord with praises honouring.
And none of all the warders checked
His entrance for their great respect
Of him well known, in place so high,
Still fain their king to gratify.
He stood beside the royal chief,
Unwitting of his deadly grief,
And with sweet words began to sing
The praises of his lord and king:
"As, when the sun begins to rise,
The sparkling sea delights our eyes,
Wake, calm with gentle soul, and thus

Give rapture, mighty King, to us.
As Mátali this selfsame hour
Sang lauds of old to Indra's power,
When he the Titan hosts o'erthrew,
So hymn I thee with praises due.
The Vedas, with their kindred lore,
Brahmá their soul-born Lord adore,
With all the doctrines of the wise,
And bid him, as I bid thee, rise.
As, with the moon, the Lord of Day
Wakes with the splendour of his ray
Prolific Earth, who neath him lies,

So, mighty King, I bid thee rise.
With blissful words, O Lord of men,
Rise, radiant in thy form, as when
The sun ascending darts his light
From Meru's everlasting height.
May Śiva, Agni, Sun, and Moon
Bestow on thee each choicest boon,
Kuvera, Varuṇa, Indra bless
Kakutstha's son with all success.
Awake, the holy night is fled,
The happy light abroad is spread;
Awake, O best of kings, and share
The glorious task that claims thy care.
The holy sage Vaśishṭha waits,
With all his Bráhmans, at the gate.
Give thy decree, without delay,
To consecrate thy son today.
As armies, by no captain led,
As flocks that feed unshepherded,
Such is the fortune of a state
Without a king and desolate."

Such were the words the bard addressed,
With weight of sage advice impressed;
And, as he heard, the hapless king
Felt deeper yet his sorrow's sting.
At length, all joy and comfort fled,
He raised his eyes with weeping red,
And, mournful for his Ráma's sake,
The good and glorious monarch spake:
"Why seek with idle praise to greet
The wretch for whom no praise is meet?
Thy words mine aching bosom tear,
And plunge me deeper in despair."

Sumantra heard the sad reply,
And saw his master's tearful eye.
With reverent palm to palm applied
He drew a little space aside.
Then, as the king, with misery weak,
With vain endeavour strove to speak,

Kaikeyí, skilled in plot and plan,
To sage Sumantra thus began:
"The king, absorbed in joyful thought
For his dear son, no rest has sought:
Sleepless to him the night has past,
And now o'erwatched he sinks at last.
Then go, Sumantra, and with speed
The glorious Ráma hither lead:
Go, as I pray, nor longer wait;
No time is this to hesitate."
"How can I go, O Lady fair,
Unless my lord his will declare?"
"Fain would I see him," cried the king,
"Quick, quick, my beauteous Ráma bring."
Then rose the happy thought to cheer
The bosom of the charioteer,
"The king, I ween, of pious mind,
The consecration has designed."
Sumantra for his wisdom famed,
Delighted with the thought he framed,
From the calm chamber, like a bay
Of crowded ocean, took his way.
He turned his face to neither side,
But forth he hurried straight;
Only a little while he eyed
The guards who kept the gate.
He saw in front a gathered crowd
Of men of every class,
Who, parting as he came, allowed
The charioteer to pass.

CANTO
XV

The Preparations

There slept the Bráhmans, deeply read
In Scripture, till the night had fled;
Then, with the royal chaplains, they
Took each his place in long array.
There gathered fast the chiefs of trade,
Nor peer nor captain long delayed,
Assembling all in order due
The consecrating rite to view.

The morning dawned with cloudless ray
On Pushya's high auspicious day,
And Cancer with benignant power
Looked down on Ráma's natal hour.
The twice-born chiefs, with zealous heed,
Made ready what the rite would need.
The well-wrought throne of holy wood
And golden urns in order stood.
There was the royal car whereon
A tiger's skin resplendent shone;
There water, brought for sprinkling thence
Where, in their sacred confluence,
Blend Jumná's waves with Gangá's tide,
From many a holy flood beside,
From brook and fountain far and near,
From pool and river, sea and mere.
And there were honey, curd, and oil,
Parched rice and grass, the garden's spoil,
Fresh milk, eight girls in bright attire,
An elephant with eyes of fire;
And urns of gold and silver made,
With milky branches overlaid,

318

All brimming from each sacred flood,
And decked with many a lotus bud.

And dancing-women fair and free,
Gay with their gems, were there to see,
Who stood in bright apparel by
With lovely brow and witching eye.
White flashed the jewelled chouri there,
And shone like moonbeams through the air;
The white umbrella overhead
A pale and moonlike lustre shed,
Wont in pure splendour to precede,
And in such rites the pomp to lead.
There stood the charger by the side
Of the great bull of snow-white hide;
There was all music soft and loud,
And bards and minstrels swelled the crowd.
For now the monarch bade combine
Each custom of his ancient line
With every rite Ayodhyá's state
Observed, her kings to consecrate.

Then, summoned by the king's behest,
The multitudes together pressed,
And, missing still the royal sire,
Began, impatient, to inquire:
"Who to our lord will tidings bear
That all his people throng the square?
Where is the king? the sun is bright,
And all is ready for the rite."

As thus they spoke, Sumantra, tried
In counsel, to the chiefs replied,
Gathered from lands on every side:
"To Ráma's house I swiftly drave,
For so the king his mandate gave.
Our aged lord and Ráma too
In honour high hold all of you:
I in your words (be long your days!)
Will ask him why he thus delays."

Thus spoke the peer in Scripture read,
And to the ladies' bower he sped.
Quick through the gates Sumantra hied,
Which access ne'er to him denied.
Behind the curtained screen he drew,
Which veiled the chamber from the view.
In benediction loud he raised
His voice, and thus the monarch praised:
"Sun, Moon, Kuvera, Śiva bless
Kakutstha's son with high success!
The Lords of air, flood, fire decree
The victory, my King, to thee!
The holy night has past away,
Auspicious shines the morning's ray.
Rise, Lord of men, thy part to take
In the great rite. Awake! awake!
Bráhmans and captains, chiefs of trade,
All wait in festive garb arrayed;
For thee they look with eager eyes:
O Raghu's son, awake! arise."

To him in holy Scripture read,
Who hailed him thus, the monarch said,
Upraising from his sleep his head:
"Go, Ráma, hither lead as thou
Wast ordered by the queen but now.
Come, tell me why my mandate laid
Upon thee thus is disobeyed.
Away! and Ráma hither bring;
I sleep not: make no tarrying."

Thus gave the king command anew:
Sumantra from his lord withdrew;
With head in lowly reverence bent,
And filled with thoughts of joy, he went.
The royal street he traversed, where
Waved flag and pennon to the air,
And, as with joy the car he drove,
He let his eyes delighted rove.
On every side, where'er he came,
He heard glad words, their theme the same,

As in their joy the gathered folk
Of Ráma and the throning spoke.
Then saw he Ráma's palace bright
And vast as Mount Kailása's height,
That glorious in its beauty showed
As Indra's own supreme abode:
With folding doors both high and wide;
With hundred porches beautified:
Where golden statues towering rose
O'er gemmed and coralled porticoes.
Bright like a cave in Meru's side,
Or clouds through Autumn's sky that ride:
Festooned with length of bloomy twine,
Flashing with pearls and jewels' shine,
While sandal-wood and aloe lent
The mingled riches of their scent;
With all the odorous sweets that fill
The breezy heights of Dardar's hill.
There by the gate the Sáras screamed,
And shrill-toned peacocks' plumage gleamed.
Its floors with deftest art inlaid,
Its sculptured wolves in gold arrayed,
With its bright sheen the palace took
The mind of man and chained the look,
For like the sun and moon it glowed,
And mocked Kuvera's loved abode.
Circling the walls a crowd he viewed
Who stood in reverent attitude,
With throngs of countrymen who sought
Acceptance of the gifts they brought.
The elephant was stationed there,
Appointed Ráma's self to bear;
Adorned with pearls, his brow and cheek
Were sandal-dyed in many a streak,
While he, in stature, bulk, and pride,
With Indra's own Airávat vied.
Sumantra, borne by coursers fleet,
Flashing a radiance o'er the street,
To Ráma's palace flew,
And all who lined the royal road,
Or thronged the prince's rich abode,

Rejoiced as near he drew.
And with delight his bosom swelled
As onward still his course he held

Through many a sumptuous court
Like Indra's palace nobly made,
Where peacocks revelled in the shade,
And beasts of silvan sort.
Through many a hall and chamber wide,
That with Kailása's splendour vied.
Or mansions of the Blest,
While Ráma's friends, beloved and tried,
Before his coming stepped aside,
Still on Sumantra pressed.
He reached the chamber door, where stood
Around his followers young and good,
Bard, minstrel, charioteer,
Well skilled the tuneful chords to sweep,
With soothing strain to lull to sleep,
Or laud their master dear.
Then, like a dolphin darting through
Unfathomed depths of ocean's blue
With store of jewels decked,
Through crowded halls that rock-like rose,
Or as proud hills where clouds repose,
Sumantra sped unchecked—
Halls like the glittering domes on high
Reared for the dwellers of the sky
By heavenly architect.

CANTO
XVI

Ráma Summoned

So through the crowded inner door
Sumantra, skilled in ancient lore,
On to the private chambers pressed
Which stood apart from all the rest.
There youthful warriors, true and bold,
Whose ears were ringed with polished gold,
All armed with trusty bows and darts,
Watched with devoted eyes and hearts.
And hoary men, a faithful train,
Whose aged hands held staves of cane,
The ladies' guard, apparelled fair
In red attire, were stationed there.
Soon as they saw Sumantra nigh,
Each longed his lord to gratify,
And from his seat beside the door
Up sprang each ancient servitor.
Then to the warders quickly cried
The skilled Sumantra, void of pride:
"Tell Ráma that the charioteer
Sumantra waits for audience here."
The ancient men with one accord
Seeking the pleasure of their lord,
Passing with speed the chamber door
To Ráma's ear the message bore.
Forthwith the prince with duteous heed
Called in the messenger with speed,
For 'twas his sire's command, he knew,
That sent him for the interview.
Like Lord Kuvera, well arrayed,
He pressed a couch of gold,
Wherefrom a covering of brocade

Hung down in many a fold.
Oil and the sandal's fragrant dust
Had tinged his body o'er
Dark as the stream the spearman's thrust
Drains from the wounded boar.
Him Sítá watched with tender care,
A chouri in her hand,
As Chitrá, ever fond in fair,
Beside the Moon will stand.
Him glorious with unborrowed light,
A liberal lord, of sunlike might,
Sumantra hailed in words like these,
Well skilled in gentle courtesies,
As, with joined hands in reverence raised,
Upon the beauteous prince he gazed:
"Happy Kauśalyá! Blest is she,
The Mother of a son like thee.
Now rise, O Ráma, speed away.
Go to thy sire without delay:
For he and Queen Kaikeyí seek
An interview with thee to speak."

The lion-lord of men, the best
Of splendid heroes, thus addressed,
To Sítá spake with joyful cheer:
"The king and queen, my lady dear,
Touching the throning, for my sake
Some salutary counsel take.
The lady of the full black eye
Would fain her husband gratify,
And, all his purpose understood,
Counsels the monarch to my good.
A happy fate is mine, I ween,
When he, consulting with his queen,
Sumantra on this charge, intent
Upon my gain and good, has sent.
An envoy of so noble sort
Well suits the splendour of the court.
The consecration rite this day
Will join me in imperial sway.
To meet the lord of earth, for so

324

His order bids me, I will go.
Thou, lady, here in comfort stay,
And with thy maidens rest or play."

Thus Ráma spake. For meet reply
The lady of the large black eye
Attended to the door her lord,
And blessings on his head implored:
"The majesty and royal state
Which holy Bráhmans venerate,
The consecration and the rite
Which sanctifies the ruler's might,
And all imperial powers should be
Thine by thy father's high decree,
As He, the worlds who formed and planned,
The kingship gave to Indra's hand.

Then shall mine eyes my king adore
When lustral rites and fast are o'er,
And black deer's skin and roebuck's horn
Thy lordly limbs and hand adorn.
May He whose hands the thunder wield
Be in the east thy guard and shield;
May Yáma's care the south befriend,
And Varuṇ's arm the west defend;
And let Kuvera, Lord of Gold,
The north with firm protection hold."

Then Ráma spoke a kind farewell,
And hailed the blessings as they fell
From Sítá's gentle lips; and then,
As a young lion from his den
Descends the mountain's stony side,
So from the hall the hero hied.
First Lakshmaṇ at the door he viewed
Who stood in reverent attitude,
Then to the central court he pressed
Where watched the friends who loved him best.
To all his dear companions there
He gave kind looks and greeting fair.
On to the lofty car that glowed

325

Like fire the royal tiger strode.
Bright as himself its silver shone:
A tiger's skin was laid thereon.
With cloudlike thunder, as it rolled,
It flashed with gems and burnished gold,
And, like the sun's meridian blaze,
Blinded the eye that none could gaze.
Like youthful elephants, tall and strong,
Fleet coursers whirled the car along:
In such a car the Thousand-eyed
Borne by swift horses loves to ride.
So like Parjanya, when he flies
Thundering through the autumn skies,
The hero from the palace sped,
As leaves the moon some cloud o'erhead.
Still close to Ráma Lakshmaṇ kept,
Behind him to the car he leapt,
And, watching with fraternal care,
Waved the long chouri's silver hair,
As from the palace gate he came
Up rose the tumult of acclaim.
While loud huzza and jubilant shout
Pealed from the gathered myriads out.
Then elephants, like mountains vast,
And steeds who all their kind surpassed,
Followed their lord by hundreds, nay
By thousands, led in long array.
First marched a band of warriors trained,
With sandal dust and aloe stained;
Well armed was each with sword and bow,
And every breast with hope aglow,
And ever, as they onward went,
Shouts from the warrior train,
And every sweet-toned instrument
Prolonged the minstrel strain.
On passed the tamer of his foes,
While well clad dames, in crowded rows,
Each chamber lattice thronged to view,
And chaplets on the hero threw.
Then all, of peerless face and limb,
Sang Ráma's praise for love of him,

And blent their voices, soft and sweet,
From palace high and crowded street:
"Now, sure, Kauśalyá's heart must swell
To see the son she loves so well,
Thee Ráma, thee, her joy and pride,
Triumphant o'er the realm preside."
Then—for they knew his bride most fair
Of all who part the soft dark hair,
His love, his life, possessed the whole
Of her young hero's heart and soul:—
"Be sure the lady's fate repays
Some mighty vow of ancient days,
For blest with Ráma's love is she
As, with the Moon's, sweet Rohiní."

Such were the witching words that came
From lips of many a peerless dame
Crowding the palace roofs to greet
The hero as he gained the street.

CANTO
XVII

Ráma's Approach

As Ráma, rendering blithe and gay
His loving friends, pursued his way,
He saw on either hand a press
Of mingled people numberless.
The royal street he traversed, where
Incense of aloe filled the air,
Where rose high palaces, that vied
With paly clouds, on either side;
With flowers of myriad colours graced.
And food for every varied taste,
Bright as the glowing path o'erhead

Which feet of Gods celestial tread,
Loud benedictions, sweet to hear,
From countless voices soothed his ear.
While he to each gave due salute
His place and dignity to suit:
"Be thou," the joyful people cried,
"Be thou our guardian, lord and guide.
Throned and anointed king to-day,
Thy feet set forth upon the way
Wherein, each honoured as a God,
Thy fathers and forefathers trod.
Thy sire and his have graced the throne,
And loving care to us have shown:
Thus blest shall we and ours remain,
Yea still more blest in Ráma's reign.

No more of dainty fare we need,
And but one cherished object heed,
That we may see our prince today
Invested with imperial sway."

Such were the words and pleasant speech
That Ráma heard, unmoved, from each
Of the dear friends around him spread,
As onward through the street he sped,
For none could turn his eye or thought
From the dear form his glances sought,
With fruitless ardour forward cast
Even when Raghu's son had past.
And he who saw not Ráma nigh,
Nor caught a look from Ráma's eye,
A mark for scorn and general blame,
Reproached himself in bitter shame.
For to each class his equal mind
With sympathy and love inclined
Most fully of the princely four,
So greatest love to him they bore.

His circling course the hero bent
Round shrine and altar, reverent,
Round homes of Gods, where cross-roads met,

Where many a sacred tree was set.
Near to his father's house he drew
Like Indra's beautiful to view,
And with the light his glory gave
Within the royal palace drave.
Through three broad courts, where bowmen kept
Their watch and ward, his coursers swept,
Then through the two remaining went
On foot the prince preëminent.
Through all the courts the hero passed,
And gained the ladies' bower at last;
Then through the door alone withdrew,
And left without his retinue.
When thus the monarch's noble boy
Had gone his sire to meet,
The multitude, elate with joy,
Stood watching in the street,
And his return with eager eyes
Expected at the gates,
As for his darling moon to rise
The King of Rivers waits.

CANTO

XVIII

The Sentence

With hopeless eye and pallid mien
There sat the monarch with the queen.
His father's feet with reverence due
He clasped, and touched Kaikeyí's too.
The king, with eyes still brimming o'er,
Cried Ráma! and could do no more.
His voice was choked, his eye was dim,
He could not speak or look on him.
Then sudden fear made Ráma shake

329

As though his foot had roused a snake,
Soon as his eyes had seen the change
So mournful, terrible, and strange.
For there his reason well-nigh fled,
Sighing, with soul disquieted,
To torturing pangs a prey,
Dismayed, despairing, and distraught,
In a fierce whirl of wildering thought
The hapless monarch lay,
Like Ocean wave-engarlanded
Storm-driven from his tranquil bed,
The Sun-God in eclipse,
Or like a holy seer, heart-stirred
With anguish, when a lying word
Has passed his heedless lips.
The sight of his dear father, pained
With woe and misery unexplained
Filled Ráma with unrest,
As Ocean's pulses rise and swell
When the great moon he loves so well
Shines full upon his breast.
So grieving for his father's sake,
To his own heart the hero spake:
"Why will the king my sire to-day
No kindly word of greeting say?
At other times, though wroth he be,
His eyes grow calm that look on me.
Then why does anguish wring his brow
To see his well-beloved now?"
Sick and perplexed, distraught with woe,
To Queen Kaikeyí bowing low,
While pallor o'er his bright cheek spread,
With humble reverence he said:
"What have I done, unknown, amiss
To make my father wroth like this?
Declare it, O dear Queen, and win
His pardon for my heedless sin.
Why is the sire I ever find
Filled with all love to-day unkind?
With eyes cast down and pallid cheek
This day alone he will not speak.

Or lies he prostrate neath the blow
Of fierce disease or sudden woe?
For all our bliss is dashed with pain,
And joy unmixt is hard to gain.
Does stroke of evil fortune smite
Dear Bharat, charming to the sight,
Or on the brave Śatrughna fall,
Or consorts, for he loves them all?
Against his words when I rebel,
Or fail to please the monarch well,
When deeds of mine his soul offend,
That hour I pray my life may end.
How should a man to him who gave
His being and his life behave?
The sire to whom he owes his birth
Should be his deity on earth.
Hast thou, by pride and folly moved,

With bitter taunt the king reproved?
Has scorn of thine or cruel jest
To passion stirred his gentle breast?
Speak truly, Queen, that I may know
What cause has changed the monarch so."

Thus by the high-souled prince addressed,
Of Raghu's sons the chief and best,
She cast all ruth and shame aside,
And bold with greedy words replied:
"Not wrath, O Ráma, stirs the king,
Nor misery stabs with sudden sting;
One thought that fills his soul has he,
But dares not speak for fear of thee.
Thou art so dear, his lips refrain
From words that might his darling pain.
But thou, as duty bids, must still
The promise of thy sire fulfil.
He who to me in days gone by
Vouchsafed a boon with honours high,
Dares now, a king, his word regret,
And caitiff-like disowns the debt.
The lord of men his promise gave

To grant the boon that I might crave,
And now a bridge would idly throw
When the dried stream has ceased to flow.
His faith the monarch must not break
In wrath, or e'en for thy dear sake.
From faith, as well the righteous know,
Our virtue and our merits flow.
Now, be they good or be they ill,
Do thou thy father's words fulfil:
Swear that his promise shall not fail,
And I will tell thee all the tale.
Yes, Ráma, when I hear that thou
Hast bound thee by thy father's vow,
Then, not till then, my lips shall speak,
Nor will he tell what boon I seek."
He heard, and with a troubled breast
This answer to the queen addressed:
"Ah me, dear lady, canst thou deem
That words like these thy lips beseem?
I, at the bidding of my sire,
Would cast my body to the fire,
A deadly draught of poison drink,
Or in the waves of ocean sink:
If he command, it shall be done,—
My father and my king in one.
Then speak and let me know the thing
So longed for by my lord the king.
It shall be done: let this suffice;
Ráma ne'er makes a promise twice."

He ended. To the princely youth
Who loved the right and spoke the truth,
Cruel, abominable came
The answer of the ruthless dame:
"When Gods and Titans fought of yore,
Transfixed with darts and bathed in gore
Two boons to me thy father gave
For the dear life 'twas mine to save.
Of him I claim the ancient debt,
That Bharat on the throne be set,
And thou, O Ráma, go this day

To Daṇḍak forest far away.
Now, Ráma, if thou wilt maintain
Thy father's faith without a stain,
And thine own truth and honour clear,
Then, best of men, my bidding hear.
Do thou thy father's word obey,
Nor from the pledge he gave me stray.
Thy life in Daṇḍak forest spend
Till nine long years and five shall end.
Upon my Bharat's princely head
Let consecrating drops be shed,
With all the royal pomp for thee
Made ready by the king's decree.
Seek Daṇḍak forest and resign
Rites that would make the empire thine,
For twice seven years of exile wear
The coat of bark and matted hair.
Then in thy stead let Bharat reign
Lord of his royal sire's domain,
Rich in the fairest gems that shine,
Cars, elephants, and steeds, and kine.
The monarch mourns thy altered fate
And vails his brow compassionate:
Bowed down by bitter grief he lies
And dares not lift to thine his eyes.
Obey his word: be firm and brave,
And with great truth the monarch save."
While thus with cruel words she spoke,
No grief the noble youth betrayed;
But forth the father's anguish broke,
At his dear Ráma's lot dismayed.

CANTO
XIX

Ráma's Promise

Calm and unmoved by threatened woe
The noble conqueror of the foe
Answered the cruel words she spoke,
Nor quailed beneath the murderous stroke:

"Yea, for my father's promise sake
I to the wood my way will take,
And dwell a lonely exile there
In hermit dress with matted hair.
One thing alone I fain would learn,
Why is the king this day so stern?
Why is the scourge of foes so cold,
Nor gives me greeting as of old?
Now let not anger flush thy cheek:
Before thy face the truth I speak,
In hermit's coat with matted hair
To the wild wood will I repair.
How can I fail his will to do,
Friend, master, grateful sovereign too?
One only pang consumes my breast:
That his own lips have not expressed
His will, nor made his longing known
That Bharat should ascend the throne.

To Bharat I would yield my wife,
My realm and wealth, mine own dear life,
Unasked I fain would yield them all:
More gladly at my father's call,
More gladly when the gift may free
His honour and bring joy to thee.
Thus, lady, his sad heart release

334

From the sore shame, and give him peace.
But tell me, O, I pray thee, why
The lord of men, with downcast eye,
Lies prostrate thus, and one by one
Down his pale cheek the tear-drops run.
Let couriers to thy father speed
On horses of the swiftest breed,
And, by the mandate of the king,
Thy Bharat to his presence bring.
My father's words I will not stay
To question, but this very day
To Daṇḍak's pathless wild will fare,
For twice seven years an exile there."

When Ráma thus had made reply
Kaikeyí's heart with joy beat high.
She, trusting to the pledge she held,
The youth's departure thus impelled:
"'Tis well. Be messengers despatched
On coursers ne'er for fleetness matched,
To seek my father's home and lead
My Bharat back with all their speed.
And, Ráma, as I ween that thou
Wilt scarce endure to linger now,
So surely it were wise and good
This hour to journey to the wood.
And if, with shame cast down and weak,
No word to thee the king can speak,
Forgive, and from thy mind dismiss
A trifle in an hour like this.
But till thy feet in rapid haste
Have left the city for the waste,
And to the distant forest fled,
He will not bathe nor call for bread."

"Woe! woe!" from the sad monarch burst,
In surging floods of grief immersed;
Then swooning, with his wits astray,
Upon the gold-wrought couch he lay,
And Ráma raised the aged king:
But the stern queen, unpitying,

Checked not her needless words, nor spared
The hero for all speed prepared,
But urged him with her bitter tongue,
Like a good horse with lashes stung,
She spoke her shameful speech. Serene
He heard the fury of the queen,
And to her words so vile and dread
Gently, unmoved in mind, he said:
"I would not in this world remain
A grovelling thrall to paltry gain,
But duty's path would fain pursue,
True as the saints themselves are true.
From death itself I would not fly
My father's wish to gratify,
What deed soe'er his loving son
May do to please him, think it done.
Amid all duties, Queen, I count
This duty first and paramount,
That sons, obedient, aye fulfil
Their honoured fathers' word and will.
Without his word, if thou decree,
Forth to the forest will I flee,
And there shall fourteen years be spent
Mid lonely wilds in banishment.
Methinks thou couldst not hope to find
One spark of virtue in my mind,
If thou, whose wish is still my lord,
Hast for this grace the king implored.
This day I go, but, ere we part,
Must cheer my Sítá's tender heart,
To my dear mother bid farewell;
Then to the woods, a while to dwell.
With thee, O Queen, the care must rest
That Bharat hear his sire's behest,
And guard the land with righteous sway,
For such the law that lives for aye."

In speechless woe the father heard,
Wept with loud cries, but spoke no word.
Then Ráma touched his senseless feet,
And hers, for honour most unmeet;

336

Round both his circling steps he bent,
Then from the bower the hero went.
Soon as he reached the gate he found
His dear companions gathered round.
Behind him came Sumitrá's child
With weeping eyes so sad and wild.
Then saw he all that rich array
Of vases for the glorious day.
Round them with reverent stops he paced,
Nor vailed his eye, nor moved in haste.
The loss of empire could not dim
The glory that encompassed him.
So will the Lord of Cooling Rays
On whom the world delights to gaze,
Through the great love of all retain
Sweet splendour in the time of wane.
Now to the exile's lot resigned
He left the rule of earth behind:
As though all worldly cares he spurned
No trouble was in him discerned.
The chouries that for kings are used,
And white umbrella, he refused,
Dismissed his chariot and his men,
And every friend and citizen.
He ruled his senses, nor betrayed
The grief that on his bosom weighed,
And thus his mother's mansion sought
To tell the mournful news he brought.
Nor could the gay-clad people there
Who flocked round Ráma true and fair,
One sign of altered fortune trace
Upon the splendid hero's face.
Nor had the chieftain, mighty-armed,
Lost the bright look all hearts that charmed,

As e'en from autumn moons is thrown
A splendour which is all their own.
With his sweet voice the hero spoke
Saluting all the gathered folk,
Then righteous-souled and great in fame
Close to his mother's house he came.

Lakshman the brave, his brother's peer
In princely virtues, followed near,
Sore troubled, but resolved to show
No token of his secret woe.
Thus to the palace Ráma went
Where all were gay with hope and joy;
But well he knew the dire event
That hope would mar, that bliss destroy.
So to his grief he would not yield
Lest the sad change their hearts might rend,
And, the dread tiding unrevealed,
Spared from the blow each faithful friend.

CANTO

XX

Kausalyá's Lament

But in the monarch's palace, when
Sped from the bower that lord of men,
Up from the weeping women went
A mighty wail and wild lament:
"Ah, he who ever freely did
His duty ere his sire could bid,
Our refuge and our sure defence,
This day will go an exile hence,
He on Kauśalyá loves to wait
Most tender and affectionate,
And as he treats his mother, thus
From childhood has he treated us.
On themes that sting he will not speak,
And when reviled is calm and meek.
He soothes the angry, heals offence:
He goes to-day an exile hence.
Our lord the king is most unwise,
And looks on life with doting eyes,

338

Who in his folly casts away
The world's protection, hope, and stay."

Thus in their woe, like kine bereaved
Of their young calves, the ladies grieved,
And ever as they wept and wailed
With keen reproach the king assailed.
Their lamentation, mixed with tears,
Smote with new grief the monarch's ears,
Who, burnt with woe too great to bear,
Fell on his couch and fainted there.

Then Ráma, smitten with the pain
His heaving heart could scarce restrain,
Groaned like an elephant and strode
With Lakshmaṇ to the queen's abode.
A warder there, whose hoary eld
In honour high by all was held,
Guarding the mansion, sat before
The portal, girt with many more.
Swift to their feet the warders sprang,
And loud the acclamation rang,
Hail, Ráma! as to him they bent,
Of victor chiefs preëminent.
One court he passed, and in the next
Saw, masters of each Veda text,
A crowd of Bráhmans, good and sage,
Dear to the king for lore and age.
To these he bowed his reverent head,
Thence to the court beyond he sped.
Old dames and tender girls, their care
To keep the doors, were stationed there.
And all, when Ráma came in view,
Delighted to the chamber flew,
To bear to Queen Kauśalyá's ear
The tidings that she loved to hear.
The queen, on rites and prayer intent,
In careful watch the night had spent,
And at the dawn, her son to aid,
To Vishṇu holy offerings made.
Firm in her vows, serenely glad,

339

In robes of spotless linen clad,
As texts prescribe, with grace implored,
Her offerings in the fire she poured.
Within her splendid bower he came,
And saw her feed the sacred flame.
There oil, and grain, and vases stood,
With wreaths, and curds, and cates, and wood,
And milk, and sesamum, and rice,
The elements of sacrifice.
She, worn and pale with many a fast
And midnight hours in vigil past,
In robes of purest white arrayed,
To Lakshmí Queen drink-offerings paid.
So long away, she flew to meet
The darling of her soul:
So runs a mare with eager feet
To welcome back her foal.
He with his firm support upheld
The queen, as near she drew,
And, by maternal love impelled,
Her arms around him threw.
Her hero son, her matchless boy
She kissed upon the head:
She blessed him in her pride and joy
With tender words, and said:

"Be like thy royal sires of old,
The nobly good, the lofty-souled!
Their lengthened days and fame be thine,
And virtue, as beseems thy line!
The pious king, thy father, see
True to his promise made to thee:
That truth thy sire this day will show,
And regent's power on thee bestow."

She spoke. He took the proffered seat,
And as she pressed her son to eat,
Raised reverent bands, and, touched with shame,
Made answer to the royal dame:
"Dear lady, thou hast yet to know
That danger threats, and heavy woe:

A grief that will with sore distress
On Sítá, thee, and Lakshmaṇ press.
What need of seats have such as I?
This day to Daṇḍak wood I fly.
The hour is come, a time, unmeet
For silken couch and gilded seat.
I must to lonely wilds repair,
Abstain from flesh, and living there
On roots, fruit, honey, hermit's food,
Pass twice seven years in solitude.
To Bharat's hand the king will yield
The regent power I thought to wield,
And me, a hermit, will he send
My days in Daṇḍak wood to spend."

As when the woodman's axe has lopped
A Śal branch in the grove, she dropped:
So from the skies a Goddess falls
Ejected from her radiant halls.

When Ráma saw her lying low,
Prostrate by too severe a blow,
Around her form his arms he wound
And raised her fainting from the ground.
His hand upheld her like a mare
Who feels her load too sore to bear,
And sinks upon the way o'ertoiled,
And all her limbs with dust are soiled.
He soothed her in her wild distress
With loving touch and soft caress.
She, meet for highest fortune, eyed
The hero watching by her side,
And thus, while Lakshmaṇ bent to hear,
Addressed her son with many a tear!
"If, Ráma, thou had ne'er been born
My child to make thy mother mourn,
Though reft of joy, a childless queen,
Such woe as this I ne'er had seen.
Though to the childless wife there clings
One sorrow armed with keenest stings,
"No child have I: no child have I,"

No second misery prompts the sigh.
When long I sought, alas, in vain,
My husband's love and bliss to gain,
In Ráma all my hopes I set
And dreamed I might be happy yet.
I, of the consorts first and best,
Must bear my rivals' taunt and jest,
And brook, though better far than they,
The soul distressing words they say.
What woman can be doomed to pine
In misery more sore than mine,
Whose hopeless days must still be spent
In grief that ends not and lament?
They scorned me when my son was nigh;
When he is banished I must die.
Me, whom my husband never prized,
Kaikeyí's retinue despised
With boundless insolence, though she
Tops not in rank nor equals me.
And they who do me service yet,
Nor old allegiance quite forget,
Whene'er they see Kaikeyí's son,
With silent lips my glances shun.
How, O my darling, shall I brook
Each menace of Kaikeyí's look,
And listen, in my low estate,
To taunts of one so passionate?
For seventeen years since thou wast born
I sat and watched, ah me, forlorn!
Hoping some blessed day to see
Deliverance from my woes by thee.
Now comes this endless grief and wrong,
So dire I cannot bear it long,
Sinking, with age and sorrow worn,
Beneath my rivals' taunts and scorn.
How shall I pass in dark distress
My long lone days of wretchedness
Without my Ráma's face, as bright
As the full moon to cheer my sight?
Alas, my cares thy steps to train,
And fasts, and vows, and prayers are vain.

Hard, hard, I ween, must be this heart
To hear this blow nor burst apart,
As some great river bank, when first
The floods of Rain-time on it burst.
No, Fate that speeds not will not slay,
Nor Yama's halls vouchsafe me room,
Or, like a lion's weeping prey,
Death now had borne me to my doom.
Hard is my heart and wrought of steel
That breaks not with the crushing blow,
Or in the pangs this day I feel
My lifeless frame had sunk below.
Death waits his hour, nor takes me now:
But this sad thought augments my pain,
That prayer and largess, fast and vow,
And Heavenward service are in vain.
Ah me, ah me! with fruitless toil
Of rites austere a child I sought:
Thus seed cast forth on barren soil
Still lifeless lies and comes to naught.
If ever wretch by anguish grieved
Before his hour to death had fled,
I mourning, like a cow bereaved,
Had been this day among the dead."

CANTO

XXI

Kausalyá Calmed

While thus Kauśalyá wept and sighed,
    With timely words sad Lakshmaṇ cried:
    "O honoured Queen I like it ill
That, subject to a woman's will,
Ráma his royal state should quit
And to an exile's doom submit.

The aged king, fond, changed, and weak,
Will as the queen compels him speak.
But why should Ráma thus be sent
To the wild woods in banishment?
No least offence I find in him,
I see no fault his fame to dim.
Not one in all the world I know,
Not outcast wretch, not secret foe,
Whose whispering lips would dare assail
His spotless life with slanderous tale.
Godlike and bounteous, just, sincere,
E'en to his very foemen dear:
Who would without a cause neglect
The right, and such a son reject?
And if a king such order gave,
In second childhood, passion's slave,
What son within his heart would lay
The senseless order, and obey?
Come, Ráma, ere this plot be known
Stand by me and secure the throne.
Stand like the King who rules below,
Stand aided by thy brother's bow:
How can the might of meaner men
Resist thy royal purpose then?
My shafts, if rebels court their fate,
Shall lay Ayodhyá desolate.
Then shall her streets with blood be dyed
Of those who stand on Bharat's side:
None shall my slaughtering hand exempt,
For gentle patience earns contempt.
If, by Kaikeyí's counsel changed,
Our father's heart be thus estranged,
No mercy must our arm restrain,
But let the foe be slain, be slain.
For should the guide, respected long,
No more discerning right and wrong,
Turn in forbidden paths to stray,
'Tis meet that force his steps should stay.
What power sufficient can he see,
What motive for the wish has he,
That to Kaikeyí would resign

344

The empire which is justly thine?
Can he, O conqueror of thy foes,
Thy strength and mine in war oppose?
Can he entrust, in our despite,
To Bharat's hand thy royal right?
I love this brother with the whole
Affection of my faithful soul.
Yea Queen, by bow and truth I swear,
By sacrifice, and gift, and prayer,
If Ráma to the forest goes,
Or where the burning furnace glows,
First shall my feet the forest tread,
The flames shall first surround my head.
My might shall chase thy grief and tears,
As darkness flies when morn appears.
Do thou, dear Queen, and Ráma too
Behold what power like mine can do.
My aged father I will kill,
The vassal of Kaikeyí's will,
Old, yet a child, the woman's thrall,
Infirm, and base, the scorn of all."

Thus Lakshman cried, the mighty-souled:
Down her sad cheeks the torrents rolled,
As to her son Kauśalyá spake:

"Now thou hast heard thy brother, take
His counsel if thou hold it wise,
And do the thing his words advise,
Do not, my son, with tears I pray,
My rival's wicked word obey,
Leave me not here consumed with woe,
Nor to the wood, an exile, go.
If thou, to virtue ever true,
Thy duty's path would still pursue,
The highest duty bids thee stay
And thus thy mother's voice obey.
Thus Kaśyap's great ascetic son
A seat among the Immortals won:
In his own home, subdued, he stayed,
And honour to his mother paid.

345

If reverence to thy sire be due,
Thy mother claims like honour too,
And thus I charge thee, O my child,
Thou must not seek the forest wild.
Ah, what to me were life and bliss,
Condemned my darling son to miss?
But with my Ráma near, to eat
The very grass itself were sweet.
But if thou still wilt go and leave
Thy hapless mother here to grieve,
I from that hour will food abjure,
Nor life without my son endure.
Then it will be thy fate to dwell
In depth of world-detested hell.
As Ocean in the olden time
Was guilty of an impious crime
That marked the lord of each fair flood
As one who spills a Bráhman's blood."

Thus spake the queen, and wept, and sighed:
Then righteous Ráma thus replied:
"I have no power to slight or break
Commandments which my father spake.
I bend my head, dear lady, low,
Forgive me, for I needs must go.
Once Kaṇḍu, mighty saint, who made
His dwelling in the forest shade,

A cow—and duty's claims he knew—
Obedient to his father, slew.
And in the line from which we spring,
When ordered by their sire the king,
Through earth the sons of Sagar cleft,
And countless things of life bereft.
So Jamadagní's son obeyed
His sire, when in the wood he laid
His hand upon his axe, and smote
Through Renuká his mother's throat.
The deeds of these and more beside.
Peers of the Gods, my steps shall guide,
And resolute will I fulfil

My father's word, my father's will.
Nor I, O Queen, unsanctioned tread
This righteous path, by duty led:
The road my footsteps journey o'er
Was traversed by the great of yore.
This high command which all accept
Shall faithfully by me be kept,
For duty ne'er will him forsake
Who fears his sire's command to break."

Thus to his mother wild with grief:
Then thus to Lakshmaṇ spake the chief
Of those by whom the bow is bent,
Mid all who speak, most eloquent:
"I know what love for me thou hast,
What firm devotion unsurpassed:
Thy valour and thy worth I know,
And glory that appals the foe.
Blest youth, my mother's woe is great,
It bends her 'neath its matchless weight:
No claims will she, with blinded eyes,
Of truth and patience recognize.
For duty is supreme in place,
And truth is duty's noblest base.
Obedient to my sire's behest
I serve the cause of duty best.
For man should truly do whate'er
To mother, Bráhman, sire, he sware:
He must in duty's path remain,
Nor let his word be pledged in vain.
And, O my brother, how can I
Obedience to this charge deny?
Kaikeyí's tongue my purpose spurred,
But 'twas my sire who gave the word.
Cast these unholy thoughts aside
Which smack of war and Warriors' pride;
To duty's call, not wrath attend,
And tread the path which I commend."

Ráma by fond affection moved
His brother Lakshmaṇ thus reproved;

Then with joined hands and reverent head
Again to Queen Kauśalyá said:

"I needs must go—do thou consent—
To the wild wood in banishment.
O give me, by my life I pray,
Thy blessing ere I go away.
I, when the promised years are o'er,
Shall see Ayodhyá's town once more.
Then, mother dear, thy tears restrain,
Nor let thy heart be wrung by pain:
In time, my father's will obeyed,
Shall I return from greenwood shade.
My dear Videhan, thou, and I,
Lakshmaṇ, Sumitrá, feel this tie,
And must my father's word obey,
As duty bids that rules for aye.
Thy preparations now forgo,
And lock within thy breast thy woe,
Nor be my pious wish withstood
To go an exile to the wood."

Calm and unmoved the prince explained
His duty's claim and purpose high,
The mother life and sense regained,
Looked on her son and made reply:
"If reverence be thy father's due,
The same by right and love is mine:
Go not, my charge I thus renew,
Nor leave me here in woe to pine,
What were such lonely life to me,
Rites to the shades, or deathless lot?
More dear, my son, one hour with thee
Than all the world where thou art not."
As bursts to view, when brands blaze high,
Some elephant concealed by night,
So, when he heard his mother's cry,
Burnt Ráma's grief with fiercer might.
Thus to the queen, half senseless still,
And Lakshmaṇ, burnt with heart-felt pain,
True to the right, with steadfast will,

His duteous speech he spoke again:
"Brother, I know thy loving mind,
Thy valour and thy truth I know,
But now to claims of duty blind
Thou and my mother swell my woe.
The fruits of deeds in human life
Make love, gain, duty, manifest,
Dear when they meet as some fond wife
With her sweet babes upon her breast.
But man to duty first should turn
Whene'er the three are not combined:
For those who heed but gain we spurn,
And those to pleasure all resigned.
Shall then the virtuous disobey
Hosts of an aged king and sire,
Though feverous joy that father sway,
Or senseless love or causeless ire?
I have no power, commanded thus,
To slight his promise and decree:
The honoured sire of both of us,
My mother's lord and life is he.
Shall she, while yet the holy king
Is living, on the right intent,—
Shall she, like some poor widowed thing,
Go forth with me to banishment?
Now, mother, speed thy parting son,
And let thy blessing soothe my pain,

That I may turn, mine exile done,
Like King Yayáti, home again.
Fair glory and the fruit she gives,
For lust of sway I ne'er will slight:
What, for the span a mortal lives.
Were rule of faith without the right?"
He soothed her thus, firm to the last
His counsel to his brother told:
Then round the queen in reverence passed,
And held her in his loving hold.

CANTO
XXII

Lakshman Calmed

So Ráma kept unshaken still
His noble heart with iron will.
To his dear brother next he turned,
Whose glaring eyes with fury burned,
Indignant, panting like a snake,
And thus again his counsel spake:
"Thine anger and thy grief restrain,
And firm in duty's path remain.
Dear brother, lay thy scorn aside,
And be the right thy joy and pride.
Thy ready zeal and thoughtful care
To aid what rites should grace the heir,—
These 'tis another's now to ask;
Come, gird thee for thy noble task,
That Bharat's throning rites may he
Graced with the things prepared for me.
And with thy gentle care provide
That her fond heart, now sorely tried
With fear and longing for my sake,
With doubt and dread may never ache.
To know that thoughts of coming ill
One hour that tender bosom fill
With agony and dark despair
Is grief too great for me to bear.
I cannot, brother, call to mind
One wilful fault or undesigned,
When I have pained in anything
My mothers or my sire the king.
The right my father keeps in view,
In promise, word, and action true;
Let him then all his fear dismiss,

Nor dread the loss of future bliss.
He fears his truth herein will fail:
Hence bitter thoughts his heart assail.
He trembles lest the rites proceed,
And at his pangs my heart should bleed.
So now this earnest wish is mine,
The consecration to resign,
And from this city turn away
To the wild wood with no delay.
My banishment to-day will free
Kaikeyí from her cares, that she,
At last contented and elate,
May Bharat's throning celebrate.
Then will the lady's trouble cease,
Then will her heart have joy and peace,
When wandering in the wood I wear
Deerskin, and bark, and matted hair.
Nor shall by me his heart be grieved
Whose choice approved, whose mind conceived
This counsel which I follow. No,
Forth to the forest will I go.
'Tis Fate, Sumitrás son, confess,
That sends me to the wilderness.
'Tis Fate alone that gives away
To other hands the royal sway.
How could Kaikeyí's purpose bring
On me this pain and suffering,
Were not her change of heart decreed
By Fate whose will commands the deed?
I know my filial love has been
The same throughout for every queen,
And with the same affection she
Has treated both her son and me.
Her shameful words of cruel spite
To stay the consecrating rite,
And drive me banished from the throne,—
These I ascribe to Fate alone,
How could she, born of royal race,
Whom nature decks with fairest grace,
Speak like a dame of low degree
Before the king to torture me?

But Fate, which none may comprehend,
To which all life must bow and bend,
In her and me its power has shown,
And all my hopes are overthrown.
What man, Sumitrá's darling, may
Contend with Fate's resistless sway,
Whose all-commanding power we find
Our former deeds alone can bind?
Our life and death, our joy and pain,
Anger and fear, and loss and gain,
Each thing that is, in every state,
All is the work of none but Fate.
E'en saints, inspired with rigid zeal,
When once the stroke of Fate they feel,
In sternest vows no more engage,
And fall enslaved by love and rage.
So now the sudden stroke whose weight
Descends unlooked for, comes of Fate,
And with unpitying might destroys
The promise of commencing joys.
Weigh this true counsel in thy soul:
With thy firm heart thy heart control;
Then, brother, thou wilt cease to grieve
For hindered rites which now I leave.
So cast thy needless grief away,
And strictly my commands obey.
Those preparations check with speed,
Nor let my throning rites proceed.
Those urns that stand prepared to shed
King-making drops upon my head,
Shall, with their pure lustrations now
Inaugurate my hermit's vow.

Yet what have I to do with things
That touch the state and pomp of kings?
These hands of mine shall water take
To sanctify the vow I make.
Now Lakshmaṇ, let thy heart no more
My fortune changed and lost deplore.
A forest life more joys may bring
Than those that wait upon a king,

352

Now though her arts successful mar
My consecrating rite,
Let not the youngest queen too far
Thy jealous fear excite.
Nor let one thought suggesting ill
Upon our father fall,
But let thy heart remember still
That Fate is lord of all."

CANTO

XXIII

Lakshman's Anger

Thus Ráma to his brother said;
 And Lakshman bent his drooping head.
 In turns by grief and pride impelled,
A middle course of thought he held,
Then in a frown of anger, bent
His brows that chief most excellent,
And like a serpent in his hole,
Breathed fierce and fast in wrath of soul.
His threatening brows so darkly frowned,
His eyes so fiercely glanced around,
They made his glare, which none might brook,
Like some infuriate lion's look.
Like some wild elephant, full oft
He raised and shook his hand aloft.
Now turned his neck to left and right
Now bent, now raised its stately height.
Now in his rage that sword he felt
Which mangling wounds to foemen dealt,
With sidelong glance his brother eyed,
And thus in burning words replied:
"Thy rash resolve, thy eager haste,
Thy mighty fear, are all misplaced:

353

No room is here for duty's claim,
No cause to dread the people's blame.
Can one as brave as thou consent
To use a coward's argument?
The glory of the Warrior race
With craven speech his lips debase?
Can one like thee so falsely speak,
Exalting Fate, confessed so weak?
Canst thou, undoubting still restrain?
Suspicions of those sinful twain?
Canst thou, most duteous, fail to know
Their hearts are set on duty's show?
They with deceit have set their trains,
And now the fruit rewards their pains.
Had they not long ago agreed,
O Ráma, on this treacherous deed,
That promised boon, so long retained,
He erst had given and she had gained.
I cannot, O my brother, bear
To see another throned as heir
With rites which all our people hate:
Then, O, this passion tolerate.
This vaunted duty which can guide
Thy steps from wisdom's path aside,
And change the counsel of thy breast,
O lofty-hearted, I detest.
Wilt thou, when power and might are thine,
Submit to this abhorred design?
Thy father's impious hest fulfil,
That vassal of Kaikeyí's will?
But if thou still wilt shut thine eyes,
Nor see the guile herein that lies,
My soul is sad, I deeply mourn,
And duty seems a thing to scorn.
Canst thou one moment think to please
This pair who live for love and ease,
And 'gainst thy peace, as foes, allied,
With tenderest names their hatred hide?
Now if thy judgment still refers
To Fate this plot of his and hers,
My mind herein can ne'er agree:

And O, in this be ruled by me.
Weak, void of manly pride are they
Who bend to Fate's imputed sway:
The choicest souls, the nobly great
Disdain to bow their heads to Fate.
And he who dares his Fate control
With vigorous act and manly soul,
Though threatening Fate his hopes assail,
Unmoved through all need never quail.
This day mankind shall learn aright
The power of Fate and human might,
So shall the gulf that lies between
A man and Fate be clearly seen.
The might of Fate subdued by me
This hour the citizens shall see,
Who saw its intervention stay
Thy consecrating rites to-day.
My power shall turn this Fate aside,
That threatens, as, with furious stride,
An elephant who scorns to feel,
In rage unchecked, the driver's steel.
Not the great Lords whose sleepless might
Protects the worlds, shall stay the rite
Though earth, hell, heaven combine their powers:
And shall we fear this sire of ours?
Then if their minds are idly bent
To doom thee, King, to banishment,
Through twice seven years of exile they

Shall in the lonely forest stay.
I will consume the hopes that fire
The queen Kaikeyí and our sire,
That to her son this check will bring
Advantage, making Bharat king.
The power of Fate will ne'er withstand
The might that arms my vigorous hand;
If danger and distress assail,
My fearless strength will still prevail.
A thousand circling years shall flee:
The forest then thy home shall be,
And thy good sons, succeeding, hold

The empire which their sire controlled.
The royal saints, of old who reigned,
For aged kings this rest ordained:
These to their sons their realm commit
That they, like sires, may cherish it.
O pious soul, if thou decline
The empire which is justly thine,
Lest, while the king distracted lies,
Disorder in the state should rise,
I,—or no mansion may I find
In worlds to hero souls assigned,—
The guardian of thy realm will be,
As the sea-bank protects the sea.
Then cast thine idle fears aside:
With prosperous rites be sanctified.
The lords of earth may strive in vain:
My power shall all their force restrain.
My pair of arms, my warrior's bow
Are not for pride or empty show:
For no support these shafts were made;
And binding up ill suits my blade:
To pierce the foe with deadly breach—
This is the work of all and each.
But small, methinks the love I show
For him I count my mortal foe.
Soon as my trenchant steel is bare,
Flashing its lightning through the air,
I heed no foe, nor stand aghast
Though Indra's self the levin cast.
Then shall the ways be hard to pass,
Where chariots lie in ruinous mass;
When elephant and man and steed
Crushed in the murderous onslaught bleed,
And legs and heads fall, heap on heap,
Beneath my sword's tremendous sweep.
Struck by my keen brand's trenchant blade,
Thine enemies shall fall dismayed,
Like towering mountains rent in twain,
Or lightning clouds that burst in rain.
When armed with brace and glove I stand,
And take my trusty bow in hand,

Who then shall vaunt his might? who dare
Count him a man to meet me there?
Then will I loose my shafts, and strike
Man, elephant, and steed alike:
At one shall many an arrow fly,
And many a foe with one shall die.
This day the world my power shall see,
That none in arms can rival me:
My strength the monarch shall abase,
And set thee, lord, in lordliest place.
These arms which breathe the sandal's scent,
Which golden bracelets ornament,
These hands which precious gifts bestow,
Which guard the friend and smite the foe,
A nobler service shall assay,
And fight in Ráma's cause to-day,
The robbers of thy rights to stay.
Speak, brother, tell thy foeman's name
Whom I, in conquering strife,
May strip of followers and fame,
Of fortune, or of life.
Say, how may all this sea-girt land
Be brought to own thy sway:
Thy faithful servant here I stand
To listen and obey."
Then strove the bride of Raghu's race
Sad Lakshman's heart to cheer,
While slowly down the hero's face,
Unchecked, there rolled a tear.
"The orders of my sire," he cried,
"My will shall ne'er oppose:
I follow still, whate'er betide,
The path which duty shows."

Kausalyá Calmed

But when Kauśalyásaw that he
Resolved to keep his sire's decree,
While tears and sobs her utterance broke,
Her very righteous speech she spoke:
"Can he, a stranger yet to pain,
Whose pleasant words all hearts enchain,
Son of the king and me the queen,
Live on the grain his hands may glean;
Can he, whose slaves and menials eat
The finest cakes of sifted wheat—
Can Ráma in the forest live
On roots and fruit which woodlands give;
Who will believe, who will not fear
When the sad story smites his ear,
That one so dear, so noble held,
Is by the king his sire expelled?
Now surely none may Fate resist,
Which orders all as it may list,
If, Ráma, in thy strength and grace,
The woods become thy dwelling-place.
A childless mother long I grieved,
And many a sigh for offspring heaved,
With wistful longing weak and worn
Till thou at last, my son, wast born.
Fanned by the storm of that desire
Deep in my soul I felt the fire,
Whose offerings flowed from weeping eyes,
With fuel fed of groans and sighs,

While round the flame the smoke grew hot
Of tears because thou camest not.

Now reft of thee, too fiery fierce
The flame of woe my heart will pierce,
As, when the days of spring return,
The sun's hot beams the forest burn.
The mother cow still follows near
The wanderings of her youngling dear.
So close to thine my feet shall be,
Where'er thou goest following thee."

Ráma, the noblest lord of men,
Heard his fond mother's speech, and then
In soothing words like these replied
To the sad queen who wept and sighed:
"Nay, by Kaikeyí's art beguiled,
When I am banished to the wild,
If thou, my mother, also fly,
The aged king will surely die.
When wedded dames their lords forsake,
Long for the crime their souls shall ache.
Thou must not e'en in thought within
Thy bosom frame so dire a sin.
Long as Kakutstha's son, who reigns
Lord of the earth, in life remains,
Thou must with love his will obey:
This duty claims, supreme for aye.
Yes, mother, thou and I must be
Submissive to my sire's decree,
King, husband, sire is he confessed,
The lord of all, the worthiest.
I in the wilds my days will spend
Till twice seven years have reached an end,
Then with great joy will come again,
And faithful to thy hests remain."

Kauśalyá by her son addressed,
With love and passion sore distressed,
Afflicted, with her eyes bedewed,
To Ráma thus her speech renewed:
"Nay, Ráma, but my heart will break
If with these queens my home I make.
Lead me too with thee; let me go

And wander like a woodland roe."
Then, while no tear the hero shed,
Thus to the weeping queen he said:
"Mother, while lives the husband, he
Is woman's lord and deity.
O dearest lady, thou and I
Our lord and king must ne'er deny;
The lord of earth himself have we
Our guardian wise and friend to be.
And Bharat, true to duty's call,
Whose sweet words take the hearts of all,
Will serve thee well, and ne'er forget
The virtuous path before him set.
Be this, I pray, thine earnest care,
That the old king my father ne'er,
When I have parted hence, may know,
Grieved for his son, a pang of woe.
Let not this grief his soul distress,
To kill him with the bitterness.
With duteous care, in every thing,
Love, comfort, cheer the aged king.
Though, best of womankind, a spouse
Keeps firmly all her fasts and vows,
Nor yet her husband's will obeys,
She treads in sin's forbidden ways.
She to her husband's will who bends,
Goes to high bliss that never ends,
Yea, though the Gods have found in her
No reverential worshipper.
Bent on his weal, a woman still
Must seek to do her husband's will:
For Scripture, custom, law uphold
This duty Heaven revealed of old.
Honour true Bráhmans for my sake,
And constant offerings duly make,
With fire-oblations and with flowers,
To all the host of heavenly powers.
Look to the coming time, and yearn
For the glad hour of my return.
And still thy duteous course pursue,
Abstemious, humble, kind, and true.

The highest bliss shalt thou obtain
When I from exile come again,
If, best of those who keep the right,
The king my sire still see the light."

The queen, by Ráma thus addressed,
Still with a mother's grief oppressed,
While her long eyes with tears were dim,
Began once more and answered him:
"Not by my pleading may be stayed
The firm resolve thy soul has made.
My hero, thou wilt go; and none
The stern commands of Fate may shun.
Go forth, dear child whom naught can bend,
And may all bliss thy steps attend.
Thou wilt return, and that dear day
Will chase mine every grief away.
Thou wilt return, thy duty done,
Thy vows discharged, high glory won;
From filial debt wilt thou be free,
And sweetest joy will come on me.
My son, the will of mighty Fate
At every time must dominate,
If now it drives thee hence to stray
Heedless of me who bid thee stay.
Go, strong of arm, go forth, my boy,
Go forth, again to come with joy,
And thine expectant mother cheer
With those sweet tones she loves to hear.
O that the blessed hour were nigh
When thou shalt glad this anxious eye,
With matted hair and hermit dress
returning from the wilderness."
Kauśalyá's conscious soul approved,
As her proud glance she bent
On Ráma constant and unmoved,
Resolved on banishment.
Such words, with happy omens fraught
To her dear son she said,
Invoking with each eager thought
A blessing on his head.

CANTO
XXV

Kausalyá's Blessing

Her grief and woe she cast aside,
Her lips with water purified,
And thus her benison began
That mother of the noblest man:
"If thou wilt hear no words of mine,
Go forth, thou pride of Raghu's line.
Go, darling, and return with speed,
Walking where noble spirits lead.
May virtue on thy steps attend,
And be her faithful lover's friend.
May Those to whom thy vows are paid
In temple and in holy shade,
With all the mighty saints combine
To keep that precious life of thine.
The arms wise Viśvámitra gave
Thy virtuous soul from danger save.
Long be thy life: thy sure defence
Shall be thy truthful innocence,
And that obedience, naught can tire,
To me thy mother and thy sire.
May fanes where holy fires are fed,
Altars with grass and fuel spread,
Each sacrificial ground, each tree,
Rock, lake, and mountain, prosper thee.
Let old Viráj, and Him who made
The universe, combine to aid;
Let Indra and each guardian Lord
Who keeps the worlds, their help afford,
And be thy constant friend the Sun,
Lord Púshá, Bhaga, Aryuman.
Fortnights and seasons, nights and days,

362

Years, months, and hours, protect thy ways,
Vrihaspati shall still be nigh,
The War-God, and the Moon on high,
And Nárad and the sainted seven
Shall watch thee from their starry heaven.
The mountains, and the seas which ring
The world, and Varuṇa the King,
Sky, ether, and the wind, whate'er
Moves not or moves, for thee shall care.
Each lunar mansion be benign,
With happier light the planets shine;
All gods, each light in heaven that glows,
Protect my child where'er he goes.
The twilight hours, the day and night,
Keep in the wood thy steps aright.
Watch, minute, instant, as they flee,
Shall all bring happiness to thee.
Celestials and the Titan brood
Protect thee in thy solitude,
And haunt the mighty wood to bless
The wanderer in his hermit dress.
Fear not, by mightier guardians screened,
The giant or night-roving fiend;
Nor let the cruel race who tear
Man's flesh for food thy bosom scare.
Far be the ape, the scorpion's sting,
Fly, gnat, and worm, and creeping thing.
Thee shall the hungry lion spare,
The tiger, elephant, and bear:
Safe, from their furious might repose,
Safe from the horned buffaloes.
Each savage thing the forests breed,
That love on human flesh to feed,
Shall for my child its rage abate,
When thus its wrath I deprecate.
Blest be thy ways: may sweet success
The valour of my darling bless.
To all that Fortune can bestow,
Go forth, my child, my Ráma, go.
Go forth, O happy in the love
Of all the Gods below, above;

And in those guardian powers confide
Thy paths who keep, thy steps who guide.
May Śukra, Yáma, Sun, and Moon,
And He who gives each golden boon,
Won by mine earnest prayers, be good
To thee, my son, in Daṇḍak wood.
Fire, wind, and smoke, each text and spell
From mouths of holy seers that fell,
Guard Ráma when his limbs he dips,
Or with the stream makes pure his lips!
May the great saints and He, the Lord
Who made the worlds, by worlds adored,
And every God in heaven beside
My banished Ráma keep and guide."

Thus with due praise the long-eyed dame,
Ennobled by her spotless fame,
With wreaths of flowers and precious scent
Worshipped the Gods, most reverent.
A high-souled Bráhman lit the fire,
And offered, at the queen's desire,
The holy oil ordained to burn
For Ráma's weal and safe return.
Kauśalyá best of dames, with care
Set oil, wreaths, fuel, mustard, there.
Then when the rites of fire had ceased,
For Ráma's bliss and health, the priest,
Standing without gave what remained
In general offering, as ordained.

Dealing among the twice-horn train
Honey, and curds, and oil, and grain,
He bade each heart and voice unite
To bless the youthful anchorite.
Then Ráma's mother, glorious dame
Bestowed, to meet the Bráhman's claim,
A lordly fee for duty done:
And thus again addressed her son:

"Such blessings as the Gods o'erjoyed
Poured forth, when Vritra was destroyed,

On Indra of the thousand eyes,
Attend, my child, thine enterprise!
Yea, such as Vinatá once gave
To King Suparṇa swift and brave,
Who sought the drink that cheers the skies,
Attend, my child, thine enterprise!
Yea, such as, when the Amrit rose,
And Indra slew his Daitya foes,
The royal Aditi bestowed
On Him whose hand with slaughter glowed
Of that dire brood of monstrous size,
Attend, my child, thine enterprise!
E'en such as peerless Vishṇu graced,
When with his triple step he paced,
Outbursting from the dwarf's disguise,
Attend, my child, thine enterprise!
Floods, isles, and seasons as they fly,
Worlds, Vedas, quarters of the sky,
Combine, O mighty-armed, to bless
Thee destined heir of happiness!"

The long-eyed lady ceased: she shed
Pure scent and grain upon his head.
And that prized herb whose sovereign power
Preserves from dark misfortune's hour,
Upon the hero's arm she set,
To be his faithful amulet.
While holy texts she murmured low,
And spoke glad words though crushed by woe,
Concealing with obedient tongue
The pangs with which her heart was wrung.
She bent, she kissed his brow, she pressed
Her darling to her troubled breast:
"Firm in thy purpose, go," she cried,
"Go Ráma, and may bliss betide.
Attain returning safe and well,
Triumphant in Ayodhyá, dwell.
Then shall my happy eyes behold
The empire by thy will controlled.
Then grief and care shall leave no trace,
Joy shall light up thy mother's face,

And I shall see my darling reign,
In moonlike glory come again.
These eyes shall fondly gaze on thee
So faithful to thy sire's decree,
When thou the forest wild shalt quit
On thine ancestral throne to sit.
Yea, thou shalt turn from exile back,
Nor choicest blessings ever lack,
Then fill with rapture ever new
My bosom and thy consort's too.
To Śiva and the heavenly host
My worship has been paid,
To mighty saint, to godlike ghost,
To every wandering shade.
Forth to the forest thou wilt hie,
Therein to dwell so long:
Let all the quarters of the sky
Protect my child from wrong."
Her blessings thus the queen bestowed;
Then round him fondly paced,
And often, while her eyes o'erflowed,
Her dearest son embraced.
Kauśalyá's honoured feet he pressed,
As round her steps she bent,
And radiant with her prayers that blessed,
To Sítá's home he went.

Alone With Sítá

S o Ráma, to his purpose true,
To Queen Kauśalyá bade adieu,
Received the benison she gave,
And to the path of duty clave.

As through the crowded street he passed,
A radiance on the way he cast,
And each fair grace, by all approved,
The bosoms of the people moved.

Now of the woeful change no word
The fair Videhan bride had heard;
The thought of that imperial rite
Still filled her bosom with delight.
With grateful heart and joyful thought
The Gods in worship she had sought,
And, well in royal duties learned,
Sat longing till her lord returned,
Not all unmarked by grief and shame
Within his sumptuous home he came,
And hurried through the happy crowd
With eye dejected, gloomy-browed.
Up Sítá sprang, and every limb
Trembled with fear at sight of him.
She marked that cheek where anguish fed,
Those senses care-disquieted.
For, when he looked on her, no more
Could his heart hide the load it bore,
Nor could the pious chief control
The paleness o'er his cheek that stole.
His altered cheer, his brow bedewed
With clammy drops, his grief she viewed,
And cried, consumed with fires of woe,
"What, O my lord, has changed thee so?

Vrihaspati looks down benign,
And the moon rests in Pushya's sign,
As Bráhmans sage this day declare:
Then whence, my lord, this grief and care?
Why does no canopy, like foam
For its white beauty, shade thee home,
Its hundred ribs spread wide to throw
Splendour on thy fair head below?
Where are the royal fans, to grace
The lotus beauty of thy face,
Fair as the moon or wild-swan's wing,

And waving round the new-made king?
Why do no sweet-toned bards rejoice
To hail thee with triumphant voice?
No tuneful heralds love to raise
Loud music in their monarch's praise?
Why do no Bráhmans, Scripture-read,
Pour curds and honey on thy head,
Anointed, as the laws ordain,
With holy rites, supreme to reign?
Where are the chiefs of every guild?
Where are the myriads should have filled
The streets, and followed home their king
With merry noise and triumphing?
Why does no gold-wrought chariot lead
With four brave horses, best for speed?
No elephant precede the crowd
Like a huge hill or thunder cloud,
Marked from his birth for happy fate,
Whom signs auspicious decorate?
Why does no henchman, young and fair,
Precede thee, and delight to bear
Entrusted to his reverent hold
The burthen of thy throne of gold?
Why, if the consecrating rite
Be ready, why this mournful plight?
Why do I see this sudden change,
This altered mien so sad and strange?"

To her, as thus she weeping cried,
Raghu's illustrious son replied:
"Sítá, my honoured sire's decree
Commands me to the woods to flee.
O high-born lady, nobly bred
In the good paths thy footsteps tread,
Hear, Janak's daughter, while I tell
The story as it all befell.
Of old my father true and brave
Two boons to Queen Kaikeyí gave.
Through these the preparations made
For me to-day by her are stayed,
For he is bound to disallow

368

This promise by that earlier vow.
In Daṇḍak forest wild and vast
Must fourteen years by me be passed.
My father's will makes Bharat heir,
The kingdom and the throne to share.
Now, ere the lonely wild I seek,
I come once more with thee to speak.
In Bharat's presence, O my dame,
Ne'er speak with pride of Ráma's name:
Another's eulogy to hear
Is hateful to a monarch's ear.
Thou must with love his rule obey
To whom my father yields the sway.
With love and sweet observance learn
His grace, and more the king's, to earn.
Now, that my father may not break
The words of promise that he spake,
To the drear wood my steps are bent:
Be firm, good Sítá, and content.
Through all that time, my blameless spouse,
Keep well thy fasts and holy vows.
Rise from thy bed at break of day,
And to the Gods due worship pay.
With meek and lowly love revere
The lord of men, my father dear,
And reverence to Kauśalyá show,
My mother, worn with eld and woe:
By duty's law, O best of dames,
High worship from thy love she claims,
Nor to the other queens refuse
Observance, rendering each her dues:
By love and fond attention shown
They are my mothers like mine own.
Let Bharat and Śatrughna bear
In thy sweet love a special share:
Dear as my life, O let them be
Like brother and like son to thee.
In every word and deed refrain
From aught that Bharat's soul may pain:
He is Ayodhyá's king and mine,
The head and lord of all our line.

For those who serve and love them much
With weariless endeavour, touch
And win the gracious hearts of kings.
While wrath from disobedience springs.
Great monarchs from their presence send
Their lawful sons who still offend,
And welcome to the vacant place
Good children of an alien race.
Then, best of women, rest thou here,
And Bharat's will with love revere.
Obedient to thy king remain,
And still thy vows of truth maintain.
To the wide wood my steps I bend:
Make thou thy dwelling here;
See that thy conduct ne'er offend,
And keep my words, my dear."

CANTO
XXVII

★

Sítá's Speech

His sweetly-speaking bride, who best
Deserved her lord, he thus addressed.
Then tender love bade passion wake,
And thus the fair Videhan spake:
"What words are these that thou hast said?
Contempt of me the thought has bred.
O best of heroes, I dismiss
With bitter scorn a speech like this:

Unworthy of a warrior's fame
It taints a monarch's son with shame,
Ne'er to be heard from those who know
The science of the sword and bow.

My lord, the mother, sire, and son
Receive their lots by merit won;
The brother and the daughter find
The portions to their deeds assigned.
The wife alone, whate'er await,
Must share on earth her husband's fate.
So now the king's command which sends
Thee to the wild, to me extends.
The wife can find no refuge, none,
In father, mother, self, or son:
Both here, and when they vanish hence,
Her husband is her sole defence.
If, Raghu's son, thy steps are led
Where Daṇḍak's pathless wilds are spread,
My foot before thine own shall pass
Through tangled thorn and matted grass.
Dismiss thine anger and thy doubt:
Like refuse water cast them out,
And lead me, O my hero, hence—
I know not sin—with confidence.
Whate'er his lot, 'tis far more sweet
To follow still a husband's feet
Than in rich palaces to lie,
Or roam at pleasure through the sky.
My mother and my sire have taught
What duty bids, and trained each thought,
Nor have I now mine ear to turn
The duties of a wife to learn.
I'll seek with thee the woodland dell
And pathless wild where no men dwell,
Where tribes of silvan creatures roam,
And many a tiger makes his home.
My life shall pass as pleasant there
As in my father's palace fair.
The worlds shall wake no care in me;
My only care be truth to thee.
There while thy wish I still obey,
True to my vows with thee I'll stray,
And there shall blissful hours be spent
In woods with honey redolent.

371

In forest shades thy mighty arm
Would keep a stranger's life from harm,
And how shall Sítá think of fear
When thou, O glorious lord, art near?
Heir of high bliss, my choice is made,
Nor can I from my will be stayed.
Doubt not; the earth will yield me roots,
These will I eat, and woodland fruits;
And as with thee I wander there
I will not bring thee grief or care.
I long, when thou, wise lord, art nigh,
All fearless, with delighted eye
To gaze upon the rocky hill,
The lake, the fountain, and the rill;
To sport with thee, my limbs to cool,
In some pure lily-covered pool,
While the white swan's and mallard's wings
Are plashing in the water-springs.
So would a thousand seasons flee
Like one sweet day, if spent with thee.
Without my lord I would not prize
A home with Gods above the skies:
Without my lord, my life to bless,
Where could be heaven or happiness?
Forbid me not: with thee I go
The tangled wood to tread.
There will I live with thee, as though
This roof were o'er my head.
My will for thine shall be resigned;
Thy feet my steps shall guide.
Thou, only thou, art in my mind:
I heed not all beside.
Thy heart shall ne'er by me be grieved;
Do not my prayer deny:
Take me, dear lord; of thee bereaved
Thy Sítá swears to die."
These words the duteous lady spake,
Nor would he yet consent
His faithful wife with him to take
To share his banishment.

The devotee must be content
To live, severely abstinent,
On what the chance of fortune shows:
The wood, my love, is full of woes.
Hunger afflicts him evermore:
The nights are black, the wild winds roar;
And there are dangers worse than those:
The wood, my love, is full of woes.
There creeping things in every form
Infest the earth, the serpents swarm,
And each proud eye with fury glows:
The wood, my love, is full of woes.
The snakes that by the rives hide
In sinuous course like rivers glide,
And line the path with deadly foes:
The wood, my love, is full of woes.
Scorpions, and grasshoppers, and flies
Disturb the wanderer as he lies,
And wake him from his troubled doze:
The wood, my love, is full of woes.
Trees, thorny bushes, intertwined,
Their branched ends together bind,
And dense with grass the thicket grows:
The wood, my dear, is full of woes,
With many ills the flesh is tried,
When these and countless fears beside
Vex those who in the wood remain:
The wilds are naught but grief and pain.
Hope, anger must be cast aside,
To penance every thought applied:
No fear must be of things to fear:
Hence is the wood for ever drear.
Enough, my love: thy purpose quit:
For forest life thou art not fit.
As thus I think on all, I see
The wild wood is no place for thee."

CANTO
XXIX

Sítá's Appeal

Thus Ráma spake. Her lord's address
The lady heard with deep distress,
And, as the tear bedimmed her eye,
In soft low accents made reply:
"The perils of the wood, and all
The woes thou countest to appal,
Led by my love I deem not pain;
Each woe a charm, each loss a gain.
Tiger, and elephant, and deer,
Bull, lion, buffalo, in fear,
Soon as thy matchless form they see,
With every silvan beast will flee.
With thee, O Ráma, I must go:
My sire's command ordains it so.
Bereft of thee, my lonely heart
Must break, and life and I must part.
While thou, O mighty lord, art nigh,
Not even He who rules the sky,
Though He is strongest of the strong,
With all his might can do me wrong.
Nor can a lonely woman left
By her dear husband live bereft.
In my great love, my lord, I ween,
The truth of this thou mayst have seen.
In my sire's palace long ago
I heard the chief of those who know,
The truth-declaring Bráhmans, tell
My fortune, in the wood to dwell.
I heard their promise who divine
The future by each mark and sign,
And from that hour have longed to lead

The forest life their lips decreed.
Now, mighty Ráma, I must share
Thy father's doom which sends thee there;
In this I will not be denied,
But follow, love, where thou shalt guide.
O husband, I will go with thee,
Obedient to that high decree.
Now let the Bráhmans' words be true,
For this the time they had in view.
I know full well the wood has woes;
But they disturb the lives of those
Who in the forest dwell, nor hold
Their rebel senses well controlled.

In my sire's halls, ere I was wed,
I heard a dame who begged her bread
Before my mother's face relate
What griefs a forest life await.
And many a time in sport I prayed
To seek with thee the greenwood shade,
For O, my heart on this is set,
To follow thee, dear anchoret.
May blessings on thy life attend:
I long with thee my steps to bend,
For with such hero as thou art
This pilgrimage enchants my heart.
Still close, my lord, to thy dear side
My spirit will be purified:
Love from all sin my soul will free:
My husband is a God to me.
So, love, with thee shall I have bliss
And share the life that follows this.
I heard a Bráhman, dear to fame,
This ancient Scripture text proclaim:
"The woman whom on earth below
Her parents on a man bestow,
And lawfully their hands unite
With water and each holy rite,
She in this world shall be his wife,
His also in the after life."
Then tell me, O beloved, why

377

Thou wilt this earnest prayer deny,
Nor take me with thee to the wood,
Thine own dear wife so true and good.
But if thou wilt not take me there
Thus grieving in my wild despair,
To fire or water I will fly,
Or to the poisoned draught, and die."

So thus to share his exile, she
Besought him with each earnest plea,
Nor could she yet her lord persuade
To take her to the lonely shade.
The answer of the strong-armed chief
Smote the Videhan's soul with grief,
And from her eyes the torrents came
bathing the bosom of the dame.

CANTO
XXX

The Triumph of Love

The daughter of Videha's king,
While Ráma strove to soothe the sting
Of her deep anguish, thus began
Once more in furtherance of her plan:
And with her spirit sorely tried
By fear and anger, love and pride,
With keenly taunting words addressed
Her hero of the stately breast:
"Why did the king my sire, who reigns
O'er fair Videha's wide domains,
Hail Ráma son with joy unwise,
A woman in a man's disguise?
Now falsely would the people say,
By idle fancies led astray,

That Ráma's own are power and might,
As glorious as the Lord of Light.
Why sinkest thou in such dismay?
What fears upon thy spirit weigh,
That thou, O Ráma, fain wouldst flee
From her who thinks of naught but thee?
To thy dear will am I resigned
In heart and body, soul and mind,
As Sávitrí gave all to one,
Satyaván, Dyumatsena's son.
Not e'en in fancy can I brook
To any guard save thee to look:
Let meaner wives their houses shame,
To go with thee is all my claim.
Like some low actor, deemst thou fit
Thy wife to others to commit—
Thine own, espoused in maiden youth,
Thy wife so long, unblamed for truth?
Do thou, my lord, his will obey
For whom thou losest royal sway,
To whom thou wouldst thy wife confide—
Not me, but thee, his wish may guide.
Thou must not here thy wife forsake,
And to the wood thy journey make,
Whether stern penance, grief, and care,
Or rule or heaven await thee there.
Nor shall fatigue my limbs distress
When wandering in the wilderness:
Each path which near to thee I tread
Shall seem a soft luxurious bed.
The reeds, the bushes where I pass,
The thorny trees, the tangled grass
Shall feel, if only thou be near,
Soft to my touch as skins of deer.
When the rude wind in fury blows,
And scattered dust upon me throws,
That dust, beloved lord, to me
Shall as the precious sandal be.
And what shall be more blest than I,
When gazing on the wood I lie
In some green glade upon a bed

With sacred grass beneath us spread?
The root, the leaf, the fruit which thou
Shalt give me from the earth or bough,
Scanty or plentiful, to eat,
Shall taste to me as Amrit sweet.
As there I live on flowers and roots
And every season's kindly fruits,
I will not for my mother grieve,
My sire, my home, or all I leave.
My presence, love, shall never add
One pain to make the heart more sad;

I will not cause thee grief or care,
Nor be a burden hard to bear.
With thee is heaven, where'er the spot;
Each place is hell where thou art not.
Then go with me, O Ráma; this
Is all my hope and all my bliss.
If thou wilt leave thy wife who still
Entreats thee with undaunted will,
This very day shall poison close
The life that spurns the rule of foes.
How, after, can my soul sustain
The bitter life of endless pain,
When thy dear face, my lord, I miss?
No, death is better far than this.
Not for an hour could I endure
The deadly grief that knows not cure,
Far less a woe I could not shun
For ten long years, and three, and one."

While fires of woe consumed her, such
Her sad appeal, lamenting much;
Then with a wild cry, anguish-wrung,
About her husband's neck she clung.
Like some she-elephant who bleeds
Struck by the hunter's venomed reeds,
So in her quivering heart she felt
The many wounds his speeches dealt.
Then, as the spark from wood is gained,
Down rolled the tear so long restrained:

The crystal moisture, sprung from woe,
From her sweet eyes began to flow,
As runs the water from a pair
Of lotuses divinely fair.
And Sítá's face with long dark eyes,
Pure as the moon of autumn skies,
Faded with weeping, as the buds
Of lotuses when sink the floods.
Around his wife his arms he strained,
Who senseless from her woe remained,
And with sweet words, that bade her wake
To life again, the hero spake:
"I would not with thy woe, my Queen,
Buy heaven and all its blissful sheen.
Void of all fear am I as He,
The self-existent God, can be.
I knew not all thy heart till now,
Dear lady of the lovely brow,
So wished not thee in woods to dwell;
Yet there mine arm can guard thee well.
Now surely thou, dear love, wast made
To dwell with me in green wood shade.
And, as a high saint's tender mind
Clings to its love for all mankind,
So I to thee will ever cling,
Sweet daughter of Videha's king.
The good, of old, O soft of frame,
Honoured this duty's sovereign claim,
And I its guidance will not shun,
True as light's Queen is to the Sun.
I cannot, pride of Janak's line,
This journey to the wood decline:
My sire's behest, the oath he sware,
The claims of truth, all lead me there.
One duty, dear the same for aye,
Is sire and mother to obey:
Should I their orders once transgress
My very life were weariness.
If glad obedience be denied
To father, mother, holy guide,
What rites, what service can be done

That stern Fate's favour may be won?
These three the triple world comprise,
O darling of the lovely eyes.
Earth has no holy thing like these
Whom with all love men seek to please.
Not truth, or gift, or bended knee,
Not honour, worship, lordly fee,
Storms heaven and wins a blessing thence
Like sonly love and reverence.
Heaven, riches, grain, and varied lore,
With sons and many a blessing more,
All these are made their own with ease
By those their elders' souls who please.
The mighty-souled, who ne'er forget,
Devoted sons, their filial debt,
Win worlds where Gods and minstrels are,
And Brahmá's sphere more glorious far.
Now as the orders of my sire,
Who keeps the way of truth, require,
So will I do, for such the way
Of duty that endures for aye:
To take thee, love, to Daṇḍak's wild
My heart at length is reconciled,
For thee such earnest thoughts impel
To follow, and with me to dwell.
O faultless form from feet to brows,
Come with me, as my will allows,
And duty there with me pursue,
Trembler, whose bright eyes thrill me through.
In all thy days, come good come ill,
Preserve unchanged such noble will,
And thou, dear love, wilt ever be
The glory of thy house and me.
Now, beauteous-armed, begin the tasks
The woodland life of hermits asks.
For me the joys of heaven above
Have charms no more without thee, love.
And now, dear Sítá, be not slow:
Food on good mendicants bestow,
And for the holy Bráhmans bring
Thy treasures and each precious thing.

Thy best attire and gems collect,
The jewels which thy beauty decked,
And every ornament and toy
Prepared for hours of sport and joy:
The beds, the cars wherein I ride,
Among our followers, next, divide."

She conscious that her lord approved
Her going, with great rapture moved,

Hastened within, without delay,
Prepared to give their wealth away.

CANTO

XXXI

Lakshman's Prayer

When Lakshmaṇ, who had joined them there,
Had heard the converse of the pair,
His mien was changed, his eyes o'erflowed,
His breast no more could bear its load.
The son of Raghu, sore distressed,
His brother's feet with fervour pressed,
While thus to Sítá he complained,
And him by lofty vows enchained:
"If thou wilt make the woods thy home,
Where elephant and roebuck roam,
I too this day will take my bow
And in the path before thee go.
Our way will lie through forest ground
Where countless birds and beasts are found,
I heed not homes of Gods on high,
I heed not life that cannot die,
Nor would I wish, with thee away,
O'er the three worlds to stretch my sway."

Thus Lakshmaṇ spake, with earnest prayer
His brother's woodland life to share.
As Ráma still his prayer denied
With soothing words, again he cried:
"When leave at first thou didst accord,
Why dost thou stay me now, my lord?
Thou art my refuge: O, be kind,
Leave me not, dear my lord, behind.
Thou canst not, brother, if thou choose
That I still live, my wish refuse."

The glorious chief his speech renewed
To faithful Lakshmaṇ as he sued,
And on the eyes of Ráma gazed
Longing to lead, with hands upraised:
"Thou art a hero just and dear,
Whose steps to virtue's path adhere,
Loved as my life till life shall end,
My faithful brother and my friend.
If to the woods thou take thy way
With Sítá and with me to-day,
Who for Kauśalyá will provide,
And guard the good Sumitrá's side?
The lord of earth, of mighty power,
Who sends good things in plenteous shower,
As Indra pours the grateful rain,
A captive lies in passion's chain.
The power imperial for her son
Has Aśvapati's daughter won,
And she, proud queen, will little heed
Her miserable rivals' need.
So Bharat, ruler of the land,
By Queen Kaikeyí's side will stand,
Nor of those two will ever think,
While grieving in despair they sink.
Now, Lakshmaṇ, as thy love decrees,
Or else the monarch's heart to please,
Follow this counsel and protect
My honoured mother from neglect.
So thou, while not to me alone

Thy great affection will be shown,
To highest duty wilt adhere
By serving those thou shouldst revere.
Now, son of Raghu, for my sake
Obey this one request I make,
Or, of her darling son bereft,
Kaúsalyá has no comfort left."

The faithful Lakshman, thus addressed
In gentle words which love expressed,
To him in lore of language learned,
His answer, eloquent, returned:

"Nay, through thy might each queen will share
Attentive Bharat's love and care,
Should Bharat, raised as king to sway
This noblest realm, his trust betray,
Nor for their safety well provide,
Seduced by ill-suggesting pride,
Doubt not my vengeful hand shall kill
The cruel wretch who counsels ill—
Kill him and all who lend him aid,
And the three worlds in league arrayed.
And good Kaúsalyá well can fee
A thousand champions like to me.
A thousand hamlets rich in grain
The station of that queen maintain.
She may, and my dear mother too,
Live on the ample revenue.
Then let me follow thee: herein:
Is naught that may resemble sin.
So shall I in my wish succeed,
And aid, perhaps, my brother's need.
My bow and quiver well supplied
With arrows hanging at my side,
My hands shall spade and basket bear,
And for thy feet the way prepare.
I'll bring thee roots and berries sweet.
And woodland fare which hermits eat.
Thou shall with thy Videhan spouse

385

Recline upon the mountain's brows;
Be mine the toil, be mine to keep
Watch o'er thee waking or asleep."

Filled by his speech with joy and pride,
Ráma to Lakshmaṇ thus replied:
"Go then, my brother, bid adieu
To all thy friends and retinue.
And those two bows of fearful might,
Celestial, which, at that famed rite,
Lord Varuṇ gave to Janak, king
Of fair Vedeha with thee bring,
With heavenly coats of sword-proof mail,
Quivers, whose arrows never fail,

And golden-hilted swords so keen,
The rivals of the sun in sheen.
Tended with care these arms are all
Preserved in my preceptor's hall.
With speed, O Lakshmaṇ, go, produce,
And bring them hither for our use."
So on a woodland life intent,
To see his faithful friends he went,
And brought the heavenly arms which lay
By Ráma's teacher stored away.
And Raghu's son to Ráma showed
Those wondrous arms which gleamed and glowed,
Well kept, adorned with many a wreath
Of flowers on case, and hilt, and sheath.
The prudent Ráma at the sight
Addressed his brother with delight:
"Well art thou come, my brother dear,
For much I longed to see thee here.
For with thine aid, before I go,
I would my gold and wealth bestow
Upon the Bráhmans sage, who school
Their lives by stern devotion's rule.
And for all those who ever dwell
Within my house and serve me well,
Devoted servants, true and good,
Will I provide a livelihood.

Quick, go and summon to this place
The good Vaśishṭha's son,
Suyajṅa, of the Bráhman race
The first and holiest one.
To all the Bráhmans wise and good
Will I due reverence pay,
Then to the solitary wood
With thee will take my way."

XXXII

The Gift of The Treasures

That speech so noble which conveyed
His friendly wish, the chief obeyed,
With steps made swift by anxious thought
The wise Suyajṅa's home he sought.
Him in the hall of Fire he found,
And bent before him to the ground:
"O friend, to Ráma's house return,
Who now performs a task most stern."
He, when his noonday rites were done,
Went forth with fair Sumitrá's son,
And came to Ráma's bright abode
Rich in the love which Lakshmí showed.
The son of Raghu, with his dame,
With joined hands met him as he came,
Showing to him who Scripture knew
The worship that is Agni's due.
With armlets, bracelets, collars, rings,
With costly pearls on golden strings,
With many a gem for neck and limb
The son of Raghu honoured him.
Then Ráma, at his wife's request,
The wise Suyajṅa thus addressed:

"Accept a necklace too to deck
With golden strings thy spouse's neck.
And Sítá here, my friend, were glad
A girdle to her gift to add.
And many a bracelet wrought with care,
And many an armlet rich and rare,
My wife to thine is fain to give,
Departing in the wood to live.
A bed by skilful workmen made,
With gold and various gems inlaid—
This too, before she goes, would she
Present, O saintly friend, to thee.
Thine be my elephant, so famed,
My uncle's present, Victor named;
And let a thousand coins of gold,
Great Bráhman, with the gift be told."
Thus Ráma spoke: nor he declined
The noble gifts for him designed.
On Ráma, Lakshmaṇ, Sítá he
Invoked all high felicity.

In pleasant words then Ráma gave
His best to Lakshmaṇ prompt and brave,
As Brahmá speaks for Him to hear
Who rules the Gods' celestial sphere:
"To the two best of Bráhmans run;
Agastya bring, and Kuśik's son,
And precious gifts upon them rain,
Like fostering floods upon the grain.
O long-armed Prince of Raghu's line,
Delight them with a thousand kine,
And many a fair and costly gem,
With gold and silver, give to them.
To him, so deep in Scripture, who,
To Queen Kauśalyá, ever true,
Serves her with blessing and respect,
Chief of the Taittiríya sect—
To him, with women-slaves, present
A chariot rich with ornament,
And costly robes of silk beside,
Until the sage be satisfied.

On Chitraratha, true and dear,
My tuneful bard and charioteer,
Gems, robes, and plenteous wealth confer—
Mine ancient friend and minister.
And these who go with staff in hand,
Grammarians trained, a numerous band,
Who their deep study only prize,
Nor think of other exercise,
Who toil not, loving dainty fare,
Whose praises e'en the good declare—
On these be eighty cars bestowed,
And each with precious treasures load.

A thousand bulls for them suffice,
Two hundred elephants of price,
And let a thousand kine beside
The dainties of each meal provide.
The throng who sacred girdles wear,
And on Kauśalyá wait with care—
A thousand golden coins shall please,
Son of Sumitrá, each of these.
Let all, dear Lakshmaṇ of the train
These special gifts of honour gain:
My mother will rejoice to know
Her Bráhmans have been cherished so."

Then Raghu's son addressed the crowd
Who round him stood and wept aloud,
When he to all who thronged the court
Had dealt his wealth for their support:
"In Lakshman's house and mine remain,
And guard them till I come again."
To all his people sad with grief,
In loving words thus spoke their chief,
Then bade his treasure-keeper bring
Gold, silver, and each precious thing.
Then straight the servants went and bore
Back to their chief the wealth in store.
Before the people's eyes it shone,
A glorious pile to look upon.
The prince of men with Lakshman's aid

Parted the treasures there displayed,
Gave to the poor, the young, the old,
And twice-born men, the gems and gold.

A Bráhman, long in evil case,
Named Trijaṭ, born of Garga's race,
Earned ever toiling in a wood
With spade and plough his livelihood.
The youthful wife, his babes who bore,
Their indigence felt more and more.
Thus to the aged man she spake:
"Hear this my word: my counsel take.
Come, throw thy spade and plough away;
To virtuous Ráma go to-day,
And somewhat of his kindness pray."

He heard the words she spoke: around
His limbs his ragged cloth he wound,
And took his journey by the road
That led to Ráma's fair abode.
To the fifth court he made his way;
Nor met the Bráhman check or stay.
Brighu, Angiras could not be
Brighter with saintly light than he.
To Ráma's presence on he pressed,
And thus the noble chief addressed:
"O Ráma, poor and weak am I,
And many children round me cry.
Scant living in the woods I earn:
On me thine eye of pity turn."
And Ráma, bent on sport and jest,
The suppliant Bráhman thus addressed:
"O aged man, one thousand kine,
Yet undistributed, are mine.
The cows on thee will I bestow
As far as thou thy staff canst throw."

The Bráhman heard. In eager haste
He bound his cloth around his waist.
Then round his head his staff he whirled,
And forth with mightiest effort hurled.

390

Cast from his hand it flew, and sank
To earth on Sarjú's farther bank,
Where herds of kine in thousands fed
Near to the well-stocked bullock shed.
And all the cows that wandered o'er
The meadow, far as Sarjú's shore,
At Ráma's word the herdsmen drove
To Trijaṭ's cottage in the grove.
He drew the Bráhman to his breast,
And thus with calming words addressed:
"Now be not angry, Sire. I pray:
This jest of mine was meant in play.
These thousand kine, but not alone.
Their herdsmen too, are all thine own.
And wealth beside I give thee: speak,
Thine shall be all thy heart can seek."

Thus Ráma spake. And Trijaṭ prayed
For means his sacrifice to aid.
And Ráma gave much wealth, required
To speed his offering as desired.

C A N T O

XXXIII

The People's Lament

Thus Sítá and the princes brave
Much wealth to all the Bráhmans gave.
Then to the monarch's house the three
Went forth the aged king to see.
The princes from two servants took
Those heavenly arms of glorious look,
Adorned with garland and with band
By Sítá's beautifying hand.
On each high house a mournful throng

Had gathered ere they passed along,
Who gazed in pure unselfish woe
From turret, roof, and portico.
So dense the crowd that blocked the ways,
The rest, unable there to gaze,
Were fain each terrace to ascend,
And thence their eyes on Ráma bend.
Then as the gathered multitude
On foot their well-loved Ráma viewed,
No royal shade to screen his head,
Such words, disturbed in grief, they said:
"O look, our hero, wont to ride
Leading a host in perfect pride—
Now Lakshmaṇ, sole of all his friends,
With Sítá on his steps attends.
Though he has known the sweets of power,
And poured his gifts in liberal shower,
From duty's path he will not swerve,

But, still his father's truth preserve.
And she whose form so soft and fair
Was veiled from spirits of the air,
Now walks unsheltered from the day,
Seen by the crowds who throng the way.
Ah, for that gently-nurtured form!
How will it fade with sun and storm!
How will the rain, the cold, the heat
Mar fragrant breast and tinted feet!
Surely some demon has possessed
His sire, and speaks within his breast,
Or how could one that is a king
Thus send his dear son wandering?
It were a deed unkindly done
To banish e'en a worthless son:
But what, when his pure life has gained
The hearts of all, by love enchained?
Six sovereign virtues join to grace
Ráma the foremost of his race:
Tender and kind and pure is he,
Docile, religious, passion-free.
Hence misery strikes not him alone:

And Sítá also follow me.
With truthful pleas I sought to bend
Their purpose; but no ear they lend.
Now cast this sorrow from thy heart,
And let us all, great King, depart.
As Brahmá sends his children, so
Let Lakshman, me, and Sítá go."

He stood unmoved, and watched intent
Until the king should grant consent.
Upon his son his eyes he cast,
And thus the monarch spake at last:
"O Ráma, by her arts enslaved,
I gave the boons Kaikeyí craved,
Unfit to reign, by her misled:
Be ruler in thy father's stead."
Thus by the lord of men addressed,
Ráma, of virtue's friends the best,
In lore of language duly learned,
His answer, reverent, thus returned:
"A thousand years, O King, remain
O'er this our city still to reign.
I in the woods my life will lead:
The lust of rule no more I heed.
Nine years and five I there will spend,
And when the portioned days shall end,
Will come, my vows and exile o'er,
And clasp thy feet, my King, once more."

A captive in the snare of truth,
Weeping, distressed with woe and ruth,
Thus spake the monarch, while the queen
Kaikeyí urged him on unseen:
"Go then, O Ráma, and begin
Thy course unvext by fear and sin:
Go, my beloved son, and earn
Success, and joy, and safe return.
So fast the bonds of duty bind.
O Raghu's son, thy truthful mind,
That naught can turn thee back, or guide
Thy will so strongly fortified.

But O, a little longer stay,
Nor turn thy steps this night away,
That I one little day——alas!
One only——with my son may pass.
Me and thy mother do not slight,
But stay, my son, with me to-night;
With every dainty please thy taste,
And seek to-morrow morn the waste.
Hard is thy task, O Raghu's son,
Dire is the toil thou wilt not shun,
Far to the lonely wood to flee,
And leave thy friends for love of me.
I swear it by my truth, believe,
For thee, my son, I deeply grieve,
Misguided by the traitress dame
With hidden guile like smouldering flame.
Now, by her wicked counsel stirred,
Thou fain wouldst keep my plighted word.
No marvel that my eldest born
Would hold me true when I have sworn."

Then Ráma having calmly heard
His wretched father speak each word,
With Lakshman standing by his side
Thus, humbly, to the King replied:
"If dainties now my taste regale,
To-morrow must those dainties fail.
This day departure I prefer
To all that wealth can minister.
O'er this fair land, no longer mine,
Which I, with all her realms, resign,

Her multitudes of men, her grain,
Her stores of wealth, let Bharat reign.
And let the promised boon which thou
Wast pleased to grant the queen ere now,
Be hers in full. Be true, O King,
Kind giver of each precious thing.
Thy spoken word I still will heed,
Obeying all thy lips decreed:
And fourteen years in woods will dwell

With those who live in glade and dell.
No hopes of power my heart can touch,
No selfish joys attract so much
As son of Raghu, to fulfil
With heart and soul my father's will.
Dismiss, dismiss thy needless woe,
Nor let those drowning torrents flow:
The Lord of Rivers in his pride
Keeps to the banks that bar his tide.
Here in thy presence I declare;
By thy good deeds, thy truth, I swear;
Nor lordship, joy, nor lands I prize;
Life, heaven, all blessings I despise.
I wish to see thee still remain
Most true, O King, and free from stain.
It must not, Sire, it must not be:
I cannot rest one hour with thee.
Then bring this sorrow to an end,
For naught my settled will can bend.
I gave a pledge that binds me too,
And to that pledge I still am true.
Kaikeyí bade me speed away:
She prayed me, and I answered yea.
Pine not for me, and weep no more;
The wood for us has joy in store,
Filled with the wild deer's peaceful herds
And voices of a thousand birds.
A father is the God of each,
Yea, e'en of Gods, so Scriptures teach:
And I will keep my sire's decree,
For as a God I honour thee.
O best of men, the time is nigh,
The fourteen years will soon pass by
And to thine eyes thy son restore:
Be comforted, and weep no more.
Thou with thy firmness shouldst support
These weeping crowds who throng the court;
Then why, O chief of high renown,
So troubled, and thy soul cast down?"

Kaikeyí Reproached

Wild with the rage he could not calm,
    Sumantra, grinding palm on palm,
    His head in quick impatience shook,
And sighed with woe he could not brook.
He gnashed his teeth, his eyes were red,
From his changed face the colour fled.
In rage and grief that knew no law,
The temper of the king he saw.
With his word-arrows swift and keen
He shook the bosom of the queen.
With scorn, as though its lightning stroke
Would blast her body, thus he spoke:
"Thou, who, of no dread sin afraid,
Hast Daśaratha's self betrayed,
Lord of the world, whose might sustains
Each thing that moves or fixed remains,
What direr crime is left thee now?
Death to thy lord and house art thou,
Whose cruel deeds the king distress,
Mahendra's peer in mightiness,
Firm as the mountain's rooted steep,
Enduring as the Ocean's deep.
Despise not Daśaratha, he
Is a kind lord and friend to thee.
A loving wife in worth outruns
The mother of ten million sons.
Kings, when their sires have passed away,
Succeed by birthright to the sway.
Ikshváku's son still rules the state,
Yet thou this rule wouldst violate.
Yea, let thy son, Kaikeyí, reign,

Let Bharat rule his sire's domain.
Thy will, O Queen, shall none oppose:
We all will go where Ráma goes.
No Bráhman, scorning thee, will rest
Within the realm thou governest,
But all will fly indignant hence:
So great thy trespass and offence.
I marvel, when thy crime I see,
Earth yawns not quick to swallow thee;
And that the Bráhman saints prepare
No burning scourge thy soul to scare,
With cries of shame to smite thee, bent
Upon our Ráma's banishment.
The Mango tree with axes fell,
And tend instead the Neem tree well,
Still watered with all care the tree
Will never sweet and pleasant be.
Thy mother's faults to thee descend,
And with thy borrowed nature blend.
True is the ancient saw: the Neem
Can ne'er distil a honeyed stream.
Taught by the tale of long ago
Thy mother's hateful sin we know.
A bounteous saint, as all have heard,
A boon upon thy sire conferred,
And all the eloquence revealed
That fills the wood, the flood, the field.
No creature walked, or swam, or flew,
But he its varied language knew.
One morn upon his couch he heard
The chattering of a gorgeous bird.
And as he marked its close intent
He laughed aloud in merriment.
Thy mother furious with her lord,
And fain to perish by the cord,
Said to her husband: "I would know,
O Monarch, why thou laughest so."

The king in answer spake again:
"If I this laughter should explain,
This very hour would be my last,

401

For death, be sure would follow fast."
Again thy mother, flushed with ire,
To Kekaya spake, thy royal sire:
"Tell me the cause; then live or die:
I will not brook thy laugh, not I."
Thus by his darling wife addressed,
The king whose might all earth confessed,
To that kind saint his story told
Who gave the wondrous gift of old.
He listened to the king's complaint,
And thus in answer spoke the saint:
"King, let her quit thy home or die,
But never with her prayer comply."
The saint's reply his trouble stilled,
And all his heart with pleasure filled.
Thy mother from his home he sent,
And days like Lord Kuvera's spent.
So thou wouldst force the king, misled
By thee, in evil paths to tread,
And bent on evil wouldst begin,
Through folly, this career of sin.
Most true, methinks, in thee is shown
The ancient saw so widely known:
The sons their fathers' worth declare
And girls their mothers' nature share.
So be not thou. For pity's sake
Accept the word the monarch spake.
Thy husband's will, O Queen, obey,
And be the people's hope and stay,
O, do not, urged by folly, draw
The king to tread on duty's law.
The lord who all the world sustains,
Bright as the God o'er Gods who reigns.
Our glorious king, by sin unstained,
Will never grant what fraud obtained;
No shade of fault in him is seen:
Let Ráma be anointed, Queen.
Remember, Queen, undying shame
Will through the world pursue thy name,
If Ráma leave the king his sire,
And, banished, to the wood retire.

Come, from thy breast this fever fling:
Of his own realm be Ráma king.
None in this city e'er can dwell
To tend and love thee half so well.
When Ráma sits in royal place,
True to the custom of his race
Our monarch of the mighty bow
A hermit to the woods will go."

Sumantra thus, palm joined to palm,
Poured forth his words of bane and balm,
With keen reproach, with pleading kind,
Striving to move Kaikeyí's mind.
In vain he prayed, in vain reproved,
She heard unsoftened and unmoved.
Nor could the eyes that watched her view
One yielding look, one change of hue.

CANTO
XXXVI

Siddhárth's Speech

Ikshváku's son with anguish torn
For the great oath his lips had sworn,
With tears and sighs of sharpest pain
Thus to Sumantra spake again:
"Prepare thou quick a perfect force,
Cars, elephants, and foot, and horse,
To follow Raghu's scion hence
Equipped with all magnificence.
Let traders with the wealth they sell,
And those who charming stories tell,
And dancing-women fair of face,
The prince's ample chariots grace.
On all the train who throng his courts,

And those who share his manly sports,
Great gifts of precious wealth bestow,
And bid them with their master go.
Let noble arms, and many a wain,
And townsmen swell the prince's train;
And hunters best for woodland skill
Their places in the concourse fill.
While elephants and deer he slays,
Drinking wood honey as he strays,
And looks on streams each fairer yet,
His kingdom he may chance forget.
Let all my gold and wealth of corn
With Ráma to the wilds be borne;
For it will soothe the exile's lot
To sacrifice in each pure spot,
Deal ample largess forth, and meet
Each hermit in his calm retreat.
The wealth shall Ráma with him bear,
Ayodhyá shall be Bharat's share."

As thus Kakutstha's offspring spoke,
Fear in Kaikeyí's breast awoke.
The freshness of her face was dried,
Her trembling tongue was terror-tied.
Alarmed and sad, with bloodless cheek,
She turned to him and scarce could speak:
"Nay, Sire, but Bharat shall not gain
An empty realm where none remain.
My Bharat shall not rule a waste
Reft of all sweets to charm the taste—
The wine-cup's dregs, all dull and dead,
Whence the light foam and life are fled."

Thus in her rage the long-eyed dame
Spoke her dire speech untouched by shame.

Then, answering, Daśaratha spoke:
"Why, having bowed me to the yoke,
Dost thou, must cruel, spur and goad
Me who am struggling with the load?

404

Why didst thou not oppose at first
This hope, vile Queen, so fondly nursed?"

Scarce could the monarch's angry speech
The ears of the fair lady reach,
When thus, with double wrath inflamed,
Kaikeyí to the king exclaimed:

"Sagar, from whom thy line is traced,
Drove forth his eldest son disgraced,
Called Asamanj, whose fate we know:
Thus should thy son to exile go."

"Fie on thee, dame!" the monarch said;
Each of her people bent his head,
And stood in shame and sorrow mute:
She marked not, bold and resolute.
Then great Siddhárth, inflamed with rage,
The good old councillor and sage
On whose wise rede the king relied,
To Queen Kaikeyí thus replied:
"But Asamanj the cruel laid
His hands on infants as they played,
Cast them to Sarjú's flood, and smiled
For pleasure when he drowned a child."
The people saw, and, furious, sped
Straight the the king his sire and said:
"Choose us, O glory of the throne,
Choose us, or Asamanj alone."
"Whence comes this dread?" the monarch cried;
And all the people thus replied:
"In folly, King, he loves to lay
Fierce hands upon our babes at play,
Casts them to Sarjú's flood and joys
To murder our bewildered boys."
With heedful ear the king of men
Heard each complaining citizen.
To please their troubled minds he strove,
And from the state his son he drove.
With wife and gear upon a car

He placed him quick, and sent him far.
And thus he gave commandment, "He
Shall all his days an exile be."
With basket and with plough he strayed
O'er mountain heights, through pathless shade,
Roaming all lands a weary time,
An outcast wretch defiled with crime.
Sagar, the righteous path who held,
His wicked offspring thus expelled.
But what has Ráma done to blame?
Why should his sentence be the same?
No sin his stainless name can dim;
We see no fault at all in him.
Pure as the moon, no darkening blot
On his sweet life has left a spot.
If thou canst see one fault, e'en one,
To dim the fame of Raghu's son,
That fault this hour, O lady, show,
And Ráma to the wood shall go.
To drive the guiltless to the wild,
Truth's constant lover, undefiled,
Would, by defiance of the right,
The glory e'en of Indra blight.
Then cease, O lady, and dismiss
Thy hope to ruin Ráma's bliss,
Or all thy gain, O fair of face,
Will be men's hatred, and disgrace."

The Coats of Bark

Thus spake the virtuous sage: and then
Ráma addressed the king of men.
In laws of meek behaviour bred,
Thus to his sire he meekly said:

"King, I renounce all earthly care,
And live in woods on woodland fare.
What, dead to joys, have I to do
With lordly train and retinue!
Who gives his elephant and yet
Upon the girths his heart will set?
How can a cord attract his eyes
Who gives away the nobler prize?
Best of the good, with me be led
No host, my King with banners spread.
All wealth, all lordship I resign:
The hermit's dress alone be mine.
Before I go, have here conveyed
A little basket and a spade.
With these alone I go, content,
For fourteen years of banishment."

With her own hands Kaikeyí took
The hermit coats of bark, and, "Look,"
She cried with bold unblushing brow
Before the concourse, "Dress thee now."
That lion leader of the brave
Took from her hand the dress she gave,
Cast his fine raiment on the ground,

And round his waist the vesture bound.
Then quick the hero Lakshmaṇ too
His garment from his shoulders threw,
And, in the presence of his sire,
Indued the ascetic's rough attire.
But Sítá, in her silks arrayed,
Threw glances, trembling and afraid,
On the bark coat she had to wear,
Like a shy doe that eyes the snare.
Ashamed and weeping for distress
From the queen's hand she took the dress.
The fair one, by her husband's side
Who matched heaven's minstrel monarch, cried:
"How bind they on their woodland dress,
Those hermits of the wilderness?"

There stood the pride of Janak's race
Perplexed, with sad appealing face.
One coat the lady's fingers grasped,
One round her neck she feebly clasped,
But failed again, again, confused
By the wild garb she ne'er had used.
Then quickly hastening Ráma, pride
Of all who cherish virtue, tied
The rough bark mantle on her, o'er
The silken raiment that she wore.

Then the sad women when they saw
Ráma the choice bark round her draw,
Rained water from each tender eye,
And cried aloud with bitter cry:
"O, not on her, beloved, not
On Sítá falls thy mournful lot.
If, faithful to thy father's will,
Thou must go forth, leave Sítá still.
Let Sítá still remaining here
Our hearts with her loved presence cheer.
With Lakshmaṇ by thy side to aid
Seek thou, dear son, the lonely shade.
Unmeet, one good and fair as she
Should dwell in woods a devotee.

Let not our prayers be prayed in vain:
Let beauteous Sítá yet remain;
For by thy love of duty tied
Thou wilt not here thyself abide."

Then the king's venerable guide
Vaśishṭha, when he saw each coat
Enclose the lady's waist and throat,
Her zeal with gentle words repressed,
And Queen Kaikeyí thus addressed:
"O evil-hearted sinner, shame
Of royal Kekaya's race and name;
Who matchless in thy sin couldst cheat
Thy lord the king with vile deceit;
Lost to all sense of duty, know
Sítá to exile shall not go.
Sítá shall guard, as 'twere her own,
The precious trust of Ráma's throne.
Those joined by wedlock's sweet control
Have but one self and common soul.
Thus Sítá shall our empress be,
For Ráma's self and soul is she.
Or if she still to Ráma cleave
And for the woods the kingdom leave:
If naught her loving heart deter,
We and this town will follow her.
The warders of the queen shall take
Their wives and go for Ráma's sake,
The nation with its stores of grain,
The city's wealth shall swell his train.
Bharat, Śatrughna both will wear
Bark mantles, and his lodging share,
Still with their elder brother dwell
In the wild wood, and serve him well.
Rest here alone, and rule thy state
Unpeopled, barren, desolate;
Be empress of the land and trees,
Thou sinner whom our sorrows please.
The land which Ráma reigns not o'er
Shall bear the kingdom's name no more:
The woods which Ráma wanders through

409

Shall be our home and kingdom too.
Bharat, be sure, will never deign
O'er realms his father yields, to reign.
Nay, if the king's true son he be,
He will not, sonlike, dwell with thee.
Nay, shouldst thou from the earth arise,
And send thy message from the skies,
To his forefathers' custom true
No erring course would he pursue.
So hast thou, by thy grievous fault,
Offended him thou wouldst exalt.
In all the world none draws his breath
Who loves not Ráma, true to death.
This day, O Queen, shalt thou behold
Birds, deer, and beasts from lea and fold
Turn to the woods in Ráma's train.
And naught save longing trees remain."

CANTO

XXXVIII

Care for Kausalyá

Then when the people wroth and sad
Saw Sítá in bark vesture clad,
Though wedded, like some widowed thing,
They cried out, "Shame upon thee, King!"
Grieved by their cry and angry look
The lord of earth at once forsook
All hope in life that still remained,
In duty, self, and fame unstained.
Ikshváku's son with burning sighs
On Queen Kaikeyí bent his eyes,
And said: "But Sítá must not flee
In garments of a devotee.

My holy guide has spoken truth:
Unfit is she in tender youth,

So gently nurtured, soft and fair,
The hardships of the wood to share.
How has she sinned, devout and true,
The noblest monarch's child,
That she should garb of bark indue
And journey to the wild?
That she should spend her youthful days
Amid a hermit band,
Like some poor mendicant who strays
Sore troubled, through the land?
Ah, let the child of Janak throw
Her dress of bark aside,
And let the royal lady go
With royal wealth supplied.
Not such the pledge I gave before,
Unfit to linger here:
The oath, which I the sinner swore
Is kept, and leaves her clear.
Won from her childlike love this too
My instant death would be,
As blossoms on the old bamboo
Destroy the parent tree.
If aught amiss by Ráma done
Offend thee, O thou wicked one,
What least transgression canst thou find
In her, thou worst of womankind?
What shade of fault in her appears,
Whose full soft eye is like the deer's?
What canst thou blame in Janak's child,
So gentle, modest, true, and mild?
Is not one crime complete, that sent
My Ráma forth to banishment?
And wilt thou other sins commit,
Thou wicked one, to double it?
This is the pledge and oath I swore,
What thou besoughtest, and no more,
Of Ráma—for I heard thee, dame—

When he for consecration came.
Now with this limit not content,
In hell should be thy punishment,
Who fain the Maithil bride wouldst press
To clothe her limbs with hermit dress."

Thus spake the father in his woe;
And Ráma, still prepared to go,
To him who sat with drooping head
Spake in return these words and said:

"Just King, here stands my mother dear,
Kauśalyá, one whom all revere.
Submissive, gentle, old is she,
And keeps her lips from blame of thee,
For her, kind lord, of me bereft
A sea of whelming woe is left.
O, show her in her new distress
Still fonder love and tenderness.
Well honoured by thine honoured hand
Her grief for me let her withstand,
Who wrapt in constant thought of me
In me would live a devotee.
Peer of Mahendra, O, to her be kind,
And treat I pray, my gentle mother so,
That, when I dwell afar, her life resigned,
She may not pass to Yáma's realm for woe."

CANTO
XXXIX

Counsel to Sítá

Scarce had the sire, with each dear queen,
Heard Ráma's pleading voice, and seen
His darling in his hermit dress
Ere failed his senses for distress.
Convulsed with woe, his soul that shook,
On Raghu's son he could not look;
Or if he looked with failing eye
He could not to the chief reply.
By pangs of bitter grief assailed,
The long-armed monarch wept and wailed,
Half dead a while and sore distraught,
While Ráma filled his every thought.
"This hand of mine in days ere now
Has reft her young from many a cow,
Or living things has idly slain:
Hence comes, I ween, this hour of pain.
Not till the hour is come to die
Can from its shell the spirit fly.
Death comes not, and Kaikeyí still
Torments the wretch she cannot kill,
Who sees his son before him quit
The fine soft robes his rank that fit,
And, glorious as the burning fire,
In hermit garb his limbs attire.
Now all the people grieve and groan
Through Queen Kaikeyí's deed alone,
Who, having dared this deed of sin,
Strives for herself the gain to win."

He spoke. With tears his eyes grew dim,
His senses all deserted him.

He cried, O Ráma, once, then weak
And fainting could no further speak.
Unconscious there he lay: at length
Regathering his sense and strength,
While his full eyes their torrents shed,
To wise Sumantra thus he said:
"Yoke the light car, and hither lead
Fleet coursers of the noblest breed,
And drive this heir of lofty fate
Beyond the limit of the state.
This seems the fruit that virtues bear,
The meed of worth which texts declare—
The sending of the brave and good
By sire and mother to the wood.'"

He heard the monarch, and obeyed,
With ready feet that ne'er delayed,
And brought before the palace gate
The horses and the car of state.
Then to the monarch's son he sped,
And raising hands of reverence said

That the light car which gold made fair,
With best of steeds, was standing there.
King Daśaratha called in haste
The lord o'er all his treasures placed.
And spoke, well skilled in place and time,
His will to him devoid of crime:
"Count all the years she has to live
Afar in forest wilds, and give
To Sítá robes and gems of price
As for the time may well suffice."
Quick to the treasure-room he went,
Charged by that king most excellent,
Brought the rich stores, and gave them all
To Sítá in the monarch's hall.
The Maithil dame of high descent
Received each robe and ornament,
And tricked those limbs, whose lines foretold
High destiny, with gems and gold.
So well adorned, so fair to view,

A glory through the hall she threw:
So, when the Lord of Light upsprings,
His radiance o'er the sky he flings.
Then Queen Kauśalyá spake at last,
With loving arms about her cast,
Pressed lingering kisses on her head,
And to the high-souled lady said:
"Ah, in this faithless world below
When dark misfortune comes and woe,
Wives, loved and cherished every day,
Neglect their lords and disobey.
Yes, woman's nature still is this:—
After long days of calm and bliss
When some light grief her spirit tries,
She changes all her love, or flies.
Young wives are thankless, false in soul,
With roving hearts that spurn control.
Brooding on sin and quickly changed,
In one short hour their love estranged.
Not glorious deed or lineage fair,
Not knowledge, gift, or tender care
In chains of lasting love can bind
A woman's light inconstant mind.
But those good dames who still maintain
What right, truth, Scripture, rule ordain—
No holy thing in their pure eyes
With one beloved husband vies.
Nor let thy lord my son, condemned
To exile, be by thee contemned,
For be he poor or wealthy, he
Is as a God, dear child, to thee."

When Sítá heard Kauśalyá's speech
Her duty and her gain to teach,
She joined her palms with reverent grace
And gave her answer face to face:
"All will I do, forgetting naught,
Which thou, O honoured Queen, hast taught.
I know, have heard, and deep have stored
The rules of duty to my lord.
Not me, good Queen, shouldst thou include

415

Among the faithless multitude.
Its own sweet light the moon shall leave
Ere I to duty cease to cleave.
The stringless lute gives forth no strain,
The wheelless car is urged in vain;
No joy a lordless dame, although
Blest with a hundred sons, can know.
From father, brother, and from son
A measured share of joy is won:
Who would not honour, love, and bless
Her lord, whose gifts are measureless?
Thus trained to think, I hold in awe
Scripture's command and duty's law.
Him can I hold in slight esteem?
Her lord is woman's God, I deem."
Kauśalyá heard the lady's speech,
Nor failed those words her heart to reach.
Then, pure in mind, she gave to flow
The tear that sprang of joy and woe.
Then duteous Ráma forward came
And stood before the honoured dame,
And joining reverent hands addressed
The queen in rank above the rest:
"O mother, from these tears refrain;
Look on my sire and still thy pain.
To thee my days afar shall fly
As if sweet slumber closed thine eye,
And fourteen years of exile seem
To thee, dear mother, like a dream.
On me returning safe and well,
Girt by my friends, thine eyes shall dwell."

Thus for their deep affection's sake
The hero to his mother spake,
Then to the half seven hundred too,
Wives of his sire, paid reverence due.
Thus Daśaratha's son addressed
That crowd of matrons sore distressed:
"If from these lips, while here I dwelt,
One heedless taunt you e'er have felt,
Forgive me, pray. And now adieu,

416

I bid good-bye to all of you."
Then straight, like curlews' cries, upwent
The voices of their wild lament,
While, as he bade farewell, the crowd
Of royal women wept aloud,
And through the ample hall's extent.
Where erst the sound of tabour, blent
With drum and shrill-toned instrument,
In joyous concert rose,
Now rang the sound of wailing high,
The lamentation and the cry,
The shriek, the choking sob, the sigh
That told the ladies' woes.

CANTO
XL

Ráma's Departure

Then Ráma, Sítá, Lakshmaṇ bent
   At the king's feet, and sadly went
Round him with slow steps reverent.
When Ráma of the duteous heart
Had gained his sire's consent to part,
With Sítá by his side he paid
Due reverence to the queen dismayed.
And Lakshmaṇ, with affection meet,
Bowed down and clasped his mother's feet.
Sumitrá viewed him as he pressed
Her feet, and thus her son addressed:
"Neglect not Ráma wandering there,
But tend him with thy faithful care.
In hours of wealth, in time of woe,
Him, sinless son, thy refuge know.
From this good law the just ne'er swerve,

That younger sons the eldest serve,
And to this righteous rule incline
All children of thine ancient line—
Freely to give, reward each rite,
Nor spare their bodies in the fight.
Let Ráma Daśaratha be,
Look upon Sítá as on me,
And let the cot wherein you dwell
Be thine Ayodhyá. Fare thee well."
Her blessing thus Sumitrá gave
To him whose soul to Ráma clave,
Exclaiming, when her speech was done,
"Go forth, O Lakshmaṇ, go, my son.
Go forth, my son to win success,
High victory and happiness.
Go forth thy foemen to destroy,
And turn again at last with joy."

As Mátali his charioteer
Speaks for the Lord of Gods to hear,
Sumantra, palm to palm applied,
In reverence trained, to Ráma cried:
"O famous Prince, my car ascend,—
May blessings on thy course attend,—
And swiftly shall my horses flee
And place thee where thou biddest me.
The fourteen years thou hast to stay
Far in the wilds, begin to-day;
For Queen Kaikeyí cries, Away."
Then Sítá, best of womankind,
Ascended, with a tranquil mind,
Soon as her toilet task was done,
That chariot brilliant as the sun.
Ráma and Lakshmaṇ true and bold
Sprang on the car adorned with gold.
The king those years had counted o'er,
And given Sítá robes and store
Of precious ornaments to wear
When following her husband there.
The brothers in the car found place
For nets and weapons of the chase,

There warlike arms and mail they laid,
A leathern basket and a spade.
Soon as Sumantra saw the three
Were seated in the chariot, he
Urged on each horse of noble breed,
Who matched the rushing wind in speed.
As thus the son of Raghu went
Forth for his dreary banishment,
Chill numbing grief the town assailed,
All strength grew weak, all spirit failed,
Ayodhyá through her wide extent
Was filled with tumult and lament:
Steeds neighed and shook the bells they bore,
Each elephant returned a roar.
Then all the city, young and old,
Wild with their sorrow uncontrolled,
Rushed to the car, as, from the sun
The panting herds to water run.
Before the car, behind, they clung,
And there as eagerly they hung,
With torrents streaming from their eyes,
Called loudly with repeated cries:
"Listen, Sumantra: draw thy rein;
Drive gently, and thy steeds restrain.
Once more on Ráma will we gaze,
Now to be lost for many days.
The queen his mother has, be sure,
A heart of iron, to endure
To see her godlike Ráma go,
Nor feel it shattered by the blow.
Sítá, well done! Videha's pride,
Still like his shadow by his side;
Rejoicing in thy duty still
As sunlight cleaves to Meru's hill.
Thou, Lakshmaṇ, too, hast well deserved,
Who from thy duty hast not swerved,
Tending the peer of Gods above,
Whose lips speak naught but words of love.
Thy firm resolve is nobly great,
And high success on thee shall wait.
Yea, thou shalt win a priceless meed—

Thy path with him to heaven shall lead."
As thus they spake, they could not hold
The tears that down their faces rolled,
While still they followed for a space
Their darling of Ikshváku's race.

There stood surrounded by a ring
Of mournful wives the mournful king;
For, "I will see once more," he cried,
"Mine own dear son," and forth he hied.
As he came near, there rose the sound
Of weeping, as the dames stood round.
So the she-elephants complain
When their great lord and guide is slain.
Kakutstha's son, the king of men,
The glorious sire, looked troubled then,
As the full moon is when dismayed
By dark eclipse's threatening shade.
Then Daśaratha's son, designed
For highest fate of lofty mind,
Urged to more speed the charioteer,
"Away, away! why linger here?
Urge on thy horses," Rama cried,
And "Stay, O stay," the people sighed.
Sumantra, urged to speed away,
The townsmen's call must disobey,
Forth as the long-armed hero went,

The dust his chariot wheels up sent
Was laid by streams that ever flowed
From their sad eyes who filled the road.
Then, sprung of woe, from eyes of all
The women drops began to fall,
As from each lotus on the lake
The darting fish the water shake.
When he, the king of high renown,
Saw that one thought held all the town,
Like some tall tree he fell and lay,
Whose root the axe has hewn away.
Then straight a mighty cry from those
Who followed Ráma's car arose,

Who saw their monarch fainting there
Beneath that grief too great to bear.
Then "Ráma, Ráma!" with the cry
Of "Ah, his mother!" sounded high,
As all the people wept aloud
Around the ladies' sorrowing crowd.
When Ráma backward turned his eye,
And saw the king his father lie
With troubled sense and failing limb,
And the sad queen, who followed him,
Like some young creature in the net,
That will not, in its misery, let
Its wild eyes on its mother rest,
So, by the bonds of duty pressed,
His mother's look he could not meet.
He saw them with their weary feet,
Who, used to bliss, in cars should ride,
Who ne'er by sorrow should be tried,
And, as one mournful look he cast,
"Drive on," he cried, "Sumantra, fast."
As when the driver's torturing hook
Goads on an elephant, the look
Of sire and mother in despair
Was more than Ráma's heart could bear.
As mother kine to stalls return
Which hold the calves for whom they yearn,
So to the car she tried to run
As a cow seeks her little one.
Once and again the hero's eyes
Looked on his mother, as with cries
Of woe she called and gestures wild,
"O Sítá, Lakshmaṇ, O my child!"
"Stay," cried the king, "thy chariot stay:"
"On, on," cried Ráma, "speed away."
As one between two hosts, inclined
To neither was Sumantra's mind.
But Ráma spake these words again:
"A lengthened woe is bitterest pain.
On, on; and if his wrath grow hot,
Thine answer be, 'I heard thee not.'"
Sumantra, at the chief's behest,

Dismissed the crowd that toward him pressed,
And, as he bade, to swiftest speed
Urged on his way each willing steed.
The king's attendants parted thence,
And paid him heart-felt reverence:
In mind, and with the tears he wept,
Each still his place near Ráma kept.
As swift away the horses sped,
His lords to Daśaratha said:
"To follow him whom thou again
Wouldst see returning home is vain."
With failing limb and drooping mien
He heard their counsel wise:
Still on their son the king and queen
Kept fast their lingering eyes.

CANTO

XLI

The Citizens' Lament

The lion chief with hands upraised
    Was born from eyes that fondly gazed.
    But then the ladies' bower was rent
With cries of weeping and lament:
"Where goes he now, our lord, the sure
Protector of the friendless poor,
In whom the wretched and the weak
Defence and aid were wont to seek?
All words of wrath he turned aside,
And ne'er, when cursed, in ire replied.
He shared his people's woe, and stilled
The troubled breast which rage had filled.
Our chief, on lofty thoughts intent,
In glorious fame preëminent:
As on his own dear mother, thus

He ever looked on each of us.
Where goes he now? His sire's behest,
By Queen Kaikeyí's guile distressed,
Has banished to the forest hence
Him who was all the world's defence.
Ah, senseless King, to drive away
The hope of men, their guard and stay,
To banish to the distant wood
Ráma the duteous, true, and good!"
The royal dames, like cows bereaved
Of their young calves, thus sadly grieved.
The monarch heard them as they wailed,
And by the fire of grief assailed
For his dear son, he bowed his head,
And all his sense and memory fled.

Then were no fires of worship fed,
Thick darkness o'er the sun was spread.
The cows their thirsty calves denied,
And elephants flung their food aside.

Triśanku, Jupiter looked dread,
And Mercury and Mars the red,
In direful opposition met,
The glory of the moon beset.
The lunar stars withheld their light,
The planets were no longer bright,
But meteors with their horrid glare,
And dire Viśákhás lit the air.
As troubled Ocean heaves and raves
When Doom's wild tempest sweeps the waves,
Thus all Ayodhyá reeled and bent
When Ráma to the forest went.
And chilling grief and dark despair
Fell suddenly on all men there.
Their wonted pastime all forgot,
Nor thought of food, or touched it not.
Crowds in the royal street were seen
With weeping eye and troubled mien:
No more a people gay and glad,
Each head and heart was sick and sad.

No more the cool wind softly blew,
The moon no more was fair to view,
No more the sun with genial glow
Cherished the world now plunged in woe.
Sons, brothers, husbands, wedded wives
Forgot the ties that joined their lives;
No thought for kith and kin was spared,
But all for only Ráma cared.
And Ráma's friends who loved him best,
Their minds disordered and distressed.
By the great burthen of their woes
Turned not to slumber or repose.
Like Earth with all her hills bereft
Of Indra's guiding care.
Ayodhyá in her sorrow left
By him, the high souled heir,
Was bowed by fear and sorrow's force,
And shook with many a throe,
While warrior, elephant, and horse
Sent up the cry of woe.

CANTO
XLII

Dasaratha's Lament

While yet the dust was seen afar
That marked the course of Ráma's car,
The glory of Ikshváku's race
Turned not away his eager face.
While yet his duteous son he saw
He could not once his gaze withdraw,
But rooted to the spot remained
With eyes that after Ráma strained.
But when that dust no more he viewed,
Fainting he fell by grief subdued.

To his right hand Kauśalyá went,
And ready aid the lady lent,
While Bharat's loving mother tried
To raise him on the other side.
The king, within whose ordered soul
Justice and virtue held control,
To Queen Kaikeyí turned and said,
With every sense disquieted:
"Touch me not, thou whose soul can plot
All sin. Kaikeyí, touch me not.
No loving wife, no friend to me,
I ne'er again would look on thee;
Ne'er from this day have aught to do
With thee and all thy retinue;
Thee whom no virtuous thoughts restrain,
Whose selfish heart seeks only gain.
The hand I laid in mine, O dame,
The steps we took around the flame,
And all that links thy life to mine
Here and hereafter I resign.
If Bharat too, thy darling son,
Joy in the rule thy art has won,
Ne'er may the funeral offerings paid
By his false hand approach my shade."

Then while the dust upon him hung,
The monarch to Kauśalyá clung,
And she with mournful steps and slow
Turned to the palace, worn with woe.
As one whose hand has touched the fire,
Or slain a Bráhman in his ire,
He felt his heart with sorrow torn
Still thinking of his son forlorn.
Each step was torture, as the road
The traces of the chariot showed,
And as the shadowed sun grows dim
So care and anguish darkened him.
He raised a cry, by woe distraught,
As of his son again he thought.
And judging that the car had sped
Beyond the city, thus he said:

425

"I still behold the foot-prints made
By the good horses that conveyed
My son afar: these marks I see,
But high-souled Ráma, where is he?
Ah me, my son! my first and best,
On pleasant couches wont to rest,
With limbs perfumed with sandal, fanned
By many a beauty's tender hand:
Where will he lie with log or stone
Beneath him for a pillow thrown,
To leave at morn his earthy bed,
Neglected, and with dust o'erspread,
As from the flood with sigh and pant
Comes forth the husband elephant?
The men who make the woods their home
Shall see the long-armed hero roam
Roused from his bed, though lord of all,
In semblance of a friendless thrall.
Janak's dear child who ne'er has met

With aught save joy and comfort yet,
Will reach to-day the forest, worn
And wearied with the brakes of thorn.
Ah, gentle girl, of woods unskilled,
How will her heart with dread be filled
At the wild beasts' deep roaring there,
Whose voices lift the shuddering hair!
Kaikeyí, glory in thy gain,
And, widow queen, begin to reign:
No will, no power to live have I
When my brave son no more is nigh."

Thus pouring forth laments, the king
Girt by the people's crowded ring,
Entered the noble bower like one
New-bathed when funeral rites are done.
Where'er he looked naught met his gaze
But empty houses, courts, and ways.
Closed were the temples: countless feet
No longer trod the royal street,

426

And thinking of his son he viewed
Men weak and worn and woe-subdued.
As sinks the sun into a cloud,
So passed he on, and wept aloud,
Within that house no more to be
The dwelling of the banished three,
Brave Ráma, his Vedehan bride,
And Lakshmaṇ by his brother's side:
Like broad still waters, when the king
Of all the birds that ply the wing
Has swooped from heaven and borne away
The glittering snakes that made them gay.
With choking sobs and voice half spent
The king renewed his sad lament:
With broken utterance faint and low
Scarce could he speak these words of woe:
"My steps to Ráma's mother guide,
And place me by Kauśalyá's side:
There, only there my heart may know
Some little respite from my woe."

The warders of the palace led
The monarch, when his words were said,
To Queen Kauśalyá's bower, and there
Laid him with reverential care.
But while he rested on the bed
Still was his soul disquieted.
In grief he tossed his arms on high
Lamenting with a piteous cry:
"O Ráma, Ráma," thus said he,
"My son, thou hast forsaken me.
High bliss awaits those favoured men
Left living in Ayodhyá then,
Whose eyes shall see my son once more
Returning when the time is o'er."
Then came the night, whose hated gloom
Fell on him like the night of doom.
At midnight Daśaratha cried
To Queen Kauśalyá by his side:
"I see thee not, Kauśalyá; lay

427

Thy gentle hand in mine, I pray.
When Ráma left his home my sight
Went with him, nor returns to-night."

CANTO

XLIII

Kausalyá's Lament

Kauśalyá saw the monarch lie
With drooping frame and failing eye,
And for her banished son distressed
With these sad words her lord addressed:
"Kaikeyí, cruel, false, and vile
Has cast the venom of her guile
On Ráma lord of men, and she
Will ravage like a snake set free;
And more and more my soul alarm,
Like a dire serpent bent on harm,
For triumph crowns each dark intent,
And Ráma to the wild is sent.
Ah, were he doomed but here to stray
Begging his food from day to day,
Or do, enslaved, Kaikeyí's will,
This were a boon, a comfort still.
But she, as chose her cruel hate,
Has hurled him from his high estate,
As Bráhmans when the moon is new
Cast to the ground the demons' due.
The long-armed hero, like the lord
Of Nágas, with his bow and sword
Begins, I ween, his forest life
With Lakshmaṇ and his faithful wife.
Ah, how will fare the exiles now,
Whom, moved by Queen Kaikeyí, thou
Hast sent in forests to abide,

Bred in delights, by woe untried?
Far banished when their lives are young,
With the fair fruit before them hung,
Deprived of all their rank that suits,
How will they live on grain and roots?
O, that my years of woe were passed,
And the glad hour were come at last
When I shall see my children dear,
Ráma, his wife, and Lakshman here!
When shall Ayodhyá, wild with glee,
Again those mighty heroes see,
And decked with wreaths her banners wave
To welcome home the true and brave?
When will the beautiful city view
With happy eyes the lordly two
Returning, joyful as the main
When the dear moon is full again?
When, like some mighty bull who leads
The cow exulting through the meads,
Will Ráma through the city ride,
Strong-armed, with Sítá at his side?
When will ten thousand thousand meet
And crowd Ayodhyá's royal street,
And grain in joyous welcome throw
Upon my sons who tame the foe?
When with delight shall youthful bands
Of Bráhman maidens in their hands

Bear fruit and flowers in goodly show,
And circling round Ayodhyá go?
With ripened judgment of a sage,
And godlike in his blooming age,
When shall my virtuous son appear,
Like kindly rain, our hearts to cheer?
Ah, in a former life, I ween,
This hand of mine, most base and mean,
Has dried the udders of the kine
And left the thirsty calves to pine.
Hence, as the lion robs the cow,
Kaikeyí makes me childless now,
Exulting from her feebler foe

429

To rend the son she cherished so.
I had but him, in Scripture skilled,
With every grace his soul was filled.
Now not a joy has life to give,
And robbed of him I would not live:
Yea, all my days are dark and drear
If he, my darling, be not near,
And Lakshmaṇ brave, my heart to cheer.
As for my son I mourn and yearn,
The quenchless flames of anguish burn
And kill me with the pain,
As in the summer's noontide blaze
The glorious Day-God with his rays
Consumes the parching plain."

CANTO
XLIV

Sumitrá's Speech

Kauśalyá ceased her sad lament,
    Of beauteous dames most excellent.
    Sumitrá who to duty clave,
In righteous words this answer gave:
"Dear Queen, all noble virtues grace
Thy son, of men the first in place.
Why dost thou shed these tears of woe
With bitter grief lamenting so?
If Ráma, leaving royal sway
Has hastened to the woods away,
'Tis for his high-souled father's sake
That he his premise may not break.
He to the path of duty clings
Which lordly fruit hereafter brings—
The path to which the righteous cleave—
For him, dear Queen, thou shouldst not grieve.

And Lakshmaṇ too, the blameless-souled,
The same high course with him will hold,
And mighty bliss on him shall wait,
So tenderly compassionate.
And Sítá, bred with tender care,
Well knows what toils await her there,
But in her love she will not part
From Ráma of the virtuous heart.
Now has thy son through all the world
The banner of his fame unfurled;
True, modest, careful of his vow,
What has he left to aim at now?
The sun will mark his mighty soul,
His wisdom, sweetness, self-control,
Will spare from pain his face and limb,
And with soft radiance shine for him.
For him through forest glades shall spring
A soft auspicious breeze, and bring
Its tempered heat and cold to play
Around him ever night and day.
The pure cold moonbeams shall delight
The hero as he sleeps at night,
And soothe him with the soft caress
Of a fond parent's tenderness.
To him, the bravest of the brave,
His heavenly arms the Bráhman gave,
When fierce Suváhu dyed the plain
With his life-blood by Ráma slain.
Still trusting to his own right arm
Thy hero son will fear no harm:
As in his father's palace, he
In the wild woods will dauntless be.
Whene'er he lets his arrows fly
His stricken foemen fall and die:
And is that prince of peerless worth
Too weak to keep and sway the earth?
His sweet pure soul, his beauty's charm,
His hero heart, his warlike arm,
Will soon redeem his rightful reign
When from the woods he comes again.
The Bráhmans on the prince's head

431

King-making drops shall quickly shed,
And Sítá, Earth, and Fortune share
The glories which await the heir.
For him, when forth his chariot swept,
The crowd that thronged Ayodhyá wept,
With agonizing woe distressed.
With him in hermít's mantle dressed
In guise of Sítá Lakshmí went,
And none his glory may prevent.
Yea, naught to him is high or hard,
Before whose steps, to be his guard,
Lakshmaṇ, the best who draws the bow,
With spear, shaft, sword rejoiced to go.
His wanderings in the forest o'er,
Thine eyes shall see thy son once more,
Quit thy faint heart, thy grief dispel,
For this, O Queen, is truth I tell.
Thy son returning, moonlike, thence,
Shall at thy feet do reverence,
And, blest and blameless lady, thou
Shalt see his head to touch them bow,
Yea, thou shalt see thy son made king
When he returns with triumphing,
And how thy happy eyes will brim
With tears of joy to look on him!
Thou, blameless lady, shouldst the whole
Of the sad people here console:
Why in thy tender heart allow
This bitter grief to harbour now?
As the long banks of cloud distil
Their water when they see the hill,

So shall the drops of rapture run
From thy glad eyes to see thy son
Returning, as he lowly bends
To greet thee, girt by all his friends."

Thus soothing, kindly eloquent,
With every hopeful argument
Kauśalyá's heart by sorrow rent,
Fair Queen Sumitrá ceased.

432

Kauśalyá heard each pleasant plea,
And grief began to leave her free,
As the light clouds of autumn flee,
Their watery stores decreased.

CANTO
XLV

The Tamasá

Their tender love the people drew
To follow Ráma brave and true,
The high-souled hero, as he went
Forth from his home to banishment.
The king himself his friends obeyed,
And turned him homeward as they prayed.
But yet the people turned not back,
Still close on Ráma's chariot track.
For they who in Ayodhyá dwelt
For him such fond affection felt,
Decked with all grace and glories high,
The dear full moon of every eye.
Though much his people prayed and wept,
Kakutstha's son his purpose kept,
And still his journey would pursue
To keep the king his father true.
Deep in the hero's bosom sank
Their love, whose signs his glad eye drank.
He spoke to cheer them, as his own
Dear children, in a loving tone:
"If ye would grant my fond desire,
Give Bharat now that love entire
And reverence shown to me by all
Who dwell within Ayodhyá's wall.
For he, Kaikeyí's darling son,
His virtuous career will run,

433

And ever bound by duty's chain
Consult your weal and bliss and gain.
In judgment old, in years a child,
With hero virtues meek and mild,
A fitting lord is he to cheer
His people and remove their fear.
In him all kingly gifts abound,
More noble than in me are found:
Imperial prince, well proved and tried—
Obey him as your lord and guide.
And grant, I pray, the boon I ask:
To please the king be still your task,
That his fond heart, while I remain
Far in the wood, may feel no pain."

The more he showed his will to tread
The path where filial duty led,
The more the people, round him thronged,
For their dear Ráma's empire longed.
Still more attached his followers grew,
As Ráma, with his brother, drew
The people with his virtues' ties,
Lamenting all with tear-dimmed eyes.
The saintly twice-born, triply old
In glory, knowledge, seasons told,
With hoary heads that shook and bowed,
Their voices raised and spake aloud:
"O steeds, who best and noblest are,
Who whirl so swiftly Ráma's car,
Go not, return: we call on you:
Be to your master kind and true.
For speechless things are swift to hear,
And naught can match a horse's ear,
O generous steeds, return, when thus
You hear the cry of all of us.
Each vow he keeps most firm and sure,
And duty makes his spirit pure.
Back with our chief! not wood-ward hence;
Back to his royal residence!"

434

Soon as he saw the aged band.
Exclaiming in their misery, stand,
And their sad cries around him rang,
Swift from his chariot Ráma sprang.
Then, still upon his journey bent,
With Sítá and with Lakshmaṇ went
The hero by the old men's side
Suiting to theirs his shortened stride.
He could not pass the twice-born throng
As weariedly they walked along:
With pitying heart, with tender eye,
He could not in his chariot fly.
When the steps of Ráma viewed
That still his onward course pursued,
Woe shook the troubled heart of each,
And burnt with grief they spoke this speech—

"With thee, O Ráma, to the wood
All Bráhmans go and Bráhmanhood:
Borne on our aged shoulders, see,
Our fires of worship go with thee.
Bright canopies that lend their shade
In Vájapeya rites displayed,
In plenteous store are borne behind
Like cloudlets in the autumn wind.
No shelter from the sun hast thou,
And, lest his fury burn thy brow,
These sacrificial shades we bear
Shall aid thee in the noontide glare.
Our hearts, who ever loved to pore
On sacred text and Vedic lore,
Now all to thee, beloved, turn,
And for a life in forests yearn.
Deep in our aged bosoms lies
The Vedas' lore, the wealth we prize,
There still, like wives at home, shall dwell,
Whose love and truth protect them well.

To follow thee our hearts are bent;
We need not plan or argument.

435

All else in duty's law we slight,
For following thee is following right.
O noble Prince, retrace thy way:
O, hear us, Ráma, as we lay,
With many tears and many prayers,
Our aged heads and swan-white hairs
Low in the dust before thy feet;
O, hear us, Ráma, we entreat.
Full many of these who with thee run,
Their sacred rites had just begun.
Unfinished yet those rites remain;
But finished if thou turn again.
All rooted life and things that move
To thee their deep affection prove.
To them, when warmed by love, they glow
And sue to thee, some favour show,
Each lowly bush, each towering tree
Would follow too for love of thee.
Bound by its root it must remain;
But—all it can—its boughs complain,
As when the wild wind rushes by
It tells its woe in groan and sigh.
No more through air the gay birds flit,
But, foodless, melancholy sit
Together on the branch and call
To thee whose kind heart feels for all."

As wailed the aged Bráhmans, bent
To turn him back, with wild lament,
Seemed Tamasá herself to aid,
Checking his progress, as they prayed.
Sumantra from the chariot freed
With ready hand each weary steed;
He groomed them with the utmost heed,

Their limbs he bathed and dried,
Then led them forth to drink and feed
At pleasure in the grassy mead
That fringed the river side.

CANTO
XLVI

The Halt

When Ráma, chief of Raghu's race,
   Arrived at that delightful place,
   He looked on Sítá first, and then
To Lakshmaṇ spake the lord of men:
"Now first the shades of night descend
Since to the wilds our steps we bend.
Joy to thee, brother! do not grieve
For our dear home and all we leave.
The woods unpeopled seem to weep
Around us, as their tenants creep
Or fly to lair and den and nest,
Both bird and beast, to seek their rest.
Methinks Ayodhyá's royal town
Where dwells my sire of high renown,
With all her men and dames to-night
Will mourn us vanished from their sight,
For, by his virtues won, they cling
In fond affection to their king,
And thee and me, O brave and true,
And Bharat and Śatrughna too.
I for my sire and mother feel
Deep sorrow o'er my bosom steal,
Lest mourning us, oppressed with fears,
They blind their eyes with endless tears.
Yet Bharat's duteous love will show
Sweet comfort in their hours of woe,
And with kind words their hearts sustain,
Suggesting duty, bliss, and gain.
I mourn my parents now no more:
I count dear Bharat's virtues o'er,

And his kind love and care dispel
The doubts I had, and all is well.
And thou thy duty wouldst not shun,
And, following me, hast nobly done;
Else, bravest, I should need a band
Around my wife as guard to stand.
On this first night, my thirst to slake,
Some water only will I take:
Thus, brother, thus my will decides,
Though varied store the wood provides."

Thus having said to Lakshmaṇ, he
Addressed in turn Sumantra: "Be
Most diligent to-night, my friend,
And with due care thy horses tend."
The sun had set: Sumantra tied
His noble horses side by side,
Gave store of grass with liberal hand,
And rested near them on the strand.
Each paid the holy evening rite,
And when around them fell the night,
The charioteer, with Lakshmaṇ's aid,
A lowly bed for Ráma laid.
To Lakshmaṇ Ráma bade adieu,
And then by Sítá's side he threw
His limbs upon the leafy bed
Their care upon the bank had spread.
When Lakshmaṇ saw the couple slept,
Still on the strand his watch he kept,
Still with Sumantra there conversed,
And Ráma's varied gifts rehearsed.
All night he watched, nor sought repose,
Till on the earth the sun arose:
With him Sumantra stayed awake,
And still of Ráma's virtues spake.
Thus, near the river's grassy shore
Which herds unnumbered wandered o'er,
Repose, untroubled, Ráma found,
And all the people lay around.
The glorious hero left his bed,

Looked on the sleeping crowd, and said
To Lakshmaṇ, whom each lucky line
Marked out for bliss with surest sign:

"O brother Lakshmaṇ, look on these
Reclining at the roots of trees;
All care of house and home resigned,
Caring for us with heart and mind,
These people of the city yearn

To see us to our home return:
To quit their lives will they consent,
But never leave their firm intent.
Come, while they all unconscious sleep,
Let us upon the chariot leap,
And swiftly on our journey speed
Where naught our progress may impede,
That these fond citizens who roam
Far from Ikshváku's ancient home,
No more may sleep 'neath bush and tree,
Following still for love of me.
A prince with tender care should heal
The self-brought woes his people feel,
And never let his subjects share
The burthen he is forced to bear."

Then Lakshmaṇ to the chief replied,
Who stood like Justice by his side:
"Thy rede, O sage, I well commend:
Without delay the car ascend."
Then Ráma to Sumantra spoke:
"Thy rapid steeds, I pray thee, yoke.
Hence to the forest will I go:
Away, my lord, and be not slow."

Sumantra, urged to utmost speed,
Yoked to the car each generous steed,
And then, with hand to hand applied,
He came before the chief and cried:
"Hail, Prince, whom mighty arms adorn,

Hail, bravest of the chariot-borne!
With Sítá and thy brother thou
Mayst mount: the car is ready now."

The hero clomb the car with haste:
His bow and gear within were placed,
And quick the eddying flood he passed
Of Tamasá whose waves run fast.
Soon as he touched the farther side,
That strong-armed hero, glorified,
He found a road both wide and clear,
Where e'en the timid naught could fear.
Then, that the crowd might be misled,
Thus Ráma to Sumantra said:
"Speed north a while, then hasten back,
Returning in thy former track,
That so the people may not learn
The course I follow: drive and turn."
Sumantra, at the chief's behest,
Quick to the task himself addressed;
Then near to Ráma came, and showed
The chariot ready for the road.
With Sítá, then, the princely two,
Who o'er the line of Raghu threw
A glory ever bright and new,
Upon the chariot stood.
Sumantra fast and faster drove
His horses, who in fleetness strove
Still onward to the distant grove,
The hermit-haunted wood.

CANTO

XLVII

The Citizens' Return

The people, when the morn shone fair,
Arose to find no Ráma there.
Then fear and numbing grief subdued
The senses of the multitude.
The woe-born tears were running fast
As all around their eyes they cast,
And sadly looked, but found no trace
Of Ráma, searching every place.
Bereft of Ráma good and wise,
With drooping cheer and weeping eyes,
Each woe-distracted sage gave vent
To sorrow in his wild lament:
"Woe worth the sleep that stole our sense
With its beguiling influence,
That now we look in vain for him
Of the broad chest and stalwart limb!
How could the strong-armed hero, thus
Deceiving all, abandon us?
His people so devoted see,
Yet to the woods, a hermit, flee?
How can he, wont our hearts to cheer,
As a fond sire his children dear,—
How can the pride of Raghu's race
Fly from us to some desert place!
Here let us all for death prepare,
Or on the last great journey fare;
Of Ráma our dear lord bereft,
What profit in our lives is left?
Huge trunks of trees around us lie,
With roots and branches sere and dry,
Come let us set these logs on fire

441

And throw our bodies on the pyre.
What shall we speak? How can we say
We followed Ráma on his way,
The mighty chief whose arm is strong,
Who sweetly speaks, who thinks no wrong?
Ayodhyá's town with sorrow dumb,
Without our lord will see us come,
And hopeless misery will strike
Elder, and child, and dame alike.
Forth with that peerless chief we came,
Whose mighty heart is aye the same:
How, reft of him we love, shall we
Returning dare that town to see?"

Complaining thus with varied cry
They tossed their aged arms on high,
And their sad hearts with grief were wrung,
Like cows who sorrow for their young.
A while they followed on the road
Which traces of his chariot showed,
But when at length those traces failed,
A deep despair their hearts assailed.

The chariot marks no more discerned,
The hopeless sages backward turned:
"Ah, what is this? What can we more?
Fate stops the way, and all is o'er."
With wearied hearts, in grief and shame
They took the road by which they came,
And reached Ayodhyá's city, where
From side to side was naught but care.
With troubled spirits quite cast down
They looked upon the royal town,
And from their eyes, oppressed with woe,
Their tears again began to flow.
Of Ráma reft, the city wore
No look of beauty as before,
Like a dull river or a lake
By Garuḍ robbed of every snake.
Dark, dismal as the moonless sky,
Or as a sea whose bed is dry,

So sad, to every pleasure dead,
They saw the town, disquieted.
On to their houses, high and vast,
Where stores of precious wealth were massed,
The melancholy Bráhmans passed,
  Their hearts with anguish cleft:
Aloof from all, they came not near
To stranger or to kinsman dear,
Showing in faces blank and drear
  That not one joy was left.

CANTO

XLVIII

The Women's Lament

When those who forth with Ráma went
  Back to the town their steps had bent,
  It seemed that death had touched and chilled
Those hearts which piercing sorrow filled.
Each to his several mansion came,
And girt by children and his dame,
From his sad eyes the water shed
That o'er his cheek in torrents spread.
All joy was fled: oppressed with cares
No bustling trader showed his wares.
Each shop had lost its brilliant look,
Each householder forbore to cook.
No hand with joy its earnings told,
None cared to win a wealth of gold,
And scarce the youthful mother smiled
To see her first, her new-born child.
In every house a woman wailed,
And her returning lord assailed
With keen taunt piercing like the steel
That bids the tusked monster kneel:

"What now to them is wedded dame,
What house and home and dearest aim,
Or son, or bliss, or gathered store,
Whose eyes on Ráma look no more!
There is but one in all the earth,
One man alone of real worth,
Lakshmaṇ, who follows, true and good,
Ráma, with Sítá, through the wood.
Made holy for all time we deem
Each pool and fountain, lake and stream,
If great Kakutstha's son shall choose
Their water for his bath to use.
Each forest, dark with lovely trees,
Shall yearn Kakutstha's son to please;
Each mountain peak and woody hill,
Each mighty flood and mazy rill,
Each rocky height, each shady grove
Where the blest feet of Ráma rove,
Shall gladly welcome with the best
Of all they have their honoured guest.
The trees that clustering blossoms bear,
And bright-hued buds to gem their hair,
The heart of Ráma shall delight,
And cheer him on the breezy height.
For him the upland slopes will show
The fairest roots and fruit that grow,
And all their wealth before him fling
Ere the due hour of ripening.
For him each earth-upholding hill
Its crystal water shall distil,
And all its floods shall be displayed
In many a thousand-hued cascade.
Where Ráma stands is naught to fear,
No danger comes if he be near;
For all who live on him depend,
The world's support, and lord, and friend.
Ere in too distant wilds he stray,
Let us to Ráma speed away,
For rich reward on those will wait
Who serve a prince of soul so great.

We will attend on Sítá there;
Be Raghu's son your special care."

The city dames, with grief distressed,
Thus once again their lords addressed:
"Ráma shall be your guard and guide,
And Sítá will for us provide.
For who would care to linger here,
Where all is sad and dark and drear?
Who, mid the mourners, hope for bliss
In a poor soulless town like this?
If Queen Kaikeyí's treacherous sin,
Our lord expelled, the kingdom win,
We heed not sons or golden store,
Our life itself we prize no more.
If she, seduced by lust of sway,
Her lord and son could cast away,
Whom would she leave unharmed, the base
Defiler of her royal race?
We swear it by our children dear,
We will not dwell as servants here;
If Queen Kaikeyí live to reign,
We will not in her realm remain.
Bowed down by her oppressive hand,
The helpless, lordless, godless land,
Cursed for Kaikeyí's guilt will fall,
And swift destruction seize it all.

For, Ráma forced from home to fly,
The king his sire will surely die,
And when the king has breathed his last
Ruin will doubtless follow fast.
Sad, robbed of merits, drug the cup
And drink the poisoned mixture up,
Or share the exiled Ráma's lot,
Or seek some land that knows her not.
No reason, but a false pretence
Drove Ráma, Sítá, Lakshmaṇ hence,
And we to Bharat have been given
Like cattle to the shambles driven."

While in each house the women, pained
At loss of Ráma, still complained,
Sank to his rest the Lord of Day,
And night through all the sky held sway.
The fires of worship all were cold,
No text was hummed, no tale was told,
And shades of midnight gloom came down
Enveloping the mournful town.
Still, sick at heart, the women shed,
As for a son or husband fled,
For Ráma tears, disquieted:
No child was loved as he.
And all Ayodhyá, where the feast,
Music, and song, and dance had ceased,
And merriment and glee,
Where every merchant's store was closed
That erst its glittering wares exposed,
Was like a dried up sea.

CANTO
XLIX

The Crossing of the Rivers

N ow Ráma, ere the night was fled,
O'er many a league of road had sped,
Till, as his course he onward held,
The morn the shades of night dispelled.
The rites of holy dawn he paid,
And all the country round surveyed.
He saw, as still he hurried through
With steeds which swift as arrows flew,
Hamlets and groves with blossoms fair,
And fields which showed the tillers' care,
While from the clustered dwellings near
The words of peasants reached his ear:

"Fie on our lord the king, whose soul
Is yielded up to love's control!
Fie on the vile Kaikeyí! Shame
On that malicious sinful dame,
Who, keenly bent on cruel deeds,
No bounds of right and virtue heeds,
But with her wicked art has sent
So good a prince to banishment,
Wise, tender-hearted, ruling well
His senses, in the woods to dwell.
Ah cruel king! his heart of steel
For his own son no love could feel,
Who with the sinless Ráma parts,
The darling of the people's hearts."

These words he heard the peasants say,
Who dwelt in hamlets by the way,
And, lord of all the realm by right,
Through Kośala pursued his flight.
Through the auspicious flood, at last,
Of Vedaśrutí's stream he passed,
And onward to the place he sped
By Saint Agastya tenanted.
Still on for many an hour he hied,
And crossed the stream whose cooling tide
Rolls onward till she meets the sea,
The herd-frequented Gomatí.
Borne by his rapid horses o'er,
He reached that river's further shore.
And Syandiká's, whose swan-loved stream
Resounded with the peacock's scream.
Then as he journeyed on his road
To his Videhan bride he showed
The populous land which Manu old
To King Ikshváku gave to hold.
The glorious prince, the lord of men
Looked on the charioteer, and then
Voiced like a wild swan, loud and clear,
He spake these words and bade him hear:
"When shall I, with returning feet
My father and my mother meet?

When shall I lead the hunt once more
In bloomy woods on Sarjú's shore?
Most eagerly I long to ride
Urging the chase on Sarjú's side.
For royal saints have seen no blame
In this, the monarch's matchless game."

Thus speeding on,—no rest or stay,—
Ikshváku's son pursued his way.
Oft his sweet voice the silence broke,
And thus on varied themes he spoke.

CANTO
L

The Halt Under the Ingudí

So through the wide and fair extent
Of Kośala the hero went.
Then toward Ayodhyá back he gazed,
And cried, with suppliant hands upraised:
"Farewell, dear city, first in place,
Protected by Kakutstha's race!
And Gods, who in thy temples dwell,
And keep thine ancient citadel!
I from his debt my sire will free,
Thy well-loved towers again will see,
And, coming from my wild retreat,
My mother and my father meet."

Then burning grief inflamed his eye,
As his right arm he raised on high,
And, while hot tears his cheek bedewed,
Addressed the mournful multitude:
"By love and tender pity moved,
Your love for me you well have proved;

Now turn again with joy, and win
Success in all your hands begin."
Before the high souled chief they bent,
With circling steps around him went,
And then with bitter wailing, they
Departed each his several way.
Like the great sun engulfed by night,
The hero sped beyond their sight,
While still the people mourned his fate
And wept aloud disconsolate.
The car-borne chieftain passed the bound
Of Kośala's delightful ground,
Where grain and riches bless the land,
And people give with liberal hand:
A lovely realm unvexed by fear,
Where countless shrines and stakes appear:
Where mango-groves and gardens grow,
And streams of pleasant water flow:
Where dwells content a well-fed race,
And countless kine the meadows grace:
Filled with the voice of praise and prayer:
Each hamlet worth a monarch's care.
Before him three-pathed Gangá rolled
Her heavenly waters bright and cold;
O'er her pure breast no weeds were spread,
Her banks were hermit-visited.
The car-borne hero saw the tide
That ran with eddies multiplied,
And thus the charioteer addressed:
"Here on the bank to-day we rest.
Not distant from the river, see!
There grows a lofty Ingudí
With blossoms thick on every spray:
There rest we, charioteer, to-day.
I on the queen of floods will gaze,
Whose holy stream has highest praise,
Where deer, and bird, and glittering snake,
God, Daitya, bard their pastime take."

Sumantra, Lakshman gave assent,
And with the steeds they thither went.

449

When Ráma reached the lovely tree,
With Sítá and with Lakshman, he
Alighted from the car: with speed
Sumantra loosed each weary steed.
And, hand to hand in reverence laid,
Stood near to Ráma in the shade.
Ráma's dear friend, renowned by fame,
Who of Nisháda lineage came,
Guha, the mighty chief, adored
Through all the land as sovereign lord,
Soon as he heard that prince renowned
Was resting on Nisháda ground,
Begirt by counsellor and peer
And many an honoured friend drew near.
Soon as the monarch came in view,
Ráma and Lakshman toward him flew.
Then Guha, at the sight distressed,
His arms around the hero pressed,
Laid both his hands upon his head
Bowed to those lotus feet, and said:
"O Ráma, make thy wishes known,
And be this kingdom as thine own.
Who, mighty-armed, will ever see
A guest so dear as thou to me?"

He placed before him dainty fare
Of every flavour, rich and rare,
Brought forth the gift for honoured guest,
And thus again the chief addressed:
"Welcome, dear Prince, whose arms are strong;
These lands and all to thee belong.
Thy servants we, our lord art thou;
Begin, good king, thine empire now.
See, various food before thee placed,
And cups to drink and sweets to taste
For thee soft beds are hither borne,
And for thy horses grass and corn."

To Guha as he pressed and prayed,
Thus Raghu's son his answer made:
"'Twas aye thy care my heart to please

With honour, love, and courtesies,
And friendship brings thee now to greet
Thy guest thus humbly on thy feet."

Again the hero spake, as round
The king his shapely arms he wound:
"Guha, I see that all is well
With thee and those who with thee dwell;
That health and bliss and wealth attend
Thy realm, thyself, and every friend.
But all these friendly gifts of thine,
Bound to refuse, I must decline.
Grass, bark, and hide my only wear,
And woodland roots and fruit my fare,
On duty all my heart is set;
I seek the woods, an anchoret.
A little grass and corn to feed
The horses—this is all I need.
So by this favour, King, alone
Shall honour due to me be shown.
For these good steeds who brought me here
Are to my sire supremely dear;
And kind attention paid to these
Will honour me and highly please."

Then Guha quickly bade his train
Give water to the steeds, and grain.
And Ráma, ere the night grew dark,
Paid evening rites in dress of bark,
And tasted water, on the strand,
Drawn from the stream by Lakshmaṇ's hand.
And Lakshmaṇ with observance meet
Bathed his beloved brother's feet,

Who rested with his Maithil spouse:
Then sat him down 'neath distant boughs.
And Guha with his bow sat near
To Lakshmaṇ and the charioteer,
And with the prince conversing kept
His faithful watch while Ráma slept.
As Daśaratha's glorious heir,

Of lofty soul and wisdom rare,
Reclining with his Sítá there
Beside the river lay—
He who no troubles e'er had seen,
Whose life a life of bliss had been—
That night beneath the branches green
Passed pleasantly away.

CANTO

LI

Lakshman's Lament

As Lakshmaṇ still his vigil held
By unaffected love impelled,
Guha, whose heart the sight distressed,
With words like these the prince addressed:
"Beloved youth, this pleasant bed
Was brought for thee, for thee is spread;
On this, my Prince, thine eyelids close,
And heal fatigue with sweet repose.
My men are all to labour trained,
But hardship thou hast ne'er sustained.
All we this night our watch will keep
And guard Kakutstha's son asleep.
In all the world there breathes not one
More dear to me than Raghu's son.
The words I speak, heroic youth,
Are true: I swear it by my truth.
Through his dear grace supreme renown
Will, so I trust, my wishes crown.
So shall my life rich store obtain
Of merit, blest with joy and gain.
While Raghu's son and Sítá lie
Entranced in happy slumber, I
Will, with my trusty bow in hand,

Guard my dear friend with all my band.
To me, who oft these forests range,
Is naught therein or new or strange.
We could with equal might oppose
A four-fold army led by foes."

Then royal Lakshmaṇ made reply:
"With thee to stand as guardian nigh,
Whose faithful soul regards the right,
Fearless we well might rest to-night.
But how, when Ráma lays his head
With Sítá on his lowly bed,—
How can I sleep? how can I care
For life, or aught that's bright and fair?
Behold the conquering chief, whose might
Is match for Gods and fiends in fight;
With Sítá now he rests his head
Asleep on grass beneath him spread.
Won by devotion, text, and prayer,
And many a rite performed with care,
Chief of our father's sons he shines
Well marked, like him, with favouring signs.
Brief, brief the monarch's life will be
Now his dear son is forced to flee;
And quickly will the widowed state
Mourn for her lord disconsolate.
Each mourner there has wept her fill;
The cries of anguish now are still:
In the king's hall each dame, o'ercome
With weariness of woe is dumb.
This first sad night of grief, I ween,
Will do to death each sorrowing queen:
Scarce is Kauśalyá left alive;
My mother, too, can scarce survive.
If when her heart is fain to break,
She lingers for Śatrughna's sake,
Kauśalyá, mother of the chief,
Must sink beneath the chilling grief.
That town which countless thousands fill,
Whose hearts with love of Ráma thrill,—
The world's delight, so rich and fair,—

Grieved for the king, his death will share.
The hopes he fondly cherished, crossed
Ayodhyá's throne to Ráma lost,—
With mournful cries, Too late, too late!
The king my sire will meet his fate.
And when my sire has passed away,
Most happy in their lot are they,
Allowed, with every pious care,
Part in his funeral rites to bear.
And O, may we with joy at last,—
These years of forest exile past,—
Turn to Ayodhyá's town to dwell
With him who keeps his promise well!"

While thus the hero mighty-souled,
In wild lament his sorrow told,
Faint with the load that on him lay,
The hours of darkness passed away.
As thus the prince, impelled by zeal
For his loved brother, prompt to feel
Strong yearnings for the people's weal,
His words of truth outspake,
King Guha grieved to see his woe,
Heart-stricken, gave his tears to flow,
Tormented by the common blow,
Sad, as a wounded snake.

CANTO
LII

The Crossing of Gangá

Soon as the shades of night had fled,
Uprising from his lowly bed,
Ráma the famous, broad of chest,
His brother Lakshmaṇ thus addressed:

"Now swift upsprings the Lord of Light,
And fled is venerable night.

That dark-winged bird the Koïl now
Is calling from the topmost bough,
And sounding from the thicket nigh
Is heard the peacock's early cry.
Come, cross the flood that seeks the sea,
The swiftly flowing Jáhnaví."

King Guha heard his speech, agreed,
And called his minister with speed:
"A boat," he cried, "swift, strong, and fair,
With rudder, oars, and men, prepare,
And place it ready by the shore
To bear the pilgrims quickly o'er."
Thus Guha spake: his followers all
Bestirred them at their master's call;
Then told the king that ready manned
A gay boat waited near the strand.
Then Guha, hand to hand applied,
With reverence thus to Ráma cried:
"The boat is ready by the shore:
How, tell me, can I aid thee more?
O lord of men, it waits for thee
To cross the flood that seeks the sea.
O godlike keeper of thy vow,
Embark: the boat is ready now."

Then Ráma, lord of glory high,
Thus to King Guha made reply:
"Thanks for thy gracious care, my lord:
Now let the gear be placed on board."
Each bow-armed chief, in mail encased,
Bound sword and quiver to his waist,
And then with Sítá near them hied
Down the broad river's shelving side.
Then with raised palms the charioteer,
In lowly reverence drawing near,
Cried thus to Ráma good and true:
"Now what remains for me to do?"

With his right hand, while answering
The hero touched his friend:
"Go back," he said, "and on the king
With watchful care attend.
Thus far, Sumantra, thou wast guide;
Now to Ayodhyá turn," he cried:
"Hence seek we leaving steeds and car,
On foot the wood that stretches far."

Sumantra, when, with grieving heart,
He heard the hero bid him part,
Thus to the bravest of the brave,
Ikshváku's son, his answer gave:
"In all the world men tell of naught,
To match thy deed, by heroes wrought—
Thus with thy brother and thy wife
Thrall-like to lead a forest life.
No meet reward of fruit repays
Thy holy lore, thy saintlike days,
Thy tender soul, thy love of truth,
If woe like this afflicts thy youth.
Thou, roaming under forest boughs
With thy dear brother and thy spouse
Shalt richer meed of glory gain
Than if three worlds confessed thy reign.
Sad is our fate, O Ráma: we,
Abandoned and repelled by thee,
Must serve as thralls Kaikeyí's will,
Imperious, wicked, born to ill."

Thus cried the faithful charioteer,
As Raghu's son, in rede his peer,
Was fast departing on his road,—
And long his tears of anguish flowed.
But Ráma, when those tears were dried
His lips with water purified,
And in soft accents, sweet and clear,
Again addressed the charioteer:
"I find no heart, my friend, like thine,
So faithful to Ikshváku's line.
Still first in view this object keep,

456

That ne'er for me my sire may weep.
For he, the world's far-ruling king,
Is old, and wild with sorrow's sting;
With love's great burthen worn and weak:
Deem this the cause that thus I speak
Whate'er the high-souled king decrees
His loved Kaikeyí's heart to please,
Yea, be his order what it may,
Without demur thou must obey,
For this alone great monarchs reign,
That ne'er a wish be formed in vain.
Then, O Sumantra, well provide
That by no check the king be tried:
Nor let his heart in sorrow pine:
This care, my faithful friend, be thine.
The honoured king my father greet,
And thus for me my words repeat
To him whose senses are controlled,
Untired till now by grief, and old;
"I, Sítá, Lakshmaṇ sorrow not,
O Monarch, for our altered lot:
The same to us, if here we roam,
Or if Ayodhyá be our home,
The fourteen years will quickly fly,
The happy hour will soon be nigh
When thou, my lord, again shalt see
Lakshmaṇ, the Maithil dame, and me."
Thus having soothed, O charioteer,
My father and my mother dear,
Let all the queens my message learn,
But to Kaikeyí chiefly turn.
With loving blessings from the three,
From Lakshmaṇ, Sítá, and from me,
My mother, Queen Kauśalyá, greet
With reverence to her sacred feet.
And add this prayer of mine: "O King;
Send quickly forth and Bharat bring,
And set him on the royal throne
Which thy decree has made his own.
When he upon the throne is placed,
When thy fond arms are round him laced,

Thine aged heart will cease to ache
With bitter pangs for Ráma's sake."

And say to Bharat: "See thou treat
The queens with all observance meet:
What care the king receives, the same
Show thou alike to every dame.
Obedience to thy father's will
Who chooses thee the throne to fill,
Will earn for thee a store of bliss
Both in the world to come and this.'"

Thus Ráma bade Sumantra go
With thoughtful care instructed so.
Sumantra all his message heard,
And spake again, by passion stirred:
"O, should deep feeling mar in aught
The speech by fond devotion taught,
Forgive whate'er I wildly speak:
My love is strong, my tongue is weak.
How shall I, if deprived of thee,
Return that mournful town to see:
Where sick at heart the people are
Because their Ráma roams afar.
Woe will be theirs too deep to brook
When on the empty car they look,
As when from hosts, whose chiefs are slain,
One charioteer comes home again.
This very day, I ween, is food
Forsworn by all the multitude,
Thinking that thou, with hosts to aid,
Art dwelling in the wild wood's shade.
The great despair, the shriek of woe
They uttered when they saw thee go,
Will, when I come with none beside,
A hundred-fold be multiplied.
How to Kauśalyá can I say:
"O Queen, I took thy son away,
And with thy brother left him well:
Weep not for him; thy woe dispel?"
So false a tale I cannot frame,

Yet how speak truth and grieve the dame?
How shall these horses, fleet and bold,
Whom not a hand but mine can hold,
Bear others, wont to whirl the car
Wherein Ikshváku's children are!
Without thee, Prince, I cannot, no,
I cannot to Ayodhyá go.
Then deign, O Ráma, to relent,
And let me share thy banishment.
But if no prayers can move thy heart,
If thou wilt quit me and depart,
The flames shall end my car and me,
Deserted thus and reft of thee.
In the wild wood when foes are near,
When dangers check thy vows austere,
Borne in my car will I attend,
All danger and all care to end.
For thy dear sake I love the skill
That guides the steed and curbs his will:
And soon a forest life will be
As pleasant, for my love of thee.
And if these horses near thee dwell,
And serve thee in the forest well,
They, for their service, will not miss
The due reward of highest bliss.
Thine orders, as with thee I stray,
Will I with heart and head obey,
Prepared, for thee, without a sigh,
To lose Ayodhyá or the sky.
As one defiled with hideous sin,
I never more can pass within
Ayodhyá, city of our king,
Unless beside me thee I bring.
One wish is mine, I ask no more,
That, when thy banishment is o'er
I in my car may bear my lord,
Triumphant, to his home restored.
The fourteen years, if spent with thee,
Will swift as light-winged moments flee;
But the same years, without thee told,
Were magnified a hundred-fold.

Do not, kind lord, thy servant leave,
Who to his master's son would cleave,
And the same path with him pursue,
Devoted, tender, just and true."

Again, again Sumantra made
His varied plaint, and wept and prayed.
Him Raghu's son, whose tender breast
Felt for his servants, thus addressed:
"O faithful servant, well my heart
Knows how attached and true thou art.
Hear thou the words I speak, and know
Why to the town I bid thee go.
Soon as Kaikeyí, youngest queen,
Thy coming to the town has seen,
No doubt will then her mind oppress
That Ráma roams the wilderness.
And so the dame, her heart content
With proof of Ráma's banishment,
Will doubt the virtuous king no more
As faithless to the oath he swore.
Chief of my cares is this, that she,
Youngest amid the queens, may see
Bharat her son securely reign
O'er rich Ayodhyá's wide domain.
For mine and for the monarch's sake
Do thou thy journey homeward take,
And, as I bade, repeat each word
That from my lips thou here hast heard."

Thus spake the prince, and strove to cheer
The sad heart of the charioteer,
And then to royal Guha said
These words most wise and spirited:
"Guha, dear friend, it is not meet
That people throng my calm retreat:
For I must live a strict recluse,
And mould my life by hermits' use.
I now the ancient rule accept
By good ascetics gladly kept.

460

I go: bring fig-tree juice that I
In matted coils my hair may tie."

Quick Guha hastened to produce,
For the king's son, that sacred juice.
Then Ráma of his long locks made,
And Lakshmaṇ's too, the hermit braid.

And the two royal brothers there
With coats of bark and matted hair,
Transformed in lovely likeness stood
To hermit saints who love the wood.
So Ráma, with his brother bold,
A pious anchorite enrolled,
Obeyed the vow which hermits take,
And to his friend, King Guha, spake:
"May people, treasure, army share,
And fenced forts, thy constant care:
Attend to all: supremely hard
The sovereign's task, to watch and guard."

Ikshváku's son, the good and brave,
This last farewell to Guha gave,
And then, with Lakshmaṇ and his bride,
Determined, on his way he hied.
Soon as he viewed, upon the shore,
The bark prepared to waft them o'er
Impetuous Gangá's rolling tide,
To Lakshmaṇ thus the chieftain cried:
"Brother, embark; thy hand extend,
Thy gentle aid to Sítá lend:
With care her trembling footsteps guide,
And place the lady by thy side."
When Lakshmaṇ heard, prepared to aid,
His brother's words he swift obeyed.
Within the bark he placed the dame,
Then to her side the hero came.
Next Lakshmaṇ's elder brother, lord
Of brightest glory, when on board,
Breathing a prayer for blessings, meet

For priest or warrior to repeat,
Then he and car-borne Lakshmaṇ bent,
Well-pleased, their heads, most reverent,
Their hands, with Sítá, having dipped,
As Scripture bids, and water sipped,
Farewell to wise Sumantra said,
And Guha, with the train he led.
So Ráma took, on board, his stand,
And urged the vessel from the land.
Then swift by vigorous arms impelled
Her onward course the vessel held,
And guided by the helmsman through
The dashing waves of Gangá flew.
Half way across the flood they came,
When Sítá, free from spot and blame,
Her reverent hands together pressed,
The Goddess of the stream addressed:
"May the great chieftain here who springs
From Daśaratha, best of kings,
Protected by thy care, fulfil
His prudent father's royal will.
When in the forest he has spent
His fourteen years of banishment,
With his dear brother and with me
His home again my lord shall see.
Returning on that blissful day,
I will to thee mine offerings pay,
Dear Queen, whose waters gently flow,
Who canst all blessed gifts bestow.
For, three-pathed Queen, though wandering here,
Thy waves descend from Brahmá's sphere,
Spouse of the God o'er floods supreme,
Though rolling here thy glorious stream.
To thee, fair Queen, my head shall bend,
To thee shall hymns of praise ascend,
When my brave lord shall turn again,
And, joyful, o'er his kingdom reign.
To win thy grace, O Queen divine,
A hundred thousand fairest kine,
And precious robes and finest meal
Among the Bráhmans will I deal.

A hundred jars of wine shall flow,
When to my home, O Queen, I go;
With these, and flesh, and corn, and rice,
Will I, delighted, sacrifice.
Each hallowed spot, each holy shrine
That stands on these fair shores of thine,
Each fane and altar on thy banks
Shall share my offerings and thanks.
With me and Lakshmaṇ, free from harm,
May he the blameless, strong of arm,
Reseek Ayodhyá from the wild,
O blameless Lady undefiled!"
As, praying for her husband's sake,
The faultless dame to Gangá spake,
To the right bank the vessel flew
With her whose heart was right and true.
Soon as the bark had crossed the wave,
The lion leader of the brave,
Leaving the vessel on the strand,
With wife and brother leapt to land.
Then Ráma thus the prince addressed
Who filled with joy Sumitrá's breast:
"Be thine alike to guard and aid
In peopled spot, in lonely shade.
Do thou, Sumitrá's son, precede:
Let Sítá walk where thou shalt lead.
Behind you both my place shall be,
To guard the Maithil dame and thee.
For she, to woe a stranger yet,
No toil or grief till now has met;
The fair Videhan will assay
The pains of forest life to-day.
To-day her tender feet must tread
Rough rocky wilds around her spread:
No tilth is there, no gardens grow,
No crowding people come and go."

The hero ceased: and Lakshmaṇ led
Obedient to the words he said:
And Sítá followed him, and then
Came Raghu's pride, the lord of men.

With Sítá walking o'er the sand
They sought the forest, bow in hand,
But still their lingering glances threw
Where yet Sumantra stood in view.
Sumantra, when his watchful eye
The royal youths no more could spy,
Turned from the spot whereon he stood
Homeward with Guha from the wood.

Still on the brothers forced their way
Where sweet birds sang on every spray,
Though scarce the eye a path could find
Mid flowering trees where creepers twined.
Far on the princely brothers pressed,
And stayed their feet at length to rest
Beneath a fig tree's mighty shade
With countless pendent shoots displayed.
Reclining there a while at ease,
They saw, not far, beneath fair trees
A lake with many a lotus bright
That bore the name of Lovely Sight.
Ráma his wife's attention drew,
And Lakshman's, to the charming view:
"Look, brother, look how fair the flood
Glows with the lotus, flower and bud!"

They drank the water fresh and clear,
And with their shafts they slew a deer.
A fire of boughs they made in haste,
And in the flame the meat they placed.
So Raghu's sons with Sítá shared
The hunter's meal their hands prepared,
Then counselled that the spreading tree
Their shelter and their home should be.

CANTO

LIII

Ráma's Lament

When evening rites were duly paid,
   Reclined beneath the leafy shade,
   To Lakshmaṇ thus spake Ráma, best
Of those who glad a people's breast:
"Now the first night has closed the day
That saw us from our country stray,
And parted from the charioteer;
Yet grieve not thou, my brother dear.
Henceforth by night, when others sleep,
Must we our careful vigil keep,
Watching for Sítá's welfare thus,
For her dear life depends on us.
Bring me the leaves that lie around,
And spread them here upon the ground,
That we on lowly beds may lie,
And let in talk the night go by."

So on the ground with leaves o'erspread,
He who should press a royal bed,
Ráma with Lakshmaṇ thus conversed,
And many a pleasant tale rehearsed:
"This night the king," he cried, "alas!
In broken sleep will sadly pass.
Kaikeyí now content should be,
For mistress of her wish is she.
So fiercely she for empire yearns,
That when her Bharat home returns,
She in her greed, may even bring
Destruction on our lord the king.
What can he do, in feeble eld,
Reft of all aid and me expelled,

465

His soul enslaved by love, a thrall
Obedient to Kaikeyí's call?
As thus I muse upon his woe
And all his wisdoms overthrow,
Love is, methinks, of greater might
To stir the heart than gain and right.
For who, in wisdom's lore untaught,
Could by a beauty's prayer be bought
To quit his own obedient son,
Who loves him, as my sire has done!
Bharat, Kaikeyí's child, alone
Will, with his wife, enjoy the throne,
And blissfully his rule maintain
O'er happy Kośala's domain.
To Bharat's single lot will fall
The kingdom and the power and all,
When fails the king from length of days,
And Ráma in the forest strays.
Whoe'er, neglecting right and gain,
Lets conquering love his soul enchain,
To him, like Daśaratha's lot,
Comes woe with feet that tarry not.
Methinks at last the royal dame,
Dear Lakshmaṇ, has secured her aim,
To see at once her husband dead,
Her son enthroned, and Ráma fled.
Ah me! I fear, lest borne away
By frenzy of success, she slay
Kauśalyá, through her wicked hate
Of me, bereft, disconsolate;
Or her who aye for me has striven
Sumitrá, to devotion given.
Hence, Lakshmaṇ, to Ayodhyá speed,
Returning in the hour of need.
With Sítá I my steps will bend
Where Daṇḍak's mighty woods extend.
No guardian has Kauśalyá now:
O, be her friend and guardian thou.
Strong hate may vile Kaikeyí lead
To many a base unrighteous deed,
Treading my mother 'neath her feet

466

When Bharat holds the royal seat.
Sure in some antenatal time
Were children, by Kauśalyá's crime,
Torn from their mothers' arms away,
And hence she mourns this evil day.
She for her child no toil would spare
Tending me long with pain and care;
Now in the hour of fruitage she
Has lost that son, ah, woe is me.
O Lakshman, may no matron e'er
A son so doomed to sorrow bear
As I, my mother's heart who rend
With anguish that can never end.
The Sáriká, methinks, possessed
More love than glows in Ráma's breast.
Who, as the tale is told to us,
Addressed the stricken parrot thus:

"Parrot, the capturer's talons tear,
While yet alone thou flutterest there,
Before his mouth has closed on me:"
So cried the bird, herself to free.
Reft of her son, in childless woe,
My mother's tears for ever flow:
Ill-fated, doomed with grief to strive,
What aid can she from me derive?
Pressed down by care, she cannot rise
From sorrow's flood wherein she lies.
In righteous wrath my single arm
Could, with my bow, protect from harm
Ayodhyá's town and all the earth:
But what is hero prowess worth?
Lest breaking duty's law I sin,
And lose the heaven I strive to win,
The forest life today I choose,
And kingly state and power refuse."
Thus mourning in that lonely spot
The troubled chief bewailed his lot,
And filled with tears, his eyes ran o'er;
Then silent sat, and spake no more.
To him, when ceased his loud lament,

Like fire whose brilliant might is spent,
Or the great sea when sleeps the wave,
Thus Lakshmaṇ consolation gave:
"Chief of the brave who bear the bow,
E'en now Ayodhyá, sunk in woe,
By thy departure reft of light
Is gloomy as the moonless night.
Unfit it seems that thou, O chief,
Shouldst so afflict thy soul with grief,
So with thou Sítá's heart consign
To deep despair as well as mine.
Not I, O Raghu's son, nor she
Could live one hour deprived of thee:
We were, without thine arm to save,
Like fish deserted by the wave.
Although my mother dear to meet,
Śatrughna, and the king, were sweet,
On them, or heaven, to feed mine eye
Were nothing, if thou wert not by."

Sitting at ease, their glances fell
Upon the beds, constructed well,
And there the sons of virtue laid
Their limbs beneath the fig tree's shade.

CANTO
LIV

Bharadvája's Hermitage

S o there that night the heroes spent
Under the boughs that o'er them bent,
And when the sun his glory spread,
Upstarting, from the place they sped.
On to that spot they made their way,

Through the dense wood that round them lay,
Where Yamuná's swift waters glide
To blend with Gangá's holy tide.
Charmed with the prospect ever new
The glorious heroes wandered through
Full many a spot of pleasant ground,
Rejoicing as they gazed around,
With eager eye and heart at ease,
On countless sorts of flowery trees.
And now the day was half-way sped
When thus to Lakshmaṇ Ráma said:
"There, there, dear brother, turn thine eyes;
See near Prayág that smoke arise:
The banner of our Lord of Flames
The dwelling of some saint proclaims.
Near to the place our steps we bend
Where Yamuná and Gangá blend.
I hear and mark the deafening roar
When chafing floods together pour.
See, near us on the ground are left
Dry logs, by labouring woodmen cleft,
And the tall trees, that blossom near
Saint Bharadvája's home, appear."

The bow-armed princes onward passed,
And as the sun was sinking fast
They reached the hermit's dwelling, set
Near where the rushing waters met.
The presence of the warrior scared
The deer and birds as on he fared,
And struck them with unwonted awe:
Then Bharadvája's cot they saw.
The high-souled hermit soon they found
Girt by his dear disciples round:
Calm saint, whose vows had well been wrought,
Whose fervent rites keen sight had bought.
Duly had flames of worship blazed
When Ráma on the hermit gazed:
His suppliant hands the hero raised,
Drew nearer to the holy man

469

With his companions, and began,
Declaring both his name and race
And why they sought that distant place:
"Saint, Daśaratha's children we,
Ráma and Lakshman, come to thee.
This my good wife from Janak springs,
The best of fair Videha's kings;
Through lonely wilds, a faultless dame,
To this pure grove with me she came.
My younger brother follows still
Me banished by my father's will:
Sumitrá's son, bound by a vow,—
He roams the wood beside me now.
Sent by my father forth to rove,
We seek, O Saint, some holy grove,
Where lives of hermits we may lead,
And upon fruits and berries feed."

When Bharadvája, prudent-souled,
Had heard the prince his tale unfold,
Water he bade them bring, a bull,
And honour-gifts in dishes full,

And drink and food of varied taste,
Berries and roots, before him placed,
And then the great ascetic showed
A cottage for the guests' abode.
The saint these honours gladly paid
To Ráma who had thither strayed,
Then compassed sat by birds and deer
And many a hermit resting near.
The prince received the service kind,
And sat him down rejoiced in mind.
Then Bharadvája silence broke,
And thus the words of duty spoke:
"Kakutstha's royal son, that thou
Hadst sought this grove I knew ere now.
Mine ears have heard thy story, sent
Without a sin to banishment.
Behold, O Prince, this ample space
Near where the mingling floods embrace,

470

Holy, and beautiful, and clear:
Dwell with us, and be happy here."

By Bharadvája thus addressed,
Ráma whose kind and tender breast
All living things would bless and save,
In gracious words his answer gave:

"My honoured lord, this tranquil spot,
Fair home of hermits, suits me not:
For all the neighbouring people here
Will seek us when they know me near:
With eager wish to look on me,
And the Videhan dame to see,
A crowd of rustics will intrude
Upon the holy solitude.
Provide, O gracious lord, I pray,
Some quiet home that lies away,
Where my Videhan spouse may dwell
Tasting the bliss deserved so well."

The hermit heard the prayer he made:
A while in earnest thought he stayed,
And then in words like these expressed
His answer to the chief's request:
"Ten leagues away there stands a hill
Where thou mayst live, if such thy will:
A holy mount, exceeding fair;
Great saints have made their dwelling there:
There great Langúrs in thousands play,
And bears amid the thickets stray;
Wide-known by Chitrakúṭa's name,
It rivals Gandhamádan's fame.
Long as the man that hill who seeks
Gazes upon its sacred peaks,
To holy things his soul he gives
And pure from thought of evil lives.
There, while a hundred autumns fled,
Has many a saint with hoary head
Spent his pure life, and won the prize,
By deep devotion, in the skies:

471

Best home, I ween, if such retreat,
Far from the ways of men, be sweet:
Or let thy years of exile flee
Here in this hermitage with me."

Thus Bharadvája spake, and trained
In lore of duty, entertained
The princes and the dame, and pressed
His friendly gifts on every guest.

Thus to Prayág the hero went,
Thus saw the saint preëminent,
And varied speeches heard and said:
Then holy night o'er heaven was spread.
And Ráma took, by toil oppressed,
With Sítá and his brother, rest;
And so the night, with sweet content,
In Bharadvája's grove was spent.
But when the dawn dispelled the night,
Ráma approached the anchorite,
And thus addressed the holy sire
Whose glory shone like kindled fire:
"Well have we spent, O truthful Sage,
The night within thy hermitage:
Now let my lord his guests permit
For their new home his grove to quit."

Then, as he saw the morning break,
In answer Bharadvája spake:
"Go forth to Chitrakúṭa's hill,
Where berries grow, and sweets distil:
Full well, I deem, that home will suit
Thee, Ráma, strong and resolute.
Go forth, and Chitrakúṭa seek,
Famed mountain of the Varied Peak.
In the wild woods that gird him round
All creatures of the chase are found:
Thou in the glades shalt see appear
Vast herds of elephants and deer.
With Sítá there shalt thou delight
To gaze upon the woody height;

There with expanding heart to look
On river, table-land, and brook,
And see the foaming torrent rave
Impetuous from the mountain cave.
Auspicious hill! where all day long
The lapwing's cry, the Koïl's song
Make all who listen gay:
Where all is fresh and fair to see,
Where elephants and deer roam free,
There, as a hermit, stay."

CANTO
LV

The Passage of Yamuná

The princely tamers of their foes
Thus passed the night in calm repose,
Then to the hermit having bent
With reverence, on their way they went.
High favour Bharadvája showed,
And blessed them ready for the road.

With such fond looks as fathers throw
On their own sons, before they go.
Then spake the saint with glory bright
To Ráma peerless in his might:
"First, lords of men, direct your feet
Where Yamuná and Gangá meet;
Then to the swift Kálindí go,
Whose westward waves to Gangá flow.
When thou shalt see her lovely shore
Worn by their feet who hasten o'er,
Then, Raghu's son, a raft prepare,
And cross the Sun born river there.
Upon her farther bank a tree,

Near to the landing wilt thou see.
The blessed source of varied gifts,
There her green boughs that Fig-tree lifts:
A tree where countless birds abide,
By Śyáma's name known far and wide.
Sítá, revere that holy shade:
There be thy prayers for blessing prayed.
Thence for a league your way pursue,
And a dark wood shall meet your view,
Where tall bamboos their foliage show,
The Gum-tree and the Jujube grow.
To Chitrakúṭa have I oft
Trodden that path so smooth and soft,
Where burning woods no traveller scare,
But all is pleasant, green, and fair."

When thus the guests their road had learned,
Back to his cot the hermit turned,
And Ráma, Lakshmaṇ, Sítá paid
Their reverent thanks for courteous aid.
Thus Ráma spake to Lakshmaṇ, when
The saint had left the lords of men:
"Great store of bliss in sooth is ours
On whom his love the hermit showers."
As each to other wisely talked,
The lion lords together walked
On to Kálindí's woody shore;
And gentle Sítá went before.
They reached that flood, whose waters flee
With rapid current to the sea;
Their minds a while to thought they gave
And counselled how to cross the wave.
At length, with logs together laid,
A mighty raft the brothers made.
Then dry bamboos across were tied,
And grass was spread from side to side.
And the great hero Lakshmaṇ brought
Cane and Rose-Apple boughs and wrought,
Trimming the branches smooth and neat,
For Sítá's use a pleasant seat.
And Ráma placed thereon his dame

Touched with a momentary shame,
Resembling in her glorious mien
All-thought-surpassing Fortune's Queen.
Then Ráma hastened to dispose,
Each in its place, the skins and bows,
And by the fair Videhan laid
The coats, the ornaments, and spade.
When Sítá thus was set on board,
And all their gear was duly stored,
The heroes each with vigorous hand,
Pushed off the raft and left the land.
When half its way the raft had made,
Thus Sítá to Kálindí prayed:
"Goddess, whose flood I traverse now,
Grant that my lord may keep his vow.
For thee shall bleed a thousand kine,
A hundred jars shall pour their wine,
When Ráma sees that town again
Where old Ikshváku's children reign."
Thus to Kálindí's stream she sued
And prayed in suppliant attitude.
Then to the river's bank the dame,
Fervent in supplication, came.
They left the raft that brought them o'er,
And the thick wood that clothed the shore,
And to the Fig-tree Śyáma made
Their way, so cool with verdant shade.
Then Sítá viewed that best of trees,
And reverent spake in words like these:
"Hail, hail, O mighty tree! Allow
My husband to complete his vow;
Let us returning, I entreat,
Kauśalyá and Sumitrá meet."
Then with her hands together placed
Around the tree she duly paced.
When Ráma saw his blameless spouse
A suppliant under holy boughs,
The gentle darling of his heart,
He thus to Lakshman spake apart:
"Brother, by thee our way be led;
Let Sítá close behind thee tread:

I, best of men, will grasp my bow,
And hindmost of the three will go.
What fruits soe'er her fancy take,
Or flowers half hidden in the brake,
For Janak's child forget not thou
To gather from the brake or bough."

Thus on they fared. The tender dame
Asked Ráma, as they walked, the name
Of every shrub that blossoms bore,
Creeper, and tree unseen before:
And Lakshmaṇ fetched, at Sítá's prayer,
Boughs of each tree with clusters fair.
Then Janak's daughter joyed to see
The sand-discoloured river flee,
Where the glad cry of many a bird,
The sáras and the swan, was heard.
A league the brothers travelled through
The forest noble game they slew:
Beneath the trees their meal they dressed
And sat them down to eat and rest.
A while in that delightful shade
Where elephants unnumbered strayed,
Where peacocks screamed and monkeys played,

They wandered with delight.
Then by the river's side they found
A pleasant spot of level ground,
Where all was smooth and fair around,
Their lodging for the night.

CANTO
LVI

Chitrakúta

Then Ráma, when the morning rose,
 Called Lakshmaṇ gently from repose:
 "Awake, the pleasant voices hear
Of forest birds that warble near.
Scourge of thy foes, no longer stay;
The hour is come to speed away."

The slumbering prince unclosed his eyes
When thus his brother bade him rise,
Compelling, at the timely cry,
Fatigue, and sleep, and rest to fly.
The brothers rose and Sítá too;
Pure water from the stream they drew,
Paid morning rites, then followed still
The road to Chitrakúṭa's hill.
Then Ráma as he took the road
With Lakshmaṇ, while the morning, glowed,
To the Videhan lady cried,
Sítá the fair, the lotus-eyed:
"Look round thee, dear; each flowery tree
Touched with the fire of morning see:
The Kinśuk, now the Frosts are fled,—
How glorious with his wreaths of red!
The Bel-trees see, so loved of men,
Hanging their boughs in every glen.
O'erburthened with their fruit and flowers:
A plenteous store of food is ours.
See, Lakshmaṇ, in the leafy trees,
Where'er they make their home.
Down hangs, the work of labouring bees
The ponderous honeycomb.

In the fair wood before us spread
The startled wild-cock cries:
Hark, where the flowers are soft to tread,
The peacock's voice replies.
Where elephants are roaming free,
And sweet birds' songs are loud,
The glorious Chitrakúṭa see:
His peaks are in the cloud.
On fair smooth ground he stands displayed,
Begirt by many a tree:
O brother, in that holy shade
How happy shall we be!"
Then Ráma, Lakshmaṇ, Sítá, each
Spoke raising suppliant hands this speech
To him, in woodland dwelling met,
Válmíki, ancient anchoret:
"O Saint, this mountain takes the mind,
With creepers, trees of every kind,
With fruit and roots abounding thus,
A pleasant life it offers us:
Here for a while we fain would stay,
And pass a season blithe and gay."

Then the great saint, in duty trained,
With honour gladly entertained:
He gave his guests a welcome fair,
And bade them sit and rest them there,
Ráma of mighty arm and chest
His faithful Lakshmaṇ then addressed:
"Brother, bring hither from the wood
Selected timber strong and good,
And build therewith a little cot;
My heart rejoices in the spot
That lies beneath the mountain's side,
Remote, with water well supplied."

Sumitrá's son his words obeyed,
Brought many a tree, and deftly made,
With branches in the forest cut,
As Ráma bade, a leafy hut.
Then Ráma, when the cottage stood

478

Fair, firmly built, and walled with wood,
To Lakshmaṇ spake, whose eager mind
To do his brother's will inclined:
"Now, Lakshmaṇ as our cot is made,
Must sacrifice be duly paid
By us, for lengthened life who hope,
With venison of the antelope.
Away, O bright-eyed Lakshmaṇ, speed:
Struck by thy bow a deer must bleed:
As Scripture bids, we must not slight
The duty that commands the rite."
Lakshmaṇ, the chief whose arrows laid
His foemen low, his word obeyed;
And Ráma thus again addressed
The swift performer of his hest:
"Prepare the venison thou hast shot,
To sacrifice for this our cot.
Haste, brother dear, for this the hour,
And this the day of certain power."
Then glorious Lakshmaṇ took the buck
His arrow in the wood had struck;
Bearing his mighty load he came,
And laid it in the kindled flame.

Soon as he saw the meat was done,
And that the juices ceased to run
From the broiled carcass, Lakshmaṇ then
Spoke thus to Ráma best of men:
"The carcass of the buck, entire,
Is ready dressed upon the fire.
Now be the sacred rites begun
To please the God, thou godlike one."

Ráma the good, in ritual trained,
Pure from the bath, with thoughts restrained,
Hasted those verses to repeat
Which make the sacrifice complete.
The hosts celestial came in view,
And Ráma to the cot withdrew,
While a sweet sense of rapture stole
Through the unequalled hero's soul.

He paid the Viśvedevas due.
And Rudra's right, and Vishṇu's too,
Nor wonted blessings, to protect
Their new-built home, did he neglect.
With voice repressed he breathed the prayer,
Bathed duly in the river fair,
And gave good offerings that remove
The stain of sin, as texts approve.
And many an altar there he made,
And shrines, to suit the holy shade,
All decked with woodland chaplets sweet,
And fruit and roots and roasted meat,
With muttered prayer, as texts require,
Water, and grass and wood and fire.
So Ráma, Lakshmaṇ, Sítá paid
Their offerings to each God and shade,
And entered then their pleasant cot
That bore fair signs of happy lot.
They entered, the illustrious three,
The well-set cottage, fair to see,
Roofed with the leaves of many a tree,
And fenced from wind and rain:
So, at their Father Brahmá's call,
The Gods of heaven, assembling all,
To their own glorious council hall
Advance in shining train.
So, resting on that lovely hill,
Near the fair lily-covered rill,
The happy prince forgot,
Surrounded by the birds and deer,
The woe, the longing, and the fear
That gloom the exile's lot.

CANTO
LVII

Sumantra's Return

When Ráma reached the southern bank,
    King Guha's heart with sorrow sank:
    He with Sumantra talked, and spent
With his deep sorrow, homeward went.
Sumantra, as the king decreed,
Yoked to the car each noble steed,
And to Ayodhyá's city sped
With his sad heart disquieted.
On lake and brook and scented grove
His glances fell, as on he drove:
City and village came in view
As o'er the road his coursers flew.
On the third day the charioteer,
When now the hour of night was near,
Came to Ayodhyá's gate, and found
The city all in sorrow drowned.
To him, in spirit quite cast down,
Forsaken seemed the silent town,
And by the rush of grief oppressed
He pondered in his mournful breast:
"Is all Ayodhyá burnt with grief,
Steed, elephant, and man, and chief?
Does her loved Ráma's exile so
Afflict her with the fires of woe?"
Thus as he mused, his steeds flew fast,
And swiftly through the gate he passed.
On drove the charioteer, and then
In hundreds, yea in thousands, men
Ran to the car from every side,
And, "Ráma, where is Ráma?" cried.

481

Sumantra said: "My chariot bore
The duteous prince to Gangá's shore;
I left him there at his behest,
And homeward to Ayodhyá pressed."
Soon as the anxious people knew
That he was o'er the flood they drew
Deep sighs, and crying, Ráma! all
Wailed, and big tears began to fall.
He heard the mournful words prolonged,
As here and there the people thronged:
"Woe, woe for us, forlorn, undone,
No more to look on Raghu's son!
His like again we ne'er shall see,
Of heart so true, of hand so free,
In gifts, in gatherings for debate,
When marriage pomps we celebrate,
What should we do? What earthly thing
Can rest, or hope, or pleasure bring?"

Thus the sad town, which Ráma kept
As a kind father, wailed and wept.
Each mansion, as the car went by,
Sent forth a loud and bitter cry,
As to the window every dame,
Mourning for banished Ráma, came.
As his sad eyes with tears o'erflowed,
He sped along the royal road
To Daśaratha's high abode.
There leaping down his car he stayed;
Within the gates his way he made;
Through seven broad courts he onward hied
Where people thronged on every side.
From each high terrace, wild with woe,
The royal ladies flocked below:

He heard them talk in gentle tone,
As each for Ráma made her moan:
"What will the charioteer reply
To Queen Kauśalyá's eager cry?
With Ráma from the gates he went;

Homeward alone, his steps are bent.
Hard is a life with woe distressed,
But difficult to win is rest,
If, when her son is banished, still
She lives beneath her load of ill."

Such was the speech Sumantra heard
From them whom grief unfeigned had stirred.
As fires of anguish burnt him through,
Swift to the monarch's hall he drew,
Past the eighth court; there met his sight,
The sovereign in his palace bright,
Still weeping for his son, forlorn,
Pale, faint, and all with sorrow worn.
As there he sat, Sumantra bent
And did obeisance reverent,
And to the king repeated o'er
The message he from Ráma bore.
The monarch heard, and well-nigh brake
His heart, but yet no word he spake:
Fainting to earth he fell, and dumb,
By grief for Ráma overcome.
Rang through the hall a startling cry,
And women's arms were tossed on high,
When, with his senses all astray,
Upon the ground the monarch lay.
Kauśalyá, with Sumitrá's aid,
Raised from the ground her lord dismayed:
"Sire, of high fate," she cried, "O, why
Dost thou no single word reply
To Ráma's messenger who brings
News of his painful wanderings?
The great injustice done, art thou
Shame-stricken for thy conduct now?
Rise up, and do thy part: bestow
Comfort and help in this our woe.
Speak freely, King; dismiss thy fear,
For Queen Kaikeyí stands not near,
Afraid of whom thou wouldst not seek
Tidings of Ráma: freely speak."

When the sad queen had ended so,
She sank, insatiate in her woe,
And prostrate lay upon the ground,
While her faint voice by sobs was drowned.
When all the ladies in despair
Saw Queen Kauśalyá wailing there,
And the poor king oppressed with pain,
They flocked around and wept again.

CANTO
LVIII

Ráma's Message

The king a while had senseless lain,
    When care brought memory back again.
        Then straight he called, the news to hear
Of Ráma, for the charioteer,
With reverent hand to hand applied
He waited by the old man's side,
Whose mind with anguish was distraught
Like a great elephant newly caught.
The king with bitter pain distressed
The faithful charioteer addressed,
Who, sad of mien, with flooded eye,
And dust upon his limbs, stood by:
"Where will be Ráma's dwelling now
At some tree's foot, beneath the bough;
Ah, what will be the exile's food,
Bred up with kind solicitude?
Can he, long lapped in pleasant rest,
Unmeet for pain, by pain oppressed,
Son of earth's king, his sad night spend
Earth-couched, as one that has no friend?
Behind him, when abroad he sped,

Cars, elephant, and foot were led:
Then how shall Ráma dwell afar
In the wild woods where no men are?
How, tell me, did the princes there,
With Sítá good and soft and fair,
Alighting from the chariot, tread
The forest wilds around them spread?
A happy lot is thine, I ween,
Whose eyes my two dear sons have seen
Seeking on foot the forest shade,
Like the bright Twins to view displayed,
The heavenly Aśvins, when they seek
The woods that hang 'neath Mandar's peak.
What words, Sumantra, quickly tell,
From Ráma, Lakshman, Sítá fell?
How in the wood did Ráma eat?
What was his bed, and what his seat?
Full answer to my questions give,
For I on thy replies shall live,
As with the saints Yayáti held
Sweet converse, from the skies expelled."

Urged by the lord of men to speak,
Whose sobbing voice came faint and weak,
Thus he, while tears his utterance broke,
In answer to the monarch spoke:
"Hear then the words that Ráma said,
Resolved in duty's path to tread.
Joining his hands, his head he bent,
And gave this message, reverent:
"Sumantra, to my father go,
Whose lofty mind all people know:
Bow down before him, as is meet,
And in my stead salute his feet.
Then to the queen my mother bend,
And give the greeting that I send:
Ne'er may her steps from duty err,
And may it still be well with her.
And add this word: "O Queen, pursue
Thy vows with faithful heart and true;

And ever at due season turn
Where holy fires of worship burn.
And, lady, on our lord bestow

Such honour as to Gods we owe.
Be kind to every queen: let pride
And thought of self be cast aside.
In the king's fond opinion raise
Kaikeyí, by respect and praise.
Let the young Bharat ever be
Loved, honoured as the king by thee:
Thy king-ward duty ne'er forget:
High over all are monarchs set."

And Bharat, too, for me address:
Pray that all health his life may bless.
Let every royal lady share,
As justice bids, his love and care.
Say to the strong-armed chief who brings
Joy to Iksváku's line of kings:
"As ruling prince thy care be shown
Of him, our sire, who holds the throne.
Stricken in years he feels their weight;
But leave him in his royal state.
As regent heir content thee still,
Submissive to thy father's will.'"
Ráma again his charge renewed,
As the hot flood his cheek bedewed:
"Hold as thine own my mother dear
Who drops for me the longing tear."
Then Lakshman, with his soul on fire,
Spake breathing fast these words of ire:
"Say, for what sin, for what offence
Was royal Ráma banished thence?
He is the cause, the king: poor slave
To the light charge Kaikeyí gave.
Let right or wrong the motive be,
The author of our woe is he.
Whether the exile were decreed
Through foolish faith or guilty greed,
For promises or empire, still

486

The king has wrought a grievous ill.
Grant that the Lord of all saw fit
To prompt the deed and sanction it,
In Ráma's life no cause I see
For which the king should bid him flee.
His blinded eyes refused to scan
The guilt and folly of the plan,
And from the weakness of the king
Here and hereafter woe shall spring.
No more my sire: the ties that used
To bind me to the king are loosed.
My brother Ráma, Raghu's son,
To me is lord, friend, sire in one.
The love of men how can he win,
Deserting, by the cruel sin,
Their joy, whose heart is swift to feel
A pleasure in the people's weal?
Shall he whose mandate could expel
The virtuous Ráma, loved so well,
To whom his subjects' fond hearts cling—
Shall he in spite of them be king?"

But Janak's child, my lord, stood by,
And oft the votaress heaved a sigh.
She seemed with dull and wandering sense,
Beneath a spirit's influence.
The noble princess, pained with woe
Which till that hour she ne'er could know,
Tears in her heavy trouble shed,
But not a word to me she said.
She raised her face which grief had dried
And tenderly her husband eyed,
Gazed on him as he turned to go
While tear chased tear in rapid flow."

CANTO
LIX

Dasaratha's Lament

As thus Sumantra, best of peers,
Told his sad tale with many tears,
The monarch cried, "I pray thee, tell
At length again what there befell."
Sumantra, at the king's behest,
Striving with sobs he scarce repressed,
His trembling voice at last controlled,
And thus his further tidings told:
"Their locks in votive coils they wound,
Their coats of bark upon them bound,
To Gangá's farther shore they went,
Thence to Prayág their steps were bent.
I saw that Lakshman walked ahead
To guard the path the two should tread.
So far I saw, no more could learn,
Forced by the hero to return.
Retracing slow my homeward course,
Scarce could I move each stubborn horse:
Shedding hot tears of grief he stood
When Ráma turned him to the wood.
As the two princes parted thence
I raised my hands in reverence,
Mounted my ready car, and bore
The grief that stung me to the core.
With Guha all that day I stayed,
Still by the earnest hope delayed
That Ráma, ere the time should end,
Some message from the wood might send.
Thy realms, great Monarch, mourn the blow,
And sympathize with Ráma's woe.

Each withering tree hangs low his head,
And shoot, and bud, and flower are dead.
Dried are the floods that wont to fill
The lake, the river, and the rill.
Drear is each grove and garden now,
Dry every blossom on the bough.
Each beast is still, no serpents crawl:
A lethargy of woe on all.
The very wood is silent: crushed
With grief for Ráma, all is hushed.
Fair blossoms from the water born,
Gay garlands that the earth adorn,
And every fruit that gleams like gold,
Have lost the scent that charmed of old.
Empty is every grove I see,
Or birds sit pensive on the tree.
Where'er I look, its beauty o'er,
The pleasance charms not as before.
I drove through fair Ayodhyá's street:
None flew with joy the car to meet.
They saw that Ráma was not there,
And turned them sighing in despair.
The people in the royal way
Wept tears of bitter grief, when they
Beheld me coming, from afar,
No Ráma with me in the car.
From palace roof and turret high
Each woman bent her eager eye;
She looked for Ráma, but in vain;
Gazed on the car and shrieked for pain.
Their long clear eyes with sorrow drowned
They, when this common grief was found,
Looked each on other, friend and foe,
In sympathy of levelling woe:
No shade of difference between
Foe, friend, or neutral, there was seen.
Without a joy, her bosom rent
With grief for Ráma's banishment,
Ayodhyá like the queen appears
Who mourns her son with many tears."

489

He ended: and the king, distressed.
With sobbing voice that lord addressed:
"Ah me, by false Kaikeyí led,
Of evil race, to evil bred,
I took no counsel of the sage,
Nor sought advice from skill and age,
I asked no lord his aid to lend,
I called no citizen or friend.
Rash was my deed, bereft of sense
Slave to a woman's influence.
Surely, my lord, a woe so great
Falls on us by the will of Fate;
It lays the house of Raghu low,
For Destiny will have it so.
I pray thee, if I e'er have done
An act to please thee, yea, but one,
Fly, fly, and Ráma homeward lead:
My life, departing, counsels speed.
Fly, ere the power to bid I lack,
Fly to the wood: bring Ráma back.
I cannot live for even one
Short hour bereaved of my son.
But ah, the prince, whose arms are strong,
Has journeyed far: the way is long:
Me, me upon the chariot place,
And let me look on Ráma's face.
Ah me, my son, mine eldest-born,
Where roams he in the wood forlorn,
The wielder of the mighty bow,
Whose shoulders like the lion's show?
O, ere the light of life be dim,
Take me to Sítá and to him.
O Ráma, Lakshmaṇ, and O thou
Dear Sítá, constant to thy vow,
Beloved ones, you cannot know
That I am dying of my woe."

The king to bitter grief a prey,
That drove each wandering sense away,
Sunk in affliction's sea, too wide
To traverse, in his anguish cried:

490

"Hard, hard to pass, my Queen, this sea
Of sorrow raging over me:
No Ráma near to soothe mine eye,
Plunged in its lowest deeps I lie.
Sorrow for Ráma swells the tide,
And Sítá's absence makes it wide:
My tears its foamy flood distain,
Made billowy by my sighs of pain:
My cries its roar, the arms I throw
About me are the fish below,
Kaikeyí is the fire that feeds
Beneath: my hair the tangled weeds:
Its source the tears for Ráma shed:
The hump-back's words its monsters dread:
The boon I gave the wretch its shore,
Till Ráma's banishment be o'er.
Ah me, that I should long to set
My eager eyes to-day
On Raghu's son, and he be yet
With Lakshman far away!"
Thus he of lofty glory wailed,
And sank upon the bed.
Beneath the woe his spirit failed,
And all his senses fled.

CANTO

LX

Kausalyá Consoled

As Queen Kauśalyá, trembling much,
As blighted by a goblin's touch,
Still lying prostrate, half awoke
To consciousness, 'twas thus she spoke:
"Bear me away, Sumantra, far,
Where Ráma, Sítá, Lakshman are.

Bereft of them I have no power
To linger on a single hour.

Again, I pray, thy steps retrace,
And me in Daṇḍak forest place,
For after them I needs must go,
Or sink to Yama's realms below."

His utterance choked by tears that rolled
Down from their fountains uncontrolled,
With suppliant hands the charioteer
Thus spake, the lady's heart to cheer:
"Dismiss thy grief, despair, and dread
That fills thy soul, of sorrow bred,
For pain and anguish thrown aside,
Will Ráma in the wood abide.
And Lakshmaṇ, with unfailing care
Will guard the feet of Ráma there,
Earning, with governed sense, the prize
That waits on duty in the skies.
And Sítá in the wild as well
As in her own dear home will dwell;
To Ráma all her heart she gives,
And free from doubt and terror lives.
No faintest sign of care or woe
The features of the lady show:
Methinks Videha's pride was made
For exile in the forest shade.
E'en as of old she used to rove
Delighted in the city's grove,
Thus, even thus she joys to tread
The woodlands uninhabited.
Like a young child, her face as fair
As the young moon, she wanders there.
What though in lonely woods she stray
Still Ráma is her joy and stay:
All his the heart no sorrow bends,
Her very life on him depends.
For, if her lord she might not see,
Ayodhyá like the wood would be.
She bids him, as she roams, declare

492

The names of towns and hamlets there,
Marks various trees that meet her eye,
And many a brook that hurries by,
And Janak's daughter seems to roam
One little league away from home
When Ráma or his brother speaks
And gives the answer that she seeks.
This, Lady, I remember well,
Nor angry words have I to tell:
Reproaches at Kaikeyí shot,
Such, Queen, my mind remembers not."
The speech when Sítá's wrath was high,
Sumantra passed in silence by,
That so his pleasant words might cheer
With sweet report Kauśalyá's ear.
"Her moonlike beauty suffers not
Though winds be rude and suns be hot:
The way, the danger, and the toil
Her gentle lustre may not soil.
Like the red lily's leafy crown
Or as the fair full moon looks down,
So the Videhan lady's face
Still shines with undiminished grace.
What if the borrowed colours throw
O'er her fine feet no rosy glow,
Still with their natural tints they spread
A lotus glory where they tread.
In sportive grace she walks the ground
And sweet her chiming anklets sound.
No jewels clasp the faultless limb:
She leaves them all for love of him.
If in the woods her gentle eye
A lion sees, or tiger nigh,
Or elephant, she fears no ill
For Ráma's arm supports her still.
No longer be their fate deplored,
Nor thine, nor that of Kośal's lord,
For conduct such as theirs shall buy
Wide glory that can never die.
For casting grief and care away,
Delighting in the forest, they

493

With joyful spirits, blithe and gay,
Set forward on the ancient way
Where mighty saints have led:
Their highest aim, their dearest care
To keep their father's honour fair,
Observing still the oath he sware,
They roam, on wild fruit fed."
Thus with persuasive art he tried
To turn her from her grief aside,
By soothing fancies won.
But still she gave her sorrow vent:
"Ah Ráma," was her shrill lament,
"My love, my son, my son!"

CANTO

LXI

Kausalyá's Lament

When, best of all who give delight,
    Her Ráma wandered far from sight,
    Kauśalyá weeping, sore distressed,
The king her husband thus addressed:
"Thy name, O Monarch, far and wide
Through the three worlds is glorified:
Yet Ráma's is the pitying mind,
His speed is true, his heart is kind.
How will thy sons, good lord, sustain
With Sítá, all their care and pain?
How in the wild endure distress,
Nursed in the lap of tenderness?
How will the dear Videhan bear
The heat and cold when wandering there
Bred in the bliss of princely state,
So young and fair and delicate?

The large-eyed lady, wont to eat
The best of finely seasoned meat—
How will she now her life sustain
With woodland fare of self-sown grain?
Will she, with joys encompassed long,
Who loved the music and the song,
In the wild wood endure to hear
The ravening lion's voice of fear?
Where sleeps my strong-armed hero, where,

Like Lord Mahendra's standard, fair?
Where is, by Lakshman's side, his bed,
His club-like arm beneath his head?
When shall I see his flower-like eyes,
And face that with the lotus vies,
Feel his sweet lily breath, and view
His glorious hair and lotus hue?
The heart within my breast, I feel,
Is adamant or hardest steel,
Or, in a thousand fragments split,
The loss of him had shattered it,
When those I love, who should be blest,
Are wandering in the wood distressed,
Condemned their wretched lives to lead
In exile, by thy ruthless deed.
If, when the fourteen years are past,
Ráma reseeks his home at last,
I think not Bharat will consent
To yield the wealth and government.
At funeral feasts some mourners deal
To kith and kin the solemn meal,
And having duly fed them all
Some Bráhmans to the banquet call.
The best of Bráhmans, good and wise,
The tardy summoning despise,
And, equal to the Gods, disdain
Cups, e'en of Amrit, thus to drain.
Nay e'en when Bráhmans first have fed,
They loathe the meal for others spread,
And from the leavings turn with scorn,

495

As bulls avoid a fractured horn.
So Ráma, sovereign lord of men,
Will spurn the sullied kingship then:
He born the eldest and the best,
His younger's leavings will detest,
Turning from tasted food away,
As tigers scorn another's prey.
The sacred post is used not twice,
Nor elements, in sacrifice.
But once the sacred grass is spread,
But once with oil the flame is fed:
So Ráma's pride will ne'er receive
The royal power which others leave,
Like wine when tasteless dregs are left,
Or rites of Soma juice bereft.
Be sure the pride of Raghu's race
Will never stoop to such disgrace:
The lordly lion will not bear
That man should beard him in his lair.
Were all the worlds against him ranged
His dauntless soul were still unchanged:
He, dutiful, in duty strong,
Would purge the impious world from wrong.
Could not the hero, brave and bold,
The archer, with his shafts of gold,
Burn up the very seas, as doom
Will in the end all life consume?
Of lion's might, eyed like a bull,
A prince so brave and beautiful,
Thou hast with wicked hate pursued,
Like sea-born tribes who eat their brood.
If thou, O Monarch, hadst but known
The duty all the Twice-born own,
If the good laws had touched thy mind,
Which sages in the Scriptures find,
Thou ne'er hadst driven forth to pine
This brave, this duteous son of thine.
First on her lord the wife depends,
Next on her son and last on friends:
These three supports in life has she,
And not a fourth for her may be.

Thy heart, O King, I have not won;
In wild woods roams my banished son;
Far are my friends: ah, hapless me,
Quite ruined and destroyed by thee."

CANTO

LXII

Dasaratha Consoled

The queen's stern speech the monarch heard,
As rage and grief her bosom stirred,
And by his anguish sore oppressed
Reflected in his secret breast.
Fainting and sad, with woe distraught,
He wandered in a maze of thought;
At length the queller of the foe
Grew conscious, rallying from his woe.
When consciousness returned anew
Long burning sighs the monarch drew,
Again immersed in thought he eyed
Kauśalyá standing by his side.
Back to his pondering soul was brought
The direful deed his hand had wrought,
When, guiltless of the wrong intent,
His arrow at a sound was sent.
Distracted by his memory's sting,
And mourning for his son, the king
To two consuming griefs a prey,
A miserable victim lay.
The double woe devoured him fast,
As on the ground his eyes he cast,
Joined supplant hands, her heart to touch,
And spake in the answer, trembling much:
"Kauśalyá, for thy grace I sue,
Joining these hands as suppliants do.

Thou e'en to foes hast ever been
A gentle, good, and loving queen.
Her lord, with noble virtues graced,
Her lord, by lack of all debased,
Is still a God in woman's eyes,
If duty's law she hold and prize.
Thou, who the right hast aye pursued,
Life's changes and its chances viewed,
Shouldst never launch, though sorrow-stirred,
At me distressed, one bitter word."

She listened, as with sorrow faint
He murmured forth his sad complaint:
Her brimming eyes with tears ran o'er,
As spouts the new fallen water pour;

His suppliant hands, with fear dismayed
She gently clasped in hers, and laid,
Like a fair lotus, on her head,
And faltering in her trouble said:
"Forgive me; at thy feet I lie,
With low bent head to thee I cry.
By thee besought, thy guilty dame
Pardon from thee can scarcely claim.
She merits not the name of wife
Who cherishes perpetual strife
With her own husband good and wise,
Her lord both here and in the skies.
I know the claims of duty well,
I know thy lips the truth must tell.
All the wild words I rashly spoke,
Forth from my heart, through anguish, broke;
For sorrow bends the stoutest soul,
And cancels Scripture's high control.
Yea, sorrow's might all else o'erthrows
The strongest and the worst of foes.
'Tis thus with all: we keenly feel,
Yet bear the blows our foemen deal,
But when a slender woe assails
The manliest spirit bends and quails.
The fifth long night has now begun

498

Since the wild woods have lodged my son:
To me whose joy is drowned in tears,
Each day a dreary year appears.
While all my thoughts on him are set
Grief at my heart swells wilder yet:
With doubled might thus Ocean raves
When rushing floods increase his waves."

As from Kaúsalyá reasoning well
The gentle words of wisdom fell,
The sun went down with dying flame,
And darkness o'er the landscape came.
His lady's soothing words in part
Relieved the monarch's aching heart,
Who, wearied out by all his woes,
Yielded to sleep and took repose.

CANTO
LXIII

The Hermit's Son

But soon by rankling grief oppressed
The king awoke from troubled rest,
And his sad heart was tried again
With anxious thought where all was pain.
Ráma and Lakshman's mournful fate
On Daśaratha, good and great
As Indra, pressed with crushing weight,
As when the demon's might assails
The Sun-God, and his glory pales.
Ere yet the sixth long night was spent,
Since Ráma to the woods was sent,
The king at midnight sadly thought
Of the old crime his hand had wrought,
And thus to Queen Kaúsalyá cried

Who still for Ráma moaned and sighed:
"If thou art waking, give, I pray,
Attention to the words I say.
Whate'er the conduct men pursue,
Be good or ill the acts they do,
Be sure, dear Queen, they find the meed
Of wicked or of virtuous deed.
A heedless child we call the man
Whose feeble judgment fails to scan
The weight of what his hands may do,
Its lightness, fault, and merit too.
One lays the Mango garden low,
And bids the gay Palásas grow:
Longing for fruit their bloom he sees,
But grieves when fruit should bend the trees.
Cut by my hand, my fruit-trees fell,
Palása trees I watered well.
My hopes this foolish heart deceive,
And for my banished son I grieve.
Kauśalyá, in my youthful prime
Armed with my bow I wrought the crime,
Proud of my skill, my name renowned,
An archer prince who shoots by sound.
The deed this hand unwitting wrought
This misery on my soul has brought,
As children seize the deadly cup
And blindly drink the poison up.
As the unreasoning man may be
Charmed with the gay Palása tree,
I unaware have reaped the fruit
Of joying at a sound to shoot.
As regent prince I shared the throne,
Thou wast a maid to me unknown,
The early Rain-time duly came,
And strengthened love's delicious flame.
The sun had drained the earth that lay
All glowing 'neath the summer day,
And to the gloomy clime had fled
Where dwell the spirits of the dead.
The fervent heat that moment ceased,
The darkening clouds each hour increased

And frogs and deer and peacocks all
Rejoiced to see the torrents fall.
Their bright wings heavy from the shower,
The birds, new-bathed, had scarce the power
To reach the branches of the trees
Whose high tops swayed beneath the breeze.
The fallen rain, and falling still,
Hung like a sheet on every hill,
Till, with glad deer, each flooded steep
Showed glorious as the mighty deep.
The torrents down its wooded side
Poured, some unstained, while others dyed

Gold, ashy, silver, ochre, bore
The tints of every mountain ore.
In that sweet time, when all are pleased,
My arrows and my bow I seized;
Keen for the chase, in field or grove,
Down Sarjú's bank my car I drove.
I longed with all my lawless will
Some elephant by night to kill,
Some buffalo that came to drink,
Or tiger, at the river's brink.
When all around was dark and still,
I heard a pitcher slowly fill,
And thought, obscured in deepest shade,
An elephant the sound had made.
I drew a shaft that glittered bright,
Fell as a serpent's venomed bite;
I longed to lay the monster dead,
And to the mark my arrow sped.
Then in the calm of morning, clear
A hermit's wailing smote my ear:
"Ah me, ah me," he cried, and sank,
Pierced by my arrow, on the bank.
E'en as the weapon smote his side,
I heard a human voice that cried:
"Why lights this shaft on one like me,
A poor and harmless devotee?
I came by night to fill my jar
From this lone stream where no men are.

501

Ah, who this deadly shaft has shot?
Whom have I wronged, and knew it not?
Why should a boy so harmless feel
The vengeance of the winged steel?
Or who should slay the guiltless son
Of hermit sire who injures none,
Who dwells retired in woods, and there
Supports his life on woodland fare?
Ah me, ah me, why am I slain,
What booty will the murderer gain?
In hermit coils I bind my hair,
Coats made of skin and bark I wear.
Ah, who the cruel deed can praise
Whose idle toil no fruit repays,
As impious as the wretch's crime
Who dares his master's bed to climb?
Nor does my parting spirit grieve
But for the life which thus I leave:
Alas, my mother and my sire,—
I mourn for them when I expire.
Ah me, that aged, helpless pair,
Long cherished by my watchful care,
How will it be with them this day
When to the Five I pass away?
Pierced by the self-same dart we die,
Mine aged mother, sire, and I.
Whose mighty hand, whose lawless mind
Has all the three to death consigned?"

When I, by love of duty stirred,
That touching lamentation heard,
Pierced to the heart by sudden woe,
I threw to earth my shafts and bow.
My heart was full of grief and dread
As swiftly to the place I sped,
Where, by my arrow wounded sore,
A hermit lay on Sarjú's shore.
His matted hair was all unbound,
His pitcher empty on the ground,
And by the fatal arrow pained,
He lay with dust and gore distained.

I stood confounded and amazed:
His dying eyes to mine he raised,
And spoke this speech in accents stern,
As though his light my soul would burn:
"How have I wronged thee, King, that I
Struck by thy mortal arrow die?
The wood my home, this jar I brought,
And water for my parents sought.
This one keen shaft that strikes me through
Slays sire and aged mother too.
Feeble and blind, in helpless pain,
They wait for me and thirst in vain.
They with parched lips their pangs must bear,
And hope will end in blank despair.
Ah me, there seems no fruit in store
For holy zeal or Scripture lore,
Or else ere now my sire would know
That his dear son is lying low.
Yet, if my mournful fate he knew,
What could his arm so feeble do?
The tree, firm-rooted, ne'er may be
The guardian of a stricken tree.
Haste to my father, and relate
While time allows, my sudden fate,
Lest he consume thee as the fire
Burns up the forest, in his ire.
This little path, O King, pursue:
My father's cot thou soon wilt view.
There sue for pardon to the sage,
Lest he should curse thee in his rage.
First from the wound extract the dart
That kills me with its deadly smart,
E'en as the flushed impetuous tide
Eats through the river's yielding side."

I feared to draw the arrow out,
And pondered thus in painful doubt:
"Now tortured by the shaft he lies,
But if I draw it forth he dies."
Helpless I stood, faint, sorely grieved:
The hermit's son my thought perceived;

As one o'ercome by direst pain
He scarce had strength to speak again.
With writhing limb and struggling breath,
Nearer and ever nearer death
"My senses undisturbed remain,
And fortitude has conquered pain:
Now from one tear thy soul be freed.
Thy hand has made a Bráhman bleed.
Let not this pang thy bosom wring:
No twice-born youth am I, O King,

For of a Vaiśya sire I came,
Who wedded with a Śúdra dame."

These words the boy could scarcely say,
As tortured by the shaft he lay,
Twisting his helpless body round,
Then trembling senseless on the ground.
Then from his bleeding side I drew
The rankling shaft that pierced him through.
With death's last fear my face he eyed,
And, rich in store of penance, died."

CANTO
LXIV

Dasaratha's Death

The son of Raghu to his queen
Thus far described the unequalled scene,
And, as the hermit's death he rued,
The mournful story thus renewed:
"The deed my heedless hand had wrought
Perplexed me with remorseful thought,
And all alone I pondered still
How kindly deed might salve the ill.

The pitcher from the ground I took,
And filled it from that fairest brook,
Then, by the path the hermit showed,
I reached his sainted sire's abode.
I came, I saw: the aged pair,
Feeble and blind, were sitting there,
Like birds with clipped wings, side by side,
With none their helpless steps to guide.
Their idle hours the twain beguiled
With talk of their returning child,
And still the cheering hope enjoyed,
The hope, alas, by me destroyed.
Then spoke the sage, as drawing near
The sound of footsteps reached his ear:
"Dear son, the water quickly bring;
Why hast thou made this tarrying?
Thy mother thirsts, and thou hast played,
And bathing in the brook delayed.
She weeps because thou camest not;
Haste, O my son, within the cot.
If she or I have ever done
A thing to pain thee, dearest son,
Dismiss the memory from thy mind:
A hermit thou, be good and kind.
On thee our lives, our all, depend:
Thou art thy friendless parents' friend.
The eyeless couple's eye art thou:
Then why so cold and silent now?"

With sobbing voice and bosom wrung
I scarce could move my faltering tongue,
And with my spirit filled with dread
I looked upon the sage, and said,
While mind, and sense, and nerve I strung
To fortify my trembling tongue,
And let the aged hermit know
His son's sad fate, my fear and woe:
"High-minded Saint, not I thy child,
A warrior, Daśaratha styled.
I bear a grievous sorrow's weight
Born of a deed which good men hate.

505

My lord, I came to Sarjú's shore,
And in my hand my bow I bore
For elephant or beast of chase
That seeks by night his drinking place.
There from the stream a sound I heard
As if a jar the water stirred.
An elephant, I thought, was nigh:
I aimed, and let an arrow fly.
Swift to the place I made my way,
And there a wounded hermit lay
Gasping for breath: the deadly dart
Stood quivering in his youthful heart.
I hastened near with pain oppressed;
He faltered out his last behest.
And quickly, as he bade me do,
From his pierced side the shaft I drew.
I drew the arrow from the rent,
And up to heaven the hermit went,
Lamenting, as from earth he passed,
His aged parents to the last.
Thus, unaware, the deed was done:
My hand, unwitting, killed thy son.
For what remains, O, let me win
Thy pardon for my heedless sin."

As the sad tale of sin I told
The hermit's grief was uncontrolled.
With flooded eyes, and sorrow-faint,
Thus spake the venerable saint:
I stood with hand to hand applied,
And listened as he spoke and sighed:
"If thou, O King, hadst left unsaid
By thine own tongue this tale of dread,
Thy head for hideous guilt accursed
Had in a thousand pieces burst.
A hermit's blood by warrior spilt,
In such a case, with purposed guilt,
Down from his high estate would bring
Even the thunder's mighty King.
And he a dart who conscious sends
Against the devotee who spends

His pure life by the law of Heaven—
That sinner's head will split in seven.
Thou livest, for thy heedless hand
Has wrought a deed thou hast not planned,
Else thou and all of Raghu's line
Had perished by this act of thine.
Now guide us," thus the hermit said,
"Forth to the spot where he lies dead.
Guide us, this day, O Monarch, we
For the last time our son would see:
The hermit dress of skin he wore
Rent from his limbs distained with gore;
His senseless body lying slain,
His soul in Yama's dark domain."

Alone the mourning pair I led,
Their souls with woe disquieted,
And let the dame and hermit lay

Their hands upon the breathless clay.
The father touched his son, and pressed
The body to his aged breast;
Then falling by the dead boy's side,
He lifted up his voice, and cried:

"Hast thou no word, my child, to say?
No greeting for thy sire to-day?
Why art thou angry, darling? why
Wilt thou upon the cold earth lie?
If thou, my son, art wroth with me,
Here, duteous child, thy mother see.
What! no embrace for me, my son?
No word of tender love—not one?
Whose gentle voice, so soft and clear,
Soothing my spirit, shall I hear
When evening comes, with accents sweet
Scripture or ancient lore repeat?
Who, having fed the sacred fire,
And duly bathed, as texts require,
Will cheer, when evening rites are done,
The father mourning for his son?

507

Who will the daily meal provide
For the poor wretch who lacks a guide,
Feeding the helpless with the best
Berries and roots, like some dear guest?
How can these hands subsistence find
For thy poor mother, old and blind?
The wretched votaress how sustain,
Who mourns her child in ceaseless pain?
Stay yet a while, my darling, stay,
Nor fly to Yama's realm to-day.
To-morrow I thy sire and she
Who bare thee, child, will go with thee.
Then when I look on Yama, I
To great Vivasvat's son will cry:
"Hear, King of justice, and restore
Our child to feed us, I implore.
Lord of the world, of mighty fame,
Faithful and just, admit my claim,
And grant this single boon to free
My soul from fear, to one like me."
Because, my son, untouched by stain,
By sinful hands thou fallest slain,
Win, through thy truth, the sphere where those
Who die by hostile darts repose.
Seek the blest home prepared for all
The valiant who in battle fall,
Who face the foe and scorn to yield,
In glory dying on the field.
Rise to the heaven where Dhundhumár
And Nahush, mighty heroes, are,
Where Janamejay and the blest
Dilípa, Sagar, Saivya, rest:
Home of all virtuous spirits, earned
By fervent rites and Scripture learned:
By those whose sacred fires have glowed,
Whose liberal hands have fields bestowed:
By givers of a thousand cows,
By lovers of one faithful spouse:
By those who serve their masters well,
And cast away this earthly shell.
None of my race can ever know

The bitter pain of lasting woe.
But doomed to that dire fate is he
Whose guilty hand has slaughtered thee."

Thus with wild tears the aged saint
Made many a time his piteous plaint,
Then with his wife began to shed
The funeral water for the dead.
But in a shape celestial clad,
Won by the merits of the lad,
The spirit from the body brake
And to the mourning parents spake:
"A glorious home in realms above
Rewards my care and filial love.
You, honoured parents, soon shall be
Partakers of that home with me."

He spake, and swiftly mounting high,
With Indra near him, to the sky
On a bright car, with flame that glowed,
Sublime the duteous hermit rode.

The father, with his consort's aid,
The funeral rites with water paid,
And thus his speech to me renewed
Who stood in suppliant attitude:
"Slay me this day, O, slay me, King,
For death no longer has a sting.
Childless am I: thy dart has done
To death my dear, my only son.
Because the boy I loved so well
Slain by thy heedless arrow fell,
My curse upon thy soul shall press
With bitter woe and heaviness.
I mourn a slaughtered child, and thou
Shalt feel the pangs that kill me now.
Bereft and suffering e'en as I,
So shalt thou mourn thy son, and die.
Thy hand unwitting dealt the blow
That laid a holy hermit low,
And distant, therefore, is the time

509

When thou shalt suffer for the crime.
The hour shall come when, crushed by woes
Like these I feel, thy life shall close:
A debt to pay in after days
Like his the priestly fee who pays."

This curse on me the hermit laid,
Nor yet his tears and groans were stayed.
Then on the pyre their bodies cast
The pair; and straight to heaven they passed.
As in sad thought I pondered long
Back to my memory came the wrong
Done in wild youth, O lady dear,
When 'twas my boast to shoot by ear.

The deed has borne the fruit, which now
Hangs ripe upon the bending bough:
Thus dainty meats the palate please,
And lure the weak to swift disease.
Now on my soul return with dread
The words that noble hermit said,
That I for a dear son should grieve,
And of the woe my life should leave."
Thus spake the king with many a tear;
Then to his wife he cried in fear:
"I cannot see thee, love; but lay
Thy gentle hand in mine, I pray.
Ah me, if Ráma touched me thus,
If once, returning home to us,
He bade me wealth and lordship give,
Then, so I think, my soul would live.
Unlike myself, unjust and mean
Have been my ways with him, my Queen,
But like himself is all that he,
My noble son, has done to me.
His son, though far from right he stray,
What prudent sire would cast away?
What banished son would check his ire,
Nor speak reproaches of his sire?
I see thee not: these eyes grow blind,
And memory quits my troubled mind.

510

Angels of Death are round me: they
Summon my soul with speed away.
What woe more grievous can there be,
That, when from light and life I flee,
I may not, ere I part, behold
My virtuous Ráma, true and bold?
Grief for my son, the brave and true,
Whose joy it was my will to do,
Dries up my breath, as summer dries
The last drop in the pool that lies.
Not men, but blessed Gods, are they
Whose eyes shall see his face that day;
See him, when fourteen years are past,
With earrings decked return at last.
My fainting mind forgets to think:
Low and more low my spirits sink.
Each from its seat, my senses steal:
I cannot hear, or taste, or feel.
This lethargy of soul o'ercomes
Each organ, and its function numbs:
So when the oil begins to fail,
The torch's rays grow faint and pale.
This flood of woe caused by this hand
Destroys me helpless and unmanned,
Resistless as the floods that bore
A passage through the river shore.
Ah Raghu's son, ah mighty-armed,
By whom my cares were soothed and charmed,
My son in whom I took delight,
Now vanished from thy father's sight!
Kauśalyá, ah, I cannot see;
Sumitrá, gentle devotee!
Alas, Kaikeyí, cruel dame,
My bitter foe, thy father's shame!"

Kauśalyá and Sumitrá kept
Their watch beside him as he wept.
And Daśaratha moaned and sighed,
And grieving for his darling died.

CANTO
LXV

The Women's Lament

And now the night had past away,
And brightly dawned another day;
The minstrels, trained to play and sing,
Flocked to the chamber of the king:
Bards, who their gayest raiment wore,
And heralds famed for ancient lore:
And singers, with their songs of praise,
Made music in their several ways.
There as they poured their blessings choice
And hailed their king with hand and voice,
Their praises with a swelling roar
Echoed through court and corridor.
Then as the bards his glory sang,
From beaten palms loud answer rang,
As glad applauders clapped their hands,
And told his deeds in distant lands.
The swelling concert woke a throng
Of sleeping birds to life and song:
Some in the branches of the trees,
Some caged in halls and galleries.
Nor was the soft string music mute;
The gentle whisper of the lute,
And blessings sung by singers skilled
The palace of the monarch filled.
Eunuchs and dames of life unstained,
Each in the arts of waiting trained,
Drew near attentive as before,
And crowded to the chamber door:
These skilful when and how to shed
The lustral stream o'er limb and head,
Others with golden ewers stood

Of water stained with sandal wood.
And many a maid, pure, young, and fair,
Her load of early offerings bare,
Cups of the flood which all revere,
And sacred things, and toilet gear.
Each several thing was duly brought
As rule of old observance taught,
And lucky signs on each impressed
Stamped it the fairest and the best.
There anxious, in their long array,
All waited till the shine of day:
But when the king nor rose nor spoke,
Doubt and alarm within them woke.
Forthwith the dames, by duty led,
Attendants on the monarch's bed,
Within the royal chamber pressed
To wake their master from his rest.
Skilled in the lore of dreaming, they
First touched the bed on which he lay.
But none replied; no sound was heard,

Nor hand, nor head, nor body stirred.
They trembled, and their dread increased,
Fearing his breath of life had ceased,
And bending low their heads, they shook
Like the tall reeds that fringe the brook.
In doubt and terror down they knelt,
Looked on his face, his cold hand felt,
And then the gloomy truth appeared
Of all their hearts had darkly feared.
Kauśalyá and Sumitrá, worn
With weeping for their sons, forlorn,
Woke not, but lay in slumber deep
And still as death's unending sleep.
Bowed down by grief, her colour fled,
Her wonted lustre dull and dead,
Kauśalyá shone not, like a star
Obscured behind a cloudy bar.
Beside the king's her couch was spread,
And next was Queen Sumitrá's bed,
Who shone no more with beauty's glow,

513

Her face bedewed with tears of woe.
There lapped in sleep each wearied queen,
There as in sleep, the king was seen;
And swift the troubling thought came o'er
Their spirits that he breathed no more.
At once with wailing loud and high
The matrons shrieked a bitter cry,
As widowed elephants bewail
Their dead lord in the woody vale.
At the loud shriek that round them rang,
Kauśalyá and Sumitrá sprang
Awakened from their beds, with eyes
Wide open in their first surprise.
Quick to the monarch's side they came,
And saw and touched his lifeless frame;
One cry, O husband! forth they sent,
And prostrate to the ground they went.
The king of Kośal's daughter there
Writhed, with the dust on limb and hair
Lustreless, as a star might lie
Hurled downward from the glorious sky.
When the king's voice in death was stilled,
The women who the chamber filled
Saw, like a widow elephant slain,
Kauśalyá prostrate in her pain.
Then all the monarch's ladies led
By Queen Kaikeyí at their head,
Poured forth their tears, and weeping so,
Sank on the ground, consumed by woe.
The cry of grief so long and loud
Went up from all the royal crowd,
That, doubled by the matron train,
It made the palace ring again.
Filled with dark fear and eager eyes,
Anxiety and wild surmise;
Echoing with the cries of grief
Of sorrowing friends who mourned their chief,
Dejected, pale with deep distress,
Hurled from their height of happiness:
Such was the look the palace wore
Where lay the king who breathed no more.

CANTO
LXVI

The Embalming

Kauśalyá's eyes with tears o'erflowed,
Weighed down by varied sorrows' load;
On her dead lord her gaze she bent,
Who lay like fire whose might is spent,
Like the great deep with waters dry,
Or like the clouded sun on high.
Then on her lap she laid his head.
And on Kaikeyí looked and said:
"Triumphant now enjoy thy reign
Without a thorn thy side to pain.
Thou hast pursued thy single aim,
And killed the king, O wicked dame.
Far from my sight my Ráma flies,
My perished lord has sought the skies.
No friend, no hope my life to cheer,
I cannot tread the dark path here.
Who would forsake her husband, who
That God to whom her love is due,
And wish to live one hour, but she
Whose heart no duty owns, like thee?
The ravenous sees no fault: his greed
Will e'en on poison blindly feed.
Kaikeyí, through a hump-back maid,
This royal house in death has laid.
King Janak, with his queen, will hear
Heart rent like me the tidings drear
Of Ráma banished by the king,
Urged by her impious counselling.
No son has he, his age is great,
And sinking with the double weight,
He for his darling child will pine,

515

And pierced with woe his life resign.
Sprung from Videha's monarch, she
A sad and lovely devotee,
Roaming the wood, unmeet for woe,
Will toil and trouble undergo.
She in the gloomy night with fear
The cries of beast and bird will hear,
And trembling in her wild alarm
Will cling to Ráma's sheltering arm.
Ah, little knows my duteous son
That I am widowed and undone—
My Ráma of the lotus eye,
Gone hence, gone hence, alas, to die.
Now, as a living wife and true,
I, e'en this day, will perish too:
Around his form these arms will throw
And to the fire with him will go."

Clasping her husband's lifeless clay
A while the weeping votaress lay,
Till chamberlains removed her thence

O'ercome by sorrow's violence.
Then in a cask of oil they laid
Him who in life the world had swayed,
And finished, as the lords desired,
All rites for parted souls required.
The lords, all-wise, refused to burn
The monarch ere his son's return;
So for a while the corpse they set
Embalmed in oil, and waited yet.
The women heard: no doubt remained,
And wildly for the king they plained.
With gushing tears that drowned each eye
Wildly they waved their arms on high,
And each her mangling nails impressed
Deep in her head and knee and breast:
"Of Ráma reft,—who ever spake
The sweetest words the heart to take,
Who firmly to the truth would cling,—
Why dost thou leave us, mighty King?

How can the consorts thou hast left
Widowed, of Raghu's son bereft,
Live with our foe Kaikeyí near,
The wicked queen we hate and fear?
She threw away the king, her spite
Drove Ráma forth and Lakshman's might,
And gentle Sítá: how will she
Spare any, whosoe'er it be?"

Oppressed with sorrow, tear-distained,
The royal women thus complained.
Like night when not a star appears,
Like a sad widow drowned in tears,
Ayodhyá's city, dark and dim,
Reft of her lord was sad for him.
When thus for woe the king to heaven had fled,
And still on earth his lovely wives remained.
With dying light the sun to rest had sped,
And night triumphant o'er the landscape reigned.

CANTO
LXVII

The Praise of Kings

That night of sorrow passed away,
And rose again the God of Day.
Then all the twice-born peers of state
Together met for high debate.
Jáválí, lord of mighty fame.
And Gautam, and Kátyáyan came,
And Márkandeya's reverend age,
And Vámadeva, glorious sage:
Sprung from Mudgalya's seed the one,
The other ancient Kaśyap's son.
With lesser lords these Bráhmans each

Spoke in his turn his several speech,
And turning to Vaśishṭha, best
Of household priests him thus addressed:
"The night of bitter woe has past,
Which seemed a hundred years to last,
Our king, in sorrow for his son,
Reunion with the Five has won.
His soul is where the blessed are,
While Ráma roams in woods afar,
And Lakshmaṇ, bright in glorious deeds,
Goes where his well-loved brother leads.
And Bharat and Śatrughna, they
Who smite their foes in battle fray,
Far in the realm of Kekaya stay,
Where their maternal grandsire's care
Keeps Rájagriha's city fair.
Let one of old Ikshváku's race
Obtain this day the sovereign's place,
Or havoc and destruction straight
Our kingless land will devastate.
In kingless lands no thunder's voice,
No lightning wreaths the heart rejoice,
Nor does Parjanya's heavenly rain
Descend upon the burning plain.
Where none is king, the sower's hand
Casts not the seed upon the land;
The son against the father strives.
And husbands fail to rule their wives.
In kingless realms no princes call
Their friends to meet in crowded hall;
No joyful citizens resort
To garden trim or sacred court.
In kingless realms no Twice-born care
To sacrifice with text and prayer,
Nor Bráhmans, who their vows maintain,
The great solemnities ordain.
The joys of happier days have ceased:
No gathering, festival, or feast
Together calls the merry throng
Delighted with the play and song.
In kingless lands it ne'er is well

518

With sons of trade who buy and sell:
No men who pleasant tales repeat
Delight the crowd with stories sweet.
In kingless realms we ne'er behold
Young maidens decked with gems and gold,
Flock to the gardens blithe and gay
To spend their evening hours in play.
No lover in the flying car
Rides with his love to woods afar.
In kingless lands no wealthy swain
Who keeps the herd and reaps the grain,
Lies sleeping, blest with ample store,
Securely near his open door.
Upon the royal roads we see
No tusked elephant roaming free,
Of three-score years, whose head and neck
Sweet tinkling bells of silver deck.
We hear no more the glad applause
When his strong bow each rival draws,
No clap of hands, no eager cries
That cheer each martial exercise.
In kingless realms no merchant bands
Who travel forth to distant lands,
With precious wares their wagons load,

And fear no danger on the road.
No sage secure in self-control,
Brooding on God with mind and soul,
In lonely wanderings finds his home
Where'er at eve his feet may roam.
In kingless realms no man is sure
He holds his life and wealth secure.
In kingless lands no warriors smite
The foeman's host in glorious fight.
In kingless lands the wise no more,
Well trained in Scripture's holy lore,
In shady groves and gardens meet
To argue in their calm retreat.
No longer, in religious fear,
Do they who pious vows revere,
Bring dainty cates and wreaths of flowers

As offerings to the heavenly powers.
No longer, bright as trees in spring,
Shine forth the children of the king
Resplendent in the people's eyes
With aloe wood and sandal dyes.
A brook where water once has been,
A grove where grass no more is green,
Kine with no herdsman's guiding hand—
So wretched is a kingless land.
The car its waving banner rears,
Banner of fire the smoke appears:
Our king, the banner of our pride,
A God with Gods is glorified.
In kingless lands no law is known,
And none may call his wealth his own,
Each preys on each from hour to hour,
As fish the weaker fish devour.
Then fearless, atheists overleap
The bounds of right the godly keep,
And when no royal powers restrain,
Preëminence and lordship gain.
As in the frame of man the eye
Keeps watch and ward, a careful spy,
The monarch in his wide domains
Protects the truth, the right maintains.
He is the right, the truth is he,
Their hopes in him the well-born see.
On him his people's lives depend,
Mother is he, and sire, and friend.
The world were veiled in blinding night,
And none could see or know aright,
Ruled there no king in any state
The good and ill to separate.
We will obey thy word and will
As if our king were living still:
As keeps his bounds the faithful sea,
So we observe thy high decree.
O best of Bráhmans, first in place,
Our kingless land lies desolate:
Some scion of Ikshváku's race
Do thou as monarch consecrate."

CANTO

LXVIII

The Envoys

Vaśishṭha heard their speech and prayer,
And thus addressed the concourse there,
Friends, Bráhmans, counsellors, and all
Assembled in the palace hall:
"Ye know that Bharat, free from care,
Still lives in Rájagriha where
The father of his mother reigns:
Śatrughna by his side remains.
Let active envoys, good at need,
Thither on fleetest horses speed,
To bring the hero youths away:
Why waste the time in dull delay?"

Quick came from all the glad reply:
"Vaśishṭha, let the envoys fly!"
He heard their speech, and thus renewed
His charge before the multitude:
"Nandan, Aśok, Siddhárth, attend,
Your ears, Jayanta, Vijay, lend:
Be yours, what need requires, to do:
I speak these words to all of you.
With coursers of the fleetest breed
To Rájagriha's city speed.
Then rid your bosoms of distress,
And Bharat thus from me address:
"The household priest and peers by us
Send health to thee and greet thee thus:
Come to thy father's home with haste:
Thine absent time no longer waste."
But speak no word of Ráma fled,
Tell not the prince his sire is dead,

521

Nor to the royal youth the fate
That ruins Raghu's race relate.
Go quickly hence, and with you bear
Fine silken vestures rich and rare,
And gems and many a precious thing
As gifts to Bharat and the king."

With ample stores of food supplied,
Each to his home the envoys hied,
Prepared, with steeds of swiftest race,
To Kekaya's land their way to trace.
They made all due provision there,
And every need arranged with care,
Then ordered by Vaśishṭha, they
Went forth with speed upon their way.
Then northward of Pralamba, west
Of Apartála, on they pressed,
Crossing the Máliní that flowed
With gentle stream athwart the road.
They traversed Gangá's holy waves

Where she Hástinapura laves,
Thence to Panchála westward fast
Through Kurujángal's land they passed.
On, on their course the envoys held
By urgency of task impelled.
Quick glancing at each lucid flood
And sweet lake gay with flower and bud.
Beyond, they passed unwearied o'er,
Where glad birds fill the flood and shore
Of Śaradaṇḍá racing fleet
With heavenly water clear and sweet,
Thereby a tree celestial grows
Which every boon on prayer bestows:
To its blest shade they humbly bent,
Then to Kulingá's town they went.
Then, having passed the Warrior's Wood,
In Abhikála next they stood,
O'er sacred Ikshumatí came,
Their ancient kings' ancestral claim.
They saw the learned Bráhmans stand,

Each drinking from his hollowed hand,
And through Báhíka journeying still
They reached at length Sudáman's hill:
There Vishṇu's footstep turned to see,
Vipáśá viewed, and Śálmalí,
And many a lake and river met,
Tank, pool, and pond, and rivulet.
And lions saw, and tigers near,
And elephants and herds of deer,
And still, by prompt obedience led,
Along the ample road they sped.
Then when their course so swift and long,
Had worn their steeds though fleet and strong,
To Girivraja's splendid town
They came by night, and lighted down.
To please their master, and to guard
The royal race, the lineal right,
The envoys, spent with riding hard,
To that fair city came by night.

CANTO
LXIX

Bharat's Dream

The night those messengers of state
Had past within the city's gate,
In dreams the slumbering Bharat saw
A sight that chilled his soul with awe.
The dream that dire events foretold
Left Bharat's heart with horror cold,

And with consuming woes distraught,
Upon his aged sire he thought.
His dear companions, swift to trace
The signs of anguish on his face,

Drew near, his sorrow to expel,
And pleasant tales began to tell.
Some woke sweet music's cheering sound,
And others danced in lively round.
With joke and jest they strove to raise
His spirits, quoting ancient plays;
But Bharat still, the lofty-souled,
Deaf to sweet tales his fellows told,
Unmoved by music, dance, and jest,
Sat silent, by his woe oppressed.
To him, begirt by comrades near,
Thus spoke the friend he held most dear:
"Why ringed around by friends, art thou
So silent and so mournful now?"
"Hear thou," thus Bharat made reply,
"What chills my heart and dims mine eye.
I dreamt I saw the king my sire
Sink headlong in a lake of mire
Down from a mountain high in air,
His body soiled, and loose his hair.
Upon the miry lake he seemed
To lie and welter, as I dreamed;
With hollowed hands full many a draught
Of oil he took, and loudly laughed.
With head cast down I saw him make
A meal on sesamum and cake;
The oil from every member dripped,
And in its clammy flood he dipped.
The ocean's bed was bare and dry,
The moon had fallen from the sky,
And all the world lay still and dead,
With whelming darkness overspread.
The earth was rent and opened wide,
The leafy trees were scorched, and died;
I saw the seated mountains split,
And wreaths of rising smoke emit.
The stately beast the monarch rode
His long tusks rent and splintered showed;
And flames that quenched and cold had lain
Blazed forth with kindled light again.
I looked, and many a handsome dame,

524

Arrayed in brown and sable came
And bore about the monarch, dressed,
On iron stool, in sable vest.
And then the king, of virtuous mind,
A blood-red wreath around him twined,
Forth on an ass-drawn chariot sped,
As southward still he bent his head.
Then, crimson-clad, a dame appeared
Who at the monarch laughed and jeered;
And a she-monster, dire to view,
Her hand upon his body threw.
Such is the dream I dreamt by night,
Which chills me yet with wild affright:
Either the king or Ráma, I
Or Lakshmaṇ now must surely die.
For when an ass-drawn chariot seems
To bear away a man in dreams,
Be sure above his funeral pyre
The smoke soon rears its cloudy spire.
This makes my spirit low and weak,
My tongue is slow and loth to speak:
My lips and throat are dry for dread,
And all my soul disquieted.
My lips, relaxed, can hardly speak,
And chilling dread has changed my cheek
I blame myself in aimless fears,
And still no cause of blame appears.
I dwell upon this dream of ill
Whose changing scenes I viewed,
And on the startling horror still
My troubled thoughts will brood.
Still to my soul these terrors cling,
Reluctant to depart,
And the strange vision of the king
Still weighs upon my heart."

CANTO
LXX

Bharat's Departure

While thus he spoke, the envoys borne
On horses faint and travel-worn
Had gained the city fenced around
With a deep moat's protecting bound.
An audience of the king they gained,
And honours from the prince obtained;
The monarch's feet they humbly pressed,
To Bharat next these words addressed:
"The household priest and peers by us
Send health to thee and greet thee thus:
"Come to thy father's house with haste:
Thine absent time no longer waste."
Receive these vestures rich and rare,
These costly gems and jewels fair,
And to thy uncle here present
Each precious robe and ornament.
These for the king and him suffice—
Two hundred millions is their price—
These, worth a hundred millions, be
Reserved, O large-eyed Prince, for thee."

Loving his friends with heart and soul,
The joyful prince received the whole,
Due honour to the envoys paid,
And thus in turn his answer made:
"Of Daśaratha tidings tell:
Is the old king my father well?
Is Ráma, and is Lakshmaṇ, he
Of the high-soul, from sickness free?
And she who walks where duty leads,

Kauśalyá, known for gracious deeds,
Mother of Ráma, loving spouse,
Bound to her lord by well kept vows?
And Lakshman's mother too, the dame
Sumitrá skilled in duty's claim,
Who brave Śatrughna also bare,
Second in age,—her health declare.

And she, in self-conceit most sage,
With selfish heart most prone to rage,
My mother, fares she well? has she
Sent message or command to me?"

Thus Bharat spake, the mighty-souled,
And they in brief their tidings told:
"All they of whom thou askest dwell,
O lion lord, secure and well:
Thine all the smiles of fortune are:
Make ready; let them yoke the car."

Thus by the royal envoys pressed,
Bharat again the band addressed:
"I go with you: no long delay,
A single hour I bid you stay."
Thus Bharat, son of him who swayed
Ayodhyás realm, his answer made,
And then bespoke, his heart to please,
His mother's sire in words like these:
"I go to see my father, King,
Urged by the envoys' summoning;
And when thy soul desires to see
Thy grandson, will return to thee."

The king his grandsire kissed his head,
And in reply to Bharat said:
"Go forth, dear child: how blest is she,
The mother of a son like thee!
Greet well thy sire, thy mother greet,
O thou whose arms the foe defeat;
The household priest, and all the rest

Amid the Twice-born chief and best;
And Ráma and brave Lakshman, who
Shoot the long shaft with aim so true."

To him the king high honour showed,
And store of wealth and gifts bestowed,
The choicest elephants to ride,
And skins and blankets deftly dyed,
A thousand strings of golden beads,
And sixteen hundred mettled steeds:
And boundless wealth before him piled
Gave Kekaya to Kaikeyí's child.
And men of counsel, good and tried,
On whose firm truth he aye relied,
King Aśvapati gave with speed
Prince Bharat on his way to lead.
And noble elephants, strong and young,
From sires of Indraśira sprung,
And others tall and fair to view
Of great Airávat's lineage true:
And well yoked asses fleet of limb
The prince his uncle gave to him.
And dogs within the palace bred,
Of body vast and massive head,
With mighty fangs for battle, brave,
The tiger's match in strength, he gave.
Yet Bharat's bosom hardly glowed
To see the wealth the king bestowed;
For he would speed that hour away,
Such care upon his bosom lay:
Those eager envoys urged him thence,
And that sad vision's influence.
He left his court-yard, crowded then
With elephants and steeds and men,
And, peerless in immortal fame,
To the great royal street he came.
He saw, as farther still he went,
The inner rooms most excellent,
And passed the doors, to him unclosed,
Where check nor bar his way opposed.
There Bharat stayed to bid adieu

To grandsire and to uncle too,
Then, with Śatrughna by his side,
Mounting his car, away he hied.
The strong-wheeled cars were yoked, and they
More than a hundred, rolled away:
Servants, with horses, asses, kine,
Followed their lord in endless line.
So, guarded by his own right hand,
Forth high-souled Bharat hied,
Surrounded by a lordly band
On whom the king relied.
Beside him sat Śatrughna dear,
The scourge of trembling foes:
Thus from the light of Indra's sphere
A saint made perfect goes.

CANTO
LXXI

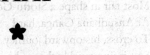

Bharat's Return

Then Bharat's face was eastward bent
As from the royal town he went.
He reached Sudámá's farther side,
And glorious, gazed upon the tide;
Passed Hládiní, and saw her toss
Her westering billows hard to cross.
Then old Ikshváku's famous son
O'er Śatadrú his passage won,
Near Ailadhána on the strand,
And came to Aparparyat's land.
O'er Śilá's flood he hurried fast,
Akurvatí's fair stream he passed,
Crossed o'er Ágneya's rapid rill,
And Śalyakartan onward still.
Śilávahá's swift stream he eyed,

True to his vows and purified,
Then crossed the lofty hills, and stood
In Chaitraratha's mighty wood.
He reached the confluence where meet
Sarasvatí and Gangá fleet,
And through Bhárunda forest, spread
Northward of Viramatsya, sped.
He sought Kálinda's child, who fills

The soul with joy, begirt by hills,
Reached Yamuná, and passing o'er,
Rested his army on the shore:
He gave his horses food and rest,
Bathed reeking limb and drooping crest.
They drank their fill and bathed them there,
And water for their journey bare.
Thence through a mighty wood he sped
All wild and uninhabited,
As in fair chariot through the skies,
Most fair in shape a Storm-God flies.
At Anśudhána Gangá, hard
To cross, his onward journey barred,
So turning quickly thence he came
To Prágvat's city dear to fame.
There having gained the farther side
To Kutikoshtiká he hied:
The stream he crossed, and onward then
To Dharmavardhan brought his men.
Thence, leaving Toran on the north,
To Jambuprastha journeyed forth.
Then onward to a pleasant grove
By fair Varútha's town he drove,
And when a while he there had stayed,
Went eastward from the friendly shade.
Eastward of Ujjihámá where
The Priyak trees are tall and fair,
He passed, and rested there each steed
Exhausted with the journey's speed.
There orders to his men addressed,
With quickened pace he onward pressed,
A while at Sarvatírtha spent,

Then o'er Uttánuká he went.
O'er many a stream beside he sped
With coursers on the mountains bred,
And passing Hastiprishṭhak, took
The road o'er Kuṭiká's fair brook.
Then, at Lohitya's village, he
Crossed o'er the swift Kapívatí,
Then passed, where Ekaśála stands,
The Sthánumatí's flood and sands,
And Gomatí of fair renown
By Vinata's delightful town.
When to Kalinga near he drew,
A wood of Sal trees charmed the view;
That passed, the sun began to rise,
And Bharat saw with happy eyes,
Ayodhyá's city, built and planned
By ancient Manu's royal hand.
Seven nights upon the road had passed,
And when he saw the town at last
Before him in her beauty spread,
Thus Bharat to the driver said:
"This glorious city from afar,
Wherein pure groves and gardens are,
Seems to my eager eyes to-day
A lifeless pile of yellow clay.
Through all her streets where erst a throng
Of men and women streamed along,
Uprose the multitudinous roar:
To-day I hear that sound no more.
No longer do mine eyes behold
The leading people, as of old,
On elephants, cars, horses, go
Abroad and homeward, to and fro.
The brilliant gardens, where we heard
The wild note of each rapturous bird,
Where men and women loved to meet,
In pleasant shades, for pastime sweet,—
These to my eyes this day appear
Joyless, and desolate, and drear:
Each tree that graced the garden grieves,
And every path is spread with leaves.

531

The merry cry of bird and beast,
That spake aloud their joy, has ceased:
Still is the long melodious note
That charmed us from each warbling throat.
Why blows the blessed air no more,
The incense-breathing air that bore
Its sweet incomparable scent
Of sandal and of aloe blent?
Why are the drum and tabour mute?
Why is the music of the lute
That woke responsive to the quill,
Loved by the happy, hushed and still?
My boding spirit gathers hence
Dire sins of awful consequence,
And omens, crowding on my sight,
Weigh down my soul with wild affright.
Scarce shall I find my friends who dwell
Here in Ayodhyá safe and well:
For surely not without a cause
This crushing dread my soul o'erawes."

Heart sick, dejected, every sense
Confused by terror's influence,
On to the town he quickly swept
Which King Ikshváku's children kept.
He passed through Vaijayanta's gate,
With weary steeds, disconsolate,
And all who near their station held,
His escort, crying Victory, swelled,
With heart distracted still he bowed
Farewell to all the following crowd,
Turned to the driver and began
To question thus the weary man:
"Why was I brought, O free from blame,
So fast, unknown for what I came?
Yet fear of ill my heart appals,
And all my wonted courage falls.
For I have heard in days gone by
The changes seen when monarchs die;
And all those signs, O charioteer,
I see to-day surround me here:

Tell the great chief that I am here:
Brother, and sire, and friend, and all
Is he, and I his trusty thrall.
For noble hearts, to virtue true,
Their sires in elder brothers view.
To clasp his feet I fain would bow:
He is my hope and refuge now.
What said my glorious sire, who knew
Virtue and vice, so brave and true?
Firm in his vows, dear lady, say,
What said he ere he passed away?
What was his rede to me? I crave
To hear the last advice he gave."

Thus closely questioned by the youth,
Kaikeyí spoke the mournful truth:
"The high-souled monarch wept and sighed,
For Ráma, Sítá, Lakshmaṇ, cried,
Then, best of all who go to bliss,
Passed to the world which follows this.
"Ah, blessed are the people who
Shall Ráma and his Sítá view,
And Lakshmaṇ of the mighty arm,
Returning free from scathe and harm."
Such were the words, the last of all,
Thy father, ere he died, let fall,
By Fate and Death's dread coils enwound,
As some great elephant is bound."

He heard, yet deeper in despair,
Her lips this double woe declare,
And with sad brow that showed his pain
Questioned his mother thus again:
"But where is he, of virtue tried,
Who fills Kauśalyá's heart with pride,
Where is the noble Ráma? where
Is Lakshmaṇ brave, and Sítá fair?"

Thus pressed, the queen began to tell
The story as each thing befell,
And gave her son in words like these,

537

The mournful news she meant to please:
"The prince is gone in hermit dress
To Daṇḍak's mighty wilderness,
And Lakshmaṇ brave and Sítá share
The wanderings of the exile there."

Then Bharat's soul with fear was stirred
Lest Ráma from the right had erred,
And jealous for ancestral fame,
He put this question to the dame:
"Has Ráma grasped with lawless hold
A Bráhman's house, or land, or gold?
Has Ráma harmed with ill intent
Some poor or wealthy innocent?
Was Ráma, faithless to his vows,
Enamoured of anothers spouse?
Why was he sent to Daṇḍak's wild,
Like one who kills an unborn child?"

He questioned thus: and she began
To tell her deeds and crafty plan.
Deceitful-hearted, fond, and blind
As is the way of womankind:
"No Bráhman's wealth has Ráma seized,
No dame his wandering fancy pleased;
His very eyes he ne'er allows
To gaze upon a neighbour's spouse.
But when I heard the monarch planned
To give the realm to Ráma's hand,
I prayed that Ráma hence might flee,
And claimed the throne, my son, for thee.
The king maintained the name he bare,
And did according to my prayer,
And Ráma, with his brother, sent,
And Sítá, forth to banishment.
When his dear son was seen no more,
The lord of earth was troubled sore:
Too feeble with his grief to strive,
He joined the elemental Five.
Up then, most dutiful! maintain
The royal state, arise, and reign.

For thee, my darling son, for thee
All this was planned and wrought by me.
Come, cast thy grief and pain aside,
With manly courage fortified.
This town and realm are all thine own,
And fear and grief are here unknown.
Come, with Vaśishṭha's guiding aid,
And priests in ritual skilled
Let the king's funeral dues be paid,
And every claim fulfilled.
Perform his obsequies with all
That suits his rank and worth,
Then give the mandate to install
Thyself as lord of earth."

CANTO

LXXIII

Kaikeyí Reproached

But when he heard the queen relate
His brothers' doom, his father's fate,
Thus Bharat to his mother said
With burning grief disquieted:

"Alas, what boots it now to reign,
Struck down by grief and well-nigh slain?
Ah, both are gone, my sire, and he
Who was a second sire to me.
Grief upon grief thy hand has made,
And salt upon gashes laid:
For my dear sire has died through thee,
And Ráma roams a devotee.
Thou camest like the night of Fate
This royal house to devastate.
Unwitting ill, my hapless sire

Placed in his bosom coals of fire,
And through thy crimes his death he met,
O thou whose heart on sin is set.
Shame of thy house! thy senseless deed
Has reft all joy from Raghu's seed.
The truthful monarch, dear to fame,
Received thee as his wedded dame,
And by thy act to misery doomed
Has died by flames of grief consumed.
Kauśalyá and Sumitrá too
The coming of my mother rue,
And if they live oppressed by woe,
For their dear sons their sad tears flow.
Was he not ever good and kind,—
That hero of the duteous mind?
Skilled in all filial duties, he
As a dear mother treated thee.
Kauśalyá too, the eldest queen,
Who far foresees with insight keen,
Did she not ever show thee all
A sister's love at duty's call?
And hast thou from the kingdom chased
Her son, with bark around his waist,
To the wild wood, to dwell therein,
And dost not sorrow for thy sin?
The love I bare to Raghu's son
Thou knewest not, ambitious one,
If thou hast wrought this impious deed
For royal sway, in lawless greed.
With him and Lakshmaṇ far away,
What power have I the realm to sway?
What hope will fire my bosom when
I see no more these lords of men?
The holy king, who loved the right
Relied on Ráma's power and might,
His guardian and his glory, so
Joys Meru in his woods below.
How can I bear, a steer untrained,
The load his mightier strength sustained?
What power have I to brook alone
This weight on feeble shoulders thrown?

But if the needful power were bought
By strength of mind and brooding thought,
No triumph shall attend the dame
Who dooms her son to lasting shame.
Now should no doubt that son prevent
From quitting thee on evil bent.
But Ráma's love o'erpowers my will,
Who holds thee as his mother still.
Whence did the thought, O thou whose eyes
Are turned to sinful deeds, arise—
A plan our ancient sires would hate,
O fallen from thy virtuous state?
For in the line from which we spring
The eldest is anointed king:
No monarchs from the rule decline,
And, least of all, Ikshváku's line.
Our holy sires, to virtue true,
Upon our race a lustre threw,
But with subversive frenzy thou
Hast marred our lineal honour now,
Of lofty birth, a noble line
Of previous kings is also thine:
Then whence this hated folly? whence
This sudden change that steals thy sense?
Thou shalt not gain thine impious will,
O thou whose thoughts are bent on ill,
Thou from whose guilty hand descend
These sinful blows my life to end.
Now to the forest will I go,
Thy cherished plans to overthrow,
And bring my brother, free from stain,
His people's darling, home again.
And Ráma, when again he turns,
Whose glory like a beacon burns,
In me a faithful slave shall find
To serve him with contented mind."

CANTO
LXXIV

Bharat's Lament

When Bharat's anger-sharpened tongue
Reproaches on the queen had flung,
Again, with mighty rage possessed,
The guilty dame he thus addressed:
"Flee, cruel, wicked sinner, flee,
Let not this kingdom harbour thee.
Thou who hast thrown all right aside,
Weep thou for me when I have died.
Canst thou one charge against the king,
Or the most duteous Ráma bring?
The one thy sin to death has sent,
The other chased to banishment.
Our line's destroyer, sin defiled
Like one who kills an unborn child,
Ne'er with thy lord in heaven to dwell,
Thy portion shall be down in hell
Because thy hand, that stayed for naught,
This awful wickedness has wrought,
And ruined him whom all held dear,
My bosom too is stirred with fear.
My father by thy sin is dead,
And Ráma to the wood is fled;
And of thy deed I bear the stain,
And fameless in the world remain.
Ambitious, evil-souled, in show
My mother, yet my direst foe.
My throning ne'er thine eyes shall bless,
Thy husband's wicked murderess.

Thou art not Aśvapati's child,
That righteous king most sage and mild,

542

But thou wast born a fiend, a foe
My father's house to overthrow.
Thou who hast made Kauśalyá, pure,
Gentle, affectionate, endure
The loss of him who was her bliss,—
What worlds await thee, Queen, for this?
Was it not patent to thy sense
That Ráma was his friends' defence,
Kauśalyá's own true child most dear,
The eldest and his father's peer?
Men in the son not only trace
The father's figure, form, and face,
But in his heart they also find
The offspring of the father's mind;
And hence, though dear their kinsmen are,
To mothers sons are dearer far.
There goes an ancient legend how
Good Surabhí, the God-loved cow,
Saw two of her dear children strain,
Drawing a plough and faint with pain.
She saw them on the earth outworn,
Toiling till noon from early morn,
And as she viewed her children's woe,
A flood of tears began to flow.
As through the air beneath her swept
The Lord of Gods, the drops she wept,
Fine, laden with delicious smell,
Upon his heavenly body fell.
And Indra lifted up his eyes
And saw her standing in the skies,
Afflicted with her sorrow's weight,
Sad, weeping, all disconsolate.
The Lord of Gods in anxious mood
Thus spoke in suppliant attitude:
"No fear disturbs our rest, and how
Come this great dread upon thee now?
Whence can this woe upon thee fall,
Say, gentle one who lovest all?"

Thus spake the God who rules the skies,
Indra, the Lord supremely wise;

543

And gentle Surabhí, well learned
In eloquence, this speech returned:
"Not thine the fault, great God, not thine
And guiltless are the Lords divine:
I mourn two children faint with toil,
Labouring hard in stubborn soil.
Wasted and sad I see them now,
While the sun beats on neck and brow,
Still goaded by the cruel hind,—
No pity in his savage mind.
O Indra, from this body sprang
These children, worn with many a pang.
For this sad sight I mourn, for none
Is to the mother like her son."
He saw her weep whose offspring feed
In thousands over hill and mead,
And knew that in a mother's eye
Naught with a son, for love, can vie.
He deemed her, when the tears that came
From her sad eyes bedewed his frame,
Laden with their celestial scent,
Of living things most excellent.
If she these tears of sorrow shed
Who many a thousand children bred,
Think what a life of woe is left
Kauśalyá, of her Ráma reft.
An only son was hers and she
Is rendered childless now by thee.
Here and hereafter, for thy crime,
Woe is thy lot through endless time.
And now, O Queen, without delay,
With all due honour will I pay
Both to my brother and my sire
The rites their several fates require.
Back to Ayodhyá will I bring
The long-armed chief, her lord and king,
And to the wood myself betake
Where hermit saints their dwelling make.
For, sinner both in deed and thought!
This hideous crime which thou hast wrought
I cannot bear, or live to see

Betray the suppliants who complain,
And make the hopeful hope in vain.
Long may his wife his kiss expect,
And pine away in cold neglect.
May he his lawful love despise,
And turn on other dames his eyes,
Fool, on forbidden joys intent,
Whose will allowed the banishment.
His sin who deadly poison throws
To spoil the water as it flows,
Lay on the wretch its burden dread
Who gave consent when Ráma fled."

Thus with his words he undeceived
Kauśalyá's troubled heart, who grieved
For son and husband reft away;
Then prostrate on the ground he lay.
Him as he lay half-senseless there,
Freed by the mighty oaths he sware,
Kauśalyá, by her woe distressed,
With melancholy words addressed:
"Anew, my son, this sorrow springs
To rend my heart with keener stings:
These awful oaths which thou hast sworn
My breast with double grief have torn.
Thy soul, and faithful Lakshmaṇ's too,
Are still, thank Heaven! to virtue true.
True to thy promise, thou shalt gain
The mansions which the good obtain."
Then to her breast that youth she drew,
Whose sweet fraternal love she knew,
And there in strict embraces held
The hero, as her tears outwelled.
And Bharat's heart grew sick and faint
With grief and oft-renewed complaint,
And all his senses were distraught
By the great woe that in him wrought.
Thus he lay and still bewailed
With sighs and loud lament
Till all his strength and reason failed,
The hours of night were spent.

549

CANTO
LXXVI

The Funeral

The saint Vaśishṭha, best of all
   Whose words with moving wisdom fall,
   Bharat, Kaikeyí's son, addressed,
Whom burning fires of grief distressed:
"O Prince, whose fame is widely spread,
Enough of grief: be comforted.
The time is come: arise, and lay
Upon the pyre the monarch's clay."

He heard the words Vaśishṭha spoke,
And slumbering resolution woke.
Then skilled in all the laws declare,
He bade his friends the rites prepare.
They raised the body from the oil,
And placed it, dripping, on the soil;
Then laid it on a bed, whereon
Wrought gold and precious jewels shone.
There, pallor o'er his features spread,
The monarch, as in sleep, lay dead.
Then Bharat sought his father's side,
And lifted up his voice and cried:
"O King, and has thy heart designed
To part and leave thy son behind?
Make Ráma flee, who loves the right,
And Lakshmaṇ of the arm of might?
Whither, great Monarch, wilt thou go
And leave this people in their woe,
Mourning their hero, wild with grief,
Of Ráma reft, their lion chief?
Ah, who will guard the people well
Who in Ayodhyá's city dwell,

550

When thou, my sire, hast sought the sky,
And Ráma has been forced to fly?
In widowed woe, bereft of thee,
The land no more is fair to see:
The city, to my aching sight,
Is gloomy as a moonless night."

Thus, with o'erwhelming sorrow pained,
Sad Bharat by the bed complained:
And thus Vaśishṭha, holy sage,
Spoke his deep anguish to assuage:
"O Lord of men, no longer stay;
The last remaining duties pay:
Haste, mighty-armed, as I advise,
The funeral rites to solemnize."

And Bharat heard Vaśishṭha's rede
With due attention and agreed.
He summoned straight from every side
Chaplain, and priest, and holy guide.
The sacred fires he bade them bring
Forth from the chapel of the king,
Wherein the priests in order due,
And ministers, the offerings threw.
Distraught in mind, with sob and tear,
They laid the body on a bier,
And servants, while their eyes brimmed o'er
The monarch from the palace bore.
Another band of mourners led
The long procession of the dead:
Rich garments in the way they cast,
And gold and silver, as they passed.
Then other hands the corse bedewed
With fragrant juices that exude
From sandal, cedar, aloe, pine,
And every perfume rare and fine.
Then priestly hands the mighty dead
Upon the pyre deposited.
The sacred fires they tended next,
And muttered low each funeral text;
And priestly singers who rehearse

551

The Śaman sang their holy verse.
Forth from the town in litters came,
Or chariots, many a royal dame,
And honoured so the funeral ground,
With aged followers ringed around.
With steps in inverse order bent,
The priests in sad procession went
Around the monarch's burning pyre
Who well had nursed each sacred fire:
With Queen Kauśalyá and the rest,
Their tender hearts with woe distressed.
The voice of women, shrill and clear
As screaming curlews, smote the ear,
As from a thousand voices rose
The shriek that tells of woman's woes.
Then weeping, faint, with loud lament,
Down Sarjú's shelving bank they went.
There standing on the river side
With Bharat, priest, and peer,
Their lips the women purified
With water fresh and clear.
Returning to the royal town,
Their eyes with tear-drops filled,
Ten days on earth they laid them down,
And wept till grief was stilled.

CANTO

LXXVII

The Gathering of the Ashes

T he tenth day passed: the prince again
        Was free from every legal stain.
        He bade them on the twelfth the great
Remaining honour celebrate.
Much gold he gave, and gems, and food,

To all the Bráhman multitude,
And goats whose hair was white and fine,
And many a thousand head of kine:
Slaves, men and damsels, he bestowed,
And many a car and fair abode:
Such gifts he gave the Bráhman race
His father's obsequies to grace.
Then when the morning's earliest ray
Appeared upon the thirteenth day,
Again the hero wept and sighed
Distraught and sorrow-stupefied;
Drew, sobbing in his anguish, near,
The last remaining debt to clear,
And at the bottom of the pyre,
He thus bespake his royal sire:
"O father, hast thou left me so,
Deserted in my friendless woe,
When he to whom the charge was given
To keep me, to the wood is driven?
Her only son is forced away
Who was his helpless mother's stay:
Ah, whither, father, art thou fled;
Leaving the queen uncomforted?"

He looked upon the pile where lay
The bones half-burnt and ashes grey,
And uttering a piteous moan,
Gave way, by anguish overthrown.
Then as his tears began to well,
Prostrate to earth the hero fell;
So from its seat the staff they drag,
And cast to earth some glorious flag.
The ministers approached again
The prince whom rites had freed from stain;
So when Yayáti fell, each seer,
In pity for his fate, drew near.
Śatrughna saw him lying low
O'erwhelmed beneath the crush of woe,
And as upon the king he thought,
He fell upon the earth distraught.
When to his loving memory came

Those noble gifts, that kingly frame,
He sorrowed, by his woe distressed,
As one by frenzied rage possessed:
"Ah me, this surging sea of woe
Has drowned us with its overflow:
The source is Manthará, dire and dark,
Kaikeyí is the ravening shark:
And the great boons the monarch gave
Lend conquering might to every wave.
Ah, whither wilt thou go, and leave
Thy Bharat in his woe to grieve,
Whom ever 'twas thy greatest joy
To fondle as a tender boy?
Didst thou not give with thoughtful care
Our food, our drink, our robes to wear?
Whose love will now for us provide,
When thou, our king and sire, hast died?
At such a time bereft, forlorn,
Why is not earth in sunder torn,
Missing her monarch's firm control,
His love of right, his lofty soul?
Ah me, for Ráma roams afar,
My sire is where the Blessed are;
How can I live deserted? I
Will pass into the fire and die.
Abandoned thus, I will not brook
Upon Ayodhyá's town to look,
Once guarded by Ikshváku's race:
The wood shall be my dwelling place."

Then when the princes' mournful train
Heard the sad brothers thus complain,
And saw their misery, at the view
Their grief burst wilder out anew.
Faint with lamenting, sad and worn,
Each like a bull with broken horn,
The brothers in their wild despair
Lay rolling, mad with misery, there.
Then old Vaśishṭha good and true,
Their father's priest, all lore who knew,
Raised weeping Bharat on his feet,

554

And thus bespake with counsel meet:
"Twelve days, my lord, have past away

Since flames consumed thy father's clay:
Delay no more: as rules ordain,
Gather what bones may yet remain.
Three constant pairs are ever found
To hem all mortal creatures round:
Then mourn not thus, O Prince, for none
Their close companionship may shun."

Sumantra bade Śatrughna rise,
And soothed his soul with counsel wise,
And skilled in truth, his hearer taught
How all things are and come to naught.
When rose each hero from the ground,
A lion lord of men, renowned,
He showed like Indra's flag, whereon
Fierce rains have dashed and suns have shone.
They wiped their red and weeping eyes,
And gently made their sad replies:
Then, urged to haste, the royal pair
Performed the rites that claimed their care.

CANTO
LXXVIII

Manthará Punished

Śatrughna thus to Bharat spake
Who longed the forest road to take:
"He who in woe was wont to give
Strength to himself and all that live—
Dear Ráma, true and pure in heart,
Is banished by a woman's art.
Yet here was Lakshmaṇ, brave and strong,

Could not his might prevent the wrong?
Could not his arm the king restrain,
Or make the banished free again?
One loving right and fearing crime
Had checked the monarch's sin in time,
When, vassal of a woman's will,
His feet approached the path of ill."

While Lakshman's younger brother, dread
Śatrughna, thus to Bharat said,
Came to the fronting door, arrayed
In glittering robes, the hump-back maid.
There she, with sandal-oil besmeared,
In garments meet for queens appeared:
And lustre to her form was lent
By many a gem and ornament.
She girdled with her broidered zone,
And many a chain about her thrown,
Showed like a female monkey round
Whose body many a string is bound.
When on that cause of evil fell
The quick eye of the sentinel,
He grasped her in his ruthless hold,
And hastening in, Śatrughna told:
"Here is the wicked pest," he cried,
"Through whom the king thy father died,
And Ráma wanders in the wood:
Do with her as thou deemest good."
The warder spoke: and every word
Śatrughna's breast to fury stirred:
He called the servants, all and each.
And spake in wrath his hasty speech:
"This is the wretch my sire who slew,
And misery on my brothers drew:
Let her this day obtain the meed,
Vile sinner, of her cruel deed."
He spake; and moved by fury laid
His mighty hand upon the maid,
Who as her fellows ringed her round,
Made with her cries the hall resound.
Soon as the gathered women viewed

Śatrughna in his angry mood,
Their hearts disturbed by sudden dread,
They turned and from his presence fled.
"His rage," they cried, "on us will fall,
And ruthless, he will slay us all.
Come, to Kauśalyá let us flee:
Our hope, our sure defence is she,
Approved by all, of virtuous mind,
Compassionate, and good, and kind."

His eyes with burning wrath aglow,
Śatrughna, shatterer of the foe,
Dragged on the ground the hump-back maid
Who shrieked aloud and screamed for aid.
This way and that with no remorse
He dragged her with resistless force,
And chains and glittering trinkets burst
Lay here and there with gems dispersed,
Till like the sky of Autumn shone
The palace floor they sparkled on.
The lord of men, supremely strong,
Haled in his rage the wretch along:
Where Queen Kaikeyí dwelt he came,
And sternly then addressed the dame.
Deep in her heart Kaikeyí felt
The stabs his keen reproaches dealt,
And of Śatrughna's ire afraid,
To Bharat flew and cried for aid.
He looked and saw the prince inflamed
With burning rage, and thus exclaimed:
"Forgive! thine angry arm restrain:
A woman never may be slain.
My hand Kaikeyí's blood would spill,
The sinner ever bent on ill,
But Ráma, long in duty tried,
Would hate the impious matricide:
And if he knew thy vengeful blade
Had slaughtered e'en this hump-back maid,
Never again, be sure, would he
Speak friendly word to thee or me."

557

Auspicious answer to their lord:
"Be royal Fortune aye benign
To thee for this good speech of thine,
Who wishest still thine elder's hand
To rule with kingly sway the land."
Their glorious speech, their favouring cries
Made his proud bosom swell:
And from the prince's noble eyes
The tears of rapture fell.

CANTO

LXXX

The Way Prepared

All they who knew the joiner's art,
Or distant ground in every part;
Each busied in his several trade,
To work machines or ply the spade;
Deft workmen skilled to frame the wheel,
Or with the ponderous engine deal;
Guides of the way, and craftsmen skilled,
To sink the well, make bricks, and build;
And those whose hands the tree could hew,
And work with slips of cut bamboo,
Went forward, and to guide them, they
Whose eyes before had seen the way.
Then onward in triumphant mood
Went all the mighty multitude.
Like the great sea whose waves leap high
When the full moon is in the sky.
Then, in his proper duty skilled,
Each joined him to his several guild,
And onward in advance they went
With every tool and implement.
Where bush and tangled creeper lay

With trenchant steel they made the way;
They felled each stump, removed each stone,
And many a tree was overthrown.
In other spots, on desert lands,
Tall trees were reared by busy hands.
Where'er the line of road they took,
They plied the hatchet, axe, and hook.

Others, with all their strength applied,
Cast vigorous plants and shrubs aside,
In shelving valleys rooted deep,
And levelled every dale and steep.
Each pit and hole that stopped the way
They filled with stones, and mud, and clay,
And all the ground that rose and fell
With busy care was levelled well.
They bridged ravines with ceaseless toil,
And pounded fine the flinty soil.
Now here, now there, to right and left,
A passage through the ground they cleft,
And soon the rushing flood was led
Abundant through the new-cut bed,
Which by the running stream supplied
With ocean's boundless waters vied.
In dry and thirsty spots they sank
Full many a well and ample tank,
And altars round about them placed
To deck the station in the waste.
With well-wrought plaster smoothly spread,
With bloomy trees that rose o'erhead,
With banners waving in the air,
And wild birds singing here and there,
With fragrant sandal-water wet,
With many a flower beside it set,
Like the Gods' heavenly pathway showed
That mighty host's imperial road.
Deft workmen, chosen for their skill
To do the high-souled Bharat's will,
In every pleasant spot where grew
Trees of sweet fruit and fair to view,
As he commanded, toiled to grace

561

With all delights his camping-place.
And they who read the stars, and well
Each lucky sign and hour could tell,
Raised carefully the tented shade
Wherein high-minded Bharat stayed.
With ample space of level ground,
With broad deep moat encompassed round;
Like Mandar in his towering pride,
With streets that ran from side to side;
Enwreathed with many a palace tall
Surrounded by its noble wall;
With roads by skilful workmen made,
Where many a glorious banner played;
With stately mansions, where the dove
Sat nestling in her cote above.
Rising aloft supremely fair
Like heavenly cars that float in air,
Each camp in beauty and in bliss
Matched Indra's own metropolis.
As shines the heaven on some fair night,
With moon and constellations filled,
The prince's royal road was bright,
Adorned by art of workmen skilled.

CANTO
LXXXI

The Assembly

Ere yet the dawn had ushered in
The day should see the march begin,
Herald and bard who rightly knew
Each nice degree of honour due,
Their loud auspicious voices raised,
And royal Bharat blessed and praised.
With sticks of gold the drum they smote,

Which thundered out its deafening note,
Blew loud the sounding shell, and blent
Each high and low-toned instrument.
The mingled sound of drum and horn
Through all the air was quickly borne,
And as in Bharat's ear it rang,
Gave the sad prince another pang.

Then Bharat, starting from repose,
Stilled the glad sounds that round him rose,
"I am not king; no more mistake:"
Then to Śatrughna thus he spake:
"O see what general wrongs succeed
Sprung from Kaikeyī's evil deed!
The king my sire has died and thrown
Fresh miseries on me alone.
The royal bliss, on duty based,
Which our just high-souled father graced,
Wanders in doubt and sore distress
Like a tossed vessel rudderless.
And he who was our lordly stay
Roams in the forest far away,
Expelled by this my mother, who
To duty's law is most untrue."
As royal Bharat thus gave vent
To bitter grief in wild lament,
Gazing upon his face the crowd
Of pitying women wept aloud.
His lamentation scarce was o'er,
When Saint Vaśishṭha, skilled in lore
Of royal duty, dear to fame,
To join the great assembly came.
Girt by disciples ever true
Still nearer to that hall he drew,
Resplendent, heavenly to behold,
Adorned with wealth of gems and gold:
E'en so a man in duty tried
Draws near to meet his virtuous bride.
He reached his golden seat o'erlaid
With coverlet of rich brocade,
There sat, in all the Vedas read,

And called the messengers, and said:
"Go forth, let Bráhman, Warrior, peer,
And every captain gather here:
Let all attentive hither throng:
Go, hasten: we delay too long.
Śatrughna, glorious Bharat bring,
The noble children of the king,

Yudhájit and Sumantra, all
The truthful and the virtuous call."

He ended: soon a mighty sound
Of thickening tumult rose around,
As to the hall they bent their course
With car, and elephant, and horse,
The people all with glad acclaim
Welcomed Prince Bharat as he came:
E'en as they loved their king to greet,
Or as the Gods Lord Indra meet.
The vast assembly shone as fair
With Bharat's kingly face
As Daśaratha's self were there
To glorify the place.
It gleamed like some unruffled lake
Where monsters huge of mould
With many a snake their pastime take
O'er shells, sand, gems, and gold.

CANTO
LXXXII

The Departure

The prudent prince the assembly viewed
Thronged with its noble multitude,
Resplendent as a cloudless night
When the full moon is in his height;
While robes of every varied hue
A glory o'er the synod threw.
The priest in lore of duty skilled
Looked on the crowd the hall that filled,
And then in accents soft and grave
To Bharat thus his counsel gave:
"The king, dear son, so good and wise,
Has gone from earth and gained the skies,
Leaving to thee, her rightful lord,
This rich wide land with foison stored.
And still has faithful Ráma stood
Firm to the duty of the good,
And kept his father's hest aright,
As the moon keeps its own dear light.
Thus sire and brother yield to thee
This realm from all annoyance free:
Rejoice thy lords: enjoy thine own:
Anointed king, ascend the throne.
Let vassal Princes hasten forth
From distant lands, west, south, and north,
From Kerala, from every sea,
And bring ten million gems to thee."
As thus the sage Vaśishṭha spoke,
A storm of grief o'er Bharat broke.
And longing to be just and true,
His thoughts to duteous Ráma flew.
With sobs and sighs and broken tones,

565

E'en as a wounded mallard moans,
He mourned with deepest sorrow moved,
And thus the holy priest reproved:
"O, how can such as Bharat dare
The power and sway from him to tear,
Wise, and devout, and true, and chaste,
With Scripture lore and virtue graced?
Can one of Daśaratha's seed
Be guilty of so vile a deed?
The realm and I are Ráma's: thou,
Shouldst speak the words of justice now.
For he, to claims of virtue true,
Is eldest born and noblest too:
Nahush, Dilípa could not be
More famous in their lives than he.
As Daśaratha ruled of right,
So Ráma's is the power and right.
If I should do this sinful deed
And forfeit hope of heavenly meed,
My guilty act would dim the shine
Of old Ikshváku's glorious line.
Nay, as the sin my mother wrought
Is grievous to my inmost thought,
I here, my hands together laid,
Will greet him in the pathless shade.
To Ráma shall my steps be bent,
My King, of men most excellent,
Raghu's illustrious son, whose sway
Might hell, and earth, and heaven obey."

That righteous speech, whose every word
Bore virtue's stamp, the audience heard;
On Ráma every thought was set,
And with glad tears each eye was wet.
"Then, if the power I still should lack
To bring my noble brother back,
I in the wood will dwell, and share
His banishment with Lakshmaṇ there.
By every art persuasive I
To bring him from the wood will try,
And show him to your loving eyes,

566

O Bráhmans noble, good, and wise.
E'en now, the road to make and clear,
Each labourer pressed, and pioneer
Have I sent forward to precede
The army I resolve to lead."

Thus, by fraternal love possessed,
His firm resolve the prince expressed,
Then to Sumantra, deeply read
In holy texts, he turned and said:
"Sumantra, rise without delay,
And as I bid my words obey.
Give orders for the march with speed,
And all the army hither lead."

The wise Sumantra, thus addressed,
Obeyed the high-souled chief's behest.
He hurried forth with joy inspired
And gave the orders he desired.
Delight each soldier's bosom filled,
And through each chief and captain thrilled,

To hear that march proclaimed, to bring
Dear Ráma back from wandering.
From house to house the tidings flew:
Each soldier's wife the order knew,
And as she listened blithe and gay
Her husband urged to speed away.
Captain and soldier soon declared
The host equipped and all prepared
With chariots matching thought for speed,
And wagons drawn by ox and steed.
When Bharat by Vaśishṭha's side,
His ready host of warriors eyed,
Thus in Sumantra's ear he spoke:
"My car and horses quickly yoke."
Sumantra hastened to fulfil
With ready joy his master's will,
And quickly with the chariot sped
Drawn by fleet horses nobly bred.
Then glorious Bharat, true, devout,

Whose genuine valour none could doubt,
Gave in fit words his order out;
For he would seek the shade
Of the great distant wood, and there
Win his dear brother with his prayer:
"Sumantra, haste! my will declare
The host be all arrayed.
I to the wood my way will take,
To Ráma supplication make,
And for the world's advantage sake,
Will lead him home again."
Then, ordered thus, the charioteer
Who listened with delighted ear,
Went forth and gave his orders clear
To captains of the train.
He gave the popular chiefs the word,
And with the news his friends he stirred,
And not a single man deferred
Preparing for the road.
Then Bráhman, Warrior, Merchant, thrall,
Obedient to Sumantra's call,
Each in his house arose, and all
Yoked elephant or camel tall,
Or ass or noble steed in stall,
And full appointed showed.

CANTO
LXXXIII

The Journey Begun

Then Bharat rose at early morn,
And in his noble chariot borne
Drove forward at a rapid pace
Eager to look on Ráma's face.
The priests and lords, a fair array,

In sun-bright chariots led the way.
Behind, a well appointed throng,
Nine thousand elephants streamed along.
Then sixty thousand cars, and then,
With various arms, came fighting men.
A hundred thousand archers showed
In lengthened line the steeds they rode—
A mighty host, the march to grace
Of Bharat, pride of Raghu's race.
Kaikeyí and Sumitrá came,
And good Kauśalyá, dear to fame:
By hopes of Ráma's coming cheered
They in a radiant car appeared.
On fared the noble host to see
Ráma and Lakshmaṇ, wild with glee,
And still each other's ear to please,
Of Ráma spoke in words like these:
"When shall our happy eyes behold
Our hero true, and pure, and bold,
So lustrous dark, so strong of arm,
Who keeps the world from woe and harm?
The tears that now our eyeballs dim
Will vanish at the sight of him,
As the whole world's black shadows fly
When the bright sun ascends the sky."

Conversing thus their way pursued
The city's joyous multitude,
And each in mutual rapture pressed
A friend or neighbour to his breast.
Thus every man of high renown,
And every merchant of the town,
And leading subjects, joyous went
Toward Ráma in his banishment.
And those who worked the potter's wheel,
And artists skilled in gems to deal;
And masters of the weaver's art,
And those who shaped the sword and dart;
And they who golden trinkets made,
And those who plied the fuller's trade;
And servants trained the bath to heat,

And they who dealt in incense sweet;
Physicians in their business skilled,
And those who wine and mead distilled;
And workmen deft in glass who wrought,
And those whose snares the peacock caught;
With them who bored the ear for rings,
Or sawed, or fashioned ivory things;
And those who knew to mix cement,
Or lived by sale of precious scent;
And men who washed, and men who sewed,
And thralls who mid the herds abode;
And fishers of the flood, and they
Who played and sang, and women gay;
And virtuous Bráhmans, Scripture-wise,
Of life approved in all men's eyes;
These swelled the prince's lengthened train,
Borne each in car or bullock wain.
Fair were the robes they wore upon
Their limbs where red-hued unguents shone.
These all in various modes conveyed
Their journey after Bharat made;
The soldiers' hearts with rapture glowed,
Following Bharat on his road,
Their chief whose tender love would fain
Bring his dear brother home again.
With elephant, and horse, and car,
The vast procession travelled far,

And came where Gangá's waves below
The town of Śringavera flow.
There, with his friends and kinsmen nigh,
Dwelt Guha, Ráma's dear ally,
Heroic guardian of the land
With dauntless heart and ready hand.
There for a while the mighty force
That followed Bharat stayed its course,
Gazing on Gangá's bosom stirred
By many a graceful water-bird.
When Bharat viewed his followers there,
And Gangá's water, blest and fair,
The prince, who lore of words possessed,

His councillors and lords addressed:
"The captains of the army call:
Proclaim this day a halt for all,
That so to-morrow, rested, we
May cross this flood that seeks the sea.
Meanwhile, descending to the shore,
The funeral stream I fain would pour
From Gangá's fair auspicious tide
To him, my father glorified."

Thus Bharat spoke: each peer and lord
Approved his words with one accord,
And bade the weary troops repose
In separate spots where'er they chose.
There by the mighty stream that day,
Most glorious in its vast array
The prince's wearied army lay
In various groups reclined.
There Bharat's hours of night were spent,
While every eager thought he bent
On bringing home from banishment
His brother, great of mind.

CANTO
LXXXIV

Guha's Anger

King Guha saw the host spread o'er
The wide expanse of Gangá's shore,
With waving flag and pennon graced,
And to his followers spoke in haste:
"A mighty army meets my eyes,
That rivals Ocean's self in size:
Where'er I look my very mind
No limit to the host can find.

Sure Bharat with some evil thought
His army to our land has brought.
See, huge of form, his flag he rears,
That like an Ebony-tree appears.
He comes with bonds to take and chain,
Or triumph o'er our people slain:
And after, Ráma will he slay,—
Him whom his father drove away:
The power complete he longs to gain,
And—task too hard—usurp the reign.
So Bharat comes with wicked will
His brother Ráma's blood to spill.
But Ráma's slave and friend am I;
He is my lord and dear ally.
Keep here your watch in arms arrayed
Near Gangá's flood to lend him aid,
And let my gathered servants stand
And line with troops the river strand.
Here let the river keepers meet,
Who flesh and roots and berries eat;
A hundred fishers man each boat
Of the five hundred here afloat,
And let the youthful and the strong
Assemble in defensive throng.
But yet, if, free from guilty thought
'Gainst Ráma, he this land have sought,
The prince's happy host to-day
Across the flood shall make its way."

He spoke: then bearing in a dish
A gift of honey, meat, and fish,
The king of the Nishádas drew
Toward Bharat for an interview.
When Bharat's noble charioteer
Observed the monarch hastening near,
He duly, skilled in courteous lore,
The tidings to his master bore:
"This aged prince who hither bends
His footsteps with a thousand friends,
Knows, firm ally of Ráma, all
That may in Daṇḍak wood befall:

572

Therefore, Kakutstha's son, admit
The monarch, as is right and fit:
For doubtless he can clearly tell
Where Ráma now and Lakshmaṇ dwell."

When Bharat heard Sumantra's rede,
To his fair words the prince agreed:
"Go quickly forth," he cried, "and bring
Before my face the aged king."
King Guha, with his kinsmen near,
Rejoiced the summoning to hear:
He nearer drew, bowed low his head,
And thus to royal Bharat said:
"No mansions can our country boast,
And unexpected comes thy host:
But what we have I give thee all:
Rest in the lodging of thy thrall.
See, the Nishádas here have brought
The fruit and roots their hands have sought:
And we have woodland fare beside,
And store of meat both fresh and dried.
To rest their weary limbs, I pray
This night at least thy host may stay:
Then cheered with all we can bestow
To-morrow thou with it mayst go."

CANTO

LXXXV

Guha And Bharat

Thus the Nishádas' king besought:
The prince with spirit wisdom-fraught
Replied in seemly words that blent
Deep matter with the argument:

"Thou, friend of him whom I revere,
With honours high hast met me here,
For thou alone wouldst entertain
And feed to-day so vast a train."
In such fair words the prince replied,
Then, pointing to the path he cried:
"Which way aright will lead my feet
To Bharadvája's calm retreat;
For all this land near Gangá's streams
Pathless and hard to traverse seems?"

Thus spoke the prince: King Guha heard
Delighted every prudent word,
And gazing on that forest wide,
Raised suppliant hands, and thus replied:
"My servants, all the ground who know,
O glorious Prince, with thee shall go
With constant care thy way to guide,
And I will journey by thy side.
But this thy host so wide dispread
Wakes in my heart one doubt and dread,
Lest, threatening Ráma good and great,
Ill thoughts thy journey stimulate."

But when King Guha, ill at ease,
Declared his fear in words like these,
As pure as is the cloudless sky
With soft voice Bharat made reply:
"Suspect me not: ne'er come the time
For me to plot so foul a crime!
He is my eldest brother, he
Is like a father dear to me.
I go to lead my brother thence
Who makes the wood his residence.
No thought but this thy heart should frame:
This simple truth my lips proclaim."

Then with glad cheer King Guha cried,
With Bharat's answer gratified:
"Blessed art thou: on earth I see
None who may vie, O Prince, with thee,

574

Who canst of thy free will resign
The kingdom which unsought is thine.
For this, a name that ne'er shall die,
Thy glory through the worlds shall fly,
Who fain wouldst balm thy brother's pain
And lead the exile home again."

As Guha thus, and Bharat, each
To other spoke in friendly speech,
The Day-God sank with glory dead,
And night o'er all the sky was spread.
Soon as King Guha's thoughtful care
Had quartered all the army there,
Well honoured, Bharat laid his head
Beside Śatrughna on a bed.
But grief for Ráma yet oppressed
High-minded Bharat's faithful breast—
Such torment little was deserved
By him who ne'er from duty swerved.
The fever raged through every vein
And burnt him with its inward pain:
So when in woods the flames leap free
The fire within consumes the tree.
From heat of burning anguish sprung
The sweat upon his body hung,
As when the sun with fervid glow
On high Himálaya melts the snow.
As, banished from the herd, a bull
Wanders alone and sorrowful.
Thus sighing and distressed,
In misery and bitter grief,
With fevered heart that mocked relief,
Distracted in his mind, the chief
Still mourned and found no rest.

CANTO
LXXXVI

Guha's Speech

Guha the king, acquainted well
With all that in the wood befell,
To Bharat the unequalled told
The tale of Lakshmaṇ mighty-souled:
"With many an earnest word I spake
To Lakshmaṇ as he stayed awake,
And with his bow and shaft in hand
To guard his brother kept his stand:
"Now sleep a little, Lakshmaṇ, see
This pleasant bed is strewn for thee:
Hereon thy weary body lay,
And strengthen thee with rest, I pray,
Inured to toil are men like these,
But thou hast aye been nursed in ease.
Rest, duteous-minded! I will keep
My watch while Ráma lies asleep:
For in the whole wide world is none
Dearer to me than Raghu's son.
Harbour no doubt or jealous fear:
I speak the truth with heart sincere:
For from the grace which he has shown
Will glory on my name be thrown:
Great store of merit shall I gain,
And duteous, form no wish in vain.
Let me enforced by many a row
Of followers, armed with shaft and bow
For well-loved Ráma's weal provide
Who lies asleep by Sítá's side.
For through this wood I often go,
And all its shades conceal I know:
And we with conquering arms can meet

A four-fold host arrayed complete."
"With words like these I spoke, designed
To move the high-souled Bharat's mind,
But he upon his duty bent,
Plied his persuasive argument:
"O, how can slumber close mine eyes
When lowly couched with Sítá lies
The royal Ráma? can I give
My heart to joy, or even live?
He whom no mighty demon, no,
Nor heavenly God can overthrow,
See, Guha, how he lies, alas,

With Sítá couched on gathered grass.
By varied labours, long, severe,
By many a prayer and rite austere,
He, Daśaratha's cherished son,
By Fortune stamped, from Heaven was won.
Now as his son is forced to fly,
The king ere long will surely die:
Reft of his guardian hand, forlorn
In widowed grief this land will mourn.
E'en now perhaps, with toil o'erspent,
The women cease their loud lament,
And cries of woe no longer ring
Throughout the palace of the king.
But ah for sad Kauśalyá! how
Fare she and mine own mother now?
How fares the king? this night, I think,
Some of the three in death will sink.
With hopes upon Śatrughna set
My mother may survive as yet,
But the sad queen will die who bore
The hero, for her grief is sore.
His cherished wish that would have made
Dear Ráma king, so long delayed,
"Too late! too late!" the king will cry,
And conquered by his misery die.
When Fate has brought the mournful day
Which sees my father pass away,
How happy in their lives are they

577

Allowed his funeral rites to pay.
Our exile o'er, with him who ne'er
Turns from the oath his lips may swear,
May we returning safe and well
gain in fair Ayodhyá dwell."
Thus Bharat stood with many a sigh
Lamenting, and the night went by.
Soon as the morning light shone fair
In votive coils both bound their hair.
And then I sent them safely o'er
And left them on the farther shore.
With Sítá then they onward passed,
Their coats of bark about them cast,
Their locks like hermits' bound,
The mighty tamers of the foe,
Each with his arrows and his bow,
Went over the rugged ground,
Proud in their strength and undeterred
Like elephants that lead the herd,
And gazing oft around."

CANTO

LXXXVII

Guha's Story

That speech of Guha Bharat heard
With grief and tender pity stirred,
And as his ears the story drank,
Deep in his thoughtful heart it sank.
His large full eyes in anguish rolled,
His trembling limbs grew stiff and cold;
Then fell he, like a tree uptorn,
In woe too grievous to be borne.
When Guha saw the long-armed chief

Whose eye was like a lotus leaf,
With lion shoulders strong and fair,
High-mettled, prostrate in despair,—
Pale, bitterly afflicted, he
Reeled as in earthquake reels a tree.
But when Śatrughna standing nigh
Saw his dear brother helpless lie,
Distraught with woe his head he bowed,
Embraced him oft and wept aloud.
Then Bharat's mothers came, forlorn
Of their dear king, with fasting worn,
And stood with weeping eyes around
The hero prostrate on the ground.
Kauśalyá, by her woe oppressed,
The senseless Bharat's limbs caressed,
As a fond cow in love and fear
Caresses oft her youngling dear:
Then yielding to her woe she said,
Weeping and sore disquieted:
"What torments, O my son, are these
Of sudden pain or swift disease?
The lives of us and all the line
Depend, dear child, on only thine.
Ráma and Lakshman forced to flee,
I live by naught but seeing thee:
For as the king has past away
Thou art my only help to-day.
Hast thou, perchance, heard evil news
Of Lakshman, which thy soul subdues,
Or Ráma dwelling with his spouse—
My all is he—neath forest boughs?"

Then slowly gathering sense and strength
The weeping hero rose at length,
And words like these to Guha spake,
That bade Kauśalyá comfort take:
"Where lodged the prince that night? and where
Lakshman the brave, and Sítá fair?
Show me the couch whereon he lay,
Tell me the food he ate, I pray."

Then Guha the Nishádas' king
Replied to Bharat's questioning:
"Of all I had I brought the best
To serve my good and honoured guest
Food of each varied kind I chose,
And every fairest fruit that grows.
Ráma the hero truly brave
Declined the gift I humbly gave:
His Warrior part he ne'er forgot,
And what I brought accepted not:
"No gifts, my friend, may we accept:
Our law is, Give, and must be kept."
The high-souled chief, O Monarch, thus
With gracious words persuaded us.
Then calm and still, absorbed in thought,
He drank the water Lakshman brought,
And then, obedient to his vows,
He fasted with his gentle spouse.
So Lakshman too from food abstained,

And sipped the water that remained:
Then with ruled lips, devoutly staid,
The three their evening worship paid.
Then Lakshman with unwearied care
Brought heaps of sacred grass, and there
With his own hands he quickly spread,
For Ráma's rest, a pleasant bed,
And faithful Sítá's too, where they
Reclining each by other lay.
Then Lakshman bathed their feet, and drew
A little distance from the two.
Here stands the tree which lent them shade,
Here is the grass beneath it laid,
Where Ráma and his consort spent
The night together ere they went.
Lakshman, whose arms the foeman quell,
Watched all the night as sentinel,
And kept his great bow strung:
His hand was gloved, his arm was braced,
Two well-filled quivers at his waist,
With deadly arrows, hung.

I took my shafts and trusty bow,
And with that tamer of the foe
Stood ever wakeful near,
And with my followers, bow in hand,
Behind me ranged, a ready band,
Kept watch o'er Indra's peer."

LXXXVIII

The Ingudí Tree

When Bharat with each friend and peer
Had heard that tale so full and clear,
They went together to the tree
The bed which Ráma pressed to see.
Then Bharat to his mothers said:
"Behold the high-souled hero's bed:
These tumbled heaps of grass betray
Where he that night with Sítá lay:
Unmeet, the heir of fortune high
Thus on the cold bare earth should lie,
The monarch's son, in counsel sage,
Of old imperial lineage.
That lion-lord whose noble bed
With finest skins of deer was spread,—
How can he now endure to press
The bare earth, cold and comfortless!
This sudden fall from bliss to grief
Appears untrue, beyond belief:
My senses are distraught: I seem
To view the fancies of a dream.
There is no deity so great,
No power in heaven can master Fate,
If Ráma, Daśaratha's heir,
Lay on the ground and slumbered there;

581

And lovely Sítá, she who springs
From fair Videha's ancient kings,
Ráma's dear wife, by all adored,
Lay on the earth beside her lord.
Here was his couch, upon this heap
He tossed and turned in restless sleep:
On the hard soil each manly limb
Has stamped the grass with signs of him.
That night, it seems, fair Sítá spent
Arrayed in every ornament,
For here and there my eyes behold
Small particles of glistering gold.
She laid her outer garment here,
For still some silken threads appear,
How dear in her devoted eyes
Must be the bed where Ráma lies,
Where she so tender could repose
And by his side forget her woes.
Alas, unhappy, guilty me!
For whom the prince was forced to flee,
And chief of Raghu's sons and best,
A bed like this with Sítá pressed.
Son of a royal sire whose hand
Ruled paramount o'er every land,
Could he who every joy bestows,
Whose body like the lotus shows,
The friend of all, who charms the sight,
Whose flashing eyes are darkly bright,
Leave the dear kingdom, his by right,
Unmeet for woe, the heir of bliss,
And lie upon a bed like this?
Great joy and happy fate are thine,
O Lakshman, marked with each fair sign,
Whose faithful footsteps follow still
Thy brother in his hour of ill.
And blest is Sítá, nobly good,
Who dwells with Ráma in the wood.
Ours is, alas, a doubtful fate
Of Ráma reft and desolate.
My royal sire has gained the skies,
In woods the high-souled hero lies;

The state is wrecked and tempest-tossed,
A vessel with her rudder lost.
Yet none in secret thought has planned
With hostile might to seize the land:
Though forced in distant wilds to dwell,
The hero's arm protects it well.
Unguarded, with deserted wall,
No elephant or steed in stall,
My father's royal city shows
Her portals open to her foes,
Of bold protectors reft and bare,
Defenceless in her dark despair:
But still her foes the wish restrain,
As men from poisoned cates refrain.
I from this hour my nights will pass
Couched on the earth or gathered grass,
Eat only fruit and roots, and wear
A coat of bark, and matted hair.
I in the woods will pass, content,
For him the term of banishment;
So shall I still unbroken save
The promise which the hero gave.

While I remain for Ráma there,
Śatrughna will my exile share,
And Ráma in his home again,
With Lakshman, o'er Ayodhyá reign,
for him, to rule and guard the state,
The twice-born men shall consecrate.
O, may the Gods I serve incline
To grant this earnest wish of mine!
If when I bow before his feet
And with all moving arts entreat,
He still deny my prayer,
Then with my brother will I live:
He must, he must permission give,
Roaming in forests there."

CANTO
LXXXIX

The Passage of Gangá

That night the son of Raghu lay
On Gangá's bank till break of day:
Then with the earliest light he woke
And thus to brave Śatrughna spoke.
"Rise up, Śatrughna, from thy bed:
Why sleepest thou the night is fled.
See how the sun who chases night
Wakes every lotus with his light.
Arise, arise, and first of all
The lord of Śringavera call,
For he his friendly aid will lend
Our army o'er the flood to send."
Thus urged, Śatrughna answered: "I,
Remembering Ráma, sleepless lie."
As thus the brothers, each to each,
The lion-mettled, ended speech,
Came Guha, the Nishádas' king,
And spoke with kindly questioning:
"Hast thou in comfort passed," he cried,
"The night upon the river side?
With thee how fares it? and are these,
Thy soldiers, healthy and at ease?"
Thus the Nishádas' lord inquired
In gentle words which love inspired,
And Bharat, Ráma's faithful slave,
Thus to the king his answer gave:
"The night has sweetly passed, and we
Are highly honoured, King, by thee.
Now let thy servants boats prepare,
Our army o'er the stream to bear."

The speech of Bharat Guha heard,
And swift to do his bidding stirred.
Within the town the monarch sped
And to his ready kinsmen said:
"Awake, each kinsman, rise, each friend!
May every joy your lives attend.
Gather each boat upon the shore
And ferry all the army o'er."
Thus Guha spoke: nor they delayed,
But, rising quick, their lord obeyed,
And soon, from every side secured,
Five hundred boats were ready moored.
Some reared aloft the mystic sign,
And mighty bells were hung in line:
Of firmest build, gay flags they bore,
And sailors for the helm and oar.
One such King Guha chose, whereon,
Of fair white cloth, an awning shone,
And sweet musicians charmed the ear,—
And bade his servants urge it near.
Then Bharat swiftly sprang on board,
And then Śatrughna, famous lord,
To whom, with many a royal dame,
Kauśalyá and Sumitrá came.
The household priest went first in place,
The elders, and the Bráhman race,
And after them the monarch's train
Of women borne in many a wain.
Then high to heaven the shouts of those
Who fired the army's huts, arose,
With theirs who bathed along the shore,
Or to the boats the baggage bore.
Full freighted with that mighty force
The boats sped swiftly on their course,
By royal Guha's servants manned,
And gentle gales the banners fanned.
Some boats a crowd of dames conveyed,
In others noble coursers neighed;
Some chariots and their cattle bore,
Some precious wealth and golden store.
Across the stream each boat was rowed,

There duly disembarked its load,
And then returning on its way,
Sped here and there in merry play.
Then swimming elephants appeared
With flying pennons high upreared.
And as the drivers urged them o'er,
The look of winged mountains wore.
Some men in barges reached the strand,
Others on rafts came safe to land:
Some buoyed with pitchers crossed the tide,
And others on their arms relied.
Thus with the help the monarch gave
The army crossed pure Gangá's wave:
Then in auspicious hour it stood
Within Prayága's famous wood.
The prince with cheering words addressed
His weary men, and bade them rest
Where'er they chose and he,
With priest and deacon by his side,
To Bharadvája's dwelling hied
That best of saints to see.

CANTO

XC

The Hermitage

The prince of men a league away
    Saw where the hermit's dwelling lay,
    Then with his lords his path pursued,
And left his warrior multitude.
On foot, as duty taught his mind,
He left his warlike gear behind;
Two robes of linen cloth he wore,
And bade Vaśishṭha walk before.
Then Bharat from his lords withdrew

When Bharadvája came in view,
And toward the holy hermit went
Behind Vaśishṭha, reverent.
When Bharadvája, saint austere,
Saw good Vaśishṭha drawing near,
He cried, upspringing from his seat,
"The grace-gift bring, my friend to greet."
When Saint Vaśishṭha near him drew,
And Bharat paid the reverence due,
The glorious hermit was aware
That Daśaratha's son was there.
The grace-gift, water for their feet
He gave, and offered fruit to eat;
Then, duty-skilled, with friendly speech
In seemly order questioned each:
"How fares it in Ayodhyá now
With treasury and army? how
With kith and kin and friends most dear,
With councillor, and prince, and peer?"
But, for he knew the king was dead,
Of Daśaratha naught he said.
Vaśishṭha and the prince in turn
Would of the hermit's welfare learn:
Of holy fires they fain would hear,
Of pupils, trees, and birds, and deer.
The glorious saint his answer made
That all was well in holy shade:
Then love of Ráma moved his breast,
And thus he questioned of his guest:
"Why art thou here, O Prince, whose band
With kingly sway protects the land?
Declare the cause, explain the whole,
For yet some doubt disturbs my soul.
He whom Kauśalyá bare, whose might
The foemen slays, his line's delight,
He who with wife and brother sent
Afar now roam in banishment,
Famed prince, to whom his father spake
This order for a woman's sake:
"Away! and in the forest spend
Thy life till fourteen years shall end"—

Has thou the wish to harm him, bent
On sin against the innocent?
Wouldst thou thine elder's realm enjoy
Without a thorn that can annoy?"

With sobbing voice and tearful eye
Thus Bharat sadly made reply:
"Ah lost am I, if thou, O Saint,
Canst thus in thought my heart attaint:
No warning charge from thee I need;
Ne'er could such crime from me proceed.
The words my guilty mother spake
When fondly jealous for my sake—
Think not that I, to triumph moved,
Those words approve or e'er approved.
O Hermit, I have sought this place
To win the lordly hero's grace,
To throw me at my brother's feet
And lead him to his royal seat.
To this, my journey's aim and end,
Thou shouldst, O Saint, thy favour lend:
Where is the lord of earth? do thou,
Most holy, say, where roams he now?"

Then, by the saint Vaśishṭha pressed,
And all the gathered priests beside,
To Bharat's dutiful request
The hermit graciously replied:
"Worthy of thee, O Prince, this deed,
True son of Raghu's ancient seed.
I know thee reverent, well-controlled,
The glory of the good of old.
I grant thy prayer: in this pursuit
I know thy heart is resolute.
'Tis for thy sake those words I said
That wider still thy fame may spread.
I know where Ráma, duty-tried,
His brother, and his wife abide.
Where Chitrakúṭa's heights arise
Thy brother Ráma's dwelling lies.
Go thither with the morning's light,

And stay with all thy lords tonight:
For I would show thee honour high,
And do not thou my wish deny."

XCI

Bharadvája's Feast

Soon as he saw the prince's mind
   To rest that day was well inclined,
   He sought Kaikeyí's son to please
With hospitable courtesies.
Then Bharat to the saint replied:
"Our wants are more than satisfied.
The gifts which honoured strangers greet,
And water for our weary feet
Hast thou bestowed with friendly care,
And every choice of woodland fare."

Then Bharadvája spoke, a smile
Playing upon his lips the while:
"I know, dear Prince, thy friendly mind
Will any fare sufficient find,
But gladly would I entertain
And banquet all thine armed train:
Such is my earnest wish: do thou
This longing of my heart allow,
Why hast thou hither bent thy way,
And made thy troops behind thee stay?

Why unattended? couldst thou not
With friends and army seek this spot?"

Bharat, with reverent hands raised high,
To that great hermit made reply:

"My troops, for awe of thee, O Sage,
I brought not to thy hermitage:
Troops of a king or monarch's son
A hermit's home should ever shun.
Behind me comes a mighty train
Wide spreading o'er the ample plain,
Where every chief and captain leads
Men, elephants, and mettled steeds.
I feared, O reverend Sage, lest these
Might harm the holy ground and trees,
Springs might be marred and cots o'erthrown,
So with the priests I came alone."

"Bring all thy host," the hermit cried,
And Bharat, to his joy, complied.
Then to the chapel went the sire,
Where ever burnt the sacred fire,
And first, in order due, with sips
Of water purified his lips:
To Viśvakarmá, then he prayed,
His hospitable feast to aid:
"Let Viśvakarmá hear my call,
The God who forms and fashions all:
A mighty banquet I provide,
Be all my wants this day supplied.
Lord Indra at their head, the three
Who guard the worlds I call to me:
A mighty host this day I feed,
Be now supplied my every need.
Let all the streams that eastward go,
And those whose waters westering flow,
Both on the earth and in the sky,
Flow hither and my wants supply.
Be some with ardent liquor filled,
And some with wine from flowers distilled,
While some their fresh cool streams retain
Sweet as the juice of sugar-cane.
I call the Gods, I call the band
Of minstrels that around them stand:
I call the Háhá and Huhú,
I call the sweet Viśvávasu,

I call the heavenly wives of these
With all the bright Apsarases,
Alambúshá of beauty rare,
The charmer of the tangled hair,
Ghritáchí and Viśváchi fair,
Hemá and Bhímá sweet to view,
And lovely Nágadantá too,
And all the sweetest nymphs who stand
By Indra or by Brahmá's hand—
I summon these with all their train
And Tumburu to lead the strain.
Here let Kuvera's garden rise
Which far in Northern Kuru lies:
For leaves let cloth and gems entwine,
And let its fruit be nymphs divine.
Let Soma give the noblest food
To feed the mighty multitude,
Of every kind, for tooth and lip,
To chew, to lick, to suck, and sip.
Let wreaths, where fairest flowers abound,
Spring from the trees that bloom around.
Each sort of wine to woo the taste,
And meats of every kind be placed."

Thus spake the hermit self-restrained,
With proper tone by rules ordained,
On deepest meditation bent,
In holy might preëminent.
Then as with hands in reverence raised
Absorbed in thought he eastward gazed,
The deities he thus addressed
Came each in semblance manifest.
Delicious gales that cooled the frame
From Malaya and Dardar came,
That kissed those scented hills and threw
Auspicious fragrance where they blew.
Then falling fast in sweetest showers
Came from the sky immortal flowers,
And all the airy region round
With heavenly drums was made to sound.
Then breathed a soft celestial breeze,

Then danced the bright Apsarases,
The minstrels and the Gods advanced,
And warbling lutes the soul entranced.
The earth and sky that music filled,
And through each ear it softly thrilled,
As from the heavenly quills it fell
With time and tune attempered well.
Soon as the minstrels ceased to play
And airs celestial died away,
The troops of Bharat saw amazed
What Viśvakarmá's art had raised.
On every side, five leagues around,
All smooth and level lay the ground,
With fresh green grass that charmed the sight
Like sapphires blent with lazulite.
There the Wood-apple hung its load,
The Mango and the Citron glowed,
The Bel and scented Jak were there,
And Apelá with fruitage fair.
There, brought from Northern Kuru, stood
Rich in delights, the glorious wood,
And many a stream was seen to glide

With flowering trees along its side.
There mansions rose with four wide halls,
And elephants and chargers' stalls,
And many a house of royal state,
Triumphal arc and bannered gate.
With noble doorways, sought the sky,
Like a pale cloud, a palace high,
Which far and wide rare fragrance shed,
With wreaths of white engarlanded.
Square was its shape, its halls were wide,
With many a seat and couch supplied,
Drink of all kinds, and every meat
Such as celestial Gods might eat.
Then at the bidding of the seer
Kaikeyí's strong-armed son drew near,
And passed within that fair abode
Which with the noblest jewels glowed.
Then, as Vaśishṭha led the way,

The councillors, in due array,
Followed delighted and amazed
And on the glorious structure gazed.
Then Bharat, Raghu's son, drew near
The kingly throne, with prince and peer,
Whereby the chouri in the shade
Of the white canopy was laid.
Before the throne he humbly bent
And honoured Ráma, reverent,
Then in his hand the chouri bore,
And sat where sits a councillor.
His ministers and household priest
Sat by degrees from chief to least,
Then sat the captain of the host
And all the men he honoured most.
Then when the saint his order gave,
Each river with enchanted wave
Rolled milk and curds divinely sweet
Before the princely Bharat's feet;
And dwellings fair on either side,
With gay white plaster beautified,
Their heavenly roofs were seen to lift,
The Bráhman Bharadvája's gift.
Then straight by Lord Kuvera sent,
Gay with celestial ornament
Of bright attire and jewels' shine,
Came twenty thousand nymphs divine:
The man on whom those beauties glanced
That moment felt his soul entranced.
With them from Nandan's blissful shades
Came twenty thousand heavenly maids.
Tumburu, Nárad, Gopa came,
And Sutanu, like radiant flame,
The kings of the Gandharva throng,
And ravished Bharat with their song.
Then spoke the saint, and swift obeyed
Alambúshá, the fairest maid,
And Miśrakeśí bright to view,
Ramaná, Puṇḍríká too,
And danced to him with graceful ease
The dances of Apsarases.

All chaplets that by Gods are worn,
Or Chaitraratha's graves adorn,
Bloomed by the saint's command arrayed
On branches in Prayága's shade.
When at the saint's command the breeze
Made music with the Vilva trees,
To wave in rhythmic beat began
The boughs of each Myrobolan,
And holy fig-trees wore the look
Of dancers, as their leaflets shook.
The fair Tamála, palm, and pine,
With trees that tower and plants that twine,
The sweetly varying forms displayed
Of stately dame or bending maid.
Here men the foaming winecup quaffed,
Here drank of milk full many a draught,
And tasted meats of every kind,
Well dressed, whatever pleased their mind.
Then beauteous women, seven or eight,
Stood ready by each man to wait:
Beside the stream his limbs they stripped
And in the cooling water dipped.
And then the fair ones, sparkling eyed,
With soft hands rubbed his limbs and dried,
And sitting on the lovely bank
Held up the winecup as he drank.
Nor did the grooms forget to feed
Camel and mule and ox and steed,
For there were stores of roasted grain,
Of honey and of sugar-cane.
So fast the wild excitement spread
Among the warriors Bharat led,
That all the mighty army through
The groom no more his charger knew,
And he who drove might seek in vain
To tell his elephant again.
With every joy and rapture fired,
Entranced with all the heart desired,
The myriads of the host that night
Revelled delirious with delight.
Urged by the damsels at their side

594

In wild delight the warriors cried:
"Ne'er will we seek Ayodhyá, no,
Nor yet to Daṇḍak forest go:
Here will we stay: may happy fate
On Bharat and on Ráma wait."
Thus cried the army gay and free
Exulting in their lawless glee,
Both infantry and those who rode
On elephants, or steeds bestrode,
Ten thousand voices shouting, "This
Is heaven indeed for perfect bliss."
With garlands decked they idly strayed,
And danced and laughed and sang and played.
At length as every soldier eyed,
With food like Amrit satisfied,
Each dainty cate and tempting meat,
No longer had he care to eat.
Thus soldier, servant, dame, and slave
Received whate'er the wish might crave.
As each in new-wrought clothes arrayed
Enjoyed the feast before him laid.

Each man was seen in white attire
Unstained by spot or speck of mire:
None was athirst or hungry there,
And none had dust upon his hair.
On every side in woody dells
Was milky food in bubbling wells,
And there were all-supplying cows
And honey dropping from the boughs.
Nor wanted lakes of flower-made drink
With piles of meat upon the brink,
Boiled, stewed, and roasted, varied cheer,
Peachick and jungle-fowl and deer,
There was the flesh of kid and boar,
And dainty sauce in endless store,
With juice of flowers concocted well,
And soup that charmed the taste and smell,
And pounded fruits of bitter taste,
And many a bath was ready placed
Down by each river's shelving side

There stood great basins well supplied,
And laid therein, of dazzling sheen,
White brushes for the teeth were seen,
And many a covered box wherein
Was sandal powdered for the skin.
And mirrors bright with constant care,
And piles of new attire were there,
And store of sandals and of shoes,
Thousands of pairs, for all to choose:
Eye-unguents, combs for hair and beard,
Umbrellas fair and bows appeared.
Lakes gleamed, that lent digestive aid,
And some for pleasant bathing made,
With waters fair, and smooth incline
For camels, horses, mules, and kine.
There saw they barley heaped on high
The countless cattle to supply:
The golden grain shone fair and bright
As sapphires or the lazulite.
To all the gathered host it seemed
As if that magic scene they dreamed,
And wonder, as they gazed, increased
At Bharadvája's glorious feast.

Thus in the hermit's grove they spent
That night in joy and merriment,
Blest as the Gods who take their ease
Under the shade of Nandan's trees.
Each minstrel bade the saint adieu,
And to his blissful mansion flew,
And every stream and heavenly dame
Returned as swiftly as she came.

Bharat's Farewell

So Bharat with his army spent
The watches of the night content,
And gladly, with the morning's light
Drew near his host the anchorite.
When Bharadvája saw him stand
With hand in reverence joined to hand,
When fires of worship had been fed,
He looked upon the prince and said:
"O blameless son, I pray thee tell,
Did the past night content thee well?
Say if the feast my care supplied
Thy host of followers gratified."
His hands he joined, his head he bent
And spoke in answer reverent
To the most high and radiant sage
Who issued from his hermitage:
"Well have I passed the night: thy feast
Gave joy to every man and beast;
And I, great lord, and every peer
Were satisfied with sumptuous cheer,
Thy banquet has delighted all
From highest chief to meanest thrall,
And rich attire and drink and meat
Banished the thought of toil and heat.
And now, O Hermit good and great,
A boon of thee I supplicate.
To Ráma's side my steps I bend:
Do thou with friendly eye commend.
O tell me how to guide my feet
To virtuous Ráma's lone retreat:

Great Hermit, I entreat thee, say
How far from here and which the way."

Thus by fraternal love inspired
The chieftain of the saint inquired:
Then thus replied the glorious seer
Of matchless might, of vows austere:
"Ere the fourth league from here be passed,
Amid a forest wild and vast,
Stands Chitrakúṭa's mountain tall,
Lovely with wood and waterfall.
North of the mountain thou wilt see
The beauteous stream Mandákiní,
Where swarm the waterfowl below,
And gay trees on the margin grow.
Then will a leafy cot between
The river and the hill be seen:
'Tis Ráma's, and the princely pair
Of brothers live for certain there.
Hence to the south thine army lead,
And then more southward still proceed,
So shalt thou find his lone retreat,
And there the son of Raghu meet."

Soon as the ordered march they knew,
The widows of the monarch flew,
Leaving their cars, most meet to ride,
And flocked to Bharadvája's side.
There with the good Sumitrá Queen
Kauśalyá, sad and worn, was seen,
Caressing, still with sorrow faint,
The feet of that illustrious saint,
Kaikeyí too, her longings crossed,
Reproached of all, her object lost,
Before the famous hermit came,

And clasped his feet, o'erwhelmed with shame.
With circling steps she humbly went
Around the saint preëminent,
And stood not far from Bharat's side
With heart oppressed, and heavy-eyed.

Then the great seer, who never broke
One holy vow, to Bharat spoke:
"Speak, Raghu's son: I fain would learn
The story of each queen in turn."

Obedient to the high request
By Bharadvája thus addressed,
His reverent hands together laid,
He, skilled in speech, his answer made:
"She whom, O Saint, thou seest here
A Goddess in her form appear,
Was the chief consort of the king,
Now worn with fast and sorrowing.
As Aditi in days of yore
The all-preserving Vishṇu bore,
Kauśalyá bore with happy fate
Lord Ráma of the lion's gait.
She who, transfixed with torturing pangs,
On her left arm so fondly hangs,
As when her withering leaves decay
Droops by the wood the Cassia spray,
Sumitrá, pained with woe, is she,
The consort second of the three:
Two princely sons the lady bare,
Fair as the Gods in heaven are fair.
And she, the wicked dame through whom
My brothers' lives are wrapped in gloom,
And mourning for his offspring dear,
The king has sought his heavenly sphere,—
Proud, foolish-hearted, swift to ire,
Self-fancied darling of my sire,
Kaikeyí, most ambitious queen,
Unlovely with her lovely mien,
My mother she, whose impious will
Is ever bent on deeds of ill,
In whom the root and spring I see
Of all this woe which crushes me."

Quick breathing like a furious snake,
With tears and sobs the hero spake,
With reddened eyes aglow with rage.

599

And Bharadvája, mighty sage,
Supreme in wisdom, calm and grave,
In words like these good counsel gave:
"O Bharat, hear the words I say;
On her the fault thou must not lay:
For many a blessing yet will spring
From banished Ráma's wandering."
And Bharat, with that promise cheered,
Went circling round that saint revered,
He humbly bade farewell, and then
Gave orders to collect his men.
Prompt at the summons thousands flew
To cars which noble coursers drew,
Bright-gleaming, glorious to behold,
Adorned with wealth of burnished gold.
Then female elephants and male,
Gold-girthed, with flags that wooed the gale,
Marched with their bright bells' tinkling chime
Like clouds when ends the summer time:
Some cars were huge and some were light,
For heavy draught or rapid flight,
Of costly price, of every kind,
With clouds of infantry behind.
The dames, Kauśalyá at their head,
Were in the noblest chariots led,
And every gentle bosom beat
With hope the banished prince to meet.
The royal Bharat, glory-crowned,
With all his retinue around,
Borne in a beauteous litter rode,
Like the young moon and sun that glowed.
The army as it streamed along,
Cars, elephants, in endless throng,
Showed, marching on its southward way,
Like autumn clouds in long array.

Chitrakúta in Sight

As through the woods its way pursued
That mighty bannered multitude,
Wild elephants in terror fled
With all the startled herds they led,
And bears and deer were seen on hill,
In forest glade, by every rill.
Wide as the sea from coast to coast,
The high-souled Bharat's mighty host
Covered the earth as cloudy trains
Obscure the sky when fall the rains.
The stately elephants he led,
And countless steeds the land o'erspread,
So closely crowded that between
Their serried ranks no ground was seen.
Then when the host had travelled far,
And steeds were worn who drew the car,
The glorious Bharat thus addressed
Vaśishṭha, of his lords the best:
"The spot, methinks, we now behold
Of which the holy hermit told,
For, as his words described, I trace
Each several feature of the place:
Before us Chitrakúṭa shows,
Mandákiní beside us flows:
Afar umbrageous woods arise
Like darksome clouds that veil the skies.
Now tread these mountain-beasts of mine
On Chitrakúṭa's fair incline.
The trees their rain of blossoms shed
On table-lands beneath them spread,
As from black clouds the floods descend

When the hot days of summer end.
Śatrughna, look, the mountain see
Where heavenly minstrels wander free,

And horses browse beneath the steep,
Countless as monsters in the deep.
Scared by my host the mountain deer
Starting with tempest speed appear
Like the long lines of cloud that fly
In autumn through the windy sky.
See, every warrior shows his head
With fragrant blooms engarlanded;
All look like southern soldiers who
Lift up their shields of azure hue.
This lonely wood beneath the hill,
That was so dark and drear and still,
Covered with men in endless streams
Now like Ayodhyá's city seems.
The dust which countless hoofs excite
Obscures the sky and veils the light;
But see, swift winds those clouds dispel
As if they strove to please me well.
See, guided in their swift career
By many a skilful charioteer,
Those cars by fleetest coursers drawn
Race onward over glade and lawn.
Look, startled as the host comes near
The lovely peacocks fly in fear,
Gorgeous as if the fairest blooms
Of earth had glorified their plumes.
Look where the sheltering covert shows
The trooping deer, both bucks and does,
That occupy in countless herds
This mountain populous with birds.
Most lovely to my mind appears
This place which every charm endears:
Fair as the road where tread the Blest;
Here holy hermits take their rest.
Then let the army onward press
And duly search each green recess

For the two lion-lords, till we
Ráma once more and Lakshmaṇ see."

Thus Bharat spoke: and hero bands
Of men with weapons in their hands
Entered the tangled forest: then
A spire of smoke appeared in ken.
Soon as they saw the rising smoke
To Bharat they returned and spoke:
"No fire where men are not: 'tis clear
That Raghu's sons are dwelling here.
Or if not here those heroes dwell
Whose mighty arms their foeman quell,
Still other hermits here must be
Like Ráma, true and good as he."

His ears attentive Bharat lent
To their resistless argument,
Then to his troops the chief who broke
His foe's embattled armies spoke:
"Here let the troops in silence stay;
One step beyond they must not stray.
Come Dhrishṭi and Sumantra, you
With me alone the path pursue."
Their leader's speech the warriors heard,
And from his place no soldier stirred,
And Bharat bent his eager eyes
Where curling smoke was seen to rise.

The host his order well obeyed,
And halting there in silence stayed
Watching where from the thicket's shade
They saw the smoke appear.
And joy through all the army ran,
"Soon shall we meet," thought every man,
"The prince we hold so dear."

Chitrakúta

There long the son of Raghu dwelt
And love for hill and wood he felt.
Then his Videhan spouse to please
And his own heart of woe to ease,
Like some Immortal—Indra so
Might Swarga's charms to Śachí show—
Drew her sweet eyes to each delight
Of Chitrakúṭa's lovely height:
"Though reft of power and kingly sway,
Though friends and home are far away,
I cannot mourn my altered lot,
Enamoured of this charming spot.
Look, darling, on this noble hill
Which sweet birds with their music fill,
Bright with a thousand metal dyes
His lofty summits cleave the skies.
See, there a silvery sheen is spread,
And there like blood the rocks are red.
There shows a streak of emerald green,
And pink and yellow glow between.
There where the higher peaks ascend,
Crystal and flowers and topaz blend,
And others flash their light afar
Like mercury or some fair star:
With such a store of metals dyed
The king of hills is glorified.
There through the wild birds' populous home
The harmless bear and tiger roam:
Hyænas range the woody slopes
With herds of deer and antelopes.

See, love, the trees that clothe his side
All lovely in their summer pride,
In richest wealth of leaves arrayed,
With flower and fruit and light and shade,
Look where the young Rose-apple glows;
What loaded boughs the Mango shows;
See, waving in the western wind
The light leaves of the Tamarind,
And mark that giant Peepul through
The feathery clump of tall bamboo.

Look, on the level lands above,
Delighting in successful love
In sweet enjoyment many a pair
Of heavenly minstrels revels there,
While overhanging boughs support
Their swords and mantles as they sport:
Then see that pleasant shelter where
Play the bright Daughters of the Air.
The mountain seems with bright cascade
And sweet rill bursting from the shade,
Like some majestic elephant o'er
Whose burning head the torrents pour.
Where breathes the man who would not feel
Delicious languor o'er him steal,
As the young morning breeze that springs
From the cool cave with balmy wings,
Breathes round him laden with the scent
Of bud and blossom dew-besprent?
If many autumns here I spent
With thee, my darling innocent,
And Lakshmaṇ, I should never know
The torture of the fires of woe,
This varied scene so charms my sight,
This mount so fills me with delight,
Where flowers in wild profusion spring,
And ripe fruits glow and sweet birds sing.
My beauteous one, a double good
Springs from my dwelling in the wood:
Loosed is the bond my sire that tied,

And Bharat too is gratified.
My darling, dost thou feel with me
Delight from every charm we see,
Of which the mind and every sense
Feel the enchanting influence?
My fathers who have passed away,
The royal saints, were wont to say,
That life in woodland shades like this
Secures a king immortal bliss.
See, round the hill at random thrown,
Huge masses lie of rugged stone
Of every shape and many a hue,
Yellow and white and red and blue.
But all is fairer still by night:
Each rock reflects a softer light,
When the whole mount from foot to crest
In robes of lambent flame is dressed;
When from a million herbs a blaze
Of their own luminous glory plays,
And clothed in fire each deep ravine,
Each pinnacle and crag is seen.
Some parts the look of mansions wear,
And others are as gardens fair,
While others seem a massive block
Of solid undivided rock.
Behold those pleasant beds o'erlaid
With lotus leaves, for lovers made,
Where mountain birch and costus throw
Cool shadows on the pair below.
See where the lovers in their play
Have cast their flowery wreaths away,
And fruit and lotus buds that crowned
Their brows lie trodden on the ground.
North Kuru's realm is fair to see,
Vasvaukasárá, Naliní,
But rich in fruit and blossom still
More fair is Chitrakúṭa's hill.
Here shall the years appointed glide
With thee, my beauty, by my side,
And Lakshmaṇ ever near;
Here shall I live in all delight,

606

Make my ancestral fame more bright,
Tread in their path who walk aright,
And to my oath adhere."

CANTO

XCV

Mandákiní

Then Ráma, like the lotus eyed,
  Descended from the mountain side,
  And to the Maithil lady showed
The lovely stream that softly flowed.
And thus Ayodhyá's lord addressed
His bride, of dames the loveliest,
Child of Videha's king, her face
Bright with the fair moon's tender grace:
"How sweetly glides, O darling, look,
Mandákiní's delightful brook,
Adorned with islets, blossoms gay,
And sárases and swans at play!

The trees with which her banks are lined
Show flowers and fruit of every kind:
The match in radiant sheen is she
Of King Kuvera's Naliní.
My heart exults with pleasure new
The shelving band and ford to view,
Where gathering herds of thirsty deer
Disturb the wave that ran so clear.
Now look, those holy hermits mark
In skins of deer and coats of bark;
With twisted coils of matted hair,
The reverend men are bathing there,
And as they lift their arms on high
The Lord of Day they glorify:

607

These best of saints, my large-eyed spouse,
Are constant to their sacred vows.
The mountain dances while the trees
Bend their proud summits to the breeze,
And scatter many a flower and bud
From branches that o'erhang the flood.
There flows the stream like lucid pearl,
Round islets here the currents whirl,
And perfect saints from middle air
Are flocking to the waters there.
See, there lie flowers in many a heap
From boughs the whistling breezes sweep,
And others wafted by the gale
Down the swift current dance and sail.
Now see that pair of wild-fowl rise,
Exulting with their joyful cries:
Hark, darling, wafted from afar
How soft their pleasant voices are.
To gaze on Chitrakúṭa's hill,
To look upon this lovely rill,
To bend mine eyes on thee, dear wife,
Is sweeter than my city life.
Come, bathe we in the pleasant rill
Whose dancing waves are never still,
Stirred by those beings pure from sin,
The sanctities who bathe therein:
Come, dearest, to the stream descend,
Approach her as a darling friend,
And dip thee in the silver flood
Which lotuses and lilies stud.
Let this fair hill Ayodhyá seem,
Its silvan things her people deem,
And let these waters as they flow
Our own beloved Sarjú show.
How blest, mine own dear love, am I;
Thou, fond and true, art ever nigh,
And duteous, faithful Lakshman stays
Beside me, and my word obeys.
Here every day I bathe me thrice,
Fruit, honey, roots for food suffice,
And ne'er my thoughts with longing stray

608

To distant home or royal sway.
For who this charming brook can see
Where herds of roedeer wander free,
And on the flowery-wooded brink
Apes, elephants, and lions drink,
Nor feel all sorrow fly?"
Thus eloquently spoke the pride
Of Raghu's children to his bride,
And wandered happy by her side
Where Chitrakúṭa azure-dyed
Uprears his peaks on high.

CANTO

XCVI

The Magic Shaft

Thus Ráma showed to Janak's child
The varied beauties of the wild,
The hill, the brook and each fair spot,
Then turned to seek their leafy cot.
North of the mountain Ráma found
A cavern in the sloping ground,
Charming to view, its floor was strown
With many a mass of ore and stone,
In secret shadow far retired
Where gay birds sang with joy inspired,
And trees their graceful branches swayed
With loads of blossom downward weighed.
Soon as he saw the cave which took
Each living heart and chained the look,
Thus Ráma spoke to Sítá who
Gazed wondering on the silvan view:
"Does this fair cave beneath the height,
Videhan lady, charm thy sight?
Then let us resting here a while

The languor of the way beguile.
That block of stone so smooth and square
Was set for thee to rest on there,
And like a thriving Keśar tree
This flowery shrub o'ershadows thee."
Thus Ráma spoke, and Janak's child,
By nature ever soft and mild,
In tender words which love betrayed
Her answer to the hero made:
"O pride of Raghu's children, still
My pleasure is to do thy will.
Enough for me thy wish to know:
Far hast thou wandered to and fro."

Thus Sítá spake in gentle tone,
And went obedient to the stone,
Of perfect face and faultless limb
Prepared to rest a while with him.
And Ráma, as she thus replied,
Turned to his spouse again and cried:
"Thou seest, love, this flowery shade
For silvan creatures' pleasure made,
How the gum streams from trees and plants
Torn by the tusks of elephants!

Through all the forest clear and high
Resounds the shrill cicala's cry.
Hark how the kite above us moans,
And calls her young in piteous tones;
So may my hapless mother be
Still mourning in her home for me.
There mounted on that lofty Sál
The loud Bhringráj repeats his call:
How sweetly now he tunes his throat
Responsive to the Koïl's note.
Or else the bird that now has sung
May be himself the Koïl's young,
Linked with such winning sweetness are
The notes he pours irregular.
See, round the blooming Mango clings
That creeper with her tender rings,

So in thy love, when none is near,
Thine arms are thrown round me, my dear."

Thus in his joy he cried; and she,
Sweet speaker, on her lover's knee,
Of faultless limb and perfect face,
Grew closer to her lord's embrace.
Reclining in her husband's arms,
A goddess in her wealth of charms,
She filled his loving breast anew
With mighty joy that thrilled him through.
His finger on the rock he laid,
Which veins of sanguine ore displayed,
And painted o'er his darling's eyes
The holy sign in mineral dyes.
Bright on her brow the metal lay
Like the young sun's first gleaming ray,
And showed her in her beauty fair
As the soft light of morning's air.
Then from the Keśar's laden tree
He picked fair blossoms in his glee,
And as he decked each lovely tress,
His heart o'erflowed with happiness.
So resting on that rocky seat
A while they spent in pastime sweet,
Then onward neath the shady boughs
Went Ráma with his Maithil spouse.
She roaming in the forest shade
Where every kind of creature strayed
Observed a monkey wandering near,
And clung to Ráma's arm in fear.
The hero Ráma fondly laced
His mighty arms around her waist,
Consoled his beauty in her dread,
And scared the Monkey till he fled.
That holy mark of sanguine ore
That gleamed on Sítá's brow before,
Shone by that close embrace impressed
Upon the hero's ample chest.
Then Sítá, when the beast who led
The monkey troop, afar had fled,

Laughed loudly in light-hearted glee
That mark on Ráma's chest to see.
A clump of bright Aśokas fired
The forest in their bloom attired:
The restless blossoms as they gleamed
A host of threatening monkeys seemed.
Then Sítá thus to Ráma cried,
As longingly the flowers she eyed:
"Pride of thy race, now let us go
Where those Aśoka blossoms grow."
He on his darling's pleasure bent
With his fair goddess thither went
And roamed delighted through the wood
Where blossoming Aśokas stood,
As Śiva with Queen Umá roves
Through Himaván's majestic groves.
Bright with purpureal glow the pair
Of happy lovers sported there,
And each upon the other set
A flower-inwoven coronet.
There many a crown and chain they wove
Of blooms from that Aśoka grove,
And in their graceful sport the two
Fresh beauty o'er the mountain threw.
The lover let his love survey
Each pleasant spot that round them lay,
Then turned they to their green retreat
Where all was garnished, gay, and neat.
By brotherly affection led,
Sumitrá's son to meet them sped,
And showed the labours of the day
Done while his brother was away.
There lay ten black-deer duly slain
With arrows pure of poison stain,
Piled in a mighty heap to dry,
With many another carcass nigh.
And Lakshmaṇ's brother saw, o'erjoyed,
The work that had his hands employed,
Then to his consort thus he cried:
"Now be the general gifts supplied."
Then Sítá, fairest beauty, placed

612

The food for living things to taste,
And set before the brothers meat
And honey that the pair might eat.
They ate the meal her hands supplied,
Their lips with water purified:
Then Janak's daughter sat at last
And duly made her own repast.
The other venison, to be dried,
Piled up in heaps was set aside,
And Ráma told his wife to stay
And drive the flocking crows away.
Her husband saw her much distressed
By one more bold than all the rest,
Whose wings where'er he chose could fly,
Now pierce the earth, now roam the sky.
Then Ráma laughed to see her stirred
To anger by the plaguing bird:
Proud of his love the beauteous dame
With burning rage was all aflame.
Now here, now there, again, again,
She chased the crow, but all in vain,
Enraging her, so quick to strike

With beak and wing and claw alike:
Then how the proud lip quivered, how
The dark frown marked her angry brow!
When Ráma saw her cheek aglow
With passion, he rebuked the crow.
But bold in impudence the bird,
With no respect for Ráma's word,
Fearless again at Sítá flew:
Then Ráma's wrath to fury grew.
The hero of the mighty arm
Spoke o'er a shaft the mystic charm,
Laid the dire weapon on his bow
And launched it at the shameless crow.
The bird, empowered by Gods to spring
Through earth itself on rapid wing,
Through the three worlds in terror fled
Still followed by that arrow dread.
Where'er he flew, now here now there,

A cloud of weapons filled the air.
Back to the high-souled prince he fled
And bent at Ráma's feet his head,
And then, as Sítá looked, began
His speech in accents of a man:
"O pardon, and for pity's sake
Spare, Ráma, spare my life to take!
Where'er I turn, where'er I flee,
No shelter from this shaft I see."
The chieftain heard the crow entreat
Helpless and prostrate at his feet,
And while soft pity moved his breast,
With wisest speech the bird addressed:
"I took the troubled Sítá's part,
And furious anger filled my heart.
Then on the string my arrow lay
Charmed with a spell thy life to slay.
Thou seekest now my feet, to crave
Forgiveness and thy life to save.
So shall thy prayer have due respect:
The suppliant I must still protect.
But ne'er in vain this dart may flee;
Yield for thy life a part of thee,
What portion of thy body, say,
Shall this mine arrow rend away?
Thus far, O bird, thus far alone
On thee my pity may be shown.
Forfeit a part thy life to buy:
'Tis better so to live than die."
Thus Ráma spoke: the bird of air
Pondered his speech with anxious care,
And wisely deemed it good to give
One of his eyes that he might live.
To Raghu's son he made reply:
"O Ráma, I will yield an eye.
So let me in thy grace confide
And live hereafter single-eyed."
Then Ráma charged the shaft, and lo,
Full in the eye it smote the crow.
And the Videhan lady gazed
Upon the ruined eye amazed.

The crow to Ráma humbly bent,
Then where his fancy led he went.
Ráma with Lakshmaṇ by his side
With needful work was occupied.

Lakshman's Anger

Thus Ráma showed his love the rill
Whose waters ran beneath the hill,
Then resting on his mountain seat
Refreshed her with the choicest meat.
So there reposed the happy two:
Then Bharat's army nearer drew:
Rose to the skies a dusty cloud,
The sound of trampling feet was loud.
The swelling roar of marching men
Drove the roused tiger from his den,
And scared amain the serpent race
Flying to hole and hiding-place.
The herds of deer in terror fled,
The air was filled with birds o'erhead,
The bear began to leave his tree,
The monkey to the cave to flee.
Wild elephants were all amazed
As though the wood around them blazed.
The lion oped his ponderous jaw,
The buffalo looked round in awe.
The prince, who heard the deafening sound,
And saw the silvan creatures round
Fly wildly startled from their rest,
The glorious Lakshmaṇ thus addressed:
"Sumitrá's noble son most dear,
Hark, Lakshmaṇ, what a roar I hear,

615

The tumult of a coming crowd,
Appalling, deafening, deep, and loud!
The din that yet more fearful grows
Scares elephants and buffaloes,
Or frightened by the lions, deer
Are flying through the wood in fear.
I fain would know who seeks this place
Comes prince or monarch for the chase?
Or does some mighty beast of prey
Frighten the silvan herds away?
'Tis hard to reach this mountain height,
Yea, e'en for birds in airy flight.
Then fain, O Lakshmaṇ, would I know
What cause disturbs the forest so."

Lakshmaṇ in haste, the wood to view,
Climbed a high Sál that near him grew,
The forest all around he eyed,
First gazing on the eastern side.
Then northward when his eyes he bent
He saw a mighty armament
Of elephants, and cars, and horse,
And men on foot, a mingled force,
And banners waving in the breeze,
And spoke to Ráma words like these:
"Quick, quick, my lord, put out the fire,
Let Sítá to the cave retire.

Thy coat of mail around thee throw,
Prepare thine arrows and thy bow."

In eager haste thus Lakshmaṇ cried,
And Ráma, lion lord, replied:
"Still closer be the army scanned,
And say who leads the warlike band."
Lakshmaṇ his answer thus returned,
As furious rage within him burned,
Exciting him like kindled fire
To scorch the army in his ire:
"'Tis Bharat: he has made the throne
By consecrating rites his own:

616

To gain the whole dominion thus
He comes in arms to slaughter us.
I mark tree-high upon his car
His flagstaff of the Kovidár,
I see his glittering banner glance,
I see his chivalry advance:
I see his eager warriors shine
On elephants in lengthened line.
Now grasp we each the shafts and bow,
And higher up the mountain go.
Or in this place, O hero, stand
With weapons in each ready hand.
Perhaps beneath our might may fall
This leader of the standard tall,
And Bharat I this day may see
Who brought this mighty woe on thee,
Sítá, and me, who drove away
My brother from the royal sway.
Bharat our foe at length is nigh,
And by this hand shall surely die:
Brother, I see no sin at all
If Bharat by my weapon fall.
No fault is his who slays the foe
Whose hand was first to strike the blow:
With Bharat now the crime begins
Who against thee and duty sins.
The queen athirst for royal sway
Will see her darling son to-day
Fall by this hand, like some fair tree
Struck by an elephant, slain by me.
Kaikeyí's self shall perish too
With kith and kin and retinue,
And earth by my avenging deed
Shall from this mass of sin be freed.
This day my wrath, too long restrained,
Shall fall upon the foe, unchained,
Mad as the kindled flame that speeds
Destroying through the grass and reeds.
This day mine arrows keen and fierce
The bodies of the foe shall pierce:
The woods on Chitrakúṭa's side

617

Shall run with torrents crimson-dyed.
The wandering beasts of prey shall feed
On heart-cleft elephant and steed,
And drag to mountain caves away
The bodies that my arrows slay.
Doubt not that Bharat and his train
Shall in this mighty wood be slain:
So shall I pay the debt my bow
And these my deadly arrows owe."

CANTO

XCVIII

Lakshman Calmed

Then Ráma nobly calm allayed
The wrath that Lakshman's bosom swayed:
"What need have we the sword to wield,
To bend the bow or lift the shield,
If Bharat brave, and wise, and good,
Himself has sought this sheltering wood?
I sware my father's will to do,
And if I now my brother slew
What gain in kingship should I find,
Despised and scorned by all mankind?
Believe me, e'en as I would shrink
From poisoned meat or deadly drink,
No power or treasure would I win
By fall of friend or kith or kin.
Brother, believe the words I speak:
For your dear sakes alone I seek
Duty and pleasure, wealth and gain:
A holy life, a happy reign.
If royal sway my heart desires,
My brothers' weal the wish inspires:
Their bliss and safety is my care,

By this uplifted bow I swear.
'Twere not so hard for me to gain
This broad land girdled by the main,
But even Indra's royal might
Should ne'er be mine in duty's spite.
If any bliss my soul can see
Deprived of dear Satrughna, thee,
And Bharat, may the flame destroy
With ashy gloom the selfish joy.
Far dearer than this life of mine,
Knowing the custom of our line,
His heart with fond affection fraught,
Bharat Ayodhyá's town resought
And hearing when he came that I,
With thee and Sítá, forced to fly
With matted hair and hermit dress
Am wandering in the wilderness.
While grief his troubled senses storms,
And tender love his bosom warms,
From every thought of evil clear,
Is come to meet his brother here.
Some grievous words perchance he spoke
Kaikeyí's anger to provoke,
Then won the king, and comes to lay
Before my feet the royal sway.
Hither, methinks, in season due
Comes Bharat for an interview,
Nor in his secret heart has he
One evil thought 'gainst thee or me.
What has he done ere now, reflect!
How failed in love or due respect

To make thee doubt his faith and lay
This evil to his charge to-day?
Thou shouldst not join with Bharat's name
So harsh a speech and idle blame.
The blows thy tongue at Bharat deals,
My sympathizing bosom feels.
How, urged by stress of any ill,
Should sons their father's life-blood spill,
Or brother slay in impious strife

A brother dearer than his life?
If thou these cruel words hast said
By strong desire of empire led,
My brother Bharat will I pray
To give to thee the kingly sway.
"Give him the realm," my speech shall be,
And Bharat will, methinks, agree."

Thus spoke the prince whose chief delight
Was duty, and to aid the right:
And Lakshman keenly felt the blame,
And shrank within himself for shame:
And then his answer thus returned,
With downcast eye and cheek that burned:
"Brother, I ween, to see thy face
Our sire himself has sought this place."
Thus Lakshman spoke and stood ashamed,
And Ráma saw and thus exclaimed:
"It is the strong-armed monarch: he
Is come, methinks, his sons to see,
To bid us both the forest quit
For joys for which he deems us fit:
He thinks on all our care and pain,
And now would lead us home again.
My glorious father hence will bear
Sítá who claims all tender care.
I see two coursers fleet as storms,
Of noble breed and lovely forms.
I see the beast of mountain size
Who bears the king our father wise,
The aged Victor, march this way
In front of all the armed array.
But doubt and fear within me rise,
For when I look with eager eyes
I see no white umbrella spread,
World-famous, o'er the royal head.
Now, Lakshman, from the tree descend,
And to my words attention lend."

Thus spoke the pious prince: and he
Descended from the lofty tree,

And reverent hand to hand applied,
Stood humbly by his brother's side.

The host, compelled by Bharat's care,
The wood from trampling feet to spare,
Dense crowding half a league each way
Encamped around the mountain lay.
Below the tall hill's shelving side
Gleamed the bright army far and wide
Spread o'er the ample space,
By Bharat led who firmly true
In duty from his bosom threw
All pride, and near his brother drew
To win the hero's grace.

CANTO

XCIX

Bharat's Approach

Soon as the warriors took their rest
Obeying Bharat's high behest,
Thus Bharat to Śatrughna spake:
"A band of soldiers with thee take,
And with these hunters o'er and o'er
The thickets of the wood explore.
With bow, sword, arrows in their hands
Let Guha with his kindred bands
Within this grove remaining trace
The children of Kakutstha's race.
And I meanwhile on foot will through
This neighbouring wood my way pursue,
With elders and the twice-born men,
And every lord and citizen.
There is, I feel, no rest for me
Till Ráma's face again I see,

Lakshman, in arms and glory great,
And Sítá born to happy fate:
No rest, until his cheek as bright
As the fair moon rejoice my sight,
No rest until I see the eye
With which the lotus petals vie;
Till on my head those dear feet rest
With signs of royal rank impressed;
None, till my kingly brother gain
His old hereditary reign,
Till o'er his limbs and noble head
The consecrating drops be shed.
How blest is Janak's daughter, true
To every wifely duty, who
Cleaves faithful to her husband's side
Whose realm is girt by Ocean's tide!
This mountain too above the rest
E'en as the King of Hills is blest,—
Whose shades Kakutstha's scion hold
As Nandan charms the Lord of Gold.
Yea, happy is this tangled grove
Where savage beasts unnumbered rove,
Where, glory of the Warrior race,
King Ráma finds a dwelling-place."

Thus Bharat, strong-armed hero spake,
And walked within the pathless brake.
O'er plains where gay trees bloomed he went,
Through boughs in tangled net-work bent,
And then from Ráma's cot appeared
The banner which the flame upreared.
And Bharat joyed with every friend
To mark those smoky wreaths ascend:
"Here Ráma dwells," he thought; "at last
The ocean of our toil is passed."
Then sure that Ráma's hermit cot
Was on the mountain's side
He stayed his army on the spot,
And on with Guha hied.

CANTO

C

The Meeting

Then Bharat to Śatrughna showed
The spot, and eager onward strode,
First bidding Saint Vaśishṭha bring
The widowed consorts of the king.
As by fraternal love impelled
His onward course the hero held,
Sumantra followed close behind
Śatrughna with an anxious mind:
Not Bharat's self more fain could be
To look on Rāma's face than he.
As, speeding on, the spot he neared,
Amid the hermits' homes appeared
His brother's cot with leaves o'erspread,
And by its side a lowly shed.
Before the shed great heaps were left
Of gathered flowers and billets cleft,
And on the trees hung grass and bark
Rāma and Lakshmaṇ's path to mark:
And heaps of fuel to provide
Against the cold stood ready dried.
The long-armed chief, as on he went
In glory's light preëminent,
With joyous words like these addressed
The brave Śatrughna and the rest:
"This is the place, I little doubt,
Which Bharadvája pointed out,
Not far from where we stand must be
The woodland stream, Mandákiní.
Here on the mountain's woody side
Roam elephants in tusked pride,
And ever with a roar and cry

Each other, as they meet, defy.
And see those smoke-wreaths thick and dark:
The presence of the flame they mark,
Which hermits in the forest strive
By every art to keep alive.
O happy me! my task is done,
And I shall look on Raghu's son,
Like some great saint, who loves to treat
His elders with all reverence meet."

Thus Bharat reached that forest rill,
Thus roamed on Chitrakúṭa's hill;
Then pity in his breast awoke,
And to his friends the hero spoke:
"Woe, woe upon my life and birth!
The prince of men, the lord of earth
Has sought the lonely wood to dwell
Sequestered in a hermit's cell.
Through me, through me these sorrows fall
On him the splendid lord of all:
Through me resigning earthly bliss
He hides him in a home like this.
Now will I, by the world abhorred,
Fall at the dear feet of my lord,
And at fair Sítá's too, to win
His pardon for my heinous sin."

As thus he sadly mourned and sighed,
The son of Daśaratha spied
A bower of leafy branches made,
Sacred and lovely in the shade,
Of fair proportions large and tall,
Well roofed with boughs of palm, and Sál,
Arranged in order due o'erhead
Like grass upon an altar spread.
Two glorious bows were gleaming there,
Like Indra's in the rainy air,
Terror of foemen, backed with gold,
Meet for the mightiest hand to hold:
And quivered arrows cast a blaze
Bright gleaming like the Day-God's rays:

Thus serpents with their eyes aglow
Adorn their capital below.
Great swords adorned the cottage, laid
Each in a case of gold brocade;
There hung the trusty shields, whereon
With purest gold the bosses shone.
The brace to bind the bowman's arm,
The glove to shield his hand from harm,
A lustre to the cottage lent
From many a golden ornament:
Safe was the cot from fear of men
As from wild beasts the lion's den.
The fire upon the altar burned,
That to the north and east was turned.
Bharat his eager glances bent
And gazed within the cot intent;
In deerskin dress, with matted hair,
Ráma his chief was sitting there:
With lion-shoulders broad and strong,
With lotus eyes, arms thick and long.
The righteous sovereign, who should be
Lord paramount from sea to sea,
High-minded, born to lofty fate,
Like Brahmá's self supremely great;
With Lakshmaṇ by his side, and her,
Fair Sítá, for his minister.
And Bharat gazing, overcome
By sorrow for a while was dumb,
Then, yielding to his woe, he ran
To Ráma and with sobs began:
"He who a royal seat should fill
With subjects round to do his will,
My elder brother,—see him here,
With silvan creatures waiting near.
The high-souled hero, wont to wear
The costliest robes exceeding fair,
Now banished, in a deerskin dress,
Here keeps the path of righteousness.
How brooks the son of Raghu now
The matted locks which load his brow,
Around whose princely head were twined

Sweet blossoms of the rarest kind?
The prince whose merits grew, acquired

By rites performed as he desired,
Would now a store of merit gain
Bought by his body's toil and pain.
Those limbs to which pure sandal lent
The freshness of its fragrant scent,
Exposed to sun, and dust, and rain,
Are now defiled with many a stain.
And I the wretched cause why this
Falls on the prince whose right is bliss!
Ah me, that ever I was born
To be the people's hate and scorn!"

Thus Bharat cried: of anguish sprung,
Great drops upon his forehead hung.
He fell o'erpowered—his grief was such—
Ere he his brother's feet could touch.
As on the glorious prince he gazed
In vain his broken voice he raised:
"Dear lord"—through tears and sobbing came,
The only words his lips could frame.
And brave Śatrughna wept aloud,
As low at Ráma's feet he bowed.
Then Ráma, while his tears ran fast,
His arms around his brothers cast.
Guha, Sumantra came to meet
The princes in their wild retreat.
Vrihaspati and Śukra bright
Their greeting thus rejoice to pay
To the dear Lord who brings the night,
And the great God who rules the day.
Then wept the dwellers of the shade,
Whose eyes the princes, meet to ride
On mighty elephants, surveyed;
And cast all thought of joy aside.

Bharata Questioned

Then Ráma gazed, and scarcely knew
  Bharat so worn and changed in hue.
  He raised him, kissed him on the head,
Embraced him, and thus kindly said:
"Where was thy father, brother dear,
That thou art come to seek me here?
Unmeet, if he be living yet,
Thy feet within the wood to set.
I pray thee now the cause declare
Why thou hast left the kingdom there,
With matted locks and deerskin dress
To roam the distant wilderness."

Thus questioned by the prince, at length
Kaikeyí's son regained his strength,
And hand to hand in reverence laid,
To Ráma thus his answer made:
"The great-armed monarch, O my lord,
Has dared to do a thing abhorred,
Left us, and grieving for his son,
A home among the Gods has won.
My mother Queen Kaikeyí gave
The order to the king her slave,
And at the bidding of the dame
He wrought the sin which mars his fame.
Athirst for sway, her hopes are crossed,
She mourns her son, her husband lost,
And through her impious crime will go
For punishment to hell below.
Now O my lord, forgive me all;
Be gracious to thy lowly thrall:

627

Anointed king, accept to-day
Like Indra's self, the royal sway.
Be gracious, Prince, to lord and peer,
And widowed queens who seek thee here
Accept the kingdom thine by right,
And so thy faithful friends delight.
Let the broad land no longer be
All widowed and forlorn of thee:
Let the full moon of autumn reign
Triumphant o'er the night again.
These lords and I before thee bend:
O Ráma, to our prayer attend.
O do not thou this grace deny:
Thy brother, pupil, slave am I.
Look on this venerable ring,
Advisers of our sire the king,
From age to age so honoured: thou
Shouldst grant their supplication now."

As weeping thus the hero prayed,
His head at Ráma's feet he laid.
Like a mad elephant he sighed:
And Ráma gazed and thus replied:
"How, brother, can a man of worth,
True to his vows, of noble birth—
A man like me, commit a sin
The lordship of the land to win?
No slightest shade of fault I see,
O tamer of thy foes, in thee.
But ne'er shouldst thou in childish thought
The queen thy mother blame in aught.
O brother wise and sinless, know
The sacred laws would have it so,
That from good wife and son require
Obedience to their lord and sire.
And we are all the king's, for thus
The virtuous ever reckon us:
Yea brother, be it known to thee,
His wives, and sons, and pupils we.
His is the right, if he deem fit,
To bid me, throned as monarch, sit,

628

Or in a coat of bark expel,
And deerskin, in the wood to dwell.
And O remember, best of all
Who act as claims of duty call,
As to a virtuous sire is due,
Such honour claims a mother too.
So they whose lives have ever been
By duty led, the king and queen,
Said, "Ráma, seek the forest shade:"
And I (what could I else?) obeyed.
Thou must the royal power retain,

And o'er the famed Ayodhyá reign:
I dressed in bark my days will spend
Where Daṇḍak's forest wilds extend.
So Daśaratha spoke, our king,
His share to each apportioning
Before his honoured servants' eyes:
Then, heir of bliss, he sought the skies.
The righteous monarch's honoured will,
Whom all revered, must guide thee still,
And thou must still enjoy the share
Assigned thee by our father's care.
So I till twice seven years are spent
Will roam this wood in banishment,
Contented with the lot which he,
My high-souled sire, has given me.
The charge the monarch gave, endeared
To all mankind, by all revered,
Peer of the Lord Supreme,
Far better, richer far in gain
Of every blessing than to reign
O'er all the worlds I deem."

CANTO
CII

Bharat's Tidings

He spoke: and Bharat thus replied:
"If, false to every claim beside,
I ne'er in kingly duties fail,
What will my royal life avail?
Still should the custom be observed,
From which our line has never swerved,
Which to the younger son ne'er gives
The kingdom while the elder lives.
Now to Ayodhyá rich and fair
With me, O Raghu's son, repair,
And to protect and gladden all
Our house, thyself as king install.
A king the world's opinion deems
A man: to me a God he seems,
Whose life in virtuous thoughts and deeds
The lives of other men exceeds.
When I in distant Kekaya stayed,
And thou hadst sought the forest shade,
Our father died, the saints' delight,
So constant in each holy rite.
Scarce with thy wife and Lakshmaṇ thou
Hadst journeyed forth to keep the vow,
When mourning for his son, forspent,
To heavenly rest the monarch went.
Then up, O lord of men, away!
His funeral rites of water pay:
I and Śatrughna, ere we came,
Neglected not the sacred claim.
But in the spirit-world, they say,
That gift alone is fresh for aye
Which best beloved hands have poured;

And thou his dearest art, my lord.
For thee he longed, for thee he grieved,
His every thought on thee was bent,
And crushed by woe, of thee bereaved,
He thought of thee as hence he went."

CIII

The Funeral Libation

When Ráma heard from Bharat each
Dark sorrow of his mournful speech,
And tidings of his father dead,
His spirits fell, his senses fled.
For the sad words his brother spoke
Struck on him like a thunder stroke,
Fierce as the bolt which Indra throws,
The victor of his Daitya foes.
Raising his arms in anguish, he,
As when the woodman hews a tree
With its fair flowery branches crowned,
Fainted and fell upon the ground.
Lord of the earth to earth he sank,
Helpless, as when a towering bank
With sudden ruin buries deep
An elephant who lay asleep.
Then swift his wife and brothers flew,
And water, weeping, o'er him threw.
As slowly sense and strength he gained,
Fast from his eyes the tears he rained,
And then in accents sad and weak
Kakutstha's son began to speak,
And mourning for the monarch dead,
With righteous words to Bharat said:
"What calls me home, when he, alas,

631

Has gone the way which all must pass?
Of him, the best of kings bereft
What guardian has Ayodhyá left?
How may I please his spirit? how
Delight the high-souled monarch now,
Who wept for me and went above
By me ungraced with mourning love?
Ah, happy brothers! you have paid
Due offerings to his parting shade.
E'en when my banishment is o'er,
Back to my home I go no more,
To look upon the widowed state
Reft of her king, disconsolate.
E'en then, O tamer of the foe,
If to Ayodhyá's town I go,
Who will direct me as of old,
Now other worlds our father hold?
From whom, my brother, shall I hear
Those words which ever charmed mine ear
And filled my bosom with delight
Whene'er he saw me act aright?"

Thus Ráma spoke: then nearer came
And looking on his moonbright dame,
"Sítá, the king is gone," he said:
"And Lakshman, know thy sire is dead,

And with the Gods on high enrolled:
This mournful news has Bharat told."
He spoke: the noble youths with sighs
Rained down the torrents from their eyes.
And then the brothers of the chief
With words of comfort soothed his grief:
"Now to the king our sire who swayed
The earth be due libations paid."
Soon as the monarch's fate she knew,
Sharp pangs of grief smote Sítá through:
Nor could she look upon her lord
With eyes from which the torrents poured.
And Ráma strove with tender care
To soothe the weeping dame's despair,

And then, with piercing woe distressed,
The mournful Lakshmaṇ thus addressed:
"Brother, I pray thee bring for me
The pressed fruit of the Ingudí,
And a bark mantle fresh and new,
That I may pay this offering due.
First of the three shall Sítá go,
Next thou, and I the last: for so
Moves the funereal pomp of woe."

Sumantra of the noble mind,
Gentle and modest, meek and kind,
Who, follower of each princely youth,
To Ráma clung with constant truth,
Now with the royal brothers' aid
The grief of Ráma soothed and stayed,
And lent his arm his lord to guide
Down to the river's holy side.
That lovely stream the heroes found,
With woods that ever blossomed crowned,
And there in bitter sorrow bent
Their footsteps down the fair descent.
Then where the stream that swiftly flowed
A pure pellucid shallow showed,
The funeral drops they duly shed,
And "Father, this be thine," they said.
But he, the lord who ruled the land,
Filled from the stream his hollowed hand,
And turning to the southern side
Stretched out his arm and weeping cried:
"This sacred water clear and pure,
An offering which shall aye endure
To thee, O lord of kings, I give:
Accept it where the spirits live!"

Then, when the solemn rite was o'er,
Came Ráma to the river shore,
And offered, with his brothers' aid,
Fresh tribute to his father's shade.
With jujube fruit he mixed the seed
Of Ingudís from moisture freed,

And placed it on a spot o'erspread
With sacred grass, and weeping said:
"Enjoy, great King, the cake which we
Thy children eat and offer thee!
For ne'er do blessed Gods refuse
To share the food which mortals use."

Then Ráma turned him to retrace
The path that brought him to the place,
And up the mountain's pleasant side
Where lovely lawns lay fair, he hied.
Soon as his cottage door he gained
His brothers to his breast he strained.
From them and Sítá in their woes
So loud the cry of weeping rose,
That like the roar of lions round
The mountain rolled the echoing sound.
And Bharat's army shook with fear
The weeping of the chiefs to hear.
"Bharat," the soldiers cried, "'tis plain,
His brother Ráma meets again,
And with these cries that round us ring
They sorrow for their sire the king."
Then leaving car and wain behind,
One eager thought in every mind,
Swift toward the weeping, every man,
As each could find a passage, ran.
Some thither bent their eager course
With car, and elephant, and horse,
And youthful captains on their feet
With longing sped their lord to meet,
As though the new-come prince had been
An exile for long years unseen.
Earth beaten in their frantic zeal
By clattering hoof and rumbling wheel,
Sent forth a deafening noise as loud
As heaven when black with many a cloud.
Then, with their consorts gathered near,
Wild elephants in sudden fear
Rushed to a distant wood, and shed
An odour round them as they fled.

And every silvan thing that dwelt
Within those shades the terror felt,
Deer, lion, tiger, boar and roe,
Bison, wild-cow, and buffalo.
And when the tumult wild they heard,
With trembling pinions flew each bird,
From tree, from thicket, and from lake,
Swan, koïl, curlew, crane, and drake.
With men the ground was overspread,
With startled birds the sky o'erhead.
Then on his sacrificial ground
The sinless, glorious chief was found.
Loading with curses deep and loud
The hump-back and the queen, the crowd
Whose cheeks were wet, whose eyes were dim,
In fond affection ran to him.
While the big tears their eyes bedewed,
He looked upon the multitude,

And then as sire and mother do,
His arms about his loved ones threw.
Some to his feet with reverence pressed,
Some in his arms he strained:
Each friend, with kindly words addressed,
Due share of honour gained.
Then, by their mighty woe o'ercome,
The weeping heroes' cry
Filled, like the roar of many a drum,
Hill, cavern, earth, and sky.

The Meeting with the Queens

Vaśishṭha with his soul athirst
   To look again on Ráma, first
   In line the royal widows placed,
And then the way behind them traced.
The ladies moving, faint and slow,
Saw the fair stream before them flow,
And by the bank their steps were led
Which the two brothers visited.
Kauśalyá with her faded cheek
And weeping eyes began to speak,
And thus in mournful tones addressed
The queen Sumitrá and the rest:
"See in the wood the bank's descent,
Which the two orphan youths frequent,
Whose noble spirits never fall,
Though woes surround them, reft of all.
Thy son with love that never tires
Draws water hence which mine requires.
This day, for lowly toil unfit,
His pious task thy son should quit."

As on the long-eyed lady strayed,
On holy grass, whose points were laid
Directed to the southern sky,
The funeral offering met her eye.
When Ráma's humble gift she spied
Thus to the queens Kauśalyá cried:
"The gift of Ráma's hand behold,
His tribute to the king high-souled,
Offered to him, as texts require,
Lord of Ikshváku's line, his sire!

Not such I deem the funeral food
Of kings with godlike might endued.
Can he who knew all pleasures, he
Who ruled the earth from sea to sea,
The mighty lord of monarchs, feed
On Ingudí's extracted seed?
In all the world there cannot be
A woe, I ween, more sad to see,
Than that my glorious son should make
His funeral gift of such a cake.
The ancient text I oft have heard
This day is true in every word:
"Ne'er do the blessed Gods refuse
To eat the food their children use.'"

The ladies soothed the weeping dame:
To Ráma's hermitage they came,
And there the hero met their eyes
Like a God fallen from the skies.
Him joyless, reft of all, they viewed,
And tears their mournful eyes bedewed.
The truthful hero left his seat,
And clasped the ladies' lotus feet,
And they with soft hands brushed away
The dust that on his shoulders lay.
Then Lakshmaṇ, when he saw each queen
With weeping eyes and troubled mien,
Near to the royal ladies drew
And paid them gentle reverence too.
He, Daśaratha's offspring, signed
The heir of bliss by Fortune kind,
Received from every dame no less
Each mark of love and tenderness.
And Sítá came and bent before
The widows, while her eyes ran o'er,
And pressed their feet with many a tear.
They when they saw the lady dear
Pale, worn with dwelling in the wild,
Embraced her as a darling child:
"Daughter of royal Janak, bride
Of Daśaratha's son," they cried,

"How couldst thou, offspring of a king,
Endure this woe and suffering
In the wild forest? When I trace
Each sign of trouble on thy face—
That lotus which the sun has dried,
That lily by the tempest tried,
That gold whereon the dust is spread,
That moon whence all the light is fled—
Sorrow assails my heart, alas!
As fire consumes the wood and grass."

Then Ráma, as she spoke distressed,
The feet of Saint Vaśishṭha pressed,
Touched them with reverential love,
Then near him took his seat:
Thus Indra clasps in realms above
The Heavenly Teacher's feet.
Then with each counsellor and peer,
Bharat of duteous mind,
With citizens and captains near,
Sat humbly down behind.
When with his hands to him upraised,
In devotee's attire,
Bharat upon his brother gazed
Whose glory shone like fire,
As when the pure Mahendra bends
To the great Lord of Life,
Among his noble crowd of friends
This anxious thought was rife:
"What words to Raghu's son to-day
Will royal Bharat speak,
Whose heart has been so prompt to pay
Obeisance fond and meek?"
Then steadfast Ráma, Lakshmaṇ wise,
Bharat for truth renowned,

Shone like three fires that heavenward rise
With holy priests around.

CANTO
CV

Ráma's Speech

Awhile they sat, each lip compressed,
　　Then Bharat thus his chief addressed:
　　"My mother here was made content;
To me was given the government.
This now, my lord, I yield to thee:
Enjoy it, from all trouble free.
Like a great bridge the floods have rent,
Impetuous in their wild descent,
All other hands but thine in vain
Would strive the burthen to maintain.
In vain the ass with steeds would vie,
With Tárkshya, birds that wing the sky;
So, lord of men, my power is slight
To rival thine imperial might.
Great joys his happy days attend
On whom the hopes of men depend,
But wretched is the life he leads
Who still the aid of others needs.
And if the seed a man has sown,
With care and kindly nurture grown,
Rear its huge trunk and spring in time
Too bulky for a dwarf to climb,
Yet, with perpetual blossom gay,
No fruit upon its boughs display,
Ne'er can that tree, thus nursed in vain,
Approval of the virtuous gain.
The simile is meant to be
Applied, O mighty-armed, to thee,
Because, our lord and leader, thou
Protectest not thy people now.
O, be the longing wish fulfilled

639

Of every chief of house and guild,
To see again their sun-bright lord
Victorious to his realm restored!
As thou returnest through the crowd
Let roars of elephants be loud.
And each fair woman lift her voice
And in her new-found king rejoice."
The people all with longing moved,
The words that Bharat spoke approved,
And crowding near to Ráma pressed
The hero with the same request.
The steadfast Ráma, when he viewed
His glorious brother's mournful mood,
With each ambitious thought controlled,
Thus the lamenting prince consoled:
"I cannot do the things I will,
For Ráma is but mortal still.
Fate with supreme, resistless law
This way and that its slave will draw,
All gathered heaps must waste away,
All lofty lore and powers decay.
Death is the end of life, and all,
Now firmly joined, apart must fall.
One fear the ripened fruit must know,
To fall upon the earth below;
So every man who draws his breath
Must fear inevitable death.
The pillared mansion, high, compact,
Must fall by Time's strong hand attacked;
So mortal men, the gradual prey
Of old and ruthless death, decay.
The night that flies no more returns:
Yamuná for the Ocean yearns:
Swift her impetuous waters flee,
But roll not backward from the sea.
The days and nights pass swiftly by
And steal our moments as they fly,
E'en as the sun's unpitying rays
Drink up the floods in summer blaze.
Then for thyself lament and leave
For death of other men to grieve,

For if thou go or if thou stay,
Thy life is shorter day by day.
Death travels with us; death attends
Our steps until our journey ends,
Death, when the traveller wins the goal,
Returns with the returning soul.
The flowing hair grows white and thin,
And wrinkles mark the altered skin.
The ills of age man's strength assail:
Ah, what can mortal power avail?
Men joy to see the sun arise,
They watch him set with joyful eyes:
But ne'er reflect, too blind to see,
How fast their own brief moments flee.
With lovely change for ever new
The seasons' sweet return they view,
Nor think with heedless hearts the while
That lives decay as seasons smile.
As haply on the boundless main
Meet drifting logs and part again,
So wives and children, friends and gold,
Ours for a little time we hold:
Soon by resistless laws of fate
To meet no more we separate.
In all this changing world not one
The common lot of all can shun:
Then why with useless tears deplore
The dead whom tears can bring no more?
As one might stand upon the way
And to a troop of travellers say:
"If ye allow it, sirs, I too
Will travel on the road with you:"
So why should mortal man lament
When on that path his feet are bent
Which all men living needs must tread,
Where sire and ancestors have led?
Life flies as torrents downward fall
Speeding away without recall,
So virtue should our thoughts engage,
For bliss is mortals' heritage.

By ceaseless care and earnest zeal
For servants and for people's weal,
By gifts, by duty nobly done,
Our glorious sire the skies has won.
Our lord the king, o'er earth who reigned,
A blissful home in heaven has gained
By wealth in ample largess spent,
And many a rite magnificent:
With constant joy from first to last
A long and noble life he passed,
Praised by the good, no tears should dim
Our eyes, O brother dear, for him.
His human body, worn and tried
By length of days, he cast aside,
And gained the godlike bliss to stray
In Brahmá's heavenly home for aye.
For such the wise as we are, deep
In Veda lore, should never weep.
Those who are firm and ever wise
Spurn vain lament and idle sighs.
Be self-possessed: thy grief restrain:
Go, in that city dwell again.
Return, O best of men, and be
Obedient to our sire's decree,
While I with every care fulfil
Our holy father's righteous will,
Observing in the lonely wood
His charge approved by all the good."
Thus Ráma of the lofty mind
To Bharat spoke his righteous speech,
By every argument designed
Obedience to his sire to teach.

CANTO
CVI

Bharat's Speech

Good Bharat, by the river side,
To virtuous Ráma's speech replied,
And thus with varied lore addressed
The prince, while nobles round him pressed:
"In all this world whom e'er can we
Find equal, scourge of foes, to thee?
No ill upon thy bosom weighs,
No thoughts of joy thy spirit raise.
Approved art thou of sages old,
To whom thy doubts are ever told.
Alike in death and life, to thee
The same to be and not to be.
The man who such a soul can gain
Can ne'er be crushed by woe or pain.
Pure as the Gods, high-minded, wise,
Concealed from thee no secret lies.
Such glorious gifts are all thine own,
And birth and death to thee are known,
That ill can ne'er thy soul depress
With all-subduing bitterness.
O let my prayer, dear brother, win
Thy pardon for my mother's sin.
Wrought for my sake who willed it not
When absent in a distant spot.
Duty alone with binding chains
The vengeance due to crime restrains,
Or on the sinner I should lift
My hand in retribution swift.
Can I who know the right, and spring
From Daśaratha, purest king—
Can I commit a heinous crime,

643

Abhorred by all through endless time?
The aged king I dare not blame,
Who died so rich in holy fame,
My honoured sire, my parted lord,
E'en as a present God adored.
Yet who in lore of duty skilled
So foul a crime has ever willed,
And dared defy both gain and right
To gratify a woman's spite?
When death draws near, so people say,
The sense of creatures dies away;
And he has proved the ancient saw
By acting thus in spite of law.
But O my honoured lord, be kind,
Dismiss the trespass from thy mind,
The sin the king committed, led
By haste, his consort's wrath, and dread.
For he who veils his sire's offence
With tender care and reverence—
His sons approved by all shall live:
Not so their fate who ne'er forgive.
Be thou, my lord, the noble son,
And the vile deed my sire has done,
Abhorred by all the virtuous, ne'er
Resent, lest thou the guilt too share.
Preserve us, for on thee we call,
Our sire, Kaikeyí, me and all
Thy citizens, thy kith and kin;
Preserve us and reverse the sin.
To live in woods a devotee
Can scarce with royal tasks agree,
Nor can the hermit's matted hair
Suit fitly with a ruler's care.
Do not, my brother, do not still
Pursue this life that suits thee ill.
Mid duties of a king we count
His consecration paramount,
That he with ready heart and hand
May keep his people and his land.
What Warrior born to royal sway
From certain good would turn away,

A doubtful duty to pursue,
That mocks him with the distant view?
Thou wouldst to duty cleave, and gain
The meed that follows toil and pain.
In thy great task no labour spare:
Rule the four castes with justest care.
Mid all the four, the wise prefer
The order of the householder:

Canst thou, whose thoughts to duty cleave,
The best of all the orders leave?
My better thou in lore divine,
My birth, my sense must yield to thine:
While thou, my lord, art here to reign,
How shall my hands the rule maintain?
O faithful lover of the right,
Take with thy friends the royal might,
Let thy sires' realm, from trouble free,
Obey her rightful king in thee.
Here let the priests and lords of state
Our monarch duly consecrate,
With prayer and holy verses blessed
By saint Vaśishṭha and the rest.
Anointed king by us, again
Seek fair Ayodhyá, there to reign,
And like imperial Indra girt
By Gods of Storm, thy might assert.
From the three debts acquittance earn,
And with thy wrath the wicked burn,
O'er all of us thy rule extend,
And cheer with boons each faithful friend.
Let thine enthronement, lord, this day
Make all thy lovers glad and gay,
And let all those who hate thee flee
To the ten winds for fear of thee.
Dear lord, my mother's words of hate
With thy sweet virtues expiate,
And from the stain of folly clear
The father whom we both revere.
Brother, to me compassion show,
I pray thee with my head bent low,

And to these friends who on thee call,—
As the Great Father pities all.
But if my tears and prayers be vain,
And thou in woods wilt still remain,
I will with thee my path pursue
And make my home in forests too."

Thus Bharat strove to bend his will
With suppliant head, but he,
Earth's lord, inexorable still
Would keep his sire's decree.
The firmness of the noble chief
The wondering people moved,
And rapture mingling with their grief,
All wept and all approved.
"How firm his steadfast will," they cried,
"Who Keeps his promise thus!
Ah, to Ayodhyá's town," they sighed,
"He comes not back with us."
The holy priest, the swains who tilled
The earth, the sons of trade,
And e'en the mournful queens were filled
With joy as Bharat prayed,
And bent their heads, then weeping stilled
A while, his prayer to aid.

CANTO

CVII

Ráma's Speech

Thus, by his friends encompassed round,
He spoke, and Ráma, far renowned,
To his dear brother thus replied,
Whom holy rites had purified:

"O thou whom Queen Kaikeyí bare
The best of kings, thy words are fair,
Our royal father, when of yore
He wed her, to her father swore
The best of kingdoms to confer,
A noble dowry meet for her;
Then, grateful, on the deadly day
Of heavenly Gods' and demons' fray,
A future boon on her bestowed
To whose sweet care his life he owed.
She to his mind that promise brought,
And then the best of kings besought
To bid me to the forest flee,
And give the rule, O Prince, to thee.
Thus bound by oath, the king our lord
Gave her those boons of free accord,
And bade me, O thou chief of men,
Live in the woods four years and ten.
I to this lonely wood have hied
With faithful Lakshman by my side,
And Sítá by no tears deterred,
Resolved to keep my father's word.
And thou, my noble brother, too
Shouldst keep our father's promise true:
Anointed ruler of the state
Maintain his word inviolate.
From his great debt, dear brother, free
Our lord the king for love of me,
Thy mother's breast with joy inspire,
And from all woe preserve thy sire.
'Tis said, near Gayá's holy town
Gayá, great saint of high renown,
This text recited when he paid
Due rites to each ancestral shade:
"A son is born his sire to free
From Put's infernal pains:
Hence, saviour of his father, he
The name of Puttra gains."
Thus numerous sons are sought by prayer,
In Scripture trained with graces fair,

That of the number one some day
May funeral rites at Gayá pay.
The mighty saints who lived of old
This holy doctrine ever hold.
Then, best of men, our sire release
From pains of hell, and give him peace.
Now Bharat, to Ayodhyá speed,
The brave Śatrughna with thee lead,
Take with thee all the twice-born men,
And please each lord and citizen.
I now, O King, without delay
To Daṇḍak wood will bend my way,
And Lakshmaṇ and the Maithil dame
Will follow still, our path the same.
Now, Bharat, lord of men be thou,
And o'er Ayodhyá reign:
The silvan world to me shall bow,
King of the wild domain.
Yea, let thy joyful steps be bent
To that fair town to-day,
And I as happy and content,
To Daṇḍak wood will stray.
The white umbrella o'er thy brow
Its cooling shade shall throw:
I to the shadow of the bough
And leafy trees will go.
Śatrughna, for wise plans renowned,
Shall still on thee attend;
And Lakshmaṇ, ever faithful found,
Be my familiar friend.
Let us his sons, O brother dear,
The path of right pursue,
And keep the king we all revere
Still to his promise true."

CANTO
CVIII

Jáváli's Speech

Thus Ráma soothed his brother's grief:
Then virtuous Jáváli, chief
Of twice-born sages, thus replied
In words that virtue's law defied:
"Hail, Raghu's princely son, dismiss
A thought so weak and vain as this.
Canst thou, with lofty heart endowed,
Think with the dull ignoble crowd?
For what are ties of kindred? can
One profit by a brother man?
Alone the babe first opes his eyes,
And all alone at last he dies.
The man, I ween, has little sense
Who looks with foolish reverence
On father's or on mother's name:
In others, none a right may claim.
E'en as a man may leave his home
And to a distant village roam,
Then from his lodging turn away
And journey on the following day,
Such brief possession mortals hold
In sire and mother, house and gold,
And never will the good and wise
The brief uncertain lodging prize.
Nor, best of men, shouldst thou disown
Thy sire's hereditary throne,
And tread the rough and stony ground
Where hardship, danger, woes abound.
Come, let Ayodhyá rich and bright
See thee enthroned with every rite:
Her tresses bound in single braid

649

She waits thy coming long delayed.
O come, thou royal Prince, and share
The kingly joys that wait thee there,
And live in bliss transcending price
As Indra lives in Paradise.
The parted king is naught to thee,
Nor right in living man has he:
The king is one, thou, Prince of men,
Another art: be counselled then.
Thy royal sire, O chief, has sped
On the long path we all must tread.
The common lot of all is this,
And thou in vain art robbed of bliss.
For those—and only those—I weep
Who to the path of duty keep;
For here they suffer ceaseless woe,
And dying to destruction go.
With pious care, each solemn day,
Will men their funeral offerings pay:
See, how the useful food they waste:
He who is dead no more can taste.
If one is fed, his strength renewed
Whene'er his brother takes his food,
Then offerings to the parted pay:
Scarce will they serve him on his way.
By crafty knaves these rules were framed,
And to enforce men's gifts proclaimed:
"Give, worship, lead a life austere,
Keep lustral rites, quit pleasures here."
There is no future life: be wise,
And do, O Prince, as I advise.
Enjoy, my lord, the present bliss,
And things unseen from thought dismiss.
Let this advice thy bosom move,
The counsel sage which all approve;
To Bharat's earnest prayer incline,
And take the rule so justly thine."

The Praises of Truth

By sage Jáváli thus addressed,
Ráma of truthful hearts the best,
With perfect skill and wisdom high
Thus to his speech made fit reply:
"Thy words that tempt to bliss are fair,
But virtue's garb they falsely wear.
For he from duty's path who strays
To wander in forbidden ways,
Allured by doctrine false and vain,
Praise from the good can never gain.
Their lives the true and boaster show,
Pure and impure, and high and low,
Else were no mark to judge between
Stainless and stained and high and mean;
They to whose lot fair signs may fall
Were but as they who lack them all,
And those to virtuous thoughts inclined
Were but as men of evil mind.
If in the sacred name of right
I do this wrong in duty's spite;
The path of virtue meanly quit,
And this polluting sin commit,
What man who marks the bounds between
Virtue and vice with insight keen,
Would rank me high in after time
Stained with this soul destroying crime?
Whither could I, the sinner, turn,
How hope a seat in heaven to earn,
If I my plighted promise break,
And thus the righteous path forsake?

This world of ours is ever led
To walk the ways which others tread,
And as their princes they behold,
The subjects too their lives will mould.
That truth and mercy still must be
Beloved of kings, is Heaven's decree.
Upheld by truth the monarch reigns,
And truth the very world sustains.
Truth evermore has been the love
Of holy saints and Gods above,
And he whose lips are truthful here
Wins after death the highest sphere.
As from a serpent's deadly tooth,
We shrink from him who scorns the truth.
For holy truth is root and spring
Of justice and each holy thing,
A might that every power transcends,
Linked to high bliss that never ends.
Truth is all virtue's surest base,
Supreme in worth and first in place.
Oblations, gifts men offer here,
Vows, sacrifice, and rites austere,
And Holy Writ, on truth depend:
So men must still that truth defend.
Truth, only truth protects the land,
By truth unharmed our houses stand;
Neglect of truth makes men distressed,
And truth in highest heaven is blessed.
Then how can I, rebellious, break
Commandments which my father spake—
I ever true and faithful found,
And by my word of honour bound?
My father's bridge of truth shall stand
Unharmed by my destructive hand:
Not folly, ignorance, or greed
My darkened soul shall thus mislead.
Have we not heard that God and shade
Turn from the hated offerings paid
By him whose false and fickle mind
No pledge can hold, no promise bind?
Truth is all duty: as the soul,

It quickens and supports the whole.
The good respect this duty: hence
Its sacred claims I reverence.
The Warrior's duty I despise
That seeks the wrong in virtue's guise:
Those claims I shrink from, which the base,
Cruel, and covetous embrace.
The heart conceives the guilty thought,
Then by the hand the sin is wrought,
And with the pair is leagued a third,
The tongue that speaks the lying word.
Fortune and land and name and fame
To man's best care have right and claim;
The good will aye to truth adhere,
And its high laws must men revere.
Base were the deed thy lips would teach,
Approved as best by subtle speech.
Shall I my plighted promise break,
That I these woods my home would make?
Shall I, as Bharat's words advise,
My father's solemn charge despise?
Firm stands the oath which then before
My father's face I soothly swore,
Which Queen Kaikeyí's anxious ear
Rejoiced with highest joy to hear.
Still in the wood will I remain,
With food prescribed my life sustain,
And please with fruit and roots and flowers
Ancestral shades and heavenly powers.
Here every sense contented, still
Heeding the bounds of good and ill,
My settled course will I pursue,
Firm in my faith and ever true.
Here in this wild and far retreat
Will I my noble task complete;
And Fire and Wind and Moon shall be
Partakers of its fruit with me.
A hundred offerings duly wrought
His rank o'er Gods for Indra bought,
And mighty saints their heaven secured
By torturing years on earth endured."

That scoffing plea the hero spurned,
And thus he spake once more,
Chiding, the while his bosom burned,
Jáváli's impious lore:
"Justice, and courage ne'er dismayed,
Pity for all distressed,
Truth, loving honour duly paid
To Bráhman, God, and guest—
In these, the true and virtuous say,
Should lives of men be passed:
They form the right and happy way
That leads to heaven at last.

My father's thoughtless act I chide
That gave thee honoured place,
Whose soul, from virtue turned aside,
Is faithless, dark, and base.
We rank the Buddhist with the thief,
And all the impious crew
Who share his sinful disbelief,
And hate the right and true.
Hence never should wise kings who seek
To rule their people well,
Admit, before their face to speak,
The cursed infidel.
But twice-born men in days gone by,
Of other sort than thou,
Have wrought good deeds, whose glories high
Are fresh among us now:
This world they conquered, nor in vain
They strove to win the skies:
The twice-born hence pure lives maintain,
And fires of worship rise.
Those who in virtue's path delight,
And with the virtuous live,—
Whose flames of holy zeal are bright,
Whose hands are swift to give,
Who injure none, and good and mild
In every grace excel,
Whose lives by sin are undefiled,
We love and honour well."

Thus Ráma spoke in righteous rage
Jáváli's speech to chide,
When thus again the virtuous sage
In truthful words replied:
"The atheist's lore I use no more,
Not mine his impious creed:
His words and doctrine I abhor,
Assumed at time of need.
E'en as I rose to speak with thee,
The fit occasion came
That bade me use the atheist's plea
To turn thee from thine aim.
The atheist creed I disavow,
Unsay the words of sin,
And use the faithful's language now
Thy favour, Prince, to win."

The Sons of Ikshváku

Then spake Vaśishṭha who perceived
That Ráma's soul was wroth and grieved:
"Well knows the sage Jáváli all
The changes that the world befall;
And but to lead thee to revoke
Thy purpose were the words he spoke.
Lord of the world, now hear from me
How first this world began to be.
First water was, and naught beside;
There earth was formed that stretches wide.
Then with the Gods from out the same
The Self-existent Brahmá came.
Then Brahmá in a boar's disguise
Bade from the deep this earth arise;

Then, with his sons of tranquil soul,
He made the world and framed the whole.
From subtlest ether Brahmá rose:
No end, no loss, no change he knows.
A son had he, Maríchi styled,
And Kaśyap was Maríchi's child.
From him Vivasvat sprang: from him
Manu, whose fame shall ne'er be dim.
Manu, who life to mortals gave,
Begot Ikshváku good and brave:
First of Ayodhyá's kings was he,
Pride of her famous dynasty.
From him the glorious Kukshi sprang,
Whose fame through all the regions rang.
Rival of Kukshi's ancient fame,
His heir the great Vikukshi came.
His son was Váṇa, lord of might,
His Anaraṇya, strong in fight.
No famine marred his blissful reign,
No drought destroyed the kindly grain;
Amid the sons of virtue chief,
His happy realm ne'er held a thief,
His son was Prithu, glorious name,
From him the wise Triśanku came:
Embodied to the skies he went
For love of truth preëminent.
He left a son renowned afar,
Known by the name of Dhundhumár.
His son succeeding bore the name
Of Yuvanáśva dear to fame.
He passed away. Him followed then
His son Mándhátá, king of men.
His son was blest in high emprise,
Susandhi, fortunate and wise.
Two noble sons had he, to wit
Dhruvasandhi and Prasenajit.
Bharat was Dhruvasandhi's son:
His glorious arm the conquest won,
Against his son King Asit, rose
In fierce array his royal foes,

Haihayas, Tálajanghas styled,
And Śaśivindhus fierce and wild.

Long time he strove, but forced to yield
Fled from his kingdom and the field.
The wives he left had both conceived—
So is the ancient tale believed:—
One, of her rival's hopes afraid,
Fell poison in the viands laid.
It chanced that Chyavan, Bhrigu's child,
Had wandered to the pathless wild
Where proud Himálaya's lovely height
Detained him with a strange delight.
Then came the other widowed queen
With lotus eyes and beauteous mien,
Longing a noble son to bear,
And wooed the saint with earnest prayer.
When thus Kálindí, fairest dame
With reverent supplication came,
To her the holy sage replied:
"O royal lady, from thy side
A glorious son shall spring ere long,
Righteous and true and brave and strong;
He, scourge of foes and lofty-souled,
His ancient race shall still uphold."

Then round the sage the lady went,
And bade farewell, most reverent.
Back to her home she turned once more,
And there her promised son she bore.
Because her rival mixed the bane
To render her conception vain,
And her unripened fruit destroy,
Sagar she called her rescued boy.
He, when he paid that solemn rite,
Filled living creatures with affright:
Obedient to his high decree
His countless sons dug out the sea.
Prince Asamanj was Sagar's child:
But him with cruel sin defiled

And loaded with the people's hate
His father banished from the state.
To Asamanj his consort bare
Bright Anśumán his valiant heir.
Anśumán's son, Dilípa famed,
Begot a son Bhagírath named.
From him renowned Kakutstha came:
Thou bearest still the lineal name.
Kakutstha's son was Raghu: thou
Art styled the son of Raghu now.
From him came Purushádak bold,
Fierce hero of gigantic mould:
Kalmáshapáda's name he bore,
Because his feet were spotted o'er.
Śankhan his son, to manhood grown,
Died sadly with his host o'erthrown,
But ere he perished sprang from him
Sudarśan fair in face and limb.
From beautiful Sudarśan came
Prince Agnivarṇa, bright as flame.
His son was Síghraga, for speed
Unmatched; and Maru was his seed.
Prasusruka was Maru's child:
His son was Ambarísha styled.
Nahush was Ambarísha's heir
With hand to strike and heart to dare.
His son was good Nábhág, from youth
Renowned for piety and truth.
From great Nábhág sprang children two
Aja and Suvrat pure and true.
From Aja Daśaratha came,
Whose virtuous life was free from blame.
His eldest son art thou: his throne,
O famous Ráma, is thine own.
Accept the sway so justly thine,
And view the world with eyes benign.
For ever in Ikshváku's race
The eldest takes his father's place,
And while he lives no son beside
As lord and king is sanctified.
The rule by Raghu's children kept

Thou must not spurn to-day.
This realm of peerless wealth accept,
And like thy father sway."

CANTO

CXI

Counsel to Bharat

Thus said Vaśishṭha, and again
To Ráma spake in duteous strain:
"All men the light of life who see
With high respect should look on three:
High honour ne'er must be denied
To father, mother, holy guide.
First to their sires their birth they owe,
Nursed with maternal love they grow:
Their holy guides fair knowledge teach:
So men should love and honour each.
Thy sire and thou have learned of me,
The sacred guide of him and thee,
And if my word thou wilt obey
Thou still wilt keep the virtuous way.
See, with the chiefs of every guild
And all thy friends, this place is filled:
All these, as duty bids, protect;
So still the righteous path respect.
O, for thine aged mother feel,
Nor spurn the virtuous dame's appeal:
Obey, O Prince, thy mother dear,
And still to virtue's path adhere.
Yield thou to Bharat's fond request,
With earnest supplication pressed,
So wilt thou to thyself be true,
And faith and duty still pursue."

Thus by his saintly guide addressed
With pleas in sweetest tones expressed,
The lord of men in turn replied
To wise Vaśishṭha by his side:
"The fondest son's observance ne'er
Repays the sire and mother's care:

The constant love that food provides,
And dress, and every need besides:
Their pleasant words still soft and mild,
Their nurture of the helpless child:
The words which Daśaratha spake,
My king and sire, I ne'er will break."

Then Bharat of the ample chest
The wise Sumantra thus addressed;
"Bring sacred grass, O charioteer,
And strew it on the level here.
For I will sit and watch his face
Until I win my brother's grace.
Like a robbed Bráhman will I lie,
Nor taste of food nor turn my eye,
In front of Ráma's leafy cot,
And till he yield will leave him not."

When Bharat saw Sumantra's eye
Looked up to Ráma for reply,
The Prince himself in eager haste
The sacred grass in order placed.
Him great and mighty Ráma, best
Of royal saints, in turn addressed:
"What, Bharat, have I done, that thou
Besiegest me, a suppliant now?
Thus streched, to force redress for wrongs
To men of Bráhman birth belongs,
Not those upon whose kingly head
The consecrating drops are shed.
Up, lord of men! arise, and quit
This fearful vow for thee unfit.
Go, brother, seek Ayodhyá's town,
Fair city of supreme renown."

But Bharat, as his seat he took,
Cast all around an eager look:
"O people, join your prayers with mine,
And so his stubborn heart incline."

And all the people answered thus:
"Full well is Ráma known to us.
Right is the word he speaks and he
Is faithful to his sire's decree:
Nor can we rashly venture now
To turn him from his purposed vow."

Then Ráma spoke: "O Bharat, heed
Thy virtuous friends, and mark their rede.
Mark well what I and these advise,
And duty view with clearer eyes.
Thy hand on mine, O hero, place,
Touch water, and thy sin efface."

Then Bharat rose: his hand he dipped,
And purifying water sipped:
"Each citizen," he cried, "give ear,
Attend, each counsellor and peer.
My mother planned, by me untaught,
To win the sway I never sought:
Ne'er Raghu's son could I despise,
In duty's lore supremely wise.
Now if obedience to our sire
This dwelling in the woods require,
I, till the destined years be spent,
Will dwell alone in banishment."

The virtuous Ráma, wonder-stirred,
The faithful speech of Bharat heard,
And thus the hero's feelings found
Due utterance, as he gazed around:

"Still to my father's word I hold,
Whate'er he bought, or pledged, or sold:
Ne'er shall his living promise be
Annulled by Bharat or by me.

Not thus my task will I evade,
My exile on another laid:
Most wise was Queen Kaikeyí's rede,
And just and good my father's deed.
Dear Bharat's patient soul I know,
How reverence due he loves to show;
In him, high-souled and faithful found,
Must each auspicious grace abound.
When from the woods I turn again
I with his aid shall nobly reign,
With one so good, of peerless worth,
A glorious lord of happy earth.
Her boon Kaikeyí sought and won.
I, as my father swore, have done:
And O, do thou, my brother dear,
The monarch's name from falsehood clear.

CANTO

CXII

The Sandals

High wonder mingled with delight
Took the great sages at the sight,
Thrilling their breasts who came to view
The meeting of the peerless two.
The saints and sages' holy train
Departed to their home again.
And high each holy voice was raised,
And thus the glorious brothers praised.

"High fate is his, the sire of two
Most virtuous souls, so brave and true:
With wonder and with joy intense
Our ears have heard their conference."
Then the great sages, longing all

To see the ten-necked tyrant fall,
To Bharat, bravest of the brave,
Their salutary counsel gave:

"O thou of lofty lineage born,
Whom wisdom, conduct, fame adorn,
Thou for thy honoured father's sake
Shouldst Ráma's righteous counsel take.

All debts to Queen Kaikeyí paid,
Thy sire his home in heaven has made,
So virtuous Ráma we would see
From filial obligation free."
Thus gave each royal sage advice,
High saint, and bard of Paradise;
Then quickly vanishing from view
Each to his proper home withdrew.
Then Ráma's face his rapture showed,
And his full heart with joy o'erflowed,
While, as the sages parted thence,
He paid his humble reverence.

Then Bharat shook in every limb
As suppliant thus he spake to him:
"The duty of a king respect,
Held by our race in high respect:
And O, thy gracious ear incline
To heed my mother's prayer and mine.
The mighty realm to rule and guard
For me alone is task too hard.
No power have I the love to gain
Of noble, citizen, and swain.
All those who know thee, warrior, friend,
On thee their eager glances bend,
As labouring hinds who till the plain
Look fondly for the Lord of Rain.
O wisest Prince, thy realm secure,
And make its firm foundations sure.
Kakutstha's son, thy mighty arm
Can keep the nation free from harm."
He spoke, and fell in sorrow drowned

At Ráma's feet upon the ground,
And there the hero sued and sighed,
And "Hear me, Raghu's son," he cried.

Then Ráma raised him up, and pressed
His brother to his loving breast,
And sweetly as a wild swan cried
To Bharat dark and lotus-eyed:
"So just and true thy generous soul,
Thy hand may well this earth control:
But many a sage his aid will lend,
With counsellor, and peer, and friend:
With these advise: their counsel ask,
And so perform thy arduous task.
The moon his beauty may forgo,
The cold forsake the Hills of Snow,
And Ocean o'er his banks may sweep,
But I my father's word will keep.
Now whether love of thee or greed
Thy mother led to plan the deed,
Forth from thy breast the memory throw,
And filial love and reverence show."

Thus spake Kauśalyá's son: again
Bharat replied in humble strain
To him who matched the sun in might
And lovely as the young moon's light:
"Put, noble brother, I entreat,
These sandals on thy blessed feet:
These, lord of men, with gold bedecked,
The realm and people will protect."

Then Ráma, as his brother prayed
Beneath his feet the sandals laid,
And these with fond affection gave
To Bharat's hand, the good and brave.
Then Bharat bowed his reverent head
And thus again to Ráma said:
"Through fourteen seasons will I wear
The hermit's dress and matted hair:
With fruit and roots my life sustain,

And still beyond the realm remain,
Longing for thee to come again.
The rule and all affairs of state
I to these shoes will delegate.
And if, O tamer of thy foes,
When fourteen years have reached their close,
I see thee not that day return,
The kindled fire my frame shall burn."

Then Ráma to his bosom drew
Dear Bharat and Śatrughna too:
"Be never wroth," he cried, "with her,
Kaikeyí's guardian minister:
This, glory of Ikshváku's line,
Is Sítá's earnest prayer and mine."
He spoke, and as the big tears fell,
To his dear brother bade farewell.
Round Ráma, Bharat strong and bold
In humble reverence paced,
When the bright sandals wrought with gold
Above his brows were placed.
The royal elephant who led
The glorious pomp he found,
And on the monster's mighty head
Those sandals duly bound.
Then noble Ráma, born to swell
The glories of his race,
To all in order bade farewell
With love and tender grace—
To brothers, counsellors, and peers,—
Still firm, in duty proved,
Firm, as the Lord of Snow uprears
His mountains unremoved.
No queen, for choking sobs and sighs,
Could say her last adieu:
Then Ráma bowed, with flooded eyes,
And to his cot withdrew.

Bharat's Return

Bearing the sandals on his head
Away triumphant Bharat sped,
And clomb, Śatrughna by his side,
The car wherein he wont to ride.
Before the mighty army went
The lords for counsel eminent,
Vaśishṭha, Vámadeva next,
Jáváli, pure with prayer and text.

Then from that lovely river they
Turned eastward on their homeward way:
With reverent steps from left to right
They circled Chitrakúṭa's height,
And viewed his peaks on every side
With stains of thousand metals dyed.
Then Bharat saw, not far away,
Where Bharadvája's dwelling lay,
And when the chieftain bold and sage
Had reached that holy hermitage,
Down from the car he sprang to greet
The saint, and bowed before his feet.
High rapture filled the hermit's breast,
Who thus the royal prince addressed:
"Say, Bharat, is thy duty done?
Hast thou with Ráma met, my son?"

The chief whose soul to virtue clave
This answer to the hermit gave:
"I prayed him with our holy guide:
But Raghu's son our prayer denied,
And long besought by both of us

He answered Saint Vaśishṭha thus:
"True to my vow, I still will be
Observant of my sire's decree:
Till fourteen years complete their course
That promise shall remain in force."
The saint in highest wisdom taught,
These solemn words with wisdom fraught,
To him in lore of language learned
Most eloquent himself returned:
"Obey my rede: let Bharat hold
This pair of sandals decked with gold:
They in Ayodhyá shall ensure
Our welfare, and our bliss secure."
When Ráma heard the royal priest
He rose, and looking to the east
Consigned the sandals to my hand
That they for him might guard the land.
Then from the high-souled chief's abode
I turned upon my homeward road,
Dismissed by him, and now this pair
Of sandals to Ayodhyá bear."

To him the hermit thus replied,
By Bharat's tidings gratified:
"No marvel thoughts so just and true,
Thou best of all who right pursue,
Should dwell in thee, O Prince of men,
As waters gather in the glen.
He is not dead, we mourn in vain:
Thy blessed father lives again,
Whose noble son we thus behold
Like Virtue's self in human mould."
He ceased: before him Bharat fell
To clasp his feet, and said farewell:
His reverent steps around him bent,
And onward to Ayodhyá went.
His host of followers stretching far
With many an elephant and car,
Waggon and steed, and mighty train,
Traversed their homeward way again.
O'er holy Yamuná they sped,

Fair stream, with waves engarlanded,
And then once more the rivers' queen,
The blessed Gangá's self was seen.
Then making o'er that flood his way,
Where crocodiles and monsters lay,
The king to Śringavera drew
His host and royal retinue.
His onward way he thence pursued,
And soon renowned Ayodhyá viewed.
Then burnt by woe and sad of cheer
Bharat addressed the charioteer:
"Ah, see, Ayodhyá dark and sad,
Her glory gone, once bright and glad:
Of joy and beauty reft, forlorn,
In silent grief she seems to mourn."

CANTO

CXIV

Bharat's Departure

Deep, pleasant was the chariot's sound
As royal Bharat, far renowned,
Whirled by his mettled coursers fast
Within Ayodhyá's city passed.
There dark and drear was every home
Where cats and owls had space to roam,
As when the shades of midnight fall
With blackest gloom, and cover all:
As Rohiṇí, dear spouse of him
Whom Ráhu hates, grows faint and dim,
When, as she shines on high alone
The demon's shade is o'er her thrown:
As burnt by summer's heat a rill
Scarce trickling from her parent hill,

With dying fish in pools half dried,
And fainting birds upon her side:
As sacrificial flames arise
When holy oil their food supplies,
But when no more the fire is fed
Sink lustreless and cold and dead:
Like some brave host that filled the plain,
With harness rent and captains slain,
When warrior, elephant, and steed
Mingled in wild confusion bleed:
As when, all spent her store of worth,
Rocks from her base the loosened earth:
Like a sad fallen star no more
Wearing the lovely light it wore:
So mournful in her lost estate
Was that sad town disconsolate.
Then car-borne Bharat, good and brave,
Thus spake to him the steeds who drave:
"Why are Ayodhyá's streets so mute?
Where is the voice of lyre and lute?
Why sounds not, as of old, to-day
The music of the minstrel's lay?

Where are the wreaths they used to twine?
Where are the blossoms and the wine?
Where is the cool refreshing scent
Of sandal dust with aloe blent?
The elephant's impatient roar,
The din of cars, I hear no more:
No more the horse's pleasant neigh
Rings out to meet me on my way.
Ayodhyá's youths, since Ráma's flight,
Have lost their relish for delight:
Her men roam forth no more, nor care
Bright garlands round their necks to wear.
All grieve for banished Ráma: feast,
And revelry and song have ceased:
Like a black night when floods pour down,
So dark and gloomy is the town.
When will he come to make them gay

Like some auspicious holiday?
When will my brother, like a cloud
At summer's close, make glad the crowd?"

Then through the streets the hero rode,
And passed within his sire's abode,
Like some deserted lion's den,
Forsaken by the lord of men.
Then to the inner bowers he came,
Once happy home of many a dame,
Now gloomy, sad, and drear,
Dark as of old that sunless day
When wept the Gods in wild dismay;
There poured he many a tear.

CANTO
CXV

Nandigrám

Then when the pious chief had seen
Lodged in her home each widowed queen,
Still with his burning grief oppressed
His holy guides he thus addressed:
"I go to Nandigrám: adieu,
This day, my lords to all of you:
I go, my load of grief to bear,
Reft of the son of Raghu, there.
The king my sire, alas, is dead,
And Ráma to the forest fled;
There will I wait till he, restored,
Shall rule the realm, its rightful lord."

They heard the high-souled prince's speech,
And thus with ready answer each
Of those great lords their chief addressed,

With saint Vaśishṭha and the rest:
"Good are the words which thou hast said,
By brotherly affection led,
Like thine own self, a faithful friend,
True to thy brother to the end:
A heart like thine must all approve,
Which naught from virtue's path can move."

Soon as the words he loved to hear
Fell upon Bharat's joyful ear,
Thus to the charioteer he spoke:
"My car with speed, Sumantra, yoke."
Then Bharat with delighted mien
Obeisance paid to every queen,
And with Śatrughna by his side
Mounting the car away he hied.
With lords, and priests in long array
The brothers hastened on their way.
And the great pomp the Bráhmans led
With Saint Vaśishṭha at their head.
Then every face was eastward bent
As on to Nandigrám they went.
Behind the army followed, all
Unsummoned by their leader's call,
And steeds and elephants and men
Streamed forth with every citizen.
As Bharat in his chariot rode
His heart with love fraternal glowed,
And with the sandals on his head
To Nandigrám he quickly sped.
Within the town he swiftly pressed,
Alighted, and his guides addressed:
"To me in trust my brother's hand
Consigned the lordship of the land,
When he these gold-wrought sandals gave
As emblems to protect and save."
Then Bharat bowed, and from his head
The sacred pledge deposited,
And thus to all the people cried
Who ringed him round on every side:
"Haste, for these sandals quickly bring

The canopy that shades the king.
Pay ye to them all reverence meet
As to my elder brother's feet,
For they will right and law maintain
Until King Ráma come again.
My brother with a loving mind
These sandals to my charge consigned:
I till he come will guard with care
The sacred trust for Raghu's heir.
My watchful task will soon be done,
The pledge restored to Raghu's son;
Then shall I see, his wanderings o'er,
These sandals on his feet once more.
My brother I shall meet at last,
The burthen from my shoulders cast,
To Ráma's hand the realm restore
And serve my elder as before.
When Ráma takes again this pair
Of sandals kept with pious care,
And here his glorious reign begins,
I shall be cleansed from all my sins,

When the glad people's voices ring
With welcome to the new-made king,
Joy will be mine four-fold as great
As if supreme I ruled the state."

Thus humbly spoke in sad lament
The chief in fame preëminent:
Thus, by his reverent lords obeyed,
At Nandigrám the kingdom swayed.
With hermit's dress and matted hair
He dwelt with all his army there.
The sandals of his brother's feet
Installed upon the royal seat,
He, all his powers to them referred,
Affairs of state administered.
In every care, in every task,
When golden store was brought,
He first, as though their rede to ask,
Those royal sandals sought.

CXVI

The Hermit's Speech

When Bharat took his homeward road
    Still Ráma in the wood abode:
    But soon he marked the fear and care
That darkened all the hermits there.
For all who dwelt before the hill
Were sad with dread of coming ill:
Each holy brow was lined by thought,
And Ráma's side they often sought.
With gathering frowns the prince they eyed,
And then withdrew and talked aside.

Then Raghu's son with anxious breast
The leader of the saints addressed:
"Can aught that I have done displease,
O reverend Sage, the devotees?
Why are their loving looks, O say,
Thus sadly changed or turned away?
Has Lakshmaṇ through his want of heed
Offended with unseemly deed?
Or is the gentle Sítá, she
Who loved to honour you and me—
Is she the cause of this offence,
Failing in lowly reverence?"

One sage, o'er whom, exceeding old,
Had many a year of penance rolled,
Trembling in every aged limb
Thus for the rest replied to him:
"How could we, O beloved, blame
Thy lofty-souled Videhan dame,
Who in the good of all delights,

And more than all of anchorites?
But yet through thee a numbing dread
Of fiends among our band has spread;
Obstructed by the demons' art
The trembling hermits talk apart.
For Rávaṇ's brother, overbold,
Named Khara, of gigantic mould,
Vexes with fury fierce and fell
All those in Janasthán who dwell.
Resistless in his cruel deeds,
On flesh of men the monster feeds:
Sinful and arrogant is he,
And looks with special hate on thee.
Since thou, beloved son, hast made
Thy home within this holy shade,
The fiends have vexed with wilder rage
The dwellers of the hermitage.
In many a wild and dreadful form
Around the trembling saints they swarm,
With hideous shape and foul disguise
They terrify our holy eyes.
They make our loathing souls endure
Insult and scorn and sights impure,
And flocking round the altars stay
The holy rites we love to pay.
In every spot throughout the grove
With evil thoughts the monsters rove,
Assailing with their secret might
Each unsuspecting anchorite.
Ladle and dish away they fling,
Our fires with floods extinguishing,
And when the sacred flame should burn
They trample on each water-urn.
Now when they see their sacred wood
Plagued by this impious brotherhood,
The troubled saints away would roam
And seek in other shades a home:
Hence will we fly, O Ráma, ere
The cruel fiends our bodies tear.
Not far away a forest lies
Rich in the roots and fruit we prize,

To this will I and all repair
And join the holy hermits there;
Be wise, and with us thither flee
Before this Khara injure thee.
Mighty art thou, O Ráma, yet
Each day with peril is beset.
If with thy consort by thy side
Thou in this wood wilt still abide."

He ceased: the words the hero spake
The hermit's purpose failed to break:
To Raghu's son farewell he said,
And blessed the chief and comforted;
Then with the rest the holy sage
Departed from the hermitage.

So from the wood the saints withdrew,
And Ráma bidding all adieu
In lowly reverence bent:
Instructed by their friendly speech,
Blest with the gracious love of each,
To his pure home he went.
Nor would the son of Raghu stray
A moment from that grove away
From which the saints had fled.
And many a hermit thither came
Attracted by his saintly fame
And the pure life he led.

CANTO
CXVII

Anasúyá

B ut dwelling in that lonely spot
Left by the hermits pleased him not.
"I met the faithful Bharat here,
The townsmen, and my mother dear:
The painful memory lingers yet,
And stings me with a vain regret.
And here the host of Bharat camped,
And many a courser here has stamped,
And elephants with ponderous feet
Have trampled through the calm retreat."
So forth to seek a home he hied,
His spouse and Lakshmaṇ by his side.
He came to Atri's pure retreat,
Paid reverence to his holy feet,
And from the saint such welcome won
As a fond father gives his son.
The noble prince with joy unfeigned
As a dear guest he entertained,
And cheered the glorious Lakshmaṇ too
And Sítá with observance due.
Then Anasúyá at the call
Of him who sought the good of all,
His blameless venerable spouse,
Delighting in her holy vows,
Came from her chamber to his side:
To her the virtuous hermit cried:
"Receive, I pray, with friendly grace
This dame of Maithil monarchs' race:"
To Ráma next made known his wife,
The devotee of saintliest life:
"Ten thousand years this votaress bent

On sternest rites of penance spent;
She when the clouds withheld their rain,
And drought ten years consumed the plain,
Caused grateful roots and fruit to grow
And ordered Gangá here to flow:
So from their cares the saints she freed,
Nor let these checks their rites impede,
She wrought in Heaven's behalf, and made
Ten nights of one, the Gods to aid:
Let holy Anasúyá be
An honoured mother, Prince, to thee.
Let thy Videhan spouse draw near
To her whom all that live revere,
Stricken in years, whose loving mind
Is slow to wrath and ever kind."

He ceased: and Ráma gave assent,
And said, with eyes on Sítá bent:
"O Princess, thou hast heard with me
This counsel of the devotee:
Now that her touch thy soul may bless,
Approach the saintly votaress:
Come to the venerable dame,
Far known by Anasúyá's name:
The mighty things that she has done
High glory in the world have won."

Thus spoke the son of Raghu: she
Approached the saintly devotee,
Who with her white locks, old and frail,
Shook like a plantain in the gale.
To that true spouse she bowed her head,
And "Lady, I am Sítá," said:
Raised suppliant hands and prayed her tell
That all was prosperous and well.

The aged matron, when she saw
Fair Sítá true to duty's law,
Addressed her thus: "High fate is thine
Whose thoughts to virtue still incline.
Thou, lady of the noble mind,

Hast kin and state and wealth resigned
To follow Ráma forced to tread
Where solitary woods are spread.
Those women gain high spheres above
Who still unchanged their husbands love,
Whether they dwell in town or wood,
Whether their hearts be ill or good.
Though wicked, poor, or led away
In love's forbidden paths to stray,
The noble matron still will deem
Her lord a deity supreme.
Regarding kin and friendship, I
Can see no better, holier tie,
And every penance-rite is dim
Beside the joy of serving him.
But dark is this to her whose mind
Promptings of idle fancy blind,
Who led by evil thoughts away
Makes him who should command obey.
Such women, O dear Maithil dame,
Their virtue lose and honest fame,
Enslaved by sin and folly, led
In these unholy paths to tread.
But they who good and true like thee
The present and the future see,
Like men by holy deeds will rise
To mansions in the blissful skies.
So keep thee pure from taint of sin,
Still to thy lord be true,
And fame and merit shalt thou win,
To thy devotion due."

CANTO
CXVIII

Anasúyá's Gifts

Thus by the holy dame addressed
Who banished envy from her breast,
Her lowly reverence Sítá paid,
And softly thus her answer made:
"No marvel, best of dames, thy speech
The duties of a wife should teach;

Yet I, O lady, also know
Due reverence to my lord to show.
Were he the meanest of the base,
Unhonoured with a single grace,
My husband still I ne'er would leave,
But firm through all to him would cleave:
Still rather to a lord like mine
Whose virtues high-exalted shine,
Compassionate, of lofty soul,
With every sense in due control,
True in his love, of righteous mind,
Like a dear sire and mother kind.
E'en as he ever loves to treat
Kauśalyá with observance meet,
Has his behaviour ever been
To every other honoured queen.
Nay, more, a sonlike reverence shows
The noble Ráma e'en to those
On whom the king his father set
His eyes one moment, to forget.
Deep in my heart the words are stored,
Said by the mother of my lord,
When from my home I turned away
In the lone fearful woods to stray.

The counsel of my mother deep
Impressed upon my soul I keep,
When by the fire I took my stand,
And Ráma clasped in his my hand.
And in my bosom cherished yet,
My friends' advice I ne'er forget:
Woman her holiest offering pays
When she her husband's will obeys.
Good Sávitrí her lord obeyed,
And a high saint in heaven was made,
And for the self-same virtue thou
Hast heaven in thy possession now.
And she with whom no dame could vie,
Now a bright Goddess in the sky,
Sweet Rohiṇí the Moon's dear Queen,
Without her lord is never seen:
And many a faithful wife beside
For her pure love is glorified."

Thus Sítá spake: soft rapture stole
Through Anasúyá's saintly soul:
Kisses on Sítá's head she pressed,
And thus the Maithil dame addressed:
"I by long rites and toils endured
Rich store of merit have secured:
From this my wealth will I bestow
A blessing ere I let thee go.
So right and wise and true each word
That from thy lips mine ears have heard,
I love thee: be my pleasing task
To grant the boon that thou shalt ask."

Then Sítá marvelled much, and while
Played o'er her lips a gentle smile,
"All has been done, O Saint," she cried,
"And naught remains to wish beside."

She spake; the lady's meek reply
Swelled Anasúyá's rapture high.
"Sítá," she said, "my gift to-day
Thy sweet contentment shall repay.

Accept this precious robe to wear,
Of heavenly fabric, rich and rare,
These gems thy limbs to ornament,
This precious balsam sweet of scent.
O Maithil dame, this gift of mine
Shall make thy limbs with beauty shine,
And breathing o'er thy frame dispense
Its pure and lasting influence.
This balsam on thy fair limbs spread
New radiance on thy lord shall shed,
As Lakshmí's beauty lends a grace
To Vishṇu's own celestial face."

Then Sítá took the gift the dame
Bestowed on her in friendship's name,
The balsam, gems, and robe divine,
And garlands wreathed of bloomy twine;
Then sat her down, with reverence meet,
At saintly Anasúyá's feet.
The matron rich in rites and vows
Turned her to Ráma's Maithil spouse,
And questioned thus in turn to hear
A pleasant tale to charm her ear:
"Sítá, 'tis said that Raghu's son
Thy hand, mid gathered suitors, won.
I fain would hear thee, lady, tell
The story as it all befell:
Do thou repeat each thing that passed,
Reviewing all from first to last."

Thus spake the dame to Sítá: she
Replying to the devotee,
"Then, lady, thy attention lend,"
Rehearsed the story to the end:

"King Janak, just and brave and strong,
Who loves the right and hates the wrong,
Well skilled in what the law ordains
For Warriors, o'er Videha reigns.
Guiding one morn the plough, his hand
Marked out, for rites the sacred land,

When, as the ploughshare cleft the earth,
Child of the king I leapt to birth.
Then as the ground he smoothed and cleared,
He saw me all with dust besmeared,
And on the new-found babe, amazed
The ruler of Videha gazed.
In childless love the monarch pressed
The welcome infant to his breast:
"My daughter," thus he cried, "is she:"
And as his child he cared for me.
Forth from the sky was heard o'erhead
As 'twere a human voice that said:
"Yea, even so: great King, this child
Henceforth thine own be justly styled."
Videha's monarch, virtuous souled,
Rejoiced o'er me with joy untold,
Delighting in his new-won prize,
The darling of his heart and eyes.
To his chief queen of saintly mind
The precious treasure he consigned,
And by her side she saw me grow,
Nursed with the love which mothers know.

Then as he saw the seasons fly,
And knew my marriage-time was nigh,
My sire was vexed with care, as sad
As one who mourns the wealth he had:
"Scorn on the maiden's sire must wait
From men of high and low estate:
The virgin's father all despise,
Though Indra's peer, who rules the skies."
More near he saw, and still more near,
The scorn that filled his soul with fear,
On trouble's billowy ocean tossed,
Like one whose shattered bark is lost.
My father knowing how I came,
No daughter of a mortal dame,
In all the regions failed to see
A bridegroom meet to match with me.
Each way with anxious thought he scanned,
And thus at length the monarch planned:

"The Bride's Election will I hold,
With every rite prescribed of old."
It pleased King Varuṇ to bestow
Quiver and shafts and heavenly bow
Upon my father's sire who reigned,
When Daksha his great rite ordained.
Where was the man might bend or lift
With utmost toil that wondrous gift?
Not e'en in dreams could mortal king
Strain the great bow or draw the string.
Of this tremendous bow possessed,
My truthful father thus addressed
The lords of many a region, all
Assembled at the monarch's call:
"Whoe'er this bow can manage, he
The husband of my child shall be."
The suitors viewed with hopeless eyes
That wondrous bow of mountain size,
Then to my sire they bade adieu,
And all with humbled hearts withdrew.
At length with Viśvámitra came
This son of Raghu, dear to fame,
The royal sacrifice to view.
Near to my father's home he drew,
His brother Lakshmaṇ by his side,
Ráma, in deeds heroic tried.
My sire with honour entertained
The saint in lore of duty trained,
Who thus in turn addressed the king:
"Ráma and Lakshmaṇ here who spring
From royal Daśaratha, long
To see thy bow so passing strong."

Before the prince's eyes was laid
That marvel, as the Bráhman prayed.
One moment on the bow he gazed,
Quick to the notch the string he raised,
Then, in the wandering people's view,
The cord with mighty force he drew.
Then with an awful crash as loud
As thunderbolts that cleave the cloud,

683

The bow beneath the matchless strain
Of arms heroic snapped in twain.
Thus, giving purest water, he,
My sire, to Ráma offered me.
The prince the offered gift declined
Till he should learn his father's mind;
So horsemen swift Ayodhyá sought
And back her aged monarch brought.
Me then my sire to Ráma gave,
Self-ruled, the bravest of the brave.
And Urmilá, the next to me,
Graced with all gifts, most fair to see,
My sire with Raghu's house allied,
And gave her to be Lakshmaṇ's bride.
Thus from the princes of the land
Lord Ráma won my maiden hand,
And him exalted high above
Heroic chiefs I truly love."

CANTO
CXIX

The Forest

When Anasúyá, virtuous-souled,
Had heard the tale by Sítá told,
She kissed the lady's brow and laced
Her loving arms around her waist.
"With sweet-toned words distinct and clear
Thy pleasant tale has charmed mine ear,
How the great king thy father held
That Maiden's Choice unparalleled.
But now the sun has sunk from sight,
And left the world to holy Night.
Hark! how the leafy thickets sound
With gathering birds that twitter round:

They sought their food by day, and all
Flock homeward when the shadows fall.
See, hither comes the hermit band,
Each with his pitcher in his hand:
Fresh from the bath, their locks are wet,
Their coats of bark are dripping yet.
Here saints their fires of worship tend,
And curling wreaths of smoke ascend:
Borne on the flames they mount above,
Dark as the brown wings of the dove.
The distant trees, though well-nigh bare,
Gloom thickened by the evening air,
And in the faint uncertain light
Shut the horizon from our sight.
The beasts that prowl in darkness rove
On every side about the grove,
And the tame deer, at ease reclined
Their shelter near the altars find.
The night o'er all the sky is spread,
With lunar stars engarlanded,
And risen in his robes of light
The moon is beautifully bright.
Now to thy lord I bid thee go:
Thy pleasant tale has charmed me so:
One thing alone I needs must pray,
Before me first thyself array:
Here in thy heavenly raiment shine,
And glad, dear love, these eyes of mine."

Then like a heavenly Goddess shone
Fair Sítá with that raiment on.
She bowed her to the matron's feet,
Then turned away her lord to meet.
The hero prince with joy surveyed
His Sítá in her robes arrayed,
As glorious to his arms she came
With love-gifts of the saintly dame.
She told him how the saint to show
Her fond affection would bestow
That garland of celestial twine,
Those ornaments and robes divine.

Then Ráma's heart, nor Lakshman's less,
Was filled with pride and happiness,
For honours high had Sítá gained,
Which mortal dames have scarce obtained.
There honoured by each pious sage
Who dwelt within the hermitage,
Beside his darling well content
That sacred night the hero spent.

The princes, when the night had fled,
Farewell to all the hermits said,
Who gazed upon the distant shade,
Their lustral rites and offerings paid.
The saints who made their dwelling there
In words like these addressed the pair:
"O Princes, monsters fierce and fell
Around that distant forest dwell:
On blood from human veins they feed,
And various forms assume at need,
With savage beasts of fearful power
That human flesh and blood devour.
Our holy saints they rend and tear
When met alone or unaware,
And eat them in their cruel joy:
These chase, O Ráma, or destroy.
By this one path our hermits go
To fetch the fruits that yonder grow:
By this, O Prince, thy feet should stray
Through pathless forests far away."

Thus by the reverent saints addressed,
And by their prayers auspicious blessed,
He left the holy crowd:
His wife and brother by his side,
Within the mighty wood he hied.
So sinks the Day-God in his pride
Beneath a bank of cloud.

BOOK

III

BOOK

III

The Hermitage

When Ráma, valiant hero, stood
In the vast shade of Daṇḍak wood,
His eyes on every side he bent
And saw a hermit settlement,
Where coats of bark were hung around,
And holy grass bestrewed the ground.
Bright with Bráhmanic lustre glowed
That circle where the saints abode:
Like the hot sun in heaven it shone,
Too dazzling to be looked upon.
Wild creatures found a refuge where
The court, well-swept, was bright and fair,
And countless birds and roedeer made
Their dwelling in the friendly shade.
Beneath the boughs of well-loved trees
Oft danced the gay Apsarases.
Around was many an ample shed
Wherein the holy fire was fed;
With sacred grass and skins of deer,
Ladles and sacrificial gear,
And roots and fruit, and wood to burn,
And many a brimming water-urn.
Tall trees their hallowed branches spread,
Laden with pleasant fruit, o'erhead;

And gifts which holy laws require,
And solemn offerings burnt with fire,
And Veda chants on every side
That home of hermits sanctified.
There many a flower its odour shed,
And lotus blooms the lake o'erspred.
There, clad in coats of bark and hide,—
Their food by roots and fruit supplied,—
Dwelt many an old and reverend sire
Bright as the sun or Lord of Fire,
All with each worldly sense subdued,
A pure and saintly multitude.
The Veda chants, the saints who trod
The sacred ground and mused on God,
Made that delightful grove appear
Like Brahmá's own most glorious sphere.
As Raghu's splendid son surveyed
That hermit home and tranquil shade,
He loosed his mighty bow-string, then
Drew nearer to the holy men.

With keen celestial sight endued
Those mighty saints the chieftain viewed,
With joy to meet the prince they came,
And gentle Sítá dear to fame.
They looked on virtuous Ráma, fair
As Soma in the evening air,
And Lakshman by his brother's side,
And Sítá long in duty tried,
And with glad blessings every sage
Received them in the hermitage.
Then Ráma's form and stature tall
Entranced the wondering eyes of all,—
His youthful grace, his strength of limb,
And garb that nobly sat on him.
To Lakshman too their looks they raised,
And upon Sítá's beauty gazed
With eyes that closed not lest their sight
Should miss the vision of delight.
Then the pure hermits of the wood,
Rejoicing in all creatures' good,

690

Their guest, the glorious Ráma, led
Within a cot with leaves o'erhead.
With highest honour all the best
Of radiant saints received their guest,
With kind observance, as is meet,
And gave him water for his feet.
To highest pitch of rapture wrought
Their stores of roots and fruit they brought.
They poured their blessings on his head,
And "All we have is thine," they said.
Then, reverent hand to hand applied,
Each duty-loving hermit cried:
"The king is our protector, bright
In fame, maintainer of the right.
He bears the awful sword, and hence
Deserves an elder's reverence.
One fourth of Indra's essence, he
Preserves his realm from danger free,
Hence honoured by the world of right
The king enjoys each choice delight.
Thou shouldst to us protection give,
For in thy realm, dear lord, we live:
Whether in town or wood thou be,
Thou art our king, thy people we.
Our wordly aims are laid aside,
Our hearts are tamed and purified.
To thee our guardian, we who earn
Our only wealth by penance turn."
Then the pure dwellers in the shade
To Raghu's son due honour paid,
And Lakshmaṇ, bringing store of roots,
And many a flower, and woodland fruits.
And others strove the prince to please
With all attentive courtesies.

Virádha

Thus entertained he passed the night,
Then, with the morning's early light,
To all the hermits bade adieu
And sought his onward way anew.
He pierced the mighty forest where
Roamed many a deer and pard and bear:
Its ruined pools he scarce could see.
For creeper rent and prostrate tree,
Where shrill cicada's cries were heard,
And plaintive notes of many a bird.
Deep in the thickets of the wood
With Lakshman and his spouse he stood,
There in the horrid shade he saw
A giant passing nature's law:
Vast as some mountain-peak in size,
With mighty voice and sunken eyes,
Huge, hideous, tall, with monstrous face,
Most ghastly of his giant race.
A tiger's hide the Rákshas wore
Still reeking with the fat and gore:
Huge-faced, like Him who rules the dead,
All living things he struck with dread.
Three lions, tigers four, ten deer
He carried on his iron spear,
Two wolves, an elephant's head beside
With mighty tusks which blood-drops dyed.
When on the three his fierce eye fell,
He charged them with a roar and yell
As furious as the grisly King
When stricken worlds are perishing.
Then with a mighty roar that shook

The earth beneath their feet, he took
The trembling Sítá to his side.
Withdrew a little space, and cried:
"Ha, short lived wretches, ye who dare,
In hermit dress with matted hair,
Armed each with arrows, sword, and bow,
Through Daṇḍak's pathless wood to go:
How with one dame, I bid you tell,
Can you among ascetics dwell?
Who are ye, sinners, who despise
The right, in holy men's disguise?
The great Virádha, day by day
Through this deep-tangled wood I stray,
And ever, armed with trusty steel,
I seize a saint to make my meal.
This woman young and fair of frame
Shall be the conquering giant's dame:
Your blood, ye things of evil life,
My lips shall quaff in battle strife."

He spoke: and Janak's hapless child,
Scared by his speech so fierce and wild,

Trembled for terror, as a frail
Young plantain shivers in the gale.
When Ráma saw Virádha clasp
Fair Sítá in his mighty grasp,
Thus with pale lips that terror dried
The hero to his brother cried:
"O see Virádha's arm enfold
My darling in its cursed hold,—
The child of Janak best of kings,
My spouse whose soul to virtue clings,
Sweet princess, with pure glory bright,
Nursed in the lap of soft delight.
Now falls the blow Kaikeyí meant,
Successful in her dark intent:
This day her cruel soul will be
Triumphant over thee and me.
Though Bharat on the throne is set,
Her greedy eyes look farther yet:

693

Me from my home she dared expel,
Me whom all creatures loved so well.
This fatal day at length, I ween,
Brings triumph to the younger queen.
I see with bitterest grief and shame
Another touch the Maithil dame.
Not loss of sire and royal power
So grieves me as this mournful hour."

Thus in his anguish cried the chief:
Then drowned in tears, o'erwhelmed by grief,
Thus Lakshmaṇ in his anger spake,
Quick panting like a spell-bound snake:

"Canst thou, my brother, Indra's peer,
When I thy minister am near,
Thus grieve like some forsaken thing,
Thou, every creature's lord and king?
My vengeful shaft the fiend shall slay,
And earth shall drink his blood to-day.
The fury which my soul at first
Upon usurping Bharat nursed,
On this Virádha will I wreak
As Indra splits the mountain peak.
Winged by this arm's impetuous might
My shaft with deadly force
The monster in the chest shall smite,
And fell his shattered corse."

CANTO
III

Virádha Attacked

Virádha with a fearful shout
That echoed through the wood, cried out:

"What men are ye, I bid you say,
And whither would ye bend your way?"
To him whose mouth shot fiery flame
The hero told his race and name:
"Two Warriors, nobly bred, are we,
And through this wood we wander free.
But who art thou, how born and styled,
Who roamest here in Daṇḍak's wild?"

To Ráma, bravest of the brave,
His answer thus Virádha gave:
"Hear, Raghu's son, and mark me well,
And I my name and race will tell.
Of Śatahradá born, I spring
From Java as my sire, O King:
Me, of this lofty lineage, all
Giants on earth Virádha call.
The rites austere I long maintained
From Brahmá's grace the boon have gained
To bear a charmed frame which ne'er
Weapon or shaft may pierce or tear.
Go as ye came, untouched by fear,
And leave with me this woman here:
Go, swiftly from my presence fly,
Or by this hand ye both shall die."

Then Ráma with his fierce eyes red
With fury to the giant said:

695

"Woe to thee, sinner, fond and weak,
Who madly thus thy death wilt seek!
Stand, for it waits thee in the fray:
With life thou ne'er shalt flee away."

He spoke, and raised the cord whereon
A pointed arrow flashed and shone,
Then, wild with anger, from his bow,
He launched the weapon on the foe.
Seven times the fatal cord he drew,
And forth seven rapid arrows flew,
Shafts winged with gold that left the wind
And e'en Suparṇa's self behind.
Full on the giant's breast they smote,
And purpled like the peacock's throat,
Passed through his mighty bulk and came
To earth again like flakes of flame.
The fiend the Maithil dame unclasped;
In his fierce hand his spear he grasped,
And wild with rage, pierced through and through,
At Ráma and his brother flew.
So loud the roar which chilled with fear,
So massy was the monster's spear,
He seemed, like Indra's flagstaff, dread
As the dark God who rules the dead.
On huge Virádha fierce as He
Who smites, and worlds have ceased to be,
The princely brothers poured amain
Their fiery flood of arrowy rain.
Unmoved he stood, and opening wide
His dire mouth laughed unterrified,
And ever as the monster gaped
Those arrows from his jaws escaped.
Preserving still his life unharmed,
By Brahmá's saving promise charmed,
His mighty spear aloft in air
He raised, and rushed upon the pair.
From Ráma's bow two arrows flew
And cleft that massive spear in two,

Dire as the flaming levin sent
From out the cloudy firmament.
Cut by the shafts he guided well
To earth the giant's weapon fell:
As when from Meru's summit, riven
By fiery bolts, a rock is driven.
Then swift his sword each warrior drew,
Like a dread serpent black of hue,
And gathering fury for the blow
Rushed fiercely on the giant foe.
Around each prince an arm he cast,
And held the dauntless heroes fast:
Then, though his gashes gaped and bled,
Bearing the twain he turned and fled.

Then Ráma saw the giant's plan,
And to his brother thus began:
"O Lakshman, let Virádha still
Hurry us onward as he will,
For look, Sumitrá's son, he goes
Along the path we freely chose."

He spoke: the rover of the night
Upraised them with terrific might,
Till, to his lofty shoulders swung,
Like children to his neck they clung.
Then sending far his fearful roar,
The princes through the wood he bore,—
A wood like some vast cloud to view,
Where birds of every plumage flew,
And mighty trees o'erarching threw
Dark shadows on the ground;
Where snakes and silvan creatures made
Their dwelling, and the jackal strayed
Through tangled brakes around.

Virádha's Death

But Sítá viewed with wild affright
The heroes hurried from her sight.
She tossed her shapely arms on high,
And shrieked aloud her bitter cry:
"Ah, the dread giant bears away
The princely Ráma as his prey,
Truthful and pure, and good and great,
And Lakshman shares his brother's fate.
The brindled tiger and the bear
My mangled limbs for food will tear.
Take me, O best of giants, me,
And leave the sons of Raghu free."

Then, by avenging fury spurred,
Her mournful cry the heroes heard,
And hastened, for the lady's sake,
The wicked monster's life to take.
Then Lakshman with resistless stroke
The foe's left arm that held him broke,
And Ráma too, as swift to smite,
Smashed with his heavy hand the right.
With broken arms and tortured frame
To earth the fainting giant came,
Like a huge cloud, or mighty rock
Rent, sundered by the levin's shock.
Then rushed they on, and crushed and beat
Their foe with arms and fists and feet,
And nerved each mighty limb to pound
And bray him on the level ground.
Keen arrows and each biting blade
Wide rents in breast and side had made;

In fight the cruel demon slew,
And radiant with delight
Deep in the hollowed earth they cast
The monster roaring to the last,
In their resistless might.
Thus when they saw the warrior's steel
No life-destroying blow might deal,
The pair, for lore renowned,
Deep in the pit their hands had made
The unresisting giant laid,
And killed him neath the ground.
Upon himself the monster brought
From Ráma's hand the death he sought
With strong desire to gain:
And thus the rover of the night
Told Ráma, as they strove in fight,
That swords might rend and arrows smite
Upon his breast in vain.
Thus Ráma, when his speech he heard,
The giant's mighty form interred,
Which mortal arms defied.
With thundering crash the giant fell,
And rock and cave and forest dell
With echoing roar replied.
The princes, when their task was done
And freedom from the peril won,
Rejoiced to see him die.
Then in the boundless wood they strayed,
Like the great sun and moon displayed
Triumphant in the sky.

Sarabhanga

Then Ráma, having slain in fight
Virádha of terrific might,
With gentle words his spouse consoled,
And clasped her in his loving hold.
Then to his brother nobly brave
The valiant prince his counsel gave:
"Wild are these woods around us spread;
And hard and rough the ground to tread:
We, O my brother, ne'er have viewed
So dark and drear a solitude:
To Śarabhanga let us haste,
Whom wealth of holy works has graced."

Thus Ráma spoke, and took the road
To Śarabhanga's pure abode.
But near that saint whose lustre vied
With Gods, by penance purified,
With startled eyes the prince beheld
A wondrous sight unparalleled.
In splendour like the fire and sun
He saw a great and glorious one.
Upon a noble car he rode,
And many a God behind him glowed:
And earth beneath his feet unpressed
The monarch of the skies confessed.
Ablaze with gems, no dust might dim
The bright attire that covered him.
Arrayed like him, on every side
High saints their master glorified.
Near, borne in air, appeared in view
His car which tawny coursers drew,

Like silver cloud, the moon, or sun
Ere yet the day is well begun.
Wreathed with gay garlands, o'er his head
A pure white canopy was spread,
And lovely nymphs stood nigh to hold
Fair chouris with their sticks of gold,
Which, waving in each gentle hand,
The forehead of their monarch fanned.
God, saint, and bard, a radiant ring,
Sang glory to their heavenly King:
Forth into joyful lauds they burst
As Indra with the sage conversed.
Then Ráma, when his wondering eyes
Beheld the monarch of the skies,

To Lakshmaṇ quickly called, and showed
The car wherein Lord Indra rode:
"See, brother, see that air-borne car,
Whose wondrous glory shines afar:
Wherefrom so bright a lustre streams
That like a falling sun it seems:
These are the steeds whose fame we know,
Of heavenly race through heaven they go:
These are the steeds who bear the yoke
Of Śakra, Him whom all invoke.
Behold these youths, a glorious band,
Toward every wind a hundred stand:
A sword in each right hand is borne,
And rings of gold their arms adorn.
What might in every broad deep chest
And club-like arm is manifest!
Clothed in attire of crimson hue
They show like tigers fierce to view.
Great chains of gold each warder deck,
Gleaming like fire beneath his neck.
The age of each fair youth appears
Some score and five of human years:
The ever-blooming prime which they
Who live in heaven retain for aye:
Such mien these lordly beings wear,
Heroic youths, most bright and fair.

703

Now, brother, in this spot, I pray,
With the Videhan lady stay,
Till I have certain knowledge who
This being is, so bright to view."

He spoke, and turning from the spot
Sought Śarabhanga's hermit cot.
But when the lord of Śachí saw
The son of Raghu near him draw,
He hastened of the sage to take
His leave, and to his followers spake:

"See, Ráma bends his steps this way,
But ere he yet a word can say,
Come, fly to our celestial sphere;
It is not meet he see me here.
Soon victor and triumphant he
In fitter time shall look on me.
Before him still a great emprise,
A task too hard for others, lies."

Then with all marks of honour high
The Thunderer bade the saint good-bye,
And in his car which coursers drew
Away to heaven the conqueror flew.
Then Ráma, Lakshman, and the dame,
To Śarabhanga nearer came,
Who sat beside the holy flame.
Before the ancient sage they bent,
And clasped his feet most reverent;
Then at his invitation found
A seat beside him on the ground.
Then Ráma prayed the sage would deign
Lord Indra's visit to explain;
And thus at length the holy man
In answer to his prayer began:
"This Lord of boons has sought me here
To waft me hence to Brahmá's sphere,
Won by my penance long and stern,—
A home the lawless ne'er can earn.
But when I knew that thou wast nigh,

704

To Brahmá's world I could not fly
Until these longing eyes were blest
With seeing thee, mine honoured guest.
Since thou, O Prince, hast cheered my sight,
Great-hearted lover of the right,
To heavenly spheres will I repair
And bliss supreme that waits me there.
For I have won, dear Prince, my way
To those fair worlds which ne'er decay,
Celestial seat of Brahmá's reign:
Be thine, with me, those worlds to gain."

Then master of all sacred lore,
Spake Ráma to the saint once more:

"I, even I, illustrious sage,
Will make those worlds mine heritage:
But now, I pray, some home assign
Within this holy grove of thine."

Thus Ráma, Indra's peer in might,
Addressed the aged anchorite:
And he, with wisdom well endued,
To Raghu's son his speech renewed:

"Sutíkshna's woodland home is near,
A glorious saint of life austere,
True to the path of duty; he
With highest bliss will prosper thee.
Against the stream thy course must be
Of this fair brook Mandákiní,
Whereon light rafts like blossoms glide;
Then to his cottage turn aside.
There lies thy path: but ere thou go,
Look on me, dear one, till I throw
Aside this mould that girds me in,
As casts the snake his withered skin."

He spoke, the fire in order laid
With holy oil due offerings made,
And Śarabhanga, glorious sire,

Laid down his body in the fire.
Then rose the flame above his head,
On skin, blood, flesh, and bones it fed,
Till forth, transformed, with radiant hue
Of tender youth, he rose anew,
Far-shining in his bright attire
Came Śarabhanga from the pyre:
Above the home of saints, and those
Who feed the quenchless flame, he rose:
Beyond the seat of Gods he passed,
And Brahmá's sphere was gained at last.

The noblest of the twice-born race,
For holy works supreme in place,
The Mighty Father there beheld
Girt round by hosts unparalleled;
And Brahmá joying at the sight
Welcomed the glorious anchorite.

CANTO

VI

Ráma's Promise

When he his heavenly home had found,
The holy men who dwelt around
To Ráma flocked, whose martial fame
Shone glorious as the kindled flame:
Vaikhánasas who love the wild,
Pure hermits Bálakhilyas styled,
Good Samprakshálas, saints who live
On rays which moon and daystar give:
Those who with leaves their lives sustain
And those who pound with stones their grain:
And they who lie in pools, and those
Whose corn, save teeth, no winnow knows:

Those who for beds the cold earth use,
And those who every couch refuse:
And those condemned to ceaseless pains,
Whose single foot their weight sustains:
And those who sleep neath open skies,
Whose food the wave or air supplies,
And hermits pure who spend their nights
On ground prepared for sacred rites;
Those who on hills their vigil hold,
Or dripping clothes around them fold:
The devotees who live for prayer,
Or the five fires unflinching bear.
On contemplation all intent,
With light that heavenly knowledge lent,
They came to Ráma, saint and sage,
In Śarabhanga's hermitage.
The hermit crowd around him pressed,
And thus the virtuous chief addressed:
"The lordship of the earth is thine,
O Prince of old Ikshváku's line.
Lord of the Gods is Indra, so
Thou art our lord and guide below.
Thy name, the glory of thy might,
Throughout the triple world are bright:
Thy filial love so nobly shown,
Thy truth and virtue well are known.
To thee, O lord, for help we fly,
And on thy love of right rely:
With kindly patience hear us speak,
And grant the boon we humbly seek.
That lord of earth were most unjust,
Foul traitor to his solemn trust,
Who should a sixth of all require,
Nor guard his people like a sire.
But he who ever watchful strives
To guard his subjects' wealth and lives,
Dear as himself or, dearer still,
His sons, with earnest heart and will,—
That king, O Raghu's son, secures
High fame that endless years endures,
And he to Brahmá's world shall rise,

Made glorious in the eternal skies.
Whate'er, by duty won, the meed
Of saints whom roots and berries feed,
One fourth thereof, for tender care
Of subjects, is the monarch's share.
These, mostly of the Bráhman race,
Who make the wood their dwelling-place,
Although a friend in thee they view,
Fall friendless neath the giant crew.
Come, Ráma, come, and see hard by
The holy hermits' corpses lie,
Where many a tangled pathway shows
The murderous work of cruel foes.
These wicked fiends the hermits kill—
Who live on Chitrakúṭa's hill,
And blood of slaughtered saints has dyed
Mandákiní and Pampá's side.
No longer can we bear to see
The death of saint and devotee
Whom through the forest day by day
These Rákshasas unpitying slay.
To thee, O Prince, we flee, and crave
Thy guardian help our lives to save.
From these fierce rovers of the night
Defend each stricken anchorite.
Throughout the world 'twere vain to seek
An arm like thine to aid the weak.
O Prince, we pray thee hear our call,
And from these fiends preserve us all."
The son of Raghu heard the plaint
Of penance-loving sage and saint,
And the good prince his speech renewed
To all the hermit multitude:

"To me, O saints, ye need not sue:
I wait the hests of all of you.
I by mine own occasion led
This mighty forest needs must tread,

And while I keep my sire's decree
Your lives from threatening foes will free.

708

I hither came of free accord
To lend the aid by you implored,
And richest meed my toil shall pay,
While here in forest shades I stay.
I long in battle strife to close.
And slay these fiends, the hermits' foes,
That saint and sage may learn aright
My prowess and my brother's might."
Thus to the saints his promise gave
That prince who still to virtue clave
With never-wandering thought:
And then with Lakshmaṇ by his side,
With penance-wealthy men to guide,
Sutíkshṇa's home he sought.

CANTO

VII

Sutíkshna

S o Raghu's son, his foemen's dread,
    With Sítá and his brother sped,
    Girt round by many a twice-born sage,
To good Sutíkshṇa's hermitage.
Through woods for many a league he passed,
O'er rushing rivers full and fast,
Until a mountain fair and bright
As lofty Meru rose in sight.
Within its belt of varied wood
Ikshváku's sons and Sítá stood,
Where trees of every foliage bore
Blossom and fruit in endless store.
There coats of bark, like garlands strung,
Before a lonely cottage hung,
And there a hermit, dust-besmeared,
A lotus on his breast, appeared.

Then Ráma with obeisance due
Addressed the sage, as near he drew:
"My name is Ráma, lord; I seek
Thy presence, saint, with thee to speak.
O sage, whose merits ne'er decay,
Some word unto thy servant say."

The sage his eyes on Ráma bent,
Of virtue's friends preëminent;
Then words like these he spoke, and pressed
The son of Raghu to his breast:
"Welcome to thee, illustrious youth,
Best champion of the rights of truth!
By thine approach this holy ground
A worthy lord this day has found.
I could not quit this mortal frame
Till thou shouldst come, O dear to fame:
To heavenly spheres I would not rise,
Expecting thee with eager eyes.
I knew that thou, unkinged, hadst made
Thy home in Chitrakúṭa's shade.
E'en now, O Ráma, Indra, lord
Supreme by all the Gods adored,
King of the Hundred Offerings, said,
When he my dwelling visited,
That the good works that I have done
My choice of all the worlds have won.
Accept this meed of holy vows,
And with thy brother and thy spouse,
Roam, through my favour, in the sky
Which saints celestial glorify."

To that bright sage, of penance stern,
The high-souled Ráma spake in turn,
As Vásava who rules the skies
To Brahmá's gracious speech replies:
"I of myself those worlds will win,
O mighty hermit pure from sin:
But now, O saint, I pray thee tell
Where I within this wood may dwell:
For I by Śarabhanga old,

The son of Gautama, was told
That thou in every lore art wise,
And seest all with loving eyes."

Thus to the saint, whose glories high
Filled all the world, he made reply:
And thus again the holy man
His pleasant speech with joy began:
"This calm retreat, O Prince, is blest
With many a charm: here take thy rest.
Here roots and kindly fruits abound,
And hermits love the holy ground.
Fair silvan beasts and gentle deer
In herds unnumbered wander here:
And as they roam, secure from harm,
Our eyes with grace and beauty charm:
Except the beasts in thickets bred,
This grove of ours has naught to dread."

The hermit's speech when Ráma heard,—
The hero ne'er by terror stirred,—
On his great bow his hand he laid,
And thus in turn his answer made:
"O saint, my darts of keenest steel,
Armed with their murderous barbs, would deal
Destruction mid the silvan race
That flocks around thy dwelling-place.
Most wretched then my fate would be
For such dishonour shown to thee:
And only for the briefest stay
Would I within this grove delay."

He spoke and ceased. With pious care
He turned him to his evening prayer,
Performed each customary rite,
And sought his lodging for the night,
With Sítá and his brother laid

Beneath the grove's delightful shade,
First good Sutíkshṇa, as elsewhere, when he saw
The shades of night around them draw,

With hospitable care
The princely chieftains entertained
With store of choicest food ordained
For holy hermit's fare.

CANTO

VIII

The Hermitage

So Ráma and Sumitrá's son,
  When every honour due was done,
  Slept through the night. When morning broke,
The heroes from their rest awoke.
Betimes the son of Raghu rose,
With gentle Sítá, from repose,
And sipped the cool delicious wave
Sweet with the scent the lotus gave,
Then to the Gods and sacred flame
The heroes and the lady came,
And bent their heads in honour meet
Within the hermit's pure retreat.
When every stain was purged away,
They saw the rising Lord of Day:
Then to Sutíkshṇa's side they went,
And softly spoke, most reverent:

"Well have we slept, O holy lord,
Honoured of thee by all adored:
Now leave to journey forth we pray:
These hermits urge us on our way.
We haste to visit, wandering by,
The ascetics' homes that round you lie,
And roaming Daṇḍak's mighty wood
To view each saintly brotherhood,
For thy permission now we sue,

712

With these high saints to duty true,
By penance taught each sense to tame,—
In lustre like the smokeless flame.
Ere on our brows the sun can beat
With fierce intolerable heat.
Like some unworthy lord who wins
His power by tyranny and sins,
O saint, we fain would part." The three
Bent humbly to the devotee.
He raised the princes as they pressed
His feet, and strained them to his breast;
And then the chief of devotees
Bespake them both in words like these:
"Go with thy brother, Ráma, go,
Pursue thy path untouched by woe:
Go with thy faithful Sítá, she
Still like a shadow follows thee.
Roam Daṇḍak wood observing well
The pleasant homes where hermits dwell,—
Pure saints whose ordered souls adhere
To penance rites and vows austere.
There plenteous roots and berries grow,
And noble trees their blossoms show,
And gentle deer and birds of air
In peaceful troops are gathered there.
There see the full-blown lotus stud
The bosom of the lucid flood,
And watch the joyous mallard shake
The reeds that fringe the pool and lake.
See with delighted eye the rill
Leap sparkling from her parent hill,
And hear the woods that round thee lie
Reëcho to the peacock's cry.
And as I bid thy brother, so,
Sumitrá's child, I bid thee go.
Go forth, these varied beauties see,
And then once more return to me."

Thus spake the sage Sutíkshṇa: both
The chiefs assented, nothing loth,
Round him with circling steps they paced,

713

Then for the road prepared with haste.
There Sítá stood, the dame long-eyed,
Fair quivers round their waists she tied,
And gave each prince his trusty bow,
And sword which ne'er a spot might know.
Each took his quiver from her hand.
And clanging bow and gleaming brand:
Then from the hermits' home the two
Went forth each woodland scene to view.
Each beauteous in the bloom of age,
Dismissed by that illustrious sage,
With bow and sword accoutred, hied
Away, and Sítá by their side.

CANTO

IX

Sítá's Speech

Blest by the sage, when Raghu's son
His onward journey had begun,
Thus in her soft tone Sítá, meek
With modest fear, began to speak:
"One little slip the great may lead
To shame that follows lawless deed:
Such shame, my lord, as still must cling
To faults from low desire that spring.
Three several sins defile the soul,
Born of desire that spurns control:
First, utterance of a lying word,
Then, viler both, the next, and third:
The lawless love of other's wife,
The thirst of blood uncaused by strife.
The first, O Raghu's son, in thee
None yet has found, none e'er shall see.
Love of another's dame destroys

All merit, lost for guilty joys:
Ráma, such crime in thee, I ween,
Has ne'er been found, shall ne'er be seen:
The very thought, my princely lord,
Is in thy secret soul abhorred.

For thou hast ever been the same
Fond lover of thine own dear dame,
Content with faithful heart to do
Thy father's will, most just and true:
Justice, and faith, and many a grace
In thee have found a resting-place.
Such virtues, Prince, the good may gain
Who empire o'er each sense retain;
And well canst thou, with loving view
Regarding all, each sense subdue.
But for the third, the lust that strives,
Insatiate still, for others' lives,—
Fond thirst of blood where hate is none,—
This, O my lord, thou wilt not shun.
Thou hast but now a promise made,
The saints of Daṇḍak wood to aid:
And to protect their lives from ill
The giants' blood in tight wilt spill:
And from thy promise lasting fame
Will glorify the forest's name.
Armed with thy bow and arrows thou
Forth with thy brother journeyest now,
While as I think how true thou art
Fears for thy bliss assail my heart,
And all my spirit at the sight
Is troubled with a strange affright.
I like it not—it seems not good—
Thy going thus to Daṇḍak wood:
And I, if thou wilt mark me well,
The reason of my fear will tell.
Thou with thy brother, bow in hand,
Beneath those ancient trees wilt stand,
And thy keen arrows will not spare
Wood-rovers who will meet thee there.
For as the fuel food supplies

715

That bids the dormant flame arise,
Thus when the warrior grasps his bow
He feels his breast with ardour glow.
Deep in a holy grove, of yore,
Where bird and beast from strife forbore,
Śuchi beneath the sheltering boughs,
A truthful hermit kept his vows.
Then Indra, Śachí's heavenly lord,
Armed like a warrior with a sword,
Came to his tranquil home to spoil
The hermit of his holy toil,
And left the glorious weapon there
Entrusted to the hermit's care,
A pledge for him to keep, whose mind
To fervent zeal was all resigned.
He took the brand: with utmost heed
He kept it for the warrior's need:
To keep his trust he fondly strove
When roaming in the neighbouring grove:
Whene'er for roots and fruit he strayed
Still by his side he bore the blade:
Still on his sacred charge intent,
He took his treasure when he went.
As day by day that brand he wore,
The hermit, rich in merit's store
From penance rites each thought withdrew,
And fierce and wild his spirit grew.
With heedless soul he spurned the right,
And found in cruel deeds delight.
So, living with the sword, he fell,
A ruined hermit, down to hell.
This tale applies to those who deal
Too closely with the warrior's steel:
The steel to warriors is the same
As fuel to the smouldering flame.
Sincere affection prompts my speech:
I honour where I fain would teach.
Mayst thou, thus armed with shaft and bow,
So dire a longing never know
As, when no hatred prompts the fray,
These giants of the wood to slay:

For he who kills without offence
Shall win but little glory thence.
The bow the warrior joys to bend
Is lent him for a nobler end,
That he may save and succour those
Who watch in woods when pressed by foes.
What, matched with woods, is bow or steel?
What, warrior's arm with hermit's zeal?
We with such might have naught to do:
The forest rule should guide us too.
But when Ayodhyá hails thee lord,
Be then thy warrior life restored:
So shall thy sire and mother joy
In bliss that naught may e'er destroy.
And if, resigning empire, thou
Submit thee to the hermit's vow,
The noblest gain from virtue springs,
And virtue joy unending brings.
All earthly blessings virtue sends:
On virtue all the world depends.
Those who with vow and fasting tame
To due restraint the mind and frame,
Win by their labour, nobly wise,
The highest virtue for their prize.
Pure in the hermit's grove remain,
True to thy duty, free from stain.
But the three worlds are open thrown
To thee, by whom all things are known.
Who gave me power that I should dare
His duty to my lord declare?
'Tis woman's fancy, light as air,
That moves my foolish breast.
Now with thy brother counsel take,
Reflect, thy choice with judgment make,
And do what seems the best."

717

Ráma's Reply

The words that Sítá uttered, spurred
By truest love, the hero heard:
Then he who ne'er from virtue strayed
To Janak's child his answer made:
"In thy wise speech, sweet love, I find
True impress of thy gentle mind,
Well skilled the warrior's path to trace,
Thou pride of Janak's ancient race.
What fitting answer shall I frame
To thy good words, my honoured dame?
Thou sayst the warrior bears the bow
That misery's tears may cease to flow;
And those pure saints who love the shade
Of Daṇḍak wood are sore dismayed.
They sought me of their own accord,
With suppliant prayers my aid implored:
They, fed on roots and fruit, who spend
Their lives where bosky wilds extend,
My timid love, enjoy no rest
By these malignant fiends distressed.
These make the flesh of man their meat:
The helpless saints they kill and eat.
The hermits sought my side, the chief
Of Bráhman race declared their grief.
I heard, and from my lips there fell
The words which thou rememberest well:
I listened as the hermits cried,
And to their prayers I thus replied:

"Your favour, gracious lords, I claim,
O'erwhelmed with this enormous shame

That Bráhmans, great and pure as you,
Who should be sought, to me should sue."
And then before the saintly crowd,
"What can I do?" I cried aloud.
Then from the trembling hermits broke
One long sad cry, and thus they spoke:
"Fiends of the wood, who wear at will
Each varied shape, afflict us still.
To thee in our distress we fly:
O help us, Ráma, or we die.
When sacred rites of fire are due,
When changing moons are full or new,
These fiends who bleeding flesh devour
Assail us with resistless power.
They with their cruel might torment
The hermits on their vows intent:
We look around for help and see
Our surest refuge, Prince, in thee.
We, armed with powers of penance, might
Destroy the rovers of the night:
But loth were we to bring to naught
The merit years of toil have bought.
Our penance rites are grown too hard,
By many a check and trouble barred,
But though our saints for food are slain
The withering curse we yet restrain.
Thus many a weary day distressed
By giants who this wood infest,
We see at length deliverance, thou
With Lakshman art our guardian now."

As thus the troubled hermits prayed,
I promised, dame, my ready aid,
And now—for truth I hold most dear—
Still to my word must I adhere.
My love, I might endure to be
Deprived of Lakshman, life, and thee,
But ne'er deny my promise, ne'er
To Bráhmans break the oath I sware.
I must, enforced by high constraint,
Protect them all. Each suffering saint

In me, unasked, his help had found;
Still more in one by promise bound.
I know thy words, mine own dear dame,
From thy sweet heart's affection came:
I thank thee for thy gentle speech,
For those we love are those we teach.
'Tis like thyself, O fair of face,
'Tis worthy of thy noble race:
Dearer than life, thy feet are set
In righteous paths they ne'er forget."

Thus to the Maithil monarch's child,
His own dear wife, in accents mild
The high-souled hero said:
Then to the holy groves which lay
Beyond them fair to see, their way
The bow-armed chieftain led.

CANTO
XI

Agastya

Ráma went foremost of the three,
Next Sítá, followed, fair to see,
And Lakshmaṇ with his bow in hand
Walked hindmost of the little band.
As onward through the wood they went,
With great delight their eyes were bent
On rocky heights beside the way
And lofty trees with blossoms gay;
And streamlets running fair and fast
The royal youths with Sítá passed.
They watched the sáras and the drake
On islets of the stream and lake,
And gazed delighted on the floods

Bright with gay birds and lotus buds.
They saw in startled herds the roes,
The passion-frenzied buffaloes,
Wild elephants who fiercely tore
The tender trees, and many a boar.
A length of woodland way they passed,
And when the sun was low at last
A lovely stream-fed lake they spied,
Two leagues across from side to side.
Tall elephants fresh beauty gave
To grassy bank and lilied wave,

By many a swan and sáras stirred,
Mallard, and gay-winged water-bird.
From those sweet waters, loud and long,
Though none was seen to wake the song,
Swelled high the singer's music blent
With each melodious instrument.
Ráma and car-borne Lakshman heard
The charming strain, with wonder stirred,
Turned on the margent of the lake
To Dharmabhrit the sage, and spake:

"Our longing souls, O hermit, burn
This music of the lake to learn:
We pray thee, noblest sage, explain
The cause of the mysterious strain."
He, as the son of Raghu prayed,
With swift accord his answer made,
And thus the hermit, virtuous-souled,
The story of the fair lake told:

"Through every age 'tis known to fame,
Panchápsaras its glorious name,
By holy Mándakarni wrought
With power his rites austere had bought.
For he, great votarist, intent
On strictest rule his stern life spent.
Ten thousand years the stream his bed,
Ten thousand years on air he fed.
Then on the blessed Gods who dwell

In heavenly homes great terror fell:
They gathered all, by Agni led,
And counselled thus disquieted:
"The hermit by ascetic pain
The seat of one of us would gain."
Thus with their hearts by fear oppressed
In full assembly spoke the Blest,
And bade five loveliest nymphs, as fair
As lightning in the evening air,
Armed with their winning wiles, seduce
From his stern vows the great recluse.
Though lore of earth and heaven he knew,
The hermit from his task they drew,
And made the great ascetic slave
To conquering love, the Gods to save.
Each of the heavenly five became,
Bound to the sage, his wedded dame;
And he, for his beloved's sake,
Formed a fair palace neath the lake.
Under the flood the ladies live,
To joy and ease their days they give,
And lap in bliss the hermit wooed
From penance rites to youth renewed.
So when the sportive nymphs within
Those secret bowers their play begin,
You hear the singers' dulcet tones
Blend sweetly with their tinkling zones."

"How wondrous are these words of thine!"
Cried the famed chiefs of Raghu's line,
As thus they heard the sage unfold
The marvels of the tale he told.

As Ráma spake, his eyes were bent
Upon a hermit settlement
With light of heavenly lore endued,
With sacred grass and vesture strewed.
His wife and brother by his side,
Within the holy bounds he hied,
And there, with honour entertained
By all the saints, a while remained.

In time, by due succession led,
Each votary's cot he visited,
And then the lord of martial lore,
Returned where he had lodged before.
Here for the months, content, he stayed,
There for a year his visit paid:
Here for four months his home would fix,
There, as it chanced, for five or six.
Here for eight months and there for three
The son of Raghu's stay would be:
Here weeks, there fortnights, more or less,
He spent in tranquil happiness.
As there the hero dwelt at ease
Among those holy devotees,
In days untroubled o'er his head
Ten circling years of pleasure fled.
So Raghu's son in duty trained
A while in every cot remained,
Then with his dame retraced the road
To good Sutíkshṇa's calm abode.
Hailed by the saints with honours due
Near to the hermit's home he drew,
And there the tamer of his foes
Dwelt for a time in sweet repose.
One day within that holy wood
By saint Sutíkshṇa Ráma stood,
And thus the prince with reverence meek
To that high sage began to speak:

"In the wide woodlands that extend
Around us, lord most reverend,
As frequent voice of rumour tells,
Agastya, saintliest hermit, dwells.
So vast the wood, I cannot trace
The path to reach his dwelling place,
Nor, searching unassisted, find
That hermit of the thoughtful mind.
I with my wife and brother fain
Would go, his favour to obtain,
Would seek him in his lone retreat
And the great saint with reverence greet.

This one desire, O Master, long
Cherished within my heart, is strong,
That I may pay of free accord
My duty to that hermit lord."

As thus the prince whose heart was bent
On virtue told his firm intent,
The good Sutíkshṇa's joy rose high,
And thus in turn he made reply:
"The very thing, O Prince, which thou
Hast sought, I wished to urge but now,
Bid thee with wife and brother see

Agastya, glorious devotee.
I count this thing an omen fair
That thou shouldst thus thy wish declare,
And I, my Prince, will gladly teach
The way Agastya's home to reach.
Southward, dear son, direct thy feet
Eight leagues beyond this still retreat:
Agastya's hermit brother there
Dwells in a home most bright and fair.
'Tis on a knoll of woody ground,
With many a branching Pippal crowned:
There sweet birds' voices ne'er are mute,
And trees are gay with flower and fruit.
There many a lake gleams bright and cool,
And lilies deck each pleasant pool,
While swan, and crane, and mallard's wings
Are lovely in the water-springs.
There for one night, O Ráma, stay,
And with the dawn pursue thy way.
Still farther, bending southward, by
The thicket's edge the course must lie,
And thou wilt see, two leagues from thence
Agastya's lovely residence,
Set in the woodland's fairest spot,
All varied foliage decks the cot:
There Sítá, Lakshman thou, at ease
May spend sweet hours neath shady trees,
For all of noblest growth are found

724

Luxuriant on that bosky ground.
If it be still thy firm intent
To see that saint preëminent,
O mighty counsellor, this day
Depart upon thine onward way."

The hermit spake, and Ráma bent
His head, with Lakshmaṇ, reverent,
And then with him and Janak's child
Set out to trace the forest wild.
He saw dark woods that fringed the road,
And distant hills like clouds that showed,
And, as the way he followed, met
With many a lake and rivulet.
So passing on with ease where led
The path Sutíkshṇa bade him tread,
The hero with exulting breast
His brother in these words addressed:

"Here, surely, is the home, in sight,
Of that illustrious anchorite:
Here great Agastya's brother leads
A life intent on holy deeds.
Warned of each guiding mark and sign,
I see them all herein combine:
I see the branches bending low
Beneath the flowers and fruit they show.
A soft air from the forest springs,
Fresh from the odorous grass, and brings
A spicy fragrance as it flees
O'er the ripe fruit of Pippal trees.
See, here and there around us high
Piled up in heaps cleft billets lie,
And holy grass is gathered, bright
As strips of shining lazulite.
Full in the centre of the shade
The hermits' holy fire is laid:
I see its smoke the pure heaven streak
Dense as a big cloud's dusky peak.
The twice-born men their steps retrace
From each sequestered bathing-place,

725

And each his sacred gift has brought
Of blossoms which his hands have sought.
Of all these signs, dear brother, each
Agrees with good Sutíkshṇa's speech,
And doubtless in this holy bound
Agastya's brother will be found.
Agastya once, the worlds who viewed
With love, a Deathlike fiend subdued,
And armed with mighty power, obtained
By holy works, this grove ordained
To be a refuge and defence
From all oppressors' violence.
In days of yore within this place
Two brothers fierce of demon race,
Vátápi dire and Ilval, dwelt,
And slaughter mid the Bráhmans dealt.
A Bráhman's form, the fiend to cloak,
Fierce Ilval wore, and Sanskrit spoke,
And twice-born sages would invite
To solemnize some funeral rite.
His brother's flesh, concealed within
A ram's false shape and borrowed skin,—
As men are wont at funeral feasts,—
He dressed and fed those gathered priests.
The holy men, unweeting ill,
Took of the food and ate their fill.
Then Ilval with a mighty shout
Exclaimed "Vátápi, issue out."
Soon as his brother's voice he heard,
The fiend with ram-like bleating stirred:
Rending in pieces every frame,
Forth from the dying priests he came.
So they who changed their forms at will
Thousands of Bráhmans dared to kill,—
Fierce fiends who loved each cruel deed,
And joyed on bleeding flesh to feed.
Agastya, mighty hermit, pressed
To funeral banquet like the rest,
Obedient to the Gods' appeal
Ate up the monster at a meal.
"'Tis done, 'tis done," fierce Ilval cried,

And water for his hands supplied:
Then lifting up his voice he spake:
"Forth, brother, from thy prison break."
Then him who called the fiend, who long
Had wrought the suffering Bráhmans wrong,
Thus thoughtful-souled Agastya, best
Of hermits, with a smile addressed:
"How, Rákshas, is the fiend empowered
To issue forth whom I devoured?
Thy brother in a ram's disguise
Is gone where Yáma's kingdom lies."

When from the words Agastya said
He knew his brother fiend was dead,
His soul on fire with vengeful rage,
Rushed the night-rover at the sage.
One lightning glance of fury, hot
As fire, the glorious hermit shot,
As the fiend neared him in his stride,
And straight, consumed to dust, he died.
In pity for the Bráhmans' plight
Agastya wrought this deed of might:
This grove which lakes and fair trees grace
In his great brother's dwelling place."

As Ráma thus the tale rehearsed,
And with Sumitrá's son conversed,
The setting sun his last rays shed,
And evening o'er the land was spread.
A while the princely brothers stayed
And even rites in order paid,
Then to the holy grove they drew
And hailed the saint with honour due.
With courtesy was Ráma met
By that illustrious anchoret,
And for one night he rested there
Regaled with fruit and hermit fare.
But when the night had reached its close,
And the sun's glorious circle rose,
The son of Raghu left his bed
And to the hermit's brother said:

"Well rested in thy hermit cell,
I stand, O saint, to bid farewell;
For with thy leave I journey hence
Thy brother saint to reverence."
"Go, Ráma go," the sage replied:
Then from the cot the chieftain hied.
And while the pleasant grove he viewed,
The path the hermit showed, pursued.
Of every leaf, of changing hue.
Plants, trees by hundreds round him grew,
With joyous eyes he looked on all,
Then Jak, the wild rice, and Sál;
He saw the red Hibiscus glow,
He saw the flower-tipped creeper throw
The glory of her clusters o'er
Tall trees that loads of blossom bore.
Some, elephants had prostrate laid,
In some the monkeys leapt and played,
And through the whole wide forest rang
The charm of gay birds as they sang.
Then Ráma of the lotus eye
To Lakshmaṇ turned who followed nigh,
And thus the hero youth impressed
With Fortune's favouring signs, addressed:

"How soft the leaves of every tree,
How tame each bird and beast we see!
Soon the fair home shall we behold
Of that great hermit tranquil-souled.
The deed the good Agastya wrought
High fame throughout the world has bought:
I see, I see his calm retreat
That balms the pain of weary feet.
Where white clouds rise from flames beneath,
Where bark-coats lie with many a wreath,
Where silvan things, made gentle, throng,
And every bird is loud in song.
With ruth for suffering creatures filled,
A deathlike fiend with might he killed,
And gave this southern realm to be
A refuge, from oppression free.

There stands his home, whose dreaded might
Has put the giant crew to flight,
Who view with envious eyes afar
The peaceful shades they cannot mar.
Since that most holy saint has made
His dwelling in this lovely shade,
Checked by his might the giant brood
Have dwelt in peace with souls subdued.
And all this southern realm, within
Whose bounds no fiend may entrance win,
Now bears a name which naught may dim,
Made glorious through the worlds by him.
When Vindhya, best of hills, would stay
The journey of the Lord of Day,
Obedient to the saint's behest
He bowed for aye his humbled crest.
That hoary hermit, world-renowned
For holy deeds, within this ground
Has set his pure and blessed home,
Where gentle silvan creatures roam.
Agastya, whom the worlds revere,
Pure saint to whom the good are dear,
To us his guests all grace will show,
Enriched with blessings ere we go.
I to this aim each thought will turn,
The favour of the saint to earn,
That here in comfort may be spent
The last years of our banishment.
Here sanctities and high saints stand,
Gods, minstrels of the heavenly band;
Upon Agastya's will they wait,
And serve him, pure and temperate.
The liar's tongue, the tyrant's mind
Within these bounds no home may find:
No cheat, no sinner here can be:
So holy and so good is he.
Here birds and lords of serpent race,
Spirits and Gods who haunt the place,
Content with scanty fare remain,
As merit's meed they strive to gain.
Made perfect here, the saints supreme,

On cars that mock the Day-God's gleam,—
Their mortal bodies cast aside,—
Sought heaven transformed and glorified,
Here Gods to living things, who win
Their favour, pure from cruel sin,
Give royal rule and many a good,

Immortal life and spirithood.
Now, Lakshmaṇ, we are near the place:
Do thou precede a little space,
And tell the mighty saint that I
With Sítá at my side am nigh."

CANTO
XII

The Heavenly Bow

He spoke: the younger prince obeyed:
Within the bounds his way he made,
And thus addressed, whom first he met,
A pupil of the anchoret:

"Brave Ráma, eldest born, who springs,
From Daśaratha, hither brings
His wife the lady Sítá: he
Would fain the holy hermit see.
Lakshmaṇ am I—if happy fame
E'er to thine ears has brought the name—
His younger brother, prompt to do
His will, devoted, fond, and true.
We, through our royal sire's decree,
To the dread woods were forced to flee.
Tell the great Master, I entreat,
Our earnest wish our lord to greet."

730

He spoke: the hermit rich in store
Of fervid zeal and sacred lore,
Sought the pure shrine which held the fire,
To bear his message to the sire.
Soon as he reached the saint most bright
In sanctity's surpassing might,
He cried, uplifting reverent hands:
"Lord Ráma near thy cottage stands."
Then spoke Agastya's pupil dear
The message for his lord to hear:
"Ráma and Lakshmaṇ, chiefs who spring
From Daśaratha, glorious king,
Thy hermitage e'en now have sought,
And lady Sítá with them brought.
The tamers of the foe are here
To see thee, Master, and revere.
'Tis thine thy further will to say:
Deign to command, and we obey."

When from his pupil's lips he knew
The presence of the princely two,
And Sítá born to fortune high.
The glorious hermit made reply:
"Great joy at last is mine this day
That Ráma hither finds his way,
For long my soul has yearned to see
The prince who comes to visit me.
Go forth, go forth, and hither bring
The royal three with welcoming:
Lead Ráma in and place him near:
Why stands he not already here?"

Thus ordered by the hermit, who,
Lord of his thought, all duty knew,
His reverent hands together laid,
The pupil answered and obeyed.
Forth from the place with speed he ran,
To Lakshmaṇ came and thus began:
"Where is he? let not Ráma wait,
But speed, the sage to venerate."

Then with the pupil Lakshmaṇ went
Across the hermit settlement,
And showed him Ráma where he stood
With Janak's daughter in the wood.
The pupil then his message spake
Which the kind hermit bade him take;
Then led the honoured Ráma thence
And brought him in with reverence.
As nigh the royal Ráma came
With Lakshmaṇ and the Maithil dame,
He viewed the herds of gentle deer
Roaming the garden free from fear.
As through the sacred grove he trod
He viewed the seat of many a God,
Brahmá and Agni, Sun and Moon,
And His who sends each golden boon;
Here Vishṇu's stood, there Bhaga's shrine,
And there Mahendra's, Lord divine;
Here His who formed this earthly frame,
His there from whom all beings came.
Váyu's, and His who loves to hold
The great noose, Varuṇ mighty-souled:
Here was the Vasus' shrine to see,
Here that of sacred Gáyatrí,
The king of serpents here had place,
And he who rules the feathered race.
Here Kártikeya, warrior lord,
And there was Justice King adored.
Then with disciples girt about
The mighty saint himself came out:
Through fierce devotion bright as flame
Before the rest the Master came:
And then to Lakshmaṇ, fortune blest,
Ráma these hasty words addressed:
"Behold, Agastya's self draws near,
The mighty saint, whom all revere:
With spirit raised I meet my lord
With richest wealth of penance stored."

The strong-armed hero spake, and ran
Forward to meet the sunbright man.

Before him, as he came, he bent
And clasped his feet most reverent,
Then rearing up his stately height
Stood suppliant by the anchorite,
While Lakshmaṇ's strength and Sítá's grace
Stood by the pride of Raghu's race.

The sage his arms round Ráma threw
And welcomed him with honours due,
Asked, was all well, with question sweet,
And bade the hero to a seat.
With holy oil he fed the flame,
He brought the gifts which strangers claim,
And kindly waiting on the three
With honours due to high degree,
He gave with hospitable care
A simple hermit's woodland fare.
Then sat the reverend father, first
Of hermits, deep in duty versed.
And thus to suppliant Ráma, bred
In all the lore of virtue, said:
"Did the false hermit, Prince, neglect
To hail his guest with due respect,
He must,—the doom the perjured meet,—
His proper flesh hereafter eat.
A car-borne king, a lord who sways
The earth, and virtue's law obeys,
Worthy of highest honour, thou
Hast sought, dear guest, my cottage now."
He spoke: with fruit and hermit fare,
With every bloom the branches bare,
Agastya graced his honoured guest,
And thus with gentle words addressed:
"Accept this mighty bow, divine,
Whereon red gold and diamonds shine;
'Twas by the Heavenly Artist planned
For Vishṇu's own almighty hand;
This God-sent shaft of sunbright hue,
Whose deadly flight is ever true,
By Lord Mahendra given of yore:
This quiver with its endless store.

733

Keen arrows hurtling to their aim
Like kindled fires that flash and flame:
Accept, in golden sheath encased,
This sword with hilt of rich gold graced.
Armed with this best of bows
Lord Vishṇu slew his demon foes,
And mid the dwellers in the skies
Won brilliant glory for his prize.
The bow, the quivers, shaft, and sword
Received from me, O glorious lord:
These conquest to thine arm shall bring,
As thunder to the thunder's King."

The splendid hermit bade him take
The noble weapons as he spake,
And as the prince accepted each
In words like these renewed his speech:

CANTO

XIII

Agastya's Counsel

"O Ráma, great delight I feel,
Pleased, Lakshmaṇ, with thy faithful zeal,
That you within these shades I see
With Sítá come to honour me.
But wandering through the rough rude wild
Has wearied Janak's gentle child:
With labours of the way oppressed
The Maithil lady longs for rest.
Young, delicate, and soft, and fair,
Such toils as these untrained to bear,
Her wifely love the dame has led
The forest's troubled ways to tread.
Here, Ráma, see that naught annoy

Her easy hours of tranquil joy:
A glorious task has she assayed,
To follow thee through woodland shade.
Since first from Nature's hand she came,
A woman's mood is still the same,
When Fortune smiles, her love to show,
And leave her lord in want and woe.
No pity then her heart can feel,
She arms her soul with warrior's steel,
Swift as the storm or Feathered King,
Uncertain as the lightning's wing.
Not so thy spouse: her purer mind
Shrinks from the faults of womankind;
Like chaste Arundhatí above,
A paragon of faithful love.
Let these blest shades, dear Ráma, be
A home for Lakshman, her, and thee."

With raised hands reverently meek
He heard the holy hermit speak,
And humbly thus addressed the sire
Whose glory shone like kindled fire:

"How blest am I, what thanks I owe
That our great Master deigns to show
His favour, that his heart can be
Content with Lakshman, Sítá, me.
Show me, I pray, some spot of ground
Where thick trees wave and springs abound,
That I may raise my hermit cell
And there in tranquil pleasure dwell."

Then thus replied Agastya, best
Of hermits, to the chief's request:
When for a little he had bent
His thoughts, upon that prayer intent:

"Beloved son, four leagues away
Is Panchavatí bright and gay:
Thronged with its deer, most fair it looks
With berries, fruit, and water-brooks.

There build thee with thy brother's aid
A cottage in the quiet shade,
And faithful to thy sire's behest,
Obedient to the sentence, rest.
For well, O sinless chieftain, well
I know thy tale, how all befell:
Stern penance and the love I bore
Thy royal sire supply the lore.
To me long rites and fervid zeal
The wish that stirs thy heart reveal,
And hence my guest I bade thee be,
That this pure grove might shelter thee.

So now, thereafter, thus I speak:
The shades of Panchavaṭí seek;
That tranquil spot is bright and fair,
And Sítá will be happy there.
Not far remote from here it lies,
A grove to charm thy loving eyes,
Godávarí's pure stream is nigh:
There Sítá's days will sweetly fly.
Pure, lovely, rich in many a charm,
O hero of the mighty arm,
'Tis gay with every plant and fruit,
And throngs of gay buds never mute.
Thou, true to virtue's path, hast might
To screen each trusting anchorite,
And wilt from thy new home defend
The hermits who on thee depend.
Now yonder, Prince, direct thine eyes
Where dense Madhúka woods arise:
Pierce their dark shade, and issuing forth
Turn to a fig-tree on the north:
Then onward up a sloping mead
Flanked by a hill the way will lead:
There Panchavaṭí, ever gay
With ceaseless bloom, thy steps will stay."

The hermit ceased: the princely two
With seemly honours bade adieu:

With reverential awe each youth
Bowed to the saint whose word was truth,
And then, dismissed with Sítá, they
To Panchavaṭí took their way.
Thus when each royal prince had grasped
His warrior's mighty bow, and clasped
His quiver to his side,
With watchful eyes along the road
The glorious saint Agastya showed,
Dauntless in fight the brothers strode,
And Sítá with them hied.

C A N T O

XIV

Jatáyus

Then as the son of Raghu made
His way to Panchavaṭí's shade,
A mighty vulture he beheld
Of size and strength unparalleled.
The princes, when the bird they saw,
Approached with reverence and awe,
And as his giant form they eyed,
"Tell who thou art," in wonder cried.
The bird, as though their hearts to gain,
Addressed them thus in gentlest strain;
"In me, dear sons, the friend behold
Your royal father loved of old."

He spoke: nor long did Ráma wait
His sire's dear friend to venerate:
He bade the bird declare his name
And the high race of which he came.
When Raghu's son had spoken, he

Declared his name and pedigree,
His words prolonging to disclose
How all the things that be arose:

"List while I tell, O Raghu's son,
The first-born Fathers, one by one,
Great Lords of Life, whence all in earth
And all in heaven derive their birth.
First Kardam heads the glorious race
Where Vikrit holds the second place,
With Śesha, Sanśray next in line,
And Bahuputra's might divine.
Then Sthánu and Maríchi came,
Atri, and Kratu's forceful frame.
Pulastya followed, next to him
Angiras' name shall ne'er be dim.
Prachetas, Pulah next, and then
Daksha, Vivasvat praised of men:
Aríshtanemi next, and last
Kaśyap in glory unsurpassed.
From Daksha,—fame the tale has told—:
Three-score bright daughters sprang of old.
Of these fair-waisted nymphs the great
Lord Kaśyap sought and wedded eight,
Aditi, Diti, Kálaká,
Támrá, Danú, and Analá,
And Krodhavasá swift to ire,
And Manu glorious as her sire.
Then when the mighty Kaśyap cried
Delighted to each tender bride:
"Sons shalt thou bear, to rule the three
Great worlds, in might resembling me."

Aditi, Diti, and Danú
Obeyed his will as consorts true,
And Kálaká; but all the rest
Refused to hear their lord's behest.
First Aditi conceived, and she,
Mother of thirty Gods and three,
The Vasus and Ádityas bare,
Rudras, and Aśvins, heavenly pair.

738

Of Diti sprang the Daityas: fame
Delights to laud their ancient name.
In days of yore their empire dread
O'er earth and woods and ocean spread.
Danú was mother of a child,
O hero, Aśvagríva styled,
And Narak next and Kálak came
Of Kálaká, celestial dame.
Of Támrá, too, five daughters bright
In deathless glory sprang to light.
Ennobling fame still keeps alive
The titles of the lovely five:
Immortal honour still she claims
For Kraunchí, Bhasí, Śyení's names.
And wills not that the world forget
Śukí or Dhritaráshtrí yet.
Then Kraunchí bare the crane and owl,
And Bhásí tribes of water fowl:
Vultures and hawks that race through air
With storm-fleet pinions Śyení bare.
All swans and geese on mere and brook
Their birth from Dhritaráshtrí took,
And all the river-haunting brood
Of ducks, a countless multitude.
From Śukí Nalá sprang, who bare
Dame Vinatá surpassing fair.
From fiery Krodhavaśá, ten
Bright daughters sprang, O King of men:
Mrigí and Mrigamandá named,
Hari and Bhadramadá famed,
Śárdúlí, Śvetá fair to see,
Mátangí bright, and Surabhí,
Surasá marked with each fair sign,
And Kadrumá, all maids divine.
Mrigí, O Prince without a peer,
Was mother of the herds of deer,
The bear, the yak, the mountain roe
Their birth to Mrigamandá owe;
And Bhadramadá joyed to be
Mother of fair Irávatí,
Who bare Airávat, huge of mould,

Mid warders of the earth enrolled,
From Harí lordly lions trace,
With monkeys of the wild, their race.
From the great dame Śárdúlí styled
Sprung pards, Lángúrs, and tigers wild.
Mátangí, Prince, gave birth to all
Mátangas, elephants strong and tall,
And Śvetá bore the beasts who stand
One at each wind, earth's warder band.
Next Surabhí the Goddess bore
Two heavenly maids, O Prince, of yore,
Gandharví—dear to fame is she—
And her sweet sister Rohiṇí.
With kine this daughter filled each mead,
And bright Gandharví bore the steed.
Surasá bore the serpents: all
The snakes Kadrú their mother call.
Then Manu, high-souled Kaśyap's wife,
To all the race of men gave life,
The Bráhmans first, the Kshatriya caste,
Then Vaiśyas, and the Śúdras last.
Sprang from her mouth the Bráhman race;
Her chest the Kshatriyas' natal place:
The Vaiśyas from her thighs, 'tis said,
The Śúdras from her feet were bred.
From Analá all trees that hang
Their fair fruit-laden branches sprang.
The child of beauteous Śukí bore
Vinatá, as I taught before:
And Surasá and Kadrú were
Born of one dame, a noble pair.
Kadrú gave birth to countless snakes
That roam the earth in woods and brakes.
Aruṇ and Garuḍ swift of flight
By Vinatá were given to light,
And sons of Aruṇ red as morn
Sampati first, then I was born,
Me then, O tamer of the foe,
Jaṭáyus, son of Śyení, know.
Thy ready helper will I be,
And guard thy house, if thou agree:

When thou and Lakshmaṇ urge the chase
By Sítá's side shall be my place."
With courteous thanks for promised aid,
The prince, to rapture stirred,
Bent low, and due obeisance paid,
Embraced the royal bird.

He often in the days gone by
Had heard his father tell
How, linked with him in friendship's tie,
He loved Jaṭáyus well.
He hastened to his trusted friend
His darling to confide,
And through the wood his steps to bend
By strong Jaṭáyus' side.
On to the grove, with Lakshmaṇ near,
The prince his way pursued
To free those pleasant shades from fear
And slay the giant brood.

CANTO
XV

Panchavatí

A rrived at Panchavatí's shade
Where silvan life and serpents strayed,
Ráma in words like these addressed
Lakshmaṇ of vigour unrepressed:

"Brother, our home is here: behold
The grove of which the hermit told:
The bowers of Panchavatí see
Made fair by every blooming tree.
Now, brother, bend thine eyes around;
With skilful glance survey the ground:

Here be some spot selected, best
Approved for gentle hermits' rest,
Where thou, the Maithil dame, and I
May dwell while seasons sweetly fly.
Some pleasant spot be chosen where
Pure waters gleam and trees are fair,
Some nook where flowers and wood are found
And sacred grass and springs abound."

Then Lakshmaṇ, Sítá standing by,
Raised reverent hands, and made reply:

"A hundred years shall flee, and still
Will I obey my brother's will:
Select thyself a pleasant spot;
Be mine the care to rear the cot."
The glorious chieftain, pleased to hear
That loving speech that soothed his ear,
Selected with observant care
A spot with every charm most fair.
He stood within that calm retreat,
A shade for hermits' home most meet,
And thus Sumitrá's son addressed,
While his dear hand in his he pressed:

"See, see this smooth and lovely glade
Which flowery trees encircling shade:
Do thou, beloved Lakshmaṇ rear
A pleasant cot to lodge us here.
I see beyond that feathery brake
The gleaming of a lilied lake,
Where flowers in sunlike glory throw
Fresh odours from the wave below.
Agastya's words now find we true,
He told the charms which here we view:
Here are the trees that blossom o'er
Godávarí's most lovely shore.
Whose pleasant flood from side to side
With swans and geese is beautified,
And fair banks crowded with the deer

That steal from every covert near.
The peacock's cry is loud and shrill
From many a tall and lovely hill,
Green-belted by the trees that wave
Full blossoms o'er the rock and cave.
Like elephants whose huge fronts glow
With painted streaks, the mountains show
Long lines of gold and silver sheen
With copper's darker hues between.
With every tree each hill is graced,
Where creepers blossom interlaced.
Look where the Sál's long branches sway,
And palms their fanlike leaves display;
The date-tree and the Jak are near,
And their long stems Tamálas rear.
See the tall Mango lift his head,
Aśokas all their glory spread,
The Ketak her sweet buds unfold,
And Champacs hang their cups of gold.
The spot is pure and pleasant: here
Are multitudes of birds and deer.
O Lakshmaṇ, with our father's friend
What happy hours we here shall spend!"

He spoke: the conquering Lakshmaṇ heard,
Obedient to his brother's word.
Raised by his toil a cottage stood
To shelter Ráma in the wood,
Of ample size, with leaves o'erlaid,
Of hardened earth the walls were made.
The strong bamboos his hands had felled
For pillars fair the roof upheld,
And rafter, beam, and lath supplied
Well interwrought from side to side.
Then Śamí boughs he deftly spread
Enlaced with knotted cord o'erhead,
Well thatched above from ridge to eaves
With holy grass, and reed, and leaves.
The mighty chief with careful toil
Had cleared the ground and smoothed the soil

Where now, his loving labour done,
Rose a fair home for Raghu's son.
Then when his work was duly wrought,
Godávarís sweet stream he sought,
Bathed, plucked the lilies, and a store
Of fruit and berries homeward bore.
Then sacrifice he duly paid,
And wooed the Gods their hopes to aid,
And then to Ráma proudly showed
The cot prepared for his abode.
Then Raghu's son with Sítá gazed
Upon the home his hands had raised,
And transport thrilled his bosom through
His leafy hermitage to view.
The glorious son of Raghu round
His brother's neck his arms enwound,
And thus began his sweet address
Of deep-felt joy and gentleness:
"Well pleased am I, dear lord, to see
This noble work performed by thee.
For this,—sole grace I can bestow,—
About thy neck mine arms I throw.
So wise art thou, thy breast is filled
With grateful thoughts, in duty skilled,
Our mighty father, free from stain,
In thee, his offspring, lives again."

Thus spoke the prince, who lent a grace
To fortune, pride of Raghu's race;
Then in that spot whose pleasant shade
Gave store of fruit, content he stayed.
With Lakshmaṇ and his Maithil spouse
He spent his day's neath sheltering boughs,
As happy as a God on high
Lives in his mansion in the sky.

Winter

W hile there the high-souled hero spent
His tranquil hours in sweet content,
The glowing autumn passed, and then
Came winter so beloved of men.

One morn, to bathe, at break of day
To the fair stream he took his way.
Behind him, with the Maithil dame
Bearing a pitcher Lakshmaṇ came,
And as he went the mighty man
Thus to his brother chief began:

"The time is come, to thee more dear
Than all the months that mark the year:
The gracious seasons' joy and pride,
By which the rest are glorified.
A robe of hoary rime is spread
O'er earth, with corn engarlanded.
The streams we loved no longer please,
But near the fire we take our ease.
Now pious men to God and shade
Offer young corn's fresh sprouted blade,
And purge away their sins with rice
Bestowed in humble sacrifice.
Rich stores of milk delight the swain,
And hearts are cheered that longed for gain,
Proud kings whose breasts for conquests glow
Lead bannered troops to smite the foe.
Dark is the north: the Lord of Day
To Yáma's south has turned away:
And she—sad widow—shines no more,

745

Reft of the bridal mark she wore.
Himálaya's hill, ordained of old
The treasure-house of frost and cold,
Scarce conscious of the feebler glow,
Is truly now the Lord of Snow.
Warmed by the noontide's genial rays
Delightful are the glorious days:
But how we shudder at the chill
Of evening shadows and the rill!
How weak the sun, how cold the breeze!
How white the rime on grass and trees!
The leaves are sere, the woods have lost
Their blossoms killed by nipping frost.
Neath open skies we sleep no more:
December's nights with rime are hoar:
Their triple watch in length extends
With hours the shortened daylight lends.
No more the moon's sun-borrowed rays
Are bright, involved in misty haze,
As when upon the mirror's sheen
The breath's obscuring cloud is seen.
E'en at the full the faint beams fail
To struggle through the darksome veil:
Changed like her hue, they want the grace
That parts not yet from Sítá's face.
Cold is the western wind, but how
Its piercing chill is heightened now,
Blowing at early morning twice
As furious with its breath of ice!
See how the dewy tears they weep
The barley, wheat, and woodland steep,
Where, as the sun goes up the sky,
The curlew and the sáras cry.
See where the rice plants scarce uphold
Their full ears tinged with paly gold,
Bending their ripe heads slowly down
Fair as the date tree's flowery crown.
Though now the sun has mounted high
Seeking the forehead of the sky,
Such mist obscures his struggling beams,

No bigger than the moon he seems.
Though weak at first, his rays at length
Grow pleasant in their noonday strength,
And where a while they chance to fall
Fling a faint splendour over all.

See, o'er the woods where grass is wet
With hoary drops that cling there yet,
With soft light clothing earth and bough
There steals a tender glory now.
Yon elephant who longs to drink,
Still standing on the river's brink,
Plucks back his trunk in shivering haste
From the cold wave he fain would taste.
The very fowl that haunt the mere
Stand doubtful on the bank, and fear
To dip them in the wintry wave
As cowards dread to meet the brave.
The frost of night, the rime of dawn
Bind flowerless trees and glades of lawn:
Benumbed in apathetic chill
Of icy chains they slumber still.
You hear the hidden sáras cry
From floods that wrapped in vapour lie,
And frosty-shining sands reveal
Where the unnoticed rivers steal.
The hoary rime of dewy night,
And suns that glow with tempered light
Lend fresh cool flavours to the rill
That sparkles from the topmost hill.
The cold has killed the lily's pride:
Leaf, filament, and flower have died:
With chilling breath rude winds have blown,
The withered stalk is left alone.
At this gay time, O noblest chief,
The faithful Bharat, worn by grief,
Lives in the royal town where he
Spends weary hours for love of thee.
From titles, honour, kingly sway,
From every joy he turns away:

Couched on cold earth, his days are passed
With scanty fare and hermit's fast.
This moment from his humble bed
He lifts, perhaps, his weary head,
And girt by many a follower goes
To bathe where silver Sarjú flows.
How, when the frosty morn is dim,
Shall Sarjú be a bath for him
Nursed with all love and tender care,
So delicate and young and fair.
How bright his hue! his brilliant eye
With the broad lotus leaf may vie.
By fortune stamped for happy fate,
His graceful form is tall and straight.
In duty skilled, his words are truth:
He proudly rules each lust of youth.
Though his strong arm smites down the foe,
In gentle speech his accents flow.
Yet every joy has he resigned
And cleaves to thee with heart and mind.
Thus by the deeds that he has done
A name in heaven has Bharat won,
For in his life he follows yet
Thy steps, O banished anchoret.
Thus faithful Bharat, nobly wise,
The proverb of the world belies:
"No men, by mothers' guidance led,
The footsteps of their fathers tread."
How could Kaikeyí, blest to be
Spouse of the king our sire, and see
A son like virtuous Bharat, blot
Her glory with so foul a plot!"

Thus in fraternal love he spoke,
And from his lips reproaches broke:
But Ráma grieved to hear him chide
The absent mother, and replied:

"Cease, O beloved, cease to blame
Our royal father's second dame.
Still speak of Bharat first in place

Of old Ikshváku's princely race.
My heart, so firmly bent but now
To dwell in woods and keep my vow,
Half melting as I hear thee speak
Of Bharat's love, grows soft and weak,
With tender joy I bring to mind
His speeches ever sweet and kind.
That dear as Amrit took the sense
With most enchanting influence.
Ah, when shall I, no more to part,
Meet Bharat of the mighty heart?
When, O my brother, when shall we
The good and brave Śatrughna see?"
Thus as he poured his fond lament
The son of Raghu onward went:
They reached the river, and the three
Bathed them in fair Godávarí.
Libations of the stream they paid
To every deity and shade,
With hymns of praise, the Sun on high
And sinless Gods to glorify.
Fresh from the purifying tide
Resplendent Ráma came,
With Lakshman ever by his side,
And the sweet Maithil dame.
So Rudra shines by worlds adored,
In glory undefiled,
When Nandi stands beside his lord,
And King Himálaya's child.

CANTO
XVII

Súrpanakhá

The bathing and the prayer were o'er;
   He turned him from the grassy shore,
   And with his brother and his spouse
Sought his fair home beneath the boughs.
Sítá and Lakshman by his side,
On to his cot the hero hied,
And after rites at morning due
Within the leafy shade withdrew.

Then, honoured by the devotees,
As royal Ráma sat at ease,
With Sítá near him, o'er his head
A canopy of green boughs spread,
He shone as shines the Lord of Night
By Chitrá's side, his dear delight.
With Lakshman there he sat and told
Sweet stories of the days of old,
And as the pleasant time he spent
With heart upon each tale intent,
A giantess, by fancy led,
Came wandering to his leafy shed.
Fierce Súrpanakhá,—her of yore
The Ten-necked tyrant's mother bore,—
Saw Ráma with his noble mien
Bright as the Gods in heaven are seen;
Him from whose brow a glory gleamed,
Like lotus leaves his full eyes beamed:
Long-armed, of elephantine gait,
With hair close coiled in hermit plait:
In youthful vigour, nobly framed,
By glorious marks a king proclaimed:

750

Like some bright lotus lustrous-hued,
With young Kandarpa's grace endued:
As there like Indra's self he shone,
She loved the youth she gazed upon.
She grim of eye and foul of face
Loved his sweet glance and forehead's grace:
She of unlovely figure, him
Of stately form and shapely limb:
She whose dim locks disordered hung,
Him whose bright hair on high brows clung:
She whose fierce accents counselled fear,
Him whose soft tones were sweet to hear:
She whose dire form with age was dried,
Him radiant in his youthful pride:
She whose false lips maintained the wrong,
Him in the words of virtue strong:
She cruel-hearted, stained with sin,
Him just in deed and pure within.
She, hideous fiend, a thing to hate,
Him formed each eye to captivate:
Fierce passion in her bosom woke,
And thus to Raghu's son she spoke:

"With matted hair above thy brows,
With bow and shaft and this thy spouse,
How hast thou sought in hermit dress
The giant-haunted wilderness?
What dost thou here? The cause explain:
Why art thou come, and what to gain?"
As Súrpanakhá questioned so,
Ráma, the terror of the foe,
In answer to the monster's call,
With fearless candour told her all.
"King Daśaratha reigned of old,
Like Gods celestial brave and bold.
I am his eldest son and heir,
And Ráma is the name I bear.
This brother, Lakshman, younger born,
Most faithful love to me has sworn.
My wife, this princess, dear to fame,
Is Sitá the Videhan dame.

751

Obedient to my sire's behest
And by the queen my mother pressed,
To keep the law and merit win,
I sought this wood to harbour in.
But speak, for I of thee in turn
Thy name, and race, and sire would learn.
Thou art of giant race, I ween.
Changing at will thy form and mien.
Speak truly, and the cause declare
That bids thee to these shades repair."

Thus Ráma spoke: the demon heard,
And thus replied by passion spurred:
"Of giant race, what form soe'er
My fancy wills, 'tis mine to wear.
Named Śúrpaṇakhá here I stray,
And where I walk spread wild dismay.
King Rávaṇ is my brother: fame
Has taught perchance his dreaded name,
Strong Kumbhakarṇa slumbering deep
In chains of never-ending sleep:
Vibhíshaṇ of the duteous mind,
In needs unlike his giant kind:
Dúshaṇ and Khara, brave and bold
Whose fame by every tongue is told:
Their might by mine is far surpassed;
But when, O best of men, I cast
These fond eyes on thy form, I see
My chosen love and lord in thee.
Endowed with wondrous might am I:
Where'er my fancy leads I fly.
The poor misshapen Sítá leave,
And me, thy worthier bride receive.
Look on my beauty, and prefer
A spouse more meet than one like her:
I'll eat that ill-formed woman there:
Thy brother too her fate shall share.
But come, beloved, thou shalt roam
With me through all our woodland home;
Each varied grove with me shalt seek,
And gaze upon each mountain peak."

As thus she spoke, the monster gazed
With sparkling eyes where passion blazed:
Then he, in lore of language learned,
This answer eloquent returned:

CANTO

XVIII

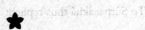

The Mutilation

On her ensnared in Káma's net
His eyes the royal Ráma set,

And thus, her passion to beguile,
Addressed her with a gentle smile:

"I have a wife: behold her here,
My Sítá ever true and dear:
And one like thee will never brook
Upon a rival spouse to look.
But there my brother Lakshmaṇ stands:
Unchained is he by nuptial bands:
A youth heroic, loved of all,
Gracious and gallant, fair and tall.
With winning looks, most nobly bred,
Unmatched till now, he longs to wed.
Meet to enjoy thy youthful charms,
O take him to thy loving arms.
Enamoured on his bosom lie,
Fair damsel of the radiant eye,
As the warm sunlight loves to rest
Upon her darling Meru's breast."

The hero spoke, the monster heard,
While passion still her bosom stirred.
Away from Ráma's side she broke,

And thus in turn to Lakshman spoke:
"Come, for thy bride take me who shine
In fairest grace that suits with thine.
Thou by my side from grove to grove
Of Dandak's wild in bliss shalt rove."

Then Lakshman, skilled in soft address,
Wooed by the amorous giantess,
With art to turn her love aside,
To Súrpanakhá thus replied:

"And can so high a dame agree
The slave-wife of a slave to be?
I, lotus-hued! in good and ill
Am bondsman to my brother's will.
Be thou, fair creature radiant-eyed,
My honoured brother's younger bride:
With faultless tint and dainty limb,
A happy wife, bring joy to him.
He from his spouse grown old and grey,
Deformed, untrue, will turn away,
Her withered charms will gladly leave,
And to his fair young darling cleave.
For who could be so fond and blind,
O loveliest of all female kind,
To love another dame and slight
Thy beauties rich in all delight?"

Thus Lakshman praised in scornful jest
The long-toothed fiend with loathly breast,
Who fondly heard his speech, nor knew
His mocking words were aught but true.
Again inflamed with love she fled
To Ráma, in his leafy shed
Where Sítá rested by his side,
And to the mighty victor cried:

"What, Ráma, canst thou blindly cling
To this old false misshapen thing?
Wilt thou refuse the charms of youth
For withered breast and grinning tooth!

Canst thou this wretched creature prize
And look on me with scornful eyes?
This aged crone this very hour
Before thy face will I devour:
Then joyous, from all rivals free.
Through Daṇḍak will I stray with thee."

She spoke, and with a glance of flame
Rushed on the fawn-eyed Maithil dame:
So would a horrid meteor mar
Fair Rohiṇí's soft beaming star.
But as the furious fiend drew near,
Like Death's dire noose which chills with fear,
The mighty chief her purpose stayed,
And spoke, his brother to upbraid:
"Ne'er should we jest with creatures rude,
Of savage race and wrathful mood.
Think, Lakshmaṇ, think how nearly slain
My dear Videhan breathes again.
Let not the hideous wretch escape
Without a mark to mar her shape.
Strike, lord of men, the monstrous fiend,
Deformed, and foul, and evil-miened."

He spoke: then Lakshmaṇ's wrath rose high,
And there before his brother's eye,
He drew that sword which none could stay,
And cleft her nose and ears away.
Noseless and earless, torn and maimed,
With fearful shrieks the fiend exclaimed,
And frantic in her wild distress
Resought the distant wilderness.
Deformed, terrific, huge, and dread,
As on she moved, her gashes bled,
And groan succeeded groan as loud
As roars, ere rain, the thunder cloud.
Still on the fearful monster passed,
While streams of blood kept falling fast,
And with a roar, and arms outspread
Within the boundless wood she fled.
To Janasthán the monster flew;

755

Fierce Khara there she found,
With chieftains of the giant crew
In thousands ranged around.
Before his awful feet she bent
And fell with piercing cries,
As when a bolt in swift descent
Comes flashing from the skies.
There for a while with senses dazed
Silent she lay and scared:
At length her drooping head she raised,
And all the tale declared,
How Ráma, Lakshmaṇ, and the dame
Had reached that lonely place:
Then told her injuries and shame,
And showed her bleeding face.

CANTO
XIX

The Rousing of Khara

When Khara saw his sister lie
    With blood-stained limbs and troubled eye,
Wild fury in his bosom woke,
And thus the monstrous giant spoke;

"Arise, my sister; cast away
This numbing terror and dismay,
And straight the impious hand declare
That marred those features once so fair.
For who his finger tip will lay
On the black snake in childish play,
And unattacked, with idle stroke
His poison-laden fang provoke?
Ill-fated fool, he little knows

Death's noose around his neck he throws,
Who rashly met thee, and a draught
Of life-destroying poison quaffed.
Strong, fierce as death, 'twas thine to choose
Thy way at will, each shape to use;
In power and might like one of us:
What hand has maimed and marred thee thus?
What God or fiend this deed has wrought,
What bard or sage of lofty thought
Was armed with power supremely great
Thy form to mar and mutilate?
In all the worlds not one I see
Would dare a deed to anger me:
Not Indra's self, the Thousand-eyed,
Beneath whose hand fierce Páka died.
My life-destroying darts this day
His guilty breath shall rend away,
E'en as the thirsty wild swan drains
Each milk-drop that the wave retains.
Whose blood in foaming streams shall burst
O'er the dry ground which lies athirst,
When by my shafts transfixed and slain
He falls upon the battle plain?
From whose dead corpse shall birds of air
The mangled flesh and sinews tear,
And in their gory feast delight,
When I have slain him in the fight?
Not God or bard or wandering ghost,
No giant of our mighty host
Shall step between us, or avail
To save the wretch when I assail.
Collect each scattered sense, recall
Thy troubled thoughts, and tell me all.
What wretch attacked thee in the way,
And quelled thee in victorious fray?"

His breast with burning fury fired,
Thus Khara of the fiend inquired:
And then with many a tear and sigh
Thus Śúrpaṇakhá made reply:
"'Tis Daśaratha's sons, a pair

757

Strong, resolute, and young, and fair:
In coats of dark and blackdeer's hide,
And like the radiant lotus eyed:
On berries roots and fruit they feed,
And lives of saintly virtue lead:
With ordered senses undefiled,
Ráma and Lakshmaṇ are they styled.
Fair as the Minstrels' King are they,
And stamped with signs of regal sway.
I know not if the heroes trace
Their line from Gods or Dánav race.
There by these wondering eyes between
The noble youths a dame was seen,
Fair, blooming, young, with dainty waist,
And all her bright apparel graced.
For her with ready heart and mind
The royal pair their strength combined,
And brought me to this last distress,
Like some lost woman, comfortless.
Perfidious wretch! my soul is fain
Her foaming blood and theirs to drain.
O let me head the vengeful fight,
And with this hand my murderers smite.
Come, brother, hasten to fulfil
This longing of my eager will.
On to the battle! Let me drink
Their lifeblood as to earth they sink."

Then Khara, by his sister pressed,
Inflamed with fury, gave his hest
To twice seven giants of his crew,
Fierce as the God of death to view:

'Two men equipped with arms, who wear
Deerskin and bark and matted hair,
Leading a beauteous dame, have strayed
To the wild gloom of Daṇḍak's shade.
These men, this cursed woman slay,
And hasten back without delay,
That this my sister's lips may be
Red with the lifeblood of the three.

Giants, my wounded sister longs
To take this vengeance for her wrongs.
With speed her dearest wish fulfil,
And with your might these creatures kill.
Soon as your matchless strength shall lay
These brothers dead in battle fray,
She in triumphant joy will laugh,
And their hearts' blood delighted quaff."

The giants heard the words he said,
And forth with Śúrpaṇakhá sped,
As mighty clouds in autumn fly
Urged by the wind along the sky.

CANTO
XX

The Giants' Death

Fierce Śúrpaṇakhá with her train
   To Ráma's dwelling came again,
   And to the eager giants showed
Where Sítá and the youths abode.
Within the leafy cot they spied
The hero by his consort's side,
And faithful Lakshmaṇ ready still
To wait upon his brother's will.

Then noble Ráma raised his eye
And saw the giants standing nigh,
And then, as nearer still they pressed.
His glorious brother thus addressed,
"Be thine a while, my brother dear,
To watch o'er Sítá's safety here,
And I will slay these creatures who
The footsteps of my spouse pursue."

He spoke, and reverent Lakshmaṇ heard
Submissive to his brother's word.
The son of Raghu, virtuous-souled,
Strung his great bow adorned with gold,
And, with the weapon in his hand,
Addressed him to the giant band:
"Ráma and Lakshmaṇ we, who spring
From Daśaratha, mighty king;
We dwell a while with Sítá here
In Daṇḍak forest wild and drear.
On woodland roots and fruit we feed,
And lives of strictest rule we lead.
Say why would ye our lives oppress
Who sojourn in the wilderness.
Sent hither by the hermits' prayer
With bow and darts unused to spare,
For vengeance am I come to slay
Your sinful band in battle fray.
Rest as ye are: remain content,
Nor try the battle's dire event.
Unless your offered lives ye spurn,
O rovers of the night, return."

They listened while the hero spoke,
And fury in each breast awoke.
The Bráhman-slayers raised on high
Their mighty spears and made reply:
They spoke with eyes aglow with ire,
While Ráma's burnt with vengeful tire,
And answered thus, in fury wild,
That peerless chief whose tones were mild:

"Nay thou hast angered, overbold,
Khara our lord, the mighty-souled,
And for thy sin, in battle strife
Shalt yield to us thy forfeit life.
No power hast thou alone to stand
Against the numbers of our band.
'Twere vain to match thy single might
Against us in the front of fight.
When we equipped for fight advance

With brandished pike and mace and lance,
Thou, vanquished in the desperate field,
Thy bow, thy strength, thy life shalt yield."
With bitter words and threatening mien
Thus furious spoke the fierce fourteen,
And raising scimitar and spear
On Ráma rushed in wild career.
Their levelled spears the giant crew
Against the matchless hero threw.
His bow the son of Raghu bent,
And twice seven shafts to meet them sent,
And every javelin sundered fell
By the bright darts he aimed so well.

The hero saw: his anger grew
To fury: from his side he drew
Fresh sunbright arrows pointed keen,
In number, like his foes, fourteen.
His bow he grasped, the string he drew,
And gazing on the giant crew,
As Indra casts the levin, so
Shot forth his arrows at the foe.
The hurtling arrows, stained with gore,
Through the fiends' breasts a passage tore,
And in the earth lay buried deep
As serpents through an ant-hill creep
Like trees uptorn by stormy blast
The shattered fiends to earth were cast,
And there with mangled bodies they,
Bathed in their blood and breathless, lay.

With fainting heart and furious eye
The demon saw her champions die.
With drying wounds that scarcely bled
Back to her brother's home she fled.
Oppressed with pain, with loud lament
At Khara's feet the monster bent.
There like a plant whence slowly come
The trickling drops of oozy gum,
With her grim features pale with pain
She poured her tears in ceaseless rain,

There routed Śúrpaṇakhá lay,
And told her brother all,
The issue of the bloody fray,
Her giant champions' fall.

XXI

The Rousing of Khara

Low in the dust he saw her lie,
　　And Khara's wrath grew fierce and high.
　　Aloud he cried to her who came
Disgracefully with baffled aim:
"I sent with thee at thy request
The bravest of my giants, best
Of all who feed upon the slain:
Why art thou weeping here again?
Still to their master's interest true,
My faithful, noble, loyal crew,
Though slaughtered in the bloody fray,
Would yet their monarch's word obey.
Now I, my sister, fain would know
The cause of this thy fear and woe,
Why like a snake thou writhest there,
Calling for aid in wild despair.
Nay, lie not thus in lowly guise:
Cast off thy weakness and arise!"

With soothing words the giant chief
Assuaged the fury of her grief.
Her weeping eyes she slowly dried
And to her brother thus replied:
"I sought thee in my shame and fear
With severed nose and mangled ear:

762

My gashes like a river bled,
I sought thee and was comforted.

Those twice seven giants, brave and strong,
Thou sentest to avenge the wrong,
To lay the savage Ráma low,
And Lakshman who misused me so.
But ah, the shafts of Ráma through
The bodies of my champions flew:
Though madly fierce their spears they plied,
Beneath his conquering might they died.
I saw them, famed for strength and speed,
I saw my heroes fall and bleed:
Great trembling seized my every limb
At the great deed achieved by him.
In trouble, horror, doubt, and dread,
Again to thee for help I fled.
While terror haunts my troubled sight,
I seek thee, rover of the night.
And canst thou not thy sister free
From this wide waste of troublous sea
Whose sharks are doubt and terror, where
Each wreathing wave is dark despair?
Low lie on earth thy giant train
By ruthless Ráma's arrows slain,
And all the mighty demons, fed
On blood, who followed me are dead.
Now if within thy breast may be
Pity for them and love for me,
If thou, O rover of the night,
Have valour and with him can fight,
Subdue the giants' cruel foe
Who dwells where Daṇḍak's thickets grow.
But if thine arm in vain assay
This queller of his foes to slay,
Now surely here before thine eyes,
Wronged and ashamed thy sister dies.
Too well, alas, too well I see
That, strong in war as thou mayst be,
Thou canst not in the battle stand

When Ráma meets thee hand to hand.
Go forth, thou hero but in name,
Assuming might thou canst not claim;
Call friend and kin, no longer stay:
Away from Janasthán, away!
Shame of thy race! the weak alone
Beneath thine arm may sink o'erthrown:
Fly Ráma and his brother: they
Are men too strong for thee to slay.
How canst thou hope, O weak and base,
To make this grove thy dwelling-place?
With Ráma's might unmeet to vie,
O'ermastered thou wilt quickly die.
A hero strong in valorous deed
Is Ráma, Daśaratha's seed:
And scarce of weaker might than he
His brother chief who mangled me."

Thus wept and wailed in deep distress
The grim misshapen giantess:
Before her brother's feet she lay
O'erwhelmed with grief, and swooned away.

Khara's Wrath

Roused by the taunting words she spoke,
The mighty Khara's wrath awoke,
And there, while giants girt him round,
In these fierce words an utterance found:

"I cannot, peerless one, contain
Mine anger at this high disdain,
Galling as salt when sprinkled o'er

The rawness of a bleeding sore.
Ráma in little count I hold,
Weak man whose days are quickly told.
The caitiff with his life to-day
For all his evil deeds shall pay.
Dry, sister, dry each needless tear,
Stint thy lament and banish fear,
For Ráma and his brother go
This day to Yáma's realm below.
My warrior's axe shall stretch him slain,
Ere set of sun, upon the plain,
Then shall thy sated lips be red
With his warm blood in torrents shed."
As Khara's speech the demon heard,
With sudden joy her heart was stirred:
She fondly praised him as the boast
And glory of the giant host.
First moved to ire by taunts and stings,
Now soothed by gentle flatterings,
To Dúshaṇ, who his armies led,
The demon Khara spoke, and said:

"Friend, from the host of giants call
Full fourteen thousand, best of all,
Slaves of my will, of fearful might,
Who never turn their backs in fight:
Fiends who rejoice to slay and mar,
Dark as the clouds of autumn are:
Make ready quickly, O my friend,
My chariot and the bows I bend.
My swords, my shafts of brilliant sheen,
My divers lances long and keen.
On to the battle will I lead
These heroes of Pulastya's seed,
And thus, O famed for warlike skill,
Ráma my wicked foeman kill."

He spoke, and ere his speech was done,
His chariot glittering like the sun,
Yoked and announced, by Dúshan's care,
With dappled steeds was ready there.

High as a peak from Meru rent
It burned with golden ornament:
The pole of lazulite, of gold
Were the bright wheels whereon it rolled.
With gold and moonstone blazoned o'er,
Fish, flowers, trees, rocks, the panels bore;
Auspicious birds embossed thereon,
And stars in costly emblem shone.
O'er flashing swords his banner hung,
And sweet bells, ever tinkling, swung.

That mighty host with sword and shield
And oar was ready for the field:
And Khara saw, and Dúshan cried,
"Forth to the fight, ye giants, ride."
Then banners waved, and shield and sword
Flashed as the host obeyed its lord.
From Janasthán they sallied out
With eager speed, and din, and shout,
Armed with the mace for close attacks,
The bill, the spear, the battle-axe,
Steel quoit and club that flashed afar,
Huge bow and sword and scimitar,
The dart to pierce, the bolt to strike,
The murderous bludgeon, lance, and pike.
So forth from Janasthán, intent
On Khara's will, the monsters went.
He saw their awful march: not far
Behind the host he drove his car.
Ware of his master's will, to speed
The driver urged each gold-decked steed.
Then forth the warrior's coursers sprang,
And with tumultuous murmur rang
Each distant quarter of the sky
And realms that intermediate lie.
High and more high within his breast
His pride triumphant rose,
While terrible as Death he pressed
Onward to slay his foes,
"More swiftly yet," as on they fled,

He cried in thundering tones
Loud as a cloud that overhead
Hails down a flood of stones.

CANTO

XXIII

The Omens

As forth upon its errand went
That huge ferocious armament,
An awful cloud, in dust and gloom,
With threatening thunders from its womb
Poured in sad augury a flood
Of rushing water mixt with blood.
The monarch's steeds, though strong and fleet,
Stumbled and fell: and yet their feet
Passed o'er the bed of flowers that lay
Fresh gathered on the royal way.
No gleam of sunlight struggled through
The sombre pall of midnight hue,
Edged with a line of bloody red,
Like whirling torches overhead.
A vulture, fierce, of mighty size.
Terrific with his cruel eyes,
Perched on the staff enriched with gold,
Whence hung the flag in many a fold.
Each ravening bird, each beast of prey
Where Janasthán's wild thickets lay,
Rose with a long discordant cry
And gathered as the host went by.
And from the south long, wild, and shrill,
Came spirit voices boding ill.
Like elephants in frantic mood,
Vast clouds terrific, sable-hued,

Hid all the sky where'er they bore
Their load of water mixt with gore.
Above, below, around were spread
Thick shades of darkness strange and dread,
Nor could the wildered glance descry
A point or quarter of the sky.
Then came o'er heaven a sanguine hue,
Though evening's flush not yet was due,
While each ill-omened bird that flies
Assailed the king with harshest cries.
There screamed the vulture and the crane,
And the loud jackal shrieked again.
Each hideous thing that bodes aright
Disaster in the coming fight,
With gaping mouth that hissed and flamed,
The ruin of the host proclaimed.
Eclipse untimely reft away
The brightness of the Lord of Day,
And near his side was seen to glow
A mace-like comet boding woe.
Then while the sun was lost to view
A mighty wind arose and blew,
And stars like fireflies shed their light,
Nor waited for the distant night.
The lilies drooped, the brooks were dried,
The fish and birds that swam them died,
And every tree that was so fair
With flower and fruit was stripped and bare.
The wild wind ceased, yet, raised on high,
Dark clouds of dust involved the sky.
In doleful twitter long sustained
The restless Sárikás complained,
And from the heavens with flash and flame
Terrific meteors roaring came.
Earth to her deep foundation shook
With rock and tree and plain and brook,
As Khara with triumphant shout,
Borne in his chariot, sallied out.
His left arm throbbed: he knew full well
That omen, and his visage fell.
Each awful sign the giant viewed,

768

And sudden tears his eye bedewed.
Care on his brow sat chill and black,
Yet mad with wrath he turned not back.
Upon each fearful sight that raised
The shuddering hair the chieftain gazed,
And laughing in his senseless pride
Thus to his giant legions cried:
"By sense of mightiest strength upborne,
These feeble signs I laugh to scorn.
I could bring down the stars that shine
In heaven with these keen shafts of mine.
Impelled by warlike fury I
Could cause e'en Death himself to die.

I will not seek my home again
Until my pointed shafts have slain
This Raghu's son so fierce in pride,
And Lakshmaṇ by his brother's side.
And she, my sister, she for whom
These sons of Raghu meet their doom,
She with delighted lips shall drain
The lifeblood of her foemen slain.
Fear not for me: I ne'er have known
Defeat, in battle overthrown.
Fear not for me, O giants; true
Are the proud words I speak to you.
The king of Gods who rules on high,
If wild Airávat bore him nigh,
Should fall before me bolt in hand:
And shall these two my wrath withstand!"

He ended and the giant host
Who heard their chief's triumphant boast,
Rejoiced with equal pride elate,
Entangled in the noose of Fate.

Then met on high in bright array,
With eyes that longed to see the fray,
God and Gandharva, sage and saint,
With beings pure from earthly taint.
Blest for good works aforetime wrought,

769

Thus each to other spake his thought:
"Now joy to Bráhmans, joy to kine,
And all whom world count half divine!
May Raghu's offspring slay in fight
Pulastya's sons who roam by night!"
In words like these and more, the best
Of high-souled saints their hopes expressed,
Bending their eager eyes from where
Car-borne with Gods they rode in air.
Beneath them stretching far, they viewed
The giants' death-doomed multitude.
They saw where, urged with fury, far
Before the host rolled Khara's car,
And close beside their leader came
Twelve giant peers of might and fame.
Four other chiefs before the rest
Behind their leader Dúshaṇ pressed.
Impetuous, cruel, dark, and dread,
All thirsting for the fray,
The hosts of giant warriors sped
Onward upon their way.
With eager speed they reached the spot
Where dwelt the princely two,—
Like planets in a league to blot
The sun and moon from view.

CANTO

XXIV

The Host in Sight

While Khara, urged by valiant rage,
Drew near that little hermitage,
Those wondrous signs in earth and sky
Smote on each prince's watchful eye.
When Ráma saw those signs of woe

Fraught with destruction to the foe,
With bold impatience scarce repressed
His brother chief he thus addressed:

"These fearful signs, my brother bold,
Which threaten all our foes, behold:
All laden, as they strike the view,
With ruin to the fiendish crew.
The angry clouds are gathering fast,
Their skirts with dusty gloom o'ercast,
And harsh with loud-voiced thunder, rain
Thick drops of blood upon the plain.
See, burning for the coming fight,
My shafts with wreaths of smoke are white,
And my great bow embossed with gold
Throbs eager for the master's hold.
Each bird that through the forest flies
Sends out its melancholy cries.
All signs foretell the dangerous strife,
The jeopardy of limb and life.
Each sight, each sound gives warning clear
That foemen meet and death is near.
But courage, valiant brother! well
The throbbings of mine arm foretell
That ruin waits the hostile powers,
And triumph in the fight is ours.
I hail the welcome omen: thou
Art bright of face and clear of brow.
For Lakshman, when the eye can trace
A cloud upon the warrior's face
Stealing the cheerful light away,
His life is doomed in battle fray.
List, brother, to that awful cry:
With shout and roar the fiends draw nigh.
With thundering beat of many a drum
The savage-hearted giants come.
The wise who value safety know
To meet, prepared, the coming blow:
In paths of prudence trained aright
They watch the stroke before it smite.
Take thou thine arrows and thy bow,

771

And with the Maithil lady go
For shelter to the mountain cave
Where thickest trees their branches wave.
I will not have thee, Lakshmaṇ, say
One word in answer, but obey.
By all thy honour for these feet
Of mine, dear brother, I entreat.
Thy warlike arm, I know could, smite
To death these rovers of the night;
But I this day would fight alone
Till all the fiends be overthrown."

He spake: and Lakshmaṇ answered naught:
His arrows and his bow he brought,
And then with Sítá following hied
For shelter to the mountain side.
As Lakshmaṇ and the lady through
The forest to the cave withdrew,
"'Tis well," cried Ráma. Then he braced
His coat of mail around his waist.
When, bright as blazing fire, upon
His mighty limbs that armour shone,
The hero stood like some great light
Uprising in the dark of night.
His dreadful shafts were by his side;
His trusty bow he bent and plied,
Prepared he stood: the bowstring rang,
Filling the welkin with the clang.

The high-souled Gods together drew
The wonder of the fight to view,
The saints made free from spot and stain,
And bright Gandharvas' heavenly train.
Each glorious sage the assembly sought,
Each saint divine of loftiest thought,
And filled with zeal for Ráma's sake.
Thus they whose deeds were holy spake:

"Now be it well with Bráhmans, now
Well with the worlds and every cow!
Let Ráma in the deadly fray

772

The fiends who walk in darkness slay,
As He who bears the discus slew
The chieftains of the Asur crew."

Then each with anxious glances viewed
His fellow and his speech renewed:
"There twice seven thousand giants stand
With impious heart and cruel hand:
Here Ráma stands, by virtue known:
How can the hero fight alone?"

Thus royal sage and Bráhman saint,
Spirit, and Virtue free from taint,
And all the Gods of heaven who rode
On golden cars, their longing showed.
Their hearts with doubt and terror rent,
They saw the giants' armament,
And Ráma clothed in warrior might,
Forth standing in the front of fight.
Lord of the arm no toil might tire,
He stood majestic in his ire,
Matchless in form as Rudra when
His wrath is fierce on Gods or men.

While Gods and saints in close array
Held converse of the coming fray,
The army of the fiends drew near
With sight and sound that counselled fear.
Long, loud and deep their war-cry pealed,
As on they rushed with flag and shield,
Each, of his proper valour proud,
Urging to fight the demon crowd.
His ponderous bow each warrior tried,
And swelled his bulk with martial pride.
'Mid shout and roar and trampling feet,
And thunder of the drums they beat,
Loud and more loud the tumult went
Throughout the forest's vast extent,
And all the life that moved within
The woodland trembled at the din.
In eager haste all fled to find

773

Some tranquil spot, nor looked behind.

With every arm of war supplied,
On-rushing wildly like the tide
Of some deep sea, the giant host
Approached where Ráma kept his post.
Then he, in battle skilled and tried,
Bent his keen eye on every side,
And viewed the host of Khara face
To face before his dwelling-place.
He drew his arrows forth, and reared
And strained that bow which foemen feared,
And yielded to the vengeful sway
Of fierce desire that host to slay.
Terrific as the ruinous fire
That ends the worlds, he glowed in ire,
And his tremendous form dismayed
The Gods who roam the forest shade.
For in the furious wrath that glowed
Within his soul the hero showed
Like Śiva when his angry might
Stayed Daksha's sacrificial rite.
Like some great cloud at dawn of day
When first the sun upsprings,
And o'er the gloomy mass each ray
A golden radiance flings:
Thus showed the children of the night,
Whose mail and chariots threw,
With gleam of bows and armlets bright,
Flashes of flamy hue.

CANTO
XXV

The Battle

When Khara with the hosts he led
Drew near to Ráma's leafy shed,
He saw that queller of the foe
Stand ready with his ordered bow.
He saw, and burning at the view
His clanging bow he raised and drew,
And bade his driver urge apace
His car to meet him face to face.
Obedient to his master's hest
His eager steeds the driver pressed
On to the spot where, none to aid,
The strong-armed chief his weapon swayed.
Soon as the children of the night
Saw Khara rushing to the fight,

His lords with loud unearthly cry
Followed their chief and gathered nigh.
As in his car the leader rode
With all his lords around, he showed
Like the red planet fiery Mars
Surrounded by the lesser stars.
Then with a horrid yell that rent
The air, the giant chieftain sent
A thousand darts in rapid shower
On Ráma matchless in his power.
The rovers of the night, impelled
By fiery rage which naught withheld,
Upon the unconquered prince, who strained
His fearful bow, their arrows rained.
With sword and club, with mace and pike,
With spear and axe to pierce and strike,

Those furious fiends on every side
The unconquerable hero plied.
The giant legions huge and strong,
Like clouds the tempest drives along,
Rushed upon Ráma with the speed
Of whirling car, and mounted steed,
And hill-like elephant, to slay
The matchless prince in battle fray.
Then upon Ráma thick and fast
The rain of mortal steel they cast,
As labouring clouds their torrents shed
Upon the mountain-monarch's head.
As near and nearer round him drew
The warriors of the giant crew,
He showed like Śiva girt by all
His spirits when night's shadows fall.
As the great deep receives each rill
And river rushing from the hill,
He bore that flood of darts, and broke
With well-aimed shaft each murderous stroke.
By stress of arrowy storm assailed,
And wounded sore, he never failed,
Like some high mountain which defies
The red bolts flashing from the skies.
With ruddy streams each limb was dyed
From gaping wounds in breast and side,
Showing the hero like the sun
'Mid crimson clouds ere day is done.
Then, at that sight of terror, faint
Grew God, Gandharva, sage, and saint,
Trembling to see the prince oppose
His single might to myriad foes.
But waxing wroth, with force unspent,
He strained his bow to utmost bent,
And forth his arrows keen and true
In hundreds, yea in thousands flew,—
Shafts none could ward, and none endure:
Death's fatal noose was scarce so sure.
As 'twere in playful ease he shot
His gilded shafts, and rested not.
With swiftest flight and truest aim

Upon the giant hosts they came.
Each smote, each stayed a foeman's breath
As fatal as the coil of Death.
Each arrow through a giant tore
A passage, and besmeared with gore,
Pursued its onward way and through
The air with flamy brilliance flew.
Unnumbered were the arrows sent
From the great bow which Ráma bent,
And every shaft with iron head
The lifeblood of a giant shed.
Their pennoned bows were cleft, nor mail
Nor shield of hide could aught avail.
For Ráma's myriad arrows tore
Through arms, and bracelets which they wore,
And severed mighty warriors' thighs
Like trunks of elephants in size,
And cut resistless passage sheer
Through gold-decked horse and charioteer,
Slew elephant and rider, slew
The horseman and the charger too,
And infantry unnumbered sent
To dwell 'neath Yáma's government.
Then rose on high a fearful yell
Of rovers of the night, who fell
Beneath that iron torrent, sore
Wounded by shafts that rent and tore.
So mangled by the ceaseless storm
Of shafts of every kind and form,
Such joy they found, as forests feel
When scorched by flame, from Ráma's steel.
The mightiest still the fight maintained,
And furious upon Ráma rained
Dart, arrow, spear, with wild attacks
Of mace, and club, and battle-axe.
But the great chief, unconquered yet,
Their weapons with his arrows met,
Which severed many a giant's head,
And all the plain with corpses spread.
With sundered bow and shattered shield
Headless they sank upon the field,

As the tall trees, that felt the blast
Of Garuḍ's wing, to earth were cast.
The giants left unslaughtered there
Where filled with terror and despair,
And to their leader Khara fled
Faint, wounded, and discomfited.
These fiery Dúshaṇ strove to cheer,
And poised his bow to calm their fear;
Then fierce as He who rules the dead,
When wroth, on angered Ráma sped.
By Dúshaṇ cheered, the demons cast
Their dread aside and rallied fast
With Sáls, rocks, palm-trees in their hands
With nooses, maces, pikes, and brands,
Again upon the godlike man
The mighty fiends infuriate ran,
These casting rocks like hail, and these
A whelming shower of leafy trees.
Wild, wondrous fight, the eye to scare,
And raise on end each shuddering hair,

As with the fiends who loved to rove
By night heroic Ráma strove!
The giants in their fury plied
Ráma with darts on every side.
Then, by the gathering demons pressed
From north and south and east and west,
By showers of deadly darts assailed
From every quarter fiercely hailed,
Girt by the foes who swarmed around,
He raised a mighty shout whose sound
Struck terror. On the giant crew
His great Gandharva arrow flew.
A thousand mortal shafts were rained
From the orbed bow the hero strained,
Till east and west and south and north
Were filled with arrows volleyed forth.
They heard the fearful shout: they saw
His mighty hand the bowstring draw,
Yet could no wounded giant's eye
See the swift storm of arrows fly.

Still firm the warrior stood and cast
His deadly missiles thick and fast.
Dark grew the air with arrowy hail
Which hid the sun as with a veil.
Fiends wounded, falling, fallen, slain,
All in a moment, spread the plain,
And thousands scarce alive were left
Mangled, and gashed, and torn, and cleft.
Dire was the sight, the plain o'erspread
With trophies of the mangled dead.
There lay, by Ráma's missiles rent,
Full many a priceless ornament,
With severed limb and broken gem,
Hauberk and helm and diadem.
There lay the shattered car, the steed,
The elephant of noblest breed,
The splintered spear, the shivered mace,
Chouris and screens to shade the face.
The giants saw with bitterest pain
Their warriors weltering on the plain,
Nor dared again his might oppose
Who scourged the cities of his foes.

CANTO
XXVI

Dúshan's Death

When Dúshan saw his giant band
Slaughtered by Ráma's conquering hand,
He called five thousand fiends, and gave
His orders. Bravest of the brave,
Invincible, of furious might,
Ne'er had they turned their backs in flight.
They, as their leader bade them seize
Spears, swords, and clubs, and rocks, and trees,

Poured on the dauntless prince again
A ceaseless shower of deadly rain.
The virtuous Ráma, undismayed,
Their missiles with his arrows stayed,
And weakened, ere it fell, the shock
Of that dire hail of tree and rock,
And like a bull with eyelids closed,
The pelting of the storm opposed.

Then blazed his ire: he longed to smite
To earth the rovers of the night.
The wrath that o'er his spirit came
Clothed him with splendour as of flame,
While showers of mortal darts he poured
Fierce on the giants and their lord.
Dúshaṇ, the foeman's dusky dread,
By frenzied rage inspirited,
On Raghu's son his missiles cast
Like Indra's bolts which rend and blast.
But Ráma with a trenchant dart
Cleft Dúshaṇ's ponderous bow apart.
And then the gold-decked steeds who drew
The chariot, with four shafts he slew.
One crescent dart he aimed which shred
Clean from his neck the driver's head;
Three more with deadly skill addressed
Stood quivering in the giant's breast.
Hurled from his car, steeds, driver slain,
The bow he trusted cleft in twain,
He seized his mace, strong, heavy, dread,
High as a mountain's towering head.
With plates of gold adorned and bound,
Embattled Gods it crushed and ground.
Its iron spikes yet bore the stains
Of mangled foemen's blood and brains.
Its heavy mass of jagged steel
Was like a thunderbolt to feel.
It shattered, as on foes it fell,
The city where the senses dwell.
Fierce Dúshaṇ seized that ponderous mace
Like monstrous form of serpent race,

And all his savage soul aglow
With fury, rushed upon the foe.
But Raghu's son took steady aim,
And as the rushing giant came,
Shore with two shafts the arms whereon
The demon's glittering bracelets shone.
His arm at each huge shoulder lopped,
The mighty body reeled and dropped,
And the great mace to earth was thrown
Like Indra's staff when storms have blown.
As some vast elephant who lies
Shorn of his tusks, and bleeding dies,
So, when his arms were rent away,
Low on the ground the giant lay.
The spirits saw the monster die,
And loudly rang their joyful cry,
"Honour to Ráma! nobly done!
Well hast thou fought, Kakutstha's son!"

But the great three, the host who led,
Enraged to see their chieftain dead,
As though Death's toils were round them cast,
Rushed upon Ráma fierce and fast,
Mahákapála seized, to strike
His foeman down, a ponderous pike:
Sthúláksha charged with spear to fling,
Pramáthi with his axe to swing.
When Ráma saw, with keen darts he
Received the onset of the three,
As calm as though he hailed a guest
In each, who came for shade and rest.
Mahákapála's monstrous head
Fell with the trenchant dart he sped.
His good right hand in battle skilled
Sthúláksha's eyes with arrows filled,
And trusting still his ready bow
He laid the fierce Pramáthi low,
Who sank as some tall tree falls down
With bough and branch and leafy crown.
Then with five thousand shafts he slew
The rest of Dúshaṇ's giant crew:

Five thousand demons, torn and rent,
To Yáma's gloomy realm he sent.

When Khara knew the fate of all
The giant band and Dúshaṇ's fall,
He called the mighty chiefs who led
His army, and in fury said:

"Now Dúshaṇ and his armèd train
Lie prostrate on the battle plain.
Lead forth an army mightier still,
Ráma this wretched man, to kill.
Fight ye with darts of every shape,
Nor let him from your wrath escape."

Thus spoke the fiend, by rage impelled,
And straight his course toward Ráma held.
With Śyenagámí and the rest
Of his twelve chiefs he onward pressed,
And every giant as he went
A storm of well-wrought arrows sent.
Then with his pointed shafts that came
With gold and diamond bright as flame,
Dead to the earth the hero threw
The remnant of the demon crew.
Those shafts with feathers bright as gold,
Like flames which wreaths of smoke enfold,
Smote down the fiends like tall trees rent
By red bolts from the firmament.
A hundred shafts he pointed well:
By their keen barbs a hundred fell:
A thousand,—and a thousand more
In battle's front lay drenched in gore.
Of all defence and guard bereft,
With sundered bows and harness cleft.
Their bodies red with bloody stain
Fell the night-rovers on the plain,
Which, covered with the loosened hair
Of bleeding giants prostrate there,
Like some great altar showed, arrayed
For holy rites with grass o'erlaid.

The darksome wood, each glade and dell
Where the wild demons fought and fell
Was like an awful hell whose floor
Is thick with mire and flesh and gore.

Thus twice seven thousand fiends, a band
With impious heart and bloody hand,
By Raghu's son were overthrown,
A man, on foot, and all alone.
Of all who met on that fierce day,
Khara, great chief, survived the fray,
The monster of the triple head,
And Raghu's son, the foeman's dread.
The other demon warriors, all
Skilful and brave and strong and tall,
In front of battle, side by side,
Struck down by Lakshman's brother died.
When Khara saw the host he led
Triumphant forth to fight
Stretched on the earth, all smitten dead,
By Ráma's nobler might,
Upon his foe he fiercely glared,
And drove against him fast,
Like Indra when his arm is bared
His thundering bolt to cast.

CANTO
XXVII

The Death of Trisirás

But Trisirás, a chieftain dread,
Marked Khara as he onward sped.
And met his car and cried, to stay
The giant from the purposed fray:
"Mine be the charge: let me attack,

And turn thee from the contest back.
Let me go forth, and thou shalt see
The strong-armed Ráma slain by me.
True are the words I speak, my lord:
I swear it as I touch my sword:
That I this Ráma's blood will spill,
Whom every giant's hand should kill.
This Ráma will I slay, or he
In battle fray shall conquer me.
Restrain thy spirit: check thy car,
And view the combat from afar.
Thou, joying o'er the prostrate foe,
To Janasthán again shalt go,
Or, if I fall in battle's chance,
Against my conqueror advance."

Thus Triśirás for death who yearned:
And Khara from the conflict turned,
"Go forth to battle," Khara cried;
And toward his foe the giant hied.
Borne on a car of glittering hue
Which harnessed coursers fleetly drew,
Like some huge hill with triple peak
He onward rushed the prince to seek.

Still, like a big cloud, sending out
His arrowy rain with many a shout
Like the deep sullen roars that come
Discordant from a moistened drum.
But Raghu's son, whose watchful eye
Beheld the demon rushing nigh,
From the great bow he raised and bent
A shower of shafts to meet him sent.
Wild grew the fight and wilder yet
As fiend and man in combat met,
As when in some dark wood's retreat
An elephant and a lion meet.

The giant bent his bow, and true
To Ráma's brow three arrows flew.
Then, raging as he felt the stroke,

These words in anger Ráma spoke:
"Heroic chief! is such the power
Of fiends who rove at midnight hour?
Soft as the touch of flowers I feel
The gentle blows thine arrows deal.
Receive in turn my shafts, and know
What arrows fly from Ráma's bow."
Thus as he spoke his wrath grew hot,
And twice seven deadly shafts he shot,
Which, dire as serpent's deadly fang,
Straight to the giant's bosom sprang.
Four arrows more,—each shaped to deal
A mortal wound with barbèd steel,—
The glorious hero shot, and slew
The four good steeds the car that drew.
Eight other shafts flew straight and fleet,
And hurled the driver from his seat,
And in the dust the banner laid
That proudly o'er the chariot played.
Then as the fiend prepared to bound
Forth from his useless car to ground,
The hero smote him to the heart,
And numbed his arm with deadly smart.
Again the chieftain, peerless-souled,
Sent forth three rapid darts, and rolled
With each keen arrow, deftly sped,
Low in the dust a monstrous head.
Then yielding to each deadly stroke,
Forth spouting streams of blood and smoke,
The headless trunk bedrenched with gore
Fell to the ground and moved no more.
The fiends who yet were left with life,
Routed and crushed in battle strife,
To Khara's side, like trembling deer
Scared by the hunter, fled in fear.
King Khara saw with furious eye
His scattered giants turn and fly;
Then rallying his broken train
At Raghu's son he drove amain,
Like Ráhu when his deadly might
Comes rushing on the Lord of Night.

XXVIII

Khara Dismounted

But when he turned his eye where bled
Both Triśirás and Dúshaṇ dead,
Fear o'er the giant's spirit came
Of Ráma's might which naught could tame.
He saw his savage legions, those
Whose force no creature dared oppose,—
He saw the leader of his train
By Ráma's single prowess slain.
With burning grief he marked the few
Still left him of his giant crew.
As Namuchi on Indra, so
Rushed the dread demon on his foe.
His mighty bow the monster strained,
And angrily on Ráma rained
His mortal arrows in a flood,
Like serpent fangs athirst for blood.
Skilled in the bowman's warlike art,
He plied the string and poised the dart.
Here, on his car, and there, he rode,
And passages of battle showed,
While all the skyey regions grew
Dark with his arrows as they flew.
Then Ráma seized his ponderous bow,
And straight the heaven was all aglow
With shafts whose stroke no life might bear
That filled with flash and flame the air,
Thick as the blinding torrents sent
Down from Parjanya's firmament.
In space itself no space remained,
But all was filled with arrows rained
Incessantly from each great bow

Wielded by Ráma and his foe.
As thus in furious combat, wrought
To mortal hate, the warriors fought,
The sun himself grew faint and pale,
Obscured behind that arrowy veil.

As when beneath the driver's steel
An elephant is forced to kneel,
So from the hard and pointed head
Of many an arrow Ráma bled.
High on his car the giant rose
Prepared in deadly strife to close,

And all the spirits saw him stand
Like Yáma with his noose in hand.
For Khara deemed in senseless pride
That he, beneath whose hand had died
The giant legions, failed at length
Slow sinking with exhausted strength.
But Ráma, like a lion, when
A trembling deer comes nigh his den,
Feared not the demon mad with hate,—
Of lion might and lion gait.
Then in his lofty car that glowed
With sunlike brilliance Khara rode
At Ráma: madly on he came
Like a poor moth that seeks the flame.
His archer skill the fiend displayed,
And at the place where Ráma laid
His hand, an arrow cleft in two
The mighty bow the hero drew.
Seven arrows by the giant sent,
Bright as the bolts of Indra, rent
Their way through mail and harness joints,
And pierced him with their iron points.
On Ráma, hero unsurpassed,
A thousand shafts smote thick and fast,
While as each missile struck, rang out
The giant's awful battle-shout.
His knotted arrows pierced and tore
The sunbright mail the hero wore,

Till, band and buckle rent away,
Glittering on the ground it lay.
Then pierced in shoulder, breast, and side,
Till every limb with blood was dyed,
The chieftain in majestic ire
Shone glorious as the smokeless fire.
Then loud and long the war-cry rose
Of Ráma, terror of his foes,
As, on the giant's death intent,
A ponderous bow he strung and bent,—
Lord Vishṇu's own, of wondrous size,—
Agastya gave the heavenly prize.
Then rushing on the demon foe,
He raised on high that mighty bow,
And with his well-wrought shafts, whereon
Bright gold between the feathers shone,
He struck the pennon fluttering o'er
The chariot, and it waved no more.
That glorious flag whose every fold
Was rich with blazonry and gold,
Fell as the sun himself by all
The Gods' decree might earthward fall.
From wrathful Khara's hand, whose art
Well knew each vulnerable part,
Four keenly-piercing arrows flew,
And blood in Ráma's bosom drew,
With every limb distained with gore
From deadly shafts which rent and tore,
From Khara's clanging bowstring shots,
The prince's wrath waxed wondrous hot.
His hand upon his bow that best
Of mighty archers firmly pressed,
And from the well-drawn bowstring, true
Each to its mark, six arrows flew.
One quivered in the giant's head,
With two his brawny shoulders bled;
Three, with the crescent heads they bore,
Deep in his breast a passage tore.
Thirteen, to which the stone had lent
The keenest point, were swiftly sent
On the fierce giant, every one

Destructive, gleaming like the sun.
With four the dappled steeds he slew;
One cleft the chariot yoke in two,
One, in the heat of battle sped,
Smote from the neck the driver's head.
The poles were rent apart by three;
Two broke the splintered axle-tree.
Then from the hand of Ráma, while
Across his lips there came a smile,
The twelfth, like thunderbolt impelled,
Cut the great hand and bow it held.
Then, scarce by Indra's self surpassed,
He pierced the giant with the last.
The bow he trusted cleft in twain,
His driver and his horses slain,
Down sprang the giant, mace in hand,
On foot against the foe to stand.
The Gods and saints in bright array
Close gathered in the skies,
The prince's might in battle-fray
Beheld with joyful eyes.
Uprising from their golden seats,
Their hands in honour raised,
They looked on Ráma's noble feats,
And blessed him as they praised.

CANTO

XXIX

Khara's Defeat

When Ráma saw the giant nigh,
     On foot, alone, with mace reared high,
     In mild reproof at first he spoke,
Then forth his threatening anger broke:
"Thou with the host 'twas thine to lead,

With elephant and car and steed,
Hast wrought an act of sin and shame,
An act which all who live must blame.
Know that the wretch whose evil mind
Joys in the grief of human kind,
Though the three worlds confess him lord,
Must perish dreaded and abhorred.
Night-rover, when a villain's deeds
Distress the world he little heeds,
Each hand is armed his life to take,
And crush him like a deadly snake.
The end is near when men begin
Through greed or lust a life of sin,
E'en as a Bráhman's dame, unwise,
Eats of the fallen hail and dies.

Thy hand has slain the pure and good,
The hermit saints of Daṇḍak wood,
Of holy life, the heirs of bliss;
And thou shalt reap the fruit of this.
Not long shall they whose cruel breasts
Joy in the sin the world detests
Retain their guilty power and pride,
But fade like trees whose roots are dried.
Yes, as the seasons come and go,
Each tree its kindly fruit must show,
And sinners reap in fitting time
The harvest of each earlier crime.
As those must surely die who eat
Unwittingly of poisoned meat,
They too whose lives in sin are spent
Receive ere long the punishment.
And know, thou rover of the night,
That I, a king, am sent to smite
The wicked down, who court the hate
Of men whose laws they violate.
This day my vengeful hand shall send
Shafts bright with gold to tear and rend,
And pass with fury through thy breast
As serpents pierce an emmet's nest.

Thou with thy host this day shalt be
Among the dead below, and see
The saints beneath thy hand who bled,
Whose flesh thy cruel maw has fed.
They, glorious on their seats of gold,
Their slayer shall in hell behold.
Fight with all strength thou callest thine,
Mean scion of ignoble line,
Still, like the palm-tree's fruit, this day
My shafts thy head in dust shall lay."

Such were the words that Ráma said:
Then Khara's eyes with wrath glowed red,
Who, maddened by the rage that burned
Within him, with a smile returned:

"Thou Daśaratha's son, hast slain
The meaner giants of my train:
And canst thou idly vaunt thy might
And claim the praise not thine by right?
Not thus in self-laudation rave
The truly great, the nobly brave:
No empty boasts like thine disgrace
The foremost of the human race.
The mean of soul, unknown to fame,
Who taint their warrior race with shame,
Thus speak in senseless pride as thou,
O Raghu's son, hast boasted now.
What hero, when the war-cry rings,
Vaunts the high race from which he springs,
Or seeks, when warriors meet and die,
His own descent to glorify?
Weakness and folly show confessed
In every vaunt thou utterest,
As when the flames fed high with grass
Detect the simulating brass.
Dost thou not see me standing here
Armed with the mighty mace I rear,
Firm as an earth upholding hill
Whose summit veins of metal fill?

Lo, here I stand before thy face
To slay thee with my murderous mace,
As Death, the universal lord,
Stands threatening with his fatal cord.
Enough of this. Much more remains
That should be said: but time constrains.
Ere to his rest the sun descend,
And shades of night the combat end,
The twice seven thousand of my band
Who fell beneath thy bloody hand
Shall have their tears all wiped away
And triumph in thy fall to-day."

He spoke, and loosing from his hold
His mighty mace ringed round with gold,
Like some red bolt alive with fire
Hurled it at Ráma, mad with ire.
The ponderous mace which Khara threw
Sent fiery flashes as it flew.
Trees, shrubs were scorched beneath the blast,
As onward to its aim it passed.
But Ráma, watching as it sped
Dire as His noose who rules the dead,
Cleft it with arrows as it came
On rushing with a hiss and flame.
Its fury spent and burnt away,
Harmless upon the ground it lay
Like a great snake in furious mood
By herbs of numbing power subdued.

Khara's Death

W hen Ráma, pride of Raghu's race,
    Virtue's dear son, had cleft the mace,
    Thus with superior smile the best
Of chiefs the furious fiend addressed:

"Thou, worst of giant blood, at length
Hast shown the utmost of thy strength,
And forced by greater might to bow,
Thy vaunting threats are idle now.
My shafts have cut thy club in twain:
Useless it lies upon the plain,
And all thy pride and haughty trust
Lie with it levelled in the dust.
The words that thou hast said to-day,
That thou wouldst wipe the tears away
Of all the giants I have slain,
My deeds shall render void and vain.
Thou meanest of the giants' breed,
Evil in thought and word and deed,
My hand shall take that life of thine
As Garuḍ seized the juice divine.

Thou, rent by shafts, this day shalt die:
Low on the ground thy corse shall lie,
And bubbles from the cloven neck
With froth and blood thy skin shall deck.
With dust and mire all rudely dyed,
Thy torn arms lying by thy side,
While streams of blood each limb shall steep,
Thou on earth's breast shalt take thy sleep
Like a fond lover when he strains

The beauty whom at length he gains.
Now when thy heavy eyelids close
For ever in thy deep repose,
Again shall Daṇḍak forest be
Safe refuge for the devotee.
Thou slain, and all thy race who held
The realm of Janasthán expelled,
Again shall happy hermits rove,
Fearing no danger, through the grove.
Within those bounds, their brethren slain,
No giant shall this day remain,
But all shall fly with many a tear
And fearing, rid the saints of fear.
This bitter day shall misery bring
On all the race that calls thee king.
Fierce as their lord, thy dames shall know,
Bereft of joys, the taste of woe.
Base, cruel wretch, of evil mind,
Plaguer of Bráhmans and mankind,
With trembling hands each devotee
Feeds holy fires in dread of thee."

Thus with wild fury unrepressed
Raghu's brave son the fiend addressed;
And Khara, as his wrath grew high,
Thus thundered forth his fierce reply:

"By senseless pride to madness wrought,
By danger girt thou fearest naught,
Nor heedest, numbered with the dead,
What thou shouldst say and leave unsaid.
When Fate's tremendous coils enfold
The captive in resistless hold,
He knows not right from wrong, each sense
Numbed by that deadly influence."
He spoke, and when his speech was done
Bent his fierce brows on Raghu's son.
With eager eyes he looked around
If lethal arms might yet be found.
Not far away and full in view
A Sál-tree towering upward grew.

794

His lips in mighty strain compressed,
He tore it up with root and crest,
With huge arms waved it o'er his head
And hurled it shouting, Thou art dead.
But Ráma, unsurpassed in might,
Stayed with his shafts its onward flight,
And furious longing seized his soul
The giant in the dust to roll.
Great drops of sweat each limb bedewed,
His red eyes showed his wrathful mood.
A thousand arrows, swiftly sent,
The giant's bosom tore and rent.
From every gash his body showed
The blood in foamy torrents flowed,
As springing from their caverns leap
Swift rivers down the mountain steep.
When Khara felt each deadened power
Yielding beneath that murderous shower,
He charged, infuriate with the scent
Of blood, in dire bewilderment.
But Ráma watched, with ready bow,
The onset of his bleeding foe,
And ere the monster reached him, drew
Backward in haste a yard or two.
Then from his side a shaft he took
Whose mortal stroke no life might brook:
Of peerless might, it bore the name
Of Brahmá's staff, and glowed with flame:
Lord Indra, ruler of the skies,
Himself had given the glorious prize.
His bow the virtuous hero drew,
And at the fiend the arrow flew.
Hissing and roaring like the blast
Of tempest through the air it passed,
And fixed, by Ráma's vigour sped,
In the foe's breast its pointed head.
Then fell the fiend: the quenchless flame
Burnt furious in his wounded frame.
So burnt by Rudra Andhak fell
In Śvetáraṇya's silvery dell:
So Namuchi and Vritra died

By steaming bolts that tamed their pride:
So Bala fell by lightning sent
By Him who rules the firmament.

Then all the Gods in close array
With the bright hosts who sing and play,
Filled full of rapture and amaze,
Sang hymns of joy in Ráma's praise,
Beat their celestial drums and shed
Rain of sweet flowers upon his head.
For three short hours had scarcely flown,
And by his pointed shafts o'erthrown
The twice seven thousand fiends, whose will
Could change their shapes, in death were still,
With Triśirás and Dúshan slain,
And Khara, leader of the train.
"O wondrous deed," the bards began,
"The noblest deed of virtuous man!
Heroic strength that stood alone,
And firmness e'en as Vishṇu's own!"

Thus having sung, the shining train
Turned to their heavenly homes again.

Then the high saints of royal race
And loftiest station sought the place,
And by the great Agastya led,
With reverence to Ráma said:

"For this, Lord Indra, glorious sire,
Majestic as the burning fire,
Who crushes cities in his rage,
Sought Śarabhanga's hermitage.
Thou wast, this great design to aid,
Led by the saints to seek this shade,
And with thy mighty arm to kill
The giants who delight in ill.
Thou Daśaratha's noble son,
The battle for our sake hast won,
And saints in Daṇḍak's wild who live

796

Their days to holy tasks can give."
Forth from the mountain cavern came
The hero Lakshmaṇ with the dame.
And rapture beaming from his face,
Resought the hermit dwelling-place.
Then when the mighty saints had paid
Due honour for the victor's aid,
The glorious Ráma honoured too
By Lakshmaṇ to his cot withdrew.
When Sítá looked upon her lord,
His foemen slain, the saints restored,
In pride and rapture uncontrolled
She clasped him in her loving hold.
On the dead fiends her glances fell:
She saw her lord alive and well,
Victorious after toil and pain,
And Janak's child was blest again.
Once more, once more with new delight
Her tender arms she threw
Round Ráma whose victorious might
Had crushed the demon crew.
Then as his grateful reverence paid
Each saint of lofty soul,
O'er her sweet face, all fears allayed,
The flush of transport stole.

CANTO

XXXI

Rávan

B ut of the host of giants one,
Akampan, from the field had run
And sped to Lanká to relate
In Rávaṇ's ear the demons' fate:

"King, many a giant from the shade
Of Janasthán in death is laid:
Khara the chief is slain, and I
Could scarcely from the battle fly."

Fierce anger, as the monarch heard,
Inflamed his look, his bosom stirred,
And while with scorching glance he eyed
The messenger, he thus replied:

"What fool has dared, already dead,
Strike Janasthán, the general dread?
Who is the wretch shall vainly try
In earth, heaven, hell, from me to fly?
Vaiśravaṇ, Indra, Vishṇu, He
Who rules the dead, must reverence me;
For not the mightiest lord of these
Can brave my will and live at ease.
Fate finds in me a mightier fate
To burn the fires that devastate.
With unresisted influence I
Can force e'en Death himself to die,
With all-surpassing might restrain
The fury of the hurricane,
And burn in my tremendous ire
The glory of the sun and fire."

As thus the fiend's hot fury blazed,
His trembling hands Akampan raised,
And with a voice which fear made weak,
Permission craved his tale to speak.
King Rávaṇ gave the leave he sought,
And bade him tell the news he brought.
His courage rose, his voice grew bold,
And thus his mournful tale he told:

"A prince with mighty shoulders, sprung
From Daśaratha, brave and young,
With arms well moulded, bears the name
Of Ráma with a lion's frame.

798

Renowned, successful, dark of limb,
Earth has no warrior equals him.
He fought in Janasthán and slew
Dúshaṇ the fierce and Khara too."

Rávaṇ the giants' royal chief.
Received Akampan's tale of grief.
Then, panting like an angry snake,
These words in turn the monarch spake:

"Say quick, did Ráma seek the shade
Of Janasthán with Indra's aid,
And all the dwellers in the skies
To back his hardy enterprise?"

Akampan heard, and straight obeyed
His master, and his answer made.
Then thus the power and might he told
Of Raghu's son the lofty-souled:

"Best is that chief of all who know
With deftest art to draw the bow.
His are strange arms of heavenly might,
And none can match him in the fight.
His brother Lakshmaṇ brave as he,
Fair as the rounded moon to see,
With eyes like night and voice that comes
Deep as the roll of beaten drums,
By Ráma's side stands ever near,
Like wind that aids the flame's career.
That glorious chief, that prince of kings,
On Janasthán this ruin brings.
No Gods were there,—dismiss the thought
No heavenly legions came and fought.
His swift-winged arrows Ráma sent,
Each bright with gold and ornament.
To serpents many-faced they turned:

The giant hosts they ate and burned.
Where'er these fled in wild dismay

Ráma was there to strike and slay.
By him O King of high estate,
Is Janasthán left desolate."

Akampan ceased: in angry pride
The giant monarch thus replied:
"To Janasthán myself will go
And lay these daring brothers low."

Thus spoke the king in furious mood:
Akampan then his speech renewed:
"O listen while I tell at length
The terror of the hero's strength.
No power can check, no might can tame
Ráma, a chief of noblest fame.
He with resistless shafts can stay
The torrent foaming on its way.
Sky, stars, and constellations, all
To his fierce might would yield and fall.
His power could earth itself uphold
Down sinking as it sank of old.
Or all its plains and cities drown,
Breaking the wild sea's barrier down;
Crush the great deep's impetuous will,
Or bid the furious wind be still.
He glorious in his high estate
The triple world could devastate,
And there, supreme of men, could place
His creatures of a new-born race.
Never can mighty Ráma be
O'ercome in fight, my King, by thee.
Thy giant host the day might win
From him, if heaven were gained by sin.
If Gods were joined with demons, they
Could ne'er, I ween, that hero slay,
But guile may kill the wondrous man;
Attend while I disclose the plan.
His wife, above all women graced,
Is Sítá of the dainty waist,
With limbs to fair proportion true,
And a soft skin of lustrous hue,

800

Round neck and arm rich gems are twined:
She is the gem of womankind.
With her no bright Gandharví vies,
No nymph or Goddess in the skies;
And none to rival her would dare
'Mid dames who part the long black hair.
That hero in the wood beguile,
And steal his lovely spouse the while.
Reft of his darling wife, be sure,
Brief days the mourner will endure."

With flattering hope of triumph moved
The giant king that plan approved,
Pondered the counsel in his breast,
And then Akampan thus addressed:
"Forth in my car I go at morn,
None but the driver with me borne,
And this fair Sítá will I bring
Back to my city triumphing."

Forth in his car by asses drawn
The giant monarch sped at dawn,
Bright as the sun, the chariot cast
Light through the sky as on it passed.
Then high in air that best of cars
Traversed the path of lunar stars,
Sending a fitful radiance pale
As moonbeams shot through cloudy veil.
Far on his airy way he flew:
Near Tádakeya's grove he drew.
Márícha welcomed him, and placed
Before him food which giants taste,
With honour led him to a seat,
And brought him water for his feet;
And then with timely words addressed
Such question to his royal guest:
"Speak, is it well with thee whose sway
The giant multitudes obey?
I know not all, and ask in fear
The cause, O King, why thou art here."

801

Ráva, the giants' mighty king,
Heard wise Márícha's questioning,
And told with ready answer, taught
In eloquence, the cause he sought:
"My guards, the bravest of my band,
Are slain by Ráma's vigorous hand,
And Janasthán, that feared no hate
Of foes, is rendered desolate.
Come, aid me in the plan I lay
To steal the conqueror's wife away."

Márícha heard the king's request,
And thus the giant chief addressed:

"What foe in friendly guise is he
Who spoke of Sítá's name to thee?
Who is the wretch whose thought would bring
Destruction on the giants' king?
Whose is the evil counsel, say,
That bids thee bear his wife away,
And careless of thy life provoke
Earth's loftiest with threatening stroke?
A foe is he who dared suggest
This hopeless folly to thy breast,
Whose ill advice would bid thee draw
The venomed fang from serpent's jaw.
By whose unwise suggestion led
Wilt thou the path of ruin tread?
Whence falls the blow that would destroy
Thy gentle sleep of ease and joy?
Like some wild elephant is he
That rears his trunk on high,
Lord of an ancient pedigree,
Huge tusks, and furious eye.
Rávan, no rover of the night
With bravest heart can brook,
Met in the front of deadly fight,
On Raghu's son to look.

The giant hosts were brave and strong,
Good at the bow and spear:

But Ráma slew the routed throng,
A lion 'mid the deer.
No lion's tooth can match his sword,
Or arrows fiercely shot:
He sleeps, he sleeps—the lion lord;
Be wise and rouse him not.
O Monarch of the giants, well
Upon my counsel think,
Lest thou for ever in the hell
Of Ráma's vengeance sink:
A hell, where deadly shafts are sent
From his tremendous-bow,
While his great arms all flight prevent,
Like deepest mire below:
Where the wild floods of battle rave
Above the foeman's head,
And each with many a feathery wave
Of shafts is garlanded.
O, quench the flames that in thy breast
With raging fury burn;
And pacified and self-possessed
To Lanká's town return.
Rest thou in her imperial bowers
With thine own wives content,
And in the wood let Ráma's hours
With Sítá still be spent."

The lord of Lanká's isle obeyed
The counsel, and his purpose stayed.
Borne on his car he parted thence
And gained his royal residence.

Rávan Roused

B ut Śúrpaṇakhá saw the plain
Spread with the fourteen thousand slain,
Doers of cruel deeds o'erthrown
By Ráma's mighty arm alone,
Add Triśirás and Dúshaṇ dead,
And Khara, with the hosts they led.
Their death she saw, and mad with pain,
Roared like a cloud that brings the rain,
And fled in anger and dismay
To Lanká, seat of Rávaṇ's sway.
There on a throne of royal state
Exalted sat the potentate,
Begirt with counsellor and peer,
Like Indra with the Storm Gods near.
Bright as the sun's full splendour shone
The glorious throne he sat upon,
As when the blazing fire is red
Upon a golden altar fed.
Wide gaped his mouth at every breath,
Tremendous as the jaws of Death.
With him high saints of lofty thought,
Gandharvas, Gods, had vainly fought.
The wounds were on his body yet
From wars where Gods and demons met.
And scars still marked his ample chest
By fierce Airávat's tusk impressed.
A score of arms, ten necks, had he,
His royal gear was brave to see.
His massive form displayed each sign
That marks the heir of kingly line.
In stature like a mountain height,

His arms were strong, his teeth were white,
And all his frame of massive mould
Seemed lazulite adorned with gold.
A hundred seams impressed each limp
Where Vishṇu's arm had wounded him,
And chest and shoulder bore the print
Of sword and spear and arrow dint,
Where every God had struck a blow
In battle with the giant foe.
His might to wildest rage could wake
The sea whose faith naught else can shake,
Hurl towering mountains to the earth,
And crush e'en foes of heavenly birth.
The bonds of law and right he spurned:
To others' wives his fancy turned.
Celestial arms he used in fight,
And loved to mar each holy rite.
He went to Bhogavatí's town,
Where Vásuki was beaten down,
And stole, victorious in the strife,
Lord Takshaka's beloved wife.
Kailása's lofty crest he sought,
And when in vain Kuvera fought,
Stole Pushpak thence, the car that through
The air, as willed the master, flew.
Impelled by furious anger, he
Spoiled Nandan's shade and Naliní,
And Chaitraratha's heavenly grove,
The haunts where Gods delight to rove.
Tall as a hill that cleaves the sky,
He raised his mighty arms on high
To check the blessed moon, and stay
The rising of the Lord of Day.
Ten thousand years the giant spent
On dire austerities intent,
And of his heads an offering, laid
Before the Self-existent, made.
No God or fiend his life could take,
Gandharva, goblin, bird, or snake:
Safe from all fears of death, except
From human arm, that life was kept.

Oft when the priests began to raise
Their consecrating hymns of praise,
He spoiled the Soma's sacred juice
Poured forth by them in solemn use.

The sacrifice his hands o'erthrew,
And cruelly the Bráhmans slew.
His was a heart that naught could melt,
Joying in woes which others felt.

She saw the ruthless monster there,
Dread of the worlds, unused to spare.
In robes of heavenly texture dressed,
Celestial wreaths adorned his breast.
He sat a shape of terror, like
Destruction ere the worlds it strike.
She saw him in his pride of place,
The joy of old Pulastya's race,
Begirt by counsellor and peer,
Rávaṇ, the foeman's mortal fear,
And terror in her features shown,
The giantess approached the throne.
Then Śúrpaṇakhá bearing yet
Each deeply printed trace
Where the great-hearted chief had set
A mark upon her face,
Impelled by terror and desire,
Still fierce, no longer bold,
To Rávaṇ of the eyes of fire
Her tale, infuriate, told.

Súrpanakhá's Speech

Burning with anger, in the ring
Of counsellors who girt their king,
To Rávaṇ, ravener of man,
With bitter words she thus began:

"Wilt thou absorbed in pleasure, still
Pursue unchecked thy selfish will:
Nor turn thy heedless eyes to see
The coming fate which threatens thee?
The king who days and hours employs
In base pursuit of vulgar joys
Must in his people's sight be vile
As fire that smokes on funeral pile.
He who when duty calls him spares
No time for thought of royal cares,
Must with his realm and people all
Involved in fatal ruin fall.
As elephants in terror shrink
From the false river's miry brink,
Thus subjects from a monarch flee
Whose face their eyes may seldom see,
Who spends the hours for toil ordained
In evil courses unrestrained.
He who neglects to guard and hold
His kingdom by himself controlled,
Sinks nameless like a hill whose head
Is buried in the ocean's bed.
Thy foes are calm and strong and wise,
Fiends, Gods, and warriors of the skies,—
How, heedless, wicked, weak, and vain,
Wilt thou thy kingly state maintain?

Thou, lord of giants, void of sense,
Slave of each changing influence,
Heedless of all that makes a king,
Destruction on thy head wilt bring.
O conquering chief, the prince, who boasts,
Of treasury and rule and hosts,
By others led, though lord of all,
Is meaner than the lowest thrall.
For this are monarchs said to be
Long-sighted, having power to see
Things far away by faithful eyes
Of messengers and loyal spies.
But aid from such thou wilt not seek:
Thy counsellors are blind and weak,
Or thou from these hadst surely known
Thy legions and thy realm o'erthrown.
Know, twice seven thousand, fierce in might,
Are slain by Ráma in the fight,
And they, the giant host who led,
Khara and Dúshaṇ, both are dead.
Know, Ráma with his conquering arm
Has freed the saints from dread of harm,
Has smitten Janasthán and made
Asylum safe in Daṇḍak's shade.
Enslaved and dull, of blinded sight,
Intoxicate with vain delight,
Thou closest still thy heedless eyes
To dangers in thy realm that rise.
A king besotted, mean, unkind,
Of niggard hand and slavish mind,
Will find no faithful followers heed
Their master in his hour of need.
The friend on whom he most relies,
In danger, from a monarch flies,
Imperious in his high estate,
Conceited, proud, and passionate;
Who ne'er to state affairs attends
With wholesome fear when woe impends.
Most weak and worthless as the grass,
Soon from his sway the realm will pass.
For rotting wood a use is found,

For clods and dust that strew the ground,
But when a king has lost his sway,
Useless he falls, and sinks for aye.
As raiment by another worn,
As faded garland crushed and torn,
So is, unthroned, the proudest king,
Though mighty once, a useless thing.
But he who every sense subdues
And each event observant views,
Rewards the good and keeps from wrong,
Shall reign secure and flourish long.
Though lulled in sleep his senses lie
He watches with a ruler's eye,
Untouched by favour, ire, and hate,
And him the people celebrate.
O weak of mind, without a trace

Of virtues that a king should grace,
Who hast not learnt from watchful spy
That low in death the giants lie.
Scorner of others, but enchained
By every base desire,
By thee each duty is disdained
Which time and place require.
Soon wilt thou, if thou canst not learn,
Ere yet it be too late,
The good from evil to discern,
Fall from thy high estate."
As thus she ceased not to upbraid
The king with cutting speech,
And every fault to view displayed,
Naming and marking each,
The monarch of the sons of night,
Of wealth and power possessed,
And proud of his imperial might,
Long pondered in his breast.

CANTO
XXXIV

Súrpanakhá's Speech

Then forth the giant's fury broke
As Śúrpaṇakhá harshly spoke.
Girt by his lords the demon king
Looked on her, fiercely questioning:

"Who is this Ráma, whence, and where?
His form, his might, his deeds declare.
His wandering steps what purpose led
To Daṇḍak forest, hard to tread?
What arms are his that he could smite
In fray the rovers of the night,
And Triśirás and Dúshaṇ lay
Low on the earth, and Khara slay?
Tell all, my sister, and declare
Who maimed thee thus, of form most fair."
Thus by the giant king addressed,
While burnt her fury unrepressed,
The giantess declared at length
The hero's form and deeds and strength:

"Long are his arms and large his eyes:
A black deer's skin his dress supplies.
King Daśaratha's son is he,
Fair as Kandarpa's self to see.
Adorned with many a golden band,
A bow, like Indra's, arms his hand,
And shoots a flood of arrows fierce
As venomed snakes to burn and pierce.
I looked, I looked, but never saw
His mighty hand the bowstring draw
That sent the deadly arrows out,

While rang through air his battle-shout.
I looked, I looked, and saw too well
How with that hail the giants fell,
As falls to earth the golden grain,
Struck by the blows of Indra's rain.
He fought, and twice seven thousand, all
Terrific giants, strong and tall,
Fell by the pointed shafts o'erthrown
Which Ráma shot on foot, alone.
Three little hours had scarcely fled,—
Khara and Dúshaṇ both were dead,
And he had freed the saints and made
Asylum sure in Daṇḍak's shade.
Me of his grace the victor spared,
Or I the giants' fate had shared.
The high-souled Ráma would not deign
His hand with woman's blood to stain.
The glorious Lakshmaṇ, justly dear,
In gifts and warrior might his peer,
Serves his great brother with the whole
Devotion of his faithful soul:
Impetuous victor, bold and wise,
First in each hardy enterprise,
Still ready by his side to stand,
A second self or better hand.
And Ráma has a large-eyed spouse,
Pure as the moon her cheek and brows,
Dearer than life in Ráma's sight,
Whose happiness is her delight.
With beauteous hair and nose the dame
From head to foot has naught to blame.
She shines the wood's bright Goddess, Queen
Of beauty with her noble mien.
First in the ranks of women placed
Is Sítá of the dainty waist.
In all the earth mine eyes have ne'er
Seen female form so sweetly fair.
Goddess nor nymph can vie with her,
Nor bride of heavenly chorister.
He who might call this dame his own,
Her eager arms about him thrown,

Would live more blest in Sítá's love
Than Indra in the world above.
She, peerless in her form and face
And rich in every gentle grace,
Is worthy bride, O King, for thee,
As thou art meet her lord to be.
I even I, will bring the bride
In triumph to her lover's side—
This beauty fairer than the rest,
With rounded limb and heaving breast.
Each wound upon my face I owe
To cruel Lakshmaṇ's savage blow.
But thou, O brother, shalt survey
Her moonlike loveliness to-day,
And Káma's piercing shafts shall smite
Thine amorous bosom at the sight.
If in thy breast the longing rise
To make thine own the beauteous prize,
Up, let thy better foot begin
The journey and the treasure win.
If, giant Lord, thy favouring eyes
Regard the plan which I advise,
Up, cast all fear and doubt away
And execute the words I say
Come, giant King, this treasure seek,
For thou art strong and they are weak.

Let Sítá of the faultless frame
Be borne away and be thy dame.
Thy host in Janasthán who dwelt
Forth to the battle hied.
And by the shafts which Ráma dealt
They perished in their pride.
Dúshaṇ and Khara breathe no more,
Laid low upon the plain.
Arise, and ere the day be o'er
Take vengeance for the slain."

Rávan's Journey

When Rávaṇ, by her fury spurred,
That terrible advice had heard,
He bade his nobles quit his side,
And to the work his thought applied.
He turned his anxious mind to scan
On every side the hardy plan:
The gain against the risk he laid,
Each hope and fear with care surveyed,
And in his heart at length decreed
To try performance of the deed.
Then steady in his dire intent
The giant to the courtyard went.
There to his charioteer he cried,
"Bring forth the car whereon I ride."
Aye ready at his master's word
The charioteer the order heard,
And yoked with active zeal the best
Of chariots at his lord's behest.
Asses with heads of goblins drew
That wondrous car where'er it flew.
Obedient to the will it rolled
Adorned with gems and glistering gold.
Then mounting, with a roar as loud
As thunder from a labouring cloud,
The mighty monarch to the tide
Of Ocean, lord of rivers, hied.
White was the shade above him spread,
White chouris waved around his head,
And he with gold and jewels bright
Shone like the glossy lazulite.
Ten necks and twenty arms had he:

His royal gear was good to see.
The heavenly Gods' insatiate foe,
Who made the blood of hermits flow,
He like the Lord of Hills appeared
With ten huge heads to heaven upreared.
In the great car whereon he rode,
Like some dark cloud the giant showed,
When round it in their close array
The cranes 'mid wreaths of lightning play.
He looked, and saw, from realms of air,
The rocky shore of ocean, where
Unnumbered trees delightful grew
With flower and fruit of every hue.
He looked on many a lilied pool
With silvery waters fresh and cool,
And shores like spacious altars meet
For holy hermits' lone retreat.
The graceful palm adorned the scene,
The plantain waved her glossy green.
There grew the sál and betel, there
On bending boughs the flowers were fair.
There hermits dwelt who tamed each sense
By strictest rule of abstinence:
Gandharvas, Kinnars, thronged the place,
Nágas and birds of heavenly race.
Bright minstrels of the ethereal quire,
And saints exempt from low desire,
With Ájas, sons of Brahmá's line,
Maríchipas of seed divine,
Vaikhánasas and Máshas strayed,
And Bálakhilyas in the shade.
The lovely nymphs of heaven were there,
Celestial wreaths confined their hair,
And to each form new grace was lent
By wealth of heavenly ornament.
Well skilled was each in play and dance
And gentle arts of dalliance.
The glorious wife of many a God
Those beautiful recesses trod,
There Gods and Dánavs, all who eat
The food of heaven, rejoiced to meet.

The swan and Sáras thronged each bay
With curlews, ducks, and divers gay,
Where the sea spray rose soft and white
O'er rocks of glossy lazulite.
As his swift way the fiend pursued
Pale chariots of the Gods he viewed,
Bearing each lord whose rites austere
Had raised him to the heavenly sphere.
Thereon celestial garlands hung,
There music played and songs were sung.
Then bright Gandharvas met his view,
And heavenly nymphs, as on he flew.
He saw the sandal woods below,
And precious trees of odorous flow,
That to the air around them lent
Their riches of delightful scent;
Nor failed his roving eye to mark
Tall aloe trees in grove and park.
He looked on wood with cassias filled,
And plants which balmy sweets distilled,
Where her fair flowers the betel showed
And the bright pods of pepper glowed.
The pearls in many a silvery heap
Lay on the margin of the deep.
And grey rocks rose amid the red
Of coral washed from ocean's bed.

High soared the mountain peaks that bore
Treasures of gold and silver ore,
And leaping down the rocky walls
Came wild and glorious waterfalls.
Fair towns which grain and treasure held,
And dames who every gem excelled,
He saw outspread beneath him far,
With steed, and elephant, and car.
That ocean shore he viewed that showed
Fair as the blessed Gods' abode
Where cool delightful breezes played
O'er levels in the freshest shade.
He saw a fig-tree like a cloud
With mighty branches earthward bowed.

It stretched a hundred leagues and made
For hermit bands a welcome shade.
Thither the feathered king of yore
An elephant and tortoise bore,
And lighted on a bough to eat
The captives of his taloned feet.
The bough unable to sustain
The crushing weight and sudden strain,
Loaded with sprays and leaves of spring
Gave way beneath the feathered king.
Under the shadow of the tree
Dwelt many a saint and devotee,
Ájas, the sons of Brahmá's line,
Máshas, Maríchipas divine.
Vaikhánasas, and all the race
Of Bálakhilyas, loved the place.
But pitying their sad estate
The feathered monarch raised the weight
Of the huge bough, and bore away
The loosened load and captured prey.
A hundred leagues away he sped,
Then on his monstrous booty fed,
And with the bough he smote the lands
Where dwell the wild Nisháda bands.
High joy was his because his deed
From jeopardy the hermits freed.
That pride for great deliverance wrought
A double share of valour brought.
His soul conceived the high emprise
To snatch the Amrit from the skies.
He rent the nets of iron first,
Then through the jewel chamber burst,
And bore the drink of heaven away
That watched in Indra's palace lay.

Such was the hermit-sheltering tree
Which Rávaṇ turned his eye to see.
Still marked where Garuḍ sought to rest,
The fig-tree bore the name of Blest.
When Rávaṇ stayed his chariot o'er

The ocean's heart-enchanting shore,
He saw a hermitage that stood
Sequestered in the holy wood.
He saw the fiend Márícha there
With deerskin garb, and matted hair
Coiled up in hermit guise, who spent
His days by rule most abstinent.
As guest and host are wont to meet,
They met within that lone retreat.
Before the king Márícha placed
Food never known to human taste.
He entertained his guest with meat
And gave him water for his feet,
And then addressed the giant king
With timely words of questioning:

"Lord, is it well with thee, and well
With those in Lanká's town who dwell?
What sudden thought, what urgent need
Has brought thee with impetuous speed?"
The fiend Márícha thus addressed
Rávan the king, his mighty guest,
And he, well skilled in arts that guide
The eloquent, in turn replied:

CANTO

XXXVI

Rávan's Speech

"Hear me, Márícha, while I speak,
And tell thee why thy home I seek.
Sick and distressed am I, and see
My surest hope and help in thee.
Of Janasthán I need not tell,

Where Śúrpaṇakhá, Khara, dwell,
And Dúshaṇ with the arm of might,
And Triśirás, the fierce in fight,
Who feeds on human flesh and gore,
And many noble giants more,
Who roam in dark of midnight through
The forest, brave and strong and true.
By my command they live at ease
And slaughter saints and devotees.
Those twice seven thousand giants, all
Obedient to their captain's call,
Joying in war and ruthless deeds
Follow where mighty Khara leads.
Those fearless warrior bands who roam
Through Janasthán their forest home,
In all their terrible array
Met Ráma in the battle fray.
Girt with all weapons forth they sped
With Khara at the army's head.
The front of battle Ráma held:
With furious wrath his bosom swelled.
Without a word his hate to show
He launched the arrows from his bow.
On the fierce hosts the missiles came,
Each burning with destructive flame,
The twice seven thousand fell o'erthrown
By him, a man, on foot, alone.
Khara the army's chief and pride,
And Dúshaṇ, fearless warrior, died,
And Triśirás the fierce was slain,
And Daṇḍak wood was free again.

He, banished by his angry sire,
Roams with his wife in mean attire.
This wretch, his Warrior tribe's disgrace
Has slain the best of giant race.

Harsh, wicked, fierce and greedy-souled,
A fool, with senses uncontrolled,
No thought of duty stirs his breast:
He joys to see the world distressed.

He sought the wood with fair pretence
Of truthful life and innocence,
But his false hand my sister left
Mangled, of nose and ears bereft.
This Ráma's wife who bears the name
Of Sítá, in her face and frame
Fair as a daughter of the skies,—
Her will I seize and bring the prize
Triumphant from the forest shade:
For this I seek thy willing aid.
If thou, O mighty one, wilt lend
Thy help and stand beside thy friend,
I with my brothers may defy
All Gods embattled in the sky.
Come, aid me now, for thine the power
To succour in the doubtful hour.
Thou art in war and time of fear,
For heart and hand, without a peer.
For thou art skilled in art and wile,
A warrior brave and trained in guile.
With this one hope, this only aim,
O Rover of the Night, I came.
Now let me tell what aid I ask
To back me in my purposed task.
In semblance of a golden deer
Adorned with silver spots appear.
Go, seek his dwelling: in the way
Of Ráma and his consort stray.
Doubt not the lady, when she sees
The wondrous deer amid the trees,
Will bid her lord and Lakshman take
The creature for its beauty's sake.
Then when the chiefs have parted thence,
And left her lone, without defence,
As Ráhu storms the moonlight, I
Will seize the lovely dame and fly.
Her lord will waste away and weep
For her his valour could not keep.
Then boldly will I strike the blow
And wreak my vengeance on the foe."

When wise Márícha heard the tale
His heart grew faint, his cheek was pale,
He stared with open orbs, and tried
To moisten lips which terror dried,
And grief, like death, his bosom rent
As on the king his look he bent.
The monarch's will he strove to stay,
Distracted with alarm,
For well he knew the might that lay
In Ráma's matchless arm.
With suppliant hands Márícha stood
And thus began to tell
His counsel for the tyrant's good,
And for his own as well:

XXXVII

Márícha's Speech

Márícha gave attentive ear
The ruler of the fiends to hear:
Then, trained in all the rules that teach
The eloquent, began his speech:
"'Tis easy task, O King, to find
Smooth speakers who delight the mind.
But they who urge and they who do
Distasteful things and wise, are few.
Thou hast not learnt, by proof untaught,
And borne away by eager thought,
That Ráma, formed for high emprise,
With Varuṇ or with Indra vies.
Still let thy people live in peace,
Nor let their name and lineage cease,
For Ráma with his vengeful hand
Can sweep the giants from the land.

O, let not Janak's daughter bring
Destruction on the giant king.
Let not the lady Sítá wake
A tempest, on thy head to break.
Still let the dame, by care untried,
Be happy by her husband's side,
Lest swift avenging ruin fall
On glorious Lanká, thee, and all.
Men such as thou with wills unchained,
Advised by sin and unrestrained,
Destroy themselves, the king, the state,
And leave the people desolate.
Ráma, in bonds of duty held,
Was never by his sire expelled.
He is no wretch of greedy mind,
Dishonour of his Warrior kind.
Free from all touch of rancorous spite,
All creatures' good is his delight.
He saw his sire of truthful heart
Deceived by Queen Kaikeyí's art,
And said, a true and duteous son,
"What thou hast promised shall be done."
To gratify the lady's will,
His father's promise to fulfil,
He left his realm and all delight
For Daṇḍak wood, an anchorite.
No cruel wretch, no senseless fool
Is Ráma, unrestrained by rule.
This groundless charge has ne'er been heard,
Nor shouldst thou speak the slanderous word.
Ráma in truth and goodness bold
Is Virtue's self in human mould,
The sovereign of the world confessed
As Indra rules among the Blest.
And dost thou plot from him to rend
The darling whom his arms defend?
Less vain the hope to steal away
The glory of the Lord of Day.

O Rávaṇ, guard thee from the fire
Of vengeful Ráma's kindled ire,—

Each spark a shaft with deadly aim,
While bow and falchion feed the flame.
Cast not away in hopeless strife
Thy realm, thy bliss, thine own dear life.
O Rávaṇ of his might beware,
A God of Death who will not spare.
That bow he knows so well to draw
Is the destroyer's flaming jaw,
And with his shafts which flash and glow
He slays the armies of the foe.
Thou ne'er canst win—the thought forego—
From the safe guard of shaft and bow
King Janak's child, the dear delight
Of Ráma unapproached in might.
The spouse of Raghu's son, confessed
Lion of men with lion chest,—
Dearer than life, through good and ill
Devoted to her husband's will,
The slender-waisted, still must be
From thy polluting touches free.
Far better grasp with venturous hand
The flame to wildest fury fanned.
What, King of giants, canst thou gain
From this attempt so wild and vain?
If in the fight his eye he bend
Upon thee, Lord, thy days must end,
So life and bliss and royal sway,
Lost beyond hope, will pass away.
Summon each lord of high estate,
And chief, Vibhishaṇ to debate.
With peers in lore of counsel tried
Consider, reason, and decide
Scan strength and weakness, count the cost,
What may be gained and what be lost.
Examine and compare aright
Thy proper power and Ráma's might,
Then if thy weal be still thy care,
Thou wilt be prudent and forbear.
O giant King, the contest shun,
Thy force is all too weak
The lord of Kosál's mighty son

In deadly fray to seek.
King of the hosts that rove at night,
O hear what I advise:
My prudent counsel do not slight;
Be patient and be wise."

<h2 style="text-align:center">CANTO</h2>

<h1 style="text-align:center">XXXVIII</h1>

<h1 style="text-align:center">Márícha's Speech</h1>

"Once in my strength and vigour's pride
I roamed this earth from side to side,
And towering like a mountain's crest,
A thousand Nágas' might possessed.
Like some vast sable cloud I showed:
My golden armlets flashed and glowed.
A crown I wore, an axe I swayed,
And all I met were sore afraid.
I roved where Daṇḍak wood is spread;
On flesh of slaughtered saints I fed.
Then Viśvámitra, sage revered,
Holy of heart, my fury feared.
To Daśaratha's court he sped
And went before the king and said:

"With me, my lord, thy Ráma send
On holy days his aid to lend.
Márícha fills my soul with dread
And keeps me sore disquieted."

The monarch heard the saint's request
And thus the glorious sage addressed:

"My boy as yet in arms untrained
The age of twelve has scarce attained.

But I myself a host will lead
To guard thee in the hour of need.
My host with fourfold troops complete,
The rover of the night shall meet,
And I, O best of saints, will kill
Thy foeman and thy prayer fulfil."
The king vouchsafed his willing aid:
The saint again this answer made:
"By Ráma's might, and his alone,
Can this great fiend be overthrown.
I know in days of yore the Blest
Thy saving help in fight confessed.
Still of thy famous deeds they tell
In heaven above, in earth, and hell,
A mighty host obeys thy hest:
Here let it still, I pray thee, rest.
Thy glorious son, though yet a boy,
Will in the fight that fiend destroy.
Ráma alone with me shall go:
Be happy, victor of the foe."

He spoke: the monarch gave assent,
And Ráma to the hermit lent.
So to his woodland home in joy
Went Viśvámitra with the boy.
With ready bow the champion stood
To guard the rites in Daṇḍak wood.
With glorious eyes, most bright to view,
Beardless as yet and dark of hue;
A single robe his only wear,
His temples veiled with waving hair,

Around his neck a chain of gold,
He grasped the bow he loved to hold;
And the young hero's presence made
A glory in the forest shade.
Thus Ráma with his beauteous mien,
Like the young rising moon was seen,
I, like a cloud which tempest brings,
My arms adorned with golden rings,
Proud of the boon which lent me might,

824

Approached where dwelt the anchorite.
But Ráma saw me venturing nigh,
Raising my murderous axe on high;
He saw, and fearless of the foe,
Strung with calm hand his trusty bow.
By pride of conscious strength beguiled,
I scorned him as a feeble child,
And rushed with an impetuous bound
On Viśvámitra's holy ground.
A keen swift shaft he pointed well,
The foeman's rage to check and quell,
And hurled a hundred leagues away
Deep in the ocean waves I lay.
He would not kill, but, nobly brave,
My forfeit life he chose to save.
So there I lay with wandering sense
Dazed by that arrow's violence.
Long in the sea I lay: at length
Slowly returned my sense and strength,
And rising from my watery bed
To Lanká's town again I sped.
Thus was I spared, but all my band
Fell slain by Ráma's conquering hand,—
A boy, untrained in warrior's skill,
Of iron arm and dauntless will.
If thou with Ráma still, in spite
Of warning and of prayer, wilt fight,
I see terrific woes impend,
And dire defeat thy days will end.
Thy giants all will feel the blow
And share the fatal overthrow,
Who love the taste of joy and play,
The banquet and the festal day.
Thine eyes will see destruction take
Thy Lanká, lost for Sítá's sake,
And stately pile and palace fall
With terrace, dome, and jewelled wall.
The good will die: the crime of kings
Destruction on the people brings:
The sinless die, as in the lake
The fish must perish with the snake.

The prostrate giants thou wilt see
Slain for this folly wrought by thee,
Their bodies bright with precious scent
And sheen of heavenly ornament;
Or see the remnant of thy train
Seek refuge far, when help is vain
And with their wives, or widowed, fly
To every quarter of the sky;
Thy mournful eyes, where'er they turn,
Will see thy stately city burn,
When royal homes with fire are red,
And arrowy nets around are spread.
A sin that tops all sins in shame
Is outrage to another's dame,
A thousand wives thy palace fill,
And countless beauties wait thy will.
O rest contented with thine own,
Nor let thy race be overthrown.
If thou, O King, hast still delight
In rank and wealth and power and might,
In noble wives, in troops of friends,
In all that royal state attends,
I warn thee, cast not all away,
Nor challenge Ráma to the fray.
If deaf to every friendly prayer,
Thou still wilt seek the strife,
And from the side of Ráma tear
His lovely Maithil wife,
Soon will thy life and empire end
Destroyed by Ráma's bow,
And thou, with kith and kin and friend,
To Yáma's realm must go."

CANTO

XXXIX

Máricha's Speech

"I told thee of that dreadful day
When Ráma smote and spared to slay.
Now hear me, Rávan, while I tell
What in the after time befell.
At length, restored to strength and pride,
I and two mighty fiends beside
Assumed the forms of deer and strayed
Through Dandak wood in lawn and glade,
I reared terrific horns: beneath
Were flaming tongue and pointed teeth.
I roamed where'er my fancy led,
And on the flesh of hermits fed,
In sacred haunt, by hallowed tree,
Where'er the ritual fires might be.
A fearful shape, I wandered through
The wood, and many a hermit slew.
With ruthless rage the saints I killed
Who in the grove their tasks fulfilled.
When smitten to the earth they sank,
Their flesh I ate, their blood I drank,
And with my cruel deeds dismayed
All dwellers in the forest shade,
Spoiling their rites in bitter hate,
With human blood inebriate.
Once in the wood I chanced to see
Ráma again, a devotee,
A hermit, fed on scanty fare,
Who made the good of all his care.
His noble wife was by his side,
And Lakshman in the battle tried.
In senseless pride I scorned the might

827

Of that illustrious anchorite,
And heedless of a hermit foe,
Recalled my earlier overthrow.

I charged him in my rage and scorn
To slay him with my pointed horn,
In heedless haste, to fury wrought
As on my former wounds I thought.
Then from the mighty bow he drew
Three foe-destroying arrows flew,
Keen-pointed, leaping from the string,
Swift as the wind or feathered king.
Dire shafts, on flesh of foemen fed,
Like rushing thunderbolts they sped,
With knots well smoothed and barbs well bent,
Shot e'en as one, the arrows went.
But I who Ráma's might had felt,
And knew the blows the hero dealt,
Escaped by rapid flight. The two
Who lingered on the spot, he slew.
I fled from mortal danger, freed
From the dire shaft by timely speed.
Now to deep thought my days I give,
And as a humble hermit live.
In every shrub, in every tree
I view that noblest devotee.
In every knotted trunk I mark
His deerskin and his coat of bark,
And see the bow-armed Ráma stand
Like Yáma with his noose in hand.
I tell thee Rávaṇ, in my fright
A thousand Rámas mock my sight,
This wood with every bush and bough
Seems all one fearful Ráma now.
Throughout the grove there is no spot
So lonely where I see him not.
He haunts me in my dreams by night,
And wakes me with the wild affright.
The letter that begins his name
Sends terror through my startled frame.
The rapid cars whereon we ride,

The rich rare jewels, once my pride,
Have names that strike upon mine ear
With hated sound that counsels fear.
His mighty strength too well I know,
Nor art thou match for such a foe.
Too strong were Raghus's son in fight
For Namuchi or Bali's might.
Then Ráma to the battle dare,
Or else be patient and forbear;
But, wouldst thou see me live in peace,
Let mention of the hero cease.
The good whose holy lives were spent
In deepest thought, most innocent,
With all their people many a time
Have perished through another's crime.
So in the common ruin, I
Must for another's folly die,
Do all thy strength and courage can,
But ne'er will I approve the plan.
For he, in might supremely great,
The giant world could extirpate,
Since, when impetuous Khara sought
The grove of Janasthán and fought
For Śúrpaṇakhá's sake, he died
By Ráma's hand in battle tried.
How has he wronged thee? Soothly swear,
And Ráma's fault and sin declare.
I warn thee, and my words are wise,
I seek thy people's weal:
But if this rede thou wilt despise,
Nor hear my last appeal,
Thou with thy kin and all thy friends
In fight this day wilt die,
When his great bow the hero bends,
And shafts unerring fly."

CANTO
XL

Rávan's Speech

But Rávaṇ scorned the rede he gave
In timely words to warn and save,
E'en as the wretch who hates to live
Rejects the herb the leeches give.
By fate to sin and ruin spurred,
That sage advice the giant heard,
Then in reproaches hard and stern
Thus to Márícha spoke in turn:

"Is this thy counsel, weak and base,
Unworthy of thy giant race?
Thy speech is fruitless, vain, thy toil
Like casting seed on barren soil.
No words of thine shall drive me back
From Ráma and the swift attack.
A fool is he, inured to sin,
And more, of human origin.
The craven, at a woman's call
To leave his sire, his mother, all
The friends he loved, the power and sway,
And hasten to the woods away!
But now his anger will I rouse,
Stealing away his darling spouse.
I in thy sight will ravish her
From Khara's cruel murderer.
Upon this plan my soul is bent,
And naught shall move my firm intent,
Not if the way through demons led
And Gods with Indra at their head.
'Tis thine, when questioned, to explain
The hope and fear, the loss and gain,

830

And, when thy king thy thoughts would know,
The triumph or the danger show.
A prudent counsellor should wait,
And speak when ordered in debate,
With hands uplifted, calm and meek,
If honour and reward he seek.
Or, when some prudent course he sees
Which, spoken, may his king displease

He should by hints of dexterous art
His counsel to his lord impart.
But prudent words are said in vain
When the blunt speech brings grief and pain.
A high-souled king will scarcely thank
The man who shames his royal rank.
Five are the shapes that kings assume,
Of majesty, of grace, and gloom:
Like Indra now, or Agni, now
Like the dear Moon, with placid brow:
Like mighty Varun now they show,
Now fierce as He who rules below.
O giant, monarchs lofty-souled
Are kind and gentle, stern and bold,
With gracious love their gifts dispense
And swiftly punish each offence.
Thus subjects should their rulers view
With all respect and honour due.
But folly leads thy heart to slight
Thy monarch and neglect his right.
Thou hast in lawless pride addressed
With bitter words thy royal guest.
I asked thee not my strength to scan,
Or loss and profit in the plan.
I only spoke to tell the deed
O mighty one, by me decreed,
And bid thee in the peril lend
Thy succour to support thy friend.
Hear me again, and I will tell
How thou canst aid my venture well.
In semblance of a golden deer
Adorned with silver drops, appear:

And near the cottage in the way
Of Ráma and his consort stray.
Draw nigh, and wandering through the brake
With thy strange form her fancy take.
The Maithil dame with wondering eyes
Will took upon thy fair disguise,
And quickly bid her husband go
And bring the deer that charms her so,
When Raghu's son has left the place,
Still pressing onward in the chase,
Cry out, "O Lakshman! Ah, mine own!"
With voice resembling Ráma's tone.
When Lakshman hears his brother's cry,
Impelled by Sítá he will fly,
Restless with eager love, to aid
The hunter in the distant shade.
When both her guards have left her side,
Even as Indra, thousand-eyed,
Clasps Śachí, will I bear away
The Maithil dame an easy prey.
When thou, my friend, this aid hast lent,
Go where thou wilt and live content.
True servant, faithful to thy vow,
With half my realm I thee endow.
Go forth, may luck thy way attend
That leads thee to the happy end.
I in my car will quickly be
In Daṇḍak wood, and follow thee.
So will I cheat this Ráma's eyes
And win without a blow the prize;
And safe return to Lanká's town
With thee, my friend, this day shall crown.
But if thou wilt not aid my will,
My hand this day thy blood shall spill.
Yea, thou must share the destined task,
For force will take the help I ask.
No bliss that rebel's life attends
Whose stubborn will his lord offends.
Thy life, if thou the task assay,
In jeopardy may stand;
Oppose me, and this very day

832

Thou diest by this hand.
Now ponder all that thou hast heard
Within thy prudent breast:
Reflect with care on every word,
And do what seems the best."

CANTO

XLI

Márícha's Reply

Against his judgment sorely pressed
By his imperious lord's behest,
Márícha threats of death defied
And thus with bitter words replied:
"Ah, who, my King, with sinful thought
This wild and wicked counsel taught,
By which destruction soon will fall
On thee, thy sons, thy realm and all?
Who is the guilty wretch who sees
With envious eye thy blissful ease,
And by this plan, so falsely shown,
Death's gate for thee has open thrown?
With souls impelled by mean desire
Thy foes against thy life conspire.
They urge thee to destruction's brink,
And gladly would they see thee sink.
Who with base thought to work thee woe
This fatal road has dared to show,
And, triumph in his wicked eye,
Would see thee enter in and die?
To all thy counsellors, untrue,
The punishment of death is due,
Who see thee tempt the dangerous way,
Nor strain each nerve thy foot to stay.
Wise lords, whose king, by passion led,

833

The path of sin begins to tread,
Restrain him while there yet is time:
But thine,—they see nor heed the crime.
These by their master's will obtain
Merit and fame and joy and gain.
'Tis only by their master's grace
That servants hold their lofty place.
But when the monarch stoops to sin
They lose each joy they strive to win,
And all the people people high and low
Fall in the common overthrow.

Merit and fame and honour spring,
Best of the mighty, from the king.
So all should strive with heart and will
To keep the king from every ill.
Pride, violence, and sullen hate
Will ne'er maintain a monarch's state,
And those who cruel deeds advise
Must perish when their master dies,
Like drivers with their cars o'erthrown
In places rough with root and stone.
The good whose holy lives were spent
On duty's highest laws intent,
With wives and children many a time
Have perished for another's crime.
Hapless are they whose sovereign lord,
Opposed to all, by all abhorred,
Is cruel-hearted, harsh, severe:
Thus might a jackal tend the deer.
Now all the giant race await,
Destroyed by thee, a speedy fate,
Ruled by a king so cruel-souled,
Foolish in heart and uncontrolled.
Think not I fear the sudden blow
That threatens now to lay me low:
I mourn the ruin that I see
Impending o'er thy host and thee.
Me first perchance will Ráma kill,
But soon his hand thy blood will spill.
I die, and if by Ráma slain

And not by thee, I count it gain.
Soon as the hero's face I see
His angry eyes will murder me,
And if on her thy hands thou lay
Thy friends and thou are dead this day.
If with my help thou still must dare
The lady from her lord to tear,
Farewell to all our days are o'er,
Lanká and giants are no more.
In vain, in vain, an earnest friend,
I warn thee, King, and pray.
Thou wilt not to my prayers attend,
Or heed the words I say
So men, when life is fleeting fast
And death's sad hour is nigh,
Heedless and blinded to the last
Reject advice and die."

CANTO
XLII

Márícha Transformed

Márícha thus in wild unrest
With bitter words the king addressed.
Then to his giant lord in dread,
"Arise, and let us go," he said.
"Ah, I have met that mighty lord
Armed with his shafts and bow and sword,
And if again that bow he bend
Our lives that very hour will end.
For none that warrior can provoke
And think to fly his deadly stroke.
Like Yáma with his staff is he,
And his dread hand will slaughter thee.
What can I more? My words can find

No passage to thy stubborn mind.
I go, great King, thy task to share,
And may success attend thee there."

With that reply and bold consent
The giant king was well content.
He strained Márícha to his breast
And thus with joyful words addressed:
"There spoke a hero dauntless still,
Obedient to his master's will,
Márícha's proper self once more:
Some other took thy shape before.
Come, mount my jewelled car that flies.
Will-governed, through the yielding skies.
These asses, goblin-faced, shall bear
Us quickly through the fields of air.
Attract the lady with thy shape,
Then through the wood, at will, escape.
And I, when she has no defence,
Will seize the dame and bear her thence."
Again Márícha made reply,
Consent and will to signify.
With rapid speed the giants two
From the calm hermit dwelling flew,
Borne in that wondrous chariot, meet
For some great God's celestial seat.
They from their airy path looked down
On many a wood and many a town,
On lake and river, brook and rill,
City and realm and towering hill.
Soon he whom giant hosts obeyed,
Márícha by his side, surveyed
The dark expanse of Daṇḍak wood
Where Ráma's hermit cottage stood.
They left the flying car, whereon
The wealth of gold and jewels shone,
And thus the giant king addressed
Márícha as his hand he pressed:

"Márícha, look! before our eyes
Round Ráma's home the plantains rise.

His hermitage is now in view:
Quick to the work we came to do!"

Thus Rávan spoke, Márícha heard
Obedient to his master's word,
Threw off his giant shape and near
The cottage strayed a beauteous deer.
With magic power, by rapid change,
His borrowed form was fair and strange.
A sapphire tipped each horn with light;
His face was black relieved with white.
The turkis and the ruby shed
A glory from his ears and head.
His arching neck was proudly raised,
And lazulites beneath it blazed.
With roseate bloom his flanks were dyed,
And lotus tints adorned his hide.
His shape was fair, compact, and slight;
His hoofs were carven lazulite.
His tail with every changing glow
Displayed the hues of Indra's bow.
With glossy skin so strangely flecked,
With tints of every gem bedecked.
A light o'er Ráma's home he sent,
And through the wood, where'er he went.
The giant clad in that strange dress
That took the soul with loveliness,
To charm the fair Videhan's eyes
With mingled wealth of mineral dyes,
Moved onward, cropping in his way,
The grass and grain and tender spray.
His coat with drops of silver bright,
A form to gaze on with delight,
He raised his fair neck as he went
To browse on bud and filament.
Now in the Cassia grove he strayed,
Now by the cot in plantains' shade.
Slowly and slowly on he came
To catch the glances of the dame,
And the tall deer of splendid hue

837

Shone full at length in Sítá's view.
He roamed where'er his fancy chose
Where Ráma's leafy cottage rose.
Now near, now far, in careless ease,
He came and went among the trees.
Now with light feet he turned to fly,
Now, reassured, again drew nigh:
Now gambolled close with leap and bound,
Now lay upon the grassy ground:
Now sought the door, devoid of fear,
And mingled with the troop of deer;
Led them a little way, and thence
Again returned with confidence.
Now flying far, now turning back
Emboldened on his former track,
Seeking to win the lady's glance
He wandered through the green expanse.
Then thronging round, the woodland deer
Gazed on his form with wondering fear;
A while they followed where he led,
Then snuffed the tainted gale and fled.
The giant, though he longed to slay
The startled quarry, spared the prey,
And mindful of the shape he wore
To veil his nature, still forbore.
Then Sítá of the glorious eye,
Returning from her task drew nigh;
For she had sought the wood to bring
Each loveliest flower of early spring.
Now would the bright-eyed lady choose
Some gorgeous bud with blending hues,
Now plucked the mango's spray, and now
The bloom from an Aśoka bough.
She with her beauteous form, unmeet
For woodland life and lone retreat,
That wondrous dappled deer beheld
Gemmed with rich pearls, unparalleled,
His silver hair the lady saw,
His radiant teeth and lips and jaw,
And gazed with rapture as her eyes
Expanded in their glad surprise.

And when the false deer's glances fell
On her whom Ráma loved so well,
He wandered here and there, and cast
A luminous beauty as he passed;
And Janak's child with strange delight
Kept gazing on the unwonted sight.

CANTO

XLIII

The Wondrous Deer

She stooped, her hands with flowers to fill,
But gazed upon the marvel still:
Gazed on its back and sparkling side
Where silver hues with golden vied.
Joyous was she of faultless mould,
With glossy skin like polished gold.
And loudly to her husband cried
And bow-armed Lakshman by his side:
Again, again she called in glee:
"O come this glorious creature see;
Quick, quick, my lord, this deer to view.
And bring thy brother Lakshman too."
As through the wood her clear tones rang,
Swift to her side the brothers sprang.
With eager eyes the grove they scanned,
And saw the deer before them stand.
But doubt was strong in Lakshman's breast,
Who thus his thought and fear expressed:

"Stay, for the wondrous deer we see
The fiend Márícha's self may be.
Ere now have kings who sought this place
To take their pastime in the chase,
Met from his wicked art defeat,

And fallen slain by like deceit.
He wears, well trained in magic guile,
The figure of a deer a while,
Bright as the very sun, or place
Where dwell the gay Gandharva race.
No deer, O Ráma, e'er was seen
Thus decked with gold and jewels' sheen.
'Tis magic, for the world has ne'er,
Lord of the world, shown aught so fair."

But Sítá of the lovely smile,
A captive to the giant's wile,
Turned Lakshmaṇ's prudent speech aside
And thus with eager words replied:
"My honoured lord, this deer I see
With beauty rare enraptures me.
Go, chief of mighty arm, and bring
For my delight this precious thing.
Fair creatures of the woodland roam
Untroubled near our hermit home.
The forest cow and stag are there,
The fawn, the monkey, and the bear,
Where spotted deer delight to play,

And strong and beauteous Kinnars stray.
But never, as they wandered by,
Has such a beauty charmed mine eye
As this with limbs so fair and slight,
So gentle, beautiful and bright.
O see, how fair it is to view
With jewels of each varied hue:
Bright as the rising moon it glows,
Lighting the wood where'er it goes.
Ah me, what form and grace are there!
Its limbs how fine, its hues how fair!
Transcending all that words express,
It takes my soul with loveliness.
O, if thou would, to please me, strive
To take the beauteous thing alive,
How thou wouldst gaze with wondering eyes
Delighted on the lovely prize!

840

And when our woodland life is o'er,
And we enjoy our realm once more,
The wondrous animal will grace
The chambers of my dwelling-place,
And a dear treasure will it be
To Bharat and the queens and me,
And all with rapture and amaze
Upon its heavenly form will gaze.
But if the beauteous deer, pursued,
Thine arts to take it still elude,
Strike it, O chieftain, and the skin
Will be a treasure, laid within.
O, how I long my time to pass
Sitting upon the tender grass,
With that soft fell beneath me spread
Bright with its hair of golden thread!
This strong desire, this eager will,
Befits a gentle lady ill:
But when I first beheld, its look
My breast with fascination took.
See, golden hair its flank adorns,
And sapphires tip its branching horns.
Resplendent as the lunar way,
Or the first blush of opening day,
With graceful form and radiant hue
It charmed thy heart, O chieftain, too."

He heard her speech with willing ear,
He looked again upon the deer.
Its lovely shape his breast beguiled
Moved by the prayer of Janak's child,
And yielding for her pleasure's sake,
To Lakshmaṇ Ráma turned and spake:

"Mark, Lakshmaṇ, mark how Sítá's breast
With eager longing is possessed.
To-day this deer of wondrous breed
Must for his passing beauty bleed,
Brighter than e'er in Nandan strayed,
Or Chaitraratha's heavenly shade.
How should the groves of earth possess

Such all-surpassing loveliness!
The hair lies smooth and bright and fine,
Or waves upon each curving line,
And drops of living gold bedeck
The beauty of his side and neck.
O look, his crimson tongue between
His teeth like flaming fire is seen,
Flashing, whene'er his lips he parts,
As from a cloud the lightning darts.
O see his sunlike forehead shine
With emerald tints and almandine,
While pearly light and roseate glow
Of shells adorn his neck below.
No eye on such a deer can rest
But soft enchantment takes the breast:
No man so fair a thing behold
Ablaze with light of radiant gold,
Celestial, bright with jewels' sheen,
Nor marvel when his eyes have seen.
A king equipped with bow and shaft
Delights in gentle forest craft,
And as in boundless woods he strays
The quarry for the venison slays.
There as he wanders with his train
A store of wealth he oft may gain.
He claims by right the precious ore,
He claims the jewels' sparkling store.
Such gains are dearer in his eyes
Than wealth that in his chamber lies,
The dearest things his spirit knows,
Dear as the bliss which Śukra chose.
But oft the rich expected gain
Which heedless men pursue in vain,
The sage, who prudent counsels know,
Explain and in a moment show.
This best of deer, this gem of all,
To yield his precious spoils must fall,
And tender Sítá by my side
Shall sit upon the golden hide.
Ne'er could I find so rich a coat
On spotted deer or sheep or goat.

No buck or antelope has such,
So bright to view, so soft to touch.
This radiant deer and one on high
That moves in glory through the sky,
Alike in heavenly beauty are,
One on the earth and one a star.
But, brother, if thy fears be true,
And this bright creature that we view
Be fierce Márícha in disguise,
Then by this hand he surely dies.
For that dire fiend who spurns control
With bloody hand and cruel soul,
Has roamed this forest and dismayed
The holiest saints who haunt the shade.
Great archers, sprung of royal race,
Pursuing in the wood the chase,
Have fallen by his wicked art,
And now my shaft shall strike his heart.
Vatápi, by his magic power

Made heedless saints his flesh devour,
Then, from within their frames he rent
Forth bursting from imprisonment.
But once his art in senseless pride
Upon the mightiest saint he tried,
Agastya's self, and caused him taste
The baited meal before him placed.
Vátápi, when the rite was o'er,
Would take the giant form he wore,
But Saint Agastya knew his wile
And checked the giant with smile.
"Vátápi, thou with cruel spite
Hast conquered many an anchorite
The noblest of the Bráhman caste,—
And now thy ruin comes at last."
Now if my power he thus defies,
This giant, like Vátápi dies,
Daring to scorn a man like me,
A self subduing devotee.
Yea, as Agastya slew the foe,
My hand shall lay Márícha low

Clad in thine arms thy bow in hand,
To guard the Maithil lady stand,
With watchful eye and thoughtful breast
Keeping each word of my behest
I go, and hunting through the brake
This wondrous deer will bring or take.
Yea surely I will bring the spoil
Returning from my hunter's toil
See, Lakshman how my consort's eyes
Are longing for the lovely prize.
This day it falls, that I may win
The treasure of so fair a skin.
Do thou and Sítá watch with care
Lest danger seize you unaware.
Swift from my bow one shaft will fly;
The stricken deer will fall and die
Then quickly will I strip the game
And bring the trophy to my dame.
Jaṭáyus, guardian good and wise,
Our old and faithful friend,
The best and strongest bird that flies,
His willing aid will lend
The Maithil lady well protect,
For every chance provide,
And in thy tender care suspect
A foe on every side."

CANTO
XLIV

Márícha's Death

Thus having warned his brother bold
He grasped his sword with haft of gold,
And bow with triple flexure bent,
His own delight and ornament;

Then bound two quivers to his side,
And hurried forth with eager stride.
Soon as the antlered monarch saw
The lord of monarchs near him draw,
A while with trembling heart he fled,
Then turned and showed his stately head.
With sword and bow the chief pursued
Where'er the fleeing deer he viewed
Sending from dell and lone recess
The splendour of his loveliness.
Now full in view the creature stood
Now vanished in the depth of wood;
Now running with a languid flight,
Now like a meteor lost to sight.
With trembling limbs away he sped;
Then like the moon with clouds o'erspread
Gleamed for a moment bright between
The trees, and was again unseen.
Thus in the magic deer's disguise
Márícha lured him to the prize,
And seen a while, then lost to view,
Far from his cot the hero drew.
Still by the flying game deceived
The hunter's heart was wroth and grieved,
And wearied with the fruitless chase
He stayed him in a shady place.
Again the rover of the night
Enraged the chieftain, full in sight,
Slow moving in the coppice near,
Surrounded by the woodland deer.
Again the hunter sought the game
That seemed a while to court his aim:
But seized again with sudden dread,
Beyond his sight the creature fled.
Again the hero left the shade,
Again the deer before him strayed.
With surer hope and stronger will
The hunter longed his prey to kill.
Then as his soul impatient grew,
An arrow from his side he drew,
Resplendent at the sunbeam's glow,

The crusher of the smitten foe.
With skillful heed the mighty lord
Fixed well shaft and strained the cord.
Upon the deer his eyes he bent,
And like a fiery serpent went
The arrow Brahma's self had framed,
Alive with sparks that hissed and flamed,
Like Indra's flashing levin, true
To the false deer the missile flew
Cleaving his flesh that wonderous dart
Stood quivering in Márícha's heart.
Scarce from the ground one foot he sprang,
Then stricken fell with deadly pang.
Half lifeless, as he pressed the ground,
He gave a roar of awful sound
And ere the wounded giant died
He threw his borrowed form aside
Remembering still his lord's behest
He pondered in his heart how best
Sítá might send her guard away,
And Rávaṇ seize the helpless prey.
The monster knew the time was nigh,
And called aloud with eager cry,
"Ho, Sítá, Lakshmaṇ" and the tone

He borrowed was like Ráma's own.

So by that matchless arrow cleft,
The deer's bright form Márícha left,
Resumed his giant shape and size
And closed in death his languid eyes.
When Ráma saw his awful foe
Gasp, smeared with blood, in deadly throe,
His anxious thoughts to Sítá sped,
And the wise words that Lakshmaṇ said,
That this was false Márícha's art,
Returned again upon his heart.
He knew the foe he triumphed o'er
The name of great Márícha bore.
"The fiend," he pondered, 'ere he died,

"Ho, Lakshmaṇ! ho, my Sítá!" cried
Ah, if that cry has reached her ear,
How dire must be my darling's fear!
And Lakshmaṇ of the mighty arm,
What thinks he in his wild alarm?
As thus he thought in sad surmise,
Each startled hair began to rise,
And when he saw the giant slain
And thought upon that cry again,
His spirit sank and terror pressed
Full sorely on the hero's breast.
Another deer he chased and struck,
He bore away the the fallen buck,
To Janasthán then turned his face
And hastened to his dwelling place.

CANTO

XLV

Lakshman's Departure

But Sítá hearing as she thought,
Her husband's cry with anguish fraught,
Called to her guardian, "Lakshmaṇ, run
And in the wood seek Raghu's son.
Scarce can my heart retain its throne,
Scarce can my life be called mine own,
As all my powers and senses fail
At that long, loud and bitter wail.
Haste to the wood with all thy speed
And save thy brother in his need.
Go, save him in the distant glade
Where loud he calls, for timely aid.
He falls beneath some giant foe—
A bull whom lions overthrow."

Deaf to her prayer, no step he stirred
Obedient to his mother's word,
Then Janak's child, with ire inflamed,
In words of bitter scorn exclaimed exclaimed

"Sumitrá's son, a friend in show,
Thou art in truth thy brother's foe,
Who canst at such any hour deny
Thy succour and neglect his cry.
Yes, Lakshmaṇ, smit with love of me
Thy brother's death thou fain wouldst see.
This guilty love thy heart has swayed
And makes thy feet so loth to aid.
Thou hast no love for Ráma, no:
Thy joy is vice, thy thoughts are low
Hence thus unmoved thou yet canst stay
While my dear lord is far away.
If aught of ill my lord betide
Who led thee here, thy chief and guide,
Ah, what will be my hapless fate
Left in the wild wood desolate!"

Thus spoke the lady sad with fear,
With many a sigh and many a tear,
Still trembling like a captured doe:
And Lakshmaṇ spoke to calm her woe:

"Videhan Queen, be sure of this,—
And at the thought thy fear dismiss,—
Thy husband's mightier power defies
All Gods and angels of the skies,
Gandharvas, and the sons of light,
Serpents, and rovers of the night.
I tell thee, of the sons of earth,
Of Gods who boast celestial birth,
Of beasts and birds and giant hosts,
Of demigods, Gandharvas, ghosts,
Of awful fiends, O thou most fair,
There lives not one whose heart would dare
To meet thy Ráma in the fight,
Like Indra's self unmatched in might.

848

Such idle words thou must not say
Thy Ráma lives whom none may slay.
I will not, cannot leave thee here
In the wild wood till he be near.
The mightiest strength can ne'er withstand
His eager force, his vigorous hand.
No, not the triple world allied
With all the immortal Gods beside.
Dismiss thy fear, again take heart,
Let all thy doubt and woe depart.
Thy lord, be sure, will soon be here
And bring thee back that best of deer.
Not his, not his that mournful cry,
Nor haply came it from the sky.
Some giant's art was busy there
And framed a castle based on air.
A precious pledge art thou, consigned
To me by him of noblest mind,
Nor can I fairest dame, forsake
The pledge which Ráma bade me take.
Upon our heads, O Queen, we drew
The giants' hate when Ráma slew
Their chieftain Khara, and the shade
Of Janasthán in ruin laid.
Through all this mighty wood they rove
With varied cries from grove to grove
On rapine bent they wander here:
But O, dismiss thy causeless fear."

Bright flashed her eye as Lakshman spoke
And forth her words of fury broke
Upon her truthful guardian, flung
With bitter taunts that pierced and stung:
"Shame on such false compassion, base
Defiler of thy glorious race!
'Twere joyous sight I ween to thee

My lord in direst strait to see.
Thou knowest Ráma sore bested,
Or word like this thou ne'er hadst said.
No marvel if we find such sin

In rivals false to kith and kin.
Wretches like thee of evil kind,
Concealing crime with crafty mind.
Thou, wretch, thine aid wilt still deny,
And leave my lord alone to die.
Has love of me unnerved thy hand,
Or Bharat's art this ruin planned?
But be the treachery his or thine,
In vain, in vain the base design.
For how shall I, the chosen bride
Of dark-hued Ráma, lotus-eyed,
The queen who once called Ráma mine,
To love of other men decline?
Believe me, Lakshmaṇ, Ráma's wife
Before thine eyes will quit this life,
And not a moment will she stay
If her dear lord have passed away."

The lady's bitter speech, that stirred
Each hair upon his frame, he heard.
With lifted hands together laid,
His calm reply he gently made:

"No words have I to answer now:
My deity, O Queen, art thou.
But 'tis no marvel, dame, to find
Such lack of sense in womankind.
Throughout this world, O Maithil dame,
Weak women's hearts are still the same.
Inconstant, urged by envious spite,
They sever friends and hate the right.
I cannot brook, Videhan Queen,
Thy words intolerably keen.
Mine ears thy fierce reproaches pain
As boiling water seethes the brain.
And now to bear me witness all
The dwellers in the wood I call,
That, when with words of truth I plead,
This harsh reply is all my meed.
Ah, woe is thee! Ah, grief, that still
Eager to do my brother's will,

Mourning thy woman's nature, I
Must see thee doubt my truth and die.
I fly to Ráma's side, and Oh,
May bliss attend thee while I go!
May all attendant wood-gods screen
Thy head from harm, O large-eyed Queen!
And though dire omens meet my sight
And fill my soul with wild affright,
May I return in peace and see
The son of Raghu safe with thee!"

The child of Janak heard him speak,
And the hot tear-drops down her cheek,
Increasing to a torrent, ran,
As thus once more the dame began:
"O Lakshman, if I widowed be
Godávarí's flood shall cover me,
Or I will die by cord, or leap,
Life weary, from yon rocky steep;
Or deadly poison will I drink,
Or 'neath the kindled flames will sink,
But never, reft of Ráma, can
Consent to touch a meaner man."

The Maithil dame with many sighs,
And torrents pouring from her eyes,
The faithful Lakshman thus addressed,
And smote her hands upon her breast.
Sumitrá's son, o'erwhelmed by fears,
Looked on the large-eyed queen:
He saw that flood of burning tears,
He saw that piteous mien.
He yearned sweet comfort to afford,
He strove to soothe her pain;
But to the brother of her lord
She spoke no word again.
His reverent hands once more he raised,
His head he slightly bent,
Upon her face he sadly gazed,
And then toward Ráma went.

CANTO
XLVI

The Guest

The angry Lakshmaṇ scarce could brook
    Her bitter words, her furious look.
    With dark forebodings in his breast
To Ráma's side he quickly pressed.

Then ten necked Rávaṇ saw the time
Propitious for his purposed crime.
A mendicant in guise he came
And stood before the Maithil dame.
His garb was red, with tufted hair
And sandalled feet a shade he bare,
And from the fiend's left shoulder slung
A staff and water-vessel hung.
Near to the lovely dame he drew,
While both the chiefs were far from view,
As darkness takes the evening air
When neither sun nor moon is there.
He bent his eye upon the dame,
A princess fair, of spotless fame:
So might some baleful planet be
Near Moon-forsaken Rohiṇí.
As the fierce tyrant nearer drew,
The trees in Janasthán that grew
Waved not a leaf for fear and woe,
And the hushed wind forbore to blow.
Godávarí's waters as they fled,
Saw his fierce eye-balls flashing red,
And from each swiftly-gliding wave
A melancholy murmur gave.
Then Rávaṇ, when his eager eye
Beheld the longed-for moment nigh,

In mendicant's apparel dressed
Near to the Maithil lady pressed.

In holy guise, a fiend abhorred,
He found her mourning for her lord.
Thus threatening draws Śaniśchar nigh
To Chitrá in the evening sky;
Thus the deep well by grass concealed
Yawns treacherous in the verdant field.
He stood and looked upon the dame
Of Ráma, queen of spotless fame
With her bright teeth and each fair limb
Like the full moon she seemed to him,
Sitting within her leafy cot,
Weeping for woe that left her not.
Thus, while with joy his pulses beat,
He saw her in her lone retreat,
Eyed like the lotus, fair to view
In silken robes of amber hue.
Pierced to the core by Káma's dart
He murmured texts with lying art,
And questioned with a soft address
The lady in her loneliness.
The fiend essayed with gentle speech
The heart of that fair dame to reach,
Pride of the worlds, like Beauty's Queen
Without her darling lotus seen:

"O thou whose silken robes enfold
A form more fair than finest gold,
With lotus garland on thy head,
Like a sweet spring with bloom o'erspread,
Who art thou, fair one, what thy name,
Beauty, or Honour, Fortune, Fame,
Spirit, or nymph, or Queen of love
Descended from thy home above?
Bright as the dazzling jasmine shine
Thy small square teeth in level line.
Like two black stars aglow with light
Thine eyes are large and pure and bright.
Thy charms of smile and teeth and hair

And winning eyes, O thou most fair,
Steal all my spirit, as the flow
Of rivers mines the bank below.
How bright, how fine each flowing tress!
How firm those orbs beneath thy dress!
That dainty waist with ease were spanned,
Sweet lady, by a lover's hand.
Mine eyes, O beauty, ne'er have seen
Goddess or nymph so fair of mien,
Or bright Gandharva's heavenly dame,
Or woman of so perfect frame.
In youth's soft prime thy years are few,
And earth has naught so fair to view.
I marvel one like thee in face
Should make the woods her dwelling-place.
Leave, lady, leave this lone retreat
In forest wilds for thee unmeet,
Where giants fierce and strong assume
All shapes and wander in the gloom.
These dainty feet were formed to tread
Some palace floor with carpets spread,
Or wander in trim gardens where
Each opening bud perfumes the air.
The richest robe thy form should deck,
The rarest gems adorn thy neck,
The sweetest wreath should bind thy hair,
The noblest lord thy bed should share.
Art thou akin, O fair of form,
To Rudras, or the Gods of storm,
Or to the glorious Vasus? How
Can less than these be bright as thou?
But never nymph or heavenly maid
Or Goddess haunts this gloomy shade.
Here giants roam, a savage race;
What led thee to so dire a place?
Here monkeys leap from tree to tree,
And bears and tigers wander free;
Here ravening lions prowl, and fell
Hyenas in the thickets yell,
And elephants infuriate roam,

Mighty and fierce, their woodland home.
Dost thou not dread, so soft and fair,
Tiger and lion, wolf and bear?
Hast thou, O beauteous dame, no fear
In the wild wood so lone and drear?
Whose and who art thou? whence and why
Sweet lady, with no guardian nigh,
Dost thou this awful forest tread
By giant bands inhabited?"

The praise the high-souled Rávaṇ spoke
No doubt within her bosom woke.
His saintly look and Bráhman guise
Deceived the lady's trusting eyes.
With due attention on the guest
Her hospitable rites she pressed.
She bade the stranger to a seat,
And gave him water for his feet.
The bowl and water-pot he bare,
And garb which wandering Bráhmans wear
Forbade a doubt to rise.
Won by his holy look she deemed
The stranger even as he seemed
To her deluded eyes.
Intent on hospitable care,
She brought her best of woodland fare,
And showed her guest a seat.
She bade the saintly stranger lave
His feet in water which she gave,
And sit and rest and eat.
He kept his eager glances bent
On her so kindly eloquent,
Wife of the noblest king;
And longed in heart to steal her thence,
Preparing by the dire offence,
Death on his head to bring.

The lady watched with anxious face
For Ráma coming from the chase
With Lakshmaṇ by his side:

855

But nothing met her wandering glance
Save the wild forest's green expanse
Extending far and wide.

CANTO
XLVII

Rávan's Wooing

As, clad in mendicant's disguise,
He questioned thus his destined prize,
She to the seeming saintly man
The story of her life began.
"My guest is he," she thought, "and I,
To 'scape his curse, must needs reply:"
"Child of a noble sire I spring
From Janak, fair Videha's king.
May every good be thine! my name
Is Sítá, Ráma's cherished dame.
Twelve winters with my lord I spent
Most happily with sweet content
In the rich home of Raghu's line,
And every earthly joy was mine.
Twelve pleasant years flew by, and then
His peers advised the king of men,
Ráma, my lord, to consecrate
Joint ruler of his ancient state.
But when the rites were scarce begun,
To consecrate Ikshváku's son,
The queen Kaikeyí, honoured dame,
Sought of her lord an ancient claim.
Her plea of former service pressed,
And made him grant her new request,
To banish Ráma to the wild
And consecrate instead her child.
This double prayer on him, the best

And truest king, she strongly pressed:
"Mine eyes in sleep I will not close,
Nor eat, nor drink, nor take repose.
This very day my death shall bring
If Ráma be anointed king."
As thus she spake in envious ire,
The aged king, my husband's sire,
Besought with fitting words; but she
Was cold and deaf to every plea.
As yet my days are few; eighteen
The years of life that I have seen;
And Ráma, best of all alive,
Has passed of years a score and five—
Ráma the great and gentle, through
All region famed as pure and true,
Large-eyed and mighty-armed and tall,
With tender heart that cares for all.
But Daśaratha, led astray
By woman's wile and passion's sway,
By his strong love of her impelled,
The consecrating rites withheld.
When, hopeful of the promised grace,
My Ráma sought his father's face,
The queen Kaikeyí, ill at ease,
Spoke to my lord brief words like these:
"Hear, son of Raghu, hear from me
The words thy father says to thee:
"I yield this day to Bharat's hand,
Free from all foes, this ancient land.
Fly from this home no longer thine,
And dwell in woods five years and nine.
Live in the forest and maintain
Mine honour pure from falsehood's stain.'"
Then Ráma spoke, untouched by dread:
"Yea, it shall be as thou hast said."
And answered, faithful to his vows,
Obeying Daśaratha's spouse:
"The offered realm I would not take,
But still keep true the words he spake."
Thus, gentle Bráhman, Ráma still
Clung to his vow with firmest will.

857

And valiant Lakshmaṇ, dear to fame,
His brother by a younger dame,
Bold victor in the deadly fray,
Would follow Ráma on his way.
On sternest vows his heart was set,
And he, a youthful anchoret,
Bound up in twisted coil his hair
And took the garb which hermits wear;
Then with his bow to guard us, he
Went forth with Ráma and with me.
By Queen Kaikeyí's art bereft
The kingdom and our home we left,
And bound by stern religious vows
We sought this shade of forest boughs.
Now, best of Bráhmans, here we tread
These pathless regions dark and dread.
But come, refresh thy soul, and rest
Here for a while an honoured guest,
For he, my lord, will soon be here
With fresh supply of woodland cheer,
Large store of venison of the buck,
Or some great boar his hand has struck.
Meanwhile, O stranger, grant my prayer:
Thy name, thy race, thy birth declare,
And why with no companion thou
Roamest in Daṇḍak forest now."

Thus questioned Sítá, Ráma's dame.
Then fierce the stranger's answer came:
"Lord of the giant legions, he
From whom celestial armies flee,—
The dread of hell and earth and sky,
Rávaṇ the Rákshas king am I.
Now when thy gold-like form I view
Arrayed in silks of amber hue,
My love, O thou of perfect mould,
For all my dames is dead and cold.
A thousand fairest women, torn
From many a land my home adorn.
But come, loveliest lady, be
The queen of every dame and me.

My city Lanká, glorious town,
Looks from a mountain's forehead down

Where ocean with his flash and foam
Beats madly on mine island home.
With me, O Sítá, shalt thou rove
Delighted through each shady grove,
Nor shall thy happy breast retain
Fond memory of this life of pain.
In gay attire, a glittering band,
Five thousand maids shall round thee stand,
And serve thee at thy beck and sign,
If thou, fair Sítá, wilt be mine."

Then forth her noble passion broke
As thus in turn the lady spoke:
"Me, me the wife of Ráma, him
The lion lord with lion's limb,
Strong as the sea, firm as the rock,
Like Indra in the battle shock.
The lord of each auspicious sign,
The glory of his princely line,
Like some fair Bodh tree strong and tall,
The noblest and the best of all,
Ráma, the heir of happy fate
Who keeps his word inviolate,
Lord of the lion gait, possessed
Of mighty arm and ample chest,
Ráma the lion-warrior, him
Whose moon bright face no fear can dim,
Ráma, his bridled passions' lord,
The darling whom his sire adored,—
Me, me the true and loving dame
Of Ráma, prince of deathless fame—
Me wouldst thou vainly woo and press?
A jackal woo a lioness!
Steal from the sun his glory! such
Thy hope Lord Ráma's wife to touch.
Ha! Thou hast seen the trees of gold,
The sign which dying eyes behold,
Thus seeking, weary of thy life,

To win the love of Ráma's wife.
Fool! wilt thou dare to rend away
The famished lion's bleeding prey,
Or from the threatening jaws to take
The fang of some envenomed snake?
What, wouldst thou shake with puny hand
Mount Mandar, towering o'er the land,
Put poison to thy lips and think
The deadly cup a harmless drink?
With pointed needle touch thine eye,
A razor to thy tongue apply,
Who wouldst pollute with impious touch
The wife whom Ráma loves so much?
Be round thy neck a millstone tied,
And swim the sea from side to side;
Or raising both thy hands on high
Pluck sun and moon from yonder sky;
Or let the kindled flame be pressed,
Wrapt in thy garment, to thy breast;
More wild the thought that seeks to win
Ráma's dear wife who knows not sin.
The fool who thinks with idle aim
To gain the love of Ráma's dame,
With dark and desperate footing makes
His way o'er points of iron stakes.
As Ocean to a bubbling spring,
The lion to a fox, the king
Of all the birds that ply the wing
To an ignoble crow
As gold to lead of little price,
As to the drainings of the rice
The drink they quaff in Paradise,
The Amrit's heavenly flow,
As sandal dust with perfume sweet
Is to the mire that soils our feet,
A tiger to a cat,
As the white swan is to the owl,
The peacock to the waterfowl,
An eagle to a bat,
Such is my lord compared with thee;
And when with bow and arrows he,

860

Mighty as Indra's self shall see
His foeman, armed to slay,
Thou, death-doomed like the fly that sips
The oil that on the altar drips,
Shalt cast the morsel from thy lips
And lose thy half-won prey."
Thus in high scorn the lady flung
The biting arrows of her tongue
In bitter words that pierced and stung
The rover of the night.
She ceased. Her gentle cheek grew pale,
Her loosened limbs began to fail,
And like a plantain in the gale
She trembled with affright.
He terrible as Death stood nigh,
And watched with fierce exulting eye
The fear that shook her frame.
To terrify the lady more,
He counted all his triumphs o'er,
Proclaimed the titles that he bore,
His pedigree and name.

CANTO

XLVIII

Rávan's Speech

With knitted brow and furious eye
The stranger made his fierce reply:
"In me O fairest dame, behold
The brother of the King of Gold.
The Lord of Ten Necks my title, named
Rávan, for might and valour famed.
Gods and Gandharva hosts I scare;
Snakes, spirits, birds that roam the air
Fly from my coming, wild with fear,

Trembling like men when Death is near.
Vaiśravaṇ once, my brother, wrought
To ire, encountered me and fought,

But yielding to superior might
Fled from his home in sore affright.
Lord of the man-drawn chariot, still
He dwells on famed Kailása's hill.
I made the vanquished king resign
The glorious car which now is mine,—
Pushpak, the far-renowned, that flies
Will-guided through the buxom skies.
Celestial hosts by Indra led
Flee from my face disquieted,
And where my dreaded feet appear
The wind is hushed or breathless is fear.
Where'er I stand, where'er I go
The troubled waters cease to flow,
Each spell-bound wave is mute and still
And the fierce sun himself is chill.
Beyond the sea my Lanká stands
Filled with fierce forms and giant bands,
A glorious city fair to see
As Indra's Amarávatí.
A towering height of solid wall,
Flashing afar, surrounds it all,
Its golden courts enchant the sight,
And gates aglow with lazulite.
Steeds, elephants, and cars are there,
And drums' loud music fills the air,
Fair trees in lovely gardens grow
Whose boughs with varied fruitage glow.
Thou, beauteous Queen, with me shalt dwell
In halls that suit a princess well,
Thy former fellows shalt forget
Nor think of women with regret,
No earthly joy thy soul shall miss,
And take its fill of heavenly bliss.
Of mortal Ráma think no more,
Whose terms of days will soon be o'er.
King Daśaratha looked in scorn

862

On Ráma though the eldest born,
Sent to the woods the weakling fool,
And set his darling son to rule.
What, O thou large-eyed dame, hast thou
To do with fallen Ráma now,
From home and kingdom forced to fly,
A wretched hermit soon to die?
Accept thy lover, nor refuse
The giant king who fondly woos.
O listen, nor reject in scorn
A heart by Káma's arrows torn.
If thou refuse to hear my prayer,
Of grief and coming woe beware;
For the sad fate will fall on thee
Which came on hapless Urvasí,
When with her foot she chanced to touch
Purúravas, and sorrowed much.
My little finger raised in fight
Were more than match for Ráma's might.
O fairest, blithe and happy be
With him whom fortune sends to thee."

Such were the words the giant said,
And Sítá's angry eyes were red.
She answered in that lonely place
The monarch of the giant race:

"Art thou the brother of the Lord
Of Gold by all the world adored,
And sprung of that illustrious seed
Wouldst now attempt this evil deed?
I tell thee, impious Monarch, all
The giants by thy sin will fall,
Whose reckless lord and king thou art,
With foolish mind and lawless heart.
Yea, one may hope to steal the wife
Of Indra and escape with life.
But he who Ráma's dame would tear
From his loved side must needs despair.
Yea, one may steal fair Sáchí, dame
Of Him who shoots the thunder flame,

May live successful in his aim
And length of day may see;
But hope, O giant King, in vain,
Though cups of Amrit thou may drain,
To shun the penalty and pain
Of wronging one like me."

CANTO
XLIX

The Rape of Sítá

The Rákshas monarch, thus addressed,
His hands a while together pressed,
And straight before her startled eyes
Stood monstrous in his giant size.
Then to the lady, with the lore
Of eloquence, he spoke once more:
"Thou scarce," he cried, "hast heard aright
The glories of my power and might.
I borne sublime in air can stand
And with these arms upheave the land,
Drink the deep flood of Ocean dry
And Death with conquering force defy,
Pierce the great sun with furious dart
And to her depths cleave earth apart.
See, thou whom love and beauty blind,
I wear each form as wills my mind."
As thus he spake in burning ire
His glowing eyes were red with fire.
His gentle garb aside was thrown
And all his native shape was shown.
Terrific, monstrous, wild, and dread
As the dark God who rules the dead,
His fiery eyes in fury rolled,
His limbs were decked with glittering gold.

Like some dark cloud the monster showed,
And his fierce breast with fury glowed.
The ten-faced rover of the night,
With twenty arms exposed to sight,
His saintly guise aside had laid
And all his giant height displayed.

Attired in robes of crimson dye
He stood and watched with angry eye
The lady in her bright array
Resplendent as the dawn of day
When from the east the sunbeams break,
And to the dark-haired lady spake:
"If thou would call that lord thine own
Whose fame in every world is known,
Look kindly on my love, and be
Bride of a consort meet for thee.
With me let blissful years be spent,
For ne'er thy choice shalt thou repent.
No deed of mine shall e'er displease
My darling as she lives at ease.
Thy love for mortal man resign,
And to a worthier lord incline.
Ah foolish lady, seeming wise
In thine own weak and partial eyes,
By what fair graces art thou held
To Ráma from his realm expelled?
Misfortunes all his life attend,
And his brief days are near their end.
Unworthy prince, infirm of mind!
A woman spoke and he resigned
His home and kingdom and withdrew
From troops of friends and retinue.
And sought this forest dark and dread
By savage beasts inhabited."

Thus Rávan urged the lady meet
For love, whose words were soft and sweet.
Near and more near the giant pressed
As love's hot fire inflamed his breast.
The leader of the giant crew

865

His arm around the lady threw:
Thus Budha with ill-omened might
Steals Rohiṇí's delicious light.
One hand her glorious tresses grasped,
One with its ruthless pressure clasped
The body of his lovely prize,
The Maithil dame with lotus eyes.
The silvan Gods in wild alarm
Marked his huge teeth and ponderous arm,
And from that Death-like presence fled,
Of mountain size and towering head.
Then seen was Rávaṇ's magic car
Aglow with gold which blazed afar,—
The mighty car which asses drew
Thundering as it onward flew.
He spared not harsh rebuke to chide
The lady as she moaned and cried,
Then with his arm about her waist
His captive in the car he placed.
In vain he threatened: long and shrill
Rang out her lamentation still,
O Ráma! which no fear could stay:
But her dear lord was far away.
Then rose the fiend, and toward the skies
Bore his poor helpless struggling prize:
Hurrying through the air above
The dame who loathed his proffered love.
So might a soaring eagle bear
A serpent's consort through the air.
As on he bore her through the sky
She shrieked aloud her bitter cry.
As when some wretch's lips complain
In agony of maddening pain;
"O Lakshmaṇ, thou whose joy is still
To do thine elder brother's will,
This fiend, who all disguises wears,
From Ráma's side his darling tears.
Thou who couldst leave bliss, fortune, all,
Yea life itself at duty's call,
Dost thou not see this outrage done
To hapless me, O Raghu's son?

'Tis thine, O victor of the foe,
To bring the haughtiest spirit low,
How canst thou such an outrage see
And let the guilty fiend go free?
Ah, seldom in a moment's time
Comes bitter fruit of sin and crime,
But in the day of harvest pain
Comes like the ripening of the grain.
So thou whom fate and folly lead
To ruin for this guilty deed,
Shalt die by Ráma's arm ere long
A dreadful death for hideous wrong.
Ah, too successful in their ends
Are Queen Kaikeyí and her friends,
When virtuous Ráma, dear to fame,
Is mourning for his ravished dame.
Ah me, ah me! a long farewell
To lawn and glade and forest dell
In Janasthán's wild region, where
The Cassia trees are bright and fair
With all your tongues to Ráma say
That Rávaṇ bears his wife away.
Farewell, a long farewell to thee,
O pleasant stream Godávarí,
Whose rippling waves are ever stirred
By many a glad wild water-bird!
All ye to Ráma's ear relate
The giant's deed and Sítá's fate.
O all ye Gods who love this ground
Where trees of every leaf abound,
Tell Ráma I am stolen hence,
I pray you all with reverence.
On all the living things beside
That these dark boughs and coverts hide,
Ye flocks of birds, ye troops of deer,
I call on you my prayer to hear.
All ye to Ráma's ear proclaim
That Rávaṇ tears away his dame
With forceful arms,—his darling wife,
Dearer to Ráma than his life.
O, if he knew I dwelt in hell,

My mighty lord, I know full well,
Would bring me, conqueror, back to-day,
Though Yáma's self reclaimed his prey."
Thus from the air the lady sent

With piteous voice her last lament,
And as she wept she chanced to see
The vulture on a lofty tree.
As Rávaṇ bore her swiftly by,
On the dear bird she bent her eye,
And with a voice which woe made faint
Renewed to him her wild complaint:

"O see, the king who rules the race
Of giants, cruel, fierce and base,
Rávaṇ the spoiler bears me hence
The helpless prey of violence.
This fiend who roves in midnight shade
By thee, dear bird, can ne'er be stayed,
For he is armed and fierce and strong
Triumphant in the power to wrong.
For thee remains one only task,
To do, kind friend, the thing I ask.
To Ráma's ear by thee be borne
How Sítá from her home is torn,
And to the valiant Lakshmaṇ tell
The giant's deed and what befell."

CANTO
L

Jatáyus

The vulture from his slumber woke
And heard the words which Sítá spoke
He raised his eye and looked on her,
Looked on her giant ravisher.
That noblest bird with pointed beak,
Majestic as a mountain peak,
High on the tree addressed the king
Of giants, wisely counselling:
"O Ten-necked lord, I firmly hold
To faith and laws ordained of old,
And thou, my brother, shouldst refrain
From guilty deeds that shame and stain.
The vulture king supreme in air,
Jaṭáyus is the name I bear.
Thy captive, known by Sítá's name,
Is the dear consort and the dame
Of Ráma, Daśaratha's heir
Who makes the good of all his care.
Lord of the world in might he vies
With the great Gods of seas and skies.
The law he boasts to keep allows
No king to touch another's spouse,
And, more than all, a prince's dame
High honour and respect may claim.
Back to the earth thy way incline,
Nor think of one who is not thine.
Heroic souls should hold it shame
To stoop to deeds which others blame,
And all respect by them is shown
To dames of others as their own.
Not every case of bliss and gain

The Scripture's holy texts explain,
And subjects, when that light is dim,
Look to their prince and follow him.
The king is bliss and profit, he
Is store of treasures fair to see,
And all the people's fortunes spring,
Their joy and misery, from the king.
If, lord of giant race, thy mind
Be fickle, false, to sin inclined,
How wilt thou kingly place retain?
High thrones in heaven no sinners gain.
The soul which gentle passions sway
Ne'er throws its nobler part away,
Nor will the mansion of the base
Long be the good man's dwelling-place.
Prince Ráma, chief of high renown,
Has wronged thee not in field or town.
Ne'er has he sinned against thee: how
Canst thou resolve to harm him now?
If moved by Śúrpaṇakhá's prayer
The giant Khara sought him there,
And fighting fell with baffled aim,
His and not Ráma's is the blame.
Say, mighty lord of giants, say
What fault on Ráma canst thou lay?
What has the world's great master done
That thou should steal his precious one?
Quick, quick the Maithil dame release;
Let Ráma's consort go in peace,
Lest scorched by his terrific eye
Beneath his wrath thou fall and die
Like Vritra when Lord Indra threw
The lightning flame that smote and slew.
Ah fool, with blinded eyes to take
Home to thy heart a venomed snake!
Ah foolish eyes, too blind to see
That Death's dire coils entangle thee!
The prudent man his strength will spare,
Nor lift a load too great to bear.
Content is he with wholesome food
Which gives him life and strength renewed,

But who would dare the guilty deed
That brings no fame or glorious meed,
Where merit there is none to win
And vengeance soon o'ertakes the sin?
My course of life, Pulastya's son,
For sixty thousand years has run.
Lord of my kind I still maintain
Mine old hereditary reign.
I, worn by years, am older far
Than thou, young lord of bow and car,
In coat of glittering mail encased
And armed with arrows at thy waist,
But not unchallenged shalt thou go,
Or steal the dame without a blow.
Thou canst not, King, before mine eyes
Bear off unchecked thy lovely prize,
Safe as the truth of Scripture bent
By no close logic's argument.
Stay if thy courage let thee, stay
And meet me in the battle fray,
And thou shalt stain the earth with gore
Falling as Khara fell before.
Soon Ráma, clothed in bark, shall smite

Thee, his proud foe, in deadly fight,—
Ráma, from whom have oft times fled
The Daitya hosts discomfited.
No power have I to kill or slay:
The princely youths are far away,
But soon shalt thou with fearful eye
Struck down beneath their arrows lie.
But while I yet have life and sense,
Thou shalt not, tyrant, carry hence
Fair Sítá, Ramá's honoured queen,
With lotus eyes and lovely mien.
Whate'er the pain, whate'er the cost,
Though in the struggle life be lost,
The will of Raghu's noblest son
And Daśaratha must be done.
Stay for a while, O Rávaṇ, stay,
One hour thy flying car delay,

And from that glorious chariot thou
Shalt fall like fruit from shaken bough,
For I to thee, while yet I live,
The welcome of a foe will give."

CANTO
LI

The Combat

Rávaṇ's red eyes in fury rolled:
Bright with his armlets' flashing gold,
In high disdain, by passion stirred
He rushed against the sovereign bird.
With clash and din and furious blows
Of murderous battle met the foes:
Thus urged by winds two clouds on high
Meet warring in the stormy sky.
Then fierce the dreadful combat raged
As fiend and bird in war engaged,
As if two winged mountains sped
To dire encounter overhead.
Keen pointed arrows thick and fast,
In never ceasing fury cast,
Rained hurtling on the vulture king
And smote him on the breast and wing.
But still that noblest bird sustained
The cloud of shafts which Rávaṇ rained,
And with strong beak and talons bent
The body of his foeman rent.
Then wild with rage the ten-necked king
Laid ten swift arrows on his string,—
Dread as the staff of Death were they,
So terrible and keen to slay.
Straight to his ear the string he drew,
Straight to the mark the arrows flew,

872

And pierced by every iron head
The vulture's mangled body bled.
One glance upon the car he bent
Where Sítá wept with shrill lament,
Then heedless of his wounds and pain
Rushed at the giant king again.
Then the brave vulture with the stroke
Of his resistless talons broke
The giant's shafts and bow whereon
The fairest pearls and jewels shone.
The monster paused, by rage unmanned:
A second bow soon armed his hand,
Whence pointed arrows swift and true
In hundreds, yea in thousands, flew.
The monarch of the vultures, plied
With ceaseless darts on every side,
Showed like a bird that turns to rest
Close covered by the branch-built nest.
He shook his pinions to repel
The storm of arrows as it fell;
Then with his talons snapped in two
The mighty bow which Rávan drew.
Next with terrific wing he smote
So fiercely on the giant's coat,
The harness, glittering with the glow
Of fire, gave way beneath the blow.
With storm of murderous strokes he beat
The harnessed asses strong and fleet,—
Each with a goblin's monstrous face
And plates of gold his neck to grace.
Then on the car he turned his ire,—
The will-moved car that shone like fire,
And broke the glorious chariot, broke
The golden steps and pole and yoke.
The chouris and the silken shade
Like the full moon to view displayed,
Together with the guards who held
Those emblems, to the ground he felled.
The royal vulture hovered o'er
The driver's head, and pierced and tore
With his strong beak and dreaded claws

His mangled brow and cheek and jaws.
With broken car and sundered bow,
His charioteer and team laid low,
One arm about the lady wound,
Sprang the fierce giant to the ground.
Spectators of the combat, all
The spirits viewed the monster's fall:
Lauding the vulture every one
Cried with glad voice, Well done! well done!
But weak with length of days, at last
The vulture's strength was failing fast.
The fiend again assayed to bear
The lady through the fields of air.
But when the vulture saw him rise
Triumphant with his trembling prize,
Bearing the sword that still was left
When other arms were lost or cleft,
Once more, impatient of repose,
Swift from the earth her champion rose,
Hung in the way the fiend would take,
And thus addressing Rávaṇ spake:
"Thou, King of giants, rash and blind,
Wilt be the ruin of thy kind,
Stealing the wife of Ráma, him
With lightning scars on chest and limb.
A mighty host obeys his will
And troops of slaves his palace fill;

His lords of state are wise and true,
Kinsmen has he and retinue.
As thirsty travellers drain the cup,
Thou drinkest deadly poison up.
The rash and careless fool who heeds
No coming fruit of guilty deeds,
A few short years of life shall see,
And perish doomed to death like thee.
Say whither wilt thou fly to loose
Thy neck from Death's entangling noose,
Caught like the fish that finds too late
The hook beneath the treacherous bait?
Never, O King—of this be sure—

Will Raghu's fiery sons endure,
Terrific in their vengeful rage,
This insult to their hermitage.
Thy guilty hands this day have done
A deed which all reprove and shun,
Unworthly of a noble chief,
The pillage loved by coward thief.
Stay, if thy heart allow thee, stay
And meet me in the deadly fray.
Soon shall thou stain the earth with gore,
And fall as Khara fell before.
The fruits of former deeds o'erpower
The sinner in his dying hour:
And such a fate on thee, O King,
Thy tyranny and madness bring.
Not e'en the Self-existent Lord,
Who reigns by all the worlds adored,
Would dare attempt a guilty deed
Which the dire fruits of crime succeed."

Thus brave Jaṭáyus, best of birds,
Addressed the fiend with moving words,
Then ready for the swift attack
Swooped down upon the giant's back.
Down to the bone the talons went;
With many a wound the flesh was rent:
Such blows infuriate drivers deal
Their elephants with pointed steel.
Fixed in his back the strong beak lay,
The talons stripped the flesh away.
He fought with claws and beak and wing,
And tore the long hair of the king.
Still as the royal vulture beat
The giant with his wings and feet,
Swelled the fiend's lips, his body shook
With furious rage too great to brook.
About the Maithil dame he cast
One huge left arm and held her fast.
In furious rage to frenzy fanned
He struck the vulture with his hand.
Jatáyus mocked the vain assay,

875

And rent his ten left arms away.
Down dropped the severed limbs: anew
Ten others from his body grew:
Thus bright with pearly radiance glide
Dread serpents from the hillock side,
Again in wrath the giant pressed
The lady closer to his breast,
And foot and fist sent blow on blow
In ceaseless fury at the foe.
So fierce and dire the battle, waged
Between those mighty champions, raged:
Here was the lord of giants, there
The noblest of the birds of air.
Thus, as his love of Ráma taught,
The faithful vulture strove and fought.
But Rávaṇ seized his sword and smote
His wings and side and feet and throat.
At mangled side and wing he bled;
He fell, and life was almost fled.
The lady saw her champion lie,
His plumes distained with gory dye,
And hastened to the vulture's side
Grieving as though a kinsman died.
The lord of Lanká's island viewed
The vulture as he lay:
Whose back like some dark cloud was hued,
His breast a paly grey,
Like ashes, when by none renewed,
The flame has died away.
The lady saw with mournful eye,
Her champion press the plain,—
The royal bird, her true ally
Whom Rávaṇ's might had slain.
Her soft arms locked in strict embrace
Around his neck she kept,
And lovely with her moon-bright face
Bent o'er her friend and wept.

Rávan's Flight

Fair as the lord of silvery rays
Whom every star in heaven obeys,
The Maithil dame her plaint renewed
O'er him by Rávan's might subdued:
"Dreams, omens, auguries foreshow
Our coming lot of weal and woe:
But thou, my Ráma, couldst not see
The grievous blow which falls on thee.
The birds and deer desert the brakes
And show the path my captor takes,
And thus e'en now this royal bird
Flew to mine aid by pity stirred.
Slain for my sake in death he lies,
The broad-winged rover of the skies.
O Ráma, haste, thine aid I crave:
O Lakshmaṇ, why delay to save?
Brave sons of old Ikshváku, hear
And rescue in this hour of fear."

Her flowery wreath was torn and rent,
Crushed was each sparkling ornament.
She with weak arms and trembling knees
Clung like a creeper to the trees,
And like some poor deserted thing
With wild shrieks made the forest ring.
But swift the giant reached her side,

As loud on Ráma's name she cried.
Fierce as grim Death one hand he laid
Upon her tresses' lovely braid.
"That touch, thou impious King, shall be

The ruin of thy race and thee."
The universal world in awe
That outrage on the lady saw,
All nature shook convulsed with dread,
And darkness o'er the land was spread.
The Lord of Day grew dark and chill,
And every breath of air was still.
The Eternal Father of the sky
Beheld the crime with heavenly eye,
And spake with solemn voice, "The deed,
The deed is done, of old decreed."
Sad were the saints within the grove,
But triumph with their sorrow strove.
They wept to see the Maithil dame
Endure the outrage, scorn, and shame:
They joyed because his life should pay
The penalty incurred that day.
Then Rávaṇ raised her up, and bare
His captive through the fields of air,
Calling with accents loud and shrill
On Ráma and on Lakshmaṇ still.
With sparkling gems on arm and breast,
In silk of paly amber dressed,
High in the air the Maithil dame
Gleamed like the lightning's flashing flame.
The giant, as the breezes blew
Upon her robes of amber hue,
And round him twined that gay attire,
Showed like a mountain girt with fire.
The lady, fairest of the fair,
Had wreathed a garland round her hair;
Its lotus petals bright and sweet
Rained down about the giant's feet.
Her vesture, bright as burning gold,
Gave to the wind each glittering fold,
Fair as a gilded cloud that gleams
Touched by the Day-God's tempered beams.
Yet struggling in the fiend's embrace,
The lady with her sweet pure face,
Far from her lord, no longer wore
The light of joy that shone before.

Like some sad lily by the side
Of waters which the sun has dried;
Like the pale moon uprising through
An autumn cloud of darkest hue,
So was her perfect face between
The arms of giant Rávaṇ seen:
Fair with the charm of braided tress
And forehead's finished loveliness;
Fair with the ivory teeth that shed
White lustre through the lips' fine red,
Fair as the lotus when the bud
Is rising from the parent flood.
With faultless lip and nose and eye,
Dear as the moon that floods the sky
With gentle light, of perfect mould,
She seemed a thing of burnished gold,
Though on her cheek the traces lay
Of tears her hand had brushed away.
But as the moon-beams swiftly fade
Ere the great Day-God shines displayed,
So in that form of perfect grace
Still trembling in the fiend's embrace,
From her beloved Ráma reft,
No light of pride or joy was left.
The lady with her golden hue
O'er the swart fiend a lustre threw,
As when embroidered girths enfold
An elephant with gleams of gold.
Fair as the lily's bending stem,—
Her arms adorned with many a gem,
A lustre to the fiend she lent
Gleaming from every ornament,
As when the cloud-shot flashes light
The shadows of a mountain height.
Whene'er the breezes earthward bore
The tinkling of the zone she wore,
He seemed a cloud of darkness hue
Sending forth murmurs as it flew.
As on her way the dame was sped
From her sweet neck fair flowers were shed,
The swift wind caught the flowery rain

And poured it o'er the fiend again.
The wind-stirred blossoms, sweet to smell,
On the dark brows of Rávan fell,
Like lunar constellations set
On Meru for a coronet.
From her small foot an anklet fair
With jewels slipped, and through the air,
Like a bright circlet of the flame
Of thunder, to the valley came.
The Maithil lady, fair to see
As the young leaflet of a tree
Clad in the tender hues of spring,
Flashed glory on the giant king,
As when a gold-embroidered zone
Around an elephant is thrown.
While, bearing far the lady, through
The realms of sky the giant flew,
She like a gleaming meteor cast
A glory round her as she passed.
Then from each limb in swift descent
Dropped many a sparkling ornament:
On earth they rested dim and pale
Like fallen stars when virtues fail.
Around her neck a garland lay
Bright as the Star-God's silvery ray:
It fell and flashed like Gangá sent
From heaven above the firmament.
The birds of every wing had flocked
To stately trees by breezes rocked:

These bowed their wind-swept heads and said:
"My lady sweet, be comforted."
With faded blooms each brook within
Whose waters moved no gleamy fin,
Stole sadly through the forest dell
Mourning the dame it loved so well.
From every woodland region near
Came lions, tigers, birds, and deer,
And followed, each with furious look,
The way her flying shadow took.
For Sítá's loss each lofty hill

CANTO
LIII

Sítá's Threats

Soon as the Maithil lady knew
    That high through air the giant flew,
    Distressed with grief and sore afraid
Her troubled spirit sank dismayed.
Then, as anew the waters welled
From those red eyes which sorrow swelled,
Forth in keen words her passion broke,
And to the fierce-eyed fiend she spoke:
"Canst thou attempt a deed so base,
Untroubled by the deep disgrace,—
To steal me from my home and fly,
When friend or guardian none was nigh?
Thy craven soul that longed to steal,
Fearing the blows that warriors deal,
Upon a magic deer relied
To lure my husband from my side,
Friend of his sire, the vulture king
Lies low on earth with mangled wing,
Who gave his aged life for me
And died for her he sought to free.
Ah, glorious strength indeed is thine,
Thou meanest of thy giant line,
Whose courage dared to tell thy name
And conquer in the fight a dame.
Does the vile deed that thou hast done
Cause thee no shame, thou wicked one—
A woman from her home to rend
When none was near his aid to lend?
Through all the worlds, O giant King,
The tidings of this deed will ring,
This deed in law and honour's spite

882

Whose tears were waterfall, and rill,
Lifting on high each arm-like steep,
Seemed in the general woe to weep.
When the great sun, the lord of day,
Saw Rávaṇ tear the dame away,
His glorious light began to fail
And all his disk grew cold and pale.
"If Rávaṇ from the forest flies
With Ráma's Sítá as his prize,
Justice and truth have vanished hence,
Honour and right and innocence."
Thus rose the cry of wild despair
From spirits as they gathered there.
In trembling troops in open lawns
Wept, wild with woe, the startled fawns,
And a strange terror changed the eyes
They lifted to the distant skies.
On silvan Gods who love the dell
A sudden fear and trembling fell,
As in the deepest woe they viewed
The lady by the fiend subdued.
Still in loud shrieks was heard afar
That voice whose sweetness naught could mar,
While eager looks of fear and woe
She bent upon the earth below.
The lady of each winning wile
With pearly teeth and lovely smile,
Seized by the lord of Lanká's isle,
Looked down for friends in vain.
She saw no friend to aid her, none,
Not Ráma nor the younger son
Of Daśaratha, and undone
She swooned with fear and pain.

By one who claims a hero's might.
Shame on thy boasted valour, shame!
Thy prowess is an empty name.
Shame, giant, on this cursed deed
For which thy race is doomed to bleed!
Thou fliest swifter than the gale,
For what can strength like thine avail?
Stay for one hour, O Rávaṇ, stay;
Thou shalt not flee with life away.
Soon as the royal chieftains' sight
Falls on the thief who roams by night,
Thou wilt not, tyrant, live one hour
Though backed by all thy legions' power.
Ne'er can thy puny strength sustain
The tempest of their arrowy rain:
Have e'er the trembling birds withstood
The wild flames raging in the wood?
Hear me, O Rávaṇ, let me go,
And save thy soul from coming woe.
Or if thou wilt not set me free,
Wroth for this insult done to me.
With his brave brother's aid my lord
Against thy life will raise his sword.
A guilty hope inflames thy breast
His wife from Ráma's home to wrest.
Ah fool, the hope thou hast is vain;
Thy dreams of bliss shall end in pain.
If torn from all I love by thee
My godlike lord no more I see,
Soon will I die and end my woes,
Nor live the captive of my foes.
Ah fool, with blinded eyes to choose
The evil and the good refuse!
So the sick wretch with stubborn will
Turns fondly to the cates that kill,
And madly draws his lips away
From medicine that would check decay.
About thy neck securely wound

The deadly coil of Fate is bound,
And thou, O Rávaṇ, dost not fear

Although the hour of death is near.
With death-doomed sight thine eyes behold
The gleaming of the trees of gold,—
See dread Vaitaraṇi, the flood
That rolls a stream of foamy blood,—
See the dark wood by all abhorred—
Its every leaf a threatening sword.
The tangled thickets thou shall tread
Where thorns with iron points are spread.
For never can thy days be long,
Base plotter of this shame and wrong
To Ráma of the lofty soul:
He dies who drinks the poisoned bowl.
The coils of death around thee lie:
They hold thee and thou canst not fly.
Ah whither, tyrant, wouldst thou run
The vengeance of my lord to shun?
By his unaided arm alone
Were twice seven thousand fiends o'erthrown:
Yes, in the twinkling of an eye
He forced thy mightiest fiends to die.
And shall that lord of lion heart,
Skilled in the bow and spear and dart,
Spare thee, O fiend, in battle strife,
The robber of his darling wife?"

These were her words, and more beside,
By wrath and bitter hate supplied.
Then by her woe and fear o'erthrown
She wept again and made her moan.
As long she wept in grief and dread,
Scarce conscious of the words she said,
The wicked giant onward fled
And bore her through the air.
As firm he held the Maithil dame,
Still wildly struggling, o'er her frame
With grief and bitter misery came
The trembling of despair.

CANTO
LIV

Lanká

He bore her on in rapid flight,
And not a friend appeared in sight.
But on a hill that o'er the wood
Raised its high top five monkeys stood.
From her fair neck her scarf she drew,
And down the glittering vesture flew.
With earring, necklet, chain, and gem,
Descending in the midst of them:
"For these," she thought, "my path may show,
And tell my lord the way I go."
Nor did the fiend, in wild alarm,
Mark when she drew from neck and arm
And foot the gems and gold, and sent
To earth each gleaming ornament.
The monkeys raised their tawny eyes
That closed not in their first surprise,
And saw the dark-eyed lady, where
She shrieked above them in the air.
High o'er their heads the giant passed
Holding the weeping lady fast.
O'er Pampa's flashing flood he sped
And on to Lanká's city fled.
He bore away in senseless joy
The prize that should his life destroy,
Like the rash fool who hugs beneath
His robe a snake with venomed teeth.
Swift as an arrow from a bow,
Speeding o'er lands that lay below,
Sublime in air his course he took
O'er wood and rock and lake and brook.
He passed at length the sounding sea

885

Where monstrous creatures wander free,—
Seat of Lord Varuṇ's ancient reign,
Controller of the eternal main.
The angry waves were raised and tossed
As Rávaṇ with the lady crossed,
And fish and snake in wild unrest
Showed flashing fin and gleaming crest.
Then from the blessed troops who dwell
In air celestial voices fell:
"O ten-necked King," they cried, "attend:
This guilty deed will bring thine end."

Then Rávaṇ speeding like the storm,
Bearing his death in human form,
The struggling Sítá, lighted down
In royal Lanká's glorious town;
A city bright and rich, that showed
Well-ordered street and noble road;
Arranged with just division, fair
With multitudes in court and square.
Thus, all his journey done, he passed
Within his royal home at last.
There in a queenly bower he placed
The black-eyed dame with dainty waist:
Thus in her chamber Máyá laid
The lovely Máyá, demon maid.
Then Rávaṇ gave command to all
The dread she-fiends who filled the hall:
"This captive lady watch and guard
From sight of man and woman barred.
But all the fair one asks beside
Be with unsparing hand supplied:
As though 'twere I that asked, withhold
No pearls or dress or gems or gold.
And she among you that shall dare
Of purpose or through want of care
One word to vex her soul to say,
Throws her unvalued life away."
Thus spake the monarch of their race
To those she-fiends who thronged the place,
And pondering on the course to take

Went from the chamber as he spake.
He saw eight giants, strong and dread,
On flesh of bleeding victims fed,
Proud in the boon which Brahmá gave,

And trusting in its power to save.
He thus the mighty chiefs addressed
Of glorious power and strength possessed:
"Arm, warriors, with the spear and bow;
With all your speed from Lanká go,
For Janasthán, our own no more,
Is now defiled with giants' gore;
The seat of Khara's royal state
Is left unto us desolate.
In your brave hearts and might confide,
And cast ignoble fear aside.
Go, in that desert region dwell
Where the fierce giants fought and fell.
A glorious host that region held,
For power and might unparalleled,
By Dúshan and brave Khara led,—
All, slain by Ráma's arrows, bled.
Hence boundless wrath that spurns control
Reigns paramount within my soul,
And naught but Ráma's death can sate
The fury of my vengeful hate.
I will not close my slumbering eyes
Till by this hand my foeman dies.
And when mine arm has slain the foe
Who laid those giant princes low,
Long will I triumph in the deed,
Like one enriched in utmost need.
Now go; that I this end may gain,
In Janasthán, O chiefs, remain.
Watch Ráma there with keenest eye,
And all his deeds and movements spy.
Go forth, no helping art neglect,
Be brave and prompt and circumspect,
And be your one endeavour still
To aid mine arm this foe to kill.
Oft have I seen your warrior might

Proved in the forehead of the fight,
And sure of strength I know so well
Send you in Janasthán to dwell."
The giants heard with prompt assent
The pleasant words he said,
And each before his master bent
For meet salute, his head.
Then as he bade, without delay,
From Lanká's gate they passed,
And hurried forward on their way
Invisible and fast.

Sítá in Prison

Thus Rávaṇ his commandment gave
To those eight giants strong and brave,
So thinking in his foolish pride
Against all dangers to provide.
Then with his wounded heart aflame
With love he thought upon the dame,
And took with hasty steps the way
To the fair chamber where she lay.
He saw the gentle lady there
Weighed down by woe too great to bear,
Amid the throng of fiends who kept
Their watch around her as she wept:
A pinnace sinking neath the wave
When mighty winds around her rave:
A lonely herd-forsaken deer,
When hungry dogs are pressing near.
Within the bower the giant passed:
Her mournful looks were downward cast.
As there she lay with streaming eyes

The giant bade the lady rise,
And to the shrinking captive showed
The glories of his rich abode,
Where thousand women spent their days
In palaces with gold ablaze;
Where wandered birds of every sort,
And jewels flashed in hall and court.
Where noble pillars charmed the sight
With diamond and lazulite,
And others glorious to behold
With ivory, crystal, silver, gold.
There swelled on high the tambour's sound,
And burnished ore was bright around
He led the mournful lady where
Resplendent gold adorned the stair,
And showed each lattice fair to see
With silver work and ivory:
Showed his bright chambers, line on line,
Adorned with nets of golden twine.
Beyond he showed the Maithil dame
His gardens bright as lightning's flame,
And many a pool and lake he showed
Where blooms of gayest colour glowed.
Through all his home from view to view
The lady sunk in grief he drew.
Then trusting in her heart to wake
Desire of all she saw, he spake:
"Three hundred million giants, all
Obedient to their master's call,
Not counting young and weak and old,
Serve me with spirits fierce and bold.
A thousand culled from all of these
Wait on the lord they long to please.
This glorious power, this pomp and sway,
Dear lady, at thy feet I lay:
Yea, with my life I give the whole,
O dearer than my life and soul.
A thousand beauties fill my hall:
Be thou my wife and rule them all.
O hear my supplication! why
This reasonable prayer deny?

Some pity to thy suitor show,
For love's hot flames within me glow.
This isle a hundred leagues in length,
Encompassed by the ocean's strength,
Would all the Gods and fiends defy
Though led by Him who rules the sky.
No God in heaven, no sage on earth,
No minstrel of celestial birth,

No spirit in the worlds I see
A match in power and might for me.
What wilt thou do with Ráma, him
Whose days are short, whose light is dim,
Expelled from home and royal sway,
Who treads on foot his weary way?
Leave the poor mortal to his fate,
And wed thee with a worthier mate.
My timid love, enjoy with me
The prime of youth before it flee.
Do not one hour the hope retain
To look on Ráma's face again.
For whom would wildest thought beguile
To seek thee in the giants' isle?
Say who is he has power to bind
In toils of net the rushing wind.
Whose is the mighty hand will tame
And hold the glory of the flame?
In all the worlds above, below,
Not one, O fair of form, I know
Who from this isle in fight could rend
The lady whom these arms defend.
Fair Queen, o'er Lanká's island reign,
Sole mistress of the wide domain.
Gods, rovers of the night like me,
And all the world thy slaves will be.
O'er thy fair brows and queenly head
Let consecrating balm be shed,
And sorrow banished from thy breast,
Enjoy my love and take thy rest.
Here never more thy soul shall know
The memory of thy former woe,

And here shall thou enjoy the meed
Deserved by every virtuous deed.
Here garlands glow of flowery twine,
With gorgeous hues and scent divine.
Take gold and gems and rich attire:
Enjoy with me thy heart's desire.
There stand, of chariots far the best,
The car my brother once possessed.
Which, victor in the stricken field,
I forced the Lord of Gold to yield.
'Tis wide and high and nobly wrought,
Bright as the sun and swift as thought.
Therein O Sítá, shalt thou ride
Delighted by thy lover's side.
But sorrow mars with lingering trace
The splendour of thy lotus face.
A cloud of woe is o'er it spread,
And all the light of joy is fled."

The lady, by her woe distressed,
One corner of her raiment pressed
To her sad cheek like moonlight clear,
And wiped away a falling tear.
The rover of the night renewed
His eager pleading as he viewed
The lady stand like one distraught,
Striving to fix her wandering thought:

"Think not, sweet lady, of the shame
Of broken vows, nor fear the blame.
The saints approve with favouring eyes
This union knit with marriage ties.
O beauty, at thy radiant feet
I lay my heads, and thus entreat.
One word of grace, one look I crave:
Have pity on thy prostrate slave.
These idle words I speak are vain,
Wrung forth by love's consuming pain,
And ne'er of Rávaṇ be it said
He wooed a dame with prostrate head."
Thus to the Maithil lady sued

The monarch of the giant brood,
And "She is now mine own," he thought,
In Death's dire coils already caught.

CANTO
LVI

Sítá's Disdain

His words the Maithil lady heard
Oppressed by woe but undeterred.
Fear of the fiend she cast aside,
And thus in noble scorn replied:
"His word of honour never stained
King Daśaratha nobly reigned,
The bridge of right, the friend of truth.
His eldest son, a noble youth,
Is Ráma, virtue's faithful friend,
Whose glories through the worlds extend.
Long arms and large full eyes has he,
My husband, yea a God to me.
With shoulders like the forest king's,
From old Ikshváku's line he springs.
He with his brother Lakshmaṇ's aid
Will smite thee with the vengeful blade.
Hadst thou but dared before his eyes
To lay thine hand upon the prize,
Thou stretched before his feet hadst lain
In Janasthán like Khara slain.
Thy boasted rovers of the night
With hideous shapes and giant might,—
Like serpents when the feathered king
Swoops down with his tremendous wing,—
Will find their useless venom fail
When Ráma's mighty arms assail.
The rapid arrows bright with gold,

Shot from the bow he loves to hold,
Will rend thy frame from flank to flank
As Gangá's waves erode the bank.
Though neither God nor fiend have power
To slay thee in the battle hour,
Yet from his hand shall come thy fate,
Struck down before his vengeful hate.
That mighty lord will strike and end
The days of life thou hast to spend.
Thy days are doomed, thy life is sped
Like victims to the pillar led.
Yea, if the glance of Ráma bright
With fury on thy form should light,
Thou scorched this day wouldst fall and die

Like Káma slain by Rudra's eye.
He who from heaven the moon could throw,
Or bid its bright rays cease to glow,—
He who could drain the mighty sea
Will set his darling Sítá free.
Fled is thy life, thy glory, fled
Thy strength and power: each sense is dead.
Soon Lanká widowed by thy guilt
Will see the blood of giants spilt.
This wicked deed, O cruel King,
No triumph, no delight will bring.
Thou with outrageous might and scorn
A woman from her lord hast torn.
My glorious husband far away,
Making heroic strength his stay,
Dwells with his brother, void of fear,
In Daṇḍak forest lone and drear.
No more in force of arms confide:
That haughty strength, that power and pride
My hero with his arrowy rain
From all thy bleeding limbs will drain.
When urged by fate's dire mandate, nigh
Comes the fixt hour for men to die.
Caught in Death's toils their eyes are blind,
And folly takes each wandering mind.
So for the outrage thou hast done

The fate is near thou canst not shun,—
The fate that on thyself and all
Thy giants and thy town shall fall.
I spurn thee: can the altar dight
With vessels for the sacred rite,
O'er which the priest his prayer has said,
Be sullied by an outcaste's tread?
So me, the consort dear and true
Of him who clings to virtue too,
Thy hated touch shall ne'er defile,
Base tyrant lord of Lanká's isle.
Can the white swan who floats in pride
Through lilies by her consort's side,
Look for one moment, as they pass,
On the poor diver in the grass?
This senseless body waits thy will,
To torture, chain, to wound or kill.
I will not, King of giants, strive
To keep this fleeting soul alive
But never shall they join the name
Of Sítá with reproach and shame."

Thus as her breast with fury burned
Her bitter speech the dame returned.
Such words of rage and scorn, the last
She uttered, at the fiend she cast.
Her taunting speech the giant heard,
And every hair with anger stirred.
Then thus with fury in his eye
He made in threats his fierce reply:
"Hear Maithil lady, hear my speech:
List to my words and ponder each.
If o'er thy head twelve months shall fly
And thou thy love wilt still deny,
My cooks shall mince thy flesh with steel
And serve it for my morning meal."

Thus with terrific threats to her
Spake Rávaṇ, cruel ravener.
Mad with the rage her answer woke
He called the fiendish train and spoke:

"Take her, ye Rákshas dames, who fright
With hideous form and mien the sight,
Who make the flesh of men your food,—
And let her pride be soon subdued."
He spoke, and at his word the band
Of fiendish monsters raised each hand
In reverence to the giant king,
And pressed round Sítá in a ring.
Rávaṇ once more with stern behest
To those she-fiends his speech addressed:
Shaking the earth beneath his tread,
He stamped his furious foot and said:
"To the Aśoka garden bear
The dame, and guard her safely there
Until her stubborn pride be bent
By mingled threat and blandishment.
See that ye watch her well, and tame,
Like some she-elephant, the dame."

They led her to that garden where
The sweetest flowers perfumed the air,
Where bright trees bore each rarest fruit,
And birds, enamoured, ne'er were mute.
Bowed down with terror and distress,
Watched by each cruel giantess,—
Like a poor solitary deer
When ravening tigresses are near,—
The hapless lady lay distraught
Like some wild thing but newly caught,
And found no solace, no relief
From agonizing fear and grief;
Not for one moment could forget
Each terrifying word and threat,
Or the fierce eyes upon her set
By those who watched around.
She thought of Ráma far away,
She mourned for Lakshmaṇ as she lay
In grief and terror and dismay
Half fainting on the ground.

Sítá Comforted

S oon as the fiend had set her down
Within his home in Lanká's town
Triumph and joy filled Indra's breast,
Whom thus the Eternal Sire addressed:

"This deed will free the worlds from woe
And cause the giants' overthrow.
The fiend has borne to Lanká's isle
The lady of the lovely smile,
True consort born to happy fate
With features fair and delicate.

She looks and longs for Ráma's face,
But sees a crowd of demon race,
And guarded by the giant's train
Pines for her lord and weeps in vain.
But Lanká founded on a steep
Is girdled by the mighty deep,
And how will Ráma know his fair
And blameless wife is prisoned there?
She on her woe will sadly brood
And pine away in solitude,
And heedless of herself, will cease
To live, despairing of release.
Yes, pondering on her fate, I see
Her gentle life in jeopardy.
Go, Indra, swiftly seek the place,
And look upon her lovely face.
Within the city make thy way:
Let heavenly food her spirit stay."

Thus Brahma spake: and He who slew
The cruel demon Páka, flew
Where Lanká's royal city lay,
And Sleep went with him on his way.
"Sleep," cried the heavenly Monarch, "close
Each giant's eye in deep repose."

Thus Indra spoke, and Sleep fulfilled
With joy his mandate, as he willed,
To aid the plan the Gods proposed,
The demons' eyes in sleep she closed.
Then Śachí's lord, the Thousand-eyed,
To the Aśoka garden hied.
He came and stood where Sítá lay,
And gently thus began to say:
"Lord of the Gods who hold the sky,
Dame of the lovely smile, am I.
Weep no more, lady, weep no more;
Thy days of woe will soon be o'er.
I come, O Janak's child, to be
The helper of thy lord and thee.
He through my grace, with hosts to aid,
This sea-girt land will soon invade.
'Tis by my art that slumbers close
The eyelids of thy giant foes.
Now I, with Sleep, this place have sought,
Videhan lady, and have brought
A gift of heaven's ambrosial food
To stay thee in thy solitude.
Receive it from my hand, and taste,
O lady of the dainty waist:
For countless ages thou shall be
From pangs of thirst and hunger free."

But doubt within her bosom woke
As to the Lord of Gods she spoke:
"How may I know for truth that thou
Whose form I see before me now
Art verily the King adored
By heavenly Gods, and Śachí's lord?
With Raghu's sons I learnt to know

897

The certain signs which Godhead show.
These marks before mine eyes display
If o'er the Gods thou bear the sway."

The heavenly lord of Śachí heard,
And did according to her word.
Above the ground his feet were raised;
With eyelids motionless he gazed.
No dust upon his raiment lay,
And his bright wreath was fresh and gay.
Nor was the lady's glad heart slow
The Monarch of the Gods to know,
And while the tears unceasing ran
From her sweet eyes she thus began:
"My lord has gained a friend in thee,
And I this day thy presence see
Shown clearly to mine eyes, as when
Ráma and Lakshmaṇ, lords of men,
Beheld it, and their sire the king,
And Janak too from whom I spring.
Now I, O Monarch of the Blest,
Will eat this food at thy behest,
Which thou hast brought me, of thy grace,
To aid and strengthen Raghu's race."

She spoke, and by his words relieved,
The food from Indra's hand received,
Yet ere she ate the balm he brought,
On Lakshmaṇ and her lord she thought.
"If my brave lord be still alive,
If valiant Lakshmaṇ yet survive,
May this my taste of heavenly food
Bring health to them and bliss renewed!"
She ate, and that celestial food
Stayed hunger, thirst, and lassitude,
And all her strength restored.
Great joy her hopeful spirit stirred
At the glad tidings newly heard
Of Lakshmaṇ and her lord.
And Indra's heart was joyful too:
He bade the Maithil dame adieu,

His saving errand done.
With Sleep beside him parting thence
He sought his heavenly residence
To prosper Raghu's son.

CANTO
LVIII

The Brothers' Meeting

When Ráma's deadly shaft had struck
The giant in the seeming buck,
The chieftain turned him from the place
His homeward way again to trace.
Then as he hastened onward, fain
To look upon his spouse again,
Behind him from a thicket nigh
Rang out a jackal's piercing cry.
Alarmed he heard the startling shriek
That raised his hair and dimmed his cheek,
And all his heart was filled with doubt
As the shrill jackal's cry rang out:
"Alas, some dire disaster seems
Portended by the jackal's screams.
O may the Maithil dame be screened
From outrage of each hungry fiend!

Alas, if Lakshman chanced to hear
That bitter cry of woe and fear
What time Márícha, as he died,
With voice that mocked my accents cried,
Swift to my side the prince would flee
And quit the dame to succour me.
Too well I see the demon band
The slaughter of my love have planned.
Me far from home and Sítá's view

899

The seeming deer Márícha drew.
He led me far through brake and dell
Till wounded by my shaft he fell,
And as he sank rang out his cry,
"O save me, Lakshmaṇ, or I die."
May it be well with both who stayed
In the great wood with none to aid,
For every fiend is now my foe
For Janasthán's great overthrow,
And many an omen seen to-day
Has filled my heart with sore dismay."

Such were the thoughts and sad surmise
Of Ráma at the jackal's cries,
And all his heart within him burned
As to his cot his steps he turned.
He pondered on the deer that led
His feet to follow where it fled,
And sad with many a bitter thought
His home in Janasthán he sought.
His soul was dark with woe and fear
When flocks of birds and troops of deer
Move round him from the left, and raised
Discordant voices as they gazed.
The omens which the chieftain viewed
The terror of his soul renewed,
When lo, to meet him Lakshmaṇ sped
With brows whence all the light had fled.
Near and more near the princes came,
Each brother's heart and look the same;
Alike on each sad visage lay
The signs of misery and dismay,
Then Ráma by his terror moved
His brother for his fault reproved
In leaving Sítá far from aid
In the wild wood where giants strayed.
Lakshmaṇ's left hand he took, and then
In gentle tones the prince of men,
Though sharp and fierce their tenour ran,
Thus to his brother chief began:
"O Lakshmaṇ, thou art much to blame

Leaving alone the Maithil dame,
And flying hither to my side:
O, may no ill my spouse betide!
But ah, I know my wife is dead,
And giants on her limbs have fed,
So strange, so terrible are all
The omens which my heart appal.
O Lakshmaṇ, may we yet return
The safety of my love to learn.
To find the child of Janak still
Alive and free from scathe and ill!
Each bird with notes of warning screams,
Though the hot sun still darts his beams.
The moan of deer, the jackal's yell
Of some o'erwhelming misery tell.
O mighty brother, still may she,
My princess, live from danger free!
That semblance of a golden deer
Allured me far away,
I followed nearer and more near,
And longed to take the prey.
I followed where the quarry fled:
My deadly arrow flew,
And as the dying creature bled,
The giant met my view.
Great fear and pain oppress my heart
That dreads the coming blow,
And through my left eye keenly dart
The throbs that herald woe.
Ah Lakshmaṇ, all these signs dismay,
My soul that sinks with dread,
I know my love is torn away,
Or, haply, she is dead."

Ráma's Return

When Ráma saw his brother stand
With none beside him, all unmanned,
Eager he questioned why he came
So far without the Maithil dame:
"Where is my wife, my darling, she
Who to the wild wood followed me?
Where hast thou left my lady, where
The dame who chose my lot to share?
Where is my love who balms my woe
As through the forest wilds I go,
Unkinged and banished and disgraced,—
My darling of the dainty waist?
She nerves my spirit for the strife,
She, only she gives zest to life,
Dear as my breath is she who vies
In charms with daughters of the skies.
If Janak's child be mine no more,
In splendour fair as virgin ore,
The lordship of the skies and earth
To me were prize of little worth.
Ah, lives she yet, the Maithil dame,
Dear as the soul within this frame?
O, let not all my toil be vain,
The banishment, the woe and pain!
O, let not dark Kaikeyí win
The guerdon of her treacherous sin,
If, Sítá lost, my days I end,
And thou without me homeward wend!
O, let not good Kauśalyá shed
Her bitter tears to mourn me dead,
Nor her proud rival's hest obey,

Strong in her son and queenly sway!
Back to my cot will I repair
If Sítá live to greet me there,

But if my wife have perished, I
Reft of my love will surely die.
O Lakshmaṇ, if I seek my cot,
Look for my love and find her not
Sweet welcome with her smile to give,
I tell thee, I will cease to live.
O answer,—let thy words be plain,—
Lives Sítá yet, or is she slain?
Didst thou thy sacred trust betray
Till ravening giants seized the prey?
Ah me, so young, so soft and fair,
Lapped in all bliss, untried by care,
Rent from her own dear husband, how
Will she support her misery now?
That voice, O Lakshmaṇ smote thine ear,
And filled, I ween, thy heart with fear,
When on thy name for succour cried
The treacherous giant ere he died.
That voice too like mine own, I ween,
Was heard by the Videhan queen.
She bade thee seek my side to aid,
And quickly was the hest obeyed,
But ah, thy fault I needs must blame,
To leave alone the helpless dame,
And let the cruel giants sate
The fury of their murderous hate.
Those blood-devouring demons all
Grieve in their souls for Khara's fall,
And Sítá, none to guard her side,
Torn by their cruel hands has died.
I sink, O tamer of thy foes,
Deep in the sea of whelming woes.
What can I now? I must endure
The mighty grief that mocks at cure."

Thus, all his thoughts on Sítá bent,
To Janasthán the chieftain went,

Hastening on with eager stride,
And Lakshmaṇ hurried by his side.
With toil and thirst and hunger worn,
His breast with doubt and anguish torn,
He sought the well-known spot.
Again, again he turned to chide
With quivering lips which terror dried:
He looked, and found her not.
Within his leafy home he sped,
Each pleasant spot he visited
Where oft his darling strayed.
"'Tis as I feared," he cried, and there,
Yielding to pangs too great to bear,
He sank by grief dismayed.

CANTO
LX

Lakshman Reproved

But Ráma ceased not to upbraid,
His brother for untimely aid,
And thus, while anguish wrung his breast,
The chief with eager question pressed:
"Why, Lakshmaṇ, didst thou hurry hence
And leave my wife without defence?
I left her in the wood with thee,
And deemed her safe from jeopardy.
When first thy form appeared in view,
I marked that Sítá came not too.
With woe my troubled soul was rent,
Prophetic of the dire event.
Thy coming steps afar I spied,
I saw no Sítá by thy side,
And felt a sudden throbbing dart
Through my left eye, and arm, and heart."

Lakshmaṇ, with Fortune's marks impressed,
His brother mournfully addressed:
"Not by my heart's free impulse led,
Leaving thy wife to thee I sped;
But by her keen reproaches sent,
O Ráma, to thine aid I went.
She heard afar a mournful cry,
"O save me, Lakshmaṇ, or I die."
The voice that spoke in moving tone
Smote on her ear and seemed thine own.
Soon as those accents reached her ear
She yielded to her woe and fear,
She wept o'ercome by grief, and cried,
"Fly, Lakshmaṇ, fly to Ráma's side."
Though many a time she bade me speed,
Her urgent prayer I would not heed.
I bade her in thy strength confide,
And thus with tender words replied:
"No giant roams the forest shade
From whom thy lord need shrink dismayed.
No human voice, believe me, spoke
Those words thy causeless fear that woke.
Can he whose might can save in woe
The heavenly Gods e'er stoop so low,
And with those piteous accents call
For succour like a caitiff thrall?
And why should wandering giants choose
The accents of thy lord to use,
In alien tones my help to crave,
And cry aloud, O Lakshmaṇ, save?
Now let my words thy spirit cheer,
Compose thy thoughts and banish fear.
In hell, in earth, or in the skies
There is not, and there cannot rise
A champion whose strong arm can slay
Thy Ráma in the battle fray.
To heavenly hosts he ne'er would yield
Though Indra led them to the field."
To soothe her thus I vainly sought:
Her heart with woe was still distraught.
While from her eyes the waters ran

905

Her bitter speech she thus began:
"Too well I see thy dark intent:
Thy lawless thoughts on me are bent.
Thou hopest, but thy hope is vain,
To win my love, thy brother slain.
Not love, but Bharat's dark decree
To share his exile counselled thee,

Or hearing now his bitter cry
Thou surely to his aid wouldst fly.
For love of me, a stealthy foe
Thou choosest by his side to go,
And now thou longest that my lord
Should die, and wilt no help afford."

Such were the words the lady said:
With angry fire my eyes were red.
With pale lips quivering in my rage
I hastened from the hermitage."
He ceased; and frenzied by his pain
The son of Raghu spoke again:
"O brother, for thy fault I grieve,
The Maithil dame alone to leave.
Thou knowest that my arm is strong
To save me from the giant throng,
And yet couldst leave the cottage, spurred
To folly by her angry word.
For this thy deed I praise thee not,—
To leave her helpless in the cot,
And thus thy sacred charge forsake
For the wild words a woman spake.
Yea thou art all to blame herein,
And very grievous is thy sin.
That anger swayed thy faithless breast
And made thee false to my behest.
An arrow speeding from my bow
Has laid the treacherous giant low,
Who lured me eager for the chase
Far from my hermit dwelling-place.
The string with easy hand I drew,
The arrow as in pastime flew,

The wounded quarry bled.
The borrowed form was cast away,
Before mine eye a giant lay
With bright gold braceleted.
My arrow smote him in the chest:
The giant by the pain distressed
Raised his loud voice on high.
Far rang the mournful sound: mine own,
It seemed, were accent, voice, and tone,
They made thee leave my spouse alone
And to my rescue fly."

CANTO
LXI

Ráma's Lament

A s Ráma sought his leafy cot
   Through his left eye keen throbbings shot,
   His wonted strength his frame forsook,
And all his body reeled and shook.
Still on those dreadful signs he thought,—
Sad omens with disaster fraught,
And from his troubled heart he cried,
"O, may no ill my spouse betide!"
Longing to gaze on Sítá's face
He hastened to his dwelling-place,
Then sinking neath his misery's weight,
He looked and found it desolate.
Tossing his mighty arms on high
He sought her with an eager cry,
From spot to spot he wildly ran
Each corner of his home to scan.
He looked, but Sítá was not there;
His cot was disolate and bare,
Like streamlet in the winter frost,

The glory of her lilies lost.
With leafy tears the sad trees wept
As a wild wind their branches swept.
Mourned bird and deer, and every flower
Drooped fainting round the lonely bower.
The silvan deities had fled
The spot where all the light was dead,
Where hermit coats of skin displayed,
And piles of sacred grass were laid.
He saw, and maddened by his pain
Cried in lament again, again:
"Where is she, dead or torn away,
Lost, or some hungry giant's prey?
Or did my darling chance to rove
For fruit and blossoms though the grove?
Or has she sought the pool or rill,
Her pitcher from the wave to fill?"
His eager eyes on fire with pain
He roamed about with maddened brain.
Each grove and glade he searched with care,
He sought, but found no Sítá there.
He wildly rushed from hill to hill;
From tree to tree, from rill to rill,
As bitter woe his bosom rent
Still Ráma roamed with fond lament:
"O sweet Kadamba say has she
Who loved thy bloom been seen by thee?
If thou have seen her face most fair,
Say, gentle tree, I pray thee, where.
O Bel tree with thy golden fruit
Round as her breast, no more be mute,
Where is my radiant darling, gay
In silk that mocks thy glossy spray?
O Arjun, say, where is she now
Who loved to touch thy scented bough?
Do not thy graceful friend forget,
But tell me, is she living yet?
Speak, Basil, thou must surely know,
For like her limbs thy branches show,—
Most lovely in thy fair array
Of twining plant and tender spray.

Sweet Tila, fairest of the trees,
Melodious with the hum of bees,
Where is my darling Sítá, tell,—
The dame who loved thy flowers so well?
Aśoka, act thy gentle part,—
Named Heartsease, give me what thou art,
To these sad eyes my darling show
And free me from this load of woe.
O Palm, in rich ripe fruitage dressed
Round as the beauties of her breast,

If thou have heart to know and feel,
My peerless consort's fate reveal.
Hast thou, Rose-apple, chanced to view
My darling bright with golden hue?
If thou have seen her quickly speak,
Where is the dame I wildly seek?
O glorious Cassia, thou art gay
With all thy loveliest bloom to-day,
Where is my dear who loved to hold
In her full lap thy flowery gold?"
To many a tree and plant beside,
To Jasmin, Mango, Sál, he cried.
"Say, hast thou seen, O gentle deer,
The fawn-eyed Sítá wandering here?
It may be that my love has strayed
To sport with fawns beneath the shade,
If thou, great elephant, have seen
My darling of the lovely mien,
Whose rounded limbs are soft and fine
As is that lissome trunk of thine,
O noblest of wild creatures, show
Where is the dame thou needs must know.
O tiger, hast thou chanced to see
My darling? very fair is she,
Cast all thy fear away, declare,
Where is my moon-faced darling, where?
There, darling of the lotus eye,
I see thee, and 'tis vain to fly,
Wilt thou not speak, dear love? I see
Thy form half hidden by the tree.

Stay if thou love me, Sítá, stay
In pity cease thy heartless play.
Why mock me now? thy gentle breast
Was never prone to cruel jest.
'Tis vain behind yon bush to steal:
Thy shimmering silks thy path reveal.
Fly not, mine eyes pursue thy way;
For pity's sake, dear Sítá, stay.
Ah me, ah me, my words are vain;
My gentle love is lost or slain.
How could her tender bosom spurn
Her husband on his home-return?
Ah no, my love is surely dead,
Fierce giants on her flesh have fed,
Rending the soft limbs of their prey
When I her lord was far away.
That moon-bright face, that polished brow,
Red lips, bright teeth—what are they now?
Alas, my darling's shapely neck
She loved with chains of gold to deck,—
That neck that mocked the sandal scent,
The ruthless fiends have grasped and rent.
Alas, 'twas vain those arms to raise
Soft as the young tree's tender sprays.
Ah, dainty meal for giants' lips
Were arms and quivering finger tips.
Ah, she who counted many a friend
Was left for fiends to seize and rend,
Was left by me without defence
From ravening giants' violence.
O Lakshman of the arm of might,
Say, is my darling love in sight?
O dearest Sítá. where art thou?
Where is my darling consort now?"

Thus as he cried in wild lament
From grove to grove the mourner went,
Here for a moment sank to rest,
Then started up and onward pressed.
Thus roaming on like one distraught
Still for his vanished love he sought,

He searched in wood and hill and glade,
By rock and brook and wild cascade.
Through groves with restless step he sped
And left no spot unvisited.
Through lawns and woods of vast extent
Still searching for his love he went
With eager steps and fast.
For many a weary hour he toiled,
Still in his fond endeavour foiled,
Yet hoping to the last.

CANTO
LXII

Ráma's Lament

When all the toil and search was vain
He sought his leafy home again.
'Twas empty still: all scattered lay
The seats of grass in disarray.
He raised his shapely arms on high
And spoke aloud with bitter cry:
"Where is the Maithil dame?" he said,
"O, whither has my darling fled?
Who can have borne away my dame,
Or feasted on her tender frame?
If, Sítá hidden by some tree,
Thou joyest still to mock at me,
Cease, cease thy cruel sport, and take
Compassion, or my heart will break.
Bethink thee, love, the gentle fawns
With whom thou playest on the lawns,
Impatient for thy coming wait
With streaming eyes disconsolate.
Reft of my love, I needs must go
Hence to the shades weighed down by woe.

The king our sire will see me there,
And cry, "O perjured Ráma, where,
Where is thy faith, that thou canst speed
From exile ere the time decreed?"

Ah Sítá, whither hast thou fled
And left me here disquieted,
A hapless mourner, reft of hope,
Too feeble with my woe to cope?
E'en thus indignant Glory flies
The wretch who stains his soul with lies.
If thou, my love, art lost to view,
I in my woe must perish too."

Thus Ráma by his grief distraught
Wept for the wife he vainly sought,
And Lakshmaṇ whose fraternal breast
Longed for his weal, the chief addressed

Whose soul gave way beneath the pain
When all his eager search was vain,
Like some great elephant who stands
Sinking upon the treacherous sands:
"Not yet, O wisest chief, despair;
Renew thy toil with utmost care.
This noble hill where trees are green
Has many a cave and dark ravine.
The Maithil lady day by day
Delighted in the woods to stray,
Deep in the grove she wanders still,
Or walks by blossom-covered rill;
Or fish-loved river stealing through
Tall clusters of the dark bamboo.
Or else the dame with arch design
To prove thy mood, O Prince, and mine,
Far in some sheltering thicket lies
To frighten ere she meet our eyes.
Then come, renew thy labour, trace
The lady to her lurking-place,
And search the wood from side to side
To know where Sítá loves to bide.

Collect thy thoughts, O royal chief,
Nor yield to unavailing grief."

Thus Lakshman, by attention stirred,
To fresh attempts his brother spurred,
And Ráma, as he ceased, began
With Lakshman's aid each spot to scan.
In eager search their way they took
Through wood, o'er hill, by pool and brook,
They roamed each mount, nor spared to seek
On ridge and crag and towering peak.
They sought the dame in every spot;
But all in vain; they found her not.
Above, below, on every side
They ranged the hill, and Ráma cried,
"O Lakshman, O my brother still
No trace of Sítá on the hill!"
Then Lakshman as he roamed the wood
Beside his glorious brother stood,
And while fierce grief his bosom burned
This answer to the chief returned:
"Thou, Ráma, after toil and pain
Wilt meet the Maithil dame again,
As Vishnu, Bali's might subdued,
His empire of the earth renewed."

Then Ráma cried in mournful tone,
His spirit by his woe o'erthrown;
"The wood is searched from side to side,
No distant spot remains untried,
No lilied pool, no streamlet where
The lotus buds are fresh and fair.
Our eyes have searched the hill with all
His caves and every waterfall,—
But ah, not yet I find my wife,
More precious than the breath of life."

As thus he mourned his vanished dame
A mighty trembling seized his frame,
And by o'erpowering grief assailed,
His troubled senses reeled and failed.

913

Too great to bear his misery grew,
And many a long hot sigh he drew,
Then as he wept and sobbed and sighed,
"O Sítá, O my love!" he cried.
Then Lakshman, joining palm to palm,
Tried every art his woe to calm.
But Ráma in his anguish heard
Or heeded not one soothing word,
Still for his spouse he mourned, and shrill
Rang out his lamentation still.

CANTO
LXIII

Ráma's Lament

Thus for his wife in vain he sought:
Then, his sad soul with pain distraught,
The hero of the lotus eyes
Filled all the air with frantic cries.
O'erpowered by love's strong influence, he
His absent wife still seemed to see,
And thus with accents weak and faint
Renewed with tears his wild complaint:

"Thou, fairer than their bloom, my spouse,
Art hidden by Aśoka boughs.
Those blooms have power to banish care,
But now they drive me to despair.
Thine arms are like the plantain's stem:
Why let the plantain cover them?
Thou art not hidden, love; thy feet
Betray thee in thy dark retreat.
Thou runnest in thy girlish sport
To flowery trees, thy dear resort.
But cease, O cease, my love, I pray,

To vex me with thy cruel play.
Such mockery in a holy spot
Where hermits dwell beseems thee not.
Ah, now I see thy fickle mind
To scornful mood too much inclined,
Come, large-eyed beauty, I implore;
Lone is the cot so dear before.

No, she is slain by giants; they
Have stolen or devoured their prey,
Or surely at my mournful cry
My darling to her lord would fly.
O Lakshmaṇ, see those troops of deer:
In each sad eye there gleams a tear.
Those looks of woe too clearly say
My consort is the giants' prey.
O noblest, fairest of the fair,
Where art thou, best of women, where?
This day will dark Kaikeyí find
Fresh triumph for her evil mind,
When I, who with my Sítá came
Return alone, without my dame.
But ne'er can I return to see
Those chambers where my queen should be
And hear the scornful people speak

Of Ráma as a coward weak.
For mine will be the coward's shame
Who let the foeman steal his dame.
How can I seek my home, or brook
Upon Videha's king to look?
How listen, when he bids me tell,
My wanderings o'er, that all is well?
He, when I meet his eager view,
Will mark that Sítá comes not too,
And when he hears the mournful tale
His wildered sense will reel and fail.
"O Daśaratha" will he cry,
"Blest in thy mansion in the sky!"
Ne'er to that town my steps shall bend,
That town which Bharat's arms defend,

For e'en the blessed homes above
Would seem a waste without my love.
Leave me, my brother, here, I pray;
To fair Ayodhyá bend thy way.
Without my love I cannot bear
To live one hour in blank despair.
Round Bharat's neck thy fond arms twine,
And greet him with these words of mine:
"Dear brother, still the power retain,
And o'er the land as monarch reign."
With salutation next incline
Before thy mother, his, and mine.
Still, brother, to my words attend,
And with all care each dame befriend.
To my dear mother's ear relate
My mournful tale and Sítá's fate."

Thus Ráma gave his sorrow vent,
And from a heart which anguish rent,
Mourned for his wife in loud lament,—
Her of the glorious hair,
From Lakshmaṇ's cheek the colour fled,
And o'er his heart came sudden dread,
Sick, faint, and sore disquieted
By woe too great to bear.

CANTO
LXIV

Ráma's Lament

Reft of his love, the royal chief,
Weighed down beneath his whelming grief,
Desponding made his brother share
His grievous burden of despair.

Over his sinking bosom rolled
The flood of sorrow uncontrolled.

And as he wept and sighed,
In mournful accents faint and slow
With words congenial to his woe,

To Lakshmaṇ thus he cried:
"Brother, I ween, beneath the sun,
Of all mankind there lives not one
So full of sin, whose hand has done
Such cursed deeds as mine.
For my sad heart with misery bleeds,
As, guerdon of those evil deeds,
Still greater woe to woe succeeds
In never-ending line.
A life of sin I freely chose,
And from my past transgression flows
A ceaseless flood of bitter woes
My folly to repay.
The fruit of sin has ripened fast,
Through many a sorrow have I passed,
And now the crowning grief at last
Falls on my head to-day.
From all my faithful friends I fled,
My sire is numbered with the dead,
My royal rank is forfeited,
My mother far away.
These woes on which I sadly think
Fill, till it raves above the brink,
The stream of grief in which I sink,—
The flood which naught can stay.
Ne'er, brother, ne'er have I complained;
Though long by toil and trouble pained,
Without a murmur I sustained
The woes of woodland life.
But fiercer than the flames that rise
When crackling wood the food supplies,—
Flashing a glow through evening skies,—
This sorrow for my wife.

Some cruel fiend has seized the prey
And torn my trembling love away,
While, as he bore her through the skies,
She shrieked aloud with frantic cries,
In tones of fear which, wild and shrill,
Retained their native sweetness still.
Ah me, that breast so soft and sweet,
For sandal's precious perfume meet,
Now all detained with dust and gore,
Shall meet my fond caress no more.
That face, whose lips with tones so clear
Made pleasant music, sweet to hear,—
With soft locks plaited o'er the brow,—
Some giant's hand is on it now.
It smiles not, as the dear light fails
When Ráhu's jaw the moon assails.
Ah, my true love! that shapely neck
She loved with fairest chains to deck,
The cruel demons rend, and drain
The lifeblood from each mangled vein.
Ah, when the savage monsters came
And dragged away the helpless dame,
The lady of the long soft eye
Called like a lamb with piteous cry.
Beneath this rock, O Lakshmaṇ, see,
My peerless consort sat with me,
And gently talked to thee the while,
Her sweet lips opening with a smile.
Here is that fairest stream which she
Loved ever, bright Godávarí.
Ne'er can the dame have passed this way:
So far alone she would not stray,
Nor has my darling, lotus-eyed,
Sought lilies by the river's side,
For without me she ne'er would go

To streamlets where the wild flowers grow,
Tell me not, brother, she has strayed
To the dark forest's distant shade
Where blooming boughs are gay and sweet,
And bright birds love the cool retreat.

Alone my love would never dare,—
My timid love,—to wander there.

O Lord of Day whose eye sees all
We act and plan, on thee I call:
For naught is hidden from thy sight,—
Great witness thou of wrong and right.
Where is she, lost or torn away?
Dispel my torturing doubt and say.
And O thou Wind who blowest free,
The worlds have naught concealed from thee.
List to my prayer, reveal one trace
Of her, the glory of her race.
Say, is she stolen hence, or dead,
Or do her feet the forest tread?"
Thus with disordered senses, faint
With woe he poured his sad complaint,
And then, a better way to teach,
Wise Lakshman spoke in seemly speech:
"Up, brother dear, thy grief subdue,
With heart and soul thy search renew.
When woes oppress and dangers threat
Brave effort ne'er was fruitless yet."

He spoke, but Ráma gave no heed
To valiant Lakshman's prudent rede.
With double force the flood of pain
Rushed o'er his yielding soul again.

CANTO

LXV

Ráma's Wrath

With piteous voice, by woe subdued,
Thus Raghu's son his speech renewed:

"Thy steps, my brother, quickly turn
To bright Godávarí and learn
If Sítá to the stream have hied
To cull the lilies on its side."

Obedient to the words he said,
His brother to the river sped.
The shelving banks he searched in vain,
And then to Ráma turned again.

"I searched, but found her not," he cried;
"I called aloud, but none replied.
Where can the Maithil lady stray,
Whose sight would chase our cares away?
I know not where, her steps untraced,
Roams Sítá of the dainty waist."

When Ráma heard the words he spoke
Again he sank beneath the stroke,
And with a bosom anguish-fraught
Himself the lovely river sought.
There standing on the shelving side,
"O Sítá, where art thou?" he cried.
No spirit voice an answer gave,
No murmur from the trembling wave
Of sweet Godávarí declared
The outrage which the fiend had dared.
"O speak!" the pitying spirits cried,

But yet the stream their prayer denied,
Nor dared she, coldly mute, relate
To the sad chief his darling's fate
Of Rávaṇ's awful form she thought,
And the dire deed his arm had wrought,
And still withheld by fear dismayed,
The tale for which the mourner prayed.
When hope was none, his heart to cheer,
That the bright stream his cry would hear
While sorrow for his darling tore
His longing soul he spake once more:
"Though I have sought with tears and sighs
Godárvarí no word replies,
O say, what answer can I frame
To Janak, father of my dame?
Or how before her mother stand
Leading no Sítá by the hand?
Where is my loyal love who went
Forth with her lord to banishment?
Her faith to me she nobly held
Though from my realm and home expelled,—
A hermit, nursed on woodland fare,—
She followed still and soothed my care.
Of all my friends am I bereft,
Nor is my faithful consort left.
How slowly will the long nights creep
While comfortless I wake and weep!
O, if my wife may yet be found,
With humble love I'll wander round
This Janasthán, Praśravaṇ's hill,
Mandákiní's delightful rill.
See how the deer with gentle eyes
Look on my face and sympathize.
I mark their soft expression: each
Would soothe me, if it could, with speech."

A while the anxious throng he eyed.
And "Where is Sítá, where?" he cried.
Thus while hot tears his utterance broke
The mourning son of Raghu spoke.
The deer in pity for his woes

Obeyed the summons and arose.
Upon his right thy stood, and raised
Their sad eyes up to heaven and gazed
Each to that quarter bent her look
Which Rávaṇ with his captive took.
Then Raghu's son again they viewed,
And toward that point their way pursued.
Then Lakshmaṇ watched their looks intent
As moaning on their way they went,
And marked each sign which struck his sense
With mute expressive influence,
Then as again his sorrow woke
Thus to his brother chief he spoke:
"Those deer thy eager question heard

And rose at once by pity stirred:
See, in thy search their aid they lend,
See, to the south their looks they bend.
Arise, dear brother, let us go
The way their eager glances show,
If haply sign or trace descried
Our footsteps in the search may guide."

The son of Raghu gave assent,
And quickly to the south they went;
With eager eyes the earth he scanned,
And Lakshmaṇ followed close at hand.
As each to other spake his thought,
And round with anxious glances sought,
Scattered before them in the way,
Blooms of a fallen garland lay.
When Ráma saw that flowery rain
He spoke once more with bitterest pain:
"O Lakshmaṇ every flower that lies
Here on the ground I recognize.
I culled them in the grove, and there
My darling twined them in her hair.
The sun, the earth, the genial breeze
Have spared these flowers my soul to please."

Then to that woody hill he prayed,
Whence flashed afar each wild cascade:
"O best of mountains, hast thou seen
A dame of perfect form and mien
In some sweet spot with trees o'ergrown,—
My darling whom I left alone?"
Then as a lion threats a deer
He thundered with a voice of fear:
"Reveal her, mountain, to my view
With golden limbs and golden hue.
Where is my darling Sítá? speak
Before I rend thee peak from peak."

The mountain seemed her track to show,
But told not all he sought to know.
Then Daśaratha's son renewed
His summons as the mount he viewed:
"Soon as my flaming arrows fly,
Consumed to ashes shall thou lie
Without a herb or bud or tree,
And birds no more shall dwell in thee.
And if this stream my prayer deny,
My wrath this day her flood shall dry,
Because she lends no aid to trace
My darling of the lotus face."

Thus Ráma spake as though his ire
Would scorch them with his glance of fire;
Then searching farther on the ground
The footprint of a fiend he found,
And small light traces here and there,
Where Sítá in her great despair,
Shrieking for Ráma's help, had fled
Before the giant's mighty tread.
His careful eye each trace surveyed
Which Sítá and the fiend had made,—
The quivers and the broken bow
And ruined chariot of the foe,—
And told, distraught by fear and grief,
His tidings to his brother chief:

"O Lakshmaṇ, here," he cried "behold
My Sítá's earrings dropped with gold.
Here lie her garlands torn and rent,
Here lies each glittering ornament.
O look, the ground on every side
With blood-like drops of gold is dyed.
The fiends who wear each strange disguise
Have seized, I ween, the helpless prize.
My lady, by their hands o'erpowered,
Is slaughtered, mangled, and devoured.
Methinks two fearful giants came
And waged fierce battle for the dame.
Whose, Lakshmaṇ, was this mighty bow
With pearls and gems in glittering row?
Cast to the ground the fragments lie,
And still their glory charms the eye.
A bow so mighty sure was planned
For heavenly God or giant's hand.
Whose was this coat of golden mail
Which, though its lustre now is pale,
Shone like the sun of morning, bright
With studs of glittering lazulite?
Whose, Lakshmaṇ, was this bloom-wreathed shade
With all its hundred ribs displayed?
This screen, most meet for royal brow,
With broken staff lies useless now.
And these tall asses, goblin-faced,
With plates of golden harness graced,
Whose hideous forms are stained with gore
Who is the lord whose yoke they bore?
Whose was this pierced and broken car
That shoots a flame-like blaze afar?
Whose these spent shafts at random spread,
Each fearful with its iron head,—
With golden mountings fair to see,
Long as a chariot's axle-tree?
These quivers see, which, rent in twain,
Their sheaves of arrows still contain.
Whose was this driver? Dead and cold,
His hands the whip and reins still hold.
See, Lakshmaṇ, here the foot I trace

Of man, nay, one of giant race.
The hatred that I nursed of old
Grows mightier now a hundred fold
Against these giants, fierce of heart,
Who change their forms by magic art.
Slain, eaten by the giant press,
Or stolen is the votaress,
Nor could her virtue bring defence
To Sítá seized and hurried hence.
O, if my love be slain or lost
All hope of bliss for me is crossed.
The power of all the worlds were vain
To bring one joy to soothe my pain.
The spirits with their blinded eyes
Would look in wonder, and despise
The Lord who made the worlds, the great
Creator when compassionate.
And so, I ween, the Immortals turn
Cold eyes upon me now, and spurn

The weakling prompt at pity's call,
Devoted to the good of all.
But from this day behold me changed,
From every gentle grace estranged.
Now be it mine all life to slay,
And sweep these cursed fiends away.
As the great sun leaps up the sky,
And the cold moonbeams fade and die,
So vengeance rises in my breast,
One passion conquering all the rest.
Gandharvas in their radiant place,
The Yakshas, and the giant race,
Kinnars and men shall look in vain
For joy they ne'er shall see again.
The anguish of my great despair,
O Lakshman, fills the heaven and air;
And I in wrath all life will slay
Within the triple world to-day.
Unless the Gods in heaven who dwell
Restore my Sítá safe and well,
I armed with all the fires of Fate,

The triple world will devastate.
The troubled stars from heaven shall fall,
The moon be wrapped in gloomy pall,
The fire be quenched, the wind be stilled,
The radiant sun grow dark and chilled;
Crushed every mountain's towering pride,
And every lake and river dried,
Dead every creeper, plant, and tree,
And lost for aye the mighty sea.
Thou shalt the world this day behold
In wild disorder uncontrolled,
With dying life which naught defends
From the fierce storm my bowstring sends.
My shafts this day, for Sítá's sake,
The life of every fiend shall take.
The Gods this day shall see the force
That wings my arrows on their course,
And mark how far that course is held,
By my unsparing wrath impelled.
No God, not one of Daitya strain,
Goblin or Rákshas shall remain.
My wrath shall end the worlds, and all
Demons and Gods therewith shall fall.
Each world which Gods, the Dánav race,
And giants make their dwelling place,
Shall fall beneath my arrows sent
In fury when my bow is bent.
The arrows loosened from my string
Confusion on the worlds shall bring.
For she is lost or breathes no more,
Nor will the Gods my love restore.
Hence all on earth with life and breath
This day I dedicate to death.
All, till my darling they reveal,
The fury of my shafts shall feel."

Thus as he spake by rage impelled,
Red grew his eyes, his fierce lips swelled.
His bark coat round his form he drew
And coiled his hermit braids anew,
Like Rudra when he yearned to slay

The demon Tripur in the fray.
So looked the hero brave and wise,
The fury flashing from his eyes.
Then Ráma, conqueror of the foe,
From Lakshmaṇ's hand received his bow,
Strained the great string, and laid thereon
A deadly dart that flashed and shone,
And spake these words as fierce in ire
As He who ends the worlds with fire:

"As age and time and death and fate
All life with checkless power await,
So Lakshmaṇ in my wrath to-day
My vengeful might shall brook no stay,
Unless this day I see my dame
In whose sweet form is naught to blame,—
Yea, as before, my love behold
Fair with bright teeth and perfect mould,
This world shall feel a deadly blow
Destroyed with ruthless overthrow,
And serpent lords and Gods of air,
Gandharvas, men, the doom shall share."

CANTO
LXVI

Lakshman's Speech

He stood incensed with eyes of flame,
Still mourning for his ravished dame,
Determined, like the fire of Fate,
To leave the wide world desolate.
His ready bow the hero eyed,
And as again, again he sighed,
The triple world would fain consume
Like Hara in the day of doom.

Then Lakshmaṇ moved with sorrow viewed
His brother in unwonted mood,
And reverent palm to palm applied,
Thus spoke with lips which terror dried
"Thy heart was ever soft and kind,
To every creature's good inclined.
Cast not thy tender mood away,
Nor yield to anger's mastering sway.
The moon for gentle grace is known,
The sun has splendour all his own,
The restless wind is free and fast,
And earth in patience unsurpassed.
So glory with her noble fruit
Is thine eternal attribute.
O, let not, for the sin of one,
The triple world be all undone.
I know not whose this car that lies
In fragments here before our eyes,
Nor who the chiefs who met and fought,
Nor what the prize the foemen sought;
Who marked the ground with hoof and wheel,

Or whose the hand that plied the steel
Which left this spot, the battle o'er,
Thus sadly dyed with drops of gore.
Searching with utmost care I view
The signs of one and not of two.
Where'er I turn mine eyes I trace
No mighty host about the place.
Then mete not out for one offence
This all-involving recompense.
For kings should use the sword they bear,
But mild in time should learn to spare,
Thou, ever moved by misery's call,
Wast the great hope and stay of all.
Throughout this world who would not blame
This outrage on thy ravished dame?
Gandharvas, Dánavs, Gods, the trees,
The rocks, the rivers, and the seas,
Can ne'er in aught thy soul offend,
As one whom holiest rites befriend.

928

But him who dared to steal the dame
Pursue, O King, with ceaseless aim,
With me, the hermits' holy band,
And thy great bow to arm thy hand
By every mighty flood we'll seek,
Each wood, each hill from base to peak.
To the fair homes of Gods we'll fly,
And bright Gandharvas in the sky,
Until we reach, where'er he be,
The wretch who stole thy spouse from thee.
Then if the Gods will not restore
Thy Sítá when the search is o'er,
Then, royal lord of Kośal's land,
No longer hold thy vengeful hand.
If meekness, prayer, and right be weak
To bring thee back the dame we seek,
Up, brother, with a deadly shower
Of gold-bright shafts thy foes o'erpower,
Fierce as the flashing levin sent
From King Mahendra's firmament.

CANTO

LXVII

Ráma Appeased

As Ráma, pierced by sorrow's sting,
Lamented like a helpless thing,
And by his mighty woe distraught
Was lost in maze of troubled thought,
Sumitrá's son with loving care
Consoled him in his wild despair,
And while his feet he gently pressed
With words like these the chief addressed:
"For sternest vow and noblest deed
Was Daśaratha blessed with seed.

Thee for his son the king obtained,
Like Amrit by the Gods regained.
Thy gentle graces won his heart,
And all too weak to live apart
The monarch died, as Bharat told,
And lives on high mid Gods enrolled.
If thou, O Ráma, wilt not bear
This grief which fills thee with despair,
How shall a weaker man e'er hope,
Infirm and mean, with woe to cope?
Take heart, I pray thee, noblest chief:
What man who breathes is free from grief?
Misfortunes come and burn like flame,
Then fly as quickly as they came.
Yayáti son of Nahush reigned
With Indra on the throne he gained.
But falling for a light offence
He mourned a while the consequence.
Vaśishṭha, reverend saint and sage,
Priest of our sire from youth to age,
Begot a hundred sons, but they
Were smitten in a single day.
And she, the queen whom all revere,
The mother whom we hold so dear,
The earth herself not seldom feels
Fierce fever when she shakes and reels.
And those twin lights, the world's great eyes,
On which the universe relies,—
Does not eclipse at times assail
Their brilliance till their fires grow pale?
The mighty Powers, the Immortal Blest
Bend to a law which none contest.
No God, no bodied life is free
From conquering Fate's supreme decree.
E'en Śakra's self must reap the meed
Of virtue and of sinful deed.
And O great lord of men, wilt thou
Helpless beneath thy misery bow?
No, if thy dame be lost or dead,
O hero, still be comforted,
Nor yield for ever to thy woe

O'ermastered like the mean and low.
Thy peers, with keen far-reaching eyes,
Spend not their hours in ceaseless sighs;
In dire distress, in whelming ill
Their manly looks are hopeful still.
To this, great chief, thy reason bend,
And earnestly the truth perpend.
By reason's aid the wisest learn
The good and evil to discern.
With sin and goodness scarcely known
Faint light by chequered lives is shown;
Without some clear undoubted deed
We mark not how the fruits succeed.
In time of old, O thou most brave,
To me thy lips such counsel gave.
Vṛihaspati can scarcely find
New wisdom to instruct thy mind.
For thine is wit and genius high
Meet for the children of the sky.
I rouse that heart benumbed by pain
And call to vigorous life again.
Be manly godlike vigour shown;
Put forth that noblest strength, thine own.

Strive, best of old Ikshváku's strain,
Strive till the conquered foe be slain.
Where is the profit or the joy
If thy fierce rage the worlds destroy?
Search till thou find the guilty foe,
Then let thy hand no mercy show."

Jatáyus

Thus faithful Lakshmaṇ strove to cheer
The prince with counsel wise and clear.
Who, prompt to seize the pith of all,
Let not that wisdom idly fall.
With vigorous effort he restrained
The passion in his breast that reigned,
And leaning on his bow for rest
His brother Lakshmaṇ thus addressed:
"How shall we labour now, reflect;
Whither again our search direct?
Brother, what plan canst thou devise
To bring her to these longing eyes?"

To him by toil and sorrow tried
The prudent Lakshmaṇ thus replied:
"Come, though our labour yet be vain,
And search through Janasthán again,—
A realm where giant foes abound,
And trees and creepers hide the ground.
For there are caverns deep and dread,
By deer and wild birds tenanted,
And hills with many a dark abyss,
Grotto and rock and precipice.
There bright Gandharvas love to dwell,
And Kinnars in each bosky dell.
With me thy eager search to aid
Be every hill and cave surveyed.
Great chiefs like thee, the best of men,
Endowed with sense and piercing ken,
Though tried by trouble never fail,
Like rooted hills that mock the gale."

Then Ráma, pierced by anger's sting,
Laid a keen arrow on his string,
And by the faithful Lakshman's side
Roamed through the forest far and wide.
Jaṭáyus there with blood-drops dyed,
Lying upon the ground he spied,
Huge as a mountain's shattered crest,
Mid all the birds of air the best.
In wrath the mighty bird he eyed,
And thus the chief to Lakshman cried:

"Ah me, these signs the truth betray;
My darling was the vulture's prey.
Some demon in the bird's disguise
Roams through the wood that round us lies.
On large-eyed Sítá he has fed,
And rests him now with wings outspread.
But my keen shafts whose flight is true,
Shall pierce the ravenous monster through."

An arrow on the string he laid,
And rushing near the bird surveyed,
While earth to ocean's distant side
Trembled beneath his furious stride.
With blood and froth on neck and beak
The dying bird essayed to speak,
And with a piteous voice, distressed,
Thus Daśaratha's son addressed:

"She whom like some sweet herb of grace
Thou seekest in this lonely place,
Fair lady, is fierce Rávaṇ's prey,
Who took, beside, my life away.
Lakshman and thou had parted hence
And left the dame without defence.
I saw her swiftly borne away
By Rávaṇ's might which none could stay.
I hurried to the lady's aid,
I crushed his car and royal shade,
And putting forth my warlike might
Hurled Rávaṇ to the earth in fight.

Here, Ráma, lies his broken bow,
Here lie the arrows of the foe.
There on the ground before thee are
The fragments of his battle car.
There bleeds the driver whom my wings
Beat down with ceaseless buffetings.
When toil my aged strength subdued,
His sword my weary pinions hewed.
Then lifting up the dame he bare
His captive through the fields of air.
Thy vengeful blows from me restrain,
Already by the giant slain."

When Ráma heard the vulture tell
The tale that proved his love so well,
His bow upon the ground he placed,
And tenderly the bird embraced:
Then to the earth he fell o'erpowered,
And burning tears both brothers showered,
For double pain and anguish pressed
Upon the patient hero's breast.
The solitary bird he eyed
Who in the lone wood gasped and sighed,
And as again his anguish woke
Thus Ráma to his brother spoke:

"Expelled from power the woods I tread,
My spouse is lost, the bird is dead.
A fate so sad, I ween, would tame
The vigour of the glorious flame.
If I to cool my fever tried
To cross the deep from side to side,
The sea,—so hard my fate,—would dry
His waters as my feet came nigh.
In all this world there lives not one
So cursed as I beneath the sun;
So strong a net of misery cast
Around me holds the captive fast,
Best of all birds that play the wing,
Loved, honoured by our sire the king,

The vulture, in my fate enwound,
Lies bleeding, dying on the ground."

Then Ráma and his brother stirred

By pity mourned the royal bird,
And, as their hands his limbs caressed,
Affection for a sire expressed.
And Ráma to his bosom strained
The bird with mangled wings distained,
With crimson blood-drops dyed.
He fell, and shedding many a tear,
"Where is my spouse than life more dear?
Where is my love?" he cried.

CANTO
LXIX

The Death of Jatáyus

As Ráma viewed with heart-felt pain
The vulture whom the fiend had slain,
In words with tender love impressed
His brother chief he thus addressed:
"This royal bird with faithful thought
For my advantage strove and fought.
Slain by the fiend in mortal strife
For me he yields his noble life.
See, Lakshmaṇ, how his wounds have bled;
His struggling breath will soon have fled.
Faint is his voice, and near to die,
He scarce can lift his trembling eye.
Jaṭáyus, if thou still can speak,
Give, give the answer that I seek.
The fate of ravished Sítá tell,

And how thy mournful chance befell.
Say why the giant stole my dame:
What have I done that he could blame?
What fault in me has Rávaṇ seen
That he should rob me of my queen?
How looked the lady's moon-bright cheek?
What were the words she found to speak?
His strength, his might, his deeds declare:
And tell the form he loves to wear.
To all my questions make reply:
Where does the giant's dwelling lie?"

The noble bird his glances bent
On Ráma as he made lament,
And in low accents faint and weak
With anguish thus began to speak:
"Fierce Rávaṇ, king of giant race,
Stole Sítá from thy dwelling-place.
He calls his magic art to aid
With wind and cloud and gloomy shade.
When in the fight my power was spent
My wearied wings he cleft and rent.
Then round the dame his arms he threw,
And to the southern region flew.
O Raghu's son, I gasp for breath,
My swimming sight is dim in death.
E'en now before my vision pass
Bright trees of gold with hair of grass,
The hour the impious robber chose
Brings on the thief a flood of woes.
The giant in his haste forgot
'Twas Vinda's hour, or heeded not.
Those robbed at such a time obtain
Their plundered store and wealth again.
He, like a fish that takes the bait,
In briefest time shall meet his fate.
Now be thy troubled heart controlled
And for thy lady's loss consoled,
For thou wilt slay the fiend in fight
And with thy dame have new delight."

With senses clear, though sorely tried,
The royal vulture thus replied,
While as he sank beneath his pain
Forth rushed the tide of blood again.
"Him, brother of the Lord of Gold,
Viśravas' self begot of old."
Thus spoke the bird, and stained with gore
Resigned the breath that came no more.

"Speak, speak again!" thus Ráma cried,
With reverent palm to palm applied,
But from the frame the spirit fled
And to the skiey regions sped.
The breath of life had passed away.
Stretched on the ground the body lay.

When Ráma saw the vulture lie,
Huge as a hill, with darksome eye,
With many a poignant woe distressed
His brother chief he thus addressed:
"Amid these haunted shades content
Full many a year this bird has spent.
His life in home of giants passed,
In Daṇḍak wood he dies at last.
The years in lengthened course have fled
Untroubled o'er the vulture's head,
And now he lies in death, for none
The stern decrees of Fate may shun.
See, Lakshmaṇ, how the vulture fell
While for my sake he battled well.
And strove to free with onset bold
My Sítá from the giant's hold.
Supreme amid the vulture kind
His ancient rule the bird resigned,
And conquered in the fruitless strife
Gave for my sake his noble life.
O Lakshmaṇ, many a time we see
Great souls who keep the law's decree,
With whom the weak sure refuge find,
In creatures of inferior kind.
The loss of her, my darling queen,

937

Strikes with a pang less fiercely keen
Than now this slaughtered bird to see
Who nobly fought and died for me.
As Daśaratha, good and great,
Was glorious in his high estate,
Honoured by all, to all endeared,
So was this royal bird revered.
Bring fuel for the funeral rite:
These hands the solemn fire shall light

And on the burning pyre shall lay
The bird who died for me to-day.
Now on the gathered wood shall lie
The lord of all the birds that fly,
And I will burn with honours due
My champion whom the giant slew.
O royal bird of noblest heart,
Graced with all funeral rites depart
To bright celestial seats above,
Rewarded for thy faithful love.
Dwell in thy happy home with those
Whose constant fires of worship rose.
Live blest amid the unyielding brave,
And those who land in largess gave."
Sore grief upon his bosom weighed
As on the pyre the bird he laid,
And bade the kindled flame ascend
To burn the body of his friend.
Then with his brother by his side
The hero to the forest hied.
There many a stately deer he slew,
The flesh around the bird to strew.
The venison into balls he made,
And on fair grass before him laid.
Then that the parted soul might rise
And find free passage to the skies,
Each solemn word and text he said
Which Bráhmans utter o'er the dead.
Then hastening went the princely pair
To bright Godávarí, and there
Libations of the stream they poured

938

In honour of the vulture lord,
With solemn ritual to the slain,
As scripture's holy texts ordain.
Thus offerings to the bird they gave
And bathed their bodies in the wave.

The vulture monarch having wrought
A hard and glorious feat,
Honoured by Ráma sage in thought,
Soared to his blissful seat.
The brothers, when each rite was paid
To him of birds supreme,
Their hearts with new-found comfort stayed,
And turned them from the stream.
Like sovereigns of celestial race
Within the wood they came,
Each pondering the means to trace,
The captor of the dame.

CANTO
LXX

Kabandha

W hen every rite was duly paid
    The princely brothers onward strayed,
    And eager in the lady's quest
They turned their footsteps to the west.
Through lonely woods that round them lay
Ikshváku's children made their way,
And armed with bow and shaft and brand
Pressed onward to the southern land.
Thick trees and shrubs and creepers grew
In the wild grove they hurried through.
'Twas dark and drear and hard to pass
For tangled thorns and matted grass.

Still onward with a southern course
They made their way with vigorous force,
And passing through the mazes stood
Beyond that vast and fearful wood.
With toil and hardship yet unspent
Three leagues from Janasthán they went,
And speeding on their way at last
Within the wood of Krauncha passed:
A fearful forest wild and black
As some huge pile of cloudy rack,
Filled with all birds and beasts, where grew
Bright blooms of every varied hue.
On Sítá bending every thought
Through all the mighty wood they sought,
And at the lady's loss dismayed
Here for a while and there they stayed.
Then turning farther eastward they
Pursued three leagues their weary way,
Passed Krauncha's wood and reached the grove
Where elephants rejoiced to rove.
The chiefs that awful wood surveyed
Where deer and wild birds filled each glade,
Where scarce a step the foot could take
For tangled shrub and tree and brake.
There in a mountain's woody side
A cave the royal brothers spied,
With dread abysses deep as hell,
Where darkness never ceased to dwell.
When, pressing on, the lords of men
Stood near the entrance of the den,
They saw within the dark recess
A huge misshapen giantess;
A thing the timid heart that shook
With fearful shape and savage look.
Terrific fiend, her voice was fierce,
Long were her teeth to rend and pierce.
The monster gorged her horrid feast
Of flesh of many a savage beast,
While her long locks, at random flung,
Dishevelled o'er her shoulders hung.
Their eyes the royal brothers raised,

940

And on the fearful monster gazed.
Forth from her den she came and glanced
At Lakshmaṇ as he first advanced,
Her eager arms to hold him spread,
And "Come and be my love" she said,
Then as she held him to her breast,
The prince in words like these addressed:
"Behold thy treasure fond and fair:
Ayomukhi the name I bear.

In thickets of each lofty hill,
On islets of each brook and rill,
With me delighted shalt thou play,
And live for many a lengthened day."

Enraged he heard the monster woo;
His ready sword he swiftly drew,
And the sharp steel that quelled his foes
Cut through her breast and ear and nose.
Thus mangled by his vengeful sword
In rage and pain the demon roared,
And hideous with her awful face
Sped to her secret dwelling place.
Soon as the fiend had fled from sight,
The brothers, dauntless in their might,
Reached a wild forest dark and dread
Whose tangled ways were hard to tread.
Then bravest Lakshmaṇ, virtuous youth,
The friend of purity and truth,
With reverent palm to palm applied
Thus to his glorious brother cried:

"My arm presaging throbs amain,
My troubled heart is sick with pain,
And cheerless omens ill portend
Where'er my anxious eyes I bend.
Dear brother, hear my words: advance
Resolved and armed for every chance,
For every sign I mark to-day
Foretells a peril in the way.
This bird of most ill-omened note,

941

Loud screaming with discordant throat,
Announces with a warning cry
That strife and victory are nigh."
Then as the chiefs their search pursued
Throughout the dreary solitude,
They heard amazed a mighty sound
That broke the very trees around,
As though a furious tempest passed
Crushing the wood beneath its blast.
Then Ráma raised his trusty sword,
And both the hidden cause explored.
There stood before their wondering eyes
A fiend broad-chested, huge of size.
A vast misshapen trunk they saw
In height surpassing nature's law.
It stood before them dire and dread
Without a neck, without a head.
Tall as some hill aloft in air,
Its limbs were clothed with bristling hair,
And deep below the monster's waist
His vast misshapen mouth was placed.
His form was huge, his voice was loud
As some dark-tinted thunder cloud.
Forth from his ample chest there came
A brilliance as of gushing flame.
Beneath long lashes, dark and keen
The monster's single eye was seen.
Deep in his chest, long, fiercely bright,
It glittered with terrific light.
He swallowed down his savage fare
Of lion, bird, and slaughtered bear,
And with huge teeth exposed to view
O'er his great lips his tongue he drew.
His arms unshapely, vast and dread,
A league in length, he raised and spread.
He seized with monstrous hands a herd
Of deer and many a bear and bird.
Among them all he picked and chose,
Drew forward these, rejected those.
Before the princely pair he stood
Barring their passage through the wood.

A league of shade the chiefs had passed
When on the fiend their eyes they cast.
A monstrous shape without a head
With mighty arms before him spread,
They saw that hideous trunk appear
That struck the trembling eye with fear.
Then, stretching to their full extent
His awful arms with fingers bent,
Round Raghu's princely sons he cast
Each grasping limb and held them fast.
Though strong of arm and fierce in fight,
Each armed with bow and sword to smite,
The royal brothers, brave and bold,
Were helpless in the giant's hold.
Then Raghu's son, heroic still,
Felt not a pang his bosom thrill;
But young, with no protection near,
His brother's heart was sad with fear,
And thus with trembling tongue he said
To Ráma, sore disquieted:

"Ah me, ah me, my days are told:
O see me in the giant's hold.
Fly, son of Raghu, swiftly flee,
And thy dear self from danger free.
Me to the fiend an offering give;
Fly at thine ease thyself and live.
Thou, great Kakutstha's son, I ween,
Wilt find ere long thy Maithil queen,
And when thou holdest, throned again,
Thine old hereditary reign,
With servants prompt to do thy will,
O think upon thy brother still."
As thus the trembling Lakshman cried,
The dauntless Ráma thus replied:
"Brother, from causeless dread forbear.
A chief like thee should scorn despair."
He spoke to soothe his wild alarm:
Then fierce Kabandha long of arm,
Among the Dánavs first and best,
The sons of Raghu thus addressed:

"What men are you, whose shoulders show
Broad as a bull's, with sword and bow,
Who roam this dark and horrid place,
Brought by your fate before my face?
Declare by what occasion led
These solitary wilds you tread,
With swords and bows and shafts to pierce,

Like bulls whose horns are strong and fierce.
Why have you sought this forest land
Where wild with hunger's pangs I stand?
Now as your steps my path have crossed
Esteem your lives already lost."

The royal brothers heard with dread
The words which fierce Kabandha said.
And Ráma to his brother cried,
Whose cheek by blanching fear was dried:
"Alas, we fall, O valiant chief,
From sorrow into direr grief,
Still mourning her I hold so dear
We see our own destruction near.
Mark, brother, mark what power has time
O'er all that live, in every clime.
Now, lord of men, thyself and me
Involved in fatal danger see.
'Tis not, be sure, the might of Fate
That crushes all with deadly weight.
Ne'er can the brave and strong, who know
The use of spear and sword and bow,
The force of conquering time withstand,
But fall like barriers built of sand."

Thus in calm strength which naught could shake
The son of Daśaratha spake,
With glory yet unstained
Upon Sumitrá's son he bent
His eyes, and firm in his intent
His dauntless heart maintained.

Kabandha's Speech

Kabandha saw each chieftain stand
Imprisoned by his mighty hand,
Which like a snare around him pressed
And thus the royal pair addressed:
"Why, warriors, are your glances bent
On me whom hungry pangs torment?
Why stand with wildered senses? Fate
Has brought you now my maw to sate."

When Lakshmaṇ heard, a while appalled,
His ancient courage he recalled,
And to his brother by his side
With seasonable counsel cried:

"This vilest of the giant race
Will draw us to his side apace.
Come, rouse thee; let the vengeful sword
Smite off his arms, my honoured lord.
This awful giant, vast of size,
On his huge strength of arm relies,
And o'er the world victorious, thus
With mighty force would slaughter us.
But in cold blood to slay, O King,
Discredit on the brave would bring,
As when some victim in the rite
Shuns not the hand upraised to smite."

The monstrous fiend, to anger stirred,
The converse of the brothers heard.
His horrid mouth he opened wide
And drew the princes to his side.

945

They, skilled due time and place to note
Unsheathed their glittering swords and smote,
Till from the giant's shoulders they
Had hewn the mighty arms away.
His trenchant falchion Ráma plied
And smote him on the better side,
While valiant Lakshman on the left
The arm that held him prisoned cleft.
Then to the earth dismembered fell
The monster with a hideous yell,
And like a cloud's his deep roar went
Through earth and air and firmament.
Then as the giant's blood flowed fast,
On his cleft limbs his eye he cast,
And called upon the princely pair
Their names and lineage to declare.
Him then the noble Lakshman, blest
With fortune's favouring marks, addressed,
And told the fiend his brother's name
And the high blood of which he came:
"Ikshváku's heir here Ráma stands,
Illustrious through a hundred lands.
I, younger brother of the heir,
O fiend, the name of Lakshman bear.
His mother stole his realm away
And drove him forth in woods to stray.
Thus through the mighty forest he
Roamed with his royal wife and me.
While glorious as a God he made
His dwelling in the greenwood shade,
Some giant stole away his dame,
And seeking her we hither came.
But tell me who thou art, and why
With headless trunk that towered so high,
With flaming face beneath thy chest,
Thou liest crushed in wild unrest."

He heard the words that Lakshman spoke,
And memory in his breast awoke,
Recalling Indra's words to mind
He spoke in gentle tones and kind:

946

"O welcome best of men, are ye
Whom, blest by fate, this day I see.
A blessing on each trenchant blade
That low on earth these arms has laid!
Thou, lord of men, incline thine ear
The story of my woe to hear,
While I the rebel pride declare
Which doomed me to the form I wear."

CANTO
LXXII

Kabandha's Tale

"Lord of the mighty arm, of yore
A shape transcending thought I wore,
And through the triple world's extent
My fame for might and valour went.

Scarce might the sun and moon on high,
Scarce Śakra, with my beauty vie.
Then for a time this form I took,
And the great world with trembling shook.
The saints in forest shades who dwelt
The terror of my presence felt.
But once I stirred to furious rage
Great Sthúlaśiras, glorious sage.
Culling in woods his hermit food
My hideous shape with fear he viewed.
Then forth his words of anger burst
That bade me live a thing accursed:
"Thou, whose delight is others' pain,
This grisly form shalt still retain."

Then when I prayed him to relent
And fix some term of punishment,—

947

Prayed that the curse at length might cease,
He bade me thus expect release:
"Let Ráma cleave thine arms away
And on the pyre thy body lay,
And then shalt thou, set free from doom,
Thine own fair shape once more assume."
O Lakshmaṇ, hear my words: in me
The world-illustrious Danu see.
By Indra's curse, subdued in fight,
I wear this form which scares the sight.
By sternest penance long maintained
The mighty Father's grace I gained.
When length of days the God bestowed,
With foolish pride my bosom glowed.
My life, of lengthened years assured,
I deemed from Śakra's might secured.
Let by my senseless pride astray
I challenged Indra to the fray.
A flaming bolt with many a knot
With his terrific arm he shot,
And straight my head and thighs compressed
Were buried in my bulky chest.
Deaf to each prayer and piteous call
He sent me not to Yáma's hall.
"Thy prayers and cries," he said "are vain:
The Father's word must true remain."
"But how may lengthened life be spent
By one the bolt has torn and rent?
How can I live," I cried, "unfed,
With shattered face and thighs and head?"
As thus I spoke his grace to crave,
Arms each a league in length he gave,
And opened in my chest beneath
This mouth supplied with fearful teeth.
So my huge arms I used to cast
Round woodland creatures as they passed,
And fed within the forest here
On lion, tiger, pard, and deer.
Then Indra spake to soothe my grief:
"When Ráma and his brother chief

948

From thy huge bulk those arms shall cleave,
Then shall the skies thy soul receive."
Disguised in this terrific shape
I let no woodland thing escape,
And still my longing soul was pleased
Whene'er my arms a victim seized,
For in these arms I fondly thought
Would Ráma's self at last be caught.
Thus hoping, toiling many a day
I yearned to cast my life away,
And here, my lord, thou standest now:
Blessings be thine! for none but thou
Could cleave my arms with trenchant stroke:
True are the words the hermit spoke.
Now let me, best of warriors, lend
My counsel, and thy plans befriend,
And aid thee with advice in turn
If thou with fire my corse wilt burn."

As thus the mighty Danu prayed
With offer of his friendly aid,
While Lakshmaṇ gazed with anxious eye,
The virtuous Ráma made reply:
"Lakshmaṇ and I through forest shade
From Janasthán a while had strayed.
When none was near her, Rávaṇ came
And bore away my glorious dame,
The giant's form and size unknown,
I learn as yet his name alone.
Not yet the power and might we know
Or dwelling of the monstrous foe.
With none our helpless feet to guide
We wander here by sorrow tried.
Let pity move thee to requite
Our service in the funeral rite.
Our hands shall bring the boughs that, dry
Where elephants have rent them, lie,
Then dig a pit, and light the fire
To burn thee as the laws require.
Do thou as meed of this declare

Who stole my spouse, his dwelling where.
O, if thou can, I pray thee say,
And let this grace our deeds repay."

Danu had lent attentive ear
The words which Ráma spoke to hear,
And thus, a speaker skilled and tried,
To that great orator replied:
"No heavenly lore my soul endows,
Naught know I of thy Maithil spouse.
Yet will I, when my shape I wear,
Him who will tell thee all declare.
Then, Ráma, will my lips disclose
His name who well that giant knows.
But till the flames my corse devour
This hidden knowledge mocks my power.
For through that curse's withering taint
My knowledge now is small and faint.
Unknown the giant's very name
Who bore away the Maithil dame.
Cursed for my evil deeds I wore
A shape which all the worlds abhor.
Now ere with wearied steeds the sun
Through western skies his course have run,
Deep in a pit my body lay

And burn it in the wonted way.
When in the grave my corse is placed,
With fire and funeral honours graced,
Then I, great chief, his name will tell
Who knows the giant robber well.
With him, who guides his life aright,
In league of trusting love unite,
And he, O valiant prince, will be
A faithful friend and aid to thee.
For, Ráma, to his searching eyes
The triple world uncovered lies.
For some dark cause of old, I ween,
Through all the spheres his ways have been."

950

LXXIII

Kabandha's Counsel

The monster ceased: the princely pair
Heard great Kabandha's eager prayer.
Within a mountain cave they sped,
Where kindled fire with care they fed.
Then Lakshmaṇ in his mighty hands
Brought ample store of lighted brands,
And to a pile of logs applied
The flame that ran from side to side.
The spreading glow with gentle force
Consumed Kabandha's mighty corse,
Till the unresting flames had drunk
The marrow of the monstrous trunk,
As balls of butter melt away
Amid the fires that o'er them play.
Then from the pyre, like flame that glows
Undimmed by cloudy smoke, he rose,
In garments pure of spot or speck,
A heavenly wreath about his neck.
Resplendent in his bright attire
He sprang exultant from the pyre.
While from neck, arm, and foot was sent
The flash of gold and ornament.
High on a chariot, bright of hue,
Which swans of fairest pinion drew,
He filled each region of the air
With splendid glow reflected there.
Then in the sky he stayed his car
And called to Ráma from afar:
"Hear, chieftain, while my lips explain
The means to win thy spouse again.
Six plans, O prince, the wise pursue

951

To reach the aims we hold in view.
When evils ripening sorely press
They load the wretch with new distress,
So thou and Lakshman, tried by woe,
Have felt at last a fiercer blow,
And plunged in bitterest grief to-day
Lament thy consort torn away.
There is no course but this: attend;
Make, best of friends, that chief thy friend.
Unless his prospering help thou gain
Thy plans and hopes must all be vain.
O Ráma, hear my words, and seek,
Sugríva, for of him I speak.
His brother Báli, Indra's son,
Expelled him when the fight was won.
With four great chieftains, faithful still,
He dwells on Rishyamúka's hill.—
Fair mountain, lovely with the flow
Of Pampá's waves that glide below,—
Lord of the Vánars just and true,
Strong, very glorious, bright to view,
Unmatched in counsel, firm and meek,
Bound by each word his lips may speak,
Good, splendid, mighty, bold and brave,
Wise in each plan to guide and save.
His brother, fired by lust of sway,
Drove forth the prince in woods to stray.
In all thy search for Sítá he
Thy ready friend and help will be.
With him to aid thee in thy quest
Dismiss all sorrow from thy breast.
Time is a mighty power, and none
His fixed decree can change or shun.
So rich reward thy toil shall bless,
And naught can stay thy sure success.
Speed hence, O chief, without delay,
To strong Sugríva take thy way.
This hour thy footsteps onward bend,
And make that mighty prince thy friend.
With him before the attesting flame
In solemn truth alliance frame.

Nor wilt thou, if thy heart be wise,
Sugríva, Vánar king, despise.
Of boundless strength, all shapes he wears,
He hearkens to a suppliant's prayers,
And, grateful for each kindly deed,
Will help and save in hour of need.
And you, I ween, the power possess
To aid his hopes and give redress.
He, let his cause succeed or fail,
Will help you, and you must prevail.
A banished prince, in fear and woe
He roams where Pampá's waters flow,
True offspring of the Lord of Light
Expelled by Báli's conquering might.
Go, Raghu's son, that chieftain seek
Who dwells on Rishyamúka's peak.
Before the flame thy weapons cast
And bind the bonds of friendship fast.
For, prince of all the Vánar race,
He in his wisdom knows each place
Where dwell the fierce gigantic brood
Who make the flesh of man their food.
To him, O Raghu's son, to him
Naught in the world is dark or dim,
Where'er the mighty Day-God gleams
Resplendent with a thousand beams.

He over rocky height and hill,
Through gloomy cave, by lake and rill,
Will with his Vánars seek the prize,
And tell thee where thy lady lies.
And he will send great chieftains forth
To east and west and south and north,
To seek the distant spot where she
All desolate laments for thee.
He even in Rávaṇ's halls would find
Thy Sítá, gem of womankind.
Yea, if the blameless lady lay
On Meru's loftiest steep,
Or, far removed from light of day,
Where hell is dark and deep,

That chief of all the Vánar race
His way would still explore,
Meet the cowed giants face to face
And thy dear spouse restore."

CANTO

LXXIV

Kabandha's Death

When wise Kabandha thus had taught
The means to find the dame they sought,
And urged them onward in the quest,
He thus again the prince addressed:

"This path, O Raghu's son, pursue
Where those fair trees which charm the view,
Extending westward far away,
The glory of their bloom display,
Where their bright leaves Rose-apples show,
And the tall Jak and Mango grow.
Whene'er you will, those trees ascend,
Or the long branches shake and bend,
Their savoury fruit like Amrit eat,
Then onward speed with willing feet.
Beyond this shady forest, decked
With flowering trees, your course direct.
Another grove you then will find
With every joy to take the mind,
Like Nandan with its charms displayed,
Or Northern Kuru's blissful shade;
Where trees distil their balmy juice,
And fruit through all the year produce;
Where shades with seasons ever fair
With Chaitraratha may compare:
Where trees whose sprays with fruit are bowed

Rise like a mountain or a cloud.
There, when you list, from time to time,
The loaded trees may Lakshmaṇ climb,
Or from the shaken boughs supply
Sweet fruit that may with Amrit vie.
The onward path pursuing still
From wood to wood, from hill to hill,
Your happy eyes at length will rest
On Pampá's lotus-covered breast.
Her banks with gentle slope descend,
Nor stones nor weed the eyes offend,
And o'er smooth beds of silver sand
Lotus and lily blooms expand.
There swans and ducks and curlews play,
And keen-eyed ospreys watch their prey,
And from the limpid waves are heard
Glad notes of many a water-bird.
Untaught a deadly foe to fear
They fly not when a man is near,
And fat as balls of butter they
Will, when you list, your hunger stay.
Then Lakshmaṇ with his shafts will take
The fish that swim the brook and lake,
Remove each bone and scale and fin,
Or strip away the speckled skin,
And then on iron skewers broil
For thy repast the savoury spoil.
Thou on a heap of flowers shalt rest
And eat the meal his hands have dressed,
There shalt thou lie on Pampá's brink,
And Lakshmaṇ's hand shall give thee drink,
Filling a lotus leaf with cool
Pure water from the crystal pool,
To which the opening blooms have lent
The riches of divinest scent.
Beside thee at the close of day
Will Lakshmaṇ through the woodland stray,
And show thee where the monkeys sleep
In caves beneath the mountain steep.
Loud-voiced as bulls they forth will burst
And seek the flood, oppressed by thirst;

Then rest a while, their wants supplied,
Their well-fed bands on Pampá's side.
Thou roving there at eve shalt see
Rich clusters hang on shrub and tree,
And Pampá flushed with roseate glow,
And at the view forget thy woe.
There shalt thou mark with strange delight
Each loveliest flower that blooms by night,
While lily buds that shrink from day
Their tender loveliness display.
In that far wild no hand but thine
Those peerless flowers in wreaths shall twine:
Immortal in their changeless pride,
Ne'er fade those blooms and ne'er are dried.
There erst on holy thoughts intent
Their days Matanga's pupils spent.
Once for their master food they sought,
And store of fruit and berries brought.
Then as they laboured through the dell
From limb and brow the heat-drops fell:
Thence sprang and bloomed those wondrous trees:
Such holy power have devotees.
Thus, from the hermits' heat-drops sprung,
Their growth is ever fresh and young.
There Śavarí is dwelling yet,
Who served each vanished anchoret.

Beneath the shade of holy boughs
That ancient votaress keeps her vows.
Her happy eyes on thee will fall,
O godlike prince, adored by all,
And she, whose life is pure from sin,
A blissful seat in heaven will win.
But cross, O son of Raghu, o'er,
And stand on Pampá's western shore.
A tranquil hermitage that lies
Deep in the woods will meet thine eyes.
No wandering elephants invade
The stillness of that holy shade,
But checked by saint Matanga's power
They spare each consecrated bower.

Through many an age those trees have stood
World-famous as Matanga's wood
Still, Raghu's son, pursue thy way:
Through shades where birds are vocal stray,
Fair as the blessed wood where rove
Immortal Gods, or Nandan's grove.
Near Pampá eastward, full in sight,
Stands Rishyamúka's wood-crowned height.
'Tis hard to climb that towering steep
Where serpents unmolested sleep.
The free and bounteous, formed of old
By Brahmá of superior mould,
Who sink when day is done to rest
Reclining on that mountain crest,—
What wealth or joy in dreams they view,
Awaking find the vision true.
But if a villain stained with crime
That holy hill presume to climb,
The giants in their fury sweep
From the hill top the wretch asleep.
There loud and long is heard the roar
Of elephants on Pampá's shore,
Who near Matanga's dwelling stray
And in those waters bathe and play.
A while they revel by the flood,
Their temples stained with streams like blood,
Then wander far away dispersed,
Dark as huge clouds before they burst.
But ere they part they drink their fill
Of bright pure water from the rill,
Delightful to the touch, where meet
Scents of all flowers divinely sweet,
Then speeding from the river side
Deep in the sheltering thicket hide.
Then bears and tigers shalt thou view
Whose soft skins show the sapphire's hue,
And silvan deer that wander nigh
Shall harmless from thy presence fly.
High in that mountain's wooded side
Is a fair cavern deep and wide,
Yet hard to enter: piles of rock

The portals of the cavern block.
Fast by the eastern door a pool
Gleams with broad waters fresh and cool,
Where stores of roots and fruit abound,
And thick trees shade the grassy ground.
This mountain cave the virtuous-souled
Sugríva, and his Vánars hold,
And oft the mighty chieftain seeks
The summits of those towering peaks."

Thus spake Kabandha high in air
His counsel to the royal pair.
Still on his neck that wreath he bore,
And radiance like the sun's he wore.
Their eyes the princely brothers raised
And on that blissful being gazed:
"Behold, we go: no more delay;
Begin," they cried, "thy heavenward way."
"Depart," Kabandha's voice replied,
"Pursue your search, and bliss betide."
Thus to the happy chiefs he said,
Then on his heavenward journey sped.
Thus once again Kabandha won
A shape that glittered like the sun
Without a spot or stain.
Thus bade he Ráma from the air
To great Sugríva's side repair
His friendly love to gain.

Savarí

Thus counselled by their friendly guide
On through the wood the princes hied,
Pursuing still the eastern road
To Pampá which Kabandha showed,
Where trees that on the mountains grew
With fruit like honey charmed the view.
They rested weary for the night
Upon a mountain's wooded height,
Then onward with the dawn they hied
And stood on Pampá's western side,
Where Śavarí's fair home they viewed
Deep in that shady solitude.
The princes reached the holy ground
Where noble trees stood thick around,
And joying in the lovely view
Near to the aged votaress drew.
To meet the sons of Raghu came,
With hands upraised, the pious dame,
And bending low with reverence meet
Welcomed them both and pressed their feet.
Then water, as beseems, she gave,
Their lips to cool, their feet to lave.
To that pure saint who never broke
One law of duty Ráma spoke:

"I trust no cares invade thy peace,
While holy works and zeal increase;
That thou content with scanty food
All touch of ire hast long subdued;
That all thy vows are well maintained

While peace of mind is surely gained,
That reverence of the saints who taught
Thy faithful heart due fruit has brought."

The aged votaress pure of taint,
Revered by every perfect saint,
Rose to her feet by Ráma's side
And thus in gentle tones replied:
"My penance meed this day I see
Complete, my lord, in meeting thee.
This day the fruit of birth I gain,
Nor have I served the saints in vain.
I reap rich fruits of toil and vow,
And heaven itself awaits me now,
When I, O chief of men, have done
Honour to thee the godlike one.
I feel, great lord, thy gentle eye
My earthly spirit purify,
And I, brave tamer of thy foes,
Shall through thy grace in bliss repose.
Thy feet by Chitrakúṭa strayed
When those great saints whom I obeyed,
In dazzling chariots bright of hue,
Hence to their heavenly mansions flew.
As the high saints were borne away
I heard their holy voices say:
"In this pure grove, O devotee,
Prince Ráma soon will visit thee.
When he and Lakshmaṇ seek this shade,
Be to thy guests all honour paid.
Him shalt thou see, and pass away
To those blest worlds which ne'er decay."
To me, O mighty chief, the best
Of lofty saints these words addressed.
Laid up within my dwelling lie
Fruits of each sort which woods supply,—
Food culled for thee in endless store
From every tree on Pampá's shore."

Thus to her virtuous guest she sued
And he, with heavenly lore endued,

Words such as these in turn addressed
To her with equal knowledge blest:
"Danu himself the power has told
Of thy great masters lofty-souled.
Now if thou will, mine eyes would fain
Assurance of their glories gain."

She heard the prince his wish declare:
Then rose she, and the royal pair
Of brothers through the wood she led
That round her holy dwelling spread.
"Behold Matanga's wood" she cried,
"A grove made famous far and wide.
Dark as thick clouds and filled with herds
Of wandering deer, and joyous birds.
In this pure spot each reverend sire
With offerings fed the holy fire.
See here the western altar stands
Where daily with their trembling hands
The aged saints, so long obeyed
By me, their gifts of blossoms laid.
The holy power, O Raghu's son,
By their ascetic virtue won,
Still keeps their well-loved altar bright,
Filling the air with beams of light.
And those seven neighbouring lakes behold
Which, when the saints infirm and old,
Worn out by fasts, no longer sought,
Moved hither drawn by power of thought.
Look, Ráma, where the devotees
Hung their bark mantles on the trees,
Fresh from the bath: those garments wet
Through many a day are dripping yet.
See, through those aged hermits' power
The tender spray, this bright-hued flower
With which the saints their worship paid,
Fresh to this hour nor change nor fade.
Here thou hast seen each lawn and dell,
And heard the tale I had to tell:
Permit thy servant, lord, I pray,
To cast this mortal shell away,

For I would dwell, this life resigned,
With those great saints of lofty mind,
Whom I within this holy shade
With reverential care obeyed."

When Ráma and his brother heard
The pious prayer the dame preferred,
Filled full of transport and amazed
They marvelled as her words they praised.
Then Ráma to the votaress said
Whose holy vows were perfected:
"Go, lady, where thou fain wouldst be,
O thou who well hast honoured me."
Her locks in hermit fashion tied,
Clad in bark coat and black deer-hide,
When Ráma gave consent, the dame
Resigned her body to the flame.
Then like the fire that burns and glows,
To heaven the sainted lady rose,
In all her heavenly garments dressed,
Immortal wreaths on neck and breast,
Bright with celestial gems she shone
Most beautiful to look upon,
And like the flame of lightning sent
A glory through the firmament.
That holy sphere the dame attained,
By depth of contemplation gained,
Where roam high saints with spirits pure
In bliss that shall for aye endure.

CANTO
LXXVI

Pampá

Whe n Śavarí had sought the skies
And gained her splendid virtue's prize,
Ráma with Lakshmaṇ stayed to brood
O'er the strange scenes their eyes had viewed.
His mind upon those saints was bent,
For power and might preëminent
And he to musing Lakshmaṇ spoke
The thoughts that in his bosom woke:

"Mine eyes this wondrous home have viewed
Of those great saints with souls subdued,
Where peaceful tigers dwell and birds,
And deer abound in heedless herds.
Our feet upon the banks have stood
Of those seven lakes within the wood,
Where we have duly dipped, and paid
Libations to each royal shade.
Forgotten now are thoughts of ill
And joyful hopes my bosom fill.
Again my heart is light and gay
And grief and care have passed away.
Come, brother, let us hasten where
Bright Pampá's flood is fresh and fair,
And towering in their beauty near
Mount Rishyamúka's heights appear,
Which, offspring of the Lord of Light,
Still fearing Báli's conquering might,
With four brave chiefs of Vánar race
Sugríva makes his dwelling-place.
I long with eager heart to find
That leader of the Vánar kind,

For on that chief my hopes depend
That this our quest have prosperous end."

Thus Ráma spoke, in battle tried,
And thus Sumitrá's son replied:
"Come, brother, come, and speed away:
My spirit brooks no more delay."
Thus spake Sumitrá's son, and then
Forth from the grove the king of men
With his dear brother by his side
To Pampá's lucid waters hied.
He gazed upon the woods where grew
Trees rich in flowers of every hue.
From brake and dell on every side
The curlew and the peacock cried,
And flocks of screaming parrots made
Shrill music in the bloomy shade.
His eager eyes, as on he went,
On many a pool and tree were bent.
Inflamed with love he journeyed on
Till a fair flood before him shone.
He stood upon the water's side
Which streams from distant hills supplied:
Matanga's name that water bore:
There bathed he from the shelving shore.
Then, each on earnest thoughts intent,
Still farther on their way they went.
But Ráma's heart once more gave way
Beneath his grief and wild dismay.
Before him lay the noble flood
Adorned with many a lotus bud.
On its fair banks Aśoka glowed,
And all bright trees their blossoms showed.
Green banks that silver waves confined
With lovely groves were fringed and lined.
The crystal waters in their flow
Showed level sands that gleamed below.
There glittering fish and tortoise played,
And bending trees gave pleasant shade.
There creepers on the branches hung

With lover-like embraces clung.
There gay Gandharvas loved to meet,
And Kinnars sought the calm retreat.
There wandering Yakshas found delight,
Snake-gods and rovers of the night.
Cool were the pleasant waters, gay
Each tree with creeper, flower, and spray.
There flushed the lotus darkly red,
Here their white glory lilies spread,
Here sweet buds showed their tints of blue:
So carpets gleam with many a hue.
A grove of Mangoes blossomed nigh,
Echoing with the peacock's cry.
When Ráma by his brother's side
The lovely flood of Pampá eyed,
Decked like a beauty, fair to see
With every charm of flower and tree,
His mighty heart with woe was rent
And thus he spoke in wild lament

"Here, Lakshmaṇ, on this beauteous shore,
Stands, dyed with tints of many an ore,
The mountain Rishyamúka bright
With flowery trees that crown each height.
Sprung from the chief who, famed of yore,
The name of Riksharajas bore,
Sugríva, chieftain strong and dread,
Dwells on that mountain's towering head.
Go to him, best of men, and seek
That prince of Vánars on the peak,
I cannot longer brook my pain,
Or, Sítá lost, my life retain."
Thus by the pangs of love distressed,
His thoughts on Sítá bent,
His faithful brother he addressed,
And cried in wild lament.
He reached the lovely ground that lay
On Pampá's wooded side,
And told in anguish and dismay,
The grief he could not hide.

With listless footsteps faint and slow
His way the chief pursued,
Till Pampá with her glorious show
Of flowering woods he viewed.
Through shades where every bird was found
The prince with Lakshmaṇ passed,
And Pampá with her groves around
Burst on his eyes at last.